International

SECOND EDITION

Economics

The Addison-Wesley Series in Economics

International Economics

SECOND EDITION

James Gerber
San Diego State University

Addison
Wesley

Boston San Francisco New York
London Toronto Sydney Tokyo Singapore Madrid
Mexico City Munich Paris Cape Town Hong Kong Montreal

For Monica and Elizabeth, in the hope that their 21st-century world will find peace and prosperity.

Editor-in-Chief: *Denise Clinton*
Executive Development Editor: *Sylvia Mallory*
Assistant Editor: *Christine Houde*
Senior Production Supervisor: *Juliet Silveri*
Production Services: *Kathy Smith*
Composition: *Gillian Hall, The Aardvark Group*
Text illustration: *George Nichols*
Design Supervisor: *Regina Hagen*
Text and Cover Designer: *Joyce Cosentino*
Marketing Manager: *Adrienne D'Ambrosio*
Print Buyer: *Hugh Crawford*
Cartographer: *Chris Lukinbeal*

Cover image © 2002 PhotoDisc, Inc.

Library of Congress Cataloging-in-Publication Data

Gerber, James.
   International economics / James Gerber.—2nd ed.
      p. cm.
   Includes bibliographical references and index.
   ISBN 0-201-72612-2
      1. International economic relations. 2. International economic integration.
   3. International trade. 4. Commercial policy. 5. United States–Foreign
   economic relations.
      I. Title.

HF1359.G474 2002
337—dc21

1 2 3 4 5 6 7 8 9 10—HT—0504030201

Brief Contents

Contents

Preface

International Economics is designed for a one-semester course covering both the micro and macro components of international economics. The Second Edition continues the approach of the First Edition in offering a principles-level introduction to the core theories, together with policy analysis and the institutional and historical contexts of our world's increasing international economic integration. The goal is to make economic reasoning about the international economy accessible to a diverse group of students, including both economics majors and nonmajors.

Several features of *International Economics* distinguish it from the many excellent texts in the field. First, the focus is wider than the theoretical apparatus used by economists. Economic theory is covered and its mastery is essential, but it is my belief that the average reader grasps theory more completely when it is given specific content. To this end, I have supplemented the economic theory with case studies and other content ranging across the role of economic institutions, the analysis of international economic policies, and the recent history of the world economy. Second, the objective of covering both the micro and macro sides in a one-semester course necessitates a paring back of the theory to focus on the central concepts. As all instructors are aware, many of the theoretical topics found in texts are of secondary or tertiary importance. This often poses a problem for students because they lack the needed breadth and depth of understanding to rank topics by their relative importance. Third, *International Economics* provides richer historical and institutional detail than most other texts. This material illuminates the relationships between economic theory and policy, and between economics and the other social sciences. Fourth, I have organized the final section of the text around five area studies chapters, covering North America, the European Union, Latin America, East Asia, and the transition economies. These chapters offer students the chance to broaden their understanding of world trends and to observe the intellectual power of economic theory in practice.

New to the Second Edition

The revisions in this Second Edition fall into four broad areas.

1. Trade and finance topics reorganized into two distinct parts: In the Second Edition, Part 2 of the text features international trade and commercial policy, and Part 3 covers the balance of payments, exchange rates, and other core areas of international macroeconomics.

2. Three brand-new chapters: Expanded coverage of finance topics is highlighted by an all-new Chapter 11 on open-economy macroeconomics and an all-new Chapter 12 on current international financial crises. A new Chapter 8 probes into the effects of international trade on labor and the environment.

3. Increased emphasis on the Internet: For every chapter, the text's Companion Web Site offers a set of Web links, along with detailed descriptions of the material they contain, presenting possibilities for student papers and research projects. Many of the think tanks and international organizations listed in the Web resources have a constant flow of accessible, student-friendly working papers and policy briefs that can add depth to the topics discussed in *International Economics*.

4. Thoroughly updated case studies: I have added many new case studies to the Second Edition, covering such controversial topics as the NAFTA region as an optimal currency area (Chapter 10), the Mexican peso crisis (Chapter 12), the Free Trade Area of the Americas (Chapter 13), and the euro (Chapter 14).

Content Updates

I am gratified by the positive reception accorded the First Edition of *International Economics*, and have fine-tuned the Second Edition as follows:

- *Chapters 1 and 2* provide more information on the major actors in the international economy. Chapter 1 includes a new discussion of the evidence linking trade to economic growth, and Chapter 2 introduces regional trade agreements.

- *Chapter 5* expands the discussion of economies of scale and trade, previously in Chapter 4 in the First Edition. Additionally, it condenses the material on industrial policies that was in Chapter 7 of the First Edition, and develops the link between external economies and industrial policies.

- *Chapter 8* is an entirely new chapter on labor and environmental standards. The chapter begins with a discussion of the costs and benefits of harmonizing standards and the alternatives to harmonization. It then examines labor and environmental standards and links them to the discussion of commercial policy in Chapters 6 and 7.

- *Chapter 9*'s coverage of the balance of payments incorporates the recent changes undertaken by the United States to make its international accounting methodology consistent with IMF recommendations.

- *Chapter 11* is an entirely new chapter on open-economy macroeconomics. The presentation integrates principles-level macroeconomics with exchange rates and current accounts.

- *Chapter 12*, also a new chapter, covers the important topic of international financial crisis. Two basic types of crises are described, and policies for crisis avoidance and crisis response are discussed. The chapter ends with an overview of the recent discussion of reforms in the international financial architecture.

- *Chapter 14* on the European Union includes an updated discussion of governance issues, EU expansion, and the euro, including the causes of its surprising weakness after its introduction in 1999.

Flexibility of Organization

A book requires a fixed topical sequence because it must order the chapters one after another. This is a potential problem for some instructors, as there is a wide variety of preferences for the order in which topics are taught. The Second Edition strives for flexibility in allowing instructors to find their own preferred sequence.

The two introductory chapters that make up Part 1 are designed to build student vocabulary, develop historical perspective, and provide background information about the different international organizations and the roles that they play in the world economy. Some instructors prefer to delve into the theory chapters immediately, and reserve this material for later in the course. There is no loss of continuity with this approach.

Part 2 presents the micro side of international economics, while Part 3 covers the macro. These two parts can easily be reversed in sequence if desired. Part 2's six chapters cover trade models (Chapters 3–5) and commercial policy (Chapters 6–8). A condensed treatment of this section could focus on the Ricardian model in Chapter 3, and the analysis of tariffs and quotas in Chapters 6 and 7. Chapter 8 on labor and environmental standards can stand on its own, although the preceding chapters deepen student understanding of the trade-offs.

Part 3 covers the balance of payments, exchange rates, open-economy macroeconomics, and international financial crises. Chapter 11 in Part 3, on open economy macroeconomics, is optional. It is intended for students and instructors who want a review of macroeconomics, including the concepts of fiscal and monetary policy, in a context that includes current accounts and exchange rates. If Chapter 11 is omitted, Chapter 12 remains accessible as long as students have an understanding of fiscal and monetary policy. Chapter 12 relies most heavily on Chapters 9 (balance of payments) and 10 (exchange rates and exchange rate systems).

Part 4 has five area studies chapters. These chapters use the theory in Chapters 3-12 in a way that is similar to the economics discussion that students find in the business press, congressional testimonies, speeches, and other sources intended for a broad civic audience. Where necessary, concepts such as the real rate of exchange are briefly reviewed. One or more of these chapters can be moved forward to fit the needs of a particular course.

Supplementary Materials

The following supplementary resources are available to support teaching and learning.

Companion Web Site: www.aw.com/gerber

- Kati Suominen of the University of California, San Diego, has prepared a Web-based PowerPoint presentation comprising lecture notes and most of the text's tables and figures to accompany the Second Edition. An art-only presentation is also available for instructors who wish to create their own PowerPoint presentation.

- In recognition of the importance of the Internet as a source of timely information, the Web site offers 5–7 Web links, also prepared by Kati Suominen of the University of California, San Diego, for each chapter of *International Economics*. These links, complete with descriptions of the content available at each site, provide easy access to relevant data sources.

In addition to the Companion Web site, the Web content is available in CourseCompass™ and Blackboard versions. CourseCompass™ is a nationally hosted, dynamic, interactive online course management system powered by Blackboard, leaders in the development of Internet-based learning tools. This easy-to-use and customizable program enables professors to tailor content and functionality to meet individual course needs. To see a demo, visit *www.coursecompass.com*. Please contact your local sales representative for more information on obtaining Web content in these various formats.

Instructor's Manual

Seid Hassan of Murray State University has revised the Instructor's Manual to bring it up to date with the text. Each chapter in the manual begins with an outline of the text chapter and a brief discussion of the chapter goals. The Instructor's Manual also has answers to the end-of-chapter questions and at least twenty multiple-choice questions for each chapter.

Acknowledgments

More than anyone, my wife Joan contributed to this book, both through her emotional support and the wonderful family life she created around me. I apologize for all the days and nights I neglected her and our daughters while working on this project.

Textbooks cannot be written by a single person. Without the feedback of students, colleagues, practitioners, and the publishing team at Addison-Wesley, this text would never have seen the light of day. I hope that this book can at least partly repay what I owe to them.

For all their efforts and professionalism, I am deeply grateful to Denise Clinton, Editor-in-Chief at Addison-Wesley; Christine Houde, the project manager for the Second Edition; Sylvia Mallory, Executive Development Manager; and Juliet Silveri, Production Supervisor. I would also like to thank Kathy Smith for copyediting the manuscript, and Chris Lukinbeal, whose maps have greatly enhanced *International Economics*.

Finally, my gratitude goes to the numerous reviewers who have played an essential role in the development of *International Economics*. Each of the following individuals reviewed the manuscript, many of them several times, and provided useful commentary. I cannot express how much the text has benefited from their feedback.

Mary Acker
Iona College

Jeff Ankrom
Wittenberg University

David Aschauer
Bates College

H. Somnez Atesoglu
Clarkson University

Eugene Beaulieu
University of Calgary

Ted Black
Towson University

Bruce Blonigen
University of Oregon

Lee Bour
Florida State University

Byron Brown
Southern Oregon University

Tom Carter
Oklahoma City University

Jen-Chi Cheng
Witchita State University

Don Clark
University of Tennessee

Raymond Cohn
Illinois State University

Peter Crabb
Northwest Nazarene University

David Crary
Eastern Michigan University

Al Culver
California State University, Chico

Joseph Daniels
Marquette University

Craig Depken II
University of Texas, Arlington

John Devereaux
University of Miami

K. Doroodian
Ohio University

Noel J.J. Farley
Bryn Mawr College

Lewis R. Gale IV
University of Southwest Louisiana

Ira Gang
Rutgers University

Joanne Gowa
Princeton University

Gregory Green
Idaho State University

Thomas Grennes
North Carolina State University

Winston Griffith
Bucknell University

Seid Hassan
Murray State University

Paul Jensen
Drexel University

George Karras
University of Illinois at Chicago

Kathy Kelly
University of Texas, Arlington

Abdul Khandker
University of Wisconsin, La Crosse

Jacqueline Khorassani
Marietta College

Sunghyun Henry Kim
Brandeis University

Vani Kotcherlakota
University of Nebraska at Kearney

Corrine Krupp
Michigan State University

Kishore Kulkarni
Metropolitan State College of Denver

Farrokh Langdana
Rutgers University

Daniel Y. Lee
Shippensburg University

Mary Lesser
Iona College

Susan Linz
Michigan State University

Thomas Lowinger
Washington State University

Mary McGlasson
Arizona State University

Joseph McKinney
Baylor University

Judith McKinney
Hobart & William Smith Colleges

Howard McNier
San Francisco State University

Michael O. Moore
George Washington University

Stephan Norribin
Florida State University

William H. Phillips
University of South Carolina

Donald Richards
Indiana State University

John Robertson
University of Kentucky Community College System

Jeffrey Rosensweig
Emory University

Raj Roy
University of Toledo

George Samuels
Sam Houston State University

Craig Schulman
University of Arizona

William Seyfried
Winthrop University

David Spiro
Columbia University

Richard Sprinkle
University of Texas, El Paso

Ann Sternlicht
Virginia Commonwealth University

Leonie Stone
State University of New York at Geneseo

Henry Thompson
Auburn University

Cynthia Tori
Valdosta State University

Edward Tower
Duke University

Jose Ventura
Sacred Heart University

Michael Welker
Franciscan University

Jerry Wheat
Indiana State University

Chong K. Yip
Georgia State University

Part 1

INTRODUCTION AND INSTITUTIONS

Chapter 1

THE UNITED STATES IN A GLOBAL ECONOMY

INTRODUCTION

During the summer of 1997, an economic crisis hit East Asia, beginning first in Thailand and then spreading to Indonesia, Malaysia, the Philippines, and South Korea. Currency values fell, stock markets crashed, and credit dried up. Several countries appealed to the International Monetary Fund (IMF) for emergency loans and by the fall of 1997 the IMF was spelling out the terms and conditions for its assistance. There was a sense of urgency in addressing the problem since the crisis was spreading globally. Japanese and European banks were heavily exposed with a large number of bad loans to the region, North and South American stock markets felt pressures from nervous investors, and American firms prepared for a wave of cheap imports brought on by the depreciated Asian currencies. While the crisis posed a threat to global economic stability, it was in fact only the latest in a series of episodes over the last decades. The Mexican peso collapse in 1994, speculation against the European Monetary System in 1992, the overvalued U.S. dollar in the mid-1980s, and the onset of the third-world debt crisis in 1982, all posed equally serious challenges to global financial stability.

Each of these events is a dramatic reminder that national economies are linked through extensive networks of financial and commercial relations. During the last decade, terms such as *globalization* and *integration* came into common usage as shorthand references to the strengthening of these networks and the deepening of interdependencies among national economies. While global financial crisis is one reminder of these links, several long-term trends have also fostered a growing awareness of the international economy and international economic interdependence. Japanese penetration of U.S. automobile and consumer electronics markets in the 1970s and 1980s, growing U.S.–Mexico trade ties and the start of the North American Free Trade Agreement in 1994, and the recent increase in international stock funds have all sparked Americans' interest in the international economy.

Increased awareness of the international economy has been accompanied by two kinds of extreme views. On the one hand, many people feel left out by the global changes in technology and economic relations. They see a dark future in which national economies are ruled by anonymous forces in a world market that is beyond their control. Others see a new global economy that requires completely new modes of analysis in order to understand the issues and opportunities it presents. Both views are mistaken. The global economy is new, but it is also old. Technology has shortened communication and transportation times, but so did technological developments in the second half of the 1800s. At the margin, technological improvements in communications and transportation in the second half of the 1800s may have had a greater impact than those we are experiencing today. The world today is far more integrated economically than in the recent past, but the changes are not without precedent. In the late 1800s, Midwestern wheat farmers, Chicago meatpackers, and California fruit growers were all part of an international market. Although this earlier episode was reversed by two world wars and a decade-long world depression, it tells us that our own period is perhaps not as unique as we might believe it to be.

A brief historical comparison is a useful and sobering exercise for making sense of the extraordinary changes that have taken place in the international economy over the last several decades. The advantage of a long-term perspective is that it can protect us from unrealistic enthusiasm (or fear) about recent changes in international economic relations. We begin with a closer look at a very basic issue: How important is the international economy in relation to our domestic economy?

GLOBALIZATION IN PERSPECTIVE

There is no doubt that the economy of the United States is more integrated with other national economies than at any time in the last sixty or seventy years. It is tempting to say that global economic integration is greater than at any time in history, yet that is less certain than it may seem. In the age of the Internet, e-mail, and fax machines, it is easy to lose sight of the fact that most of what we buy and sell never makes it out of our local or national markets. We are aware of the fact that the parts in our cars are made in a dozen or more countries, but we should not forget that haircuts, restaurant meals, gardens, health care, education, financial services utilities, most entertainment, and many other goods and services are domestic products. In fact, for the United States, about 87 percent of what we currently consume is made inside our borders, since imports are equal to about 13 percent of our total economic output. In 1890, we made about 92 percent of what we consumed, a larger share than today, but not radically different.

Imports and exports are one criterion by which we can judge the importance of the international economy, but they are not the only one. Integrated economies are also linked by the movement of capital and labor. Consider, for example, the fifty states of the United States. No one could claim that they are fully integrated if workers and investment flows were not free to move across state lines. This is also true of national economies where the degree of freedom in the movement of capital and labor is a key indicator of the depth of their integration. A third marker of economic integration is the movement of prices in different markets. When economies become linked to each other, price differences across markets should shrink as goods and services are allowed to move freely across international boundaries. Each of these indicators, (1) trade flows, (2) factor movements, and (3) similarity of prices, are measures of the degree of international economic integration.

The Growth of World Trade

Since the end of World War II, world trade has grown much faster than world output. World output, which is equivalent to world income, has risen about six-fold over the last fifty years, while world trade has grown about twelvefold. As a result, trade has become a larger share of most national economies. One measure of the importance of international trade in a nation's economy is the sum of exports plus imports, divided by the **gross domestic product (GDP)**, where GDP is a measure of total production. Specifically, it is the value of all final goods and services produced inside a nation during some period, usually a year. The ratio of trade to GDP is called the **index of openness**:

$$\text{Index of Openness} = (\text{Exports} + \text{Imports}) / \text{GDP}.$$

It should be stressed that openness does not tell us about a country's trade policies; that is, countries with higher openness measures do not necessarily have lower barriers to trade, although that is one possibility. Large countries are less dependent on international trade because their firms can reach an optimal production size without having to sell to foreign markets. Consequently, smaller countries tend to have higher measures of openness than big countries.

The openness indices for the United States are shown in Figure 1.1. One factor that stands out is the decline in the importance of U.S. international trade between 1890 and 1950. In 1890, the openness indicator was over 15 percent. Then, as now, recent technological innovations in communications and transportation made it easier to trade over long distances. For example, the trans-Atlantic telegraph cable (1866) increased information flows, ocean-going steamships and better navigation charts cut travel times, and new national railroad networks connected domestic markets. The British navy, which suppressed piracy and provided security on the high seas, also contributed to the increase in international commerce. By 1890, U.S. products such as grain, beef, and timber were sensitive to commodity price movements around the world.

From the start of World War I until the end of World War II, many of the gains in market integration were eroded. The two world wars and the Great Depression of the 1930s caused nations to cut their trade ties, partly for strategic military reasons and partly to protect their home industries from import competition during the Depression. High tariffs (import taxes) were enacted throughout the world and total world trade declined dramatically during the interwar period. In effect, part of the growth of trade since 1950 has simply brought our economy back to where it was at the end of the nineteenth century.

Figure 1.1 shows that the relative importance of international trade has increased by about 50 percent over its importance in 1890, but an important

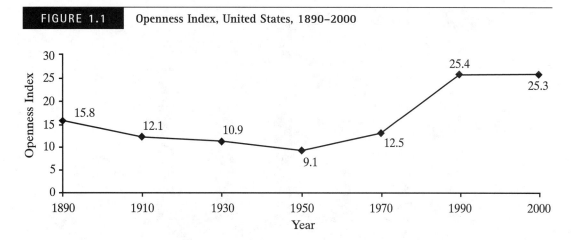

FIGURE 1.1 Openness Index, United States, 1890–2000

The openness index for the U.S. economy decreased from the 1890s until around 1950; since then it has risen to about 50 percent above its level in 1890.

trend is obscured within this data. In 1890, most U.S. trade was in agricultural products and raw materials, while today, most American exports and imports are manufactured goods. More specifically, the importance of capital goods (machinery and equipment) has increased dramatically. Consequently, producers of manufactured items are far more exposed to international competition than they were at the beginning of the twentieth century.

Figure 1.2 illustrates the increase in merchandise goods exports; it does not include services. (Services are about 25 percent of total exports.) Relative to the size of our economy (GDP), goods exports increased from their low point of 3.6 percent in 1950 to 7.7 percent by 2000. Over the same period, however, merchandise exports grew from 8.9 percent of goods production to 41.3 percent. In other words, by the criteria of international competition, U.S. manufacturers are now far more integrated into the world economy than they were in 1950 (or, for that matter, in 1890).

Capital and Labor Mobility

In addition to exports and imports, factor movements are also an indicator of economic integration. As national economies become more interdependent, labor and capital should move more easily across international boundaries. Taking the case of labor first, at the beginning of the twenty-first century, labor is much less mobile internationally than it was at the start of the twentieth century. As one indicator of this trend, in 1890 approximately 14.5 percent of the U.S. population was foreign born, while the figure for the 1990s was less

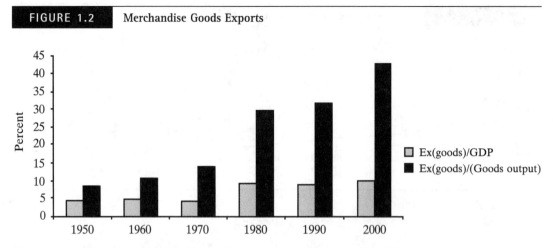

| FIGURE 1.2 | Merchandise Goods Exports |

Manufacturing is far more exposed to international competition than it was in 1950 since a larger proportion of total goods production is exported.

Source: Irwin, Douglas, "The United States in a New Global Economy? A Century's Perspective." *American Economic Review*, May 1996; and author's calculations.

than 8 percent. At the start of the twentieth century, many nations had open door immigration policies, and passport controls, immigration visas, and work permits were the exception rather than the rule. In the 1920s, the United States sharply restricted immigration and international labor mobility declined. These restrictions lasted until the 1960s, when changes in immigration laws once again encouraged foreigners to migrate to the United States, albeit at numbers far lower than in the 1800s.

On the capital side, measurement is more difficult, since there are several ways to measure capital flows. The most basic distinction is between flows of financial capital representing paper assets (stocks, bonds, currencies, bank accounts, etc.) and flows of capital representing physical assets (real estate, factories, businesses, etc.). The latter type of capital flow is called **foreign direct investment**, or **FDI**. To some extent, the distinction between the two is immaterial, because both types of capital flows represent shifts in wealth across national boundaries and both make one nation's savings available to another. Nevertheless, since FDI represents cross-border capital flows related to the purchase of land and businesses, it is longer term and less likely to reverse itself and flow out of a country on short notice.

When we compare today's trends to those of a century ago, we should keep two points in mind. First, if there were a single world capital market, then the investment rates (Investment/GDP) of any particular country would not need to be correlated with its savings rates (Savings/GDP). Capital would flow to the countries that offered the highest (risk-adjusted) rates of return. Since capital is abundant in high-income countries and relatively scarce in developing countries, we should expect to see higher risk-adjusted returns in developing countries and enormous flows into them. While capital flows to developing countries have grown significantly over the last decades, it is, however, still true that the level of investment in any country is highly correlated with its level of savings. Low-savings countries have low investment levels, and high-savings countries have high investment levels. In other words, national savings rates are a far more important determinant of a nation's investment than is the global capital market.

The second point to bear in mind is that at the end of the nineteenth century, what was true for trade flows was also true for capital flows. Late-nineteenth-century capital was mobile, partly because of the same technological improvements that increased trade flows. For example, in 1866 the first trans-Atlantic cable linked New York to the world's largest financial market in London, decreasing the time required to obtain market information and conclude a transaction from about three weeks to just one day. One effect was that the gap in interest rates and asset prices between New York and London shrank significantly.

Capital flows at the end of the nineteenth century also increased from the enormous capital demands for railroad and mine construction in the colonies and former colonies of the European powers. At the same time, the development of financial market institutions such as Wall Street and stock, bond, and commodity exchanges aided the growth of capital markets and capital flows. In the late nineteenth and early twentieth centuries, Great Britain annually supplied 5 to 10 percent of their GDP to world capital markets and at its peak invested as much abroad as it did domestically. Today, countries with large flows of foreign investment (all kinds) rarely supply more than 2 to 3 percent (net) of their GDP to world capital markets. As was the case for labor mobility and trade flows, capital mobility was also reduced by the two world wars and the Great Depression. Industrial countries began to restrict capital flows during the 1920s, and in most cases, capital mobility did not begin to recover until the 1970s and 1980s.

Three main differences separate capital flows at the beginning of the twenty-first century from those at the end of the nineteenth century. First, there are many more financial instruments available now than there were a century ago. These range from the relatively well known instruments such as stocks and mutual funds, to relatively exotic instruments such as derivatives, ADRs, currency swaps, and others. In aggregate, they represent a wide variety of instruments that can be tailored to nearly every level of income and risk tolerance. Many of these new financial instruments are complex, specialized tools designed to meet very narrow objectives in an innovative and more open global economy. By contrast, at the turn of the twentieth century, there were only a few hundred stocks listed on the New York Stock Exchange, and most international financial transactions involved the buying and selling of bonds. All the financial innovation of the late twentieth century is a sign that flows of financial capital are much larger than they were in the nineteenth century. According to the Bank for International Settlements in Geneva, Switzerland, *daily* foreign exchange transactions in 1998 were equal to $1.5 *trillion*, whereas in 1973, they were $15 billion.

The increase in financial transaction involving currency exchanges is related to the second major difference between capital flows today and those a hundred years ago. In 1900, the world operated on a fixed exchange rate standard. This means that there was little or no risk of losing money on a foreign investment because of a decrease in value of the foreign currency. By comparison, protecting against exchange rate risk is a key component of today's international financial markets and accounts for a significant share of the day-to-day international transactions of financial institutions.

The third major difference in capital flows is that the costs of foreign financial transactions have fallen significantly. Economists refer to the costs of obtaining market information, negotiating an agreement, and enforcing the agreement (if necessary) as **transaction costs**. They are an important part of any business's costs, whether it is a purely domestic enterprise, or involved in foreign markets. Due to sheer distance, as well as differences in culture, laws, and languages, transaction costs are often higher in international markets than they are in domestic ones. Today's lower transaction costs for foreign investment means that it is less expensive to move capital across international boundaries. Along with the deregulation of capital controls in the 1970s and 1980s, lower transaction costs have significantly increased capital flows.

The sometimes extremely volatile movement of financial capital into and out of national markets is often regarded as a new feature of the international economy, but this is a shortsighted view. Speculative excesses and overinvestment, followed by capital flight and bankruptcies, have occurred throughout the modern era, going back at least as far as the 1600s and probably farther. U.S. history has a number of cases. During the fifty years after 1890, at least four episodes of overspeculation and crisis hit the U.S. economy: 1890 to 1893 (speculation in silver stocks), 1907 (coffee futures and trust companies), 1920 to 1921 (agricultural land), and 1929 (U.S. stocks). As long as enough people cling to the get-rich-quick dream, and as long as domestic policymakers are subject to human error, the world will probably continue to experience episodes of volatile capital flows and speculative excess. One of the challenges of economic policymaking is to tame this type of excess without making things worse by destroying more beneficial types of capital flows.

New Features of the Global Economy

Belief in an unprecedented era of globalization is not justified by the analysis. While international economic integration has been rapid, it does not appear to be historically unprecedented. Trade, as measured by the openness index, is about 50 percent more important to the U.S. economy. Labor is less mobile than earlier in our history, but capital is somewhat more mobile. Prices in many

U.S. and foreign markets tend to be similar, although there are still significant differences (the price of a pair of denim jeans in the United States and Europe, for example). Given these patterns, is anything fundamentally different about today's economy, other than the size of capital flows and the increased amount of trade? The answer is "Yes."

New Issues in International Trade and Investment. Most high-income, industrial countries have few barriers to imports of manufactured goods. There are exceptions (e.g., processed foodstuffs, textiles, and apparel), but as a general rule, import tariffs are low and other forms of protection are uncommon. Low trade barriers are the result of a process that began at the end of World War II and that has had a slow cumulative effect in rolling back the high levels of protection that were implemented in the 1920s and 1930s. The relative absence of tariffs outside of agriculture and apparel manufacturing does not mean that there are no barriers to trade, however. As countries gradually eliminated their formal restrictions on imports, various domestic policies have become barriers to further increases in trade flows. These policies include sensitive issues such as labor conditions, environmental policy, the rules of fair economic competition, limits on investment, and government support for specific industries. As long as formal restrictions on imports kept out many goods, differences between nations in their domestic policies were unimportant. As formal barriers came down, however, purely domestic policies became hindrances to the further growth of trade flows.

Negotiations between nations can be difficult in these areas both because the rules and laws are complex and because they represent fundamental elements of domestic policy. Reducing a tax on imports is simple by comparison, particularly if other nations agree to similar cuts. When nations open their markets symmetrically, through simultaneous reductions in import taxes, it is easily understood by the electorate and appeals to their sense of fairness. A similar symmetry in changing labor standards, or investment rules, is more difficult to define. When restrictive investment rules are eliminated, for example, it may seem that there is no reciprocal action, and that foreign influence has undermined national sovereignty.

Economists refer to the elimination of **tariffs** (taxes on imports) and **quotas** (quantitative restrictions on imports) as **shallow integration**, or integration at the border. By contrast, the elimination or reduction of trade barriers that stems from domestic policies is referred to as **deep integration**.

The issues of deep integration take up a sizable part of the dialogue between nations over matters related to foreign trade and investment. Economically, it is not necessary and is often undesirable that nations should adopt the same or similar policies. Nevertheless, small countries fear that they will be forced to adopt the standards of the United States or some other industrial economy, and large countries such as the United States worry that their domestic policies will be determined by the collective action of small countries. An international dialogue on these issues is a relatively new experience.

The Role of International Organizations. At the end of World War II, the United States, Britain, and their allies created a number of international organizations that were given active roles in maintaining international economic and political stability. Although the architects of these organizations could not envision the challenges and issues that would confront the international economy over the next fifty years, they gave the institutions significant flexibility. These institutions play an important and growing role, in part as a forum for addressing the issues of deep integration.

The International Monetary Fund (IMF), the World Bank, the General Agreement on Tariffs and Trade (GATT), the United Nations (UN), the World Trade Organization (WTO began operation in 1995, but grew out of the GATT), and a host of smaller organizations have broad international participation. They serve as forums for discussing and establishing rules, as mediators of disputes, and as organizers of actions to resolve problems. All of these organizations are controversial and have come under increasing fire from critics who charge that they promote unsustainable economic policies that often destroy the environment and protect the interests of wealthy elites. Many critics argue they are also tools of the United States and other rich nations, while critics in the United States sometimes argue that they are unnecessary foreign entanglements that severely limit the scope for national action (Chapter 2 examines this issue in detail). For better or worse, these organizations represent a series of attempts at creating internationally acceptable rules for trade and commerce and at dealing with potential disputes before they spill across international borders. Without a doubt, they are an entirely new element in the international economy.

Regional Trade Agreements. Agreements between groups of nations are not new. Free-trade agreements and other forms of preferential trade have existed throughout history. What appears to be new is the significant increase in the number of **regional trade agreements** that have been signed in the last twenty years, especially in the 1990s. It is still too early to say if this is a new trend or simply a phenomenon that will soon disappear.

The formation of preferential trade agreements is controversial. Trade opponents dislike the provisions that expose more of the national economy to international competition, whereas some trade proponents dislike the preferential nature of these agreements, which invariably favors regions included in the agreement at the expense of regions outside the agreement. The North American Free Trade Agreement (NAFTA), the European Union (EU), the Mercado Común del Sur (Mercosúr), and Asia Pacific Economic Cooperation (APEC) are the largest alliances, but they are only the tip of the iceberg of regional economic alliances.

Trade and Economic Growth

It is not surprising that many people are more than a little apprehensive about increased international economic integration. The list of potential problems is a long one. More trade may give consumers lower prices and greater choice, but it also means more competition for firms and workers. Capital flows make more funds available for investment purposes, but they also increase the risk of spreading financial crises internationally. Rising immigration means higher incomes for migrants and lower labor costs for firms, but also more competition in labor markets and, inevitably, greater social tensions. International organizations may help resolve disputes, but they may also reduce national sovereignty by putting pressure on countries to make changes in the way they operate. And free-trade agreements may increase trade flows, but again, that means more competition and more pressure on domestic workers and firms. Given the pluses and minuses, it seems imperative to ask if these changes are worth it.

In general, economists remain firmly convinced that the benefits of trade outweigh the costs. While there is disagreement over the best way to achieve different goals (e.g., how to protect against the harmful effects of sudden flows of capital), the general belief in openness to the world economy as a superior policy to closing off a country is quite strong. In order to support this stance, there are three kinds of evidence that economists can point to. First, there is the casual empirical evidence of historical experience. Second, there is the evidence based on economic models and deductive reasoning. And third, there is the evidence of statistical comparisons of countries. While no one of these three is conclusive by itself, taken together they provide solid support for the idea that more open economies grow faster and prosper sooner than more closed ones.

The historical evidence examines the experiences of countries when they tried to isolate themselves from the world economy. There is the experience of the 1930s when most countries tried to protect themselves from world events by shutting out flows of goods, capital, and labor. This did not cause the Depression of the 1930s but it most likely worsened it and, ultimately, led to the misery and tragedy of World War II. There are also the parallel experiences of countries that were divided by war, with one side becoming closed to the world economy, the other side open. Germany and Korea are the best examples, but all of Eastern Europe stands in stark contrast to the prosperity and cleaner environments of Western Europe after World War II. There are also the experiences of Latin America and East Asia in the 1960s, 1970s, and 1980s. It is perhaps not too much of a generalization to say that East Asia integrated itself into the world economy and watched growth take off, while Latin America partially closed its doors and got mediocre growth and a decade of depression and crisis in the 1980s.

The logic of economic theory generally supports these examples by suggesting the causal mechanisms that lead from trade to faster growth. While it must be pointed out that trade theory also points to cases where the costs of trade may outweigh the benefits (see Chapter 5), in general, the benefits of increased innovation and access to new technologies and ideas that are fostered by trade are seen as positive factors. Trade increases the quality and quantity of machinery and equipment, and leads to more output. On the consumer side, it provides a greater variety of goods and offers them at lower prices. Both the variety and cost factors are real increases in consumer income.

The statistical evidence for the benefits of more open economies comes from comparisons of large samples of countries over different periods. While the statistical tests of the relationship between trade policy and economic growth suffer from their own technical shortcomings (usually problems of measuring trade policy), the results consistently show that more open economies grow faster. These results cannot be viewed as absolutely conclusive, but based on the historical evidence, on trade theory, and on the statistical tests taken as a whole, it would be unreasonable to believe that trade is generally bad for the economy.

ELEVEN ISSUES IN THE INTERNATIONAL ECONOMY

The chapters that follow will examine a number of these and other issues. Each of the following eleven themes raises a number of important issues for the international economy. In some cases, international economics provides a relatively straightforward method of analysis for understanding the issues. In other cases, the themes are overlapping, many-sided, and interdisciplinary. International economics cannot claim the final word on these issues, yet in the chapters that follow you will find that it provides an analytically powerful and logically consistent approach. It would be a huge mistake to dismiss the economic analysis of these issues.

The Gains from Trade (Chapters 3, 4, and 5)

Why is international trade desirable? We have already briefly addressed this issue, and will consider additional points as we go along. Given that economic analysis clearly demonstrates that the benefits of international trade outweigh the costs, it is not surprising that virtually all economists support open markets and increased trade. Recent polls of economists put the level of agreement on this issue at around 98 percent, when a general question is asked about the desirability of closed versus open markets. The benefits were first analyzed in the late 1700s, and are perhaps the oldest and strongest finding in all of economics. Given the certainty of the benefits from trade, why do many non-economists oppose it?

Wages, Jobs, and Protection (Chapters 3, 6, 7, and 8)

Whereas international trade benefits the majority of people in a national economy, it does not usually benefit every member of society. Workers in firms that cannot compete may be forced to find new jobs or to take pay cuts. The fact that consumers pay less for the goods they buy, or that exporters hire more workers, may not help them. Increased awareness of the international economy has heightened the fears of people who feel vulnerable to changes in the international economy. They are concerned that wages in the United States must fall in order to compete with workers in low-wage countries or that their jobs may be moved overseas. The solution, according to some, is to keep foreign goods out—particularly goods that are made by laborers who are paid less than American workers. One of the key issues challenging policymakers is to find the right mix of domestic policies so that the nation benefits from trade without creating a backlash from those individuals and industries that are hurt.

Trade Deficits (Chapters 9 and 11)

In 1980, a comprehensive measure of the United States's trade accounts showed that there was a slight surplus of $2.3 billion. It was all downhill from there and by 2000, the same measure had fallen to a deficit of $435 billion. Each year a country runs a trade deficit, it must borrow from abroad, essentially selling a piece of its future output in order to obtain more goods and services today. Among other things, large trade deficits have been known to cause currencies to collapse and to generate severe crises in financial systems, usually followed by deep recessions. The impact of large trade imbalances is uncertain, however, and the conditions that cause one country's deficits to disappear, and another's to turn into a deep recession, are imperfectly understood.

Regional Trade Agreements (Chapters 2, 13, and 14)

As the world economy becomes more integrated, some regions are running ahead of the general trend. Western Europeans, for example, have eliminated many of the economic barriers separating their nations, and are creating a broad political and economic union. With implementation of the North American Free Trade Agreement (NAFTA) in 1994, the United States, Canada, and Mexico are moving toward a free trade area. The largest countries in the Pacific Basin, including China, Japan, and the United States, have agreed to turn the Pacific region into a free trade area by the year 2020. The United States and thirty-three other nations in the Western Hemisphere are negotiating a hemispheric free-trade area which is targeted to begin by 2005. Country by country, Eastern Europe has applied for membership in the European Union, and the Association of South East Asian Nations (ASEAN) has moved toward the creation of a free-trade zone among its member states.

The Resolution of Trade Conflicts (Chapters 2, 7, and 8)

Commercial conflicts between nations cover a wide variety of issues and complaints. In one sense these conflicts are routine since the World Trade

Organization (WTO) provides a formal dispute resolution procedure that has the assent of most of the world's nations. The WTO process does not cover all goods and services, however, nor does it say much about a large number of practices that some nations find objectionable. The ability of nations to resolve conflicts without resorting to protectionist measures is one key to maintaining a healthy international economic environment. Disputes can become acrimonious, so it is imperative that differences of opinion not be permitted to escalate into a wider disagreement. Trade wars are not real wars, but they are harmful enough.

The Role of International Institutions (Chapters 2 and 12)

The organization with the greatest responsibility for resolving trade disagreements is the World Trade Organization (WTO). The WTO came into existence in 1995 and was an adaptation of the General Agreement on Tariffs and Trade (GATT), which was created shortly after World War II. Resolving trade disputes is only one of the new roles played by international organizations. Various organizations offer development support, technical economic advice, emergency loans in a crisis situation, and other services and assistance. These organizations perform services that were not offered before World War II (development support), or that were done by a single country (lending in a crisis)—usually the world's greatest military power. They exist today only through the mutual consent and cooperation of participating nations, and without that cooperation, they would dissolve. Their abilities are limited, however. They cannot prevent crises, and they cannot make poor countries rich. They are also controversial and are viewed by some as tools of the United States or as a threat to national independence. They are very likely to grow in function, however, as concerns grow over problems such as global warming, which lack a purely national solution.

Exchange Rates and the Macroeconomy (Chapters 10 and 11)

Twelve of the fifteen members of the European Union have given up on their own currency and have jointly adopted the new euro, which will appear in January, 2002. A number of Latin American nations have adopted the dollar (Panama, Ecuador, El Salvador). Others have put a straightjacket on their central banks and made it illegal to create new money that is not backed by something valuable such as the U.S. dollar. Throughout the world, countries are struggling to decide whether to keep their money, and to find the best exchange rate system if they do. Floating rates, fixed rates, and crawling pegs each have important implications for domestic economic policy and all serve as a two-way communication link between the domestic and world economies. When exchange-rate systems develop problems, nations sometimes fall into deep recessions.

Financial Crises and Global Contagion (Chapter 12)

As trade and investment barriers have crumbled, and as fax, e-mail, and satellite communication systems have grown, it is easier to move capital across international borders. This trend is bolstered by lower transaction costs for foreign investment and increased availability of different types of financial assets. The increase in international capital flows has created an impression that the global economy is more unstable today than it was in the past. As discussed earlier, financial crisis is an old story, but the increase in global capital flows during the 1990s has led to discussions about techniques for reducing volatile capital flows across international borders. In particular, how do countries tame the capital flows that add to instability without stopping those that create valuable new investment? Given that the volatility of international capital flows is not likely to disappear, this issue will continue to be a topic of discussion and investigation.

Crisis and Reform in Latin America (Chapter 15)

Beginning in the early 1980s, many of the nations of Latin America entered into a crisis brought on by high levels of debt owed to banks and governments outside the region. The crisis was characterized by deep recessions, high interest rates, bankruptcies, falling wages, and increasing poverty. Throughout the region, the 1980s came to be called the Lost Decade, a name that symbolized the absolute lack of progress in meeting economic development needs. Beginning in the mid-1980s, a series of policy reforms emerged out of the debt crisis and spread across Latin America. Economies that had been sheltered from international competition were opened, and the region gave up its traditional, inward-looking policies dating from the 1930s. The story of this shift in national policies, from inward- to outward-looking perspectives, is one of the most interesting and significant stories in the international economy of the late twentieth and early twenty-first centuries.

Export-Led Growth in East Asia (Chapter 16)

Throughout the late 1980s and into the 1990s, it has been hard to ignore the East Asian "miracle." While some economists have pointed out that it is not really a miracle—just a lot of hard work and sound economic policies—the growth rates of the "high-performance Asian economies" are unique in human history. Rates of growth of real GDP *per person* commonly reached 4 to 5 percent per year, with 6 to 8 percent not unusual. The crisis in East Asia, beginning in 1997, tarnished the image of the region, but it would be a mistake to lose sight of the long run. By 1999, most countries had returned to positive growth and were on their way to a full recovery. The costs have been high, but the recovery is beyond most forecasters' expectations. One of the dominant traits of the countries in East Asia is the extent to which they are outward looking and dependent on the growth of their manufactured exports.

The Integration of Ex-Socialist Countries into the World Economy (Chapter 17)

Chinese reforms and the collapse of communism are the final themes taken up in this book. China began its transition to capitalism with a set of reforms that began in 1978, while the Soviet empire broke up in 1989, and the Soviet Union itself ceased to exist at the end of 1991. All these countries are in the midst of changes that will transform their domestic economies and leave them far more integrated into the world economy. The impact on the world economy promises to be huge, and the effects are already appearing. Eastern Europe has turned west and is lobbying for admission into the European Union (EU). In all the transition economies, the demand for capital to build modern economies is growing significantly as the development of business practices and legal institutions encourages greater confidence among outside investors. China, the nations of central and eastern Europe, and all but two of the countries created out of the former Soviet Union are members of the WTO, or are negotiating their membership.

The following chapters explore each of these eleven issues in more detail. Chapter 2 begins with a discussion of the role of international institutions, while Chapters 3 through 12 develop the tools of international economic analysis. The final five chapters of the book, Chapters 13 through 17, make use of these tools to analyze important regional trends and issues.

Vocabulary

deep integration

foreign direct investment

gross domestic product (GDP)

index of openness

quotas

regional trade agreement

shallow integration

tariffs

transaction costs

Study Questions

1. How can globalization and international economic integration be measured?
2. In what sense is the U.S. economy more integrated with the world today than it was a century ago? In what ways is it less integrated?
3. What is "openness"? How is it measured? Does a low openness indicator indicate that a country is closed to trade with the outside world?
4. Describe the pattern over the last century shown by the United States's openness index.

5. Trade and capital flows were described and measured in relative terms rather than absolute. Explain the difference. Which seems more valid, relative or absolute? Why?

6. The relative size of international capital flows may not be much greater today than they were 100 years ago, although they are certainly greater than they were 50 years ago. Qualitatively, however, capital flows are different today. Explain.

7. What are the new issues in international trade and investment? In what sense do they expose national economies to outside influences?

8. Describe the three kinds of evidence economists use to support the assertion that open economies grow faster than economies that are closed to the world economy.

Chapter 2

INTERNATIONAL ECONOMIC INSTITUTIONS SINCE WORLD WAR II

INTRODUCTION: INTERNATIONAL INSTITUTIONS AND ISSUES SINCE WORLD WAR II

As World War II was drawing to a close, representatives from the United States, Great Britain, and other Allied nations met in the small New Hampshire town of Bretton Woods. The outcome of these meetings was a series of agreements that created an exchange rate system (which lasted until 1971), the International Bank for Reconstruction and Development (IBRD), also known as the World Bank, and the International Monetary Fund (IMF). In 1946, two years after Bretton Woods, twenty-three nations including the United States and Britain began talks on reducing their trade barriers, leading to the General Agreement on Tariffs and Trade (GATT), which began operation in 1948.

Chapter 2 focuses on these global economic institutions, their history, their role in the world economy, and controversies surrounding their activities. Institutions that do not have a primary economic role, such as the General Assembly of the United Nations or the North Atlantic Treaty Organization (NATO), are not included.

International Institutions

International economic institutions are an important feature of the world economy. When social scientists try to explain the increasing integration of national economies after World War II, one of the key explanations must be the increased stability and reduced uncertainty that these institutions help create. Nevertheless, as international economic integration has increased, these organizations have come under more scrutiny and received much criticism. Before we look at their impact and some of the criticisms that have been levied at them, we should define what we mean by an *institution*.

What Is an "Institution"?

Most people probably think of a formal organization when they hear the word *institution*. Economists tend to define **institutions** more broadly, however. For example, the "New Institutionalists," led by economist Douglas North, have argued that organizations are not institutions in themselves, although they may embody one. In this view, institutions are the rules that govern behavior. They tells us what is permissible and what is not; they are constraints that limit our actions.

Institutions can be formal or informal. A formal institution is a written set of rules that explicitly state what is and is not allowed. The rules may be embodied in a club, an association, or a legal system. An informal institution is a custom or tradition that tells people how to act in the same way that a law does, but without legal enforcement. For example, informal institutions include the rules of socializing, gift exchange, table manners, e-mail etiquette ("netiquette"), and so forth. In this chapter, the term *institution* refers to both rules and organizations.

A Taxonomy of International Economic Institutions

International economic institutions come in many sizes and shapes. They can be lobbying groups for a particular commodity or an international producer's association; the joint management by several nations of a common resource; trade agreements or development funds for a select group of nations; or even global associations. Although this chapter's focus is on global economic institutions, it is useful to look at a taxonomy of international economic institutions, from the most limited and specific, to the most general. Table 2.1 shows five main types.

THE IMF, THE WORLD BANK, AND THE WTO

Three global organizations play a major role in international economic relations and are central to this book: the International Monetary Fund (IMF), the World Bank, and the World Trade Organization (WTO). Two of them, the IMF and the World Bank, date from the end of World War II, while the WTO started in 1995 as a result of trade negotiations that ended in 1993. The WTO grew out of the General Agreement on Tariffs and Trade (GATT), which it deepens and broadens. Accordingly, it is useful to know the history and function of the GATT as well as the WTO.

The IMF and World Bank

During World War II, the United States and Great Britain (and a few other Allies) held regular discussions about the shape of the postwar international economic order. They wanted to avoid the mistakes of the 1920s and 1930s, when a lack of international cooperation led to the complete collapse of economic relations. The culmination of these talks was the Bretton Woods meetings in July of 1944, where the Allies created the outlines of the **International**

TABLE 2.1	A Taxonomy of International Economic Institutions, with Examples
Type	*Examples*
Commodity or industry-specific organizations: These range from trade associations, to international standards setting bodies, to powerful cartels.	■ Oil Producing and Exporting Countries (OPEC) ■ International Telecommunications Union (ITU) ■ International Sugar Organization ■ International Lead and Zinc Study Group
Commissions and agencies for managing shared resources.	■ International Boundary and Water Commission (IBWC) ■ Lake Chad Basin Commission ■ Mekong River Commission
Development funds and banks.	■ Inter-American Development Bank (IDB) ■ North American Development Bank (NADBank) ■ Asian Development Bank ■ Islamic Development Bank
International trade agreements involving a few nations (regional trade alliances or trade blocs).	■ North American Free Trade Agreement (NAFTA) ■ US-Israel Free Trade Agreement ■ Mercado Común del Sur (Mercosúr) ■ Asia-Pacific Economic Cooperation (APEC) ■ Enterprise for the Americas Initiative (EAI)
Global organizations for trade, development, and macroeconomic stability.	■ International Monetary Fund (IMF) ■ World Bank ■ World Trade Organization (WTO)

Monetary Fund (IMF) and the **International Bank for Reconstruction and Development (World Bank)**.

The IMF began operation on December 27, 1945 with a membership of twenty-nine countries. Its success is indicated by the fact that by the year 2000, it had grown to 182 members. The IMF provides loans to its members under different programs for the short, medium, and long term. Each member is charged a fee, or quota, as the price of membership, the size of the quota varying with the size of the nation's economy and the importance of its currency in world trade and payments. Currently, the IMF has nearly $300 billion in quotas. Important decisions within the IMF are made by vote with the weight of each nation's vote proportional to its quota. This gives the high-income countries of the world a voting power that is disproportionate to their population. For example, the United States alone controls almost 18 percent of the total votes, and the G-7 (the seven largest industrial economies: Canada, Italy, France, Germany, Japan, the United Kingdom, and the United States) control almost 45 percent. Some votes on IMF policy require a "super majority" of as high as 85 percent, giving the United States a veto power on those particular issues. The size of the quota also determines a country's access to loans.

The most visible role for the IMF is to intercede, by invitation, whenever a nation experiences a crisis in its international payments. For example, if a country imports more than it exports, then it may run out of its reserves of foreign exchange that are used to pay for foreign goods. **Foreign exchange reserves** are dollars, yen, pounds, German marks, or another currency (or gold) that is accepted internationally. If a country lacks reserves, it cannot pay for its imports, nor can it pay the interest and principal it owes on its international borrowings. This is one scenario that warrants a call to the IMF. The IMF makes loans to its members, but it usually extracts a price above and beyond the interest it charges. The price is an agreement by the borrower to change its policies so that the problem cannot recur. If simple economic reforms such as a cut in the value of the currency, or limits on the central bank's creation of credit, are insufficient to permanently solve the problem, then the IMF usually requires a borrower to make fundamental changes in the relationship between government and markets in order to qualify for IMF funds. These requirements are known as **IMF conditionality**.

The IMF also performs several related functions. In the current world economy, it has been an important source of both technical expertise and capital for the transitional economies of Central and Eastern Europe. These economies lack experience with open markets and large private sectors. They have had to create tax systems, social programs, and business codes from scratch, and the IMF has been a major source of information and financing. This role too, is not without controversy. The IMF has also been the main provider of funds and advice to the crisis-gripped economies of East Asia, again, with a great deal of controversy over the advice it gave and the conditions it imposed.

The **World Bank** was founded in 1944 at same time as IMF. Currently (2001), there are 183 members. Members buy shares in the Bank and, similar to the quotas that determine voting rights in the IMF, shareholding determines the weight of each member in setting the Bank's policies and practices. Originally, the World Bank was known as the International Bank for Reconstruction and Development, or IBRD. The name reflected the fact that it was primarily created to assist in the reconstruction of the war-torn areas. As the capital requirements for reconstruction grew, however, it soon became apparent that the IBRD lacked sufficient funds to do the job and, in 1948, the United States created the parallel program known as the Marshall Plan to assist Europe.

By the 1950s, the field of development economics had begun to take off. Several leading economists were able to make credible arguments that the world's less economically developed regions could grow much faster if they could get around the constraints imposed by a lack of investment capital, and the IBRD was encouraged to lend to developing economies. Today, the IBRD is one of five separate subgroups that make up the World Bank. The role of the IBRD is to lend for specific development projects such as dams, highways, and schools, and to support major adjustments in government policies that change the way they manage the economy. Other sub-groups in the World Bank are focused on the very poor, private sector development, and loan guarantee programs. Only developing countries can borrow from the World Bank.

The GATT, the Uruguay Round, and the WTO

At the end of World War II, a third global economic organization was proposed, to be named the International Trade Organization (ITO). If it had been implemented, the ITO's job would have been to establish rules relating to world trade, business practices, and international investment. U.S. opposition killed the idea of the ITO, however, and no such organization was created until 1995. Nevertheless, in 1946, while they were still considering the idea of the ITO, twenty-three countries opened negotiations over tariff reductions. These negotiations led to some 45,000 tariff reductions affecting $10 billion, or one-fifth of world trade. In addition, a number of agreements were made on rules for trade, with the expectation that the rules would become a part of the ITO. Both the tariff reductions and the rules were implemented in 1948; when the possibility of an ITO died in 1950, the agreements on tariffs and trade rules remained in force as a separate agreement, known as the **General Agreement on Tariffs and Trade**, or **GATT**. The GATT has been very successful in gradually bringing down trade barriers. One indicator is that international trade has grown more than 6 percent per year over the last fifty years, which is much faster than before the war and faster than growth in the world's total output.

The GATT functions through a series of **trade rounds** in which countries periodically negotiate a set of incremental tariff reductions. Gradually, through the Kennedy Round in the mid-1960s and the Tokyo Round of the 1970s, trade rules other than tariffs began to be addressed, including the problems of dumping (selling in a foreign market below cost or below a fair price), subsidies to industry, and nontariff barriers to trade. As tariffs came down, these nontariff issues became more prominent.

The GATT intentionally ignored the extremely contentious sectors of agriculture, textiles, and apparel. In addition, trade in services was ignored because it was not important. The accumulation of unresolved issues in these sectors, however, along with the increased importance of nontariff trade barriers, led to the demand for a new, more extensive set of negotiations. These demands culminated in the **Uruguay Round** of trade negotiations that began in 1986 and concluded in 1993. In 1994 the new agreement was signed by 125 countries, and by 2001 its membership had grown to 140 members, with approximately another 30 in the process of negotiating to join.

Every two years, trade ministers from around the world meet to set the broad policy objectives of the WTO. Day-to-day work, however, is done by the WTO's staff (General Council), under the leadership of the Director-General. The WTO's rules for trade consist of twenty-nine separate legal texts, plus more than twenty-five declarations, memoranda of understanding, and joint statements. The key concepts of all WTO agreements, however, were carried over directly from the GATT: **nondiscrimination** and **national treatment**. More broadly, these concepts are realized in the general mission of the WTO, which includes insurance of market access, promotion of fair competition, and encouragement of economic development and economic reform.

The important concept of nondiscrimination is embodied in the idea of **most favored nation status**, or **MFN**. MFN requires every member of the WTO to treat each of its trading partners as well as it treats its most favored trading partner. In effect, it prohibits one country from discriminating against another. The main exception to MFN is that it permits trade agreements such as the NAFTA (North American Free Trade Agreement) and does not require a country to extend the same treatment to countries outside the agreement. National treatment says that imports may not be treated any differently from domestically produced goods. In other words, imports must have the same market access as similar domestic goods.

The Uruguay Round and the establishment of the WTO were genuine reforms in the rules of world trade. The WTO preserves the GATT while reaching into new areas, including agriculture, textiles, and services; it replaces the GATT's dispute resolution procedure with a faster and more effective mechanism; and it monitors national trade practices more closely.

CASE STUDY

The GATT Rounds

Agreements in the GATT forum to reduce trade barriers take place in "rounds" of negotiations. Counting the first round, there have been eight rounds of negotiations, the most recent being the Uruguay Round, which ended in 1993. Originally, the GATT was an international agreement and not an organization. The failure to create the International Trade Organization in 1950, however, resulted in the gradual conversion of the GATT into a *de facto* organization by 1960, with a permanent secretariat to manage it from Geneva. Table 2.2 lists the various rounds of negotiations.

(*continues*)

TABLE 2.2	The GATT Rounds	

Round	Year	Number of Participants
Geneva I	1947	23
Annecy	1949	13
Torquay	1951	38
Geneva II	1956	26
Dillon	1960–1961	26
Kennedy	1964–1967	62
Tokyo	1973–1979	102
Uruguay	1986–1993	105

The first five rounds were organized around product-by-product negotiations. Beginning with the Kennedy Round, negotiations were simplified. Countries negotiated an across-the-board percentage reduction in all tariffs for a range of industrial products. One effect is that tariffs have never been uniform across countries. The goal has been to bring them all down, but not necessarily to create the same tariff for all countries.

The Tokyo Round is notable because it was the first round to begin to establish rules regarding subsidies. Subsidies give an industry a competitive advantage since the national government pays part of the cost of production, either through direct payment or indirectly through subsidized interest rates, artifi-cially cheap access to foreign currency, or in some other way. The Tokyo Round began the laborious process of creating rules in this area, one of the most important of which was the agreement to prohibit subsidies for exports of industrial goods (but not agricultural goods or textiles and apparel).

The subsidy issue of the Tokyo Round was carried forward into the Uruguay Round, where subsidies were defined in greater detail. The Uruguay Round accomplished many other things as well, not the least of which was the creation of the World Trade Organization as a formal organization to oversee and administer the GATT. Additional accomplishments are described in Chapter 7, which explores trade policy and trade barriers in more detail.

REGIONAL TRADE AGREEMENTS

Trade agreements between two or more countries constitute another important type of institutional structure in the world economy. Many of these have familiar names—NAFTA, the EU, etc.—but basic differences in the common types of agreements are less familiar. These regional agreements are usually classified into one of four categories of trade agreements, but they often include more than trade, and they do not fit very neatly into nonoverlapping categories. Reality is far messier than a classification scheme, and most formal agreements between nations combine incomplete elements from two or more of the categories. In addition, it is useful to recognize a fifth type of agreement, a **partial trade agreement**, that does not rise to the level of the first category. With a partial trade agreement, two or more countries agree to liberalize trade in a selected group of categories. This type of agreement has become common, particularly among developing countries, whenever there is a reluctance to completely open the economy to a set of trading partners, but all partners desire free trade for a limited group of commodities. With a partial trade agreement, for example, two countries might agree to free trade in certain manufactured goods, but maintain protectionist barriers in other areas.

Four Types of Regional Trade Agreements

As more goods are included in the partial trade agreement, it begins to look more like a **free trade area**. An example is the North American Free Trade Agreement (NAFTA), but there are many others such as the European Free Trade Area (EFTA) and the U.S.-Israel Free Trade Agreement. In a free trade area, nations are allowed to trade goods and services across international boundaries without paying a tariff and without the limitations imposed by **quotas**, which are direct limits on imports. In reality, however, most free trade areas such as NAFTA do not allow completely free trade. Nations usually reserve some restrictions for particularly sensitive items. For example, as part of its efforts to protect its culture, Canada limits the quantity of U.S. television programs that Canadian television stations may purchase. With a free-trade area, nations usually keep their own health, safety, and technical standards, and may deny entry of imports if they do not meet national standards. For example, the United States does not allow Mexican avocados to enter California (where they are grown) because farmers claim that they contain a seed weevil that would destroy the U.S. crop.

The next level of integration is called a **customs union**. A customs union is a free-trade area plus a common external tariff towards nonmembers. Between the mid-1970s and the early 1990s, the European Union was a customs union, and in today's economy, Mercosúr (Brazil, Argentina, Uruguay, and Paraguay) is one. This means that the four members have free trade with each other and the same tariff on imports from nonmembers, for example American computers. As with free-trade areas, many items are usually left out of the agreement. In the European case, each nation retained its own tariffs and quotas with respect to Japanese autos. **Common markets** are the next level beyond customs unions. A common market is a customs union plus an agreement to allow the free mobility of inputs, such as labor and capital. The clearest example, again, is the European Union in the 1990s. Soon after his election in 2000, the president of Mexico, Vicente Fox, indicated that he would like to see the NAFTA countries move toward becoming a common market, but the problems associated with allowing free mobility of labor are probably too great to think that this will happen anytime soon. Nevertheless, the three NAFTA countries have elements of a common market (without the common external tariff) since they allow capital to move freely around the region. NAFTA also grants relatively free movement to certain types of white-collar labor, such as architects, business consultants, and others.

The final level of economic integration is **economic union**. An economic union is a common market with substantial coordination of macroeconomic policies, including a common currency, and harmonization of many standards and regulations. The clearest examples are the states of the United States or the provinces of Canada. The BENELUX Union of Belgium, the Netherlands, and Luxembourg is an example of separate nations that have formed a union, and the European Union is in the process of becoming an economic union, with the euro, its common currency, and, at some point, a common defense policy and common citizenship rights.

CASE STUDY

Prominent Regional Trade Agreements

Each of the four levels of integration are examples of different kinds of **regional trade agreements (RTAs)**, or **trade blocs**. The question naturally arises as to how many there are and whether they are beneficial or harmful for the world economy. The simple question—how many?—is difficult to answer precisely. Many of the agreements do not fit neatly into any of the four categories listed above, so it is not clear if they should be counted. That is, should all partial agreements be counted when they are not quite free-trade areas, yet they have elements of free trade, customs unions, and even common markets? In addition, many of the agreements are either on paper only (have no real effect), or have yet to be fully negotiated and/or implemented. Until there is substantial implementa-

tion, there is always the possibility that the agreement will collapse, since opening an economy inevitably generates opposition from uncompetitive sectors.

Countries that have signed the GATT are obligated to notify the GATT secretariat when they form an RTA. According to the WTO, since the implementation of the GATT in 1948, they have been notified of over 200 RTAs. Some of these are defunct, but over 130 are still operating. Most of the still-functioning agreements were started in the 1990s, with 90 agreements entering into force since 1995. Europe accounts for about 65 percent of the RTAs currently in force, and about 78 percent of all RTAs involve developed countries only (43 percent) or developed and developing countries (35 percent).

The answer to the second question above—are they beneficial or harmful?—is even more difficult to ascertain. A 1995 study by the WTO concluded that in most cases "regional and multilateral integration initiatives are complements rather than alternatives." Broadly speaking, the WTO sees these agreements as helping it to further reduce trade barriers. This view is not shared by all economists, however, as any regional agreement must favor the interests of its members over the interests of outsiders. In other words, there is an element of discrimination that goes against the WTO's fundamental principle of equal treatment (most favored nation). Preferential treatment for members of the trade agreement causes most regional trade agreements to destroy some of the trade between their members and nonmembers. The WTO recognizes this problem, but argues that as long as a regional agreement creates more new trade than it destroys, the net result is beneficial. In addition, the WTO sees the regional trade agreements as places where countries can try out new arrangements, some of which will be eventually incorporated into the larger, global agreement.

Nearly all WTO members belong to at least one RTA, and many countries belong to several. For example, Mexico is a member of NAFTA, but it recently completed a free-trade agreement with the European Union, and has bilateral agreements with Chile, Venezuela, and a number of other countries. Table 2.3 lists some of the RTAs currently in force. Among the best known are the European Union, the European Free Trade Association, the North American Free Trade Agreement, MERCOSÚR in South America, the ASEAN Free Trade Area in southeast Asia, and COMESA in eastern and southern Africa. There are many more, however, ranging from tariff agreements on a subset of output to common markets and economic unions. The dates in parentheses are the dates of implementation of the agreements.

Sources: Harmsen, Richard, and Michael Leidy, "Regional Trading Arrangements," in *International Trade Policies: The Uruguay Round and Beyond. Volume II: Background Papers.* Washington, DC: International Monetary Fund. 1994.

The WTO, "Regionalism." Geneva: The World Trade Organization. *http://www.wto.org/english/thewto_e/whatis_e/tif_e/ bey3_e.htm.* Accessed October 6, 2000.

TABLE 2.3	Prominent Regional Trade Blocs

Region/Country	Objective
Africa	
COMESA—Common Market for Eastern and Southern Africa (1993)	Common market
ECCAS—Economic Community of Central African States (1992)	Common market
ECOWAS—Economic Community of West African States (1975)	Common market

(*continues*)

TABLE 2.3	Prominent Regional Trade Blocs *(continued)*	
Region/Country		*Objective*
Asia		
AFTA—ASEAN Free Trade Arrangement (1992)		Free-trade area
ANZCERTA—Australia-New Zealand Closer Economic Relations (1983)		Free-trade area
APEC—Asia-Pacific Economic Cooperation (1989)		Free-trade area
Europe		
CEFTA—Central European Free Trade Arrangement (1992)		Free-trade area
EEA—European Economic Area (1994)		Common market
EFTA—European Free Trade Association (1960)		Free-trade area
EU—European Union (1957)		Economic union
Middle East		
ACM—Arab Common Market (1964)		Customs union
AMU—Arab-Maghreb Union (1989)		Economic union
GCC—Gulf Cooperation Council (1981)		Common market
Western Hemisphere		
ANCOM—Andean Common Market (1969)		Common market
CACM—Central American Common Market (1961)		Customs union
CARICOM—Caribbean Community (1973)		Common market
MERCOSUR—Southern Cone Common Market (1991)		Common market
NAFTA—North American Free Trade Area (1994)		Free-trade area

THE ROLE OF INTERNATIONAL ECONOMIC INSTITUTIONS

In every part of the world, people rely on institutions to create order and to reduce uncertainty. By defining the constraints or limits on economic, political, and social interactions, institutions define the incentive system of a society and help to create stability. The provision of order and the reduction of uncertainty are so important that when they are absent, economies cannot develop. Within a nation, the formal rules of behavior are defined by the various levels of government. In the United States, for example, this includes cities, counties, special districts, states, and the federal government. In the international sphere, however, there are no corresponding sets of government. The establishment of rules for international trade and international macroeconomic relations are dependent on the voluntary associations of nations in international economic organizations.

The primary difference between international economic organizations and the government of a single nation is that the former have limited enforcement power. National and local governments have police powers that they can use to enforce their rules; international organizations have no police power, but they do have more subtle powers for encouraging cooperation. For example, the IMF and World Bank can withdraw lines of credit to developing countries. The withdrawal of IMF credit and its "stamp of approval" raises a red flag for private lenders and makes it more costly for uncooperative nations to gain access to capital in private markets. Likewise, the WTO can legitimize retaliatory sanctions against nations that fail to honor their trade obligations. At bottom, however, international organizations rely on moral suasion and the commitments of individual nations to remain effective. If nations choose to withdraw their support from an international organization, it dies.

The provision of order and the reduction of uncertainty are services that everyone values. This is why we pay police officers, judges, and legislators. Although public order and the lessening of uncertainty are intangibles, they are desired and valued in the same sense that more tangible material objects are. Their economic characteristics are different from most goods and services however, and they fall into the category known as **public goods**.

The Definition of Public Goods

By definition, public goods are (1) **nonexcludable** and (2) **nonrival** or **nondiminshable**. Nonexcludability means that the normal price mechanism does not work as a way of regulating access. For example, when a signal is broadcast on the airwaves by a television station, anyone with a TV set who lives in its range can pick it up. (Of course, this is not the case with cable stations, which are granted permission to scramble their signals. Signal scrambling is a clever technological solution to the problem of nonexcludability.)

The second characteristic of public goods is that they are nonrival or nondiminishable. This refers to the attribute of not being diminished by consumption. For example, if I tune in to the broadcast signal of a local TV station, all my neighbors will have the same amount available to them. Most goods get smaller, or diminish, when they are consumed, but public goods do not.

Private markets often fail to supply optimal levels of public goods because of the problem of **free riding**. Free riding means that there is no incentive to pay for public goods because people cannot be excluded from consumption. Given this characteristic, public goods will not be produced optimally by free markets unless institutional arrangements can somehow overcome the free riding. In most cases, governments step in as providers and use their powers to tax as a means to force people to pay for the good.

Maintaining Order and Reducing Uncertainty

Two of the most important functions of international economic institutions are to maintain order in international economic relations and to reduce uncertainty. Taken together, these two functions are often instrumental in the avoidance of a global economic crisis. Furthermore, if a national crisis threatens to become global, international institutions often help to bring it to a less costly end and to prevent nations from shifting the cost of national problems to other countries.

The maintenance of order and the reduction of uncertainty are general tasks that require specific rules in a number of areas of international economic interaction, although economists do not completely agree on the specific rules or the specific types of cooperation that should be provided. Nevertheless, the proponents of international institutions such as economist Charles Kindleberger, have noted several areas where institutions are needed in order to strengthen cooperation and prevent free riding in the provision of international public goods. Among the items he lists are the four public goods in Table 2.4.

TABLE 2.4	Four Examples of International Public Goods	
Public Good	*Purpose*
1. Open markets in a recession	To prevent a fall in exports from magnifying the effects of a recession.
2. Capital flows to less-developed countries (LDCs)	To assist economic development in poor countries.
3. International money—for settlement of international debts	To maintain a globally accepted system for paying debts.
4. Last resort lending	To prevent the spread of some types of financial crises.

Kindleberger and others have argued that the absence of a set of rules for providing one or more of these public goods has usually been a key part of the explanation of historical crises such as the worldwide Great Depression of the 1930s. The specific items in Table 2.4 may be debatable, but the basic point is sound. If no international institutions are available to help nations overcome the tendency to free ride, then international economic stability grows more fragile. As an illustration, consider the first item listed. During recessions, politicians begin to feel enormous pressure to close markets in order to protect jobs at home. During the 1930s, for example, most nations enacted high tariffs and restrictive quotas on imports. This set in motion waves of retaliation as the nations that lost their foreign markets followed suit and imposed their own tariffs and quotas. In the end, no one benefited and international trade collapsed.

In essence, each nation was free riding. That is, everyone prefers a situation in which all markets are open over one in which all markets are closed. Each nation tries to let other countries be the ones to stay open and to pay the price of a loss of some jobs in import-competing industries. In a recession, free riders want to close their markets to reduce imports and create more jobs. At the same time, however, they want all other nations to stay open so that they do not lose any export markets. These desires are inconsistent, and the effect of free riding behavior is that all countries retaliate by closing their markets, international trade collapses, and everyone is worse off than before. Kindleberger shows that the shift in trade policies towards high tariffs and restrictive quotas helped intensify and spread the Great Depression of the 1930s.

Kindleberger also argues that the sudden decline in capital flows to developing countries in the 1930s and the complete absence of a **lender of last resort** deepened the Depression and provides further historical evidence for the importance of international institutions. The lack of a lender of last resort was particularly critical because a number of countries with temporary financial problems soon passed into full-blown financial collapse. As it became impossible for them pay their foreign debts, the crisis spread from the indebted nations to the lending nations.

No one has tried to measure the frequency of potentially disastrous international economic events. Their occurrence is not infrequent, however, and it is relatively easy to list a number of recent events that have had the potential, if improperly handled, to turn into major global problems: the debt crisis in many developing countries in the early 1980s, the collapse of the Mexican peso in December of 1994, the transition to capitalism by the socialist countries, the Asian crisis of 1997, Russia's default on its debt in 1998—the list is fairly long.

In each crisis or potential crisis, international institutions play an important role by preventing free riding. Lacking much in the way of formal enforcement mechanisms, they overcome the free rider problem by changing each nation's expectations about every other nation. For example, if all countries are committed to open markets, in good times and bad, then during a worldwide recession, no country expects its trading partners to close their markets. As another example, if each country pays a share of the IMF's operating funds, then it overcomes the problems that arise when each country waits for the others to make risky loans during a crisis. The effectiveness of international institutions depends on the credible commitment of the world's nations. If a country agrees to a set of rules, but has a reputation for breaking its agreements, then its commitment is not credible. Institutions cannot overcome the free rider problem under those circumstances.

CASE STUDY

Bretton Woods

After World War I, the United States retreated into a relative isolationism under the mistaken belief that noninvolvement in European affairs would protect the country from entanglement in disastrous European conflicts such as the First World War. The rise of Hitler, Japanese aggression in the Pacific, and the start of World War II showed that this policy would not work.

The United States began to realize its mistake in the 1930s as it watched Hitler take over a large part of the European continent. U.S. and British cooperation and planning for the postwar era began before the United States entered the war in December, 1941, and long before the outcome was known. President Roosevelt and Prime Minister Churchill met on a battleship off the coast of Newfoundland in August, 1941. Soon after, they announced the Atlantic Charter, a program for postwar reconstruction that committed both nations to working for the fullest possible economic collaboration between all nations after the war. Concurrent with the Atlantic Charter, the United States and Britain began discussing the kinds of international institutions that might be proposed.

All parties agreed that in any postwar order, the United States would have to be the political, military, and economic leader. It had surpassed Britain in wealth and size several decades earlier, and its leadership during the war gave it prestige and credibility. In addition, the United States's physical infrastructure was not damaged by the war, and it was the only industrial nation able to provide the financial capital and physical material needed to repair the war damage.

Looking back to the 1920s and 1930s, the postwar planners recognized four serious problems that they should guard against: (1) the worldwide depression; (2) the collapse of international trade; (3) the collapse of the international monetary system; and (4) the collapse of international lending. Discussions during World War II were mainly devoted to rules, agreements, and organizations that could be created to avoid these problems. Three international institutions were viewed as central for the achievement of these goals:

1. An international organization to help stabilize exchange rates and to assist nations that are unable to pay their international debts
2. Agreements to reduce trade barriers
3. An international organization for providing relief to the war-damaged nations, and to assist with reconstruction

Plans for the postwar period were finalized at a conference held in July, 1944, in **Bretton Woods**, New Hampshire. The Bretton Woods institutions include the International Monetary Fund, the World Bank, and the Bretton Woods exchange rate system. Although it was conceived separately, the General Agreement on Tariffs and Trade is sometimes included because it embodies the goals and ideas of the Bretton Woods planners with respect to international trade. Taken together, these four are a historically unique set of international economic institutions, and each, in its own area, has played a key role in the history of the international economy since 1945.

The founding principles of the Bretton Woods institutions are relatively simple. First, trade should open in *all* countries, not just the United States alone, or the United States and the United Kingdom together. In economic terms, this was a call for multilateral opening, as opposed to unilateralism (one-sided opening) or bilateralism (two-sided opening). Second, nations should not discriminate against other nations. Whatever tariffs and quotas the United Kingdom or the United States might levy against another country, they should be the same ones imposed on everyone. Third, in order to ensure the ability of importers to purchase goods abroad, countries should not limit the buying and selling of currency when its purpose is to pay for imports. Fourth, exchange rates should be fixed but with the possibility for periodic adjustment. These four principles formed the cornerstones of the institutions.

THE OPPOSITION TO INTERNATIONAL INSTITUTIONS

The IMF, the World Bank, the WTO, and the various regional agreements have helped to open markets and to bring a degree of stability to the world economy. Still, not everyone agrees that the results are positive on balance. When the world's trade ministers met to discuss a new round of WTO negotiations in Seattle in December, 1999, they were met by tens of thousands of protesters, and when the IMF held its annual meetings in Prague in September, 2000, the demonstrators were there again. The global institutions have become targets for the uneasiness that many people feel about the rapid changes occurring in the world economy. Few people are willing to march in protest, but many people question whether the global institutions are fostering development and economic security or whether they are protecting the interests of a small group of extremely wealthy people.

It is important to distinguish between two very different critiques of global institutions. The first is a criticism of the idea of globalization (international economic integration), which is defined by the 1998 winner of the Nobel Prize in Economics, Amartya Sen, as the "intensification of the process of interaction involving trade, migration, and dissemination of knowledge that have shaped the progress of the world over millennia." It is impossible to see how the world would benefit from curtailing the interactions of people living in different nation states. In fact, most people would view the end of social and economic interactions as a gross violation of human rights. Clearly, the alternative to globalization and its interactions is separation and isolation, both of which are giant backward steps for human society.

Many critics of the global institutions are not anti-internationalists, however, because they do not argue against globalization in principle. Instead, they see it as harmful in practice, given the way it is happening. Their critique focuses on the priorities of global institutions and the way they make policy without accountability for the results. This criticism comes in many flavors, from some of the street protesters in Seattle and Prague, to politicians of different ideologies, to leading social scientists. Among these critics of the global institutions, it is possible to distinguish two overlapping but different strands of criticism. One criticizes the decision-making processes of the global institutions, including their relative lack of openness to public input, while the other is a series of technical criticisms of the institutions on the grounds that their economic analysis and policymaking is flawed. Complaints about the decision-making process and the lack of public input are discussed below, while a discussion of the debate over their technical analysis and policy is reserved for Chapter 12, after the introduction of several important concepts.

In order to put the decision-making processes of the global institutions in perspective, it is useful to recall that they were created in the 1940s to solve technical problems such as exchange rate depreciations and trade imbalances, and to overcome various free rider problems in the provision of international public goods, such as the need for a lender of last resort and a gradual, coordinated reduction of trade barriers. They have generally done a good job at building support for open markets and in bringing greater efficiency to international economic policies. What they have not done, however, is to address the inequalities of income and opportunity that persist throughout the world. To be fair, they were not created to fight discrimination, corruption, or inequality, and the world of the 1940s was much more tolerant of those violations of human and civil rights.

The world of the twenty-first century is different in this regard, however, as there is much less tolerance for inequality in all its forms. Meanwhile, the global institutions have been slow to respond to this shift in thinking. In part, this is probably a result of being run by experts who are mainly responsible to the political leaders of the countries that appoint them. Given that the institutions were designed to solve technical problems, this is a reasonable arrangement, as long as the issues are relatively narrow in scope. Building broad-based support for markets, and creating the conditions that allow them to function effectively, however, requires more than a set of techniques. Markets cannot work properly if a broad set of national and subnational institutions that support them are absent, such as education, health care, civil and human rights, access to credit, and others. When these social institutions are missing, the people of a country or a region or a social class cannot fully participate in the market economy, and the policies of the global institutions mainly support a limited subset of a nation's population. This is not to say that the policies are necessarily harmful to the rest of the population, although that is one possibility. The point is that people outside a market economy cannot take advantage of free trade, stable exchange rates, or foreign investment.

In response to the criticism that it ignores the needs of large numbers of people, the World Bank has shifted its policies toward broader support for economic security and the development of social institutions such as schools and health care systems. The World Bank is more capable of this type of adjustment since the changes are within the framework of its mission to promote development. The IMF has been less responsive to criticisms of its policies, in part because its mission is primarily defined in terms of the relatively narrow framework of international finance. Nevertheless, there is some movement toward examining the effects of its policies on the most vulnerable groups. Similarly, the role of the WTO is fairly narrow, as a promoter of trade and not as a promoter of social development. Consequently, it lacks the authority and the resources to support a worldwide development of social institutions.

Critics of the global institutions argue that one of the reasons for the failure to consider the effects of policies on vulnerable groups is that these and other institutions are relatively closed to grassroots input from civic and social organizations. In other words, there is little opportunity for subnational organizations to express their views or to provide information about the local effects of national policies. Again, this was originally by design, as the global institutions were envisioned as forums for national governments. The historical doctrine of the sovereignty of nations gives national governments the exclusive right to address issues within their national boundaries, and foreign governments or foreign interest groups have no legal right to address conditions inside another country. Yet, international integration has broken down some of these barriers, in part by creating civic and social groups, for example environmental groups, whose membership and areas of concern cross national boundaries. This has increased the demand for greater responsiveness on the part of the global institutions to the various grassroots organizations such as labor unions, environmental groups, and human rights groups. The way in which each of the global institutions will adapt to these new demands for openness and dialogue remains to be seen.

From the standpoint of the institutions, it is difficult to know who is represented by the various grassroots groups demanding a voice. This is a serious problem since the various groups are not always models of democracy either, and it would be harmful for everyone if the value system of a vocal minority were imposed on a whole nation or a group of nations. By way of illustration, consider the following hypothetical case. A developing country, with the help of World Bank loans, harvests the timber in its forests, which it sells in international markets. The logging, trucking, and milling of the logs creates jobs that are badly needed, but the logging in particular is destructive of the forests and the wildlife that lives there. An internationally based environmental group, along with local environmentalists, protest the logging and the World Bank loans that make it possible. Should the loans be curtailed? Should the logging be stopped? Who should have authority to decide whether the loans are beneficial or not—the World Bank staff, the environmentalists, the national government, or the people who benefit from the jobs?

The tension between the sovereignty of national governments on the one hand, and the demands by civic and social groups to be heard on the other, is a key part of the conflict over the role of the global institutions. The pessimistic view of this conflict is that it will roll back some of the international integration of the last decades and leave us all poorer as a result. There is a historical precedent for this view in the antiglobalization movement at the end of the nineteenth century and the beginning of the twentieth century. The optimistic view is that a greater voice for the environment and human and civic rights is a positive development because ultimately it will lead to better policies and wider participation in the benefits of international economic integration.

This is not an issue that will be resolved soon. All of the global institutions are attempting to create forums for wider civic and social input—as well as to provide more information so that their critics will be better informed about actual policies and procedures. How successful they will be in converting the critics to a more benign view of the role of global institutions, and a deeper appreciation for the benefits of international integration, remains to be seen. As of this writing, a widespread, popular backlash against these institutions remains a distinct possibility, as does the continued movement toward greater integration.

Summary

1. Institutions are the "rules of the game." They can be formal, as in a nation's constitution, or informal, as in a custom or tradition. In either case, humans depend on institutions as a mechanism for creating order and reducing uncertainty. Global institutions have played an important role in fostering the growth of international trade and investment during the last fifty years. They have defined a set of rules that have helped avoid trade wars and the problems of the 1930s.

2. The "Big 3" of international economic organizations are the International Monetary Fund, the World Bank, and the World Trade Organization. The latter grew out of the General Agreement on Tariffs and Trade. The IMF, World Bank, and GATT were created at the end of World War II with the purpose of avoiding a return to the destructive economic conditions of the interwar years (between World War I and World War II).

3. Regional trade agreements are another important type of international institution, although they are not global in scope. Formally, there are four types of regional trade agreements. In order, from less integrated to more integrated, they are free-trade areas, customs unions, common markets, and economic unions. Each level is cumulative and incorporates the features of the previous level. The real world is messier than this, however, and actual trade agreements usually combine features from two or more types.

4. International economic institutions are an attempt to overcome the problem of free riding by individual nations in the sphere of providing international public goods. The most important public goods are order and a reduction in uncertainty. Some economists believe that these goods are best provided when there are agreements that help keep markets open in recessions and in boom periods; when there

is an international lender of last resort; when there are sufficient lenders of capital to developing nations; and when there is an adequate supply of money for international payment.

5. In recent years, a popular revolt against the global institutions has developed. The critics of the global institutions complain that their decision making is closed to outside participation by civic and social groups. In addition, some critics argue that their policymaking is based on outdated economics and flawed analysis.

6. The call for greater civic and social participation in the WTO, the IMF, and the World Bank is fed by a lower tolerance of inequality, and the view that the policies of the global institutions do not benefit large numbers of people in many countries. This view is based on the observation that the global institutions have neglected the development of national and subnational institutions that are essential for well-functioning market economies, for example education, health care systems, and human and civic rights.

Vocabulary

Bretton Woods conference

common external tariff

common market

customs union

economic union

free riding

free trade area

foreign exchange reserves

General Agreement on Tariffs and Trade (GATT)

institutions

IMF conditionality

International Monetary Fund (IMF)

lender of last resort

most favored nation (MFN)

national treatment

nondiminishable

nondiscrimination

nonexcludable

nonrival

partial trade agreement

public goods

quota

regional trade agreement (RTA)

tariffs

trade bloc

trade rounds

Uruguay Round

World Bank

World Trade Organization

Study Questions

1. What is an institution? Give examples of both formal and informal institutions. Explain how they differ from organizations.

2. What are the arguments in favor of international organizations? What are the arguments against? Which do you think are stronger?

3. What are public goods and how do they differ from private ones? Give examples of each.

4. What are the main tasks or functions of (1) the International Monetary Fund, (2) The World Bank, (3) the General Agreement on Tariffs and Trade, and (4) the World Trade Organization?

5. When nations sign the GATT agreement, they bind their tariffs at their current level, or lower. Tariff binding means that they agree not to raise the tariffs except under unusual circumstances. Explain how tariff binding in the GATT prevents free riding during a global slowdown.

6. Kindleberger's study of the Great Depression of the 1930s led him to believe that market economies are sometimes unstable and that nations can get locked into prolonged downturns. Other economists are not convinced. Suppose that you disagree with Kindleberger and that you believe that market-based economies are inherently stable. How would you view the need for international institutions to address the provision of each of the public goods in Table 2.4?

7. What are the four main types of regional trade agreements and what are their primary characteristics?

8. Critics of the global institutions have a variety of complaints about the WTO, the IMF, and the World Bank. Describe the two main categories of complaints.

Part 2

INTERNATIONAL TRADE

Chapter 3

COMPARATIVE ADVANTAGE
AND THE GAINS
FROM TRADE

INTRODUCTION

This chapter introduces the theory of comparative advantage. A simple model is used to show how nations maximize their material welfare by specializing in goods and services that have the lowest relative costs of production. The improvement in national welfare is known as the **gains from trade**. The concepts of comparative advantage and the gains from trade are two of the oldest and most widely held ideas in all of economics, yet they are often misunderstood and misinterpreted. Therefore it is worth the effort to develop a clear understanding of both.

Adam Smith and the Attack on Economic Nationalism

The development of modern economic theory is intimately linked to the birth of international economics. In 1776, Adam Smith published *An Inquiry into the Nature and Causes of the Wealth of Nations*, a work that became the first modern statement of economic theory. In the process of laying out the basic ground rules for the efficient allocation of resources, Smith initiated a general attack on **mercantilism**, the system of nationalistic economics that dominated economic thought in the 1700s. Mercantilism stressed exports over imports, primarily as a way to obtain revenues for building armies and national construction projects. Although Smith successfully established modern economics, he did not end mercantilist thinking, which persists today as economic nationalism.

The key mistake in mercantilist thinking was the belief that trade was a **zero sum** activity. In the eighteenth century the term *zero sum* did not exist, but it is a convenient expression for the concept that one nation's gain is another nation's loss. A moment's reflection should be enough to see the mistake in this belief, at least as it applies to voluntary exchange. When you buy a gallon of milk, do you lose and the store wins? Why would you buy the milk if that were true? If the store loses, why would they sell it? Voluntary exchange is positive sum. Both sides must gain, or else one or both sides would withdraw from the exchange. In trade, the most accurate metaphor is not football or poker or some other zero sum competitive game but rock climbing or dance, which are positive sum activities.

40

No one in the 1770s thought they were living in the midst of an industrial revolution, but Smith was observant enough to perceive that many improvements in the standard of living had occurred during his lifetime as a result of increasing specialization in production. When he analyzed specialization, he made one of his most important contributions to economics, the discovery that specialization depends on the size of the market.

A contemporary example may be helpful. If the giant automobile manufacturer General Motors were only permitted to sell its cars and trucks in, say, Michigan, they would have much less revenue and would sell many fewer vehicles. They would hire fewer employees, and each person would be less specialized. As it is, GM's market is so large (essentially, it is the world) that it can hire engineers who are completely specialized in small, even minuscule, parts of a car—door locks, for example. Your door lock engineer will know everything there is to know about the design, production, and assembly of door locks and will be able to help GM put them into its cars in the most efficient manner possible. A firm that was limited to the Michigan market could never afford to hire such specialized skills in every area of vehicle manufacture.

One of the keys to Smith's story of wealth creation is access to foreign markets. If no one is willing to import, then every company is limited by the size of the national market. In some cases, that may be large enough (the United States or China), but in most cases it is not. Small- and medium-sized countries cannot efficiently produce every item they consume. Holland, for example, has always imported a large share of its goods and has depended on access to foreign markets in order to earn money to pay for imports.

Smith was highly critical of trade barriers because they decreased specialization, technological progress, and wealth creation. He also recognized that imports enable a country to obtain goods it either cannot make or cannot make as cheaply, while exports are made for someone else and are only useful if they lead to imports. The modern view of trade shares Smith's dislike of trade barriers for mostly the same reasons. Although international economists recognize that there are limitations to the application of theory, the vast majority of economists share a strongly held preference for free and open markets. In Chapters 5 and 6 we will examine trade barriers in greater detail, but at this point we will develop a deeper understanding of the gains from trade by means of a simple algebraic and graphical model.

A Simple Model of Production and Trade

We begin with one of the simplest models in economics. The conclusion of this analysis is that a policy of free trade maximizes a nation's material well-being. Later we will examine some of the cases where real-world conditions do not conform to the assumptions of the model and where the optimality of free trade is questionable.

The basic model is often referred to as a Ricardian model, since it first took form in the analysis of David Ricardo. The model begins by assuming that there are only two countries, producing two goods, using one input (labor). More complex models can be built with *n* countries producing *m* goods and using *k* inputs, but other than adding a layer of mathematical sophistication, the final outcome is almost the same. The Ricardian model assumes that firms are price takers, or, in other words, markets are competitive, and no firm has market power. The model is static in the sense that it assumes that technology is constant and there are no learning effects of production that might make firms and industries more productive over time. We will relax both of these assumptions in the coming chapters. Ricardo assumed that labor is perfectly mobile and can easily move back and forth between industries, another simplifying assumption that will be dropped in Chapter 4. In this chapter, we assume that labor is mobile between industries but not across national boundaries.

Absolute Productivity Advantage and the Gains from Trade

To begin we define *productivity* in the Ricardian model. Productivity is the amount of output obtained from a unit of input. Since labor is the only input, we can define **labor productivity** as

(units of output) / (hours worked)

If, for example, two loaves of bread can be produced in 1 hour, then productivity is

(2 loaves) / (1 hour)

or 2 loaves per hour. If 4 loaves are produced in 2 hours, then productivity is still

(4 loaves) / (2 hours) = 2 loaves per hour

Suppose there are two goods, bread and steel, and two countries, the United States and Canada. Suppose also that each produces according to the productivities given in Table 3.1.

The values in Table 3.1 show that Canada's productivity is greater than the United States's in bread production, and the United States's is greater in steel. Canada has an **absolute productivity advantage** in bread because it produces more loaves per hour worked (3 versus 2 in the United States). At the same time, and using the same logic, the United States has an absolute productivity advantage in steel production.

The basis of Adam Smith's support for free trade was the belief that every country would have an absolute advantage in something. Smith thought it did not really matter where the source of the advantage came from. Whether it was due to special skills in the labor force, climate and soil characteristics of the country, or the temperament of its people, there would be goods that each country could manufacture, or grow, or dig out of the ground more efficiently than its trading partner. Consequently, every country could benefit from trade.

TABLE 3.1	Output per Hour Worked	
	U.S.	*Canada*
Bread	2 loaves	3 loaves
Steel	3 tons	1 ton

Canada is more productive than the United States in bread production, but the United States is more productive at steel production.

In the numerical example outlined in Table 3.1, each loaf of bread costs the United States 1.5 tons of steel. Put another way, the **opportunity cost** of bread is 1.5 tons of steel, since each unit of bread produced requires the economy to move labor out of steel production, forfeiting 1.5 tons of steel that it could have produced instead. This follows from the fact that each hour of labor can produce either 2 loaves of bread or 3 tons of steel. We can write this ratio as the barter price of bread:

$$P_{us}^{b} = \frac{3 \text{ tons}}{2 \text{ loaves}} = 1.5 \left(\frac{\text{tons}}{\text{loaves}} \right),$$

where b is for bread and us is the country. Similarly, we can write the U.S. price of steel as the inverse:

$$P_{us}^{s} = \frac{2 \text{ loaves}}{3 \text{ tons}} = 0.67 \left(\frac{\text{loaves}}{\text{tons}} \right).$$

You should be able to verify that the Canadian price of bread will be 0.33 (tons/loaf) and that steel will cost 3 (loaves/ton).

If the United States can sell a ton of steel for more than 0.67 loaves of bread, it is better off. Similarly, if Canadians can obtain a ton of steel for fewer than 3 loaves of bread, they are better off. Each country will gain from trade if the United States agrees to sell steel for fewer than 3 loaves of bread but more than 0.67 loaves. Anywhere in that range, both Canadians and Americans will benefit. In the end, trade will occur at a price somewhere between these two limits:

$$3.0 \left(\frac{\text{loaves}}{\text{ton}} \right) > P_{w}^{s} > 0.67 \left(\frac{\text{loaves}}{\text{ton}} \right),$$

where P_{w}^{s} = the world price of steel (i.e., the trade price). Without knowing more details about the demand side of the market, it is impossible to say whether the price will settle closer to 3.0 (the Canadian opportunity cost of steel) or 0.67 (the U.S. opportunity cost). The closer the price is to 0.67, the more Canada benefits from trade, and the closer it is to 3.0, the more the United States benefits. Regardless of which country benefits more, as long as the price is between these two limits, both countries benefit from trade.

COMPARATIVE PRODUCTIVITY ADVANTAGE AND THE GAINS FROM TRADE

The obvious question to ask at this point is what happens if a country does not have an absolute productivity advantage in anything. It is not hard to imagine an extremely poor, resource-deficient nation with low literacy and scarce capital. What can these countries produce more efficiently than the United States or Germany? Why would a rich country want to trade with them when they are inefficient at everything? The answer is that even if a country lacks a single good in which it has an absolute productivity advantage, it can still benefit from trade. Perhaps even more surprising, rich, high-productivity countries also benefit from the trade. In other words, the idea that nations benefit from trade has nothing to do with whether a country has an absolute advantage in producing a particular good. In order to see this, we must first develop a few more basic concepts.

The Production Possibilities Curve

The **production possibilities curve** (**PPC**) shows the tradeoffs a country faces when it chooses its combination of bread and steel output. Figure 3.1 illustrates a hypothetical PPC for the United States. Point B on the PPC is an efficient point of production because it utilizes existing resources to obtain the maximum possible level of output. The assumption of full employment is equivalent to assuming that the United States is operating at a point like B that lies on its PPC. At point A, the economy is inside its production curve and is operating at

| FIGURE 3.1 | The United States's Production Possibilities Curve |

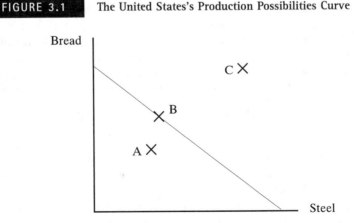

In a model with only two goods, the production possibilities curve shows the tradeoffs between them.

an inefficient level of output because it is not obtaining the maximum possible output from its available inputs. At point A, there is waste in the economy, since a greater quantity of bread and steel could be produced with the existing labor supply. Point C is infeasible since resources do not permit the production of bread and steel in the combination indicated.

The PPC in Figure 3.1 is a straight line because it is assumed that the trade-off between bread and steel does not change. This follows from the assumption that labor is homogeneous, or all the same, and that no group of workers is more skilled than another group. The tradeoff between bread and steel is another way to refer to the opportunity cost of steel. This follows from the definition of opportunity cost as the best forgone alternative: in order to produce a ton of steel, the United States gives up ⅔ a loaf of bread. In Figure 3.2, the slope of the PPC is –0.67, the number of loaves of bread forgone (Δbread) divided by the quantity of steel obtained (Δsteel):

Slope of the PPC = (Δbread output) / (Δsteel output) = opportunity cost of steel.

FIGURE 3.2	Opportunity Costs and the Slope of the PPC

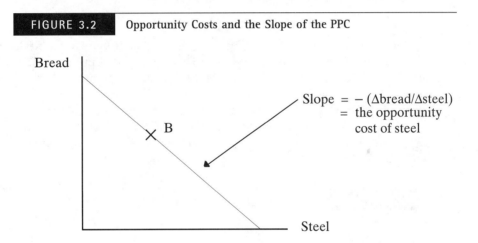

The slope of the PPC is the opportunity cost of the good on the horizontal axis. This follows from the definition of the slope as the ratio of the vertical change to the horizontal change moving along the PPC.

Relative Prices

Suppose that the slope of the PPC is –0.67, as in Figure 3.2. If the United States does not trade, it gives up 0.67 loaves of bread for an additional ton of steel. This tradeoff is called either the **relative price** of steel or the opportunity cost of steel. The term *relative price* follows from the fact that it is not in monetary units but in units of the other good. If no trade takes place, then the relative price of a good must be equal to its opportunity cost in production.

It is easy to convert the relative price of steel into the relative price of bread: simply take the inverse of the price of steel. In other words, if 0.67 loaves of bread is the price of one ton of steel in the United States, then 1.5 tons of steel is the price of one loaf of bread. By the same reasoning, 1.5 tons of steel is the opportunity cost of a loaf of bread in the United States when production is at point B in Figure 3.2.

The Price Line, or Trade Line

The complete absence of trade is called **autarky**, and in this situation, both the United States and Canada are limited in their consumption to the goods that they produce at home. Suppose that autarky prevails and the opportunity cost of steel in Canada is 3 loaves of bread per ton, and in the United States it is 0.67 loaves per ton (as given in Table 3.1). In this case both countries can raise their consumption levels if they trade. In particular, for trade to be desirable, the price of steel must settle somewhere between the opportunity costs in Canada and in the United States. That is, countries benefit if

$$3.0 \ (\text{loaves/ton}) > P_w^s > 0.67 \ (\text{loaves/ton}).$$

Suppose that the price settles at 2 loaves per ton. In the United States, the pretrade price was 0.67 loaves per ton. This is illustrated in Figure 3.3 where the United States's PPC is shown with the production point at A. The trading possibilities for the United States are illustrated by line TT, the **price line** or **trade line**. The slope of TT is −2, which is the relative price of steel, or the rate at which bread and steel can be traded for each other. TT passes through point A because this is the combination of steel and bread that is available to trade.

FIGURE 3.3   Production and Trade Before Specialization

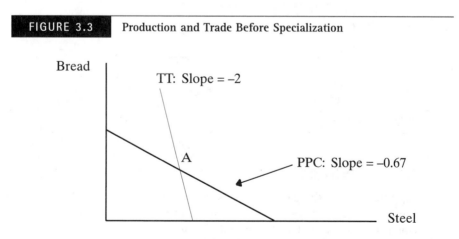

If the United States produces at A and the trade pice of steel is 2, then it can trade steel for bread and move its consumption bundle outside its PPC.

If the United States chooses to trade, it could move up TT, trading each ton of steel for two loaves of bread. This is a better tradeoff than it gets if it tries to make more bread, since along its PPC each ton brings only two-thirds more loaves of bread. While it is always impossible to produce outside the PPC, in effect, the United States can consume outside it by trading steel for bread.

The Gains from Trade

You should wonder why the United States would choose to make bread at all, since a ton of steel not produced brings in only two-thirds loaf of bread. If the United States were to specialize in steel production and trade for bread, it could do much better, since it would get 2 loaves for each ton. This possibility is illustrated in Figure 3.4. Here the United States's pretrade production point is at A. This is also its consumption point, since in the absence of trade, consumption must equal production. Point B in Figure 3.4 represents production that is completely specialized in steel. With the opening of trade, production could occur at B, and the United States could trade up along TT′, which has a slope of –2, the same as TT. If the United States produces at B and moves up TT′, it can reach a point like C, which is unambiguously superior to the consumption bundle available when production is at point A. C is superior because it represents more of both bread and steel than is available at A. Similarly, for any combination of bread and steel that is available along the PPC, or along TT if the United States produces at A and trades, there is a consumption bundle on TT′,which represents more of both goods.

The most important thing to note about production point B is that it maximizes U.S. income. This follows from the fact that it makes available the great-

| FIGURE 3.4 | Production to Maximize Income |

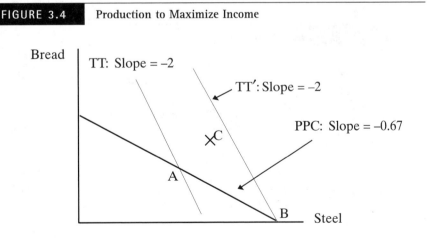

By specializing production at B and trading for bread, the United States obtains the largest possible consumption bundle.

est combinations of bread and steel. To see this, consider that no other point of production puts the United States on a price line that lies farther out from the origin. Every other production point on the U.S.'s PPC lies below TT', and every trade line with a slope of –2 that passes through the PPC at a point other than B also lies below TT'. In other words, given the U.S.'s PPC and a relative steel price of 2, the largest bundle of consumption goods is obtained when the United States specializes in steel and trades for its bread.

The United States benefits from trade, but does Canada? Unequivocally, the answer is yes. Consider Figure 3.5 where point A is Canada's pretrade production point. Along Canada's PPC, the opportunity cost of steel is 3 loaves of bread per ton. After trade, the price settles between 0.67 and 3.00, at 2 loaves per ton. With a trade price of 2 (price line TT), Canada maximizes its income by moving along its PPC to where it is completely specialized in bread production. It can then trade bread for steel at a trade price that is more favorable than its domestic tradeoff of 3 loaves per ton. Canada, too, can consume at a point on TT that is outside its PPC and above and to the right of its pretrade equilibrium at point A. Canada, like the United States, is better off, because with trade it gets a larger combination of both goods than it can produce for itself.

A numerical example will help clarify the existence of gains from trade. Suppose the relative price of steel is 2 loaves per ton. When the United States increases its steel output by 1 ton, it gives up 0.67 loaves of bread output, but it can trade the steel for 2 loaves, leaving a net gain of 1.33 loaves (2 – 0.67 = 1.33). In order to meet U.S. demand for 2 more loaves of bread, Canada must give up 0.67 ton of steel production. It trades the 2 loaves for 1 ton of steel, however, leaving a net gain of 0.33 ton (1 – 0.67 = 0.33). Hence, both countries benefit from the trade.

FIGURE 3.5	Canada's Gains from Trade

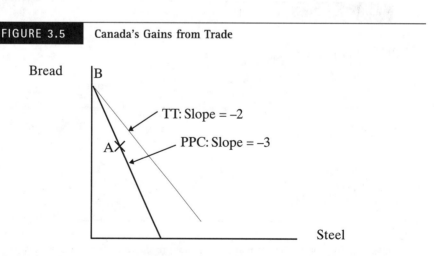

By specializing production at B and trading for steel, Canada obtains the largest possible consumption bundle.

Domestic Prices and the Trade Price

Now we know that as long as the trade price is between the pretrade domestic prices in Canada and the United States, both countries can gain from trade. What ensures that the trade price actually settles within this range, 3.0 (loaves/ton) > P_w^s > 0.67 (loaves/ton)? What would happen if, for example, P_w^s were equal to 4, or 0.5?

Consider the first case when the trade price is 4 loaves per ton of steel. At $P_w^s = 4$, the trade price of steel is greater than the production cost in each country. Clearly, the United States would want to continue to specialize in steel and trade it for bread. Nothing has changed with regard to the U.S. strategy for maximizing its consumption bundle, or income. The only difference now is that the United States gets 4 units of bread for each unit of steel, instead of 2 as before. In Canada's case, the higher price of steel makes it profitable for Canadian producers to switch to steel production. This follows because the production opportunity cost of steel is 3 loaves of bread, but each ton produced can trade for 4 loaves. By specializing in steel production and trading for bread, Canada maximizes its consumption bundle.

Finally, it should be obvious that both countries are specialized in steel production and that no one is producing bread. Both Canada and the United States will bring their excess steel to market looking to trade it for bread, but neither country has any to trade. There is a bread shortage and a glut of steel. Consequently, bread prices rise, and steel prices fall. This goes on at least until the trade price of steel falls below the opportunity cost of production in Canada, the higher-cost country. Once P_w^s is less than 3, Canadian producers switch back to bread, steel production goes down, bread is up, and trade can resume.

In the second case, where P_w^s is less than 0.67, Canada continues to specialize in bread, and the United States switches. Bread is the surplus good, steel is in short supply, and a similar dynamic causes the price to move in order to ensure both goods are produced. The equilibrium trade price, then, has to be within the range we specified earlier, between the opportunity costs in the two countries. In our case, this is between 0.67 and 3.0 loaves per ton.

At the extreme, the trade price could be equal to the opportunity cost in one country; for example, if the trade price of steel is 0.67 loaves per ton, then the United States is indifferent about trading. It cannot be hurt by trading, but it does not gain either, since all the gains go to Canada. Similarly, if the trade price is equal to Canada's opportunity cost, then Canada is indifferent and all the gains accrue to the United States.

Without more information we cannot say much more about the trade price. Will it be close to 0.67 or to 3.0? The answer depends on the strength of demand for each good in both countries, but we have not explicitly included demand in our model, so we cannot say. We do know that if the price is closer to 0.67, the gains from trade are larger for Canada, and if it is closer to 3.0, the United States benefits more. Nevertheless, both countries gain as long as it is between the two opportunity costs, and economic forces determine that the price must be in that range.

ABSOLUTE AND COMPARATIVE PRODUCTIVITY ADVANTAGE CONTRASTED

Absolute productivity advantage is defined as having higher labor productivity. We saw that if each country has an absolute productivity advantage in one of the goods, they can both benefit by specializing in that good and trading it for the other good. Note, however, that the gains from trade we saw did not depend in any way on each country having an absolute advantage. In fact, what mattered was the pretrade opportunity costs of bread and steel in each country. The opportunity costs were derived from the productivities, but since they are a ratio, vastly different levels of productivity can lead to the same tradeoff.

A country has a **comparative productivity advantage** in a good, or simply a comparative advantage, if its opportunity costs of producing a good are lower than those of its trading partners. The concept of comparative advantage is based on the idea that nations maximize their material well-being when they use their resources where they have their highest value. In order to know the highest-valued usage for any resource, we must compare alternative uses. If, by comparison to the United States's, Canada's opportunity cost of bread is lower, then it should produce more bread and trade for steel.

The distinction between absolute and comparative productivity advantages is one of the most important in economics. It is also one of the least well understood, in spite of the fact that it is relatively simple. For example, it is common to read or hear comments about competitiveness that assume that if a country does not have an absolute advantage, it will not be able to sell its products abroad. Our model explains why this logic is erroneous and why even the least productive of nations exports some goods.

COMPARATIVE ADVANTAGE AND "COMPETITIVENESS"

The rhetoric of "competitiveness" is so common in our public discourse that it is useful to consider its relationship to comparative advantage. In the analysis so far, comparative advantage resulted from productivity differences between nations in autarky. In our simple model of a barter economy, wages, prices, and exchange rates were omitted. Real businesses do not barter steel for bread, however, and they cannot pay their workers by dividing up the firm's output.

In general, by ignoring money wages, money prices, and exchange rates, we assumed that all goods and labor were correctly priced. In other words, it is assumed that the prices of both outputs and inputs are an accurate indication of their relative scarcity. In this case, there is no difference between a nation's comparative advantage in a good and the ability of its firms to sell the good at a price that is competitive. That is, if all markets correctly value the price of inputs and outputs, then a nation's commercial advantage in a good will be determined by its comparative advantage.

Unfortunately, markets sometimes fail to produce optimal outcomes. This means that at times, outputs and inputs can be incorrectly priced. Sometimes, under- or overvaluation of a good stems from inherent difficulties in measuring its true value or in measuring its true cost of production. For example, we usually ignore the costs of air pollution when we measure the costs of driving a car. Other times, under- or overvaluation may result from government policies, as when prices are maintained at an artificially high or low level. In either case, the fact that a market price may not accurately reflect the economic value of an input or an output means that a wedge is driven between commercial or **competitive advantage** and comparative advantage.

It is often (incorrectly) argued that nations should pursue commercial advantages for their firms even if it means a misallocation of resources. In effect, this means a country follows policies that lower living standards by failing to maximize the value of national output. In terms of Figures 3.4 and 3.5, this is equivalent to asserting that the United States and Canada should each remain at point A, where the United States overestimates the value of producing its own bread and Canada overestimates the value of steel. Both countries end up with consumption bundles that are suboptimal from the standpoint of national welfare.

Consider a real-world example. Indonesia tried to develop an aircraft industry in spite of the fact that it lacks a comparative advantage in aircraft production. Nevertheless, through a combination of government policies (some of which paid people to buy the planes!) the price to foreigners has been competitive at times. From the perspective of Indonesian national welfare and the optimal use of scarce Indonesian resources, this is a mistake. From the perspective of a business, however, Indonesian policies have made it profitable to make airplanes, even though it means using resources in ways that are suboptimal from the national perspective.

This case illustrates the common mistake of equating nations with business enterprises. Indonesian plane manufacturers care about their subsidies and any other policy that makes them profitable. The national interest, however, is to achieve the most efficient allocation of resources possible within the framework of the nation's laws and values. It is possible to make individual firms highly profitable through subsidies or protection from international competition, while at the same time and through the same policies cause the nation's overall standard of living to be lower than it would be otherwise. While most American businesses do not receive subsidies, they are not in business to ensure that resources are efficiently allocated at the national level. If they can legally tip the playing field in their direction, they will not hesitate.

Another important distinction between nations and business enterprises is that nations do not compete with each other in any normal sense of the word. Economic relations between the United States and Canada, or any pair of nations, are not equivalent to the commercial competition that exists between companies such as Coke and Pepsi. If Canada grows, the United States does not go out of business or suffer in any identifiable way. In fact, Canadian growth would be a stimulus to U.S. growth and would create spillover benefits for Americans. Cola companies fight over a relatively static market size, but nations can all simultaneously increase their incomes.

CASE STUDY

The U.S. and Mexican Auto Industries

When the United States and Canada began negotiations with Mexico to include Mexico in an expanded North American free-trade zone, American and Canadian autoworkers expressed fears that they could not compete with Mexican workers, who were paid much lower wages. Union representatives of the autoworkers argued in front of Congress that Mexican autoworkers earning between $4 and $5 per hour would overwhelm U.S. workers, who earn more than $35 per hour in wages and benefits in the largest auto plants. Free trade, they argued, would result in a loss of jobs and a migration of the industry to Mexico.

As it turns out, the autoworkers and their union representatives were wrong. Since signing NAFTA, U.S. and Canadian exports of autos to Mexico have actually increased. What happened? How are the United States and Canada able to overcome such enormous disadvantages in wages (between seven to one and eight to one) and actually increase exports of cars to Mexico? The answer is a simple lesson in comparative advantage.

Mexican workers earn a lot less than U.S. and Canadian workers simply because they are a lot less productive. The primary reasons are because they have less capital at work and the surrounding Mexican economy does not function as smoothly because the transportation, water, power, and communication systems are less developed. In economic terms, Mexican workers have less capital, both at work and in the supporting economy outside their plants.

Table 3.2 shows the costs for vehicle assembly based on "good" practices (but not the "best") of each country. A plant in the United States requires about twenty hours per vehicle for assembly, and in Mexico it takes around thirty hours. In spite of the faster assembly times, U.S. labor costs are much higher ($700 versus $140) due to the higher wages paid. However, the advantage of Mexican producers in the area of labor costs is completely lost elsewhere in the assembly process. The biggest offsetting factors are component and final vehicle shipping costs, where the United States has a $700 cost advantage (($400 + $600) − ($225 + $75)). The $700 cost advantage more than compensates for the $560 ($700 − $140) labor cost disadvantage. The net result is that the application of labor and capital to auto-

TABLE 3.2	Cost Structure for Auto Assembly in the United States and Mexico, Around 1990		
		U.S.	*Mexico*
Labor		$ 700	$ 140
Parts, components, subassemblies		7,750	8,000
Component shipping costs		75	600
Finished vehicle shipping		225	400
Inventory costs		20	40
Total cost		$8,770	$9,180

Lower labor costs in Mexico are offset by higher nonlabor costs.

Source: Congress of the United States, Office of Technology Assessment, *U.S.-Mexico Trade: Pulling Together or Pulling Apart?* (1992), p. 145.

mobile assembly in the United States is more productive than using capital and labor in Mexico to assemble cars. From the perspective of economic policy, Mexico should seek to raise the productivity of its capital and labor used in automobile production, or else use its capital and labor resources in some other activity.

The key to this outcome is overall productivity, or the amount of output per unit of input. In the simple Ricardian model of trade introduced earlier, labor was the only input, and money prices did not come into the picture. In the real world, however, labor is but one input along with capital and natural resources such as energy. Also, inputs and outputs are priced in dollar terms rather than in terms of the relative prices of output. Under these more realistic conditions, it is the combination of labor, capital, and natural resources that determines overall productivity and which country can make each good with the lowest opportunity cost.

This example illustrates an important principle of international trade theory.

A country can have higher wages and still produce at a lower cost as long as its productivity is higher than its trading partner's. In this example, U.S. productivity overcomes higher U.S. wages so that the opportunity cost of car production is actually lower in the United States than in Mexico.

Should Mexico abandon car production and completely specialize in something else? Not quite. Another difference between our model and the actual world we live in is that countries do not completely specialize. There are many reasons for this, including the facts that some goods are never traded (haircuts and restaurant meals, for example) and that most industries probably have increasing costs rather than the constant costs portrayed in our straight-line PPCs. The latter fact makes the PPC a bowed-out curve rather than a straight line and leads to incomplete specialization as opposed to the total specialization of our simple Ricardian model. To understand this, however, we need to introduce some additional concepts in Chapter 4.

ECONOMIC RESTRUCTURING

Economic restructuring refers to changes in the economy that may require some industries to grow and others to shrink or even disappear altogether. For example, the United States has seen a dramatic decrease in the size of its steel industry and, some years later, a rebirth of a new industry based around smaller, more specialized steel mills. In any dynamic economy, some types of economic activity will be growing, and others will be scaling back or dying. In some cases, these changes are a direct consequence of increased openness to foreign competition. For example, the influx of Japanese cars has played a major role in the reorganization and restructuring of the U.S. auto industry.

In our simple Ricardian model, after the opening of trade the United States was able to maximize its well-being by shifting workers out of bread production and into steel production. Even though this restructuring of the economy improved overall economic welfare, it does not mean that it benefited every individual—a nation's gains from trade may be divided in different ways, and it is usually the case that some individuals benefit while others are hurt by trade. If there are net gains from opening trade (which are measured by an increase in the consumption bundle), then it means that the economic gains of the winners are greater than the economic losses of the losers, and therefore the nation as a whole is better off. Nevertheless, opening an economy to increased foreign competition is rarely painless and usually generates a number of new problems. In the model used in this chapter, it is likely that bread producers may not know much about steel production. They may not know where to go to find work, and they may leave behind a community that is dying as its most mobile and economically active citizens find work elsewhere.

When the U.S. auto industry was in its least competitive position against the Japanese in the early 1980s, our overly simplified model of comparative advantage would have counseled laid-off autoworkers to leave Michigan and move to California where they could find jobs in the booming computer and defense industries. Obviously, this is not realistic advice for most autoworkers. The fact that the U.S. economy was open to Japanese auto manufacturers certainly made consumers and firms that bought cars better off. It increased the selection of automobiles and enabled us to buy higher quality cars at lower prices. It is another matter, however, for the U.S. autoworkers who lost their jobs.

Most economists would agree that this tradeoff is worth it because the availability of Japanese cars, or foreign made goods in general, increases our choices as consumers, lowers the cost of inputs, increases competition and innovation, and enables us to obtain a greater bundle of goods with our incomes. The availability of imports puts pressure on domestic producers to improve their product quality and to hold down their costs of production. Finally, it leads to the diffusion of technological change, which benefits us all. No one would argue, for example, that if a German drug company invented a cure for AIDS or cancer that we should prohibit its importation because it may hurt the income of a lot of doctors and perhaps lead to the closing of some hospitals. The gain to the nation would vastly outweigh the losses to those adversely affected by the changes in medicine.

While it is easy to show that trade barriers are a suboptimal solution to the social problems of economic change that are caused by trade, it is uncertain what the optimal policies are. To a large extent, political assumptions about the way the world works will color the solutions offered by economists, political scientists, and other social scientists. For example, some ardent believers in less government intervention into the economy would argue that government should not have any policies for handling unemployment or the economic collapse of communities that is caused by the rapid growth of imports. They maintain that unemployment is a self-correcting problem; laid-off workers will look for new jobs and will, if necessary, accept lower wages. The argument is also frequently heard that government cannot efficiently deal with these sorts of problems; it creates inefficient, bureaucratic programs that live on long after they become unnecessary. Others make a value judgment that this sort of social problem should not be a governmental concern, that it should be left up to the private economy and individual initiative.

An alternative to this "do nothing" approach to economic restructuring is for the government to look for ways to get the winners to compensate the losers. The proponents of this view justify it on several grounds. First, the nation as a whole benefits from trade, so there are newly added resources to the economy that make compensation possible. In addition, compensation reduces the incentives for those that oppose trade to organize against imports. If industries or workers think they are unable to compete, they may organize to restrict trade. Promises of financial assistance and help in finding another job may weaken this urge. In this view, compensation is a useful tool for undermining the antitrade position.

The practice of offering **trade adjustment assistance (TAA)** is common in many countries, including the United States. These programs usually take the form of extended unemployment benefits and worker retraining, along with a temporary imposition of a tax on imports in order to create some breathing room for an industry suffering from a sudden surge in imports. For example, the U.S. government created a special program of benefits for workers who are hurt by trade with Mexico due to the signing of the North American Free Trade Agreement (NAFTA). In 1994, the first year of NAFTA, 17,000 workers qualified for TAA under the NAFTA provision. Generally, in order to qualify for the benefits, workers must demonstrate that they were laid off as a result of imports from Mexico or because their firm relocated to Mexico. Needless to say, it is sometimes difficult to establish a direct link between imports and a job loss; a poorly managed firm may have been on its way out of business with or without imports.

The important point is that trade creates change, and it may be difficult for some people, industries, or communities to deal with change. When a nation moves along its PPC toward a different mix of industries, there is a period of transition that is painful for some. Economic restructuring does not happen overnight, and although it is desirable for the higher living standard it brings, change and transformation cost time and money.

Summary

- The single most important determinant of trade patterns is the opportunity cost of producing traded goods. Countries that sacrifice the least amount of alternative production when producing a particular good have the lowest opportunity cost, or a comparative advantage. The idea of comparative advantage has been one of the most enduring concepts of economic thought and has been a central theme in international economic policy since the mid-1800s.

- Nations that produce according to their comparative advantage are maximizing the benefits they receive from trade and, consequently, their national welfare. This is the same as maximizing their gains from trade.

- Comparative advantage is often confused with absolute advantage. The latter refers to the advantage a nation has if its absolute productivity in a particular product is greater than its trading partners. It is not necessary to have an absolute advantage in order to have a comparative advantage.

- One common fallacious argument against following comparative advantage is that workers in other countries are paid less than American workers. This argument neglects the issue of productivity. Developing-country wages are lower because the value of output from one hour of labor is less. Labor productivity is less because workers are generally less skilled, they have less capital on the job, and they have less capital in the surrounding economy to support their on-the-job productivity.

- Businesspeople and economists look at the issue of trade differently because they have different objectives in mind. Businesspeople are often concerned about their ability to compete—that is, to sell a particular item in a given market at the lowest price. Their perspective is that of the firm. Economists focus on the efficient use of resources at the national or global level. The perspective is that of all firms taken together.

Vocabulary

absolute productivity advantage	economic restructuring
autarky	gains from trade
comparative productivity advantage	labor productivity
competitive advantage	mercantilism
	opportunity cost

<table>
<tr><td>price line</td><td>trade adjustment assistance</td></tr>
<tr><td>production possibilities curve (PPC)</td><td>trade line</td></tr>
<tr><td></td><td>zero sum</td></tr>
<tr><td>relative price</td><td></td></tr>
</table>

Study Questions

1. Use the information in the following table on labor productivities in France and Germany to answer the questions.

   Output per hour worked

	France	Germany
Cheese	2 kilograms	1 kilogram
Cars	0.25	0.5

   a) Which country has an absolute advantage in cheese? In cars?
   b) What is the relative price of cheese in France if it does not trade? In Germany if it does not trade?
   c) What is opportunity cost of cheese in France? In Germany?
   d) Which country has a comparative advantage in cheese? In cars? Show how you know.
   e) What is the upper and lower bound for the trade price of cheese? *range of terms of trade*
   f) Draw a hypothetical PPC for France, and label its slope. Suppose that France follows its comparative advantage in deciding where to produce on its PPC. Label its production point. If the trade price of cars is 5 kilos of cheese per car, draw a trade line showing how France can gain form trade.

2. Explain how a nation can gain from trade even though not everyone is made better off. Isn't this a contradiction?

3. Economic nationalists in America worry that international trade is destroying our economy. A common complaint is that agreements such as NAFTA (North American Free Trade Agreement) open our economy to increased trade with countries such as Mexico, where workers are paid a fraction of what they earn in the United States. Explain the faulty logic of this argument.

4. Many people believe that the goal of international trade should be to create jobs. Consequently, when they see workers laid off due to a firm's inability to compete against cheaper and better imports, they assume that trade must be bad for the economy. Is this assumption correct? Why, or why not?

5. Suppose that the United States decides to become self-sufficient in bananas and even to export them. In order to accomplish these goals, large tax incentives are granted companies that will invest in banana production. Soon, the American industry is competitive and able to sell bananas at the lowest price anywhere. Does the United States. have a comparative advantage? Why, or why not? What are the consequences for the overall economy?

Chapter 4

COMPARATIVE ADVANTAGE AND FACTOR ENDOWMENTS

INTRODUCTION

The theory presented in Chapter 3 did not consider the determinants of comparative advantage. It was assumed that countries had different levels of productivity, but the reasons why one country might be more productive than another in a particular line of production was never analyzed. In this chapter, the idea of comparative advantage is examined in more detail, beginning with the factors that determine it. We will also examine the impact of trade on income distribution. In the simple model in Chapter 3, it was assumed that everyone that wanted a job could find one and that after trade began, anyone laid off from the shrinking industry found employment in the expanding one. The opposition to expanded trade, however, often comes from people who fear that increased trade will downsize their industry, and they do not view themselves as having options for employment in the expanding sectors. We also saw that trade causes the price of the export good to rise and the price of the import good to fall, making the nation as a whole better off. In reality, we consume both export and import goods, and the fact that the nation is better off may not reflect your individual circumstances if your consumption is heavily weighted toward the export good.

MODERN TRADE THEORY

In Chapter 3, comparative advantage depended on each country's relative productivity, and those were given by assumption at the start of the exercise. Smith and Ricardo thought that each country would have its own technology, its own climate, and its own resources, and that differences between nations would give rise to productivity differences. In the twentieth century, several economists have developed a more detailed explanation of trade in which the productivity differences of each country depend on the country's endowments of the inputs (called factors of production or, simply, factors) that are used to produce each good. The theory has various names: the Heckscher-Ohlin theory (HO), the Heckscher-Ohlin-Samuelson theory, or the Factor Proportions theory. They all refer to the same set of ideas.

The Heckscher–Ohlin (HO) Trade Model

The HO trade model begins with the observation that nations are endowed with different levels of each input (factors). Furthermore, each output has a different "recipe" for its production and requires different combinations and levels of the various inputs. Steel production, for example, requires a lot of iron ore, coking material, semiskilled labor, and some expensive capital equipment. Clothing production requires unskilled and semiskilled workers with rudimentary capital equipment in the form of sewing machines.

In order to analyze how the availability of inputs creates productivity differences, we must first define **factor abundance** and **factor scarcity**. The hypothetical example in Table 4.1 illustrates these concepts. The United States's capital-labor ratio (K_{us}/L_{us}) is $^{50}/_{150}$ or $^{1}/_{3}$. In Canada, K_{can}/L_{can} is $^{5}/_{10}$ or $^{1}/_{2}$. Since Canada's capital-labor ratio is higher ($K_{can}/L_{can} > K_{us}/L_{us}$, or $^{1}/_{2} > ^{1}/_{3}$), it is the capital-abundant country. With just two inputs, Canada is also the labor-scarce country. Note that Canada is capital abundant relative to the United States even though it has only $^{1}/_{10}$ the absolute quantity of capital. However, each Canadian worker is better equipped with capital than each American worker, and this makes Canada *relatively* better endowed with capital.

Relative abundance of a factor implies that its relative cost is less than in counties where it is relatively scarcer. Conversely, relatively scarce resources are more expensive. Consequently, capital is relatively cheap in Canada and labor is relatively expensive. It follows that economies have relatively lower costs in the production of goods where the "recipe" calls for greater quantities of the abundant factor and smaller quantities of the scarce factor. In this example, the United States will have a lower opportunity cost in production that uses relatively more labor and relatively less capital, while Canada's opportunity cost will be lower in production that uses relatively more capital and less labor.

The **Heckscher-Ohlin trade theory** makes exactly this point. It asserts that a country's comparative advantage lies in the production of goods that use relatively abundant factors. In other words, comparative advantage is determined by a nation's factor endowment, and once this is determined, it should be possible to predict exported goods. (It is also possible to predict imported goods because the model is symmetric.)

TABLE 4.1	An Example of Factor Abundance	
	United States	*Canada*
Capital	50 machines	5 machines
Labor	150 workers	10 workers

Canada is capital abundant and the United States is labor abundant.

To clarify this idea, let's consider the United States. It is richly endowed with a wide variety of factors. It has natural resources in the form of rich farmland and extensive forests. It has highly skilled labor, such as scientists, engineers, and managers. Although savings rates are not very high, the wealth of the nation has enabled it to create an abundance of physical capital, both public and private. Its exports, therefore, should include agricultural products, particularly those requiring skilled labor and physical capital, and all sorts of machinery and industrial goods that require intensive input of physical capital and scientific and engineering skills.

One leading U.S. export is commercial jet aircraft—a product that requires a vast array of physical capital and scientific, engineering, and managerial talent. The United States is also a major exporter of grains and grain products, such as vegetable oils. These are produced with relatively small labor inputs, very large capital inputs (combines, tractors, etc.), farmland, and a great deal of scientific research and development that has produced hybrid seeds, pesticides, herbicides, and so forth.

Gains from Trade in the HO Model

In the Ricardian model we assumed that each country faced a constant set of tradeoffs: 2 loaves of bread for 3 tons of steel (United States) or 3 loaves of bread for 1 ton of steel (Canada). The constant costs of the Ricardian model stemmed from the fact that there was one homogeneous input: labor. Labor could be used to make bread or steel. Workers did not vary in their skills, and since there was no capital input, each worker was as productive as the next. Consequently, when labor was reallocated from bread to steel, or vice versa, the tradeoff was always at a constant rate.

In the HO model, we have a multiplicity of inputs—labor, capital, farmland, and so forth—so each worker may be equipped with a different quantity of supporting inputs, such as capital. Obviously, at the end of the day, a worker with a $5 shovel will have dug a smaller hole than one equipped with a $150,000 earth-moving machine. Furthermore, the quality of labor and capital can vary. Some labor is skilled, and some is unskilled. Certain jobs require scientific or other technical training, while others require only basic literacy or even less. Similarly, capital can be low or high tech, and resources such as farmland have different fertility and climate characteristics. In effect, each important qualitative difference can be treated as a key characteristic of a separate input, so unskilled and skilled labor can be considered different factors.

If a country has multiple inputs with various suitabilities for different tasks, we can no longer assume a PPC with constant costs. Rather, the economy is assumed to have increasing costs, implying that each country has a rising opportunity cost for each type of production. Consequently, as the United States or Canada moves labor, capital, and land into bread production, each additional unit of bread leads to a greater loss of steel output than the one before. The reason is straightforward: If more bread is wanted, resources must be taken out of steel. The optimal strategy is to move resources that are relatively good at bread production but poor at steel production. This leads to the greatest gain in bread with the smallest loss of steel. The next shift in production, toward more bread, cuts deeper into the stock of resources used for steel production, and in all likelihood there will not be resources to move that are as good at bread and as poor at steel as the previous production shift. Consequently, in order to get the same increase in bread, more steel must be given up than before. This result is symmetric, so shifts going the other way, toward more steel, cause the opportunity cost of steel to rise with each shift. Figure 4.1 illustrates a PPC with increasing costs.

As with constant costs, the tradeoff between bread and steel is equal to the slope of the PPC. Since the PPC is curved, its slope changes at every point, and we must measure the tradeoff at the point of production. For example, in Figure 4.2, if the United States is producing at point A, then the opportunity cost of an additional ton of steel is equivalent to the slope of the PPC at point A. Since the PPC is a curve rather than a straight line, the slope is measured by drawing a tangent line at the point of production and measuring its slope.

Most of the analysis of the gains from trade in Chapter 3 carry over into the HO model. In order to demonstrate this, assume that point A is the U.S. production point in autarky and that at point A the opportunity cost of steel is 0.67 loaves of bread. This means that the slope of the tangent at A is –0.67. Also assume that Canada's opportunity cost of steel is above the United States's at 3 loaves of bread per ton, the same as before. Also assume that after trade begins, the world price, or trade price, is 2 loaves of bread per ton of steel, the same as the example in Chapter 3. After trade opens, the United States can

| FIGURE 4.1 | The United States's Production Possibilities Curve with Increasing Costs |

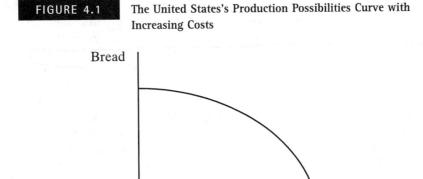

Moving from left to right, the opportunity cost of another unit of steel increases.

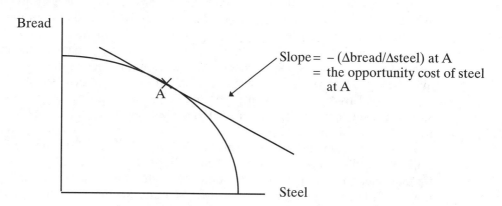

FIGURE 4.2   Opportunity Costs and the Slope of the PPC

The opportunity cost of steel is measured by the slope of the tangent at the point of production.

continue to produce at A and not trade, or it can produce at A and trade. Trade line TT in Figure 4.3 illustrates the possibilities if the United States stays at point A on its PPC.

TT is the price line with slope –2 passing through A and showing the combinations of bread and steel that are available when production is at A and trade is possible. In Figure 4.3, TT′ is a trade line that is tangent to the PPC at point B, an alternative production point to the right of A and closer to the steel axis. If the United States exploits its comparative advantage and shifts toward increased steel production, increasing costs come into play. This is the same as saying that the marginal cost of steel output is rising. As production rises, the gap between the opportunity cost of production and the trade price narrows until finally, at point B, they are equal. Further increases in steel production would push the cost above its value in trade and, therefore, are not warranted.

At point B, the opportunity cost of steel equals its trade price. Since the model is symmetric and the opportunity cost and trade price of bread are the inverse of the steel, the same equivalency holds for bread. To the left of B, the opportunity cost of steel (bread) is less (greater) than the trade price, so more (less) production is warranted. To the right of B, the opportunity cost of steel (bread) is greater (less) than the trade price, so less (more) production is warranted. Only at point B does the opportunity cost equal the trade price. Since no other changes can make the United States better off, point B is the production combination that maximizes income.

Graphically, the superiority of point B can be seen by first comparing B to A. Point B is clearly superior to A in terms of the consumption possibilities because for every point along TT there is another point on TT′ that offers more of both goods. That is, TT′ lies above and to the right of TT. Since a greater

| FIGURE 4.3 | Gains from Trade in the HO Model |

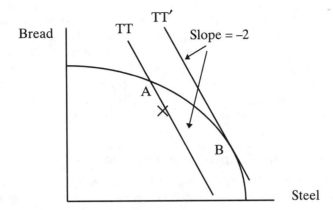

TT is the trade line if production is at A. Production at B maximizes income.

combination of both goods is available if the United States produces at B and trades, B is superior to A. Furthermore, when the trade price is 2, every other production point along the PPC leads to smaller consumption bundles. That is, at any other production point, a trade line with a slope of –2 that passes through the point will lie below and to the left of TT′, representing smaller combinations of steel and bread. Consequently, point B maximizes income by creating the largest possible consumption bundle.

The notion of gains from trade in the HO model is nearly the same as the Ricardian model. The only significant difference is that in the HO model, specialization is not complete. The United States continues to make some bread, and Canada makes some steel.

TRADE AND INCOME DISTRIBUTION

Recall that in the Ricardian model of comparative advantage, the nation as a whole gained from trade, and, by assumption, we ruled out the potentially harmful effects of trade on some members of society. When trade began, the economy shifted from one point on its production frontier to a different point. Workers that were affected by the production shift simply moved out of the declining industry and into the expanding one. Everyone had the same skills, and each type of production required only labor, so everyone had access to a job, and everyone benefited from both the fall in the price of the imported good and the rise in the price of the exported one.

The Heckscher-Ohlin trade model is a more sophisticated way to analyze the gains and losses from trade because it drops these unrealistic assumptions. Labor can be divided into two or more skill categories, other types of inputs can be included, and industries can require different mixes of the various inputs. Under these more realistic assumptions, it can be shown that while trade benefits the nation as a whole, some groups within the nation benefit more than others, and some will actually be harmed. Furthermore, it can be shown that there is a systematic relationship between the factor endowments of a country and the winners and losers from trade. Opening the discussion to an analysis of winners and losers adds an important and necessary element of realism. We are all aware that not everyone favors increased trade, and without an analysis of trade's income distribution effects, we have no basis for understanding the opposition to increased trade.

The Stolper-Samuelson Theorem

The analysis begins by recognizing that everyone's income depends on the inputs he or she supplies to the economy. Labor earns wages that may be high or low depending on the skill level; owners of capital earn profits; landowners earn rents. The amount of income earned per unit of input depends on the demand for the inputs as well as their supply. The demand for a particular input is sometimes referred to as a **derived demand**, since it is derived indirectly from the demand for the output it is used to produce. If the output is in high demand, and consequently its price is high, then the inputs that are used to produce it will benefit by receiving higher returns.

In general, any change in the economy that alters the price of outputs will have a direct impact on incomes. We have seen that trade causes output prices to change. Specifically, the price of the export good rises, while the price of the import falls. The movement of prices causes a change in the demand for each factor and leads to a change in the returns paid to each factor. Hence, trade impacts income distribution.

When trade begins and output prices change, resources leave the sector that produces imported goods and move into the sector that produces exports. In the HO model, unlike the simple Ricardian model, different goods are produced with different combinations of inputs, so the movement along the production possibilities frontier causes a change in the demand for each input. Factors that are used intensively in the imported goods sector will find that the demand for their services has shrunk—and so has their income. Conversely, factors used intensively in the export sector will experience an increase in the demand for their services and in their incomes. In sum, when trade begins, incomes of the factors used intensively in the import sector fall, and incomes of the factors used intensively in the export sector rise.

These effects are summarized in the Stolper-Samuelson theorem, which is derived from the HO theory. The **Stolper-Samuelson theorem** says that an increase in the price of a good raises the income earned by factors that are used intensively in its production. Conversely, a fall in the price of a good lowers the income of the factors it uses intensively.

Figure 4.4 illustrates these tendencies. Suppose that the United States and Canada can make bread or steel, using capital and labor. Suppose also that bread is the labor-intensive product,

$$K^b/L^b < K^s/L^s$$

and the United States is relatively well endowed with capital, compared to Canada.

$$K_{can}/L_{can} < K_{us}/L_{us}$$

According to the HO theory, the United States will have a comparative advantage in steel, which it will export in return for Canadian bread. In Figure 4.4, after trade begins, the United States moves along its PPC toward the steel axis from point A to point B.

As the United States shifts along its PPC, the change in the mix of goods produced leads to lower demands for labor and higher demands for capital. The steel industry will pick up some of the labor laid off in the bread industry, but since it is not as labor intensive as bread, its increase in labor demand is less than the fall in labor demand in the bread industry. The net result is that labor in both industries experiences a fall in demand, leading to a fall in wages and income earned. Note that Stolper-Samuelson does not state that all the factors used in the export industries are better off, nor that all the factors used in the import-competing industry get hurt. Rather, the abundant factor that is used to determine comparative advantage and exports is favored, and the scarce factor sees a decline in its income, regardless of industry.

FIGURE 4.4   An Illustration of the Stolper-Samuelson Theorem

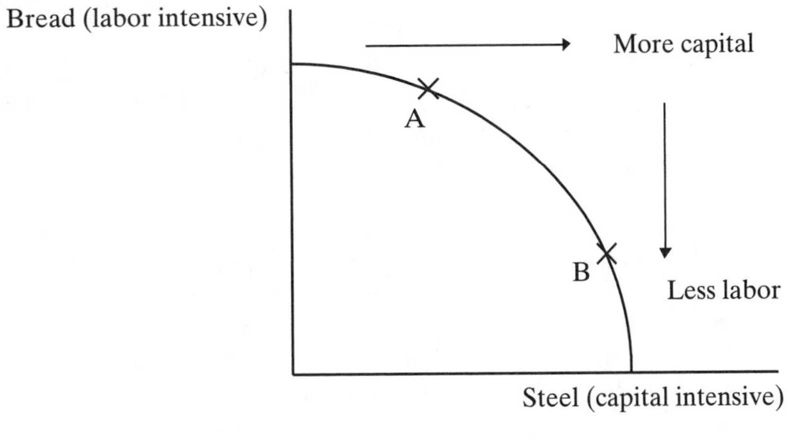

Movement along the PPC from A to B reduces the economy's demand for labor and increases its demand for capital.

The Stolper-Samuelson theorem is a starting point for understanding the income distribution effects of trade, but it only tells part of the story. An extension of the theorem, called the **magnification effect**, shows that the change in output prices has a magnified effect on factor incomes. For example, if after opening trade, bread prices declined by 75 percent, then the fall in labor income will be greater than 75 percent. Similarly, if the price of an export good (steel) rises by, say, 50 percent, incomes earned by the intensively used factors in the export sector (capital) rise more than 50 percent.

The ultimate effects on income of an opening of trade depend on the flexibility of the affected factors. If labor is stuck in bread production and unable to move to the steel sector, it could be hurt much worse than if it were completely flexible to move. Another example illustrates this point: within the debate over U.S.–Mexico free trade, there is a small but intense controversy surrounding avocado production. Mexico has a comparative advantage in avocados because it is well endowed with the necessary inputs (a particular quality of land and climate, together with unskilled labor and a little capital). If free trade were to open in the avocado market, the owners of avocado orchards in California would find their investments in land, equipment, and avocado trees worthless. Why would anyone pay $1 or more per avocado when Mexican ones sell for 25¢ or less? However, many of the California avocado groves are located in the suburbs of sprawling metropolitan regions, and presumably, if the land were worthless for avocado production, it could be put to valuable use in another line of production—for example, as housing developments. Consequently, the income of the landowners may not decline in the long run, although in the short run, they may be unable to put their land to an alternative use. In order to build these considerations into a trade model, we must turn now to a short-run version of the HO model.

The Specific Factors Model

In the short run, the ability of factors to move between different output sectors is more limited. For example, suppose stiffer competition in the world steel industry causes American steelworkers to take pay cuts, and perhaps some lose their jobs. In the long run, most of the laid-off steelworkers will find jobs outside the steel sector, but in the short run, they are stuck with cuts in pay and layoffs. Similarly, physical capital is usually dedicated to a particular use and cannot be converted into producing a different product, and, as we have seen, land is usually tied up in a particular kind of use and cannot be switched to something else instantaneously. In the long run, however, plants and equipment can be redirected to a different line of production, land can be put to different uses, and workers find jobs doing something else.

In order to highlight the ability of labor and other factors to find alternative employment in the long run but not in the short run, economists sometimes add conditions to the HO model. Suppose there are three factors—land, labor, and capital—and two goods—steel and bread. Assume that the production of steel takes capital and labor, while bread takes land and labor. In this version of the HO model, labor is called the variable factor because its use varies between both goods. Land and capital are called the specific factors because their use is specific to bread and steel, respectively.

The model just described is an example of the **specific factors model**, a special case of the HO model. The HO model assumes that factors migrate easily from one sector to another, from steel to bread, for example. In the specific factors model, each good is produced with a specific factor, whose only use is in the production of that good, and a variable factor, which is used to produce both goods. The specific factors (land and capital) are immobile and cannot move between bread and steel, while the variable factor (labor) is completely mobile between industries.

The determinants of comparative advantage with a specific factors model is similar to the analysis with an HO model. As with HO, comparative advantage depends on factor endowments. The main difference in the two models is that the specific factor plays a critical role. Suppose that Canada is relatively well endowed with land and the United States is relatively well endowed with capital. Then Canada exports bread, and the United States exports steel. The reasoning is the same as with the HO model. Since Canada is well endowed with the specific factor used to make bread, its opportunity cost of bread production is lower than it is in the United States, where land is relatively less abundant. Similarly, steel uses capital, which is abundant in the United States and relatively scarce in Canada.

The analysis of the income distribution effects of trade is straightforward. When trade opens, each country follows its comparative advantage and moves toward greater specialization. The shift in production alters the demand for the specific factor that is used in the industry that shrinks. In each country, the specific factor in the declining industry experiences a fall in income. For example, Canada cuts back on steel production in order to concentrate on bread, which it exports for steel. Canadian owners of capital are hurt, since the structure of the economy changes away from the production of capital-intensive steel, while Canadian landowners experience precisely the opposite effect. Their incomes rise as the demand for land to produce bread exports rises. In the United States, landowners lose and capital owners win.

| TABLE 4.2 | A Specific Factors Model |

	Outputs	
Inputs	Bread	Steel
Specific factors	Land	Capital
Variable factors	Labor	Labor

The specific factors of land and capital can only be used to produce one good. The variable factor of labor is used in both bread and steel production.

In this example, the income distribution effects of trade on labor, the variable factor, are indeterminate. Since labor is mobile, workers laid off in the declining sector find employment in the expanding sector. Canadian workers find that steel is cheaper, so they are better off to the extent they consume products that embody steel. On the other hand, the fact that the world price of bread is above the price Canadians paid in autarky means that they are worse off to the extent that their income goes to buy bread. The net effect on Canadian labor depends on which effect is strongest, rising bread prices or falling steel prices. U.S. workers face rising steel prices and falling bread prices, and, again, the net effect is ambiguous and depends on their consumption patterns.

CASE STUDY

Forecasts of Winners and Losers Under NAFTA

When the United States, Mexico, and Canada began negotiations over the North American Free Trade Agreement, one of the major issues in the United States was the effect of free trade on the livelihood of various groups. The Heckscher-Ohlin trade model, the Stolper-Samuelson theorem, and the specific factors model were each used to analyze this effect.

Since the United States and Canada are similarly endowed with labor, capital, and land, and since they began a free-trade arrangement in 1989 (the Canadian-United States Trade Agreement, or CUSTA), NAFTA was not expected to significantly affect U.S.–Canadian trade. Mexico, however, was a different case. Where the United States and Canada have relatively abundant supplies of skilled labor, including scientists, engineers, managers, technicians, and professionals, Mexico has shortages of skilled labor and an abundant supply of unskilled and semiskilled labor. In addition, capital is relatively abundant in the United States and Canada and relatively scarce in Mexico. Finally,

Mexico's climate and soils make it a good location to produce many kinds of fruits and vegetables, but it is a poor location for grains.

Given these simple observations, it was relatively straightforward to estimate the winners and losers in a U.S.–Mexico trade agreement. Mexican industries that were expected to pose the greatest challenge to the United States were the ones that combined the experience of Mexico's relatively scarce entrepreneurs and managers with its abundant supply of unskilled and semi-skilled labor. To the extent that these industries could avoid large inputs of capital, they were likely to be even more competitive.

One of the first industries that was expected to gain was Mexico's small, but significant, apparel industry. Clothing manufacture requires little capital, some managerial expertise to obtain orders for clothing and ensure their timely delivery to purchasers, and an abundant supply of relatively less-skilled labor. (The fashion design industry is another matter. The focus here is on basic, standardized apparel, such as undershirts or socks.) In the United States, large sections of this industry exist only as a result of U.S. quotas on imports. Consequently, many long-run forecasts of the impacts of NAFTA on U.S. garment workers were negative. Unions in the apparel industry were cognizant of this fact, and they formed one of the strongest bases of opposition to NAFTA. In effect, labor in the apparel industry viewed itself as a specific factor that, given their skills and location, was unable to shift to another line of employment.

Industries that are similar to clothing manufacturing are leather goods, furniture, and building materials (stone, clay, and glass manufacturers). Each requires some material inputs (wood, cloth, leather, stone, and so on), less capital than in more advanced manufacturing processes, and a lot of basic labor.

In the area of agriculture, it was forecast that some labor-intensive fruit and vegetable crops would expand into Mexico and contract in the United States. These included frozen vegetables such as broccoli and cauliflower, and citrus crops such as oranges for frozen juice. Not surprisingly, Florida citrus growers and California avocado growers both opposed the agreement. As owners of specific factors (citrus and avocado groves), they had no alternative uses for their land.

On the other hand, U.S. crops that were capital rather than labor intensive were expected to benefit. Notable examples are cereals, both for human and animal consumption, and oilseeds. These crops use enormous quantities of agricultural machinery, together with extensive land inputs and a favorable climate to produce grains and legumes at prices that are competitive with the best in the world. In Mexico, producers of corn opposed the agreement.

A second type of industry that feared more open competition with Mexico was basic manufacturing. Industries included in this category are automobiles, some kinds of industrial machinery (e.g., pumps, diesel engines, electrical motors), and fabricated metal products, such as screws and fasteners. The capital requirements for production are much higher in these areas, but the products are so well established that there is little input of skilled labor in scientific research or product development. The labor used in the manufacturing process is more skilled than agricultural labor but can be trained on the job as long as it is literate.

An example of the opposition to NAFTA in the area of basic manufacturing is the autoworkers' union. Automobile manufacturing requires more capital than clothing or furniture, but many autoworkers feared that under the terms of a more open North American market, U.S. automakers would relocate their capital in Mexico where unskilled and semiskilled labor are relatively abundant and inexpensive. Autoworkers viewed alternatives to their current employment as dismal, and for that reason they formed one of the strongest blocs against NAFTA. Although they were not able to stop the agreement, they were instrumental in the creation of an expanded federal program for assisting workers whose livelihoods were harmed by the agreement.

In reality, the net effect of trade opening in basic manufacturing is ambiguous. Mexico's ability to compete depends on a number of additional factors in the wider economy. For example, auto assembly requires delivery to the factory

(continues)

of thousands of parts. If they must come all the way from Detroit or Windsor, Ontario, it may be uneconomical to assemble cars in Mexico. (Forecasts are that the Mexican car industry will grow over time, but there is a debate as to whether this will be at the expense of U.S. and Canadian producers or at the expense of European and Japanese firms.) In addition to parts suppliers, these more capital-intensive manufacturing processes depend on reliable, low-cost transportation and communication systems, along with overall infrastructure, such as power systems, water delivery, and waste disposal.

In the United States and Canada, the industries that were expected to benefit included the very capital-intensive grain and oilseeds industries. In addition, it was expected that a wide variety of more advanced manufacturing industries, including telecommunications, computing, aircraft, measuring and control devices, chemicals, and so on, would see growing markets. Furthermore, a number of skilled, high-wage service industries were also expected to expand, including banking, insurance, business services, engineering services, and others. Like advanced manufacturing, each of these service industries requires highly skilled, well-educated labor.

Forecasts of NAFTA's effects on income distribution depend on a number of other assumptions. In the simplest model, the prices of goods produced with abundant unskilled labor should rise in Mexico and fall in the United States, while goods produced with abundant skilled labor and capital should do the opposite. Consequently, in the short to medium run, unskilled labor is the beneficiary in Mexico, and skilled labor and capital benefit in the United States. The losers in Mexico are owners of Mexican capital that cannot move to alternative uses and skilled Mexican labor that likewise has no alternative use. In the United States, unskilled, immobile labor loses.

Two good summaries of these issues are *North American Free Trade: Issues and Recommendations* (1992), by Jeffrey Schott and Gary Clyde Hufbauer, and *North American Free Trade: Assessing the Impact* (1992), edited by Nora Lustig, Barry P. Bosworth, and Robert Z. Lawrence. See also *U.S.–Mexico Trade: Pulling Together or Pulling Apart?* (1992), Congress of the United States, Office of Technology Assessment.

EMPIRICAL TESTS OF THE THEORY OF COMPARATIVE ADVANTAGE

All the popular theories of trade are variations on the idea of comparative advantage. In addition, each theory makes predictions about the goods that a country will export and import. Therefore, it should be relatively straightforward to test each theory by holding its predictions up to actual trade flows and seeing if the two match. Unfortunately, empirical tests of trade theories are more difficult to conduct than they are to describe. Part of the problem is that it is difficult to measure variables such as factor endowments and prices in autarky.

The trade theories presented in this chapter and in Chapter 3 are the two most popular theories: the Ricardian theory of trade, based on relative productivities, and the Heckscher-Ohlin theory, based on factor endowments. In the Ricardian theory of Chapter 3, comparative advantage depended on relative productivity. This model is easier to test because it is easier to measure labor productivity than factor endowments. Therefore, it is not surprising that statistical tests of the Ricardian theory have been more successful. In general, they have confirmed the hypothesis that trade patterns between pairs of countries are determined to a significant degree by the relative differences in their labor productivities. More specifically, as labor productivity in a particular industry increases, the greater the likelihood the country becomes a net exporter of the good.

Tests of the Heckscher-Ohlin theory of trade have been mixed. One of the problems for any researcher in this area is that it is difficult to obtain a uniform set of measurements of factor endowments. In the presentation of the model in this chapter, only two inputs were considered, although we expanded that to three when we covered the specific factors model. In reality, there are many more than three factors. There are different kinds of labor (unskilled, semi-skilled, managerial, technical, and so forth), and there are many varieties of natural resources and capital. None of these categories have standardized definitions, and consequently each type of labor, capital, and natural resource is measured differently in each country. As a result, formal statistical analyses of tests of the HO theory have concluded that measurement errors in the data are a major problem.

Nevertheless, the consensus among economists seems to be that endowments matter, although they are far from the whole story. Even if it were possible to accurately measure factor endowments, technological differences between countries would not be captured, and these can be a significant source of productivity differences. In addition to technology, other important determinants of trade patterns not considered by the factor endowment theory are economies of scale, corporate structure, and economic policy.

While the theory of trade based on factor endowments receives only mixed empirical support, it nevertheless remains the foundation of most economists' thinking about trade. This may seem curious, but there is actually a good reason for it. While factor endowments cannot explain all of the world's trade patterns, they do explain a significant part of it. Therefore it is useful to begin with factor endowments and to supplement this view with other ideas. Perhaps most importantly, the factor endowment schema is a useful way to categorize the income distribution effects of trade. For both these reasons, the HO model and its variations remain at the core of international economics.

EXTENSION OF THE HECKSCHER–OHLIN MODEL

Several alternative trade models are popular in the literature. Both of the models presented below focus on an attribute of production in an industry or group of industries that makes them unlike the simple models assumed by the

Ricardian and HO models. Both, however, are elaborations of the theory of comparative advantage. In Chapter 5 we will leave the comparative advantage framework and look at cases where trade is not determined by productivity differences or factor endowments.

The Product Cycle

The **product cycle** model of trade was developed by Raymond Vernon. The model is an insightful analysis that incorporates ideas about the evolution of manufactured goods and technology. One of its greatest strengths is that it can explain exports of sophisticated manufactured goods from countries that have shortages of skilled labor and capital.

Vernon pointed out that many manufactured products, such as automobiles, VCRs, and semiconductors, go through a product cycle in which the inputs change over time. Initially, when these goods are brand new, there is a great deal of experimentation in both the characteristics of the final product and its manufacturing process. For example, when video machines were first developed for the home market, there was a wide variety of different forms to choose from. There were laser discs, betamax, and VHS, each of which had different sets of options, often even within the same technology. That is, while betamax differed from VHS, the features on a VHS machine were not standardized either.

In this early stage of production, manufacturers need to be near a high-income market, where consumer feedback is greatest. Experimentation with basic design features requires information about the market's reaction. Consequently, there must be both a consumer base with substantial income and skilled marketing to advertise information about the product. In addition, on the input side, experimentation and improvement in design and manufacturing require scientific and engineering inputs, along with capital that is willing to risk failure and an initial period of little or no profits. Both the consumption side and the production side necessitate that product research, development, and initial production take place in industrial countries.

Over time, however, the product begins to leave the early phase of its development and production and enters the middle phase (Figures 4.5 and 4.6). The product itself begins to be standardized in size, features, and manufacturing process. Experimentation with fundamentally new designs begins to wane as product development shifts toward incremental improvements in a basic design. In the middle phase, production begins to shift to countries with low labor costs. Standardized manufacturing routines are increasingly common, using low-skilled and semiskilled labor in assembly-type operations.

Countries reach the late phase of the product cycle when consumption in high-income nations begins to exceed production. At this point, an increasing share of the world's output is moving to developing countries where abundant unskilled and semiskilled labor keep labor costs low. The pressure on high-income countries in the late phase is to turn toward innovation of new products, which starts the cycle over again.

| FIGURE 4.5 | The Product Cycle in High-Income Countries |

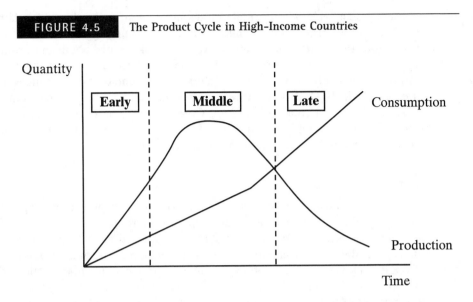

Many manufactured goods experience a product cycle of innovation, stabilization, and standardization.

| FIGURE 4.6 | The Product Cycle in Low-Income Countries |

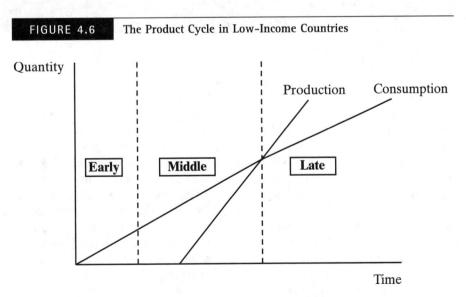

Low-income countries begin production during the period of stabilization.

The product cycle is a more elaborate story about technology than either the Ricardian or HO models. It may seem to differ fundamentally from those models, but in fact it is very similar. At its core is a story about opportunity costs. As manufacturing processes become standardized, they can be performed by relatively unskilled labor. In effect, the blend of inputs changes over time, from highly skilled scientific, engineering, and marketing elements to basic unskilled and semiskilled labor. Consequently, the opportunity cost of production in developing countries becomes lower than the cost in high-income countries. In essence, it's the Ricardian story once again.

Intra-firm Trade

Advances in transportation and communications have played an important part in the development of a product cycle. Jet aircraft, container ships, fax machines, satellite systems, and e-mail have enabled firms in Japan, Taiwan, or the United States to relocate part of their production far from their home base of operations. Goods produced in Guangdong province in China or along the U.S.–Mexican border in Ciudad Juarez, can be monitored from a home base in Chicago or Osaka. As a result, a significant share of world trade is international trade between a parent company and a foreign-owned affiliate, called **intra-firm trade**. An example is U.S. exports of Toyota Camrys from Toyota of America to Toyota in Japan.

CASE STUDY

United States–China Trade

China is the world's most populous nation, with more than 1.2 billion people in mid-2000, according to the U.S. Census Bureau. It is also one of the world's poorest nations. The World Bank puts its GNP per capita at the equivalent of $750 (at market exchange rates, 1998). About 20 percent of China's adults are estimated to be illiterate.

China's economy was substantially closed to the outside until 1978, when it began significant economic reforms. Initially, the reforms were limited to agriculture, but they quickly incorporated a number of special economic zones in the coastal regions (see Chapter 17).

China's proximity to Hong Kong, along with large populations of Chinese in Taiwan, Hong Kong, Singapore, and other regions of East Asia, enabled it to attract huge amounts of foreign investment once it became receptive to capital inflows. The net result is that its economy and, especially, its exports have grown rapidly over the last two decades.

China's resource endowment includes a huge population of unskilled and semiskilled labor and a relative scarcity of scientific and engineering talent. It is not surprising, therefore, that its exports are heavily weighted toward labor-intensive manufactured goods.

Table 4.2 lists the top ten Chinese exports to the United States in 1999. The major items are simple manufactured goods that use China's abundant labor together with a little capital: toys, shoes, apparel, and so forth. In the top ten, items 1, 2, 5, 8, 9, and 10 fall into this category. Item 7 might also be categorized as producing a relatively unsophisticated product with labor-intensive manufacturing.

Items 3, 4, and 6, however, appear to be different. These are high-tech items related to telecommunications and computing (data processing), and they also illustrate the product cycle. These Chinese exports originate in assembly operations, many of which have been set up with capital from outside China. A telephone manufacturer, for example, decides to take advantage of low wages by producing a standardized product in China. Once the assembly plant is built, only a handful of skilled workers are required to keep it running. Most workers can be quickly trained to fasten together pieces and to perform simple diagnostic tests on the product. The result is that China exports telecommunications equipment and appears to have a developing high-technology sector. No design, research, or industrial engineering takes place there, however.

Similarly, several decades ago, radio receivers and plastics (items 7 and 10) were exclusively products of industrial countries. They became standardized, along with the methods for producing them, and production migrated to places where unskilled labor was relatively more abundant. In sum, China's successful export drive has utilized two forces: a shift toward its comparative advantage and the product cycle.

TABLE 4.2	Top 10 Chinese Exports to the United States, 1999

Item	Value, Millions of $
1. Toys and sporting goods	11,639
2. Footwear	8,434
3. Automatic data processing machines	4,116
4. Telecommunications equipment	3,434
5. Furniture & bedding accessories	3,262
6. Parts for office machines & ADP machines	3,208
7. Radiobroadcast receivers	2,189
8. Women/girls coats, not knit	2,158
9. Articles of apparel of textile fabrics	2,126
10. Articles of plastics	2,111

China's labor endowment and the product cycle explain its export pattern.

Source: Department of Commerce, *United States Foreign Trade Highlights, 2000.* http://www.ita.doc.gov/otea/, October, 2000.

Intra-firm trade occurs for several reasons. When a firm spreads its production across international boundaries, it can take advantage of differences in the price of inputs. Unskilled labor is abundant in China, for example, so by locating assembly processes there, manufacturers are able to significantly reduce their direct labor costs. A second reason for intra-firm trade is to reduce the costs of intermediate inputs that are obtained in foreign markets. For example, an American manufacturer may find that it can reduce the price and secure a more continuous flow of quality inputs if it goes through a foreign subsidiary rather than buying the inputs from wholly independent foreign firms. And finally, intra-firm trade is also a means to reduce distribution costs. A manufacturer may find it cheaper to work with distributors that it owns than with independent firms.

Recent estimates indicate that in the mid-1990s about one-third of U.S. merchandise exports and about two-fifths of U.S. merchandise imports took place in the context of intra-firm trade, with the proportions varying significantly by country.

In many respects, intra-firm trade may be another elaboration of the idea of comparative advantage through the product cycle. For example, Sony and Sanyo decide to assemble televisions in Tijuana, Mexico, where labor costs are low and they are close to the large U.S. market. They keep their research and design labs at home in Japan (or in San Diego, across the border from the assembly operations), however, where engineering and scientific talent are relatively abundant. In this example, Sony and Sanyo are sharing their production globally in order to take advantage of factor price differences across international boundaries.

However, there are also reasons to believe that a significant share (no one knows how much) of intra-firm trade is not determined by comparative advantage. Firms may locate in a foreign market to deter entry by competitors; to use low production costs for one product line to subsidize production of another product line (cross-subsidization); to subsidize one region's customers by another's; or to escape taxation. In addition, firms may view multiple locations as "insurance" against unforeseen events, such as political upheavals, radical exchange rate fluctuations, and so forth.

There is little consensus among economists about the meaning of all this. On the one hand, it is simply another form of trade, and no special considerations are necessary. On the other hand, the market power and strategic behavior of multinational corporations (MNCs) cause some to argue that this type of trade is significantly different. They argue that since this trade is (partly) unrelated to resource endowments or input costs, it should be viewed through the lens of national industrial regulation and antitrust, or else markets will become less open to competition.

There is one area of agreement, however. As firms spread around the globe, developing affiliates in foreign markets, it becomes increasingly difficult for them to keep their technology proprietary. This is especially true as firms expand the amount of R&D (research and development) that they do abroad.

In this regard, there is no doubt that the expansion of MNCs has helped diffuse technology across national boundaries and has undermined the efforts of countries to keep their technology within their own borders.

THE IMPACT OF TRADE
ON WAGES AND JOBS

Since the 1960s, manufacturing in North America and Europe has become a smaller part of the economy when measured as a share of GDP and as a share of overall employment. In Europe, the assumption that a shrinking manufacturing sector is a significant problem has been emphasized by high rates of overall unemployment and very slow growth in the total number of new jobs created in the economy. At the same time, wage inequality has increased, rather slowly at first, then more rapidly in the 1980s. Wage inequality has been particularly severe in the United States and has primarily affected younger workers and workers with less schooling or fewer skills. More recently, in the late 1990s, wage inequality has stopped increasing, but it is still too early to tell if this is temporary or permanent.

Many observers question whether the rise in manufactured imports from low-wage, developing economies has something to do with these trends. Could it be that the high-wage, industrialized nations are losing jobs to developing economies and, at the same time, are having their wages forced down in order to remain competitive?

Let's take each trend separately. The first issue is whether trade has a negative impact on the number of jobs available to workers in high-wage countries. Economic theory offers some evidence on this issue. In the medium run and long run, the absolute number of jobs depends mainly on factors such as the age and size of the population, rules governing the hiring and firing of employees (labor market policies), and the generosity of the social safety net (incentives to work). In the short run, one of the primary determinants of the number of jobs is the government's macroeconomic policies, which determine variables such as interest rates, taxes, and overall government expenditures. While trade may have a short-run effect as well, particularly if firms cannot compete against imports, or if sudden opportunities for export expansion appear, these impacts are usually outweighed by macroeconomic policies affecting the entire domestic economy. By comparison, changes in trade flows usually affect one or two manufacturing industries and a small share of overall GDP. Trade will certainly affect the composition of jobs, but it is unlikely to have much impact on the overall number of jobs.

The problem of persistently high unemployment in some European countries, such as Spain and France, cannot be caused by trade. While it is possible that some of the lost manufacturing jobs throughout the industrial world have resulted from increased trade flows, the inability of laid-off workers to find new jobs must be attributed to labor market policies that restrict job creation or macroeconomic policies that restrict overall economic growth. Ten or fifteen years of high unemployment, which has been the norm in many European countries, is a long enough time period for even the most radical restructuring to occur. The fact that unemployment remains high means that new jobs are not created elsewhere in the economy.

Furthermore, a majority of the reductions in manufacturing employment in all industrial countries appears to have resulted from productivity gains, not trade. Manufacturing is easier to automate than services (e.g., automating gardening, house cleaning, or health care is very difficult, if not impossible) and as a consequence has much faster rates of productivity growth than services. In essence, because productivity grows so fast in manufacturing, it takes fewer and fewer people to produce the tangible, manufactured products we consume. Many services, on the other hand, have stagnant or very slow rates of productivity growth. Often the same number of workers is required today as it was centuries ago; one haircut, for example, still takes only one barber (who may or may not be faster), and modern musicians are no more "productive" at playing Bach's Brandenburg Concertos than they were in the 1700s. When incomes rise, we consume more services and more manufactured goods, but because the services require more or less the same number of workers per unit made, and manufactured goods can be made with fewer workers per good, a growing share of our total employment ends up in services.

The second issue concerns the impact of trade with less-developed countries (LDCs) on the wages of workers in the advanced industrial economies. This question has been studied by many economists, and the general consensus is that trade may have caused some of the decline in wages for the less skilled (and, hence, some of the increase in wage inequality), but it is responsible for only a small share of the overall changes. The primary culprit seems to be technological changes that have reduced the role of unskilled and semiskilled labor in manufacturing.

The Stolper-Samuelson theorem predicts that if the United States and other industrial countries have relatively scarce supplies of unskilled labor (by comparison to less-developed countries), then trade will cause the wages of unskilled workers to fall. Over the years, however, firms can alter their use of inputs to take advantage of cheaper ones and to conserve on more expensive ones. The key is that the time frame must be sufficiently long so that firms can alter their capital and other inputs. In the case of skilled and unskilled labor the reverse has happened. As skilled labor has become more expensive, firms have used relatively more, and as unskilled labor has become cheaper, they have used less. This trend has gone on for over two decades, so firms have had plenty of time to alter their production technologies, if they can. The only logical explanation is that technology has created larger roles for skilled labor and smaller ones for the unskilled.

While it seems the consensus of professional economic opinion is that technological change and not trade is responsible for the lion's share of both the decline in manufactured jobs and the growth of wage inequality, there is also a widespread recognition that economists really aren't sure. A small number of economists have produced controversial calculations showing that trade has played a far larger role in the growth of wage inequality than is generally recognized. At any rate, the policy conclusions are likely to be the same. Regardless of the causes, there seems to be a greater need for education and training programs targeted at the less skilled. The next two chapters will show that blocking trade to protect jobs is extraordinarily expensive, and doing so to protect wages will actually make things worse in the long run.

Summary

- The Heckscher-Ohlin model hypothesizes that comparative advantage is based on national differences in factor endowments. Countries export goods that have production requirements that are intensive in the nation's relatively abundant factors. They import goods that require intensive input from the nation's relatively scarce factors.

- The Heckscher-Ohlin model has implications for the income distribution effects of trade. The opening of trade favors the abundant factor and reduces the use of the scarce factor. Consequently, the income or returns earned by the abundant factor rises, while it falls for the scarce factor. A corollary to the Heckscher-Ohlin model, called the Stolper-Samuelson theorem, describes these effects.

- In the specific factors model, some factors of production are assumed to be immobile between different outputs. Consequently, when trade expands the production of it, the specific factor used to produce it experiences a rise in the demand for its services, and its income increases. The specific factor used to produce the import good experiences a fall in the demand for its services, and its income declines. The specific factors model can be viewed as a short- to medium-run version of the HO model.

- Empirical tests of the theory of comparative advantage give mixed results. While underlying productivity differences explain a significant share of trade, national differences in factor endowments are less successful at explaining trade patterns.

- Several alternative trade models have been hypothesized. Most are elaborations of the theory of comparative advantage. Two of the most popular alternative trade theories are the theory of the product cycle and the theory of intra-firm trade. The product cycle focuses on the speed of technological change and the life history of many manufactured items through periods of innovation, stabilization, and standardization. The theory of intra-firm trade allows a role for comparative advantage but also has industrial organization elements. It is impossible to state a general rule about the determinants of intra-firm trade.

- In the medium to long run, trade has little or no effect on the number of jobs in a country. The abundance or scarcity of jobs is a function of labor market policies, incentives to work, and the macroeconomic policies of the central bank and government. In the short run, trade may reduce jobs in an industry that suffers a loss in its competitiveness, just as it may increase jobs in an industry with growing competitiveness.

■ The consensus among economists is that trade between developing and high-income countries may have contributed slightly to the decline in real wages for unskilled workers in the industrial economies. This is consistent with the predictions of the Stolper-Samuelson theorem. The main cause of increasing wage inequality is thought to be technological changes that have reduced the demand for unskilled labor and increased it for skilled, highly educated labor. This point is not settled, however, and continues to receive a significant amount of empirical investigation.

Vocabulary

derived demand

factor abundance

factor scarcity

Heckscher-Ohlin (HO) theory

intra-firm trade

magnification effect

product cycle

specific factors model

Stolper-Samuelson theorem

Study Questions

1. According to the following table, which country is relatively more labor abundant? Explain how you know. Which country is relatively capital abundant?

	United States	*Canada*
Capital	40 machines	10 machines
Labor	200 workers	60 workers

2. Suppose that the United States and Canada have the factor endowments in the preceding table. Suppose further that the production requirements for a unit of steel is two machines and eight workers, and the requirement for a unit of bread is one machine and eight workers.
   a) Which good, bread or steel, is relatively capital intensive? Labor intensive? Explain how you know.
   b) Which country would export bread? Why?

3. Suppose that, before trade takes place, the United States is at a point on its PPC where it produces 20 bread and 20 steel. Once trade becomes possible, the price of a unit of steel is two units of bread. In response, the United States moves along its PPC to a new point where it produces 30 steel and 10 bread. Is the country better off? How do you know?

4. Given the information in questions 1 and 2, explain what happens to the returns to capital and labor after trade begins.

5. Suppose that there are three factors: capital, labor, and land. Bread requires inputs of land and labor, and steel requires capital and labor.
   a) Which factors are variable, and which are specific?
   b) Suppose Canada's endowments are 10 capital and 100 land and the United States's are 50 capital and 100 land. Which good does each country export?
   c) How does trade affect the returns to land, labor, and capital in the United States and in Canada?

6. Describe the changes in production requirements and the location of production that take place over the three phases of the product cycle.

7. Does intra-firm trade contradict the theory of comparative advantage? Why, or why not?

APPENDIX: FINDING TRADE DATA

U.S. Data

Data on U.S. trade in individual commodities are easy to find. The problem for the first-time user of U.S. data is to make sense of the classifications used to categorize goods and services. Export and import statistics are initially collected and compiled into 8000 and 14,000 commodity classifications, respectively. These classifications conform to a standard for classifying goods known as the Harmonized Commodity Description and Coding System, or the Harmonized System (HS). The HS was developed by the Customs Cooperation Council in Brussels, Belgium, and included participants from the United States, Canada, Western Europe, and Japan. A source of confusion is that the description of U.S. data in HS format bears the names TSUSA (Tariff Schedule for the United States, Annotated) for imports and Schedule B for exports.

A second system of classifying goods is also used by the United States, the United Nations, and many other nations. This is the Standard International Trade Classification (SITC). The SITC is on its third revision, so it is sometimes called the SITC-Rev. 3. The Harmonized System and the SITC are interrelated, and in effect the SITC scheme is an aggregation of the HS. For example, the United States takes its 8000 HS categories of exports and summarizes them into 3000 SITC categories, which it calls Schedule E. The HS categories for imports are rearranged in SITC codes and called Schedule A. The SITC system is useful for international comparisons and is the form in which the most commonly available U.S. publications present their data.

Table 4.A lists the names used by U.S. publications to label imports and exports, classified according to the HS or SITC system. For example, reading across the row labeled Exports, we see that HS export data is called Schedule B and that Schedule E is the rearrangement of the data into SITC format.

Three other commodity classifications are in use, and although they are of lesser importance worldwide, they are relevant for research on the United States. One is another summarization of the HS into what is called the End Use

TABLE 4.A	U.S. Names for Trade Data Classifications Schemes	
	Harmonized System (HS)	*Standard International Trade Classification (SITC)*
Exports	Schedule B	Schedule E
Imports	Tariff Schedule of the United States, Annotated (TSUSA)	Schedule A

Commodity Category. It consists of 6 principal categories and 140 broad category definitions. Several of the more commonly found U.S. publications use these commodity definitions to summarize reported data. Another classification scheme is the Standard Industrial Classification (SIC) code, which is used to classify industries. The SIC code and the associated trade data are being replaced with the North American Industrial Classification System (NAICS), which is a harmonization of the codes of Canada, Mexico, and the United States. The SIC and its replacement, the NAICS, are the primary systems for reporting information about industries. Having the trade data on the same basis allows comparisons to be made between industries and for the trade data to be linked up with the characteristics of particular industries.

There are numerous U.S. publications with trade data. They appear in various media, including hardcopy, CD-ROM, computer tape, and online. A complete description can be found in the U.S. Department of Commerce publication, *Guide to Foreign Trade Statistics*. The *Guide* describes the classification systems in use, the publications available, and how to obtain them. The government documents department of any federal depository library should have it. It is also available online through the federal government's subscription data archive, STAT-USA.

The easiest source of free online data is located on the International Trade Administration Web site (*http://www.ita.doc.gov*). The ITA offers access to annual publications, such as *United States Foreign Trade Highlights*, and several databases. You can find trade by region, by commodity (under the HS, SITC, and SIC classification schemes), and by country. In addition, the ITA site shows exports by state and city.

International Data

Most international data are presented in the SITC-Rev. 3 format. The leading sources are:

1. *International Trade Centre (ITC) (http://www.intracen.org)* The ITC is a partnership between the UN and the WTO. It provides a wide variety of free, online trade data, including export profiles of individual countries,

an index of online trade data from commercial and noncommercial sources, and five years of trade statistics for most of the world's nations, classified in SITC-Rev. 3 format.

2. *International Trade Statistics Yearbook* The *Yearbook* is published by the United Nations, along with the more general *Statistical Yearbook*. The *Yearbook* of trade statistics is more detailed in its treatment of commodity flows. Goods are classified on the basis of SITC-Rev. 3 codes. It is useful for historical data.

3. *Direction of Trade Statistics (DOTS)* DOTS is one of several sister publications of the International Monetary Fund. DOTS is an easy-to-use source of information on trade between pairs of countries. It has annual data for the most recent seven or eight years, along with percentage changes. DOTS does not disaggregate the data by commodity.

Chapter 5

BEYOND COMPARATIVE ADVANTAGE

INTRODUCTION

The idea of comparative advantage is the foundation of our understanding of the gains from trade and its potential income distribution effects. Unfortunately, trade models built exclusively on the idea of comparative advantage have a mixed record when it comes to predicting a country's trade patterns. This is an important failure since we tend to think that if we accurately measured a country's comparative advantage, we should be able to predict import and export patterns. In addition, if we knew in advance what specific products an economy could produce at the lowest relative cost, it would give policymakers and entrepreneurs a definite advantage in deciding what to produce. The problem, however, is that it is exceedingly difficult to measure a country's comparative advantage. This problem is compounded by the fact that there are many potential products an economy might export that use the same comparative advantage, and there is no way to determine which specific products will dominate. Furthermore, and perhaps most seriously, a large share of international trade is not based on comparative advantage. This chapter takes up two important exceptions to the models of the previous chapters, and examines how and why many countries try to select and plan the development of their export industries.

The first section tries to make sense of the fact that an important share of world trade consists of countries exporting the same thing they import. Canada and the United States, for example, have the largest trade relationship in the world, and a large share of it is based on both countries exporting cars and car parts to each other. This pattern is clearly at odds with the bread-for-steel examples of Chapter 3 and 4. In the second section of the chapter, we examine industrial clustering. Many traded goods and services that are essential parts of a country's exports are produced in regional clusters. For example, the U.S. advantage in entertainment products (music, television programming, movies) largely reflects the output of a handful of regions such as Hollywood and Nashville. Software reflects clusters in Silicon Valley, Seattle, and a few other spots, and biotechnology is in San Francisco, San Diego, and a handful of other places. Surprisingly, international trade can play an important role in this type of clustering and may, under certain conditions, prevent new clusters from forming.

The issue of regional clusters leads directly into a discussion of industrial policies in the third section of the chapter. Industrial policies are the tools many countries use to address the challenge of trying to plan an advantage in a particular industry or a group of products. Can countries pick the items they will export and successfully build a strong export industry? What are the costs and benefits of the policies they follow? At bottom, we are asking if comparative advantage is mutable and how nations can use their policies to shape its development.

INTRAINDUSTRY TRADE

The models of comparative advantage developed in the two previous chapters are built on the foundation of country differences. In those models, differences in productivity (Chapter 3) or factor endowments (Chapter 4) make it possible for countries to raise their living standards by specializing their production and trading. The point of these models is not to paint a detailed portrait of economic life, but rather to create a simplified abstract model of the economy that is focused on key economic relations in the area of trade. To that end, unnecessary details are omitted, and rare or exceptional cases are ignored.

It sometimes happens that rare or exceptional cases become more important over time. Such is the case with the increasing importance of **intraindustry trade** (the prefix "intra" means *within*). Intraindustry trade is the international trade of products made within the same industry, for example steel-for-steel, or bread-for-bread. The opposite of intraindustry trade is **interindustry trade** (the prefix "inter" means *between*). Interindustry trade is international trade of products between two different industries, for example bread-for-steel. The growing importance of intraindustry trade has forced economists to develop a new set of models in order to explain the reasons why countries often export the same goods they import, and to explain how they benefit from this type of trade.

Measures of Intraindustry Trade

Intraindustry trade between industrial countries is common. Empirical measures of the importance of intraindustry trade vary, however, because of the fundamental problem of defining an industry. For example, if computers are defined as office machinery, then computers and pencil sharpeners are in the same industry and a country that exports computers and imports pencil sharpeners would be engaged in intraindustry trade. In general, the broader the definition of an industry, the more trade appears to be intraindustry. Conversely, the more detailed the definition, the less trade is defined as intraindustry. Intraindustry trade is measured for each industry with a statistic called the **Grubel-Lloyd (GL) index**:

$$GL_i = 1 - \frac{|X_i - M_i|}{X_i + M_i}$$

The equation says that the index for any industry (industry "i") is calculated by taking the absolute value of the trade balance for the industry, $|X_i - M_i|$, dividing it by industry exports plus imports from the same industry, $X_i + M_i$, and subtracting the ratio from 1. If exports of a domestic industry are equal to the value of imports from the same industry ($X_i = M_i$), then the numerator in the ratio is equal to 0, and the index equals 1. In that case, all of the industry's trade is intraindustry. Conversely, if exports are not matched by any imports in the same industry, or imports have no matching exports, then either X_i or M_i will be 0. In that case, the numerator equals the denominator, the index is 0, and none of the industry's trade is intraindustry. In order to calculate the index for the whole economy and not just for one industry, both the numerator and the denominator of the ratio are summed over all industries before calculating the ratio, and the result is subtracted from 1.

Estimates of the share of total U.S. merchandise trade that is intraindustry range between one-third and two-thirds, depending on the narrowness of the definitions of industry. When narrow definitions are used, so that goods are classified together only when they are very similar, U.S. intraindustry trade is more than 50 percent of total merchandise trade (excluding services and food). This pattern is repeated for most industrial countries, and probably more than 40 percent of total world trade is intraindustry. Evidence suggests that intraindustry trade is greater in high technology industries where the rapid generation of new products leads to greater product differentiation, and is greater in countries with few barriers to trade. Intraindustry trade also grows in importance as a nation's income rises.

Characteristics of Intraindustry Trade

In the models of comparative advantage-based trade presented in Chapters 3 and 4, production costs are either constant (Chapter 3) or increasing (Chapter 4). Accordingly, each additional unit of bread produced led to the loss of a fixed or increasing amount of steel. The production of many goods, however, is characterized by **economies of scale**, or decreasing costs, over a relatively large range of output. Economies of scale can be either **internal economies** or **external economies**. Internal economies are defined as falling average costs over a relatively large range of output. In practice, this leads to larger firms because size confers a competitive advantage in the form of lower average costs. One of the distinguishing features of intraindustry trade is the presence of internal economies of scale. In the case of external economies, larger firms have no inherent advantage over smaller firms, but average costs decline for all firms as the size of the industry increases. Unlike internal economies of scale, with external economies, the size or scale effects are located in the industry and not in the firm. We will examine external economies when we look at industrial clustering later in the chapter.

Table 5.1 illustrates a firm's cost structure when it experiences increasing returns to scale. More output leads to higher costs, but the cost per unit, or average cost, declines. In most cases, with increasing production levels, average

| TABLE 5.1 | Increasing Returns to Scale for a Single Firm |

Output	Total Cost	Average Cost
100	1000	10
200	1400	7
300	1500	5
400	1600	4
500	1650	3.5
600	1950	3.25

As production increases, total costs rise, but the cost per unit falls. Bigger firms are more efficient than smaller firms.

cost begins eventually to rise. In a few cases, such as commercial jet aircraft discussed later in the chapter, the output level at which average cost starts to rise is equal to a large share of the entire world market and, consequently, large firms have enormous advantages. Increasing returns are usually based on the inherent development, engineering, or marketing aspects of production and are associated with products that have a large fixed cost component. Car companies, software, and popular household brand name products, to name a few, tend to have large fixed costs. These occur for various reasons, such as the cost of constructing a large production plant, large R&D budgets, or large marketing expenditures. Software, for example, requires large up-front expenditures on R&D to develop a product, and the more units a firm can sell, the more it can spread out those fixed R&D costs.

Internal economies of scale have important implications for the type of market that prevails. In Chapters 3 and 4, it is assumed that firms operate in competitive markets where no one firm can influence prices or overall industry output. When larger firms are more competitive, however, it reduces the number of firms in a market and leads to one of several types of market structures. In an **oligopoly**, a handful of firms produce the entire market output. The pattern of production and trade is very difficult to predict in this case, because each firm uses predictions about the actions of its competitors as it formulates its own profit-maximizing strategy. This type of response means that each firm alters its output level as it sees what its competitors are doing, and production levels and trade become less predictable. An example is presented later in the chapter in the material discussing industrial policies and strategic trade theory.

Internal economies often lead to the relatively common market structure called **monopolistic competition**. Recall that in a pure monopoly, one firm produces the entire industry output. In monopolistic competition, there is competition among many firms, but their competition is attenuated by the practice of **product differentiation**. With product differentiation, each firm produces a slightly different product. This gives rise to the monopoly element of monopolistic competition, in that each firm is the sole producer of its products. For example, only Ford can sell Ford Explorers. Unlike a pure monopoly, however, every other firm produces a close substitute and this introduces a real element of competition.

In monopolistic competition, the level of competition between firms increases whenever new firms enter the market. This has two effects. On the one hand, heightened competition will lead to lower prices. This happens because products are substitutes for each other and in the struggle to capture sales, downward pressure is placed on prices. On the other hand, when more firms divide the market, each firm on average sells fewer units of output, and so costs rise. This follows directly from the internal economies of each firm. As long as prices are above costs, more firms will enter the market, and whenever prices are below costs, firms exit.

The presence of internal economies of scale is the reason why firms want to enter export markets. Any firm that exports has a competitive advantage since it will have higher sales and be able to take advantage of the cost-reducing effects of its internal economies of scale. For any given number of firms, average costs are lower in a larger market. This follows from the economies of scale that each firm experiences and the fact that if the number of firms is held constant, each firm sells more as the size of the market expands.

The Gains from Intraindustry Trade

Intraindustry trade also creates gains from trade. While the increase in the size of the market leads to lower costs through the effect of scale economies, competition between firms forces them to pass their lower costs on to consumers in the form of lower prices. Lower prices for exports and imports stands in marked contrast to the case of comparative advantage-based trade. Recall that in the trade models of both Chapters 3 and 4, each country's consumers benefit from a reduction in the price of the good it imports, but at the same time, the price of the export rises. Higher export prices occurs because the world price with trade falls below the foreign price, but above the domestic price. Higher export prices benefit the country's producers and encourage them to expand production, but the export price movements hurt consumers. With intraindustry trade, however, prices for both imports and exports decline, leading to unambiguous benefits for consumers in both countries. The decline in prices brought on by intraindustry trade is a result of increased output under conditions of internal economies of scale. Trade enables these firms to produce at a higher level of efficiency and that raises everyone's real income through the reduction in prices.

The expansion of the market that occurs with trade ultimately leads to an increase in the number of firms. This follows from the fact that exports initially create a situation where costs are below prices. This attracts new firms into the market, and the excess profits that firms initially earn are competed away. It is indeterminate if the increase in the number of firms comes about through an increase in domestic or foreign firms, or how the increase might be divided between the two. While it is safe to say that the combined foreign and domestic industry will expand, the location of the expansion is indeterminate. It is even conceivable that foreigners might expand disproportionately and leave the domestic industry smaller than it was initially. While this cannot be ruled out, in general, intraindustry trade is usually perceived as less threatening to jobs and firms than comparative advantage-based trade. This difference is primarily due to the decline of the import sector in comparative advantage-based trade, and the need for some or all of its workers to look for work in the expanding export sector. By contrast, in intraindustry trade, there is a significant likelihood that trade expands the number of domestic firms and the quantity of domestic output. At the very least, domestic firms have an opportunity to expand, and it would be expected that well-run firms would take heed of the larger market available to them. This makes intraindustry trade inherently less threatening and less likely to lead to complaints about fairness or that foreigners are taking advantage of lower labor or environmental standards in order to expand their production. Recall also that intraindustry trade is primarily between countries of similar income and factor endowments, which also reduces the tendency toward protectionist pressure.

In addition to lower prices (higher real income) and the potential expansion of production, another benefit from intraindustry trade is that it increases consumer choices. Without trade, consumers are limited to the goods produced in the domestic market. This is not necessarily a limitation for some people, but a scan of the highways should be enough to convince anyone that many consumers prefer foreign-made goods over their domestic substitutes. The value of added choices is not easy to measure in dollar terms, but it is clearly a significant benefit for most people.

CASE STUDY

United States–Canada Trade

In 1965, the United States and Canada implemented a free-trade policy that covered autos and auto parts. The results were dramatic, particularly on the Canadian side of the border. Prior to the Auto Pact, Canada required most cars sold domestically to be made inside the country. The relatively small market in Canada meant that only a few different car models were produced, each in small batches that cost more to make since automakers could not take full advantage of economies of scale in production. After the Auto Pact, automakers refocused production on a smaller number of models that were produced for the combined Canadian and U.S. market. Canadian productivity in the automobile industry rose dramatically as the scale of production

(continues)

increased. In addition, as imports from the United States increased, Canadian consumers had many more models to choose from.

Overall, the automobile industry began to completely integrate production in the United States and Canada. Trade between the two countries rose dramatically, and eventually grew into the largest bilateral trade relationship of any two countries in the world. Table 5.2 illustrates the importance of intraindustry trade.

Four of the top seven U.S. exports to Canada and three of the top seven imports are motor vehicles or related products. In terms of value, an overwhelming share of the top seven exports and imports are car-related. Clearly, intraindustry trade is fundamental to the U.S.–Canadian trade pattern.

It is also interesting to note that the top seven U.S. imports include a number of Canadian exports that take advantage of its rich endowment of forests (paper and wood) and oil. This part of the trade relationship illustrates comparative advantage-based trade built around differing factor endowments. As a result, U.S.–Canadian trade is partly intraindustry, partly comparative advantage-based.

TABLE 5.2	U.S.–Canadian Merchandise Trade, 1999 (billions of U.S. dollars)		
Top 7 U.S. Exports	*Value*	*Top 7 U.S. Imports*	*Value*
Motor vehicle parts*	17.3	All motor vehicles*	34.2
All motor vehicles*	9.5	Misc. unclassified transactions	9.7
Internal combustion engines*	7.5	Motor vehicle parts*	9.3
Thermionic, cold cathode, photocathode valves	5.7	Special-purpose vehicles*	9.2
Data processing machinery	5.6	Paper and paperboard	7.6
Special-purpose vehicles*	4.0	Wood	7.3
Telecommunications equipment	3.9	Crude oil	6.6

Cars and car parts are the largest component of U.S.–Canadian trade.

*Represent products related to motor vehicle manufacturing.

Source: Department of Commerce, *United States Foreign Trade Highlights, 1999.* http://www.ita.doc.gov/td/industry/otea/usfth (July, 2000).

TRADE AND GEOGRAPHY

The telecommunications revolution has reduced the size of geographical barriers and lessened the importance of distance. Satellites, fiber optics, cell phones, and e-mail have dramatically reduced the cost of communicating over vast distances and enabled firms to coordinate production that is spread around the globe. At the same time, and in a somewhat contradictory manner, discussion of these developments often assumes a critically important role for geographical concentrations of technology such as Silicon Valley or the Research Triangle. Clearly, distance still matters for some things. High-tech startups may be able to locate anywhere, but a lot of them still want to be in Silicon Valley, even though housing and other costs are ridiculously high and freeways are congested. The concentration of software design, biotechnology, carpet manufacturing, and a number of other industries in just a few locations tells us that geography and distance have not been completely conquered by the recent advances in telecommunications. The fact that firms are willing to take on the higher costs of locating in Silicon Valley, for example, is strong evidence that for some types of firms there are large financial benefits to geographical clustering.

It may be obvious that the incentives for some firms to form regional concentrations, or **agglomerations**, are still very strong in spite of the recent advances in telecommunications and transportation, but it is probably not too clear what it has to do with trade and trade patterns. There are two key connections between geography and trade. First, as trade barriers come down, there are powerful incentives for some industries to reallocate production to take advantage of lower trade costs. For example, Mexico used to require firms to make cars inside the country if they wanted to sell them there, but as the North American car market became more integrated following the opening of the Mexican economy, a different pattern of automobile production emerged. Automakers now look at the entire continent as a single market, both for production and for sales. Decisions about production location and trade flows are made in response to regional variations in demand, the location of supplier industries, and the quality of transportation infrastructure, instead of in response to barriers imposed by Mexican, U.S., or Canadian policies.

A second connection between trade and geography occurs when geographical concentration gives an industry a competitive advantage. When a firm joins a regional industrial cluster, it may obtain certain advantages for itself, but it may also enhance the competitiveness of the other firms in the cluster and strengthen the country's export performance. When a country is the first to develop a particular industrial concentration, it may gain a competitive advantage over all other potential rivals and actually prevent the development of competing industries in other nations. In this case, the ability of the firms in the agglomeration to export at a low price prevents a similar concentration from developing in other countries. Cheap imports remove the incentive for new firms to enter the market, and trade actually closes the door on potential developments. In the next section, we look at the mechanisms that lead to industrial clustering.

External Economies of Scale

Geographical concentrations of industries are not a new, high-tech, phenomenon. In the twenteith century, Detroit emerged as a center of automobile production, and before that there were geographical concentrations of steel producers, textile firms, pottery manufacturers, financial service providers, and so on down a long list of economic activities. In some cases, the motivating factor behind the agglomerations was a plentiful supply of raw materials or good access to inexpensive water power, but in other cases, geographical concentration conferred advantages on the individual firm through the mechanism of external economies of scale.

External economies of scale differ from internal economies in that the advantage of larger size does not apply to the firm but rather applies to the whole industry. When external economies are present, a larger industry creates advantages for individual firms but the firms themselves have no incentive to grow so large that they can influence markets. External economies can occur in one or more ways. First, if the firms in a region produce similar products, then there are likely to be knowledge spillovers that help keep all firms abreast of the latest technology and newest developments. Close physical proximity enhances knowledge spillovers because it creates more opportunities for information exchange through formal and informal networks of people. Regional industry associations can be important, but so can soccer teams, churches, Girl Scouts, and other civic organizations that bring together people that work in different firms. Knowledge spillovers are particularly important in frontier industries undergoing rapid technological change, and they seem to be very sensitive to the face-to-face contact that is impaired by geographical distance.

A second form of external economies of scale occurs when the presence of a large number of producers in one area helps to create a deep labor market for specialized skills. If an industry is large enough to attract a steady stream of potential employees with specialized skills, it reduces the search costs of firms and also offers them the best available skills. This advantage is particularly important in industries that demand highly technical or scarce skills.

A third potential advantage to a large geographical concentration is that it can lead to a dense network of input suppliers. Manufacturers of intermediate inputs prefer to locate near the market for their products since it holds down transportation costs and may keep them better informed. In high-tech sectors, a large number of nearby supplier firms will lower the cost of finding a producer of a specialized input and will also create a wider and deeper selection of input goods and services. All of these effects hold down producer costs. The linkage from producers back to their suppliers can also occur in the other direction. If the concentrated industry manufactures intermediate goods or services, it may attract firms that use its products to make a final good or service. This gives firms more information about their market and may also lead to closer collaboration between suppliers and purchasers of intermediate inputs.

Trade and External Economies

One of the essential features of geographical concentration is that it is self-reinforcing. For example, as firms attract skilled workers or specialized input suppliers, the increase in the availability of high-quality inputs creates feedback leading to more firms in the same industry locating in the area. In turn, this leads to a stronger pull for workers and input suppliers, and so on. In effect, each of the elements act on each other to propel the system forward. At some point, as a region grows beyond its ability to provide adequate housing or other infrastructure, the high monetary cost of living in the region and the disamenities of crowding and congestion will put an end to further development, but it is probably safe to say that few regions reach this point.

One implication of these features is that small differences in initial conditions may lead to large differences in outcome. That is, a region with a small head start or other small initial advantage in attracting firms may develop significant scale economies before other regions. Once the scale advantages become significant, the gap between the lead region and its competitors can widen, and may turn into a permanent competitive advantage. The source of the initial advantage can be anything, including historical accident. For example, during World War II, as jet engines were being developed in Great Britain, the Allies decided to locate production in the United States on the West Coast where it minimized the probability that the Axis powers could destroy the factories with air raids. Ultimately, this led to a supplier industry around the major jet aircraft manufacturers (Boeing, Lockheed, and McDonnell-Douglas), and helped in the development of specialized labor skills such as aerospace engineering. As a result of an historical accident and the Allies' decisions during the war, the United States dominated the commercial jet aircraft industry for several decades, until a consortium of European governments used large subsidies and other interventions to foster a European competitor, Airbus.

Once the U.S. lead was established, then other countries with essentially the same technological ability as the United States could never catch up, even though in theory they had the capacity to achieve the same level of efficiency as the United States. The development of U.S. regional agglomerations, for example, the concentration of specialized aerospace manufacturing firms in the Seattle and Southern California regions, gave the United States a head start and a competitive advantage that could not be easily overcome. U.S. planes were always available at lower prices than a newer, less developed, industry could offer. In this instance, trade stifles the development of an industry that may be as competitive as existing producers.

In theory, it is possible that the outcome is even worse than described: trade may stifle the development of a new industry that is more efficient than the existing one. Suppose, for example, that Europeans are potentially more efficient at making commercial aircraft than Americans. Their potential can only be realized, however, after a period of experimentation and development. The initial problem they face is that the efficiency advantage goes to the United States because of its better developed linkages between suppliers and producers. In this case, trade and the initial availability of U.S. planes at a lower cost removes the incentive for Europeans to invest in their industry and prevents the development of what would be a more efficient industry. As long as U.S. planes are available at a lower price than European planes, there is no economic reason why anyone would buy European, and the lack of an initial market for their planes guarantees the Europeans a period of financial losses, thereby discouraging investment. In effect, the historical accident of locating jet aircraft production in the United States in order to avoid Hitler's bombers is locked in by trade.

The aircraft example is instructive because it illustrates a case in which trade may not be beneficial. In every other case we've examined so far, trade is beneficial. However, under the circumstances outlined above, it is potentially harmful since, in this hypothetical case, it reduces global efficiency by concentrating world production in the less efficient producer. The aircraft example also illustrates how small initial differences can cascade into large differences in outcome and how with external economies, trade patterns can be a result of completely unpredictable accidents of history.

INDUSTRIAL POLICY

Faced with a more competitive U.S. aircraft industry, what can Europeans do to get their own industry off the ground? This was the question asked several decades ago by the governments of Britain, France, Germany, and Spain. Their answer was to pool the resources of their domestic aircraft and aerospace firms, to provide generous subsidies from the four governments to help the consortium absorb the initial losses, and to develop their own industry. The result is Airbus, the large European challenger to the U.S.-based Boeing company.

The creation of Airbus is a prime example of governments using **industrial policies** to explicitly direct economic activity. As the name and example imply, industrial policies are government policies designed to create new industries or to support existing industries. Industrial policies are widely pursued around the globe, by both developed and developing countries, and they can have profound impacts on trade and trade patterns. Airbus, for example, now exports commercial aircraft around the world and has become a serious competitive force.

It should not be a surprise that industrial policies are controversial, so much so, that recent international agreements limit the scope of action that countries can take to support their industries. In addition, it is clear that in some cases they are politically motivated and end up wasting huge amounts of money. Brazil and Indonesia, for example, have also used industrial policies to develop regional commercial jet aircraft industries, targeted at the 20- to 100-passenger plane market. While Brazil has had commercial success, the Indonesian industry wasted billions of tax dollars and used a large number of engineers and other skilled workers whose talents could have been put to work developing the Indonesian economy. In the European case, however, it is clear that there are small differences between the United States and Europe. Both regions have a comparative advantage in aircraft, while Indonesia does not.

No country can have a comparative advantage in everything, and even if trade is based on economies of scale, it still requires the exporting country to be able to reach world class efficiency levels. There is no doubt that comparative advantage can change, and as educational attainment rises, as the infrastructure of roads and ports improve, and as capital becomes more abundant, the potential range of products that a country can efficiently make changes as well. Comparative advantage is not immutable. It is several steps from this observation, however, to the claim that a country can successfully pick the specific industry it wants to develop. Aircraft were beyond the reach of Indonesia at this point in time, and large-scale commercial jetliners may be beyond the reach of Brazil, but how should a country decide which industries it can successfully develop? And, even more basic, why should countries target any particular industry at all? Why not provide the basic components of a well functioning economy, such as education, stable institutions, the rule of law, and so on, and let the market decide whether to produce aircraft, high-speed trains, or some other product?

Industrial Policies and Market Failure

When the private market economy fails to deliver an optimal quantity of goods and services, it is called a **market failure**. Market failure is one of the main theoretical justifications for industrial policies. An optimal quantity is one where the value of the goods to private consumers and society is equal to its cost of production, so it follows that too little or too much of a good is a market failure. There are many different ways to approach this concept, but one of the clearest is to view market failures as a divergence between **private returns** and **social returns**. A frequent cause of a divergence between private and social returns is that some of the costs or benefits of an activity are externalized, or outside the area of concern of the economic agents engaged in the activity. For obvious reasons, economists refer to the market failure that results from the externalization of costs or benefits as an **externality**. The idea behind the concept of externalities is that not all the costs or benefits of an action go to the people or companies engaged in the economic activity. That is, they externalize the costs or benefits. For example, a steel mill that pollutes a river imposes a cost on inhabitants downstream, and parents that vaccinate their child create a benefit for their neighbor's children. In an accounting sense, the private returns are the cost and benefits to the steel mill or the parents with the vaccinated child, while the social returns include the private costs and benefits, but also take into account the costs and benefits to the rest of society—the downstream inhabitants or the neighbor's children. Note that externalized costs or benefits do not mean that they disappear and are of no consequence. From an economic viewpoint, they are as important as any other costs or benefits even though they do not fall on the individuals or firms that created them.

There are two simple rules for analyzing cases of market failure. First, when social returns are greater than private returns, a free-market economy produces less than the optimal amount. This follows from the fact that not all the benefits are captured by individuals or firms that produce the benefits, so they naturally do not consider the entire set of benefits when they decide how much to produce. The second rule is that when social returns are less than private returns, a free-market economy produces more than the optimal amount. In this case, economic agents do not take into account the costs that spill over onto others and that reduce the value to society of the good or service.

The divergence between private and social returns is illustrated in Figure 5.1. Supply and demand are plotted for a competitively produced good that generates external benefits when it is produced. The supply curve S_{priv} is a normal market supply curve, embodying all of the private costs encountered by firms that engage in production. It is labeled with the subscript "priv" to indicate that only the private costs, the costs paid by the firms producing the good, are taken into account. Since production entails some external benefits to members of the society (who are not specified in this model), we can offset some of the costs of production with the external benefits. These are subtracted from the supply curve to derive the social supply curve, S_{soc}, which embodies the private costs minus the external benefits. The supply curve S_{soc} is more comprehensive than S_{priv} since it takes into consideration all the costs and benefits to society, not simply the private ones.

As can be seen in Figure 5.1, private markets lead to output Q_1 at price P_1. From the standpoint of the social optimum, however, the price is too high and the quantity is too low. The social optimum, at P_2 and Q_2, takes into account both the costs and benefits that are external to the producing firms and their internal costs and benefits. In effect, private agents earn less than the social return, which includes the external benefit that firms cannot capture. As a

---

FIGURE 5.1   Market Failure: Externalities

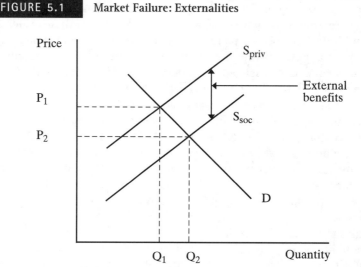

When social returns exceed private returns, markets produce less than the optimum and sell it at too high a price.

result, there is less than the socially optimal amount of investment in the activity generating the returns. For advocates of industrial policies, the solution is activist government intervention to increase the level of the desirable activity. The tools and problems associated with this type of intervention are discussed below.

There are many reasons why social returns and private returns may differ. Knowledge spillovers are a common example and are often cited as a reason for industrial policies. Social and business interactions between workers in different firms can spread knowledge about new products and new processes. In this case, the social return to the new knowledge is greater than the private return because some of the value of the knowledge spills over from the firm that created it into other firms. An important case of knowledge spillovers comes from the first entrant into a particular industry. The first firm in an industry provides valuable information about the feasibility of the industry. The first firm may also often leak marketing and technological information to other firms, and again, under any of these circumstances, the social returns are higher than the private ones.

A related knowledge spillover occurs in the area of research and development (R&D). Firms that develop new technologies may create breakthroughs that pay handsome profits. Often, before too much time goes by, the new product will be taken apart and improved upon by a competitor. In essence, the competitor benefits from the original research and development by being able to copy and improve upon it. Although the original innovator is unable to capture the full monetary benefit of its R&D, the benefits are not lost since other elements in society capture them. A variation of the effect of R&D is the problem of obtaining existing information. Often, existing technology may provide a solution to a common problem, but information about the technology may lie buried, for example, in a government research lab or in a Japanese technical journal. Firms could pay to search these sources for technical information, but once they find the answer to their problem, there is a high probability that all their competitors will be able to copy it because it is difficult to keep information within a single firm.

Another source of divergence between private and social returns is capital market imperfections. According to this argument, new firms may have difficulty attracting sufficient start-up capital. The same applies to existing firms that need to borrow to develop new products or processes. If banks and other lenders in the financial system lack the information they need to make loans, many solid prospects may not receive funding. Imperfect capital markets may also lead to market failure when economies of scale are involved. Proponents of industrial policies cite the fact that many large-scale projects require a set of interdependent investments to be made all at once. For example, a potentially competitive steel industry may require simultaneous investment in port and rail linkages. By itself, each piece may be unprofitable, but taken together the result would be a large, competitive, sector.

Strategic Trade

A second justification for industrial policies goes by the name of **strategic trade policy**. The two essential ingredients for strategic trade policy are that an industry has economies of scale and firms in the industry have market power that enables them to earn higher than normal profits. Strategic trade policy is the selective use of trade barriers and industry subsidies in order to capture some of the profits of foreign firms. Setting aside for a minute the practical difficulties of enacting strategic trade policy, in theory it is possible to convince foreign firms to leave the industry by starting a well-publicized and credible system of subsidies to new domestic firms. The size of the subsidy should be sufficient to enable the home country firms to earn profits. As long as home country firms gain a market share, their presence reduces the output of their competitors and, due to economies of scale, drives up the costs of production for foreign firms.

The following example illustrates these ideas. We return to the case of aircraft production. Regional commercial jet aircraft are smaller than the behemoths produced by Boeing and Airbus, and are used for shorter trips, with 20- to 100-seat planes, often flying between destinations inside a country. Approximately 90 percent of the world's production is evenly split between Canada's Bombardier and Brazil's Embraer. Given that these two firms can satisfy 90 percent of world demand, it can be assumed that there are significant economies of scale in production. The Brazilian firm, Embraer, is the younger of the two. It started in 1969 as a government-owned firm producing aircraft for the Brazilian military, and is gradually moving into the commercial jet business, where it has several current planes, and several more under development. In 1994, the company was privatized, but the Brazilian government retains stock shares and veto power over certain business decisions.

This example imagines a time before the entry of Embraer, when Bombardier (actually its predecessor) was a dominant firm. The problem faced by the Brazilian firm was that the capital investment required to enter the market is enormous, in the tens of billions of dollars, and this is too much to risk in a speculative venture that will certainly run into stiff competition from an already established and profitable Canadian firm.

Table 5.3 presents a set of hypothetical payoffs to Embraer and Bombardier as the former firm contemplates entering the market. As the Brazilian firm surveys its options, it notes that it has a choice of entering the market and losing −10, or staying out and losing 0. Obviously, staying out of the market is the better choice given that the Canadian firm is already in the market and is not likely to leave. The dominant strategy under these circumstances is that Bombardier stays in the market and Embraer stays out. Suppose, however, that the Brazilian government decides to offer a subsidy. The subsidy should be enough to keep its company profitable regardless of whether the Canadian company leaves the market or stays in it. Let's say that the governments offer a subsidy of 15 if Embraer enters the market. Under these conditions, the payoffs will be those detailed in Table 5.4.

TABLE 5.3	A Hypothetical Payoff Matrix	

	Brazil's Embraer (BE)	
Canada's Bombardier (CB)	Enter Market	Stay Out of Market
Stay in Market	BE (–10) CB (–10)	BE (0) CB (25)
Leave Market	BE (25) CB (0)	BE (0) CB (0)

The dominant strategy is for Embraer to stay out of the market and for Bombardier to stay in. The outcome is the payoff in the upper right corner.

With the subsidy (Table 5.4), the dominant strategy is for Brazil's Embraer to enter the market. If it stays out, it earns 0, but if it enters, it earns either 5 or 40, depending on the reaction of Canada's Bombardier. The latter, however, knows for certain that Embraer will enter the market and that consequently, its own choice is between –10 if it stays in the market, or 0 if it leaves. The rational decision for Bombardier is to leave, ensuring that the Brazilian firm captures the above normal profits that were accruing to the Canadian firm.

Is this scenario feasible? Something like this has already happened in the aircraft industry, both in the large-scale, transcontinental commercial aircraft market and in the smaller, regional aircraft market. The WTO's rules for international competition make it difficult to offer direct subsidies, but in both market segments of this industry, every firm has tried to establish that its

TABLE 5.4	The Payoff Matrix after a Subsidy of 15	

	Brazil's Embraer (BE)	
Canada's Bombardier (CB)	Enter Market	Stay Out of Market
Stay in Market	BE (5) CB (–10)	BE (0) CB (25)
Leave Market	BE (40) CB (0)	BE (0) CB (0)

The dominant strategy is for Embraer to enter the market and for Bombardier to leave it. The outcome is the payoff in the lower left corner.

competitor is subsidized. For example, Canada and Brazil each have brought the other into the dispute settlement process at the WTO, and tensions have run high over allegations of unfair competition.

While these examples illustrate how subsidies may permit a country to capture for itself or its firms, the profits of a foreign company, there are at least two practical problems that have been ignored so far. These are in addition to the fact that subsidies violate the WTO's rules for fair competition, and that using them can lead to a trade war. In addition, we assumed that governments have far more detailed information about costs and profits than is likely. Second, we assumed that there are no counter subsidies offered by the government of the company that loses out.

Industrial Policy Tools

Although there are a variety of techniques used to carry out industrial policies, they all share the same objective of channeling resources to the targeted industry. This can be accomplished in various ways, but the most obvious is to offer direct subsidies to firms in the targeted industry. As noted, this runs into the practical difficulty that Uruguay Round rules of the WTO prohibit subsidies for competitive products. Nevertheless, the rules do allow governments to subsidize "precompetitive" activities such as research, and the distinction between the two can be blurry at times. It is not necessary, however, to provide direct subsidies to targeted industries in order to support them. Governments have a wide range of options, ranging from providing information about conditions in foreign markets (many countries do this through their embassies and consulates), helping negotiate contracts, lobbying foreign governments to adopt home country technical standards, or tying foreign aid to purchases from home country firms.

One common practice used by governments in some newly industrializing countries is to sell foreign exchange to targeted firms at below-market prices, thereby enabling them to buy capital goods from abroad at below-market prices. A second common technique is to provide government loans to private firms at below-market interest rates or, alternatively, provide government guarantees on loans obtained from the private sector, thereby enabling borrowers to obtain favorable interest rates. Similarly, governments may provide special tax treatment to targeted industries. Governments also use their own purchases as a way to develop an industry. This can affect a wide range of activities, including medical equipment for state-owned hospitals, power generating equipment for state-owned utilities, telecommunications equipment for state-owned phone and broadcast media, military hardware, and so on. In some cases—for example suppliers of military hardware in the United States—firms are guaranteed a profit on the development of new products, which essentially removes all risk to the firm and spreads it across taxpayers.

Governments often support industries by encouraging firms to work together, either through the direct funding of the research done by consortia and/or through the relaxation of antitrust laws. This decreases the probability that competing firms will spend resources duplicating each other's research and development, but it increases their market power. Finally, governments may directly own firms, although this is less common after several recent waves of privatization in capitalist countries and the collapse of communism. In countries where government ownership is not unusual (France for example), the firms are often run more or less like private firms. These firms may or may not receive favorable treatment, but their track record indicates that government ownership is not an effective way to ensure international competitiveness.

Proponents of industrial policies stress that no matter which technique is used to target an industry, it is critical for governments to refrain from coercion. Firms should be allowed to refuse assistance (with the inevitable strings attached), and governments should recognize that any action they take to penalize noncooperation is likely to weaken the industry and lower the probability of a successful program.

Problems with Industrial Policies

While every economist recognizes that markets do not always produce the optimal outcome, most are skeptical about the practicality of using industrial policies to solve problems of market failure. One basic problem is that it is difficult to obtain the information necessary to measure the extent of market failure. For example, an efficient industrial policy requires governments to provide precisely the right amount of additional resources to the targeted industry. This implies that governments should keep adding resources as long as the external benefits are greater than the cost of the resources, but in most cases no one is capable of precisely measuring the benefits, particularly if they are spread throughout the economy and if they are only realized over a long period of time. Without the advantage of hard numbers, it is easy to imagine a situation where a government program spends $100 million to capture $50 million of external benefits. Similarly, the implementation of a successful strategic trade policy requires governments to know the costs of production for foreign firms and to be able to correctly anticipate their reaction when they face subsidized competition. While it is conceivable that the production costs may be known, it is impossible to know their reactions. Even if these objections could somehow be met, there remains the problem of determining which industry to target. If everyone acknowledges that a particular industry has a bright future, then entrepreneurs and investors will jump on it and government support is unnecessary. On the other hand, we know that external benefits lead markets to underinvest. Consequently, one possibility for choosing industries to target is to pick the ones that have the largest external benefits. The problem with this strategy is that the positive externalities that develop out of new technologies and inventions are usually a surprise to everyone involved and it is impossible to know beforehand that they will occur. In 1990, for example, almost no one foresaw the advent of the Internet, and over a decade later, there is still a lot of uncertainty about its direction, the benefits it will provide, and what components are key to maximizing its positive impact.

Another strategy that has been advocated for selecting the industries to target is to target high **value added** industries, where value added is the difference between the cost of materials and the value of the output. Value added is partly determined by the contribution of labor to production, and high value added industries are usually ones where wages are high. Value added is also determined by the contribution of capital, and it is really a mixture of the two—labor and capital. Therefore, value added may be high because an industry uses a lot of capital or a lot of highly skilled labor, or both. High value added industries are often selected as desirable ones to target because they tend to pay high wages or use new technologies that are viewed as important for future prosperity. The problem with this strategy for selecting an industry to target is that it often makes no sense in practice. For example, two of the highest value-added industries in the United States are petroleum refining and tobacco products. No one, to my knowledge, has argued that these industries should be targeted for future development. In any case, it is not clear why high value-added industries will not develop more efficiently through market processes. That is, there is nothing inherent in their nature that creates more external benefits than in other industries.

Another problem with industrial policies is that they encourage **rent seeking**. Rent seeking is any activity by firms, individuals, or special interests, which is designed to alter the distribution of income in their favor without adding to the amount of total income in the economy. When lobbyists persuade Congress to impose a tax on steel imports, for example, it raises the income of the U.S. steel industry, lowers the income of steel users, and leaves unchanged the total amount of income in the economy. (Note that more steel will be produced, but as a consequence, fewer other things will be produced.) If firms know that government is willing to subsidize R&D, or new investment, they will spend resources to obtain some of the subsidies. This may require the hiring of lobbyists, economists, engineers, and so on, whose job is to persuade the legislature or some other rule makers. The downside is that it uses up resources but does not add to total output.

The extent to which industrial policies encourage resources to be wasted in lobbying and other non-economically productive activities partly depends on the administrative process through which targeted industries are chosen, and the political culture of the country enacting the industrial policy. Countries that have a greater degree of corruption in their political system are likely to have a much harder time choosing between industries on the basis of scientific, technological, or economic criteria. Even in relatively corruption-free environments, however, the problem of industrial policies encouraging rent seeking is real.

Another problem with industrial policies is that it is impossible to contain the external benefits of R&D spending within national boundaries. New technologies soon spread to every nation that has the technological sophistication to take advantage of them. One set of estimates puts the benefits to foreigners of R&D spending by the home country at around one-fourth of the total benefits. This is not necessarily a problem, but if one of the purposes of the industrial policy is to enhance the competitiveness of home-based industries, it is ironic that in the end, they benefit foreign firms. Industrial policies are sometimes designed to prevent foreign firms from benefiting by excluding them from participation in joint ventures, research consortia, and other groups that are formed to carry out industrial policy objectives. For example, Sematech (Semiconductor Manufacturing Technology) is a consortium open to any U.S.-owned semiconductor manufacturer with the purpose of maintaining a U.S. lead in semiconductor manufacturing. Half its funding comes from its members and the other half comes from the U.S. government. The fact that many U.S. firms have separate joint ventures in research and production with European and Japanese firms increases the chances that a new breakthrough will spread to firms in other countries. Similarly, General Motors, Ford, and Chrysler will benefit from the Motor Vehicle Manufacturing Program (see below), but they all have corporate ties to various foreign firms such as Toyota, Mazda, and so on, and Chrysler, long an American firm, is now owned by Daimler-Benz, the manufacturer of Mercedes Benz.

U.S. INDUSTRIAL POLICIES

Throughout U.S. history and until World War II, a policy of high tariffs was a regular component of U.S. support for specific industries, but the use of direct subsidies was infrequent. Not counting the extensive involvement of state and federal governments in the development of transportation infrastructure (roads, canals, railroads, seaports, highways, and airports), the two main exceptions to U.S. avoidance of direct subsidies were agriculture and defense industries.

Agriculture experiences externalities from the ability of neighboring farms to copy each other's innovations. This is an example of external benefits where the discoveries or methods of one farmer are easily copied by everyone else. Since a farmer who innovates cannot capture all the rewards of his or her innovation, we know that the private market economy will underproduce agricultural research. This principle was intuitively understood by U.S. farmers and legislators and in 1862, the U.S. Congress passed the Morrill Act, giving federally owned lands to states for the purpose of establishing agricultural research colleges. The Morrill Act was followed in 1887 by the Hatch Act setting up agricultural research stations, and in 1914 by the Smith-Lever Act establishing a system of cooperative education for farmers.

It is difficult to disentangle the effects of these policies from several other factors that worked to create a strong agricultural sector in the United States The climate, the availability of land, soil fertility, the high level of farmer literacy, the ability to overcome labor shortages with innovations in farm machinery, and the development of a transportation infrastructure, all worked to create a comparative advantage in agriculture. In all likelihood, the United States would have emerged as a world supplier of grains and other commodities with or without the support of the universities, research stations, and extension service. These institutions undoubtedly made agriculture more productive, but it seems unlikely that they created a comparative advantage in agriculture that would not have been there otherwise.

The theoretical justification for industrial policies in the defense industry is fairly clear. Defense is a public good (if one person gets it, everyone does, whether they pay for it or not) and public goods often create market failures since the economic incentive is for everyone to free ride and let others pay. For this reason, most economists agree that it is impossible for markets to provide defense and that it must be done by governments. This does not mean, however, that governments necessarily have to be directly involved in the production of war goods. In the post–World War II era, the weapons and tools of the United States's defense forces have been produced by private firms, although the U.S. government has provided substantial resources to keep these firms in business, under the assumption that it would be detrimental to U.S. defense capability if the nation had to rely on foreign producers for major weapon systems.

Few people would disagree in general with this view, although there are disagreements about the optimal level of defense spending and the types of military equipment that are necessary. The main issue about defense spending in the context of industrial policies is that some economists argue that the United States has used the rhetoric of building a strong defense to hide a wide variety of industrial policies that are targeted at commercial developments. The research consortium Sematech is a case in point. Sematech was founded in 1987 by the Department of Defense in response to the growing use of Japanese semiconductors in U.S. jet aircraft. Its initial goal was to regain technological superiority in the manufacture of semiconductors, and it seems to have largely succeeded. Many people, however, view Sematech as simply a subsidy to IBM, Motorola, Texas Instruments, and other U.S. corporations—that was given to help restore their international competitiveness, although it was justified on the basis of a military need.

The Political Debate of the 1980s

The most common form of U.S. government support for targeted industries has been through the creation of new research and the dissemination of information. At two specific points in American history, however, the debate over commercial (i.e., nonmilitary) industrial policies has heated up. In both periods, the country felt threatened by outside economic forces. The first period was in the 1790s when the United States feared domination by Great Britain and the second period was in the 1970s and 1980s when fears of Japanese technological and manufacturing superiority began to surface. The first episode gave rise to the classic *Report on Manufactures* by Secretary of the Treasury, Alexander

Hamilton. Hamilton's report called for a national effort to develop greater manufacturing competitiveness and to lessen United States's dependence on Britain for manufactured items.

The second period of debate began in the late 1970s when U.S. steel production, then consumer electronics, autos, and semiconductors seemed to either vanish or to be on the verge of collapse as waves of Japanese imports captured increasing market shares. Looking back to the 1990s, as the Japanese economy temporarily floundered, it is difficult to understand the panic that struck U.S. corporate executives, policymakers, and workers. Lower priced, higher quality, Japanese goods that had been dismissed in the 1960s as junk, gained market share in industries that the United States had once dominated, and by the mid-1980s, the U.S. trade deficit with Japan had jumped enormously, roughly from equality of exports and imports in 1975 to a deficit for the United States of around $60 billion in 1987. At the same time, the overall U.S. trade deficit went from a slight surplus in 1975 to deficits of $150 to $170 billion in the mid-1980s (see Chapter 9).

At the same time that many U.S. industries were getting pounded by imports, technological progress began to favor skilled workers over unskilled. The effect was twofold. First, it reduced the number of workers needed to produce a given level of output, and secondly, it widened the wage differences between skilled and unskilled workers and contributed to growing inequality. Many thoughtful books and papers appeared in the early 1980s, arguing that the United States was "deindustrializing." Some analysts argued that this was a good thing because it was a sign of progress for the economy to pass through manufacturing and industry to services, and the United States was farther along in its transformation to an information-based economy than were most other economies. Consequently, the United States was certain to be a world economic leader in the twenty-first century. Alternatively, many analysts argued that the loss of manufacturing was a symptom of a much deeper problem in the U.S. economy: an inability to compete with Japan and the new industrial countries of East Asia.

From the vantage point of the start of the twenty-first century, it seems that both the optimism and the pessimism about the U.S. economy were overblown. The rise of Japan and the newly industrialized economies of East Asia has caused the United States to lose its comparative advantage in some relatively labor-intensive production such as shipbuilding and basic steel manufacturing. (This does not mean that the United States does not produce these goods, only that it produces a lot less.) At the same time, the pressures to move away from more labor-intensive production have been reinforced by technological changes that favor capital-intensive and skilled labor-intensive production.

One outcome of the experience with ballooning trade deficits and declining wages for unskilled workers was an opening of the industrial policy debate at the highest levels of U.S. economic policy. Proponents argued that the market economy of the United States was not capable of an optimal response to the challenges from abroad, while many opponents feared that resources would be wasted by another newer government bureaucracy. The opponents of industrial policies won the political debate, however, although no president openly embraced the idea. All the presidents before Clinton, however, hedged their bets by supporting industrial policies and calling them something else.

CASE STUDY

Targeting Motor Vehicle Manufacturing Processes

Although the general tendency in U.S. economic policy is to avoid direct government intervention in industry, the United States has a number of industrial policies that it supports. One of the more developed cases is the Motor Vehicle Manufacturing Technology Program, which is one of several initiatives sponsored by the Advanced Technology Program. The ATP describes the benefits of the Motor Vehicle Manufacturing Technology Program in the following terms:

Changeovers to new car, van, or truck models are engineering and manufacturing marathons, taking U.S. auto makers and their suppliers an average of 42 to 48 months to cross the finish line. With more agile equipment and processes that sharply reduce the time and cost of converting factories to new models, the nation's automotive industry can significantly reduce the span from initial design to consumer-ready vehicle and sprint ahead of the competition. . . .

The ATP focused program on motor vehicle manufacturing technology will foster innovations in manufacturing practices that could slash time-to-market to 24 months, markedly better than even the best times logged to date by foreign or domestic car makers. Sought-after advances will

lead to more versatile equipment, better control and integration of processes, and greater operational flexibility at all levels, from suppliers of parts, dies, and machine tools to assembly plants. With the reusable, modular equipment and processes envisioned by the program, the cost of retooling car-manufacturing facilities— now ranging between $1.2 billion and $2.9 billion, depending on the extent of the changeover—could be reduced by as much as tenfold. The savings would reduce the size of break-even production volumes needed to recover investment costs, making it profitable for U.S. automobile companies to compete in small-volume markets at mass-production prices. . . .

The automotive sector, which accounts for about 4 percent of the U.S. gross domestic product and employs more than 2 million people, will be the initial beneficiary of the anticipated technologies. . . . Outside the sector, a variety of other manufacturing industries, from metal furniture to precision instruments, will be able to exploit targeted improvements in machining, grinding, and other widely used processes.

The ATP ends its discussion of its Advanced Motor Vehicle Technology Program:

Domestic auto manufacturers devote the bulk of their R&D to product research. The fraction allocated to process-oriented R&D tends to focus on shorter term, incremental improvements, in contrast with the major gains in performance and capabilities that the ATP focused program will foster. Moreover, *individual car companies will not independently fund work likely to yield non-appropriable, or widely shared, benefits that competitors can profit from without having to make that same R&D investment.*

Source: http://www.atp.nist.gov/atp/focus/mvmt.htm

Summary

- Comparative advantage cannot account for a significant part of world trade. A large share, probably over 40 percent at the world level, and more than 50 percent of the trade of industrial countries is intraindustry trade.

- Intraindustry trade is not based on comparative advantage since it consists of the export and import of similar products and occurs mostly between countries that have similar productivity, technology, and factor endowments. Intraindustry trade is based on economies of scale and product differentiation.

- Economies of scale occur whenever average costs decrease as production increases. Economies of scale are an important determinant of trade patterns because they form a separate basis for trade that is in addition to comparative advantage-based trade.

- Economies of scale can be either internal, external, or both. With internal economies of scale, the gains from trade include a wider selection of consumer choices and lower prices. With external economies of scale, the gains from trade are less certain since, in theory, they can lock in production in a less efficient country and prevent the development of production in a more efficient country.

- External economies of scale lead to regional agglomerations of firms. Firms are attracted by several positive factors derived from operating in close geographical proximity to each other. The three main factors are large pools of skilled labor, specialized suppliers of inputs, and knowledge spillovers.

- Industrial policies are premised on the idea that markets may fail to develop an industry that is essential for future prosperity, or that there will be less development than is optimal if many of the benefits of an industry are external to the firms in the industry.

- Historically, governments have used a number of tools to foster the development of industries they thought were essential to future prosperity. These tools included a number of different types of direct and indirect subsidies. The Uruguay Round of the GATT agreement has made it illegal to subsidize a commercial product.

- Problems with industrial policies include the absence of a reliable method for selecting the industry to target; rent seeking; international spillovers, and the difficulty of correctly estimating the optimal amount of support to provide.

Vocabulary

agglomerations

external economies of scale

externality

Grubel-Lloyd index

industrial policy

interindustry trade

internal economies of scale

intraindustry trade

market failure

monopolistic competition

oligopoly

private returns

product differentiation

rent seeking

social returns

strategic trade policy

value added

Study Questions

1. What is intraindustry trade, how is it measured, and how does it differ from interindustry trade? Are the gains from trade similar?

2. Comparing U.S. trade with Germany and Brazil, is trade with Germany more likely to be based on comparative advantage or economies of scale? Why?

3. What are the differences between external and internal economies of scale with respect to (i) the size of firms, (ii) market structure, and (iii) gains from trade?

4. What are three key incentives for firms in a particular industry to cluster together in a geographical region?

5. How might trade hurt a country if it imports goods that are produced under conditions of external economies of scale?

6. When the United States signed a free-trade agreement with Canada (1989), no one thought twice about it. When the agreement with Mexico was signed (1994), there was significant opposition. Use the concepts of interindustry and intraindustry trade to explain the differences in opposition to the two trade agreements.

7. What are the theoretical justifications for targeting the development of specific industries?

8. What are some common problems in implementing industrial policies?

9. Figure 5.1 in the text illustrates the case of an industry that generates external social benefits with its production. Draw a supply and demand graph for an industry that creates external costs with its production. Compare and contrast the market determined price and output level with the socially optimal price and output levels.

APPENDIX: A GRAPHICAL ILLUSTRATION OF PRICES AND COSTS WITH MONOPOLISTIC COMPETITION

Figure 5.A illustrates the relationship among the number of firms in the industry, average costs, and output prices. The horizontal axis measures the number of firms in the industry, while the vertical axis measures average costs and prices. Line segment P shows the relationship between the number of firms and prices. It slopes downward to the right because as more firms enter the market, it puts downward pressure on prices. Line segment AC shows the relationship between average cost for each individual firm and the total number of firms in the market. It slopes upward because as more firms enter the market, the quantity each existing firm sells is reduced and their average cost of production increases. At prices above P_1, new firms have an incentive to enter the market since price exceeds average costs. At prices below P_1, just the opposite occurs and some firms will leave the market because their costs are greater than the market price.

Figure 5.A also makes obvious the reason why firms want to export. Any firm that exports will be at a competitive advantage since it will have the greater sales it needs to drive down its costs. This idea is illustrated in Figure 5.B, where the alternative cost curve, AC*, is identical to AC except that it belongs to a larger market. For any given number of firms, AC* shows that

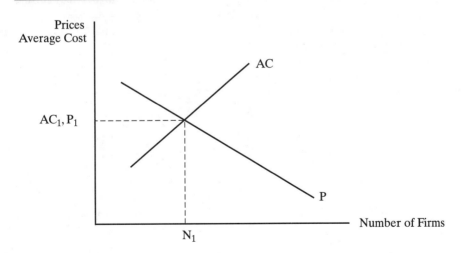

FIGURE 5.A

In monopolistic competition, an increase in the number of firms drives down prices and drives up each firm's average costs. Equilibrium occurs when price equals average cost.

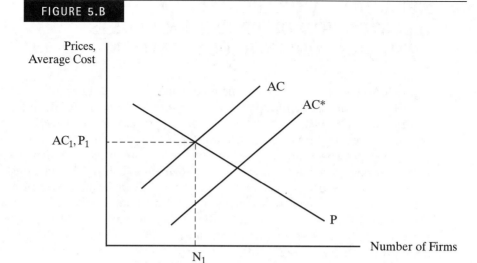

FIGURE 5.B

For any given number of firms, an increase in the size of the market through the creation of foreign sales allows economies of scale to be realized and pushes down average costs.

average costs are lower in a larger market. This follows from the economies of scale that each firm experiences and the fact that if the number of firms is held constant, each firm sells more when the size of the market expands.

Export markets enable firms to expand production and to realize their scale economies. Scale economies, together with competition between firms, leads directly to the gains from trade. Increased production causes average costs to fall, while competition forces firms to pass the cost savings on to consumers in the form of lower prices.

Chapter 6

THE THEORY OF TARIFFS AND QUOTAS

INTRODUCTION

Chapters 6 and 7 are an introduction to the theory and policy of tariffs and quotas. In the economics literature, this analysis is called commercial policy. Chapter 6 is an introduction to tariff theory, and Chapter 7 focuses on an empirical estimate of the direct costs of protectionism and the arguments used by proponents of restricted trade. The inefficiency and expense of tariffs and quotas as a means to protect industries and jobs will be apparent after measuring their direct costs.

In general, tariffs have been negotiated down to very low levels in the industrial world, with the partial exception of agriculture, textiles, and apparel. These sectors were excluded from the GATT until the Uruguay Round and continue to have relatively high trade barriers. This is an issue for developing countries that often have a comparative advantage in precisely those areas.

Analysis of a Tariff

Barriers to trade come in all shapes and sizes. Some are obvious, or **transparent** whereas others are hidden or **nontransparent**. **Quotas** directly limit the quantity of imports, while tariffs indirectly limit imports by taxing them. **Tariffs** and quotas cause consumers to switch to relatively cheaper domestic goods or to drop out of the market altogether. They also encourage domestic producers to increase their output because demand switches from foreign to domestic goods.

In the analysis that follows, we will be looking at only the effects of tariffs and quotas on the industry in which they are imposed. For example, the economy-wide effect of a tariff in, say, the steel industry will not be analyzed. In the language of economics, the analysis in Chapter 6 is known as *partial equilibrium analysis* because it considers the effects of tariffs and quotas on only a part of the economy—the market in which the trade barrier is erected. Before we turn to tariff analysis, however, we must first introduce two important concepts, consumer and producer surplus.

Consumer and Producer Surplus

What is the maximum price you would be willing to pay for a gallon of milk? The answer is likely to be different for each consumer, depending on income, how much they like milk, whether they have kids that need it, whether they can tolerate lactose or not, and a number of other factors, many of which are subjective. The subjective value that consumers place on milk is contained in the market demand curve for milk, which describes the total quantity of a good that consumers are willing and able to buy at each and every price. As the market price falls, a greater quantity is purchased because more consumers will feel that the lower price is equal to or below the value they place on the milk.

Suppose, for example, that you are willing to pay $3.50 for a gallon of milk, but the price is only $3.20. In essence, each gallon of milk you buy provides you with $0.30 of value that is "free" in the sense that it is over and above what you must pay. This excess value is called **consumer surplus**. It is the value received by consumers that is in excess of the price they pay. It occurs because not everyone values each good the same, yet for most goods, there is only one price. Consumer surplus can be measured if the demand curve is known. Since the demand curve is a summary of the value that each consumer places on a particular good, the area between the demand curve and the price line is a measurement of consumer surplus.

Figure 6.1 shows hypothetical market demand and supply curves for milk. At the market equilibrium price of $3.20 per gallon, 10,000 gallons will be supplied and demanded. Many people value milk at a higher price, however, and the value they receive in consuming milk is greater than the price they pay. If the price were to rise to $8.00 per gallon, no milk would be purchased. In Figure 6.1, consumer surplus is the area below the demand curve and above the price line of $3.20. The size or value of consumer surplus is the area of the triangle given by the formula (½) × (height) × (width), or (½) × ($4.80) ×

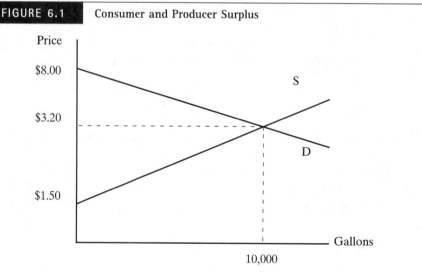

FIGURE 6.1   Consumer and Producer Surplus

Consumer surplus is the area below the demand curve and above the price line. Producer surplus is the area above the supply curve and below the price line.

(10,000), which is equal to $24,000. This equals the difference between the value of the milk consumed and the total amount consumers spent for it.

Consumer surplus is a real savings to consumers. If firms had a way to determine the maximum price that each consumer was willing to pay, then theoretically they could charge every individual a different price and thus reduce consumer surplus to zero. Luckily for those of us not in the milk business, firms usually cannot get this information without going through a long and costly interview procedure. As a result, it is usually impractical (and in some cases, illegal) for firms to charge different customers different prices. Nevertheless, some firms such as car dealers manage to charge different prices for the same goods. The easiest strategy for most firms is simply to charge everyone the same price, so consumer surplus is a real savings for most consumers in most markets.

On the production side, the analogous concept is called **producer surplus**. In our hypothetical milk example, if you owned a dairy farm and were willing and able to produce milk at $3.00 per gallon, you would be receiving producer surplus of $0.20 per gallon if you sold milk at $3.20. Recall that the supply curve for a market is the sum of supply curves for the firms in the market and that it reflects the minimum price firms will accept and still produce a given amount. In Figure 6.1, some firms are willing to produce at $2.00 per gallon, and at every price above $1.50 at least some firms will have output to sell. Every firm that is willing to sell for less than the equilibrium price of $3.20 earns revenue that is above the minimum they need. This excess or surplus revenue is their producer surplus.

As in the case of consumer surplus, we can measure producer surplus. Measurement in this case depends on knowing the parameters of the supply curve (where it crosses the price axis and its slope) because producer surplus is the area above the supply curve and below the price line. In our example, it is equal in value to the triangle given by the formula $(\frac{1}{2}) \times (\$1.70) \times (10,000)$, which equals $8,500. This is the revenue received by producers that is in excess of the minimum amount of revenue that would be required to get them to produce 10,000 gallons of milk.

The Effect of a Tariff on Prices, Output, and Consumption

We will use the concepts of producer and consumer surplus when we discuss the income distribution effects of tariffs and quotas. Before we analyze those effects, however, we must begin with a description of the effects of tariffs on prices, domestic output, and domestic consumption.

Figure 6.2 shows the domestic or national supply and demand for a good that is imported. We are assuming that there is one price for the good, which we will call the world price, or P_w, and that foreign producers are willing to supply us with all of the units of the good that we want at that price. This is equivalent to assuming that foreign supply is perfectly elastic, or that the United

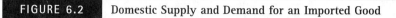

FIGURE 6.2   Domestic Supply and Demand for an Imported Good

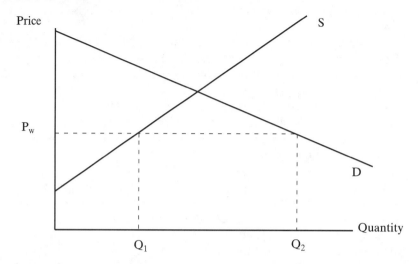

The difference between domestic demand and domestic supply, $Q_2 - Q_1$, is the quantity of world imports at price P_w.

States does not consume a large enough quantity to affect the price. We will drop this assumption below when we discuss the case of a large country. Note that the world price is below the domestic equilibrium price. This means that domestic producers are not able to satisfy all of domestic demand at the market price of P_w and that consumers depend on foreign producers for some of their consumption. Specifically, at price P_w, consumers demand Q_2, but domestic producers supply only Q_1. The difference, $Q_2 - Q_1$, or line segment Q_1Q_2, is made up by imports.

Now suppose that the government imposes a tariff of amount "t." Importers will still be able to buy the good from foreign producers for amount P_w, but they will have to pay the import tax of "t," which they tack onto the price to domestic consumers. In other words, the price to consumers rises to $P_w + t = P_t$, as shown in Figure 6.3. The price increase in the domestic market has effects on domestic consumption, domestic production, and imports. First, the price increase squeezes some people out of the market, and domestic consumption falls from Q_2 to Q_2^*. Next, on the production side, the higher price encourages domestic production to increase from Q_1 to Q_1^*. The increase in domestic production occurs because domestic firms are able to charge a slightly higher price $(P_w + t)$ in order to cover their increasing costs while remaining competitive with foreign firms. Finally, imports decrease from Q_1Q_2 to $Q_1^*Q_2^*$. To summarize, tariffs cause the domestic price to rise by the amount of the tariff, domestic consumption falls, domestic production rises, and imports fall.

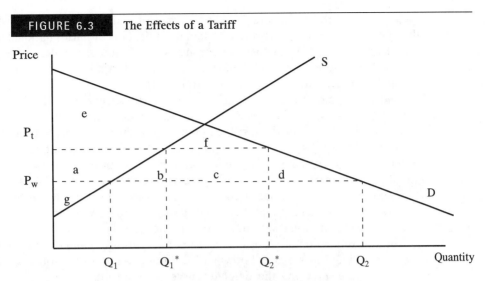

FIGURE 6.3   The Effects of a Tariff

Tariffs cause an increase in domestic prices and domestic production, and a fall in domestic consumption. They increase producer surplus and government revenue, but decrease consumer surplus.

The Effect of a Tariff on Resource Allocation and Income Distribution

Tariffs have more subtle effects than just a rise in prices and a fall in imports. The increase in domestic production requires additional resources of land, labor, and capital to be reallocated from their prior uses into the industry receiving the protection under the tariff. Also, when the price changes, so do consumer and producer surplus.

Let's consider the effect on consumer surplus first. Figure 6.3 shows both the pre- and post-tariff price and output levels. Remember that consumer surplus is the entire area above the price line and below the demand curve. When consumers pay price P_w, this is areas $a + b + c + d + e + f$. After the tariff is imposed and the price rises to P_t, consumer surplus shrinks to $e + f$. The difference, area $a + b + c + d$, represents a loss to consumers.

Unlike consumer surplus, producer surplus grows. Pre-tariff producer surplus is area g, and post-tariff is $g + a$. The difference, area a, is the additional revenue that is above the minimum necessary to encourage domestic firms to increase their output from Q_1 to Q_1^*. On net, producers are better off, and consumers worse off, but what about the nation as a whole?

If we consider the whole loss to consumers, areas $a + b + c + d$, we see that it can be subdivided into several different areas. Part of the loss, area a, is a transfer from consumer surplus to producer surplus. Although the loss makes consumers worse off, it makes producers better off by the same amount. Therefore, the nation as a whole is neither better nor worse off unless it can be established that giving the resources to producers somehow benefits or harms national welfare. This part of the lost consumer surplus is an income distribution effect of the tariff, since it rearranges national income by transferring resources from one group (consumers) to another group (producers).

Another income distribution effect of the tariff is represented by area c. Note that the height of this area is equal to the tariff, and the width is the amount of imports after the tariff is imposed. Therefore, this part of lost consumer surplus is equal to (tariff) × (imports), which is the amount of revenue collected by the government when it enacts the tariff. In this case, the income distribution effect is a transfer from consumers to the government. Again, it is assumed that there is no net effect on national welfare since the loss by consumers is exactly matched by the gain of government. As long as this transfer does not change national welfare, there is no net effect.

The two remaining areas of lost consumer surplus are b and d. Both represent net national losses, and both involve a misallocation of resources. Consider area d first. Along the demand curve between Q_2^* and Q_2, there are consumers that value the good above the cost of purchasing it at the world price. As a result of the tariff, however, they have been squeezed out of the market and are not willing or able to pay price P_t. The fact that consumers value the good above the cost of obtaining it in the world market but cannot purchase it is a net loss to the nation. Economists refer to the destruction of value that is not compensated by a gain somewhere else as a **deadweight loss**. Area d is this type of loss.

The final area to consider is b. Along the domestic supply curve between Q_1 and Q_1^*, output is increased at existing plants. Given that the supply curve slopes upward, firms can only increase their output if the price is allowed to rise. In other words, in order to obtain the additional output, domestic producers must be able to charge a higher price that will cover their rising costs for each additional unit. At the pre-tariff price of P_w, the total cost of imports $Q_1Q_1^*$ would have been the price times the quantity, or $(P_w) \times (Q_1Q_1^*)$. The cost of producing the same goods at home is equal to the cost of the imports plus area b. In other words, the triangle b is the additional cost to the nation when it tries to make the extra output $Q_1Q_1^*$ instead of buying it in the world market at price P_w. Area b is a resource misallocation and a net loss to the nation because the same goods $(Q_1Q_1^*)$ could have been acquired without giving up this amount. Area b is another deadweight loss, sometimes referred to as an **efficiency loss** because it occurs on the production side.

We can summarize the net effect of the tariff on the nation's welfare by subtracting the gains of producers and government from the losses of consumers: $(a + b + c + d - a - c) = b + d$. The two triangular areas are losses for which there are no compensating gains and, therefore, represent real losses to the nation as a whole. Table 6.1 summarizes all the effects of the tariff that we have noted.

TABLE 6.1	Economic Effects of the Tariff in Figure 6.3		
		Pre-tariff	*Post-tariff*
Price to consumers		P_w	P_t
Domestic consumption		Q_2	Q_2*
Domestic production		Q_1	Q_1*
Imports		$Q_1 Q_2$	Q_1*Q_2*
Consumer surplus		$a + b + c + d + e + f$	$e + f$
Producer surplus		g	g + a
Government revenue		0	c
Deadweight consumption loss		0	d
Deadweight production (efficiency) loss		0	b

Tariffs reallocate income from consumers to producers and government. They also create dead-weight losses, one on the consumption side and one on the production side.

Other Potential Costs

These effects of tariffs are the ones that are most predictable and quantifiable. In the next chapter, there are some actual estimates of the production and income distribution effects of tariffs and quotas for a number of industries in the United States and Japan. These are not the only effects of tariffs, however, and three others should be noted. These are the effects if trading partners retaliate, the impact of protection on domestic innovation and productivity, and the incentive for firms to engage in rent-seeking behavior. Each of these effects broadens our focus to a consideration of more than the directly affected industry.

Retaliation. Retaliation can add to the net loss of a tariff by hurting the export markets of other industries. For example, the United States imposed a tariff on European (mainly Italian) pasta a few years ago because of a number of trade practices that the United States felt discriminated against its pasta manufacturers. In return, the European Community retaliated by imposing tariffs on U.S. manufacturers of vegetable oils—corn, soybean, safflower, and other cooking oils. The cost of the U.S.-imposed tariff affected not just U.S. consumers of Italian pasta, who were forced to pay higher prices, but workers and owners of capital in the U.S. vegetable oil industry. In essence, in addition to the deadweight losses brought on by the tariff, the vegetable oil industry lost export markets. A further problem is that retaliation can quickly escalate. For example, in the 1930s, many depressed nations reduced imports through tariffs, with the result that they gained jobs in industries that competed with imports but lost jobs in industries that produced exports. In the end, no jobs were gained, trade declined, and everyone had a lower standard of living.

Innovation. A costly long run effect of tariffs is that they reduce the incentive to innovate new products or to upgrade the quality and features of existing ones. When domestic firms are isolated from foreign competition, there is less incentive to improve their products and processes. As a result, the nation misses many of the benefits of competition. It is admittedly difficult to measure this effect, but as Chapter 1 described, there are several types of evidence showing that open economies grow faster than closed ones.

Rent Seeking. Hypothetically, tariffs could stimulate product improvement if domestic producers know they are temporary and if they believe they will be removed. The reason this is often only a hypothetical effect is that while firms have tariff protection, they often hire the best lobbyists available and work to keep the protection in place. Economists use the term **rent seeking** to describe this type of behavior. Rent seeking is any activity that uses resources to try to capture more income without actually producing a good or service.

From a cost-benefit point of view, a firm might ask whether it is more profitable to hire lobbyists to work for protection or to hire scientists, engineers, and skilled managers to make the business more efficient. New products have an uncertain acceptance by consumers, and new capital equipment is expensive. In other words, the increased productivity route has costs and risks. If protection is easy to obtain, then it may be a less risky strategy. If protection is uncertain, then the hiring of lobbyists (who can also be expensive) will be a risky strategy as well. For this reason, political systems that do not easily provide protective tariffs are much more likely to avoid one source of wasted resources.

The Large Country Case

Economists distinguish between large and small countries when it comes to tariff analysis. As a practical matter there may not be much difference between the two, but in theory it is possible for large countries to actually improve their national welfare with a tariff as long as their trading partners do not retaliate. In economic terms, a large country is one that imports enough of a particular product so that if it imposes a tariff, the exporting country will reduce its price in order to keep some of the market it might otherwise lose.

The **large country case** is illustrated in Figure 6.4. Suppose that the United States, a large country, imposes a tariff of size t on its imports of oil. The fall in U.S. demand brought on by the tariff causes P_w, the world price, to fall to P_w*, offsetting some or all of the deadweight loss from the tariff.

Looking more closely at Figure 6.4, we can compare the large and small country cases. The situation before the tariff is the same as in Figure 6.3. The main difference between the two cases stems from the fact that foreign suppliers cut the price to P_w* after the tarrif is levied. Consequently, less additional domestic production occurs, and fewer consumers are squeezed out of the mar-

FIGURE 6.4   Tariffs in the Large Country Case

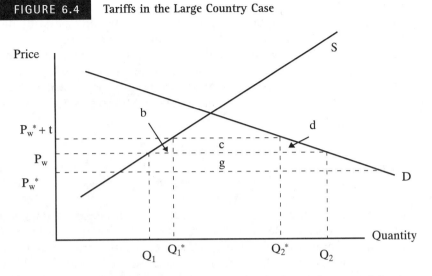

A tariff in a large country reduces demand so much that foreign producers cut their prices.

ket. In other words, areas b and d in Figure 6.4 are smaller than they would be in the small country case where there is no price drop. A smaller deadweight loss is not the only effect, however. In Figure 6.4, area g represents tariff revenue, which together with area c is the total tariff revenue collected. However, compared to the pre-tariff situation, area g is a net gain to the importing nation. Pre-tariff, area g was money paid for imports. After the tariff, and due to the price decline, it is part of the revenue collected by the government and, hence, stays within the nation.

As long as $g > b + d$, a large country can improve its welfare by imposing a tariff. This outcome, however, assumes that there is no retaliation, rent seeking, or harmful effects on innovation.

Effective Versus Nominal Rates of Protection

One of the ironies of tariff protection is that often it is not what it seems. In fact, the amount of protection given to any one product depends not only on the tariff rate but also on whether there are tariffs on the inputs used to produce it. Suppose, for example, that the United States decided to impose a tariff on imports of laptop computers. If American made laptops have foreign parts in them, then the amount of protection they receive from a tariff depends also on whether there are tariffs on their imported inputs. It is conceivable, in other words, that the protection given by a tariff on laptops could be completely undone by forcing laptop manufacturers to pay tariffs on their imported inputs.

Economists distinguish between the **effective rate of protection** and the **nominal rate of protection**. The nominal rate is what we have discussed so far in this chapter—the rate that is levied on a given product. The effective rate of protection takes into account both the nominal rate and any tariffs on intermediate inputs. Consequently, it gives a clearer picture of the overall amount of protection that any given product receives. The effective rate of protection is related to the concept of value added. **Value added** is the price of a good minus the costs of the intermediate goods used to produce it. Value added measures the contributions of capital and labor at a given stage of production. The effective rate of protection is defined as:

$$(VA^* - VA) / VA$$

where VA is the amount of domestic value added under free trade, and VA* is the amount of domestic value added after taking into account all tariffs, both on final goods and intermediate inputs.

Consider the example in Table 6.2. Suppose that laptop computers sell for $1000, and foreign producers are willing to sell the United States all it wants at that price. In order to make a laptop, American manufacturers must import $600 worth of parts, so that a domestic laptop actually has $400 of value added in the United States ($1000 − $600 = $400). If the United States imposes a 20 percent tariff, the price rises to $1200. Value added in the United States is now $600 ($1200 − $600), and the effective rate of protection is 50 percent (($600 − $400) / $400). That is, a 20 percent tariff provides 50 percent protection! This happens because a large share of the value of the final product is produced elsewhere, so all of the domestic protection falls on the share produced in the United States.

Now consider what happens if the United States decides to also protect domestic component manufacturers and levies a large tariff on intermediate

TABLE 6.2	Nominal and Effective Rates of Protection		
	No Tariff	*A 20% Tariff on the Final Product*	*A 20% Tariff Plus a 50% Tariff on Imported Inputs*
Price of a laptop computer	$1000	$1200	$1200
Value of foreign inputs	$600	$600	$900
Domestic value added	$400	$600	$300
Effective rate of protection	0	50%	−25%

Effective rates of protection are higher than nominal rates if intermediate inputs are imported tariff free. If intermediate inputs are tariffed, it reduces the effective rate of protection and can even turn it negative.

inputs. If the tariff on foreign parts is 50 percent, the cost of intermediate inputs rises from $600 to $900. With a 20 percent tariff on the value of the final product, the price of imports stays at $1200, which is the price American laptop makers must meet. Value added with the tariff on intermediate inputs is $300 (i.e., $1200 − $900), and the effective rate of protection is now −25 percent (($300 − $400) / $400). That is, even with a 20 percent tariff on foreign laptops, American laptop makers receive *negative* protection. The tariff on the final product is more than offset by the tariffs on the intermediate products, so that the overall situation leaves producers more exposed to foreign competition than if there were no tariffs levied at all.

Negative rates of effective protection are not uncommon. Part of the reason stems from the fact that tariffs are enacted in a piecemeal fashion over long periods and are not constructed in a planned and coherent way. Pressures from domestic lobbyists, considerations of strategic interests, and numerous other forces go into the shaping of national tariff systems. Consequently, it is not surprising to find contradictory tariff policies where newer tariffs undo the effects of an older one.

This discussion should add a note of caution to attempts to determine exactly which industries are protected. Clearly, the notion of effective rates of protection is more relevant than nominal rates. With tariff rates, what you see may not always be what you get.

ANALYSIS OF A QUOTA

The economic analysis of quotas is nearly identical to that of tariffs. **Quotas** are quantitative restrictions that specify a limit on the quantity of imports rather than a tax. The net result is much the same: both tariffs and quotas lead to a reduction in imports, a fall in total domestic consumption, and an increase in domestic production. The main difference between quotas and tariffs is that quotas that are not followed up with additional policy actions do not generate tariff revenue for the government. The lost tariff revenue can end up in the hands of foreign producers as they raise their prices to match demand to supply. Hence, the net loss from quotas can exceed that from tariffs.

In terms of Figure 6.3, consumers still lose area a + b + c + d, but government does not collect area c as a tax. (We will examine what happens to area c, but you might see if you can reason it out for yourself.)

Types of Quotas

The most transparent type of quota is an outright limitation on the quantity of imports. Limitations are sometimes specified in terms of the quantity of a product coming from a particular country, and at other times there is an overall limit set without regard to which country supplies the product. For example, in the apparel sector, the United States sets quotas for imports of each type of garment (men's suits, boys' shirts, socks, etc.). The quota for each good is further divided by country, so, for example, Hong Kong and Haiti have different limits on each type of apparel that they can export to the United States.

Another type of quota is an import licensing requirement. The United States uses this form infrequently, but a number of other nations have relied on these quotas for the bulk of their protection. For example, until 1989 they were the main form of protection in Mexico. As the name implies, import licensing requirements force importers to obtain government licenses for their imports. By regulating the number of licenses granted and the quantity permitted under each license, import licenses are essentially the same as quotas. They are less transparent than a quota because governments usually do not publish information on the total allowable quantity of imports, and foreign firms are left in the dark about the specific limits to their exports.

A third form of quota, and the one that has been common in U.S. commercial policy, is the **voluntary export restraint** (**VER**), also known as the *voluntary restraint agreement* (VRA). Under a VER, the exporting country "voluntarily" agrees to limit its exports for some period of time. The agreement usually occurs after a series of negotiations in which the exporter may be threatened with much more severe restrictions if they do not agree to limit exports in a specific market. Given that there is usually more than a hint of coercion, it may be a misnomer to call these restrictions "voluntary."

VERs are similar to a quota in their economic effect, but they are popular with politicians for two reasons. First, in the United States, they do not require legislative action, which makes them quick to enact. Second, they allow politicians to provide protection and claim support for free trade, satisfying both the domestic industry and the proponents of open markets. This result is dependent on the politician's ability to avoid the charge of protectionism by claiming that the agreement is a negotiated settlement and that the exporting country voluntarily agrees to restrict its shipments. Since it is a "negotiated" settlement—often with threats of market closings—it looks different from an import restriction.

Because of their political expediency, and because they are the culmination of a series of negotiations between the importing and exporting countries and therefore appear to be voluntary, VERs became popular over the last three decades. Another factor contributing to their use is the limitation placed on the use of tariffs by industrial countries. Most countries have signed the General Agreement on Tariffs and Trade binding their tariffs at current levels and agreeing not to raise them except under various extraordinary conditions. Until recently VERs were a way around these restrictions, but recent negotiations severely limited the use of VERs to protect industries from sudden import surges.

The Effect on the Profits of Foreign Producers

The main difference between tariffs and quotas is that there is no government revenue from quotas. In place of tariff revenue, there are greater profits for foreign producers. These are usually called **quota rents**.

In Figure 6.5, the world price is set at P_w, domestic production is Q_1, and imports are Q_1Q_2. Suppose that the government decides to set a quota on imports of quantity $Q_1Q_2^*$. At price P_w, demand exceeds supply, which is equal to Q_1 domestic plus $Q_1Q_2^*$ imports. Consequently, the price will rise until supply equals demand, and that happens when the gap between the domestic supply curve and the domestic demand curve is equal to $Q_1Q_2^*$. This is illustrated in Figure 6.6, where domestic supply is shown as having grown to Q_1^*, and the domestic price is P_q, which is above P_w.

Figure 6.6 looks the same as Figure 6.3, which was used to illustrate a tariff in a small country case. That is because they have nearly identical effects on production, consumption, and prices paid by consumers. Indeed, for any given quota there is some tariff that will accomplish the identical import restriction. One difference stands out, however. In the tariff case, the government earned revenue from imports, area c in Figures 6.3 and 6.6. In the quota case, no revenue is earned. Instead, area c represents the extra profits of foreign producers due to the higher prices.

A second important difference between tariffs and quotas relates to their effect on producer surplus over time, as demand for the good increases. If a quota remains fixed, an increase in consumer demand also increases the price paid by consumers and the quantity of producer surplus garnered by domestic firms. In contrast, an increase in consumer demand for an item that has an import tariff increases the quantity of imports and leaves the price intact. This assumes that the country is relatively small and the increase in its demand does

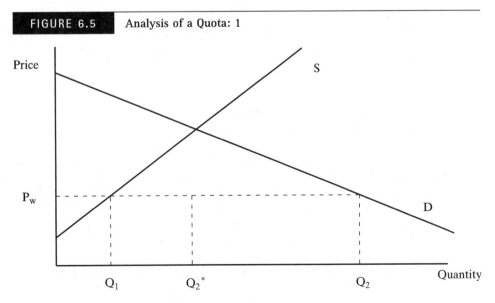

FIGURE 6.5   Analysis of a Quota: 1

A quota restricts imports to line segment $Q_1Q_2^*$ and creates excess demand equal to $Q_2^*Q_2$.

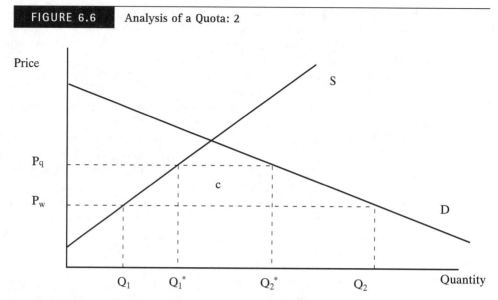

FIGURE 6.6   Analysis of a Quota: 2

The quota generates extra revenue for foreign producers in area c.

not alter the world (pre-tariff) price. Given this difference, it is not surprising that domestic firms prefer quotas over tariffs as a form of protection for their industry.

Two circumstances can mitigate or limit the ability of foreign suppliers to earn extra profits. First, if there is a large number of foreign suppliers, then competitive conditions may prevent them from raising their prices. And second, a clever government can extract the extra profits from foreign producers through the implementation of an auction for import licenses.

Suppose that the country imposing the quota decides to auction off the right to import. How much would a domestic importer be willing to pay? In Figures 6.5 and 6.6, foreign suppliers are willing to sell the amount of the quota (Q_1Q_2* in Figure 6.5, or Q_1*Q_2* in Figure 6.6) at price P_w. A domestic importer, recognizing that she can sell the good at price P_q, should be willing to pay an amount equal to something slightly less than the difference P_q minus P_w. In other words, she pays P_w for the good that she sells for P_q. If she pays anything less than $P_q - P_w$ for the right to sell in the market with the quota, she makes a profit. In equilibrium, an auction market should lead to bids for the right to sell that are more or less equal to the projected price increase. With an auction market, then, the government can potentially collect the same revenue with a quota that it would with a tariff. Of course, administrative costs of a quota may be higher, since the government must implement its auction market.

Hidden Forms of Protection

While outright quantitative restrictions, import licensing requirements, and VERs are each a form of quota, there are numerous other forms of protection that function the same as quotas. Any kind of trade barrier that reduces imports without imposing a tax functions more or less like a quota. For this reason, economists divide the different forms of protection into two main categories: tariffs and **nontariff barriers**. Nontariff barriers can be subdivided into quotas and nontariff measures. Nontariff measures are often nontransparent, or hidden, in that they are not presented as trade barriers or forms of protection even though they serve that purpose.

One type of nontariff measure is government purchasing that discriminates against foreign suppliers. It may seem fair to allow national governments to favor their own nation's suppliers. The problem occurs when major sectors of an economy (health care, transportation, communications, power generation, and so on) are wholly or partially state owned. Foreign firms are shut out of a significant share of economic activity if they cannot sell to governments. Furthermore, if one country's health care is private and another's is public, then there is an asymmetry in market access: firms in one country can supply the other but not vice versa. The asymmetry appears unfair and easily leads to trade friction, which can spill over into other markets. For this reason, nations have attempted to use international negotiations with the framework of the General Agreement on Tariffs and Trade (GATT) to open public procurement to trade. This effort has met with some success.

CASE STUDY

U.S. VERs on Japanese Autos in the 1980s

In 1980, the United States experienced a short recession. For automakers, the economic slowdown came at a bad time, since they were struggling to meet new safety and emissions regulations and ever-increasing pressure from Japanese car makers. Imports of Japanese cars jumped from 15.2 percent of the market in 1979 to 22.2 percent in 1980. The combined effects of the new auto regulations, the strength of imports, and the economic slowdown caused U.S. automakers to lose $4.7 billion in 1980—the most they had ever lost.

In June of 1980, the autoworkers' union, the United Auto Workers (UAW), appealed to the U.S. International Trade Commission (USITC) for temporary protection. The UAW was soon joined in its appeal by the Ford Motor Company. It is the job of the USITC to conduct investigations to determine if a sudden surge of imports is hurting American industries. In November of 1980, at the conclusion of their investigation, the USITC commissioners voted 3–2 against the UAW and the Ford Motor Co. The USITC found that the

(*continues*)

recession and the shift in the U.S. car market away from large, gas-guzzling cars were the main sources of problems, not imports. President Carter resisted further entreaties from the car industry, but legislation in Congress to restrict Japanese cars to 1.6 million vehicles per year for 1981–1983 moved forward. President Reagan took office in January 1981, and in May he announced a voluntary export restraint agreement that his administration had reached with Japan. The VER agreement limited the Japanese to exports of 1.82 million vehicles for 1981 and was subsequently lowered to 1.68 million when it was renewed for 1982 and 1983. The restraints were continued after 1983 but at the higher level of 1.85 million for 1984 and 1985.

The quotas pushed up the price of both domestic and imported cars. The average price increase for Japanese cars was estimated at between $725 and $960, holding constant the quality and option features, while U.S. cars went up between $360 and $425 per car. The price increase for Japanese cars is estimated to have put an extra $2 billion per year in the pockets of Japanese and European manufacturers (who also benefited from the price increase) by 1984. The total cost to consumers was estimated at around $5.8 billion in 1984. Around $2.6 billion of the loss in consumer surplus was a gain in producer surplus. An estimated 55,000 U.S. jobs were saved by the VERs, at a cost to consumers of $105,000 *per job saved* ($5.8 billion divided by 55,000 jobs).

The critics of this agreement point out that the U.S. auto industry was already adjusting to the difficulties it faced and that most of these had stemmed from poor management, not Japanese imports. Detroit lost a big share of the market when it delayed competing for the small-car market after the two periods of oil shortages and gas price hikes in 1973–1974 and 1979. By 1981, the average domestic car was more than 25 percent more fuel efficient than cars of the same weight in 1972–1973, and the car weighed 30 percent less, giving it an even greater increase in fuel efficiency.

Critics also point out that before the VERs, most Japanese car manufacturers had targeted the subcompact and entry-level car markets, but the revenue from the increase in car prices and the limits on the numbers of cars they could sell gave Japanese car companies strong incentives to enter the midsized and luxury car markets where profits per car are greater.

One final effect of the VERs and the threat of U.S. protection is that it probably strengthened the incentive for Japanese manufacturers to begin production in the United States. Between 1982 and 1991, six Japanese companies and two joint ventures between U.S. and Japanese firms invested $7.9 billion in U.S. automobile assembly plants, with a capacity to produce 2.5 million cars and employ 31,000 workers. By contrast, between 1979 and 1984, U.S. firms closed ten assembly plants and reduced their workforce by more than 170,000.

Sources: Hufbauer, Berliner, and Elliott. *Trade Protection in the United States: 31 Case Studies*, Institute for International Economics, Washington, DC: 1986; and Robert Crandall. "Import Quotas and the Automobile Industry," *The Brookings Review*, Summer 1984.

Other common forms of protection that act like quotas are esoteric or unclear safety standards, special product certification that only domestic firms seem to know how to comply with, and excessive bureaucratic regulation and red tape. It should be noted that safety standards are not trade barriers and that they are a vital part of the regulatory apparatus of a nation. In spite of this, they are often used by governments that want to limit imports and are unable to do so outright. Still other barriers require foreign firms to do something specific in order to have access to the market. For example, local content requirements force foreign manufacturers to buy or produce locally a percentage of the value of the goods they sell. This forces foreign producers to invest inside the country they are exporting to or to buy inputs from domestic firms.

CASE STUDY

Japanese Snow, U.S. Meat, and Mexican Tuna

Nontariff barriers provide some of the most unusual examples of economic reasoning in all of policy making. Nearly every country has stories about the economic excuses for trade barriers it has encountered from its trading partners. Three of them are given here. The problem with anecdotes such as these is that however interesting they may be, you can never know if they are exceptional cases of trade policy or if they represent the general tendency. Yet, while they may or may not be representative, they often give insight into how difficult it can be to get to the bottom of some trade disputes.

The first case involves Japanese snow, a weak Japanese ski equipment industry, and a strong European competitor. Japan felt that it would eventually have a comparative advantage in the manufacture of ski equipment because the country excels in the high-technology area of materials science, and snow skis are put together with advanced synthetic materials. The problem was that it is a young industry in Japan, and at current prices and levels of productivity it could not compete with the far more experienced European producers. Furthermore, under its obligations as a signatory to the GATT, placing tariffs on European equipment was not an option. Consequently, in the mid-1980s, Japanese trade officials announced that they were banning the importation of foreign snow skis as a safety precaution. Japanese snow, they claimed, is different, and foreign equipment is unsafe. Their announcement was greeted around the world with derision and legal challenges through the GATT, and Japan never went through with its planned import ban.

In the case of Japanese skis, it was clear that the safety standards were phony and that they were an attempt to protect a domestic industry without appearing to do so. In the next example, the technical legitimacy of the safety

(continues)

standard is beyond the ability of consumers (or economists) to unravel.

In January of 1988, the European Community (now called the European Union) banned the use of all growth hormones in livestock production. The ban eliminated U.S. beef and pork from the EC market. Growth hormones are used in most U.S. meat production to speed up the animals' weight gain in feedlots. Faster growth means a more rapid turnover and lower costs to U.S. meat producers. The U.S. Food and Drug Administration has certified growth hormones as safe, but the EC disputed these scientific findings. The United States claims that the ban was a subterfuge to provide protection to less efficient EC meat producers under the guise of health and safety standards. The United States says the science is clear and indisputable, but the EC disagrees. Who is right?

In the first case, the safety standards were phony, while in the second, they are at least questionable. The third case involves safety standards for nonhumans, and it reflects a difference in the environmental tradeoffs nations are willing to make. The case involves tuna caught by Mexican fishermen and sold in the United States. Fishermen plying the waters of the eastern tropical Pacific catch yellowfin tuna by following dolphins. When the yellowfin tuna are netted, dolphins tend to be trapped as well, causing many to drown. In 1988, the United States passed the U.S. Marine Mammal Protection Act, which banned imports of tuna from countries that could not certify that their harvesting of tuna minimized the harm to dolphins. In

1990, all Mexican tuna was banned from the U.S. market due to the failure of Mexico to certify its catch. Mexico claims that the mortality of dolphins in its tuna-fishing operations is below the levels set by the international agency that monitors tuna fishing (the Interamerican Tropical Tuna Commission) and wants the United States to end its ban, which has hurt several west coast ports, such as Ensenada. The International Dolphin Conservation Program, a multilateral agreement to protect dolphins and other marine species in the eastern Pacific Ocean, was signed by eight countries including the United States and Mexico on May 21, 1998. It was hoped that this would resolve the dispute, but as of mid-2001, it has not.

The Japanese snow case is an attempt to protect an uncompetitive domestic industry while trying to appear as if it is protecting the safety of its people. The U.S. meat case raises a more serious question about consumer safety, but it illustrates the way in which protection can potentially hide behind serious scientific disputes. The Mexican tuna case reflects a difference in environmental values in countries at different levels of economic development. In the growth hormone and yellowfin tuna cases, both sides make strong cases for their point of view, and the ability of negotiators to resolve the dispute on objective grounds seems limited. Both cases illustrate how difficult dispute resolution can be when protection hides behind safety or other standards and how protection often becomes intertwined with noneconomic values.

Summary

- Tariffs increase domestic production and employment at the cost of greater inefficiency and higher prices. The production and distribution effects are measured by estimating the changes in producer surplus and consumer surplus.

- In addition to short-run welfare and efficiency effects, tariffs have long-run costs of increased rent seeking, slower innovation, and the loss of export markets through the retaliation of trading partners.

- In theory, a large country can improve its welfare with a tariff. In general, welfare-improving tariffs tend to be small, and they only improve welfare if there is no retaliation by supplying nations and no external costs such as increased rent seeking.

- Economists distinguish between nominal and effective rates of protection. The effective rate is the difference in domestic value added with and without tariffs, expressed in percentage terms.

- Quotas have similar effects as tariffs, although the overall national losses are greater due to the transfer of quota rents to foreign producers. Auction markets, in which governments auction the right to import an item under a quota, can reduce the amount of quota rents and, in the limit, provide the same revenue as an equivalent tariff.

- Administratively, quotas take many forms. They can be well-specified quantitative restrictions on imports, negotiated limits on a trading partner's exports, or requirements to obtain a license to import.

Vocabulary

consumer surplus

deadweight loss

effective rate of protection

efficiency loss

large country case

nominal rate of protection

nominal tariff

nontariff barrier

nontransparent

producer surplus

transparent

quota

quota rents

rent seeking

tariff

value added

voluntary export restraint (VER)

Study Questions

1. Graph the supply and demand of a good that is produced domestically and imported. Assume that the country is not large enough to affect the world price. Illustrate the effects that a tariff on imports has. Discuss:
   a. the income distribution effects;
   b. the resource allocation effects;
   c. the effects on domestic production and consumption;
   d. the effects on government revenue;
   e. the effect on the price of the good.

2. Suppose the world price for a good is 40 and the domestic demand-and-supply curves are given by the following equations:

   Demand: $P = 80 - 2Q$

   Supply: $P = 5 + 3Q$

   a. How much is consumed?
   b. How much is produced at home?
   c. What are the values of consumer and producer surplus?
   d. If a tariff of 10 percent is imposed, by how much do consumption and domestic production change?
   e. What is the change in consumer and producer surplus?
   f. How much revenue does the government earn from the tariff?
   g. What is the net national cost of the tariff?

3. Under what conditions may a tariff actually make a country better off?

4. In addition to the production and consumption side deadweight losses, what are some of the other potential costs of tariffs?

5. The Uruguay Round of the GATT began a process of phasing out the use of voluntary export restraints. Why did they come into widespread use in the 1980s? For example, given that VERs are a form of quota, and that they create quota rents and a larger reduction in national welfare than a tariff, why did nations use them instead of tariffs?

6. The GATT strongly favors tariffs as a protective measure over quotas or other nontariff measure. One of the first things it encourages new members to do is to convert quotas to their tariff equivalents. One of the main reasons tariffs are preferred is because they are more transparent, particularly by comparison to nontariff measures. Explain the idea of transparency, and how nontariff measures may be nontransparent.

7. Suppose that bicycles are made in the United States out of a combination of domestic and foreign parts.
   a) If a bike sells for $500 but requires $300 of imported parts, what is the domestic value added?
   b) If a 20 percent tariff is levied on bikes of the same quality and with the same features, how do the price and the domestic value added change? (Assume the U.S. cannot cause the world price to change.)
   c) What is the effective rate of protection?
   d) If in addition to the 20 percent tariff on the final good, a 20 percent tariff on imported parts is also levied, what is the effective rate of protection for American bicycle manufactures?

Chapter 7

COMMERCIAL POLICY

INTRODUCTION

An argument was made in Chapter 6 that tariffs and quotas lower national welfare by creating deadweight losses. In this chapter, we examine the dollar value of the effects of tariffs and quotas in two countries. The overall level of tariffs and quotas in the United States and Japan are about average for industrial economies. They are also fairly low, implying that the total deadweight loss imposed on each country is relatively minor. The purpose of this exercise, however, is to compare the costs and benefits of trade barriers. As will be shown, even low trade barriers have a high ratio of costs to benefits, and should make you question the strategy of trying to gain jobs in this way.

After a look at the dollar costs of protection in the United States and Japan, we examine the most common reasons given for protecting specific industries. Again, the purpose is not to question the goals that nations set for themselves, but to look at the efficiency of tariffs and quotas in reaching them. Finally, the chapter ends with a discussion of the mechanisms used to provide protection.

THE COSTS OF PROTECTION IN THE UNITED STATES AND JAPAN

Between 1947 and 1992, the average U.S. tariff fell from 20 percent to 5 percent. In 1994, with the signing of the Uruguay Round agreement, the (then) 123 members of the WTO agreed to reduce their tariffs by another 40 percent so that in the first decade of the twenty-first century, the average U.S. tariff will be between 2 and 4 percent. The level of tariffs and quotas in the United States are about average for an industrial country, and rates around the industrialized world are at comparable levels. A few industries have bucked the trend, however, and in the United States, textiles and apparel continue to receive substantial protection, while Japan heavily protects agricultural goods and a few manufacturing industries such as textiles.

With the overall decline in the use of tariffs, the United States has increasingly relied on VERs and other nontariff barriers in the 1970s and 1980s. In the 1980s, these were applied to steel, autos, and machine tools, among others. Japan has also used quantitative restrictions such as import bans (e.g., rice) or VERs (e.g., Korean clothes and textiles). In addition, Japan has provided generous subsidies to industries such as dairy and vegetables.

Total Costs and Costs per Job Saved in Both Countries

In the United States, before the phase-in of the Uruguay Round tariff cuts, twenty-one industries accounted for one-half of the total cost to consumers of formal protection. Textiles and apparel are the most highly protected sector, costing each man, woman, and child an average of about $100 per year. For the year 1990, the total reduction in consumer surplus from all tariffs and quotas in the United States is estimated to have been around $64 billion, or roughly 1.3 percent of the U.S. GDP.

Estimates of the cost to Japanese consumers of their nation's trade protection are more difficult to make because tariffs and quotas are fairly low, and most observers argue that nontransparent barriers (administrative regulations, product certification requirements, and so forth) make up the bulk of Japanese protectionism. One recent study has estimated that in 1989, Japanese trade barriers, both formal and nontransparent, cost Japanese consumers between $75 and $110 billion, or between 2.6 and 3.8 percent of their GDP. Forty-seven industries accounted for all of this cost.

Table 7.1 itemizes the impact of Japanese and U.S. tariffs and quotas. Forty-seven Japanese industries and twenty-one U.S. industries making up the bulk of each country's protection are grouped together into six categories. The number in parentheses after each category is the specific number of industries with high levels of protection included in the category data. Column A is an estimate of the share of consumer surplus transferred to producers as an increase in producer surplus; column B is tariff revenue; column C is the quota rent; column D is the production side efficiency loss plus the consumption side deadweight loss; and the last column (C + D) is the net national welfare loss. Since each category of goods includes many separate items, some protected by tariffs and others by nontariff restrictions, most categories generate both tariff revenues and quota rents.

The values for the totals for each country are also presented in Figure 7.1, with the Japanese number first, followed by the U.S. value in italics.

Table 7.2 carries the analysis one step farther. The total cost to consumers is shown in the first column. This is the sum of columns A, B, C, and D in Table 7.1. The second column shows the number of jobs saved as a result of the higher U.S. or Japanese production level. The third column is the cost to consumers per job saved (column 1 divided by column 2). First note the general pattern of Table 7.2. In Japan, more than one-half of the total cost to Japanese consumers of their nation's protection is in the food and beverages sector (despite the fact that Japan is the world's largest importer of agricultural products); in the United States, the bulk of the cost is in the light manufacturing sector—clothing manufacturing and textiles, to be specific. Neither the United States nor Japan concentrates its protective barrier in high technology or other cutting edge industries of the future. Instead, older, labor-intensive industries receive the bulk of the protection in each country. Other industrial nations

| TABLE 7.1 | Japanese and American Protection (Millions of Dollars) |

	Producer Surplus Gained	*Tariff Revenue*	*Quota Rents*	*Efficiency and Consumption Deadweight Losses*	*National Welfare Loss*
Japan (1989)	**A**	**B**	**C**	**D**	**(C+D)**
Food and beverages (17)	43,210	1,086	6,909	7,189	14,098
Textiles and light industry (6)	3,341	812	3,059	1,767	4,826
Metals (7)	2,546	77	2,185	354	2,539
Chemical products (11)	8,466	135	3,866	3,033	6,899
Machinery (6)	12,286	25	4,233	5,043	9,276
Total, Japan	69,849	2,135	20,252	17,386	37,638
United States (1990)					
Food and beverages (5)	1,775	176	646	350	996
Textiles and light industry (9)	12,242	5,403	6,124	2,574	8,698
Chemical products (2)	222	232	0	30	30
Machinery (1)	157	0	350	35	385
Miscellaneous (2)	1,288	50	0	557	557
Total, United States	15,684	5,861	7,120	3,546	10,666

Before Uruguay Round cuts, the national losses to Japan and the United States were approximately $37.6 billion and $21.4 (2 × 10.7) billion, respectively.

Notes: The numbers in parentheses are the number of industries with high levels of protection included in each category. The Japanese totals make up the majority of total protection in Japan, while the U.S. figures include the twenty-one industries comprising about one-half the total protection in the United States. The sources are Sazanami, Urata, and Kawai, *Measuring the Costs of Protection in Japan*; and Hufbauer and Elliott, *Measuring the Costs of Protection in the United States.*

would undoubtedly exhibit a similar pattern (e.g., agriculture in Europe is highly protected).

The failure of industrial nations to open wide their markets in agriculture, foodstuffs, textiles, and apparel is particularly unfortunate for developing nations, as these are often the leading industries in economic development. Textiles, apparel, and food processing are less capital intensive and more labor intensive than other branches of industry, making them areas of comparative advantage for many developing countries. Historically, these are often the industries that develop, in part because of the relatively simple technology and low investment requirements. Restrictions on market access in the high-

| FIGURE 7.1 | Japan and the United States: Income Effects of Tariffs and Quotas |

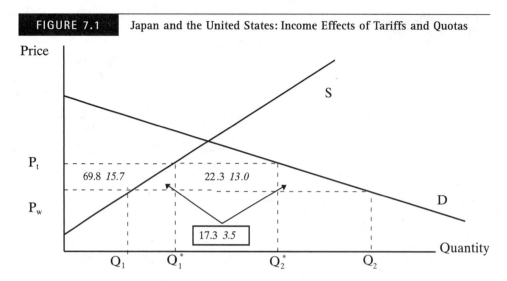

Numbers are in billions of U.S. dollars. The first number is the value for Japan; italic numbers are U.S. values. All values are from Table 7.1. Coverage for the United States is only about one-half the value of U.S. tariffs and quotas in 1990.

income countries inevitably hurts many developing countries by limiting the size of the market over which they can exercise their comparative advantage.

The total number of jobs saved in column 2 may seem like a lot, but relative to the size of the U.S. economy, it is not. Over the long run, the average number of jobs added to the U.S. economy *each month* is more than 200,000. Therefore, U.S. trade barriers in the most highly protected industries save the equivalent of one or two months' worth of new jobs at a cost to U.S. consumers of over $32 billion per year. The cost per job saved is in column 3: $169,000 per job each year in the United States and a whopping $602,000 per job per year in Japan.

In many respects, the last column of Table 7.2 is the point of this exercise. While everyone agrees that job creation is a good thing, it is important to ask how much we pay for the jobs we create. If a government agency were to implement a job-creation program at a similar cost (or even one-quarter this cost), citizens would be outraged. Because we pay for this grossly inefficient jobs program through higher prices, however, we do not associate the policy with its cost. When we pay $50 for a pair of denim jeans, we do not consider that a part of the price is because of our trade policy. The lesson we derive from Tables 7.1 and 7.2 is that trade policy is a grossly inefficient way to create jobs because it relies on too many intervening variables and does not go straight to the heart of the problem. If job creation is the issue, then tariffs and quotas are very expensive substitutes for good macroeconomic policy and flexible labor markets.

TABLE 7.2	Jobs Saved by Japanese and American Protection		
	Total Cost to Consumers (Millions of U.S. $)	*Jobs Saved*	*Cost to Consumers per Job Saved (U.S. $, 1990 Prices)*
Japan (1989)			
Food and beverages (17)	58,394	76,600	762,000
Textiles and light industry (6)	8,979	18,500	485,000
Metals (7)	5,162	5,300	974,000
Chemical products (11)	15,500	6,500	2,385,000
Machinery (6)	21,587	75,200	287,000
Total, Japan	109,622	182,100	602,000
United States (1990)			
Food and Beverages (5)	2,947	6,035	488,000
Textiles and light industry (9)	26,443	179,102	148,000
Chemical products (2)	484	514	942,000
Machinery (1)	542	1,556	348,000
Miscellaneous (2)	1,895	4,457	425,000
Total, United States	32,311	191,664	169,000

In the United States, each job saved with a tariff or quota cost U.S. consumers $169,000, on average. In Japan, the costs are higher ($602,000). The cost per job saved will not change much as tariffs fall.

Source: See Table 7.1

The Logic of Collective Action

Given that the costs to consumers are so high for each job saved, why do people tolerate tariffs and quotas? Ignorance is certainly the case for some goods, but for some tariffs and quotas, the costs have been relatively well publicized. For example, many people are aware of the fact that quotas on sugar imports cost each man, woman, and child in the United States between $5 and $10 per year. The costs are in the form of higher prices on candy bars, soft drinks, and other products containing sugar. Few of us work in the sugar industry, or any industry for that matter, that benefits from protection, so the argument that our jobs depend on it is weak at best.

In a surprising way, however, we probably permit our tariffs and quotas because of a version of the jobs argument. The economist Mancur Olson stud-

CASE STUDY

The Uruguay Round of the GATT Negotiations

The Uruguay Round of the General Agreement on Tariffs and Trade (GATT) concluded in 1993 after nearly seven years of hard negotiations. Originally, it was scheduled to be completed within four years, but because it was the most ambitious round of multilateral trade negotiations ever undertaken, it was more contentious than anticipated and took longer to complete. Most of the 123 nations that participated ratified the agreement in 1994, and it went into effect at the start of 1995. (The tariff costs in Table 7.1 are before the Uruguay Round changes.)

There are four main categories of effects created by the Uruguay Round, as summarized in Table 7.3. Trade barriers are reduced to open markets wider; trade rules were reformed in several areas but most notably in the area of subsidies; several new issues were addressed; and the institutional structure of the GATT was made stronger and placed on a more permanent footing. In addition, the agreement also committed the members to open negotiations in a number of new areas according to a timetable specified in the agreement. For example, negotiations over opening a $500 billion world telecommunications market were begun shortly after the agreement was signed, and in 1997, a telecommunications agreement was completed.

The Uruguay Round was significant in several ways. One of its biggest accomplishments was the inclusion of agriculture and textiles. While the provisions regarding these two sectors are relatively mild, a precedent has been set for future negotiations. In addition, the Uruguay Round developed separate agreements (i.e., outside of the GATT) on trade in services (GATS), intellectual property protection (TRIPS), and foreign investment (TRIMS).

Another major breakthrough was the reorganization of the institutional structure of GATT. Recall from Chapter 2 that in its original form, GATT was an agreement but not an organization. The original framers of the GATT hoped to create an International Trade Organization (ITO) that would coordinate trade agreements and oversee the implementation of the GATT. The ITO was never created, however, and the GATT established its own secretariat to administer the agreement.

The Uruguay Round creates a superstructure called the World Trade Organization (WTO) to administer all of the agreements, including the GATT. The WTO also oversees the new, more efficient dispute settlement process and the Trade Policy Review Mechanism (TPRM). The TPRM conducts periodic reviews of the trade policies of each of the WTO members and publishes the results.

The WTO's Web site provides a wealth of history and background information. It also provides access to the TPRMs it has conducted, results of dispute settlement process, news releases, and other information. It is located at: http://www.wto.org.

| TABLE 7.3 | The Uruguay Round of the GATT Negotiations |

Category	Examples
Trade barriers reduced	• Across-the-board cut of 40 percent in tariffs on most industrial products • Agriculture reduces export subsidies and some domestic production subsidies; NTBs are converted to tariffs. • Phaseout of textile quotas over ten year period; cut tariffs.
Trade rules	• Clarification of the definition of subsidies • Classification of allowable and nonallowable subsidies
New issues	• General Agreement on Trade in Services (GATS) • Agreement on Trade Related Aspects of Intellectual Property Rights (TRIPS) • Agreement on Trade Related Investment Measures (TRIMS)
Institutional reform	• Creation of the World Trade Organization (WTO) • Reorganization of the disputesettlement procedure • Creation of the Trade Policy Review Mechanism

The Uruguay Round went beyond tariff cuts and broke new ground in several important areas.

ied this problem and similar ones and noticed two important points about tariffs and quotas. First, the costs of the policy are spread over a great many people. Second, the benefits are concentrated. For example, we all pay a little more for candy bars and soft drinks, but a few sugar producers reap large benefits from our restrictions on sugar imports. In cases such as this, Olson found, there is an asymmetry in the incentives to support and to oppose the policy. With trade protection, the benefits are concentrated in a single industry. The tariff may help a few owners of capital and the workers in the industry. Consequently, it pays for the industry to commit resources to obtaining or maintaining its protection. The industry will hire lobbyists and perhaps participate directly in the political process through running candidates or supporting friendly candidates. If people in the industry think their entire livelihood depends on their ability to limit foreign competition, they have a very large incentive to become involved in setting policy.

The costs of protection are nowhere near as concentrated as the benefits because they are spread over all consumers of a product. The $5 to $10 per year that it costs each of us because of sugar quotas is hardly worth hiring a lobbyist or protesting in Washington. Thus, one side pushes hard to obtain or keep protection, and the other side is silent on the matter. Given this imbalance, an interesting question is why there are not more trade barriers.

WHY NATIONS PROTECT THEIR INDUSTRIES

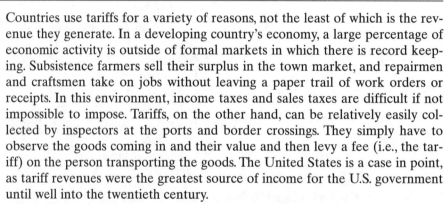

Countries use tariffs for a variety of reasons, not the least of which is the revenue they generate. In a developing country's economy, a large percentage of economic activity is outside of formal markets in which there is record keeping. Subsistence farmers sell their surplus in the town market, and repairmen and craftsmen take on jobs without leaving a paper trail of work orders or receipts. In this environment, income taxes and sales taxes are difficult if not impossible to impose. Tariffs, on the other hand, can be relatively easily collected by inspectors at the ports and border crossings. They simply have to observe the goods coming in and their value and then levy a fee (i.e., the tariff) on the person transporting the goods. The United States is a case in point, as tariff revenues were the greatest source of income for the U.S. government until well into the twentieth century.

In addition to the need for revenue, there are four broad categories of reasons that nations give for imposing trade barriers.

The Labor Argument

The labor argument is a perennial U.S. justification for trade barriers. It was used throughout the nineteenth century and, most recently, has been resurrected by the opponents of the North American Free Trade Agreement. The argument states that nations must protect their markets against imports from countries where wages are much lower because, otherwise, the advantage of lower wages will either wreck the domestic industry or force it to match the lower wages. In the debate leading up the ratification of the North American Free Trade Agreement by Congress, opponents argued that Mexico would have an unfair advantage in trade with the United States because Mexican firms pay their workers a fraction (on average, about one-eighth) of the wages paid to American workers.

The labor argument is an unsophisticated argument for protection, in that it fails to consider productivity differences. Mexican workers, for example, earn about one-eighth of the salary of U.S. workers because their productivity, on average, is about one-eighth of the level of U.S. workers. Mexico has lower productivity because the education and skill levels of its workforce are less than in the United States, Mexican workers have less capital at work than U.S. workers, and the infrastructure of the Mexican economy is not as developed as the infrastructure of the United States. As Mexican workers gain more skills and education, and as the capital available on the job and in the surrounding economy increases, their productivity will rise, and so will their wages.

The Infant Industry Argument

A much more sophisticated argument for protection is the **infant industry** argument. The argument is mainly associated with the tariff policies of developing nations that protect their "infant" industries against the competition of more mature firms in industrial countries. Although the concept is closely associated with developing nations, developed ones use this argument on occasion to justify protection in some high-technology cases. (Japanese skis are an example.) Two beliefs lie at the root of the infant industry argument. The first is that market forces will not support the development of a particular industry, usually because foreign competition is too well established, but also possibly because the industry is too risky. The second belief is that the industry in question has some spillover benefits, or positive **externalities**, that make the industry more valuable to the national economy than simply the wages and profits it might generate. Whenever there are spillover benefits, the market may not support the development of an industry to the optimum level. With positive externalities, many of the benefits of production are captured by other firms or individuals outside of the producing firm. Since the producers do not get the full benefit of their own production, they produce less than the amount that is most beneficial for society.

Positive externalities are usually argued to be in the form of linkages to other industries or of a technological nature. As an example of the linkage case, many nations have attempted to start their own steel industries because they assumed it would create a cheaper source of steel for other industries, such as cars. The problem with this argument is that it does not demonstrate that there is some inherent advantage in making something as opposed to buying it, or in other words, that the car industry will have a special advantage if it can buy steel from local producers. If the car industry is forced to buy from local producers who never manage to obtain world levels of efficiency, protection on the domestic steel industry may actually harm the car industry. This is what happened to firms in Brazil when the government tried to start a domestic computer industry by keeping out foreign producers. The policy actually had negative linkage effects on Brazilian businesses because they had to pay higher prices for computers and got lower-quality machines in the bargain. Brazil would have been better off importing its computers, as it does now.

Technological externalities can happen when workers change jobs and take the skills they have learned to their new employment, or whenever an industry creates information or technology that is useful somewhere else in the economy. As a practical matter, however, it is difficult to know in advance when there will be technological spillovers, and, accordingly, it is difficult to judge which industries should be protected.

Even if technological externalities are present, it is not enough to establish the validity of the infant industry argument. Two more conditions must hold. First, the protection that is offered must be limited in time, and second, the protected industry must experience falling costs. The time limits on protection ensure that the industry does not become a permanent recipient of transfers from consumers, and the presence of falling costs ensures that the policy will eventually pay for itself. The goal is an industry that provides a rate of return on capital that is equal to alternative investments. Given that the returns are initially too low to attract private investment, the initial excess costs must decline so that returns can rise.

The National Security Argument

Every nation protects some industries as a way to guard its national security. In trade terms, national security can be interpreted in the narrow sense of military capability or in a broader sense of cultural identity. The most obvious examples of national security in a narrow sense include weapons industries and, somewhat more broadly, strategic technologies. Some nations also include strategic minerals such as the exotic ores used in jet aircraft. Protection for the sake of making available specific minerals or other resources is not an optimal policy. A better policy is to build stockpiles of the mineral by buying large quantities in peacetime when it is cheap.

A broader definition of national security includes the cultural industries— movies, television programming, music, print media, and theater. Some nations worry that if they allow completely free trade in the cultural industries, then the most commercially viable firms will dominate, and the cultural values of the home country will be obscured and forgotten. Since the United States has the strongest presence in the movie, television, and much of the rest of the entertainment industry, the goal of protecting national cultural values is usually an argument in favor of protecting a nation's television, movie making, and music against complete domination by its U.S. counterparts. For example, the precursor to the North American Free Trade Agreement, called the Canadian–United States Free Trade Agreement (signed in 1988), established the right of Canada to require its TV and radio stations to broadcast a certain proportion of Canadian-produced programs. There are similar requirements in music, theater, and the print media. U.S. television and movie producers naturally opposed this limitation on free trade and demanded the right to sell an unlimited amount of U.S.-produced entertainment. They lost this argument, however, and they lost again when the Uruguay Round of the GATT was signed. The new multinational trade accord allows all nations to place similar requirements on their movies, television, and other cultural industries.

The issue of free trade in military and cultural industries inevitably involves noneconomic values and issues. How, for example, can we begin to assess the effects on Canadian culture and society of limitations on U.S. television programming? Given that many industries argue that their products are absolutely essential to maintaining military capability, how can we assess the strategic value of particular products or technologies? Economists tend to defer to the judgment of scientific and engineering experts on questions of strategic importance, pointing out that a less costly option is stockpiling the needed materials when possible. In the case of protection for cultural industries, economists can point out some of the tradeoffs, but they can not estimate the cultural benefits of, say, a nationally based movie industry.

The Retaliation Argument

A final category of reasons given by nations to justify trade barriers is retaliation for unfair trade practices. When a country decides that another country's trade practices unfairly discriminate against them, a common response is to impose a trade barrier. Retaliatory tariffs and quotas can provide an incentive for negotiations, but they can also lead to escalating trade wars.

Economic analysis is of limited utility in understanding this situation, since the outcome depends on political processes that determine how nations respond to pressure, their willingness to negotiate, and the outcome of negotiations. There are three camps of economists on this issue. One camp argues that free trade is beneficial regardless of the actions of a country's trading partners. If other countries choose to protect their markets, this argument goes, then it lowers their standard of living, and we would be foolish to do the same by imposing trade barriers in retaliation. Another camp argues that since free trade is beneficial, it is in everyone's interest to see it followed as widely as possible. Therefore, if a tariff today will cause other nations to open their markets tomorrow, the world economy will benefit in the long run.

A third group argues that countries that have a closed market or that restrict market access by imposing barriers to trade have an unfair advantage, particularly in high-technology products. They have a domestic market all to themselves, and they can compete freely in other markets that are more open than their own. In cases where the size of the market is important, the ability to sell to a market larger (home plus foreign) than their competitor's may give the firms in the protected market a competitive advantage. If firms in the open market are forced out of business, then the technology, skills, and expertise that go with it will exist only in the firms from the country that adopted the strategy of protecting its market. To ensure that this scenario does not play out, and

CASE STUDY

Economic Sanctions

Economic sanctions are a form of trade restriction. Unlike tariffs and quotas, which affect imports alone, sanctions are often on exports as well as imports and may include financial components as well. Access to international credit through privately owned banks or international lending agencies may be limited or blocked, as may investment by domestic firms in the country singled out for sanctions. Examples of export prohibitions included the U.S. rule during the Cold War that prohibited computer sales by domestic firms to the Soviet Union, and current prohibitions on selling goods or services to Iraq and Iran. The world community's boycott of investment in South Africa before the ending of apartheid is an example of an investment sanction as well as a trade sanction.

Economic sanctions go beyond simple trade or investment measures. In most cases they are used as one of several tactics aimed at achieving a broader policy objective—the ending of Soviet expansion or Iranian terrorism or South African apartheid. Another feature of sanctions is that they are often accompanied by additional measures, ranging from diplomatic pressure to military invasion.

The logical question to ask about sanctions is "Do they work?" In an important two-volume study of this question, three economists analyzed 120 episodes of economic sanctions throughout the world since World War I. Table 7.4 summarizes their findings. They found it useful to categorize the goals of sanctions into five separate groups: those

TABLE 7.4	Economic Sanctions Since World War I	
Goal	*Number of Cases*	*Successes*
Modest policy change	51	17
Destabilize a government	21	11
Disrupt a military adventure	18	6
Impair military potential	10	2
Other	20	5

Sanctions imposed between World War I and 1990 had about a 38 percent success rate.

Source: Gary Clyde, Hufbauer, Schott, and Kimberly Ann Elliott. *Economic Sanctions Reconsidered.* Washington, DC: Institute for International Economics. 1990; "Executive Summary," 1998. http://www.iie.com/FOCUS/SANCTION/execsum.htm#start.

designed to create a relatively modest policy change (e.g., to free a political prisoner or to limit nuclear proliferation); those intended to destabilize a government; sanctions aimed at disrupting a military adventure of another nation (e.g., stopping Iraq's invasion of Kuwait); those designed to impair another nation's military potential; and a fifth category of other goals, such as stopping apartheid, or the Arab League's boycott of oil sales to the United States in retaliation for support for Israel.

In order to be classified a success, the policy outcome must have been the one desired by the country imposing the sanctions, and the sanctions must have been a contributor to the policy outcome. Hufbauer, Schott, and Elliott find 41 successes in the 120 cases they examine, but they report a drop in the number of successes after about 1973. Sanctions are more effective when (1) the target country is small, economically weak, and politically unstable, (2) the target country is a friendly ally, (3) sanctions are imposed quickly and decisively, (4) the costs to the sending country are small, and (5) the goal is a relatively small change.

so that we do not lose critical technologies, some would argue that we should use the threat of retaliation to force open markets that are presently closed.

THE POLITICS OF PROTECTION IN THE UNITED STATES

Although U.S. trade with the rest of the world has grown, political pressures to protect domestic industries have frequently been intense. Part of the reason stems from the fact that Congressional reforms removed some of the insulation from industry lobbyists Congress enjoyed in the 1950s and 1960s. Another reason stems from the end of the Cold War and the lessening of U.S. willingness to sacrifice trade issues for the sake of maintaining close geopolitical alliances. A third reason is the rise of the export-oriented East Asian newly industrializing countries (NICs) and the pressure they have put on a number of domestic U.S. industries. Finally, the growth of the U.S. trade deficit and the widespread fear in the 1980s that the United States had lost its competitive edge also contributed to a greater reluctance to open U.S. markets without regard to the behavior of other countries and foreign firms. For each of these reasons, trade conflicts have become more open.

Protection in the United States is usually obtained either through direct action by the president (e.g., the VERs on Japanese autos in the 1980s) or through one of four different legal procedures: (1) countervailing duties; (2) antidumping duties; (3) escape clause relief; and (4) Section 301 retaliation. In each case, a firm, an industry trade association, or a government agency may petition the federal government to initiate an investigation into foreign country or foreign firm practices.

Countervailing Duties

A **countervailing duty** is a tariff that is granted to a U.S. industry that has been hurt by foreign country subsidies of its national firms. Since subsidies permit a firm to sell its goods at a lower price and still make a profit, an effect of subsidies is to make firms more competitive. The goal of a countervailing duty is to raise the U.S. price of the foreign good to a level high enough to countervail the effect of the subsidy. The idea is to level the playing field between domestic firms that receive no subsidies and foreign ones that do.

The key to countervailing duties is to define what subsidies are. The definition often seems inherently subjective and, as a consequence, is an ongoing source of tension between countries. In the past, the United States had its own definition, but it was often at odds with trading partners over the application of the definition. One of the benefits of the Uruguay Round of the GATT is that, for the first time, it provides a definition of subsidies. A **subsidy** is (1) a direct loan or transfer, (2) preferential tax treatments, such as tax credits, (3) the supply of goods or services other than general infrastructure, or (4) income and price supports.

Antidumping Duties

An **antidumping duty** is a tariff levied on an import that is selling at a price below the product's **fair value**. The determination of fair value introduces an element of subjectivity into the process of justifying an antidumping duty, as does the fact that the legal analysis and the economic analysis of dumping are not in agreement. Consequently, the growing use of antidumping duties has become a source of significant trade tension between countries, and it is not surprising that a number of countries would like to strengthen the WTO's rules regarding antidumping duties, making them harder to apply.

According to the rules of the WTO, **dumping** occurs when an exporter sells a product at a price below what it charges in its home market. It is not always possible to compare the home market and foreign market prices, however, and wholesalers, transportation costs, and other add-ons to the price may limit the usefulness of the comparison. Therefore, two other methods may be used to determine if a good is being dumped. Comparisons can be made with the price charged in third country markets, or to an estimate of the cost of production. Comparison to prices in another country is similar to the comparison between prices in the exporter's home market and the complaining country's market, and may be uninformative for the same reasons. Therefore, the WTO allows the third method whereby a country estimates the foreign firm's production costs and uses that measure to determine if dumping is occurring. In this case, an exporter does not need to sell below the cost of production to be found guilty of dumping. Dumping charges are supported if the foreign firm is not selling at a price that provides a normal rate of return on invested capital.

One final criterion must be met before antidumping duties are allowed. The country claiming dumping must also be able to show that the dumping has caused material injury to its firms. If dumping occurs, but there are no harmful effects on domestic firms, then antidumping duties are not allowed. This would happen if the dumping margin is too small to matter.

At their most basic level, antidumping duties are a tool of commercial policy that protects against predatory pricing by foreign firms. Selling below cost as a strategy to drive the competition out of business is widely perceived as unfair, and allowing it to happen can harm the economic interest of a country. This is particularly likely if it results in higher prices after the domestic producers have been driven out of the market, and in order to prevent this from happening, the WTO and many countries recognize antidumping duties as a legitimate tool of commercial policy.

Problems arise, however, because the economic theory and the legal definition are not completely in agreement. First, in order for a firm to sell in a foreign market at a price that is below its cost of production, it must have market power at home that allows it to earn higher than normal profits to subsidize its foreign sales. If a firm is not earning above average profits somewhere, it cannot maintain a price somewhere else that is below its cost. Yet, when countries investigate a dumping complaint, market structure is rarely considered. This problem is compounded by the use of estimated production costs to determine dumping, since estimated values require some guesswork about technology and other inputs, and this creates a significant margin of error.

Second, within the scope of normal commercial operations, firms often sell below cost. The most obvious case is that of goods that are likely to spoil. A fresh-fish exporter, with a load sitting on a dock somewhere, is likely to progressively lower her price as time passes. In this case, the cost of producing the shipment of fish represents sunk costs that have already been incurred, and the only option is to sell the goods for whatever is possible. Firms also sell selected items below cost as a technique for penetrating markets. This is similar to the behavior of large retail chains that offer some goods at an extremely low price in order to create a reputation as a value-oriented retailer. And finally, firms will go for extended periods selling at prices that do not cover the cost of their capital and other fixed costs as long as the costs of their variable inputs such as labor and materials are covered. Since capital costs such as interest on their loans have to be paid no matter what is produced, in the short run, the chief consideration is whether the price is high enough to cover labor costs and material input costs. In the long run, a firm that cannot sell at a high enough price to meet its capital costs will have to shut down, but in the short run, it continues to produce.

The increasing use of antidumping duties has generated a great deal of interest in defining their usage more carefully, and a number of countries have proposed that they been included in the WTO's next round of multilateral trade negotiations. As things now stand, there is a wide variation among countries in their application and their willingness to negotiate their usage. Some countries rarely apply them, and some trade agreements, such as the one between Canada and Chile, ban their usage except under exceptional circumstances. Other countries use them frequently, often it seems, as a politically expedient way to satisfy an important industry lobbying group.

In the United States, the procedure for firms to obtain protection requires that a petition be filed with the International Trade Administration in the Department of Commerce. The ITA investigates whether dumping (or subsidization in the case of a petition for countervailing duties) has occurred. If their finding is positive (dumping has occurred), the case is turned over to the United States International Trade Commission (USITC), an independent regulatory commission. The USITC conducts an additional investigation to determine if substantial harm has been done to the domestic industry and if an antidumping or countervailing duty is warranted. The relative success of U.S. firms in proving that foreign companies are dumping has encouraged a growing number of antidumping petitions in recent years.

Escape Clause Relief

Escape clause relief is so named because it refers to a clause in the U.S. and GATT trade rules that permits an industry to escape the pressure of imports by temporarily imposing a tariff. Escape clause relief is a temporary tariff on imports in order to provide a period of adjustment to a domestic industry. It is initiated when an industry or firm petitions the USITC directly for relief from a sudden surge of imports. The burden of escape clause relief is on the firm; it must establish that it is been harmed by imports and not by some other factor, such as bad management decisions. In practice, it has become so difficult to obtain relief from import competition under this procedure that few cases are filed.

Section 301 and Super 301

Section 301 of the U.S. Trade Act of 1974 requires the president's chief trade negotiator, the United States Trade Representative (USTR), to take action against any nation that persistently engages in unfair trade practices. The action usually begins with a request for negotiations with the targeted country. The goal of the negotiations is to change the policies of countries that restrict U.S. commerce in an unreasonable or unjustifiable way. Note that it is left to the United States to define unreasonable and unjustifiable restrictions on U.S. commerce.

Super 301 was passed in 1988 as part of a larger trade bill. It requires the USTR to name countries that systematically engage in unfair trade, to open negotiations with them over their practices, and to retaliate if the negotiations are not fruitful in producing changes.

Applications of Section 301 and Super 301 are widely regarded as arbitrary, often unfair, and one sided; and they are most often the result of internal U.S. political pressures to take a tough stance against a particular country. The United States usually initiates a Section 301 action by requesting consultations or negotiations with the target nation, and often the discussion does not go through the WTO dispute-resolution process. Many nations feel that this has weakened the WTO and reduced its effectiveness.

For their part, U.S. lawmakers argue that the GATT/WTO is too slow and rigid. While waiting for a decision, whole industries could disappear. Furthermore, prior to the Uruguay Round, the GATT had little to say about many new trade issues, such as trade in services, intellectual property protection, and investment restrictions. Therefore, the United States found it more expedient to go straight to the country with which it had a dispute. The World Trade Organization was designed to streamline dispute resolution and to discourage retaliation outside its forum. It remains to be seen, however, if the United States's use of Section 301 and Super 301 will be curtailed.

Summary

- Regardless of their cost or their ability to achieve a desired objective, every nation uses trade barriers. In most industrial nations, they are not used to develop comparative advantage in new industries, but rather to protect old industries that can no longer compete or to temporarily protect industries that are under pressure from new competitors. Textiles and apparel, two of the first industries established in the United States, are the most protected sectors of the U.S. economy.

- Tariffs and quotas are grossly inefficient mechanisms for creating (or keeping) jobs. Because the costs are hidden in the prices consumers pay for both foreign and domestic goods, few people realize how inefficient they are.

- The primary beneficiaries of trade barriers are producers who receive protection and governments that receive tariff revenue. The losers are consumers. Because the gains are concentrated among a relatively few people, and the losses are dispersed across many, there is usually only a small economic incentive for anyone to oppose trade barriers but a large incentive to seek them.

- The valid arguments in favor of protection involve economic returns to society that are undervalued or not counted by markets. That is, it must be the case that the market does not take into consideration the gains that spill over from production. The total value of producing a good, including any spillovers, is extremely difficult to measure, however, and it is often impossible to know the future value of the skills or technological sophistication an industry creates.

- In addition to presidential action, there are several forms of protection in the United States: countervailing duties to counter a foreign subsidy, antidumping duties to counter dumping of foreign goods, escape clause relief to counter an import surge, and 301 actions to retaliate against foreign trade practices that have been labeled as unfair by the United

States. Except for the escape clause relief, each type of tariff requires a demonstration that foreign products are competing unfairly in the U.S. market and that they have harmed domestic producers. The most common form of tariff imposition is an antidumping duty.

Vocabulary

antidumping duties

countervailing duties

dumping

escape clause relief

externality

fair value

infant industry

Section 301 and Super 301

subsidies

Study Questions

1. Which industries are more heavily protected in the United States and Japan? Are high-income or low-income nations more affected by American and Japanese trade barriers? Explain.

2. What new areas of trade and investment received coverage under the agreement signed after the Uruguay Round of the General Agreement on Tariffs and Trade?

3. Given that tariffs and quotas cost consumers and that they are grossly inefficient means for creating or preserving jobs, why do citizens allow these policies to exist?

4. What four main groups of arguments do nations use to justify protection for particular industries? Which are economic, and which are noneconomic?

5. Evaluate the labor and infant industry arguments for protection.

6. Are tariffs justified as a retaliatory measure against other nations? Justify your answer.

7. What four legal procedures do American firms have at their disposal for seeking protection? What are the conditions that would generate a request for each kind of protection?

Chapter 8

INTERNATIONAL TRADE AND LABOR AND ENVIRONMENTAL STANDARDS

INTRODUCTION

Since the end of World War II, many of the formal barriers to international trade have been removed. This was accomplished through the sustained efforts of the world's trading nations, often working through the negotiating frameworks provided by the General Agreement on Tariffs and Trade, the World Trade Organization, and more recently, the regional trade agreements springing up around the globe. Today's world economy may have the freest trading environment for manufactured goods in world history.

As trade barriers are removed, however, new obstacles to increased international economic integration begin to appear. These obstacles are driven by two distinct but equally important forces. First, it sometimes happens that national laws and regulations that were adopted for strictly domestic reasons unintentionally limit international commerce in a more integrated economic environment. For example, a law designed to capture economies of scale by giving one company a monopoly in telephone services makes it impossible for foreign telephone companies to enter the market.

A second obstacle to increased international economic integration is the conflict over standards. These extend from disputes over technical product standards, to health and safety standards, to labor and environmental standards. Issues arise in these areas for a variety of reasons. For example, the adoption of a common set of product standards gives a significant commercial advantage to firms that are already producing to the standard, and hence, each country would like to see the wider application of its own standards. Another reason behind many of the conflicts over standards is the wide variation in world income levels. When a high-income country and a low-income country increase their trading, the opportunities for gains from trade increase, but the changes in each country's pattern of specialization and production can be significant. Trade between developed and developing countries is usually based on comparative advantage and it moves countries along their production possibility curves, causing greater specialization in production. Although each nation's gains from trade may be large, greater specialization creates winners and losers inside each country, and raises questions of fairness.

Economic conditions and living standards inside developing countries are vastly different from conditions inside high-income economies such as the United States. In particular, labor and environmental standards tend to be lower and less consistently enforced in developing countries. Lower wages, longer hours, less safe working conditions, dirtier industries, and less regard for environmental degradation are relatively more common than in high-income countries. When trade occurs between countries with radically different living standards, people in higher income countries may begin to wonder about the inexpensive goods they import from low-income countries. Does their production exploit children, are working conditions safe and healthy, do workers have political and civil rights, and are the methods employed environmentally friendly? And if not, then can trade barriers such as tariffs, quotas, or complete prohibition of imports effectively pressure the exporting country into changing its practices?

SETTING STANDARDS: HARMONIZATION, MUTUAL RECOGNITION, OR SEPARATE?

Two or more economies can be deeply integrated even if they have different rules, regulations, and standards governing their individual economies. The United States is an obvious example, since individual states impose different standards on vehicle emissions, minimum wages, teacher training, food safety, construction codes, and product availability, to name just a few. Lesser forms of integration between sovereign nations, such as partial trade agreements, free-trade areas, customs unions, and common markets, are likely to vary even more with respect to rules, regulations, and standards.

Harmonization of product and process standards is one option for countries seeking to expand their commercial ties. **Harmonization of standards** refers to the case where two or more countries share a common set of standards in an area of concern, such as product safety, labor, environment, fair competition, and so forth. Another option is **mutual recognition of standards**, in which countries keep their own product and process standards, but accept the standards of others as equally valid and sufficient. For example, a medical doctor trained in a foreign country may not receive the same training as medical doctors in the home country, but under a system of mutual recognition, she is qualified to practice in either country. A third option is **separate standards**. In this case, countries keep their own standards and refuse to recognize those of anyone else. For example, if the home country has a more stringent rule for pesticide residue left on vegetables after harvest, then with separate standards they prohibit imports that are considered unsafe. Most regional trade agreements and the WTO agreements practice a combination of harmonization, mutual recognition, and separate standards.

There are no general rules to determine which approach is most efficient or fairest in all cases. Often it is the case that the harmonization of technical standards having to do with product design or performance is useful since it leads to a larger, more unified market and creates greater efficiency. Simple examples such as the number of threads per centimeter on screws, or the size of electrical plugs on home appliances are illustrations of cases where harmonization unifies a market and creates efficiency gains across the economy. In other cases, harmonization of standards may pose the potential problem of freezing into place a set of inferior standards. New technologies are a case in point, since the evolution of new products and processes is impossible to forecast, and freezing technical standards into legal requirements may have a harmful effect on future developments. In addition, there are many cases such as labor or environmental legislation where it is unclear which country has the "best" rules. Mutual recognition is a superior option under these conditions, as it allows competition between different standards, which may help clarify the costs and benefits of each one.

Harmonization of standards sometimes poses an additional problem in its failure to take into account the differences between countries. Most importantly, differences in income result in basic differences in what is possible for countries to achieve and the standards they can reasonably enforce. In some cases, this is not an issue. With many product standards, for example the size of car tires, the potential to harmonize standards is relatively unaffected by income differences among countries. In other cases, such as labor and environmental standards, income levels are a major determinant of standards. When standards across countries vary by the level of development, it is generally better to mutually recognize each other's standards, or, if that is not possible for safety or other reasons, then to maintain separate standards. While trade theory is clear on this point, many people living in high-income countries find it hard to accept, particularly with respect to labor and environmental standards.

Many citizens in high-income countries fear that in the absence of a common set of labor and environmental standards, international trade leads to an unfair and harmful outcome. Specifically, they fear that low standards abroad create competitive pressures for domestic firms to lower their standards, or to move to a foreign location in order to reduce their costs. This possibility has been labeled a **race to the bottom**, where the bottom is the lowest possible level of standards. In the following sections, we examine this issue and others, in the context of labor and environmental standards.

CASE STUDY

Income, Environment, and Society

The World Bank has four categories of income that it uses to classify countries. Table 8.1 shows world population and the level of income in each of the four categories.

Note that most of the world's population, and a majority of the countries in the world are classified as **low-income** (per capita incomes less than $755 per person in 1999) or **lower-middle income**

(*continues*)

TABLE 8.1	Income and Population by World Bank Income Categories			
Income Category	*Number of Countries*	*Estimated Population 1999 (billions)*	*Income Range (per person)*	*Average Income per Person 1999 (dollars)*
Low	58	2.4	100–754	410
Lower middle	49	2.1	755–2,995	1,200
Upper middle	27	0.6	2,996–9,265	4,900
High	27	0.9	9,266+	25,730

The World Bank classifies countries into four income categories; most of the world's population lives in low-income or lower-middle-income countries.

Source: World Bank, *World Development Report, 2000/01.*

(per capita incomes between $755 and $2,995 per person in 1999). Income differences as large as those in Table 8.1 lead to very large differences in most social, economic, and environmental indicators. Table 8.2 illustrates this with two environmental and two social indicators.

Table 8.2 displays several patterns of change. Infant mortality, measured as the number of infant deaths per 100,000 live births, shows a strong and consistent pattern of decrease with income, reflecting the increase in medical care and sanitation that accompanies income growth. Similarly, the percentage of children in the 10–14 age group who work also decreases with income. At low levels of income, nearly 1 in 5 (20 percent) children age 10 to 14 are working, but by the time per capita income reaches the range of $755 to $2,995 (lower-middle income), the number drops to 1 in 14 (7 percent).

The two environmental indicators show a mixed pattern. Carbon dioxide, CO_2, is the major greenhouse gas responsible for global warming. Consumption of energy is the major reason for CO_2 emissions, and high-income countries consume far more energy than the other categories of countries. Hence, on a per capita basis, they generate more than eleven times the carbon dioxide of people living in low-income countries. Another environmental indicator that gets consistently worse with rising incomes is the amount of solid waste (garbage). Many environmental indicators improve with income, however, although in some cases the improvement comes only after a period of deterioration. Deforestation fits into this category. As shown in Table 8.2, there is a large increase in deforestation per capita as incomes rise, followed by a decrease and, ultimately, net reforestation as countries gain income. This is the common pattern for some types of urban air pollution, for example, particulate matter and sulfur dioxide (a major cause of acid rain). Some environmental indicators, water pollution and sanitation for example, show constant improvement at almost all levels of income.

TABLE 8.2	Income Categories, Environment, and Society			
Income Category	*Infant Deaths per 100,000 Births*	*Children Age 10–14 in Labor Force, Percent of Age Group*	*CO_2 Emissions, Metric Tons per Person*	*Annual Deforestation, Square Kilometers per 100,000 People*
Low	68	19	1.1	1.8
Lower middle	35	7	3.3	1.2
Upper middle	26	6	5.5	7.2
High	6	<1	12.3	–1.3*

Infant mortality and child labor decrease with income level, while CO_2 emissions increase, and deforestation increases but then decreases.

*A negative number implies reforestation instead of deforestation.
Source: World Bank, *World Development Report, 2000/01*.

LABOR STANDARDS

Recently, the United States and other countries demanded that labor and environmental standards be included in any future trade negotiations. This is a politically charged issue that is likely to come and go over time, depending in part on the political party in power, but it also reflects rising worldwide interests in issues related to human rights and the environment. To date, the United States's trade agreements with Canada and Mexico (the North American Free Trade Agreement) and Jordan contain language on labor and environmental standards, either in the treaty itself, or as a side-agreement to the trade treaty. In each case, the language specifies that each country must enforce its own standards or face monetary fines. Many labor and environmental activists view this as inadequate and are pushing to include trade sanctions as part of the enforcement mechanism, both in existing agreements and in future agreements, including those reached by the WTO.

The complaints against trade by labor and environmental interests are relatively similar. In both cases, it is alleged that trade with countries that have lower standards creates a race to the bottom in standards, and that countries with high standards are forced to lower their standards or experience a loss of jobs and industry. Furthermore, it is alleged that this type of trade is unfair, since the failure to enact or to enforce standards gives firms in the countries with lower standards a commercial advantage. Before addressing these issues, it is useful to clarify what is meant by standards, particularly in the case of labor standards.

Defining Labor Standards

The concept of labor standards is multifaceted, since it covers a wide variety of potential rights, stretching from basic rights such as the right to be free from forced labor to civic rights such as the right to representation in a union. At present, there is no core set of work-related rights that everyone views as universal human rights.

We take as a starting point the five labor standards proposed as basic rights by the International Labor Organization (ILO, see below) and revised by the Organization for Economic Cooperation and Development (OECD):

- prohibition of forced labor;
- freedom of association;
- the right to organize and bargain collectively;
- an end to the exploitation of child labor;
- nondiscrimination in employment.

Most people would probably agree to these five rights, although there is a fair amount of ambiguity attached to each of them. For example, conditions that are considered exploitative in a high-income country might seem acceptable in a poor one. Or, cultural or religious values regarding employment opportunities for men and women may be at odds with the idea of nondiscrimination.

Other potential standards are significantly more contentious. For example, universal standards for minimum wages, limits on the number of hours someone can work in a day, and health and safety issues in the workplace are difficult to define given the wide variation in incomes and living conditions around the world. High-income countries, where unskilled labor is relatively scarce, face an entirely different set of economic constraints compared to those faced by low-income countries where unskilled labor is relatively abundant. For example, if low-income countries are forced to pay a minimum wage high enough to satisfy critics in high-income countries, many people fear that the result would be the closing down of production and a rise in unemployment rather than an increase in living standards. Too high a minimum wage, in other words, may be well intentioned, but it may reduce living standards in low-income countries. Even this is ambiguous, however, since it is no easy matter to determine how high is too high.

CASE STUDY

Child Labor

Child labor is one of the most difficult issues in the labor standards debate. In large part, the difficulty arises because nations cannot reach consensus on the policies that would effectively eliminate the worst forms of exploitation of children.

The International Labor Organization (ILO, see below) estimates that 250 million children between the ages of five and fourteen are working worldwide, and about 120 million are working full time (Figure 8.1). Geographically, they estimate that 61 percent of these children are in Asia, 32 percent are in Africa, and 7 percent are in Latin America. While Asia has the largest numbers of working children, Africa has the highest proportion, with an estimated one in three children employed (Figure 8.2). Child labor is much more common in rural areas than in urban, and three-fourths of working kids are employed in

a family-run enterprise—often a subsistence farm. This pattern is similar to the pattern of economic development in the United States.

Worldwide, most children work in activities that are oriented toward production for domestic consumption. The ILO estimates that less than 6 to 7 percent are working in export-oriented industries, such as export manufacturing, mining, or export-oriented agriculture. In general, the use of child labor declines dramatically with GDP, falling from an estimated 30 to 60 percent of children (five to fourteen years of age)

| FIGURE 8.1 | Child Labor, in Millions |

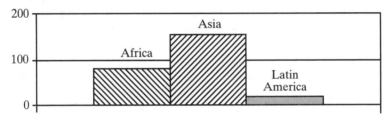

Asia has the most child labor, followed by Africa and Latin America.

| FIGURE 8.2 | Proportion of Children Working, Ages 5–14 |

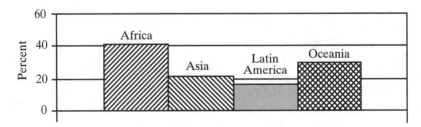

Africa has the highest proportion of its children in the labor force, followed by Oceania (excluding Australia and New Zealand) and Asia.

(continues)

in countries with $500 or less of GDP per person (1987 dollars), to 10 to 30 percent in countries with $500 to $1,000 of GDP per person (Table 8.2).

The fact that child labor is tied to poverty and agriculture is precisely what makes it a difficult policy issue. Child labor is a common family survival strategy, and if it were stopped, it would force many families deeper into poverty. We would like to believe that if children did not work, they would attend school, but unfortunately this is often not the case since many rural areas and poor countries lack enough schools to meet the needs of their children. When countries try to regulate child labor, problems stem from the fact that children often work in family enterprises and in remote areas where it is expensive to send inspectors and to maintain a system of vigilance.

Although the United States officially denies that it has a problem with child labor, and even though it is a rich country, it illustrates the difficulties involved in ending the practice. On a world scale, there is little child labor in the United States, but in remote agricultural regions, it is not uncommon. According to U.S. labor law (the Fair Labor Standards Act, or FLSA, is the primary labor code in the United States), a child is anyone age seventeen or under. The General Accounting Office (GAO) of the federal government estimates that 300,000 children work in agriculture each year. The GAO also acknowledges that this is an undercount due to methodological problems. The United Farm Workers Union estimates that the true figure is closer to 800,000. Concentrations of child farm workers can be found in Arizona, California, Florida, and Texas, although the group Human Rights Watch states that "virtually no state is without child labor in agriculture."

The main provisions of the U.S. labor code (FLSA) exempt agriculture from many of its standards. Consequently, conditions can be brutal and exploitative. For example, employers may legally hire children younger than twelve to work unlimited hours outside of school, and they may legally hire sixteen- and seventeen-year-olds to work in hazardous conditions handling toxic chemicals and dangerous machinery. Both of these practices are forbidden in the rest of the economy.

The persistence of child labor in a wealthy country such as the United States underscores the difficulty of the issue. Farm worker families are among the poorest working people in the United States. They live in rural areas and often migrate as they follow the harvest. They work in a sector of the economy that is partially outside the coverage of the main body of protective standards. And for a variety of reasons—history, the seasonal nature of the work, the legislative power of special interests, corruption, official denial of the problem—legislative reform that would effectively curtail the use of child labor has not been achieved.

Sources: Human Rights Watch, *Fingers to the Bone: United States Failure to Protect Child Farmworkers.* Human Rights Watch: New York. 2000.

International Labor Office, "Child Labour: Targeting the Intolerable." International Labor Conference. 86th Session. Geneva: Author, 1996.

_____, *Child Labour: What Is To Be Done?* Geneva: Author, 1996.

Siddiqi, Faraaz, and Harry Patrinos, "Child Labor: Issues, Causes, and Interventions," Human Capital Development and Operations Policy Working Paper 56. Washington, DC: World Bank, No date.

Labor Standards and Trade

The major source of disagreements between trade economists and labor activists is over the use of trade barriers to enforce labor standards. That is, should one country use trade barriers to pressure another country into altering its labor standards? Trade economists tend to be more skeptical about the use of trade barriers, partly for the reasons outlined in Chapter 7, where it was shown that they are expensive and grossly inefficient policies for reaching most of the goals for which they are used. In addition to the deadweight losses in consumption and production at home, the use of trade barriers to enforce standards abroad raises several other concerns for economists. These include their effectiveness in creating change in an exporting country, the hazy borderline between protectionism and concern over standards, the lack of agreement over the specific content of standards, and their potential to erupt into a wider trade war. We will examine each of these points.

Effectiveness. In addition to the deadweight losses and income redistribution effects of trade barriers, it is clear that only large countries can hope to use barriers successfully, since a small country cannot have a large enough impact on demand. That is, if a small country such as the Netherlands decides that garment producers in Haiti are exploiting children, then any trade barrier that the Netherlands erects against imports from Haiti are not likely to reduce demand enough to stop the offending Haitian practice. Only countries that constitute a significant share of the Haitian market could erect barriers that would impose costs on Haitian producers, and even then only if there are no alternative markets for Haitian goods. Nor would this necessarily lead to changes, since there are numerous examples (Cuba, Iraq, and others) where countries have suffered large costs from trade sanctions but have not altered their policies in response. In effect, the general rule here is that the effectiveness of the trade barrier increases as more countries join together to impose them. For example, the strong unity of the world's industrial economies against South Africa was at least partly responsible for ending the policy of apartheid.

In addition to the problem of creating a coalition of countries, an additional obstacle to the effectiveness of trade barriers is that in some cases they will make conditions worse rather than better. This outcome occurs when sanctions cause producers inside a country to move their facilities into the informal, unregulated, economy where it is out of sight of domestic inspectors and regulators. Some share of production in every economy takes place in the **informal economy**. The informal economy does not necessarily produce illegal goods (drugs, for example), but it is untaxed, unregulated, and uninspected. In developing countries this tends to be a relatively larger share of overall economic activity than in industrial economies, and it is typically composed of small firms operating with little capital. Employees in these enterprises usually earn less and suffer harsher working conditions. If sanctions against a country create incentives for its employers to avoid the scrutiny of labor inspectors, then a larger share of the working population could find themselves laboring under worse conditions.

Hazy Borderline between Protectionism and Concern. When does the concern over foreign labor practices become a justification for protectionism? There is no definitive way to answer this question, although it is certain that special interests sometimes use the issue of labor standards as a means to justify their real goal, which is to obtain protection against foreign competition. Indeed, this is the fear of many developing countries, and explains why their governments have so far resisted negotiating over labor standards. Developing countries tend to have abundant supplies of unskilled labor and they depend on low-wage, low-productivity jobs for a large share of their employment. In these countries, proposals to set labor standards and to use trade barriers as an enforcement mechanism are widely viewed as a new form of protectionism on the part of high-income countries. Given that most high-income countries continue to protect their markets in the two most important areas of developing country production—agriculture and textiles/apparel—there is a strong suspicion that calls for labor standards are a way to undermine the comparative advantage of low-income countries, and to close the markets of high-income countries in selected areas.

The Specific Content of Labor Standards. The problem of reaching agreement on the specific content of standards has yet to be resolved. We have seen how child labor varies by income, and even the definition of a child varies across countries. For example, disputes over the minimum age at which someone may legally enter the labor force have so far blocked international agreement on child labor, other than vague condemnations of the practice. Other standards are equally contentious, although it is always conceivable that an international consensus may develop in the long run. At the present time, however, the lack of international agreement on the specific content of labor standards, other than the relatively vague proposals from the OECD and ILO, means that trade sanctions are unilateral measures with a large potential for creating conflict and undermining international economic relations.

The Potential To Set Off a Trade War. One of the primary obligations of countries in the WTO is to treat other members the same. That is, discrimination by one WTO member against another is not allowed. There are exceptions, as in the case of national security, or in the case of the special benefits given to other members of a free-trade area, but in general, discriminatory trade practices are not allowed. Consequently, the use of trade sanctions to enforce labor standards places a country out of compliance with its WTO obligations and opens it to the risk of retaliation by the targeted country. Where this ends is indeterminate.

The purpose of this discussion is to raise questions about the efficacy of trade barriers as a tool for overturning objectionable foreign labor practices. It is not meant to imply that nothing should ever be done. Later in the chapter, a number of alternative approaches are discussed.

Evidence on Low Standards as a Predatory Practice

One of the concerns expressed by the proponents of trade sanctions is that low standards may reflect a deliberate policy to capture markets and foreign investment. There are no reasons why a country cannot use its coercive power to hold down or repress labor standards, and thereby reduce the costs of producing goods. While theoretically possible, this too has a number of issues that must be examined empirically. First, it should be noted that a country cannot simultaneously run a large trade surplus (capture markets abroad) and attract net foreign investment. The relationship between these variables will be explored in Chapter 9, but at this point it is sufficient to note that trade surpluses imply capital outflows, not capital inflows. Hence, countries cannot simultaneously capture markets and attract net foreign investment.

Additionally, there is little or no support for the view that countries use low labor standards in this way. While there is evidence that a country can reduce production costs by outlawing unions to undermine wage increases, or by some other repressive practice, there is no evidence that this type of policy has succeeded in giving any country a comparative advantage in lines of production that it did not already have. In other words, low standards can reduce production costs, but they cannot change a country's comparative advantage.

This result does not affect the case of competition between countries with the same or similar comparative advantages, and within a particular line of production, such as the clothing industry, countries may compete by lowering labor standards. This means, however, that the harmful competitive effects of low standards are on other countries with low standards, not on countries with high standards and with an entirely different comparative advantage.

While low labor standards may help a country compete against another low labor standards country, there is clear evidence that low labor standards are not a successful strategy for attracting foreign investment. The reason is simple. Low labor standards are highly correlated with a labor force that is abundant in illiterate, unskilled, labor. Furthermore, it is a sign that the nation's infrastructure of roads, ports, power supply, telecommunications, schools, and sanitation are also undeveloped. Hence, the labor cost savings of low labor standards is more than likely to be offset by higher costs everywhere else in production. Consequently, empirical studies show that countries with low labor standards are less successful at attracting foreign investment.

Finally, there is the case of intolerable practices, such as apartheid in the old South Africa, the gulags of the former Soviet Union, and slavery in Sudan and elsewhere. These types of practices raise a number of moral issues which make it unreasonable to solely rely on economic analysis. Clearly, however, the more united the world is against a particular inhumane labor practice, the more likely sanctions are to succeed. For example, the United States is isolated in imposing sanctions on Cuba, and although they have imposed significant costs on its economy, the lack of international support for U.S. policies has prevented the sanctions from successfully changing Cuban policies.

CASE STUDY

The International Labor Organization (ILO)

The **International Labor Organization** "seeks the promotion of social justice and internationally recognized human and labour rights." The ILO began in 1919 and is the only surviving element of the League of Nations, which was founded after World War I and is the precursor of the United Nations (UN). In 1946, the ILO was incorporated into the United Nations and since then, most of the world's countries have become members.

The ILO uses several tools to attain its goals. Most prominently, it develops labor standards that are embodied in specific Conventions and Recommendations. Individual countries are encouraged but not required to ratify the ILO Conventions. Currently, there are 183 Conventions, about 26 of which have been shelved and are no longer proposed, leaving 157 in force.

On June 18th, 1998, the ILO adopted the "Declaration on Fundamental Principles and Rights at Work and its Follow-up." This document specifies the eight **core labor standards** it believes all countries should respect, regardless of which Conventions they ratified. The eight core standards are:

1. Freedom of association and the right to organize;
2. The right to bargain collectively;
3–4. The abolition of forced, involuntary, labor (two separate conventions);
5. Freedom from employment discrimination;
6. The right to equal pay for equal work;
7. A minimum age for work (fourteen to sixteen, depending on the country);
8. Freedom from the worst forms of exploitation of child labor.

To date, only 42 countries have ratified all eight conventions. In cases where countries have ratified fewer than eight, the ILO can request that these countries explain how they are implementing or trying to implement the core labor standards. Figure 8.3 shows the distribution of countries by the number of conventions ratified. To date, the United States has ratified two of the eight Conventions on core labor standards.

The most serious type of complaint handled by the ILO concerns cases where worker's organizations, firms, or governments file a formal complaint that a member government is not enforcing core labor rights. The process for handling such complaints begins with a consultation with the alleged offender, followed by an official investigation if the consultation does not resolve the issue. The investigating committee may make recommendations, which the target country may appeal to the International Court of Justice. After the appeal, if there is one, the ILO can propose actions against the offending country. Economic actions such as trade sanctions are within the legal framework of options available to the ILO. It should be noted, however, that through-

FIGURE 8.3   Conventions Ratified

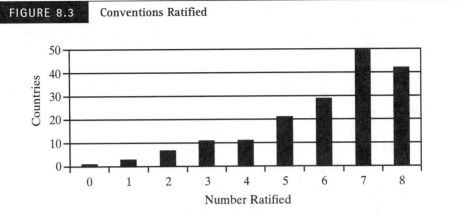

out its lengthy history, the ILO has recommended actions against only one country, and it has never proposed trade sanctions.

The ILO's reluctance to use the full extent of its power, along with the failure of some of its members to support it, results in a fairly weak organization. Changes may be in the air, however, as the ILO has shown a new energy to actually name countries that violate core labor standards and recently (1999) proposed its first actions against an offending nation. These were directed against Myanmar (Burma), which has extensively used forced labor over a long period of time.

The new willingness of the ILO to take action is probably due to the renewed support it has received from a number of countries that previously ignored it. A stronger and more aggressive ILO has gained appreciation as a useful mechanism for resolving tensions between trade and labor standards. This has generated support from politicians who see the ILO as a way to move for-

ward on trade issues. For example, in addition to defining core labor standards, the "Declaration on Fundamental Principles and Rights at Work" directs the Director General of the ILO to prepare an annual report on global labor rights, based on annual reports from individual nations. Some believe that this report will be a benchmark for judging future progress.

In addition to handling complaints and proposing Conventions, the ILO also provides technical assistance in all aspects of labor policy, including labor law, worker benefit programs, vocational training, development and administration of cooperatives, and many other areas.

Sources: International Labor Organization. http://www.ilo.org. Elliott, Kimberly Ann, "The ILO and Enforcement of Core Labor Standards." Washington, DC: Institute for International Economics. July, 2000. http://www.iie.com/NEWSLTR/ news00-6.htm. Accessed 10-9-00.

TRADE AND THE ENVIRONMENT

Over the last forty years, humans have come to the realization that our activities profoundly affect the natural environment. Unfortunately, our production and consumption choices do not always reflect the environmental costs of our decisions, and in the short run our economies too often perform as if environmental costs and limits are irrelevant. Yet, if economic agents are allowed to ignore the environmental costs of their actions, then conflict between financial and environmental interests are inevitable. Most high-income countries have a significant amount of such conflict, and trade, along with other economic activities, has received its share of environmental criticism.

Transboundary and Non-Transboundary Effects

There is a considerable overlap between environmental standards and labor standards. For example, many proponents of putting environmental standards into trade agreements believe that trade sanctions—tariffs, quotas, prohibitions on imports—should be used as enforcement mechanisms, while the critics of trade sanctions have the same concerns raised earlier: they are relatively ineffective, there is a hazy borderline between protectionism and concern for the environment, there is a lack of international agreement, and there is a potential to start trade wars.

There are some differences between labor and environmental standards, however, beginning with the fact that some but not all environmental impacts are **transboundary**. In other words, low standards in one country can degrade the environment in another country or countries. When it comes to trade policy, the distinction between transboundary and **non-transboundary** environmental impacts is an important one. We will look at non-transboundary, or exclusively national impacts first.

Trade and Environmental Impacts That Do Not Cross Borders. Proponents of trade barriers to enforce environmental standards base their analysis on two types of claims. First, they argue that environmental standards reduce industrial competitiveness. This induces an environmental race to the bottom where countries are forced to rescind standards in order to maintain employment. Second, they argue that standards in rich countries causes them to "export pollution" to developing countries by relocating their dirty industries there. Both effects are harmful to the environment, as they lead to downward pressures on environmental standards and the concentration of dirty industries in a few developing countries.

The first claim, that environmental standards reduce industrial competitiveness, is theoretically valid since standards must raise the costs of production. Essentially, environmental standards prohibit the shifting of environmental costs to the public at large and thereby force firms to take a more complete measure of all their costs of production. If the standards are correctly implemented, they raise national well-being and lead to an economically optimal level of production. This implies that the argument against standards by firms that are subject to them is an argument between their interests and the nation's interests. Clearly, the nation is better off if the production of dirty industries is curtailed somewhat, even though the workers and firms in the shrinking industry may be worse off in the short-to-medium runs. The idea that the sectional interests are so politically strong that they can force environmental deregulation (race to the bottom) or prevent the introduction of new standards altogether, may have some merit, but in general, environmental standards in most countries have gotten tougher over time, not more lax.

Countries that compete by offering foreign firms a reduced set of environmental compliance requirements are known as **pollution havens**. Note the essential similarity between the pollution haven concept and the claim that countries compete for foreign investment by lowering their labor standards. Empirically, there is evidence that some dirty industries from high-income industrial economies moved to developing countries in the 1970s when the industrial economies first began cracking down on environmental polluters. Steel and chemical industries fall into this pattern, although it is possible that the developing countries were gaining a comparative advantage in these areas as high-income countries were losing theirs. Nevertheless, there is strong evidence showing that the idea of pollution havens is invalid. That is, it is impossible to identify any country that successfully competes for new investment on the basis of low environmental standards. The fact that there are no pollution havens is good news, but it does not mean that individual firms cannot move to escape the environmental regulations of a high-standards country. Undoubtedly, there are cases of this, although numbers and overall importance are uncertain.

From a trade perspective, the issue is complicated by the fact that differences in income and preferences make the optimal set of environmental standards variable by country. An optimal set of standards in Europe, for example, might be entirely different from the optimal set in North Africa or Central Asia. The fact that budgets and regulatory abilities are limited implies that countries cannot do everything, and that they must prioritize their efforts. Biodiversity and habitat preservation may receive top priority in one place, while clean water and soil conservation are first in another. When the optimality of standards varies across countries, the introduction of trade barriers as a means of enforcing one country's standards in another country's production system would actually lower global welfare rather than raise it.

Trade and Transboundary Environmental Problems. Transboundary environmental impacts happen when one country's pollution spills over into a second country, for example, when a shared watershed is polluted by the upstream user, or industrial production in one country creates acid rain in another country. It can also happen in a mutual way, for example, when heavy truck traffic between two countries creates air pollution in both. And, finally, transboundary environmental impacts can occur as the result of similar activities in many countries leading to global impacts such as global warming and ozone depletion. There are a variety of potential actions that countries may contemplate, from tariffs on the output of the polluting industries, to embargoes, to multi-country or global negotiations.

The analysis of labor standards applies here, as unilateral actions by one country are unlikely to have any effect whatsoever except in the large country case. Even then, the more isolated it is, the lower the probability that its actions will successfully alter the policies of the offending countries, and the higher the probability that it runs afoul of the WTO rules. When small countries ignore their WTO obligations, there may be little impact on the world trading system, but when large countries do so, it undermines the stability of the entire system.

CASE STUDY

Trade Barriers and Endangered Species

The connection between trade and endangered species protection is an area where the environmental movement has been critical of the WTO. The original precedent-setting case began with the United States's ban on imports of tuna that were caught with nets that were particularly harmful to dolphins (see the Case Study in Chapter 6). Under the terms of the Endangered Species Act of 1973, the United States imposed a ban on tuna imports that were not certified as "dolphin safe." Mexico lodged a complaint, and the outcome of the investigation was a GATT ruling that countries cannot prohibit imports based on the method of production, as long as the goods are legal. Because the United States allowed tuna to be sold in its market, it could not keep out tuna harvested in a way that hurt dolphins.

The United States's prohibitions on certain shrimp imports was the next important case to draw attention to the conflict between trade and the protection of endangered species. The United States sought to protect endangered sea turtles that are harmed by shrimp trawlers that do not use turtle excluder devices (TED) on their nets. In 1987, it issued guidelines requiring shrimp trawlers to use TEDs and in 1989, it announced that beginning in May of 1991, it would ban shrimp from countries that were not certified. The guidelines applied only to the Caribbean and the Western Atlantic, and countries were given three years to come into compliance. In 1996, a number of additional conditions were placed on shrimp imports, the guidelines were extended worldwide, and countries were given four months to come into compliance.

India, Malaysia, Pakistan, and Thailand immediately protested to the WTO. The primary basis of the protest was that they were given four months to comply with the U.S. rules, while countries in the Caribbean were given three years and technical assistance. In addition, they cited the dolphin–tuna case, and argued that the GATT rules forbid discrimination against imports based on the process of production. After the United States and the Asian nations failed to resolve their dispute through informal consultations, the Asians asked the WTO's Dispute Settlement Body to establish a panel to resolve the issue. In May, 1998, the WTO dispute resolution panel concluded that the United States was in violation of its WTO commitments, mainly because its unilateral actions ignored its obligation to consult and negotiate before taking action.

The United States appealed this decision, and the Appeal Body of the WTO partially reversed the decision against the United States. The Appeal Body stated that the United States's import barriers are potentially allowable but that the failure to negotiate or confer with the affected countries placed it in violation of WTO rules. Furthermore, by giving Caribbean states three years to install TEDs, along with technical and financial assistance, while only allowing the East Asian countries four months, with no technical or financial assistance, the United States acted in a discriminatory manner. In response, the United States began a series of negotiations with the countries that filed the complaint. In the end, it revised its timetable and procedures for certification, and agreed to provide technical assistance in the use of TEDs. The case remains open, however, as the Asian countries have continued to claim discrimination against their interests.

This case is important because, in the words of the WTO, "We have *not* decided that the sovereign nations that are Members of the WTO cannot adopt effective measures to protect endangered species, such as sea turtles. Clearly, they can and should." In effect, the WTO forced a multilateral solution by arranging for the United States—which places a relatively high value on sea turtles—to assist a number of developing countries—which place a relatively higher value on their commercial fishing industries—in acquiring the technology they need. This enables the United States to extend its protection of an endangered species worldwide, while the fishing fleets of South Asia remain commercially viable.

The WTO also clarified the controversial issue of products versus processes that first began with the tuna–dolphin dispute. In its ruling, the WTO states that trade measures are permitted to protect endangered species. At the same time, the ruling stressed the need to negotiate a solution and disallowed unilateral action.

Source: World Trade Organization, "United States-Import Prohibition of Certain Shrimp and Shrimp Products," AB-1998-4. http://www.wto.org/english/tratop_e/dispu_e/58abr.doc.

ALTERNATIVES TO TRADE MEASURES

At the present moment, it is impossible to predict how, or even if, trade rules might eventually change in order to accommodate labor and environmental standards. These are new issues for the world trading system, and it is possible that they will become a permanent source of tension in international economic relations. As long as there are large income gaps between rich and poor countries, it seems unlikely that differences in standards will disappear. If trade tensions over standards are likely to continue in one form or another, then it is important to look for a ways to preserve the benefits created by world trade while simultaneously resolving the conflicts over standards.

In the search for alternatives to trade measures, it is useful to recognize the general economic principle that efficient policies go directly to the root of whatever problem they are designed to correct. This was illustrated in Chapter 7, where it was demonstrated that trade barriers are an enormously expensive way to solve the problem of job shortages in a particular industry. In the cases of environmental degradation and the exploitation of labor, the root of the problem lies in the production and/or consumption of particular goods, not in their trade. If a steel mill pollutes a river or exploits children, the cause of the environmental and human harm is the set of production standards employed by the mill, not the fact that the steel is exported. In some cases of negative environmental effects, the root of the problem is consumption instead of production, for example, air pollution caused by gas-burning cars. Given that environmental degradation and labor exploitation are by-products of production and consumption decisions, the optimal policies for addressing them is at the level of production and consumption, not at the level of trade measures, since the latter create production and consumption inefficiencies in the country that imposes them. In some cases, such as countries that still allow slavery, trade measures may be the only available option short of military intervention, but in most international conflicts over labor and environmental standards, there are more efficient policies than trade measures.

Labels for Exports

The idea of labeling is widespread and has been implemented with mixed success. This idea is a certification process producing a label that is attached to the good when it is exported. The label is designed to tell consumers that the good was produced under conditions that are humane or environmentally sustainable. This method is already in place in a few instances, although not always successfully. For example, in 1999, the United States and Cambodia agreed that the United States would increase its quota of Cambodian textiles and garments if the country allowed foreign observers to visit its factories. Cambodia agreed to the intrusion of labor inspectors because it is desperate for the export business. The initial result was a heightening of conflict between Cambodian unions and employers, and a threat by producers to move elsewhere. In another case, Starbucks Coffee signed up with an independent inspection agency that offers its services to firms that import coffee and other tropical products. This allows Starbucks to advertise that it sells at least one type of coffee that is certified as beneficial to small farmers that grow coffee. In a similar way, some cosmetic brands and retailers certify that their products are not tested on animals.

Labeling probably has an important role to play in resolving conflicts, but not in its present form. First, many countries will resist what they consider an infringement of their sovereignty. Allowing foreign inspectors to probe into the details of a country's labor and environmental conditions is likely to upset nationalistic sentiment and create resistance to the spread of labeling. A second problem is that consumers will have to be convinced that the label provides reliable information. If a sweater made in Cambodia has a label saying it was made under humane conditions, what degree of confidence should you put on that information? As the procedure of labeling becomes more widespread, it is possible that the true information value of labels will decrease. These problems are not insurmountable, but they have to be addressed before labeling is adopted on a larger scale.

Requiring Home Country Standards

A second alternative to trade measures is to require home country firms to follow home country standards whenever they open foreign operations. An example was the Sullivan Principles, which asked multinationals operating in South Africa during the apartheid era to practice nondiscrimination. In the case of labor standards, a domestic firm in a high-standards country that wants to open a plant in a developing country would be required by law to adhere to the same labor standards as the ones it must follow at home. This does not mean that wages and benefits must be the same, since the cost of labor varies, but minimum wages might be included, along with some benefits, workplace health and safety standards, child labor standards, hours of work standards, and so forth. In the environmental sphere, it is not uncommon for firms to adopt the same standards abroad as they use at home, since environmental control is often built into the technology and a least-cost strategy usually involves the adoption of one set of standards rather than multiple standards.

The advantage of this approach is that it takes care of the fear of a race to the bottom by making it impossible for a home-based company to exploit low labor or environmental standards abroad, while, at the same time, preserving access to the low-wage labor of labor abundant countries. Furthermore, this technique shifts the costs of improved standards to firms and consumers in high-income countries—which is where most of the concern originates. It might seem strange to regulate companies operating outside the nation, but it is well within the legal right of nations to impose standards on domestic firms that operate abroad, as long as the standards do not conflict with the laws of the host country. Given that the required standards are meant to be more stringent than those in the host country, this should not be a problem.

One weakness of this approach, however, is that it only addresses the problem of firms in high-standards countries that go abroad, but does not address the problem of foreign-owned and -operated firms that export into the domestic market. In other words, firms based in countries with low standards are untouched by this type of rule. More problematically, a clothing manufacturer based in a high-standards country might outsource its production through contracts with firms based in low-standards countries. This puts part of the production at arm's length and makes it more difficult to ensure that working conditions are satisfactory. Since the firms doing the actual cutting and sewing are foreign owned, they may lie completely outside the reach of the regulations governing the clothing manufacturer located in the high-standards country.

Nevertheless, regulations placed on domestic firms operating abroad address a significant share of the fears of a race to the bottom. In particular, they remove the threat by domestic firms to relocate abroad if standards are not reduced at home, and ensure that the attraction of foreign-based production is the foreign comparative advantage, not the ability to lower labor standards or ignore the environment. In addition, it avoids the problems created when high-income countries appear to be dictating labor and environmental standards for low- and middle-income countries. Each country sets its own standards, but when firms cross national boundaries, they must conform to whichever standards are higher, either those in the sending country or the receiving country.

Increasing International Negotiations

A third alternative to trade measures is to increase the level of international negotiations, using either existing international organizations such as the ILO for labor, or creating new agreements and organizations for the environment. In the labor standards arena, proponents of increased negotiations would like to see the ILO publicize examples where countries are out of compliance with core labor rights. It could do this with the information it already gathers on the labor practices of its member countries. An expanded role for the ILO is supported by the growing recognition that it has the technical capability to assess labor policies, whereas the WTO does not.

In the environmental arena, the World Trade Organization reports that there are about two hundred multilateral environmental agreements (e.g., the Montreal Protocol regulating the use of chlorofluorocarbons, the Basel Convention regulating the transportation of hazardous waste, the Convention on International Trade in Endangered Species, etc.) and that about twenty of them have the potential to affect trade. In cases where two or more countries have signed an agreement and the agreement allows trade sanctions as part of its enforcement mechanism, the WTO's position is that disputes should be resolved within the environmental agreement and not within the WTO. In cases where there are no environmental agreements, however, as with the United States's shrimp import ban, then WTO rules of nondiscrimination apply.

It is significant that the WTO has staked out a position on the issue of multilateral environmental agreements. The WTO recognizes explicitly that it is not an environmental organization and that it has no expertise in this area. However, it has left room for environmental agreements to develop their own enforcement mechanisms. This does not change the fact that trade sanctions are unlikely to be the optimal (lowest cost) technique for resolving environmental disputes, but it does leave it up to the nations involved to decide on their own methods of enforcement.

Summary

- The increase in world trade over the last fifty years has reduced tariffs and eliminated quotas, but as a result, many domestic policies have become unintentional barriers to trade. Examples include competition polices, product standards, health and safety standards, and labor and environmental standards.

- Countries do not need to harmonize standards in order to trade. In many cases, harmonization would remove some of the differences between countries and eliminate the gains from trade. Alternative treatment of standards include mutual recognition and maintaining completely separate standards.

- Differing labor and environmental standards have become a point of significant conflict between high-income and low-income countries. Standards differ primarily because of differences in income and factor endowments.

- Core labor standards defined by the OECD and the ILO include prohibitions against forced labor, freedom of association and collective bargaining, the elimination of child labor, and nondiscrimination in employment.

- Child labor is most common in Africa and Asia. Asia has the most children working, but a larger proportion of African kids under age fourteen are at work. Child labor is most common in agriculture and in small-scale, family-operated businesses.

- Proponents of using trade barriers to enforce labor and environmental standards abroad argue that differences in standards are an unfair competitive advantage for the low-standards country. They also fear that trade and foreign investment cause a race to the bottom in standards and that low environmental standards make some countries "pollution havens."

- Evidence is scarce that countries use low standards to attract industry. In reality, there is a negative correlation between low standards and foreign investment. In addition, there is no evidence of pollution havens.

- Most economists oppose the use of trade measures to enforce standards because they are relatively ineffective, do not go to the root of the problem, are not based on an agreement regarding the content of standards, encourage protectionism in the guise of support for standards, and can lead to wider trade conflict.

- Environmental problems can be transboundary or non-transboundary. International conflicts over both types of problems are similar to conflicts over labor standards. Transboundary problems, in particular, require international negotiations.

- Alternatives to trade measures include labeling, enforcement of home country standards on home country firms operating abroad, and increased international negotiations. Greater support for the ILO and increasing support for international environmental agreements are also more efficient alternatives to trade measures.

Vocabulary

core labor standards

harmonization of standards

informal economy

International Labor Organization

low, lower middle, upper middle, and high income countries

mutual recognition of standards

pollution havens

race to the bottom

separate standards

transboundary and non-transboundary environmental problems

Study Questions

1. What are the three ways for countries to handle different standards abroad? Do standards have to be the same for countries to be integrated?

2. What are the advantages and disadvantages for countries that adopt the same standards?

3. When high definition television (HDTV) was first considered a possibility in the United States, the U.S. government held a competition to select the technical standards that would be used nationwide. Why would the government see an advantage to setting one standard, and what are the pros and cons for the private businesses that were interested in producing for the United States's market?

4. Why do standards vary across countries? Illustrate your answer with examples in the area of labor standards.

5. What are labor standards, and why are arguments about labor standards confined primarily to arguments between high-income countries on the one hand, and low- and middle-income countries on the other?

6. Discuss the reasons why using trade barriers to enforce labor or environmental standards may be less efficient than other measures.

7. What are the arguments in favor of using trade barriers to enforce labor and environmental standards? Assess each argument.

8. One common critique of the WTO is that it overturns national environmental protections, and forces countries to lower their standards. For example, when the United States. tried to protect endangered sea turtles, the WTO prevented it. Assess this claim.

9. What are the alternatives to trade measures for raising labor and environmental standards? What are the strengths and weaknesses of each one?

Part 3

INTERNATIONAL FINANCE

Chapter 9

TRADE AND THE
BALANCE OF PAYMENTS

INTRODUCTION TO
THE CURRENT ACCOUNT

The international transactions of a nation are divided into three separate accounts, called the *current account*, the *capital account*, and the *financial account*. For most countries, the capital account is relatively minor, and the two most important accounts are the current and financial accounts. The **current account** tracks the flow of goods and services into and out of the country, while the **financial account** is the record of the flow of financial capital. The **capital account** is the record of some specialized types of relatively small capital flows. This chapter examines the accounting system used to keep track of a country's international transactions. One of its primary goals is to understand the accounting relationships among domestic investment, domestic savings, and international flows of goods, services, and financial assets. In addition, we will use the international accounts to examine the meaning of international indebtedness and to discuss its consequences.

The Merchandise Trade Balance

In 2000, the United States purchased $1,438.0 billion in goods and services from foreign producers. The composition of the purchases included a wide array of items, from Japanese Nintendos to Taiwanese computer parts, from Venezuelan oil to Canadian cars, and from luxury vacations in Cancun, Mexico, to Europasses on the European rail system. In the same year, U.S. firms sold to foreigners $1,069.5 billion in goods and services. The single most important item in the United States's exports was aircraft, but wheat, airplane tickets, software, and trips to Disney World also figured prominently in the total. The difference between exports and imports of goods (excluding services) is called the nation's **merchandise trade balance.** In 2000, the United States's merchandise trade balance was $773.3 billion in exports minus $1,222.7 billion in imports, or $-449.4 billion. A negative merchandise trade balance is called a **trade deficit**, while a positive balance is a **trade surplus**.

Note that the merchandise trade balance does not include **services**, a category in which the United States has a large surplus ($81.0 billion in 2000). The merchandise trade balance is calculated monthly, which is too short a time frame to get an accurate measurement of service exports and imports. Goods are tangible, they pass through ports where they can be tabulated by customs officials, and they require paperwork that reveals their content. Services, on the other hand, are intangible and do not pass under the watchful eye of customs inspectors. Hence, they are harder to measure and are reported on a less frequent basis (quarterly).

The Current Account Balance

The merchandise trade balance is the most commonly cited measurement of a nation's transactions with the rest of the world. The widespread dissemination of the monthly trade balance statistics through press releases and news articles makes it the most familiar concept in international economics as well as the basis of most people's understanding of U.S. international economic relations. In addition, it probably has an unintended effect of causing the public to concentrate too heavily on tangible, manufactured goods to the detriment of services trade.

A more comprehensive statistic that includes services and other items is the **current account balance**. The additional work required to measure the current account balance means that it is only available on a quarterly basis (every three months), but this effort also means that it is a much more comprehensive measure than the merchandise trade balance. The current account balance measures all current (non-capital) transactions between a nation and the rest of the world. It has three main items: (1) the value of goods and services exported, minus the value of imports; (2) income received from investments abroad, minus income paid to foreigners on their U.S. investments; and (3) any foreign aid or other transfers received from foreigners, minus that given to foreigners. The simplest framework for conceptualizing these three components is in terms of credits and debits, as portrayed in Table 9.1.

Each of the three items—goods and services, **investment income**, and **unilateral transfers**—has credit (positive) and debit (negative) components. If the sum of the credits is greater than the sum of the debits, the nation has a current account surplus, otherwise, it has a deficit. Note also that the investment income items are not movements of investment capital but are the income received or income paid on previous flows of investment capital. For example,

TABLE 9.1	Components of the Current Account	
	Credit	*Debit*
1. Goods and Services	Exports	Imports
2. Investment Income	Income received on foreign investments	Income paid to foreigners on their U.S. investments
3. Unilateral Transfers	Transfers received from abroad	Transfers made to foreigners

There are three main components to the current account. Each component is divided into debit and credit elements.

financial capital sent to Germany to buy a German bond would not be included, but the interest received on the bond would be. (The capital that leaves the United States is counted in the financial account).

It is useful to think of investment income flows as payments for the use of another nation's financial capital. If U.S. mutual funds invest in the Mexican stock market, for example, the initial investment will not show up directly in the current account (it will be in the financial account), but the subsequent flow of dividends back to the mutual fund manager in the United States will be counted. Conceptually, it is as if U.S. investors are receiving payment for the rental of U.S. capital to Mexican firms, which makes it similar to payments for a service. The third item in the current account balance includes payments made that are not in exchange for a good or service, such as foreign aid, or the remittances (sending home of the wages) of immigrants temporarily residing in another country. In the U.S. case these payments are usually relatively small, but they can figure very importantly in the current account balances of developing countries receiving either substantial foreign aid or large remittances from their citizens working abroad.

Table 9.2 gives a picture of the U.S. current account in 2000. The $435,377 million deficit is part of the growing trend in U.S. current account deficits, as can be seen in Figure 9.1. Large deficits in the current account began around

TABLE 9.2	U.S. Current Account Balance, 2000 (millions of dollars)	
	Credit	*Debit*
1. Goods and Services		
Exports of goods	773,304	
Exports of services	296,227	
Imports of goods		–1,222,772
Imports of services		–215,239
2. Investment Income		
Investment Income Received	345,394	
Investment Income Paid		–359,050
3. Net Unilateral Transfers		–53,241
Merchandise Trade Balance		–449,468
Goods and Services Balance		–368,480
Current Account Balance		–435,377

The U.S. current account was in deficit by $435.4 billion in 2000. The deficit is largely the result of merchandise goods imports exceeding exports. The United States has a significant surplus in services.

Source: U.S. Department of Commerce, Bureau of Economic Analysis, http://www.bea.doc.gov/bea/di/trans1.htm

| FIGURE 9.1 | U.S. Current Account Balance, 1946–2000 (Percent of GDP) |

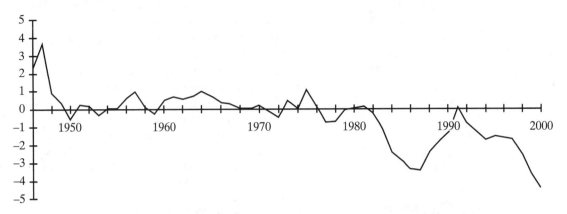

The large U.S. current account deficit began in the 1980s and has persisted since then, with the exception of 1991, a year of recession and the Gulf War.

Source: Bureau of Economic Analysis. Online at http://www.bea.doc.gov.

1982, and have been a more-or-less constant feature of the U.S. economy since then. Although the deficit turned into a small surplus of $6.6 billion in 1991 (partly due to large unilateral transfers received by the United States as payment for Operation Desert Storm), since then it has deteriorated significantly.

While the deficit looks ominous and is not sustainable in the long run, there is a serious debate over its likely consequences. We will explore this issue later, but here it should be noted that it is not simply a sign of weakness. On the contrary, through much of the 1990s, rapid economic growth has raised incomes and created a voracious appetite for imports. Meanwhile, economic growth among the United States's main trading partners ranged between negative and sluggish so that foreign incomes have not risen as rapidly. Consequently, their demand for U.S. exports has grown less rapidly than the U.S. demand for imports. Therefore, it can be argued that the current account deficit is a sign of relative U.S. economic strength. It would be a mistake to carry this argument too far, however, since everyone agrees that the deficit is not sustainable in the long run and that there is a potential for it to create serious future problems. We will look at this issue later in the chapter after a few more concepts are introduced.

INTRODUCTION TO THE FINANCIAL AND CAPITAL ACCOUNTS

The financial and capital accounts are the primary record of the international flow of financial capital and other assets. In most countries, the capital account is of lesser importance and the financial account is the primary statement of international financial flows. The capital account includes transfers of specific types of capital, such as debt forgiveness, the personal assets that migrants take with them when they cross international boundaries, and the transfer of real estate and other fixed assets, such as transfer of ownership of a military base or an embassy. The many categories of the financial account are divided into two primary ones: (1) net changes in U.S.-owned assets abroad, and (2) net changes in foreign-owned assets in the United States. Assets can be financial ones such as stocks and bonds, as well as real assets such as factories and businesses. Table 9.3 shows the capital and financial accounts in relation to the current account. Two points about the capital and financial accounts should be kept in mind. First, both accounts present the flow of assets during the year and not the stock of assets that have accumulated over time. Second, all flows are "net" changes rather than "gross" changes. Net changes are the differences

TABLE 9.3	The U.S. Balance of Payments, 2000 (millions of dollars)		
		Credit	*Debit*
Current Account			
1. Goods and services			
	Exports	1,069,531	
	Imports		–1,438,011
2. Investment income			
	Investment income received	345,394	
	Investment income paid		–359,050
3. Net unilateral transfers			–53,241
Current account balance (1 + 2 + 3)			–435,377
Capital Account			
4. Capital account transactions, net		680	
Financial Account			
5. Net change in U.S. assets abroad (increase/outflow (–))			–553,349
6. Net change in foreign assets in the United States (increase/inflow(+))		952,430	
Financial account balance (5 + 6)		399,081	
Statistical discrepancy		35,616	

The financial account measures capital inflows and outflows and is nearly the mirror image of the current account.

Source: U.S. Department of Commerce, Bureau of Economic Analysis, http://www.bea.doc.gov/bea/di/trans1.htm

between assets sold and assets bought as when, for example, U.S. residents purchase shares in the Mexican stock market while simultaneously selling Mexican bonds. The net change in U.S.-owned assets is the difference between the value of the shares purchased and the bonds sold. If the stocks and bonds are equal in value, then the net change is zero. Net changes are informative because they measure the monetary value of the change in a country's financial stake in foreign economies.

Under the accounting procedure used to tabulate credits and debits in the financial account, outflows of financial assets are a debit item while inflows are a credit item. This point is most easily understood by considering home country financial outflows as payments for the purchase of foreign-owned assets, and financial inflows as receipts from the sale of home country assets to foreigners. In this manner, the negative and positive signs of asset flows are conceptually similar to imports and exports. In other words, home country assets used to purchase foreign assets are capital outflows and debit (negative) entries in the financial account. Conversely, when foreigners purchase home country assets, there is a capital inflow and a credit (positive) entry in the financial account. In effect, any acquisition of foreign assets by home country residents represents a capital outflow, and any acquisition of home country assets by foreigners is a capital inflow.

There is a clear relationship between the current account and financial account balances. As long as the capital account balance is zero, the financial account balance must be the same as the current account balance, but with an opposite sign. If we know that a nation's current account balance is in deficit by $20 billion, its financial account balance must be a $20 billion surplus because every current account transaction (e.g., imports or exports) involves a flow of assets that are used to pay for the goods. For example, suppose that the United States has a $20 billion current account deficit. Then, in order to cover the deficit, the United States must generate net capital inflows of $20 billion. It does this by selling assets, such as stocks or bonds or factories. It is the same for individuals. You may not own factories that you can sell, but if you buy more than your current income allows, then you have to generate financial flows in order to cover the difference. Your credit card company or the department store where you made your purchases might loan you the money, or you might sell some of your wealth that you keep in your bank, or in the stock market, or some other financial institution. Regardless of the source of the financial flows, you must raise enough money to cover the difference between your income and your purchases.

A large share of a nation's financial account transactions, however, is not in response to current account flows of goods and services. For example, a London-based investment company may buy stock in a Chilean firm, lend money to the government of Thailand, and engage in any number of financial transactions that have nothing to do with the movements of goods and services on current account. In an accounting sense, these purely financial transactions must have a net value of zero. The reason they add to zero is that the purchase of an asset is simultaneously the sale of an asset of equal value. For example, if you buy a share of stock, you obtain the asset of partial ownership while the person selling the share obtains your cash. It is the same internationally. If a Canadian citizen buys shares in the Mexican stock market (capital outflow), she must sell Canadian dollars or some other asset (capital inflow). (If she pays for her shares by writing a check drawn on a Mexican bank, then it does not enter the financial account since it is a change of one foreign asset for another.) As a result, the financial account is a complete picture of net flows of financial assets during the year.

At the very bottom of Table 9.3, the last item entered is in the row labeled "**Statistical discrepancy**." Previously, it was stated that the sum of the current account, capital account, and financial account must total zero. The statistical discrepancy is the amount by which they are off. It is calculated as the sum of the current, capital, and financial accounts, with the sign reversed. In 2000 it was calculated as:

$$[(-1) \times (-435{,}377 + 680 + 399{,}081)] = 35{,}616.$$

The statistical discrepancy exists because our record of all of the transactions in the balance of payments is incomplete. Although the errors could be in any of the three accounts, it is believed that most of the errors are in the financial account since it is the hardest one to measure accurately. Financial flows are intangible, and in certain cases such as money laundering associated with the illegal drug trade, the sending or receiving agents have incentives to hide them.

Types of Financial Flows

One of the primary concerns of most governments is the form of financial flows entering and leaving their country. Some financial flows are very mobile and represent a short run outlook on the receiving economy. These flows are often the mechanism that transmits a financial crisis from one country to another, or that moves suddenly in response to a change in investor expectations about the short run prospects of an economy. The degree of mobility of financial flows and the potential of some flows to introduce a large element of volatility into an economy have turned the consideration of the type of flows a country receives into a major issue. As a first approach to a more detailed representation of the financial account, it is useful to subdivide the financial flows in Table 9.3 into categories that reference their origin in the public (governmental) or private sector. In most countries, the bulk of financial flows are private, although in times of crisis this can change. Table 9.4 shows the 2000 financial account for the United States, divided into five subcategories representing the main components of inflows and outflows in terms of public and private assets.

Official reserve assets include gold bullion and the International Monetary Fund's artificial currency, called the SDR (special drawing right), but they are mainly the currencies of the largest and most stable economies in the world,

TABLE 9.4	Components of the U.S. Financial Account, 2000 (millions of dollars)		
		Credit	*Debit*
1. *Net change in U.S. assets abroad (increase/outflow (–))*			–553,349
A. U.S. official reserve assets			–290
B. U.S. government assets, other than official reserve assets			–715
C. U.S. private assets			–552,344
2. *Net change in foreign assets in the United States (increase/inflow (+))*		952,430	
A. Foreign official assets in the United States		35,909	
B. Other foreign assets in the United States		916,521	

There are five main categories of financial flows. Each of these categories can be further subdivided.

Source: U.S. Department of Commerce, Bureau of Economic Analysis, http://www.bea.doc.gov/bea/di/trans1.htm

such as U.S. dollars, German marks (or, in 2002, the euro), British pounds, and Japanese yen. They are reserve assets because they are acceptable means of settling international debts and, consequently, central banks and treasury ministries use them as a store of value. For example, when an importer in a small country such as Chile purchases a shipload of goods from Europe, payment may be in dollars or marks or pounds, but it is unlikely that the supplier would accept Chilean pesos from the purchaser. The importer must convert some pesos into a reserve currency, such as U.S. dollars, and use them to pay for its imports. If the Chilean central bank is unable to provide dollars or another reserve currency to Chilean banks and importers, then the import business grinds to a halt unless the importer is able to secure some form of credit from the seller. Since all forms of international debts are settled with reserve assets, especially key currencies, they play a very prominent role in international finance. When they become scarce in a country, it signals that potentially serious problems are arising. For example, as discussed below, when Mexico's economy collapsed in late 1994 and early 1995, it was because Mexicans owed dollars to various international investors, but the sudden outflow of dollars from Mexico during 1994 had severely reduced the supply of dollars and, in the short run, made it impossible for firms and the government to pay their dollar denominated debts. Relief came when Mexico was able to arrange several loans from the IMF, the United States, and Canada, which replenished its supply of official reserve assets.

The fallout from the Mexican crisis of 1994–1995 was a disastrous recession and changes in the government's data reporting system so that everyone could track the inflows and outflows of reserve assets in a more timely manner. Note, however, that since the financial account reports on financial flows, it does not indicate the stock, or total supply, of assets available. Looking at Table 9.4, the United States had a debit of $290 billion for 2000 in its official reserve assets, representing a purchase of $290 billion in official reserve assets. There is no indication given, however, of the total stock of reserve assets available, so the financial account gives no idea what the total reserve holdings are. Central bank Web sites and numerous other sources, including popular media such as *The Economist* magazine, provide this information, however.

Row 1.B in Table 9.4 includes other assets acquired by the federal government. These mainly represent loans to foreign governments, the rescheduling of past loans made to foreign governments, payments received on outstanding loans, and changes in non-reserve currency holdings, such as Mexican pesos or Israeli shekels. Line 2.A of Table 9.4 is symmetrical with 1.A. When the federal government needs to borrow money in order to cover its deficit or to refinance its debt, foreign governments usually purchase a share of the Treasury bills or bonds sold, and it shows up in line 2.A. U.S. Treasury securities are equivalent to reserve assets for foreign governments because they are easily sold for dollars and the dollar is universally accepted as payment for international debt. Private foreign interests may also purchase U.S. Treasury or other securities, however, and these purchases show up in line 2.B, along with other private investments in the U.S. economy.

Row 1.C represents the largest value of any of the outflows in the upper part of the table and is conceptually similar to private inflows in row 2.B. Flows of privately owned financial assets are by far the largest element in the account. The main categories of rows 1.C and 2.B are presented in more detail in Table 9.5.

The first subcomponent of financial outflows and inflows (1.A and 2.A) is **foreign direct investment (FDI)**. FDI includes tangible items such as real estate, factories, warehouses, transportation facilities, and other physical (real) assets. The second and third subcomponents can be considered portfolio investment since they represent paper assets such as stocks, bonds, and loans. The similarity between FDI and **foreign portfolio investment** is that they both give their holders a claim on the future output of the foreign economy. They are very different, however, in their time horizons and this can have dramatic effects on the host country, where assets are located. Direct investments usually involve a longer time horizon because they are difficult to liquidate quickly and therefore represent a long-term position in the host country. Factories and other real assets cannot be sold overnight. Firms making these sorts of commitments usually take a long-term view and are willing to endure the inevitable ups and downs of the host country's economy. Portfolio investments

TABLE 9.5	Private Flows in the U.S. Financial Account, 2000 (millions of dollars)		
		Credit	*Debit*
1. *U.S. private assets abroad, net (increase/outflow(–))*			–552,344
Subcomponents:			
A. Direct investment			–161,577
B. Foreign securities			–123,606
C. Loans to foreign firms, including banks			–267,161
2. *Foreign owned assets in the United States, net (increase/inflow(+))*		916,521	
Subcomponents:			
A. Direct investment		316,527	
B. U.S. securities and currency		414,781	
C. Loans to U.S. firms, including banks		185,213	

Private asset flows are the largest part of the financial account. These are usefully divided into three symmetrical categories of inflows and outflows.

Source: U.S. Department of Commerce, Bureau of Economic Analysis, http://www.bea.doc.gov/bea/di/trans1.htm

in stocks and bonds tend to be more short term. While many investors may decide to hold their foreign securities through all the ups and downs, by their nature, stocks and bonds are much more liquid than real estate or factories. It is common, therefore, for portfolio investors to have a shorter time horizon, and to move quickly if they expect a sudden downturn. Sudden shifts in investor confidence, or sudden increases in uncertainty, can lead to large, destabilizing outflows (1.B and 1.C) as investors sell off their financial assets in the home country and move those assets elsewhere. In most of the financial crises of the last decade (Mexico, 1994; East Asia, 1997; Russia, 1998; Turkey, 2001), there were large and sudden financial outflows as both home country and foreign investors tried to take their assets out of the country before the expected crisis. In late 1994, for example, after Mexico decided to devalue its currency, there was a sudden financial outflow as Mexican stock and bond owners tried to liquidate their holdings and take the proceeds out of the country before the peso completely collapsed. The sudden sell-off put enormous pressure on the peso since sellers of Mexican stocks and bonds all tried to convert their earnings into dollars in order to insulate themselves from the collapsing peso. This drained the central bank of most of its reserve assets (dollars) and caused the peso to lose approximately one-half its dollar value. Ultimately, the economy fell into a deep recession.

The growth of stock markets around the world, particularly in the newly industrializing countries of South America and Asia, represents a worldwide expansion of the buying and selling of stocks and related assets. Much of the buying and selling is done by residents of the country, but the banking systems in some developing countries play an important role since they have conduits for acquiring loans from foreign sources. Banks in some countries (it depends on the perception of credit worthiness and economic prospects in the country) borrow abroad in order to acquire funds for lending to domestic residents who use the money to buy stocks, or speculate in real estate, or who expand their businesses. The link from foreign financial capital to domestic borrowers was a key relationship at the root of the East Asian financial crisis in 1997 and the Turkish crisis in 2001, and it highlights the importance of items 1.C and 2.C in Table 9.5. The pattern of borrowing abroad in order to lend at home was particularly damaging in the East Asian case as it created debts that mostly had to be paid in dollars while the domestic lending was in home country currency. Consequently, when the crisis hit and the value of the home country currencies collapsed, the entire banking systems of some countries were thrown into crisis. The payments received by the banks were in their devalued home country currency, which was suddenly inadequate to service their dollar denominated debts.

Limits on Financial Flows

Until a few years ago, most nations limited the movement of financial flows across their national borders. A typical pattern was to allow financial flows that were related to transactions on current account, but to severely limit and regulate financial flows related to financial account transactions. In other words, if an importer needed a foreign loan to purchase goods abroad, or if an exporter needed foreign financing in order to buy materials needed to make export goods, then these financial flows were regulated but generally allowed. Conversely, if a bank wanted to borrow abroad in order to make loans at home, for example, to real estate speculators, then the inflow of financial capital to the bank was prohibited or subjected to such onerous terms and conditions that it was undesirable. These types of restrictions on financial flows were a normal part of the international economic landscape, even in industrial economies, until the 1980s and 1990s. For example, the members of the European Union did not completely liberalize financial flows between member countries until 1993.

In the movement toward more open markets over the last decades, there has been a significant lifting of controls on financial flows across international boundaries. This change in international economic policy was seen as desirable because restrictions on financial flows limit the availability of financial capital. Developing countries, in particular, were thought to benefit from liberalization since they have the greatest scarcity of financial capital and their need to raise incomes and living standards depends greatly on access to adequate financial capital. In addition, it is difficult to disentangle financial flows related to financing current account transactions from flows that are purely financial account transactions. This makes it difficult to regulate or control international finan-

CASE STUDY

The Mexican Sexenio Crisis

The excitement surrounding the Mexican presidential elections of July 2000 was heightened by two factors, one political and one economic. On the political scorecard, the Institutional Revolutionary Party (PRI) that had been in power for 71 years faced its most serious challenge ever (it lost). On the economic side, the air was filled with the uncertainty of a possible financial collapse after the election. The end-of-term presidential transitions of the previous four presidents—Echeverría (1970–1976), Portillo (1976–1982), de la Madrid (1982–1988), and Salinas (1988–1994)—involved traumatic and destructive economic crises that were triggered by large financial account outflows. Since Mexican presidents serve a single six-year term, called a *sexenio* in Spanish, the financial crises at the end of the terms have come to be called *sexenio* crises. The severity of the *sexenio* crises varied, ranging from the relatively mild crisis at the end of de la Madrid's term in 1988, to the deep and lasting crisis at the end of Portillo's term in 1982, and the even deeper but relatively short recession after Salinas in 1994. Ernesto Zedillo, the outgoing president in 2000, promised to break this pattern.

Each of the four crises shared a set of characteristics: (1) large and sudden outflows of financial capital; (2) rapid outflows of official reserve assets such as U.S. dollars; and (3) a relatively large amount of short-term debt caused by previously large financial inflows to Mexican banks and firms. In addition, with the exception of 1988, there were:

(4) a significantly overvalued peso; and (5) a large current account deficit.

These factors are interrelated. For example, an overvalued peso leads to cheaper imports (and makes Mexican exports more expensive to foreigners), resulting in large current account deficits. The expectation that Mexico will have to devalue its currency to eliminate the current account deficit (devaluation makes imports expensive to Mexicans and Mexican goods cheaper to foreigners) causes both Mexicans and foreigners to move financial assets out of the country in an attempt to preserve the value of their investments. Large financial outflows, or *capital flight* as it is called, draw down foreign exchange reserves and make it impossible to service short-term debt. The result is a debt crisis, followed by a falling peso, then inflation and a recession as rising prices reduce real wages and income.

President Zedillo has a doctorate in economics from Yale and he clearly understood these relationships. He was adamant that Mexico would avoid another *sexenio* crisis and he took several steps to insulate the economy. First, he reduced the reliance of Mexican investors on foreign financing by putting into place policies that encouraged more domestic savings. This reduced the inflow of bank loans (item 2.C in Table 9.5). He encouraged foreign direct investment in place of portfolio or financial investment (item 2.A instead of 2.B or 2.C) as a means to finance the current account deficit and

(*continues*)

to avoid short-term borrowing. He balanced the government's budget so there would be no dependence on foreign borrowing by government. In case a crisis began to develop, he arranged $23.7 billion in stand-by lines of emergency credit from the IMF, World Bank, Inter-American Development Bank, Export-Import Bank of the United States, and a funding mechanism under NAFTA called the North American Framework Agreement.

Each step in this reform package helped raise the stock of Mexican official reserve assets while reducing the likelihood of large financial capital outflows that would drain the reserve assets and throw the country into crisis. Finally, and perhaps most important, Zedillo's administration moved the country from a controlled value of the peso to a market-based system in which the peso's value is determined by the supply and demand for the currency. We will examine the effects of this change in the next chapter. Suffice it to say that the reforms have broken the pattern in place since 1976 of a balance-of-payments-driven *sexenio* crisis.

Source: Heath, Jonathan, and Sidney Weintraub. *Mexico and the Sexenio Curse: Presidential Successions and Economic Crises in Modern Mexico.* Washington, D.C.: CSIS Press. 1999.

cial flows, and many economists argued that the attempt to do so created unnecessary red tape, bureaucratic delay and arbitrariness, and reduced economic efficiency. For over a decade, through much of the 1980s and 1990s, the consensus among economists was that it is better to allow financial capital to move freely across international borders.

More recently, the extreme volatility in some financial markets and the severe damage it has caused to a number of countries has revived interest in some form of controls or regulations to limit the damage caused by unexpectedly large financial outflows. It is easy to understand the tensions involved, however. On the one hand, foreign capital inflows are beneficial because they enable countries to increase their investments in factories and ports and other physical assets that help raise living standards and incomes. On the other hand, the sudden outward flight of foreign financial capital can generate a debt crisis and throw a country into deep depression. The key is to capture the benefits of increased investment while minimizing the risks of capital flight. At this point there is not much consensus among economists about the best policies. Chapter 12 looks at this issue in more detail after several more concepts have been introduced.

THE CURRENT ACCOUNT AND THE MACROECONOMY

There are two important practical reasons for learning about the balance of payments. One is to understand the broader implications of current account imbalances and to analyze the policies that might be used to tame a current account deficit. This is particularly important for small countries that are easily buffeted about by changes in the global economy, but it is also of interest to a big economy such as the United States, where very large current account deficits have been the norm for several years. A second practical reason for studying the balance of payments is to try to understand how countries might avoid a crisis brought on by volatile financial flows, and what policies there are to minimize the harmful affects of a crisis if it occurs. Economic analysis is still in its infancy when it comes to the problem of volatile financial flows, and there is some distance to travel before there is likely to be a consensus agreement on issues such as free versus restricted capital mobility, or the links from financial flows to economic growth. Nevertheless, there are some basic points of agreement among economists, and we will take these up in Chapters 10 and 12. Before we get there, however, we must examine the relationship of the current account to the macroeconomy. This requires a brief review of basic concepts from the principles of macroeconomics.

The National Income and Product Accounts

The internal, domestic accounting system used by countries to keep track of total production and total income are called the **national income** and **product accounts**. These accounts are very detailed presentations of income, output, and other measures of a nation's macroeconomy. We will use the most fundamental concepts from this accounting system, beginning with the concept of **gross domestic product**, or **GDP**. Recall from the principles of economics that a nation's gross domestic product is the market value of all final goods and services produced inside its borders during some time period, usually a year. GDP is the most common measure of the size of an economy, although it is widely recognized that it ignores some important considerations, such as the value of leisure time and environmental degradation that takes place during the process of producing the nation's output. In addition, GDP only includes goods that pass through organized markets, so household production (cooking, sewing, landscaping, childcare, and so forth) and other non-market-oriented production are left out. For these and other reasons, economists caution against using GDP as a sole determinant of the well-being of a society. In spite of these limitations, however, it does provide a starting point for understanding different economies.

In order to avoid the problem of double counting, GDP only includes the value of *final* goods and services. This is actually a strength of the measure, since if we added the value of steel sold to a car maker, and the value of the cars, we would be counting the steel twice, once as steel and a second time as part of the value of the car. The final part of the definition states that GDP must be measured over some time period, usually a year. Most countries measure GDP every three months, but for most purposes, including ours, the most useful time period to consider is the span of one year.

An alternative concept for measuring a nation's output is **gross national product**, or **GNP**. For most countries, the difference between the two concepts

| TABLE 9.6 | Variable Definitions |

Variable	Definition
GDP	Gross domestic product
GNP	Gross national product
C	Consumption expenditures
I	Investment expenditures
G	Government expenditures on goods and services
X	Exports of goods and services
M	Imports of goods and services
CA	Current account balance
S	Private savings (savings of households and firms)
T	Net taxes, or taxes paid minus transfer payments received

is very small since GNP is the value of all final goods and services produced by the labor, capital, and other resources of a country, regardless of where production occurred. In an accounting sense, GNP is equal to GDP plus investment income and unilateral transfers received from foreigners minus investment income and unilateral transfers paid to foreigners:

$$\text{GDP} + \text{foreign investment income received}$$
$$- \text{investment income paid to foreigners}$$
$$+ \text{net unilateral transfers} = \text{GNP}$$

Note that the difference between GNP and GDP is precisely equal to lines 2 and 3 in Tables 9.1, 9.2, and 9.3: the investment income and unilateral transfers components of the current account balance. This fact is useful since GDP includes exports minus imports and it enables us to bring the entire current account concept into the picture.

The usefulness of adding net foreign investment income (investment income received minus investment income paid) plus net unilateral transfers is apparent when we look at the definition of GDP based on its four main components. Table 9.6 defines the necessary variables GDP is equal to the sum of consumer expenditures plus investment expenditures plus government expenditures on goods and services plus exports of goods and services minus imports of goods and services:

$$\text{GDP} = C + I + G + X - M. \tag{1}$$

Given that GNP is equal to GDP plus net foreign investment income and net unilateral transfers:

$$GNP = GDP + \text{(Net foreign investment income + net transfers),} \qquad \textbf{(2)}$$

or

$$GNP = (C + I + G) + (X - M + \text{Net foreign investment income} \qquad \textbf{(3)}$$
$$+ \text{ net transfers),}$$

we can write the definition of GNP in terms of the current account balance. Rewriting equation (3) in a simpler form:

$$GNP = C + I + G + CA. \qquad \textbf{(4)}$$

Equation (4) explicitly shows the relationship between the current account and the main macroeconomic variables such as consumer spending, investment, and government purchases.

As the total value of goods and services produced by the labor, capital, and other resources of a country, GNP is also the value of income received. This follows from the fact that the production of final goods and services generates incomes that are equal in value to output and is embodied in the basic macroeconomic accounting identity stating that every economy's income must equal its output. From the point of view of the income recipients, there are three choices or obligations. They may consume their income (C), save it (S), or use it to pay taxes (T). In reality, we all do a combination of the three. This permits us to rewrite the definition of GNP in terms of income and its uses:

$$GNP = C + S + T. \qquad \textbf{(5)}$$

Since equations (4) and (5) are equivalent definitions of GNP, one in terms of the components of output, the other in terms of the uses of income, we can set them equal to each other:

$$C + I + G + CA = C + S + T. \qquad \textbf{(6)}$$

Subtracting consumption from both sides and rearranging terms:

$$I + G + CA = S + T, \qquad \textbf{(7)}$$

or

$$S + (T - G) = I + CA. \qquad \textbf{(8)}$$

Equation (8) is an accounting identity, or something that is true by definition. It is worth memorizing since it summarizes the important relationship between the current account balance, investment, and public and private savings in the economy. Equation (8) does not reveal any of the causal mechanisms through which changes in savings or investment are connected to the current account balance, but it does provide insight into the economy. For example, if total savings remains unchanged while investment increases, then the current account balance must move toward, or deeper into, deficit.

In order to see this, it is necessary to be certain that you understand the bracketed term on the left side, $(T - G)$. This is the combined (federal, state, and local) budget balances of all levels of government, or, to say it another way, government savings. It is savings because T is government revenue (or income) and G is government expenditure. A positive (T – G) states that the combined government budgets are in surplus, which in the governmental sector is equivalent to savings. Conversely, a negative (T – G) is a deficit, or dissavings. By placing governmental budget balances on the left-hand side, we are emphasizing that there are two sources of savings in an economy: the private sector, S, and the public or governmental sector, (T – G). If governments dissave (run deficits), then they must borrow from the private sector, which reduces total national savings on the left-hand side.

From equation (8) we see that a nation's savings (private plus public) is divided into two uses. First, it is a source of funds for domestic investment, or I. This role is crucial because new investments in machinery and equipment are the source of a lot of the economic growth that any country experiences. Investment is essential as the means to upgrade the skills of the labor force, to provide more capital on the job, and to improve the quality of capital by introducing new technology. According to equation (8), if government budgets are in deficit, the total supply of national savings is reduced, and, all else equal, investment will be less than it might otherwise have been. Conversely, a surplus in government budgets will augment private savings and increase the funds available for investment, all else equal.

The second use for national savings is as a source of funds for foreign investment. If the current account is in surplus, national savings finances the purchase of domestic goods by foreign users of those goods. In return, or as payment, the domestic economy acquires foreign financial assets. Recall from the discussion of the relationship between the current and financial accounts, that the financial account is more or less a mirror image of the current account. (Actually, except for the statistical discrepancy, the current account plus the capital account is equal to the financial account, with an opposite sign.) In other words, a positive current account is associated with a negative financial account, which is an outflow of financial capital. Equivalence between the outflow's magnitude and the current account surplus ensures that foreigners obtain the financial resources they need to buy more goods and services than they sell in world markets. In a sense, the surplus country provides its savings to the rest of the world, thereby enabling it (the surplus country) to sell more goods abroad than it buys. For a surplus country, a financial capital outflow is an investment because it involves the acquisition of assets that are expected to pay a future return. It is not the same as domestic investment, however, because the assets are outside the country. Hence, another name for the current account balance is *net foreign investment*. A positive balance implies positive foreign investment, while a negative balance implies negative investment (disinvestment), or a reduction in net foreign assets.

These relationships are illustrated in Figure 9.2, which traces the four variables in equation (8) for the United States from 1991 to 2000. The four variables, S, (T – G), I, and CA, are measured on the vertical axis as a percent of GNP. Over the 1990s, the United States experienced increasingly large current

| FIGURE 9.2 | U.S. Savings and Investment, 1991–2000 |

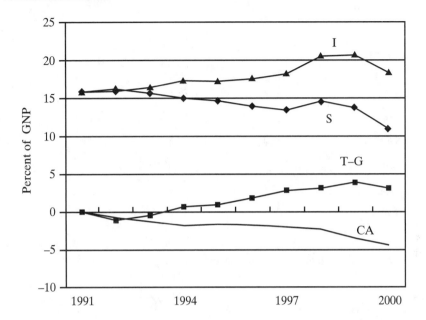

During the 1990s, private savings fell while investment rose. The gap between savings and investment was filled by increased public savings (budget surpluses), and by capital inflows, which appear as growing current account deficits.

Source: United States Bureau of Economic Analysis, http://www.bea.doc.gov

account deficits, both in absolute terms and as a share of GNP. By 2000, the deficit was nearly 4.4 percent of GNP. The causes of the large current account deficit are beyond the scope of this chapter, but looking at Figure 9.2 in the light of equation (8), we can view the performance of some of the key variables associated with the current account. Over the period from 1991 to 2000, savings have fallen while investment has risen (although, as a share of GNP, investment fell in 2000). The gap between the two was partly filled by the increase in public savings—government budgets moved into surplus—but the United States also increasingly relied on foreign capital inflows to make up the difference between savings and investment. This rise in foreign capital inflows shows up as an increasingly larger current account deficit.

Table 9.7 is an alternative way of looking at the relationship between private savings, investment, budget balances, and current account balances. Table 9.7 shows the percent of GNP in each category for two groups of countries, moderate savers and high savers.

Table 9.7 shows a general, but imperfect, relationship between private savings (S) and investment (I). The four countries with moderate savings

TABLE 9.7	Private Savings, Investment, Government Budgets, and Current Account Balances as a Percent of GNP, 1998			
	S	$T - G$	I	CA
Moderate Savings				
Chile	0.197	0.004	0.259	−0.058
Germany	0.226	−0.015	0.212	−0.002
Italy	0.239	−0.036	0.186	0.017
Mexico	0.193	−0.015	0.217	−0.038
High Savings				
South Korea	0.471	−0.039	0.302	0.130
Singapore	0.435	0.157	0.354	0.238

In general, the higher the level of savings, the higher the level of investment. There is not a one-to-one relationship, however, and moderate savings countries such as Mexico and Chile are able to invest more than Italy, which has a higher savings rate.

Source: IMF, *International Financial Statistics.* July, 2000.

levels (19 to 24 percent of GNP) have moderate investment levels as well, while high-savings countries have high rates of investment. The savings–investment relationship is not a perfect one-to-one relationship, however, because it is moderated by government budgets $(T - G)$ and the current account (CA). Private savings in Chile is about the same as Mexico's, for example, but since it has a balanced set of government budgets and a larger current account deficit, it invests nearly 4 percent more of its GNP. Korea and Singapore both have extraordinarily high savings, although in 1998, Korea's savings were nearly 4 percent more of GNP. Nevertheless, due to Singapore's enormous budget surpluses, investment was about 5 percent more of its GNP. In general, high savings and high investment rates go together, as do low savings and low investment, but government budgets and the current account intervene in this relationship so that there is no precise relationship between S and I.

Korea and Singapore are also interesting because they show that the relationship between budget balances and current account balances is not fixed. In 1998, both countries had large current account surpluses and while Korea had a moderately large budget deficit, Singapore had an extremely large budget surplus. In the 1980s, some observers argued that the large U.S. budget deficit was directly responsible for the large current account deficits that the economy experienced at the time. These were often referred to as the "Twin Deficits," and it was sometimes assumed that if the federal government eliminated its huge deficit (state and local budgets were more or less balanced) then the current account deficit would shrink as well. What we have seen in the 1990s contradicts this, as federal budget deficits have turned to surpluses and the current account deficit has widened. Singapore and Korea illustrate that there is no set relationship between T – G and CA, or, indeed, between any two of the four variables in Table 9.7 and Figure 9.2. Each of the four variables depends on the other three, not just one other one.

Are Current Account Deficits Harmful?

The relationship between the current account balance, investment, and total national savings is an identity. Consequently, it does not tell us why an economy runs a current account deficit or surplus. In equation (8)

$$S + (T - G) = I + CA,$$

the left and right sides are equal by definition. Consequently, we cannot say that the current account is in deficit because savings are too low any more than we can say it is because investment is too high.

There is a general tendency in the media and the public to interpret a current account deficit as a sign of weakness and as harmful to the nation's welfare. Another interpretation is that the deficit enables more investment than would be possible otherwise, and since higher investment is correlated with higher living standards, the current account deficit might be interpreted as beneficial. In addition, the capital inflows that are associated with current account deficits are an implicit vote of confidence by foreigners. For example, between 1980 and 1991, Japan invested more than $25 billion of its trade surplus in U.S. manufacturing. By the start of the 1990s, the Japanese owned 66 steel works, 20 rubber and tire factories, 8 major car assembly plants, and 270 auto parts suppliers, employing more than 100,000 workers. Furthermore, the investment came at a time when the three major U.S.-based auto manufacturers (Chrysler, Ford, and GM) were laying off workers and relocating production abroad. Some of the Japanese firms were acquisitions (which may have closed if they had not been bought) and many were new plants built from scratch with Japanese savings. During the deficits of the 1990s, foreign investors continued to pour in capital, enabling the United States to raise its level of investment and increase its productivity in spite of its declining savings rate. In this particular case, the current account deficit has been beneficial because, all else equal, it enabled more investment than was possible otherwise, given the savings rate.

Current account deficits can also generate problems, however. The capital inflows that occur with a current account deficit increase the stock of foreign-owned assets inside the home country, raising the possibility that a change in investor expectations about the economy's future can lead to a sudden surge in capital outflows. In the worst case scenario, capital flight is followed by a depletion of international reserves and a financial crisis. This is an experience shared by a number of developing countries since the 1980s, but it should not lead you to believe that the optimal policy for a country is to avoid current account deficits. As we have just seen, they allow countries to invest more than they could otherwise, and this is particularly important for developing countries where investment capital is especially scarce. Furthermore, current account surpluses are no guarantee that a country will be able to avoid a crisis if one develops among its trading partners. International financial crises, much like some biological diseases, tend to be contagious. When Mexico slipped into the peso crisis in late 1994 and early 1995, for example, economists and journalists began to write about the "Tequila effect" on Latin America. Similarly, when the currency of Thailand, the baht, lost a large share of its value in July of 1997, the media were filled with stories of "baht-ulism" spreading across East Asia and the rest of the developing world. In both cases, the size of a country's current account balances was not a good predictor of whether it was drawn into the crisis. (See Chapter 12 for a more detailed discussion of financial crises.)

The experiences of countries in the 1980s and 1990s has taught economists that financial crises are determined by more than the size of the current account deficit, and that there are no absolute thresholds between safe and dangerous levels of a deficit. While deficits of 3 to 4 percent of GDP begin to raise red flags, and deficits of 7 to 9 percent are considered extremely risky, there are too many other factors that must be taken into consideration before the probability of a crisis can be determined.

THE INTERNATIONAL INVESTMENT POSITION

Each year a nation runs a current account deficit, it borrows from abroad and adds to its indebtedness to foreigners. Each year it runs a current account surplus, it lends to foreigners and reduces its overall indebtedness. If the total of all domestic assets owned by foreigners is subtracted from the total of all foreign assets owned by residents of the home country, the result is the **international investment position**. If the international investment position is positive, then the home country could sell all its foreign assets and have more than enough revenue to purchase all the domestic assets owned by foreigners. If it is negative, then selling all foreign assets would not provide enough revenue to buy all the domestic assets owned by foreigners.

As an example of the international investment position, consider the United States at the end of 1999. The market value of all assets outside the United States but owned by the U.S. government, citizens, and corporations, was $7,173 billion. These included foreign factories, shares of stocks in foreign companies, foreign bonds, foreign currency, and other assets. Meanwhile, the market value of assets inside the United States that were owned by foreign individuals, businesses, and governments was valued at $8,647 billion dollars. The resulting international investment position of the United States was $–1,474 billion ($7,173 – $8,647). Equation (9) summarizes this relationship.

International investment position = Domestically owned foreign assets –
foreign owned domestic assets

$$= \$7{,}173 \text{ billion} - \$8{,}647 \text{ billion} \qquad \textbf{(9)}$$

$$= -\$1{,}474 \text{ billion}.$$

The large current account deficits of the 1980s and 1990s have eroded the United States's investment position from a positive $288.6 billion in 1983, to zero in 1989, and negative since then. Each year a country experiences a current account deficit, foreigners acquire more assets inside its boundaries than its residents acquire abroad, and the international investment position shrinks further.

Citizens in most countries are prone to worry about foreign ownership of tangible assets inside the country and that a negative international investment position gives foreign corporations and governments too much domestic economic power. This worry is not without merit, but in the case of large economies such as the United States, it is probably overblown. Data from the U.S. Bureau of Economic Analysis statistics illustrate why this should not be a worry, at least in the United States's case. In 1998, the latest year of data, foreigners owned about 3.9 percent of the U.S. capital stock:

(Total foreign direct investment in the U.S.) / (U.S. stock of fixed assets)

$$= (\$928 \text{ billion})/(\$23{,}760 \text{ billion}) = 0.039.$$

Four percent of the stock of U.S. factories, machines, and private real estate is too small a number to represent a serious erosion in national sovereignty. The leading investors in the United States are the United Kingdom (18.5 percent of total), followed by Japan (15 percent), the Netherlands (13 percent), and Canada (8 percent).

The positive effect of foreign investment on a country's overall level of investment has been discussed already. What was not mentioned was the fact that foreign investment is often a primary mechanism for transferring technology and spreading new techniques. Throughout the post–World War II period, one of the main ways in which European and Japanese companies have been able to catch up to their American counterparts is through the borrowing and adapting of technology that first came to their countries through U.S. investments. As Japanese and European engineers, scientists, and managers gained experience working in U.S. firms in sectors that were more advanced, they developed new skills and insights that could be transferred into domestically owned firms. In addition, foreign-owned firms develop networks of supplier relationships that also serve as channels through which new technology can spread. Without foreign investment, it would be much harder to learn about new processes, new production technologies, and new organizational forms. Today, this relationship is particularly important for developing countries, where a significant portion of the capital, technology, and skills that they need will come via foreign investment.

If the benefits are identifiable as greater investment levels and new technology, the costs are harder to pin down. One potential cost is that foreign investment provides a gateway into a nation's inner circles of power, since politicians are likely to give access and listen carefully to the owners of a car factory, a steel plant, or some other large business located in their district or state. In the United States, as in every nation, money and economic clout provide political access. In the case of a small, poor country, large corporations can wield proportionately greater power than in large or wealthy nations because the playing field is relatively empty and there are few countervailing powers to balance their economic clout. This is particularly the case in countries where the legal systems are less transparent, and having "friends in high places" may be sufficient to influence whatever government policy needs changing. In the case of larger and richer nations such as the United States, France, or Germany, the national sovereignty issue is much less important because the political clout of a wealthy foreign investor is diluted by the contending interests of numerous powerful domestic enterprises and interest groups.

Even if national sovereignty is not an issue, national security concerns may be. Many people wonder if foreign-owned firms might not be a liability in an international conflict. It is at least conceivable that foreign-owned firms may transfer technology or pass along sensitive information about production capabilities, if not engage in outright sabotage, during a war. Histories of United States-owned operations in Germany and German-owned operations in the United States during World War II paint a picture of minimal danger from this quarter, since enemy assets are frozen or nationalized in time of war.

The astute reader will no doubt have noticed that all the discussion of costs and benefits of foreign investment has focused on foreign direct investment, as opposed to portfolio investment. Obviously, with portfolio investment, there can be no transfer of new technologies. Other than that, many of the benefits and costs are the same. Foreigners who invest in a country's stock market, for example, provide financial capital that can be used by domestic firms to bolster their investment. Given the "hands-off" nature of financial or portfolio investment, however, there is less scope for affecting a wartime situation. And, finally, one previously mentioned cost to the host country of foreign portfolio investment is the sudden shift of foreign financial capital out of a nation. This can have severe repercussions, as a number of countries found out in the 1990s.

Summary

- Every nation's transactions with the rest of the world are summarized in its balance of payments. The balance of payments has three components: the current account, the capital account, and the financial account. The two most important components are the current and financial accounts.
- The current account is a record of a nation's trade, investment income, and transfers between it and the rest of the world

- The financial account is a record of financial capital flows between a country and the rest of the world. The financial account is equal to the current account plus the capital account, with the sign reversed. This follows from the accounting principle that every purchase or sale of a good or service must generate a payment or a receipt.

- Capital flows in the financial account are grouped together as governmental and private. Private flows are the bulk of international capital flows. They are grouped into categories of direct investment and portfolio investment. In general, direct investment is longer term and, therefore, less volatile.

- Large, sudden outflows of financial capital have created economic instability in many countries, particularly during the 1990s. This has created an active debate over the merits of restricting foreign capital flows. Economists are divided on this point, with some favoring restrictions and some favoring free capital mobility.

- There is a fundamental economic identity that total private and public savings in an economy must be equal to domestic investment plus net foreign investment. The current account balance is equal to net foreign investment, and a negative balance is equivalent to disinvestment abroad.

- During the 1990s, the United States experienced growing current account deficits.

- Current account deficits enable a country to invest more than it could otherwise, which has a beneficial effect on national income. If deficits are too large, however, they increase the vulnerability of a country to sudden outflows of financial capital.

- The international investment position is the difference between foreign-based assets owned by residents in the home country and home-based assets owned by residents of foreign countries.

- Foreign investment is controversial for the general public because it seems to many citizens that foreign interests are "taking over." The reality of that fear depends in on the size and wealth of the host country, and the stability and openness of its political system.

Vocabulary

capital account	foreign portfolio investment
current account	gross domestic product (GDP)
current account balance	gross national product (GNP)
financial account	international investment position
foreign direct investment (FDI)	investment income

merchandise trade balance

national income and product accounts

official reserve assets

services

statistical discrepancy

trade deficit

trade surplus

unilateral transfers

Study Questions

1. Use the following information to answer the questions below. Assume that the capital account is equal to 0.

Net unilateral transfers	–50
Exports of goods and services	500
Net increase in U.S. government's nonreserve foreign assists	30
Net increase in foreign ownership of U.S.-based nonreserve assets	400
Net increase in U.S. private assets abroad	250
Invest income received in the United States	200
Net increase in U.S. ownership of official reserve assets	20
Imports of goods and services	600
Net increase in foreign ownership of U.S.-based reserve assets	100
Investment income paid abroad by the United States	300

   a) What is the current account balance?

   b) Does the financial account equal the current account?

   c) What is the statistical discrepancy?

2. Look at each of the cases below from the point of view of the balance of payments for the United States. Determine the subcategory of the current account or capital account that each transaction would be classified in, and state whether it would enter as a credit or debit.

   a) The U.S. government sells gold for dollars.

   b) A migrant worker in California sends $500 dollars home to his village in Mexico.

   c) An American mutual fund manager uses the deposits of his fund investors to buy Brazilian telecommunication stocks.

   d) A mutual fund manager in New York takes the earnings of the fund's Brazilian telecommunications stocks, converts them to dollars, and pays out dividends on the fund.

   e) A Japanese firm in Tennessee buys car parts from a subsidiary in Malaysia.

   f) An Italian importer of American semiconductors deposits two billion Italian lira into the semiconductor company's foreign bank account in Milan.

   g) An American church donates five tons of rice to the Sudan to help with famine relief.

   h) An American retired couple flies from Seattle to Tokyo on Japan Airlines.

   i) The Mexican government sells pesos to the United States Treasury and buys dollars.

3. Weigh the pros and cons of a large trade deficit.

4. Is the budget deficit of a country linked to its current account balance? How so? Explain how it is possible for the United States's current account deficit to grow while the budget deficit has disappeared.

5. Compare and contrast portfolio capital flows with direct investment capital flows.

6. Why is a current account surplus equivalent to foreign investment?

APPENDIX 1: MEASURING THE INTERNATIONAL INVESTMENT POSITION

It may seem like a straightforward job to add up the value of assets, but nothing could be farther from the truth. Consider the following problem: The United States ran trade surpluses in the 1950s and 1960s and accumulated large holdings of foreign assets. In the 1980s and 1990s, the United States ran trade deficits and foreigners accumulated large holdings inside the United States. By 2000, a sizable proportion of U.S.-owned assets had been purchased decades ago when prices were much lower, and foreign-owned assets were purchased recently, after the worldwide inflation of the 1970s and the early 1980s. If asset values are tallied up using their historical cost, the price at the time of purchase, then foreign-owned assets appear more valuable, not necessarily because they are but because they were acquired more recently when world prices were higher.

It seems logical to expect that the reporting of asset values would be done on a current cost basis, rather than an historical cost basis, where current cost is the cost of purchasing the asset in the current period. Unfortunately, it does not happen like this. In the United States, firms use historical cost as the basis for valuation of assets in company records, and they use this when they report their foreign holdings to the agency that collects the data, the Bureau of Economic Analysis. The difference between current cost and historical cost does not affect the measurement of portfolio investment, which is relatively short term, but it has significant effects on the measurement of direct investment since it is held for longer time periods.

Until 1991, the United States only calculated the historical cost of U.S.-owned foreign assets. As a result, the U.S. international investment position appeared to become negative very rapidly as large trade deficits in the mid-1980s led to a rapid accumulation of new assets in the United States by foreign interests. More recently, in the 1990s, the United States began to report all assets on a current value basis. The primary deficiency in this data as it now stands is that it cannot be broken down into country-specific or industry-specific data. Therefore, we know the overall international investment position for the United States, but we cannot accurately examine the U.S.–Japan bilateral investment position, since we only have U.S. assets in Japan on a historical cost basis.

APPENDIX 2: BALANCE OF PAYMENTS DATA

Current account and international investment data are readily available for most nations of the world. Many databases are also available in electronic form over the Internet. United States and world data can also be found in the Web resources for Chapter 9. Data for other countries are usually available on their government's Web site, or in the following sources:

1. International Financial Statistics (IFS)

This is a regular publication of the International Monetary Fund. It appears quarterly, with an annual *Yearbook* at the year's end. Each of the quarterly volumes contains a subset of the world's nations, and the *Yearbook* collects them all into one volume. As the name implies, IFS focuses on financial data, but it also contains information on current accounts and international capital flows. The IFS also has the most recent estimates of GDP and its major components along with population. Coverage is of most of the world's nations, and the most recent *Yearbook* usually contains a decade of data for each country. The IMF publications are one of the sources used by many international agencies and private enterprises. Nearly all university libraries and many city libraries will have IFS.

2. Balance of Payments Statistics (BOPS)

This is a sister publication of the International Monetary Fund that complements the data in IFS. Publication format is similar, with quarterly volumes covering a selection of nations and an annual *Yearbook* that combines all countries into one large volume and a thin supplement. The BOPS has the most up-to-date and detailed current account statistics of any international data source. In addition, it contains detailed breakdowns of capital flows.

3. United Nations' Statistical Yearbook and Related Volumes

The *Statistical Yearbook* is generally somewhat less current than the IMF data listed above. It does contain a much greater variety of data, however. The *Statistical Yearbook* is a combination of data from several more specialized UN sources, including the *United Nations' National Account Statistics, Demographic Yearbook, Industrial Statistics Yearbook, Energy Statistics Yearbook*, and *International Trade Statistics Yearbook*. The *Statistical Yearbook* has the advantage of combining in one place a great quantity of data, usually going back one decade. Its major disadvantage is that it lacks the detail that can be found in the more specialized volumes. The most current data can be located in the United Nations' *Monthly Bulletin of Statistics*. Most university libraries are likely to have one or all of these volumes.

Chapter 10

EXCHANGE RATES AND EXCHANGE RATE SYSTEMS

INTRODUCTION

The topics of exchange rates and exchange rate systems are less settled than most issues examined so far. The lack of consensus is partly because countries must decide on the type of exchange rate system that best suits their conditions, and there is a fairly extensive menu of choices for selection. Some of the choices are relatively recent innovations, such as crawling pegs or target rate zones, and their performance characteristics under a wide array of economic conditions have yet to be fully analyzed. In general, the choice of an exchange rate system varies along a continuum from completely flexible rates that are determined by the market forces of supply and demand, to completely fixed rates that are set and maintained by a country's central bank. Between these two poles, there are many intermediate forms combining various degrees of fixity and flexibility in the determination of the exchange rate.

A further complication is that each type of exchange rate requires a different set of policies by government officials, and each responds differently to pressures from the world economy. All three of these factors—exchange rate system, government policy, and the world economy—interact in ways that are at times impossible to predict and, as a result, have given rise to an active set of debates over the selection and management of a country's exchange rate system.

EXCHANGE RATES AND CURRENCY TRADING

The **exchange rate** is the price of one currency stated in terms of a second currency. An exchange rate can be given in one of two ways, either as units of domestic currency per unit of foreign currency or vice versa. For example, we might give the U.S.–Mexico exchange rate as dollars per peso (0.10 dollars) or pesos per dollar (10 pesos). The custom varies with the currency. For example, the U.S. dollar–British pound exchange rate is usually quoted in terms of dollars per pound, but the U.S. dollar–Mexican peso is usually pesos per dollar. In this chapter and the rest of the book, the exchange rate is always given as the number of units of domestic currency per unit of foreign currency. For the United States, this means it is dollars per peso and dollars per pound.

Exchange rates are reported on a daily basis in the financial pages of every major newspaper and in numerous Web sites. Table 10.1 shows a selection of exchange rates taken from the April 5, 2001, daily posting by the Federal Reserve. These rates, like all the rates reported by the financial press, are wholesale prices rather than retail. In order to realize the listed exchange rate, a bank or currency trader has to purchase large quantities of the currency, typically a million dollars or more. Although Table 10.1 lists the U.S. dollar price of the Swedish krona as $0.0981 on April 5, 2001, tourists such as you and I could not have bought them at this price. However, banks, currency traders, and corporations that wanted to buy or sell millions of dollars worth of foreign exchange on that date would have found prices fairly close to those listed in the table.

TABLE 10.1	Exchange Rates for Selected Countries, April 5, 2001		
Country	*Currency*	*Units per U.S. Dollar*	*U.S. Dollars per Unit*
Australia	Dollar	2.042	0.4898
Brazil	Real	2.168	0.4613
Canada	Dollar	1.579	0.6334
China, P.R.	Yuan	8.277	0.1208
Denmark	Krone	8.316	0.1203
EMU Members	Euro	1.114	0.8976
Hong Kong	Dollar	7.799	0.1282
India	Rupee	46.640	0.0214
Japan	Yen	124.330	0.0080
Malaysia	Ringgit	3.800	0.2632
Mexico	Peso	9.388	0.1065
New Zealand	Dollar	2.476	0.4038
Norway	Krone	9.072	0.1102
Singapore	Dollar	1.809	0.5528
South Africa	Rand	8.083	0.1237
South Korea	Won	1,352.000	0.0007
Sri Lanka	Rupee	88.100	0.0114
Sweden	Krona	10.191	0.0981
Switzerland	Franc	1.702	0.5875
Taiwan	Dollar	32.900	0.0304
Thailand	Baht	45.370	0.0220
United Kingdom	Pound	0.701	1.4266
Venezuela	Bolivar	709.000	0.0014

Source: Federal Reserve, http://www.bog.frb.fed.us/releases/H10/update/h10daily.txt.

The values in Table 10.1 are in a state of constant change. Most of the countries in the table have flexible exchange rate systems that allow the value or price of its currency to be determined by supply and demand. When a currency becomes more valuable, it buys more units of another currency and is said to have **appreciated**. When it loses value, it is described as having **depreciated**. Note that since this text will define the exchange rate as the units of domestic currency per unit of foreign currency, an increase or appreciation in the home country's currency is a fall in the exchange rate. For example if the U.S. dollar appreciates against the British pound, it might move from 1.4266 dollars per pound to 1.40 dollars. This is an appreciation of the dollar because it takes fewer dollars to buy a pound—1.40 instead of 1.4266.

Reasons for Holding Foreign Currencies

Economists identify three reasons for holding foreign currency. The first is for trade and investment purposes. Traders (importers and exporters) and investors routinely transact in foreign currencies, either receiving or making payments in another country's money. Tourists are included in this category because they hold foreign exchange in order to buy foreign goods and services.

The second reason for holding foreign exchange is to take advantage of interest rate differentials, or **interest rate arbitrage**. Arbitrage conveys the idea of buying something where it is relatively cheap and selling it where it is relatively expensive. Interest rate arbitrage is similar in that arbitrageurs acquire money where interest rates are relatively low and lend it where rates are relatively high. By moving financial capital in this way, interest rate arbitrage keeps interest rates from diverging too far, and also constitutes one of the primary linkages between national economies. Capital inflows to the high interest rate countries puts downward pressure on interest rates, while the outflow from the low interest rate countries dries up the supply and puts upward pressure on rates. This drawing together of interest rates in different countries is one way in which economic conditions are transmitted across national borders. Various other factors intervene in this relationship, such as perceptions of risk, but in general, interest rate arbitrage is a powerful force in the world economy and tends to be one of the main reasons for holding foreign currency.

The third reason for holding foreign exchange is to speculate. Speculators are businesses who buy or sell a currency because they expect its price to rise or fall. They have no need for foreign exchange to buy goods or services or financial assets; rather, they hope to realize profits or avoid losses through correctly anticipating changes in a currency's market value. Speculators are often reviled in the popular press, but in fact they help to bring currencies into equilibrium after they have become over- or undervalued. If speculators view a currency as overvalued, they will sell it and, in the process, drive down its value and thereby realize the result they anticipated. If they guessed wrong, however, they tend to lose a lot of money since they placed their bets on a result that did not materialize. For this reason, some economists have argued that speculation either serves the useful function of bringing currency values into proper alignment, or its practitioners lose money and go out of business. Not everyone agrees with this view, however, and some economists feel that speculation against a currency can be destabilizing in the sense that it does not always push an exchange rate to its equilibrium value, but instead, will sometimes lead to a grossly over- or undervalued currency, which is a major problem for the country involved. Needless to say, the role of speculation in the market for foreign exchange is an issue that has not reached a consensus.

Institutions

There are four main participants in foreign currency markets: retail customers, commercial banks, foreign exchange brokers, and central banks. Of these four, commercial banks are the most important. Retail customers include firms and individuals that hold foreign exchange for any of the three reasons given above—to engage in purchases, to adjust their portfolios, or to profit from expected future currency movements. In most cases, they buy and sell through a commercial bank. Commercial banks in many parts of the world hold inventories of foreign currencies as part of the services offered to customers. Not all banks provide this service, but those that do usually have a relationship with several foreign banks where they hold their balances of foreign currencies. When a surplus accumulates, or a shortage develops, the banks trade with each other to adjust their holdings.

In the United States, foreign exchange brokers also play an important role. It is not very common for U.S. banks to trade currency with foreign banks. Instead, U.S. banks tend to go through foreign exchange brokers, who act as middlemen between buyers and sellers since they do not usually hold foreign exchange. Brokers can also serve as agents for central banks. The market, then, works as follows. An individual or firm that needs foreign exchange calls its bank. The bank quotes a price at which it will sell the currency. The price is based on one of two possible sources of supply: (1) the bank may have an account with another bank in the country where the currency is used, or, (2) it may call a foreign exchange broker. The broker keeps track of buyers and sellers of currencies and acts as a deal maker by bringing together a seller and a bank that is buying for its customer.

In most cases, currency trades take the form of credits and debits to a firm's bank accounts. For example, a local U.S. importer that must make payment in yen can call and tell its bank to transfer yen to the Japanese bank of the firm that supplies the importer with goods. The importer will have a debit to its local bank account that is equivalent to the cost of the yen. If the U.S. bank has a branch or correspondence bank in Japan, they can electronically notify it to debit the yen from the account of the U.S. bank and credit it to the Japanese bank of the supplier. If the U.S. bank goes through a currency trader instead of dealing directly with a Japanese bank, then it first buys yen that are in an account with a Japanese bank. Next, it requests that some or all of its yen assets be transferred to the bank of the Japanese supplier of the U.S. importer.

Exchange Rate Risk

Firms that do business in more than one country are subject to **exchange rate risks**. These risks stem from the fact that currencies are constantly changing in value and, as a result, expected future payments that will be made or received in a foreign currency will be a different domestic currency amount from when the contract was signed.

Suppose, for example, that a U.S. semiconductor manufacturer signs a contract to send a British computer manufacturer a shipment of microprocessors in six months. If the U.S. manufacturer agrees on a price in British pounds, it must know the value of the pound six months from now in order to know the dollar equivalent of its future revenue. If the U.S. manufacturer specifies that the microprocessors be paid for in dollars, then it shifts the exchange rate risk to the British firm. The U.S. company knows the exact dollar amount it will receive in six months, but the British firm is uncertain of the price of the dollar, and therefore the pound price of microprocessors.

Financial markets recognized this problem long ago and, in the nineteenth century they created mechanisms for dealing with it. The mechanisms are the forward exchange rate, and the forward market. The **forward exchange rate** is the price of a currency that will be delivered in the future, while the **forward market** refers to the market in which the buying and selling of currencies for future delivery takes place. Forward markets for currencies are an everyday tool for international traders, investors, and speculators because they are a way to eliminate the exchange rate risk associated with future payments and receipts. Forward foreign exchange markets allow an exporter or importer to sign a currency contract on the day they sign an agreement to ship or receive goods. The currency contract guarantees a set price for the foreign currency, usually 30, 90, or 180 days into the future. By contrast, the market for buying and selling in the present is called a **spot market**. The prices of foreign currencies quoted in Table 10.1 are "spot prices," although many newspapers also report forward market prices.

Suppose the U.S. semiconductor manufacturer signs a contract to deliver the microprocessors to the British firm in six months. Suppose also that the price is stated in British pounds. The manufacturer knows precisely how many pounds it will earn six months from now, but it does not know whether the pound will rise or fall in value, so it does not know what it will earn in dollar terms. The solution is to sign a forward contract to sell British pounds six months from now in exchange for U.S. dollars at a price agreed upon today. Using the forward market, the U.S. manufacturer avoids the risk that comes from exchange rate fluctuations.

Forward markets are important to financial investors and speculators as well as exporters and importers. We have seen that interest arbitrage is one of the primary reasons for holding foreign currencies. Bondholders and other interest rate arbitrageurs often use forward markets to protect themselves against the foreign exchange risk incurred while holding foreign bonds and other financial assets. This is called **hedging** and it is accomplished by buying a forward contract to sell foreign currency at the same time that the bond or other interest earning asset matures. When interest rate arbitrageurs use the forward market to insure against exchange rate risk, it is called **covered interest arbitrage**.

THE SUPPLY AND DEMAND FOR FOREIGN EXCHANGE

The value of one nation's money, like most things, can be analyzed by looking at its supply and demand. Under a system of flexible, or floating exchange rates, an increase in the demand for the dollar will raise its price (cause an appreciation in its value), while an increase in its supply will lower its price (cause a depreciation). Under a fixed exchange rate system, the value of the dollar is held constant through the actions of the central bank that counteract the market forces of supply and demand. Consequently, supply and demand analysis is a useful tool for understanding the pressures on a currency regardless of the type of exchange rate system adopted. For this reason, we begin with the assumption that exchange rates are completely flexible. After examining the usefulness of supply and demand analysis, we will turn to alternative systems, including gold standards and other variations on fixed exchange rates.

Supply and Demand with Flexible Exchange Rates

Figure 10.1 shows the demand for British pounds in the United States. The curve is a normal downward sloping demand curve, indicating that as the pound depreciates relative to the dollar, the quantity of pounds demanded by Americans increases. Note also that we are measuring the price of the pound— the exchange rate—on the vertical axis. Since it is dollars per pound ($/£), it is the price of a pound in terms of dollars and an increase in the exchange rate, R, is a decline in the value of the dollar. In other words, movements up the vertical axis represent an increase in the price of the pound, which is equivalent to a fall in the price of the dollar. Similarly, movements down the vertical axis represent a decrease in the price of the pound.

For Americans, British goods are less expensive when the pound is cheaper and the dollar is stronger. Hence, at depreciated values for the pound, Americans will switch from U.S. or third-party suppliers of goods and services to British suppliers. Before they can purchase goods made in Britain, however, they must first exchange dollars for British pounds. Consequently, the increased demand for British goods is simultaneously an increase in the quantity of British pounds demanded.

Figure 10.2 shows the supply side of the picture. The supply curve slopes up because British firms and consumers are willing to buy a greater quantity of American goods as the dollar becomes cheaper (i.e., as they receive more dol-

| FIGURE 10.1 | The Demand Curve for Foreign Exchange |

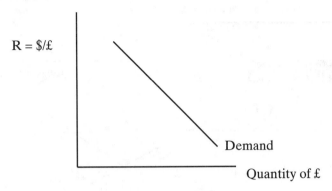

As the exchange rate falls, the dollar appreciates and the dollar price of British goods falls. The quantity of pounds demanded by the U.S. market increases as U.S. consumers and firms purchase more goods and services in Britain.

lars per pound). Before British customers can buy American goods, however, they must first convert pounds into dollars, so the increase in the quantity of American goods demanded is simultaneously an increase in the quantity of foreign currency supplied to the United States.

| FIGURE 10.2 | The Supply of Foreign Exchange |

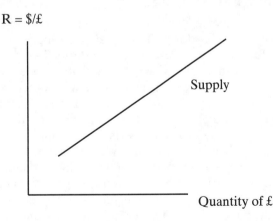

As the exchange rate rises, the dollar depreciates and the pound price of U.S. goods falls. The quantity of pounds supplied to the U.S. market is increased as British consumers and firms purchase more goods in the United States.

Figure 10.3 combines the supply and demand curves. The intersection determines the market exchange rate and the quantity of pounds supplied to the United States. At exchange rate R_1, the demand and supply of British pounds to the United States is Q_1.

FIGURE 10.3   Supply and Demand in the Foreign Exchange Market

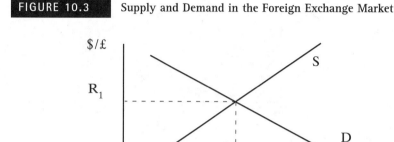

The intersection of the supply of British pounds to the U.S. market, and the U.S. demand for British pounds determines the quantity of pounds available in the United States (Q_1), and their dollar price (exchange rate R_1).

Exchange Rates in the Long Run

We have determined that the supply curve slopes up to the right and the demand curve slopes down. The next step in supply and demand analysis is to consider the factors that determine the intersection of supply and demand and the actual exchange rate. We will continue to assume that the exchange rate is completely flexible. Later in the chapter we look at exchange rates that are fixed, and at intermediate rates between fixed and flexible.

In Figure 10.4, an increase in the U.S. demand for the pound (rightward shift of the demand curve), causes a rise in the exchange rate, an appreciation in the pound, and a depreciation in the dollar. Conversely, a fall in demand would shift the demand curve left and lead to a falling pound and a rising dollar. On the supply side, an increase in the supply of pounds to the U.S. market (supply curve shifts right) is illustrated in Figure 10.5, where a new intersection for supply and demand occurs at a lower exchange rate and an appreciated dollar. A decrease in the supply of pounds shifts the curve leftward, causing the exchange rate to rise and the dollar to depreciate.

The causal factors behind the shifts in the supply and demand are easier to conceptualize if we divide the determinants of exchange rates into three peri-

FIGURE 10.4   **An Increase in Demand for British Pounds**

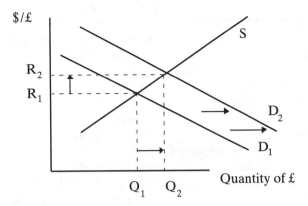

An increase in the U.S. demand for British pounds (rightward shift of the curve) causes the dollar to depreciate.

FIGURE 10.5   **An Increase in the Supply of British Pounds**

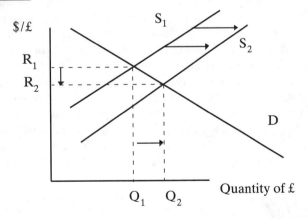

An increase in the supply of British pounds to the U.S. market (rightward shift of the curve) causes the dollar to appreciate.

ods: long run, medium run, and short run. This seems to be accurate empirically, as not all the factors that determine an exchange rate show up instantaneously. In fact, some causal factors take a very long time—a decade or more—to exert their full influence, and in the meantime, a number of short-run or medium-run factors may push in a completely opposite direction.

Looking at the long run first, **purchasing power parity** states that the equilibrium value of an exchange rate is at the level that allows a given amount of money to buy the same quantity of goods abroad that it will buy at home. By this criteria, the equilibrium exchange rate is the point where the dollar buys pounds at a rate that keeps its purchasing power over goods and services constant. That is, $100 buys the right amount of pounds to enable the purchase of the same basket of goods and services in Britain that $100 buys in the United States. Table 10.2 illustrates this idea.

In Table 10.2, a basket of goods costs $1,000 or £500, depending on the country where it is purchased. Accordingly, the long-run tendency is for the exchange rate to move to $2 per £. If it is above that, the pound is overvalued and the dollar is undervalued. An overvalued pound buys more in the United States than in Britain since it would be possible to convert £500 to more than $1,000 and buy a larger basket of goods than can be bought in Britain. Exchange rates less than 2 would imply the opposite—the pound is undervalued and the dollar overvalued.

It should be stressed that this is an underlying tendency and not a description of actual exchange rates at any point in time. Over the long run, purchasing power parity exerts influence over exchange rates, but in the short to medium run, there are significant deviations from this pattern. If you have traveled outside your home country, you are probably aware of cases where your domestic currency buys you so much foreign currency that your standard of living is higher when you travel. You might be able to stay in a better class of hotel, eat in better restaurants, and shop for items that you cannot afford at home. Or, you may be familiar with the opposite, where your standard of living declines because you get so little foreign currency in exchange for your domestic currency that everything seems inordinately expensive.

Purchasing power parity influences currency values indirectly. When a currency is over- or undervalued, it creates profit-making opportunities for merchants that can move goods across international borders. Suppose, for example, that the dollar is overvalued and that instead of $2 per pound, the exchange rate is $1.75 per pound. Prices are assumed to be the same as those in Table

TABLE 10.2	A Hypothetical Example of the Exchange Rate in the Long Run

	Cost of the Same Basket of Goods in Each Country
Price in dollars	$1,000
Price in pounds	£500
Long-run equilibrium exchange rate	($1,000/£500) = $2/£

Purchasing power parity states that dollars will tend to exchange for pounds at a rate that maintains a constant purchasing power of a given quantity of currency.

10.2. In this case, $1,000 buys £571.43 (1,000/1.75). If merchants take the £571.43 and buy British goods, then ship the goods to the United States, they can earn more than $1,000. (They earn $1,142.86 since goods prices are 2 to 1.) In the long run, the demand for British pounds increases and, as shown in Figure 10.4, the exchange rate rises. The process will continue until the exchange rate hits $2 per £, and there are no more profit-making opportunities from shipping goods from Britain to the United States.

The process just described is reinforced by the flow of goods from Britain to the United States. The supply of goods shrinks in Britain, leading to rising prices there. In the United States, supply rises and under normal competitive conditions, prices will fall. These effects will take a while to exert themselves, but they are another factor reinforcing purchasing power parity. In this case, however, prices are moving in the direction that equalizes the purchasing power of the two currencies, instead of equalization through exchange rate movement as in the previous example. In theory, it does not matter which changes—prices or exchange rates—but given that prices in many countries tend not to fall easily, while exchange rates are relatively easily moved, most of the equalization probably occurs through exchange rate movements.

The story of goods arbitrage—buying where the goods are cheaper and selling where they are more expensive—which stands behind purchasing power parity, obviously has a few unrealistic assumptions. In particular, it requires that goods flow costlessly across international borders and that all goods and services can be traded. In reality, there are transportation costs involved with moving goods. This means that our merchant who buys £571.43 of goods in Britain and sells them for $1142.86 in the United States loses some of her $142.86 profit to shipping, insurance, and other transaction costs. In addition, she pays a fee to a bank or a currency broker when she buys the needed pounds.

Nor is this the only obstacle standing in the way of her profits. Few nations have eliminated all their barriers to the entry of foreign goods and services. She may face a tariff, import license fees, inspection fees, or some other barrier at the border that adds to her cost. In the limit, imports of the goods in question may be prohibited and goods arbitrage may be impossible at any price differential. In addition, some goods and many services are not traded. For example, restaurant meals, haircuts, landscape maintenance, and a host of other services that must be consumed on the spot are rarely, if ever, traded.

Once the assumptions of purchasing power parity are examined, it is not surprising that it exerts its influence over exchange rates only in the long run. If there are significant profit-making opportunities through goods arbitrage, then in spite of today's obstacles, entrepreneurs will work to create the conditions that will allow them to take advantage of the price differentials across markets. They will look for ways to lower transport costs, to minimize the costs of compliance with import rules and regulations, and to change the rules where it is feasible. All of these steps take time, but in spite of the real obstacles to its operation, purchasing power parity remains a significant long-run force in the determination of exchange rates.

Exchange Rates in the Medium Run and Short Run

While purchasing power parity is working slowly in the background, other forces have more immediate impacts on the position of the supply and demand curves for foreign exchange. We turn first to the forces that are correlated with the business cycle, the natural but irregular rhythms of expansion and recession that every country undergoes. Given that the time period from the peak of one expansion to the next is usually several years in duration, the forces that are tied to the business cycle can be considered medium run. That is, they are pressures on an exchange rate that may last for several years, but almost always less than a decade and usually less than 5 to 7 years.

The most important medium-run force is the strength of a country's economic growth. Rapid growth implies rising incomes and increased consumption. When consumers feel secure in their jobs and at the same time experience a rapid growth in their incomes, they spend more, some of which will be on imports and travel abroad. As a result, rapid economic growth at home is translated into increased imports and an outward shift in the demand for foreign currency, as illustrated in Figure 10.4. Holding constant a host of short-run forces that may be in play at the same time, the effect of rapid economic growth at home is a depreciating currency.

The effect of growth is symmetrical, both with respect to slower growth at home, and with respect to the rate of economic growth abroad. Slower growth, such as a recession during which output declines (negative economic growth), raises consumer uncertainty about jobs and reduces many people's incomes. For the economy as a whole, as consumption expenditures fall, expenditures on imports decline as well, and the demand for foreign exchange falls. A leftward shift of the demand curve reduces the exchange rate and appreciates the currency. In other words, just as more rapid economic growth can cause a depreciation in a country's currency, slower growth sets forces in motion that lead to an appreciation.

Growth abroad does not have a direct effect on the home country's demand for foreign exchange (although it may have an indirect effect through its stimulation of the home economy), but it will directly affect the supply curve. More rapid foreign growth leads to more exports from the home country, and slower foreign growth results in fewer exports. More exports to foreigners increase the supply of foreign currency and shifts the supply curve rightward, as illustrated in Figure 10.5. Fewer exports have the opposite effect. You should practice drawing the effects of changes in the rates of home and foreign economic growth on the supply and demand curves for foreign exchange.

Turning from the medium run of the business cycle to short-run periods of a year or less, a number of forces are constantly at work shaping currency values. The foremost short-run force is the flow of financial capital. The effects of financial flows range from minor and subtle to dramatic and, at times, catastrophic. They are as capable of creating slight day-to-day variations in the value of a currency as they are of creating complete financial chaos and bringing down governments. The degree of volatility in financial flows varies greatly and is highly responsive to governmental policies and conditions in the world economy. The impact on exchange rates of large-scale, short-run, movements in financial capital has become one of the most serious issues in international economics.

Two variables in particular are responsible for a large share of short run capital flows: interest rates and expectations about future exchange rates. These two forces often influence each other and are capable of creating unpredictable interactions, as when a change in interest rates reshapes investor confidence or catalyzes speculative actions in currency markets.

The role of interest rates in the short-run determination of exchange rates is crucial. The interest rate–exchange rate relationship is summed up in the **interest parity** condition which states that the difference between any pair of countries' interest rates is approximately equal to the expected change in the exchange rate. The appendix to this chapter develops the algebra of this relationship, but the intuition is not difficult to grasp. Interest rate arbitrageurs have a choice of investing in the home country or investing abroad. For the sake of simplicity, we will compare two alternatives, which are called *Home* and *Foreign*. At Home, investors expect to earn the interest rate i, while in Foreign they can earn i*. The three possibilities are:

$$i = i^*, \tag{1}$$

$$i > i^*, \tag{2}$$

or

$$i < i^*. \tag{3}$$

In case (1), investors are indifferent between the two options. In case (2), Home investments are preferred to Foreign (Home experiences capital inflows) and in case (3) Foreign investments are preferred (Home experiences capital outflows). As long as financial capital moves across international borders, there are exchange rate risks for the sending country's investors. When international investors eventually convert back to their own currency, the exchange rate is likely to be different than the rate they paid when they moved assets out of their country. Admittedly, they might gain or lose in the conversion process, but if their original intention is to take advantage of interest rate differentials, it is unlikely that they are seeking to speculate in currencies. Therefore, interest rate arbitrageurs usually act in a similar way to merchants and sign a forward contract to sell the proceeds of their foreign currency earnings when they mature.

The difference between the forward and spot exchange rates reflects the expected appreciation or depreciation of the home currency. For example, if the forward rate for a given maturity (30 days, 180 days, etc.) is 3 percent less than the spot rate, it signals that currency markets expect the home currency to appreciate by 3 percent over the maturity period of the forward rate. As noted earlier, no one can actually predict an exchange rate 30 or 180 days into the future, but the spread between the forward and spot rates reflects the best available market information at the time the contract is signed. If Foreign investors move their financial capital into Home, they can expect a 3 percent appreciation in the value of their assets when measured in terms of Foreign's prices. In other words, they could earn 3 percent less in interest over the same period and still come out even, given that they will gain 3 percent in the conversion back into their own currency. This relationship is summarized in the following interest parity equation:

$$i - i^* \approx (F - R)/R,$$

where F stands for a forward exchange rate with the same term to maturity as the interest rates i and i*. The right-hand side is the percentage difference in the forward and spot rates. If it is positive, then $F > R$, Home currency is expected to depreciate, and Home interest rates must exceed Foreign rates by an approximately equivalent percentage. If $F < R$, an appreciation is expected in the value of Home currency and interest rates will be below Foreign rates by an approximately equivalent percentage. The algebra of this relationship is developed in the appendix.

The utility of the interest parity condition is that it brings together the reason for a significant share of international capital flows, domestic interest rate policy, and exchange rate expectations. Suppose for example, that Case (3) is operative, and Home interest rates are below Foreign: $i < i^*$. This tells us that the forward rate is below the spot rate ($F < R$) and that markets expect an appreciation in the home currency. To see why the interest parity condition is an equilibrium toward which the exchange rate will move, consider what happens if the percentage difference in the forward and spot rates is insufficient to compensate for lower interest rates. In this case, financial capital will flow out of Home and into Foreign. Suppose for example that $i < i^*$, and $F = R$. As a result, currency markets are signaling that no changes are expected in the exchange rate, and both Home and Foreign investors can do better if they invest in Foreign since the interest rate they earn is higher. Capital would flow out of Home, increasing the demand for Foreign currency, and perhaps raising the price of financial capital in Home, which is i. In addition, the supply of Foreign's currency would decline since fewer investors in Foreign would invest in Home. As a result, R rises (from the increase in the demand and decrease in the supply of Foreign's currency) and i rises (due to the decrease in the supply of financial capital to Home). Both effects work to restore an equilibrium where the interest rate differential is approximately equal to the percentage difference between forward and spot exchange rates.

Consider another example. Suppose that Home interest rates are less than Foreign ($i < i^*$) and that forward rates are less than spot rates ($F < R$) by an appropriate amount so that the interest parity condition holds. Beginning at this point, Home policymakers decide for some reason to raise their interest rates to the same level as Foreign rates: $i = i^*$. Now, investors in both Home and Foreign will invest more in Home because they earn the same rate of interest, and they expect Home's currency to appreciate in value (since $F < R$). Figure 10.6 illustrates these shifts. Note that both the demand curve for foreign's currency and the supply curve of foreign's currency shift, with demand moving in and supply moving out. Taken together, both shifts reinforce a downward movement in the spot rate. As R falls, Home's currency appreciates and the gap between F and R closes. If $i = i^*$, the process ends when $F = R$.

In addition to their impact on the forward-spot rate differential, expectations play a crucial role in the determination of exchange rates in another way. A sudden change in the expected future value of an exchange rate can have a dramatic and often self-fulfilling impact on a country's currency. For example, if investors suddenly come to believe that a currency must depreciate more than they had anticipated, it lowers the expected value of assets denominated in that currency. This can create a sudden exodus of financial capital and put enormous pressure on the country's supply of foreign exchange reserves. To a significant extent, episodes of capital flight can be self-fulfilling in their expectations about an exchange rate. If investors expect depreciation, they try to convert their assets to another currency. This raises the demand for foreign exchange and depresses the supply, fulfilling the expectation of a depreciation.

There are numerous potential causes of this type of volatility in financial capital flows and exchange rate shifts. It also seems likely that technological changes in telecommunications have altered the sensitivity of markets toward changes in expectations, although this is yet to be established definitively. Nevertheless, it is certain that a frequent cause of sudden shifts in expectations is the realization that a particular government is practicing economic policies that are internally inconsistent and unsustainable. We will examine this in more

| FIGURE 10.6 | The Effects of an Increase in Home's Interest Rate |

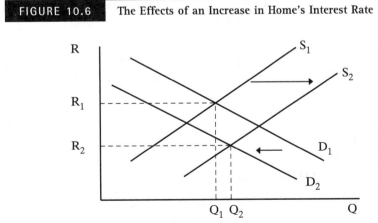

An increase in Home's interest rate causes a decrease in demand and an increase in supply of the foreign currency. Both effects cause an appreciation in the exchange rate from R_1 to R_2.

CASE STUDY

The Largest Market in the World

The daily volume of foreign exchange bought and sold in the world's currency markets was around $1,490,000,000,000 (1.49 trillion) in 1998. This is equivalent to about 17 percent of the United States's annual production of goods and services. The currency trading figure comes from the Bank for International Settlements (BIS), a "central bank for central banks." The BIS carried out a survey of foreign exchange transactions in April, 1998, and plans a follow-up survey in 2001. By the time you read this, it should be available on their Web site at http://www.bis.org.

Between 1989 and 1998, the daily volume of transactions grew from $590 billion to 1.49 trillion, a growth rate of more than 10 percent per year, and far faster than the growth of the world economy. In spite of the rapid rate of growth, the composition of currency trades remained about the same from 1989 to 1998. Eighty-seven percent of every trade in 1998 involved the U.S. dollar, either as the currency sold or the currency bought. The second most active currency was the German mark (30 percent of all trades), followed by the Japanese yen (21 percent) and the British pound (11 percent). Table 10.3 shows the main currencies.

Note that the total is 200 percent, rather than 100, because every sale is simultaneously a purchase. The dollar is so often traded because it is used as an

| **TABLE 10.3** | Composition of World Currency Trades, April, 1998 |

Currency	Percent of Total Trades
U.S. dollar	87
German mark	30
Japanese yen	21
British pound	11
French franc	5
Swiss franc	7
Canadian dollar	4
Australian dollar	3
ECU and other EU currency	17
Other	15

Source: Bank for International Settlements, "Central Bank Survey of Foreign Exchange and Derivatives Market Activity in April, 1998: Preliminary Global Data." Available: http://www.bis.org/publ/r_fx98.pdf.

international medium of exchange and because of the cross trading that occurs between pairs of currencies. That is, a Chilean importer may pay her Mexican supplier in U.S. dollars, or she may use Chilean pesos to buy dollars and the dollars to buy Mexican pesos. Since the 1998 survey, the European Union has introduced the common currency for eleven of its members, called the *euro*, and most analysts expect it to eventually replace the dollar in some uses.

The location of currency trading is concentrated in four main centers: London, New York, Tokyo, and Singapore.

London is by far the largest center of foreign exchange trading. As an illustration of this, the BIS survey discovered that more U.S. dollars and German marks are traded in London than in New York or Germany.

Given the preponderance of the U.S. dollar in currency trades and the importance of London as a trading center, it follows that most of the trades in London do not involve the British pound. According to the BIS, 82 percent of all trades in London involved two currencies, neither of which was the pound.

TABLE 10.4   **Currency Trading Centers**

Location	Percent of World Currency Trading
United Kingdom	32
United States	18
Japan	8
Singapore	7
Germany	5
Switzerland	4
France	4

Source: See Table 10.3.

---

detail in Chapters 11 and 12, but it is relatively easy to get a sense of the meaning of inconsistent policies. An example is policies that are designed to strongly stimulate the economy (more growth → more imports → more demand for foreign exchange) when the supply of foreign exchange is severely limited (not enough exports, very low interest rates).

The mechanisms from inconsistent policy to exchange rate crisis and collapse are fairly well understood, but this begs the question about the cause of a sudden shift in expectations. Many recent episodes of sudden exchange rate shifts have occurred when investors lost confidence in a particular currency.

Yet why the sudden change in investor confidence? Government policies had been in place for years in some cases, yet suddenly they were deemed unsustainable and likely to lead to a severe depreciation. In order to understand this, economists will have to develop a far deeper understanding of the subtle relationships between actual economic conditions and psychological expectations. This goal is a way off at this point.

Table 10.5 summarizes the long-, medium-, and short-run factors that have been discussed. The list is not exhaustive, but the main elements are included.

TABLE 10.5	Major Determinants of an Appreciation or Depreciation	
	R Falls: An Appreciation in the Domestic Currency	*R Rises: A Depreciation in the Domestic Currency*
Long run: Purchasing Power Parity	Home goods are less expensive than Foreign goods	Home goods are more expensive than Foreign goods
Medium run: The Business Cycle	Home's economy grows more slowly than Foreign	Home's economy grows faster than Foreign
Short run (1): Interest Parity	Home interest rates rise, or Foreign rates	Home interest rates fall, or Foreign rates rise
Short run (2): Speculation	Expectations of a future appreciation	Expectations of a future depreciation

THE REAL EXCHANGE RATE

The concept of the exchange rate that has been used so far and that is exemplified by the values in Table 10.1 does not really tell us what a foreign currency is worth. Exchange rates tells us how many units of domestic currency we give up for one unit of foreign currency, but unless we know what foreign prices are, we still do not know the purchasing power of our domestic money when it is converted to a foreign currency. As an illustration of this problem, suppose that the U.S. dollar–French franc exchange rate is $0.20 and that it stays constant over the year. However, suppose also that French inflation is 4 percent while U.S. inflation is 1 percent. After one year, the 5 francs that cost a dollar will buy 3 percent less in France than the dollar buys in the United States. The relatively higher inflation in France erodes the value of a dollar's worth of francs more rapidly than the dollar loses value at home. Consequently, when converted to francs, the real purchasing power of the dollar has declined even though the exchange rate is still $0.20 per franc.

From the point of view of tourists and business people who use foreign exchange, the key item of interest is the purchasing power they get when they convert their dollars, not the number of units of a foreign currency. An American importer trying to decide between French and Italian textiles does not really care if she gets 5 French francs per dollar or 1,500 Italian lira per dollar. The biggest concern is the volume of textiles that can be purchased in France with 5 francs and in Italy with 1,500 lira.

The **real exchange rate** is the market exchange rate (or **nominal exchange rate**) adjusted for price differences. The two are closely connected. By way of illustration, let's consider the case of a wine merchant who is trying to decide whether to stock her shop with American or French wine. Let's say that French wine of a given quality cost 600 francs and American wine of the same quality costs $180. What the merchant needs to know is the real exchange rate between French and American wine. Suppose that the nominal rate is $0.20 per franc, so that $180 is equivalent to 900 francs in the currency market. In this case, French wine costs a third less than American, and the real exchange rate is two-thirds of a case of American wine per case of French wine. The algebra is straightforward:

Real exchange rate

= [(Nominal exchange rate) × (Foreign price)] / (Domestic price),

= [($0.20 per franc) × (600 francs per case)] / ($180 per case)

= ($120 per case of French wine) / ($180 per case of American wine)

= $2/3$ case of American wine per case of French wine.

Since the real purchasing power of the dollar is much greater in France than in the United States, the choice facing the wine merchant is obvious.

In this example, the main lesson is clear. What matters most to exporters and importers is not the nominal exchange rate, but the real exchange rate—in other words, how much purchasing power they have in the countries under comparison. Let R_r symbolize the real exchange rate, R_n the nominal rate. Since we are interested in the whole economy rather than just one market such as the market for wine, we will use a price index to measure overall prices in the two countries. Price indexes are equivalent to the average price of a basket of goods and services in each economy. Let P stand for the home country price index, and P* represent foreign prices. Then, following the algebra of the wine merchant's calculation,

Real exchange rate

= [(Nominal exchange rate) × (Foreign prices)] / (Domestic prices),

or, more compactly,

$$R_r = R_n(P^*/P).$$

Suppose, for example, that the U.S. dollar–French franc nominal exchange rate is $0.20 per franc and that both price levels are initially set at 100. In this case, the cost of a basket of goods and services is the same in real terms in both countries and

$$R_r = R_n(P^*/P) = R_n(100/100) = R_n.$$

The real rate equals the nominal rate when the purchasing power is the same in both countries. Note that purchasing power parity indicates that this is the long-run equilibrium. Over time, however, if inflation is higher at home than in the foreign country, then P rises more than P^*, and R_r falls, meaning the domestic currency appreciates in real terms.

By way of illustration, suppose that the United States has 10 percent inflation while France has 0 percent. Then, the real U.S.–France exchange rate (in terms of dollars per franc) would be

$$R_r = (\$0.2 \text{ per franc}) \times (100/110) = \$0.1818 \text{ per franc.}$$

Tourists, investors, and business people can still trade dollars and francs at the nominal rate of $0.2 per franc (plus whatever commissions they pay to the seller), but the real purchasing power of the U.S. dollar has risen in France compared to what it buys at home. The real exchange rate of $0.1818 per franc tells us that French goods are now 10 percent cheaper than the U.S. goods that have risen in price. As a result, unless the nominal rate changes, the dollar goes farther in France than at home. In real terms, the franc has depreciated and the dollar has appreciated.

Changes in the value of real exchange rates play an important role in international macroeconomic relations. When countries control the value of their nominal exchange rate, for example, they must be certain that their prices do not change in relation to the prices of their trading partners. If inflation runs higher at home, then the real value of their currency appreciates. Over a period of time, if uncorrected, this can lead to a build-up in the current account deficit as imports increase and exports decrease. In a number of cases, the end result has been a currency crisis and the collapse of the nominal exchange rate. (Some examples are Mexico in December, 1994, and Thailand in July, 1997.)

Alternatives to Flexible Exchange Rates

Exchange rate systems are all modifications of two fundamental categories: fixed and floating (flexible) exchange rate systems. The differences are basic. In a **fixed system exchange rate**, the value of a nation's money is defined in terms of a fixed amount of a commodity such as gold or in terms of a fixed amount of another currency, such as the U.S. dollar. In a **flexible (floating) exchange rate system**, the value of a nation's money is allowed to "float" up and down in response to the market forces described earlier in the chapter. Through the first 70 years of the twentieth century, fixed exchange rates were the norm, often within a framework that defined the value of a country's currency in terms of a fixed amount of gold. After World War II, many nations shifted away from gold and pegged the value of their currencies to the U.S. dollar or to the currency of another country with which they had strong historical ties. For example, a number of former French colonies in sub-Sahara Africa fixed their currencies to the franc. Beginning in the 1970s, the use of fixed exchange rate systems began a swift decline, first in the high-income industrial economies, and then in many developing countries during the 1980s and 1990s. By the end of the twentieth century, flexible exchange rate systems were the norm in every region of the world.

Although the weight of current economic opinion probably favors floating exchange rates, there is widespread recognition that individual country conditions are unique and that there is no single type of exchange rate system appropriate for every country. The analysis of the pros and cons of different systems in the context of individual country conditions is a very active area of research, and no one can say whether the trend toward flexible rates during the last decades is irreversible, or if world economic conditions might not change in ways that encourage countries to return to some form of fixed exchange rate.

Fixed Exchange Rate Systems

Gold standards are a form of fixed exchange rates. Under a pure gold standard, nations keep gold as their international reserve. Gold is used to settle most international obligations and nations must be prepared to trade it for their own currency whenever foreigners attempt to "redeem" the home currency they have earned by selling goods and services. In this sense, the nation's money is backed by gold.

There are essentially three rules that countries must follow in order to maintain a gold exchange standard. First, they must fix the value of their currency unit (the dollar, the pound, the franc, etc.) in terms of gold. This fixes the exchange rate. For example, under the modified gold standard of the **Bretton Woods exchange rate system** that was developed at the end of World War II (1947–1971), the U.S. dollar was fixed at $35 per ounce and the British pound was set at £12.5 per ounce. Since both were fixed in terms of gold, they were implicitly set in terms of each other: $35 = one ounce of gold = £12.5, or 2.80 dollars per pound (2.80 = 35/12.5).

The second rule of the gold standard is that nations keep the supply of their domestic money fixed in some constant proportion to their supply of gold. This requirement is an informal one, but is necessary in order to ensure that the domestic money supply does not grow beyond the capacity of the gold supply to support it. The third rule of a gold standard is that nations must stand ready and willing to provide gold in exchange for their home country currency.

Consider what would happen if a country decided to print large quantities of money for which there is no gold backing. In the short run, purchases of domestically produced goods would rise, causing domestic prices to rise as well. As domestic prices rise, foreign goods become more attractive, since a fixed exchange rate means that they have not increased in price. As imports in the home country increase, foreigners accumulate an unwanted supply of the home country's currency. This is the point at which the gold standard would begin to become unhinged. If gold supplies are low in relation to the supply of domestic currency, at some point, the gold reserves will begin to run out as the country pays out gold in exchange for its currency. This spells crisis and a possible end to the gold standard.

Under a fixed exchange rate system, the national supply and demand for foreign currencies may vary but the nominal exchange rate does not. It is the responsibility of the monetary authorities (i.e., the central bank or treasury department) to keep the exchange rate fixed. Figure 10.7 illustrates the task before a national government when it wishes to keep its currency fixed. Suppose that the United States and United Kingdom are both on the gold standard and the U.S. demand for British pounds increases.

In the short run or medium run, a rise in demand for pounds from D_1 to D_2 is caused by one of the factors listed in Table 10.5: increased U.S. demand for U.K. goods, higher U.K. or lower U.S. interest rates, or speculation that the value of the dollar might not remain fixed for much longer. If R_1 is the fixed U.S.–U.K. exchange rate, then the United States must counter the weakening dollar and prevent the rate from depreciating to R_2. One option is to sell the United States's gold reserves in exchange for dollars. This puts gold in the hands of merchants, investors, or speculators, who are trying to obtain British pounds. The quantity of gold that must be sold is equivalent to the value of the pounds represented by line segment AB. In effect, the United States meets the

---

FIGURE 10.7   Fixed Exchange Rates and Changes in Demand

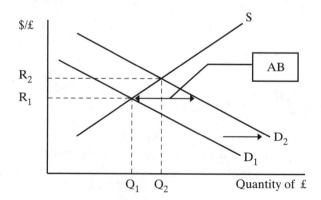

An increase in the demand for British pounds puts pressure on the exchange rate and will cause the dollar to depreciate to R_2 unless the increase in demand is countered by an increase in supply equal to line segment AB.

increased demand for British pounds by supplying international money—gold—to the market through a sale of some of its gold stock. Since gold and pounds are interchangeable, an increase in the supply of gold is equivalent to an increase in the supply of pounds, as shown in Figure 10.8, and the exchange rate stays at R_1.

Under a pure gold standard, countries hold gold as a reserve instead of foreign currencies and sell their gold reserves in exchange for their own currency. This action increases the supply of gold—which is international money—and offsets the pressure on the home currency to depreciate. Actually, there are two possibilities for the home country as it sells its gold reserves. Either the demand for gold is satisfied and the pressure on its currency eases, or it begins to run out of gold. If the latter happens, the home country may be forced into a devaluation that is accomplished by changing the gold price of its currency. As an illustration, if the dollar is fixed at $35 per ounce of gold, a devaluation would shift the price of gold to something more than $35, say $50, and each ounce of gold sold by the United States buys back a greater quantity of dollars.

Pure gold standards have been rare since the 1930s. More commonly, countries have adopted modified gold standards, such as the Bretton Woods system (1947–1971) which is discussed later, or fixed exchange rate systems called **pegged exchange rates**. Pegged exchange rate systems operate similarly to a gold standard except that instead of gold, another currency is used to "anchor" the value of the home currency. Many developing countries have experimented with pegged exchange rates as a means of avoiding fluctuations in the value of their currency against a major world currency such as the dollar.

One potential source of problems with a pegged currency is that the home currency's value is synchronized with its peg, so changes between the peg and

---

FIGURE 10.8   Selling Reserves of Pounds to Counter a Weakening Dollar

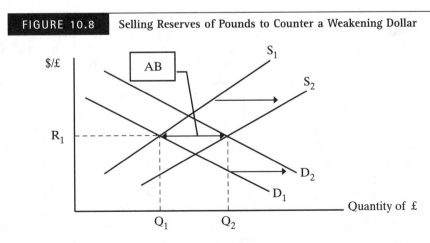

By selling gold equal in value to AB pounds, the United States prevents a depreciation in the dollar–pound exchange rate.

a third-party currency are identical for the home currency and the third party. An example will clarify. Suppose that Thailand decides to peg its currency to the U.S. dollar at the rate of 25 Thai baht per U.S. dollar. The goal of Thailand's central bank must be to supply dollars whenever it is asked to redeem its own baht. If the dollar appreciates against the Japanese yen, then so does the Thai baht, and at the same rate. Appreciation against the Japanese yen may or may not be a problem for Thailand's producers, depending on the importance of the Japan–Thailand trade relationship. In 1997, it turned out to be very important, and declining Thai competitiveness from its appreciating currency played a prominent role in triggering the Asian financial crisis of 1997–1998.

The simplest way to avoid this type of problem is to peg the currency not to one single currency, but to a group of currencies. This is, in fact, closer to Thailand's actual policy in 1997. While this is slightly more complex arithmetically, it reduces the importance of any single country's currency in the determination of the home country's currency value. Typically, countries that adopt this strategy select the currencies of their most important trading partners as elements of the basket.

Pegged exchange rates can work very well under many circumstances, but another factor that can cause them to unravel is a significant difference in inflation rates between the home country and its peg. We saw above that real exchange rates play a greater role in determining trade patterns than nominal rates. Using the United States–Thailand example, and looking at the equation that describes the relationship between real and nominal exchange rates from Thailand's point of view (as the home country),

$$R_r = (25 \text{ baht per dollar}) \times [(\text{U.S. price level})/(\text{Thai price level})]$$
$$= R_n(P^*/P).$$

Relatively high inflation in Thailand appears as a faster rate of change in P, and leads to a real appreciation in the baht. Under these circumstances, Thai producers are less competitive and U.S. producers are more so (in Thailand). If the situation persists, speculators will likely step in and begin to sell bahts in the expectation that the pegged nominal rate of 25 baht per dollar will be devalued to offset the appreciation in the real rate. Moving the nominal peg from 25 to 30 or 40 baht per dollar may be necessary to restore balance.

The most common technique for dealing with this problem is through the adoption of a **crawling peg**. Crawling pegs are fixed—i.e., pegged—exchange rates that are periodically adjusted. The idea is to offset any differences in inflation (changes in P) through regular adjustments in R_n. If correctly handled, the real exchange rate remains constant and the impact of inflation differences never shows up as a change in competitiveness.

There are several other variations on the theme of managed exchange rates. One of the key points to keep in mind is that purely fixed or purely flexible exchange rate arrangements are rare. When a currency is fixed in value, it is still subject to market pressures of supply and demand which, at times, can force governments to alter its value. Similarly, when countries adopt a flexible exchange rate system, there is usually some degree of government intervention in currency markets to try to shape its value. Consequently, many countries that claim to have a flexible exchange rate actually have adopted a **managed float** in which they occasionally sell or buy their currency as they try to nudge the exchange rate up or down.

CASE STUDY

Dollarization and Currency Boards

Dollarization is the term used to describe the adoption of the United States dollar as a country's own currency. In an abstract sense, the term has come to signify the adoption of any currency other than one's own, but for many countries, the universal acceptability of the U.S. dollar has made it the alternative currency of choice. For example, Panama dollarized its economy by pegging its currency to the dollar and then declaring the dollar to be legal tender with its own currency, the cordoba, while Ecuador went one step further in September 2000 and officially adopted the dollar as its currency, as did El Salvador in November 2000. Throughout Latin America, other countries are discussing the Ecuadorean and Salvadorean cases and thinking about using the dollar as the national currency. There is no barrier in international law that prevents countries from adopting the dollar, and about two-thirds of all dollars in circulation are outside the United States. In Latin America, Argentina, Bolivia, Peru, and Uruguay each have a greater quantity of dollar deposits in their financial systems than they have deposits of the domestic currency.

As you might imagine, there is usually a great deal of opposition to giving up so important a symbol of national sovereignty as the nation's money. Still, dollarization has proceeded on an informal basis in many countries. When it is possible to borrow long term in an emerging market, it is often in dollar terms. In Mexico, real estate is usually sold in dollars, and merchants, landlords, and many personal service providers (e.g., electricians, plumbers, etc.) in some parts of Mexico (particularly near the border and in heavy tourist areas) have adopted the dollar as their preferred currency. Considering the long U.S. embargo against Cuba, it is curious to note that Cuba has significantly dollarized its economy and many stores require U.S. dollars.

Argentina's dollarization plan highlights another possibility for exchange rate policy advocated by some economists for countries that have a difficult time controlling inflation. Technically, Argentina is not dollarized, but the effects of its policies are very similar to the adoption of the dollar as its currency unit. In the Argentine case, the peso is pegged to the dollar at approximately a one-to-one ratio. In addition, Argentina has taken the power to create new money (pesos) out of the hands of its central bank and placed it in the hands of a specially created **currency board**. Argentine laws require the currency

(continues)

board to ensure that for every peso added to the money supply, there is a dollar in reserve. Consequently, Argentina has dollarized not through the adoption of the dollar as its currency unit, but rather by limiting the creation of its domestic money, the peso, to the quantity of dollars available to back it. In many respects, it is like a traditional gold standard, where the dollar replaces gold, and there is a strict one-to-one ratio in quantity of dollars and pesos.

Why would a country adopt such stringent rules for its money supply? Argentina's recent history gives ample reasons. Through much of the 1980s, the country suffered from extremely high rates of inflation. Between 1985 and 1990, the lowest rate was achieved in 1986 when inflation hit 82 percent, but by 1989 it had skyrocketed to 4,924 percent.

Argentina tried a number of reforms in the mid-1980s. The most famous, the Austral Plan, included a currency reform in which the Argentine peso was replaced with a new currency called the austral, which used a crawling peg to try to stabilize the real exchange rate. In addition to fixing the exchange rate, the government also fixed the prices of government services, hoping that they would "anchor" prices elsewhere in the economy and prevent them from rising. When economy-wide prices rose anyway, the fixed prices for government services resulted in large budget deficits and the printing of lots of new money to cover the government's bills. The resulting inflation quickly turned into hyperinflation, the condition in which money ceases to have value and barter becomes common. Traffic fines, for example, were denominated in terms of gallons of gasoline, rather than australs.

An added problem was that despite the regular adjustments of the nominal exchange rate, the rate of inflation made it impossible to keep up with the price increases, and the real exchange rate tended to become seriously overvalued. Predictably, the overvalued exchange rate resulted in a growing trade deficit and a looming balance of payments crisis. In 1991, the government of Carlos Menem passed Argentina's Convertibility Law. The law fixed the value of the new currency, now called the peso once again, to the U.S. dollar at the rate of

TABLE 10.6	Inflation in Argentina, 1985–1994			
1985	*1986*	*1987*	*1988*	*1989*
385	82	175	388	4,924
1990	*1991*	*1992*	*1993*	*1994*
2,315	172	25	11	4

Argentina was unable to control its high inflation until it instituted a currency board in 1991.

Source: Inter-American Development Bank; Statistics and Quantitative Analysis Unit; Sebastian Edwards, *Crisis and Reform in Latin America.*

one-to-one. In order to ensure that it stayed fixed, the Convertibility Law states that no new money may be added to the money supply unless the treasury holds an equivalent amount in dollars. The problem of inadequate government revenue and a spiraling budget deficit was addressed through several measures to increase government tax revenues (including the firing of a large number of tax collectors suspected of corruption) and to reduce government expenditures. The Argentine lesson is clear. Dollarization through the use of a currency board and the adoption of strict rules for holding dollar reserves

have enabled it to control some of the worst hyperinflation in recent world history. The success of these policies depended on a number of related reforms, however, in government finance and the financial system.

A key question for research is whether official dollarization might hold an added benefit in the form of faster economic growth. There is conflicting evidence on this point. Some research points to no effect on growth and, perhaps surprisingly, no effect on trade. Other research, however, shows substantial effects. Which research is correct? It is impossible to say at this point.

CHOOSING THE RIGHT EXCHANGE RATE SYSTEM

Given the menu of choices for exchange rate systems, an active area of economic research has focused on the performance characteristics of systems under different economic conditions and institutional arrangements. For many years, economists debated the pros and cons of fixed and flexible rates, but as the variety of exchange rate options has grown, as capital mobility has increased, and as international trade and investment relations have deepened, researchers have become more concerned with understanding how varying degrees of flexibility or fixity might best serve the interests of individual countries. In particular, economists have tried to learn how different exchange rate systems might influence the core elements of a country's macroeconomy such as the rate of economic growth, the rate of inflation, and the frequency of currency crises.

Traditional views held that countries with fixed exchange rate systems were better at controlling inflation, but that they paid a price in the form of slower economic growth. The reasoning behind this view was that in order to maintain a fixed rate, governments have to be very careful about issuing new money. Since most of the episodes of hyperinflation during the second half of the twentieth century resulted from overexpanding the money supply, it seems reasonable that an exchange rate policy that limits the supply of money would also help avoid inflation. However, in the view of some economists, the limits placed on the ability of a country to manipulate its money supply also remove an important tool that governments use to help manage the rate of economic growth. Therefore, the tradeoff was lower growth for lower inflation.

More recent research, particularly with data from the 1990s, has failed to demonstrate a strong relationship between the type of exchange rate system and either inflation or economic growth. Prior to the 1990s, countries with fixed or pegged exchange rates tended to have lower rates of inflation, but during the 1990s their advantages on the inflation front diminished substantially. Similarly, there is evidence that countries with more flexible rates tend to have higher average rates of economic growth, but this result depends on the classification of the fastest growing Asian economies. Technically, many of these countries have flexible exchange rates, but at the same time they manage them very closely. When they are omitted from the analysis, there is no significant difference in the rate of growth between countries with relatively fixed and relatively flexible rates. And finally, neither fixed nor flexible rates seem to offer superior protection against a currency crisis. As a result, no particular system seems to rank above any other in its ability to provide superior macroeconomic performance.

Insofar as economists have been able to devise a set of rules for selecting an exchange rate system, they are very general and very basic. If the goal is to find the system that helps minimize negative shocks to an economy, then the source of the shock determines whether a more flexible or more fixed system should be adopted. When the shocks originate in the monetary sector—for example, a central bank that goes overboard in printing new money—a fixed rate is better, and Argentina is a good example. On the other hand, if the shocks to an economy originate in the external environment—for example, a sudden change in the price of imported oil—then relatively more flexibility in the exchange rate enables the country to adapt to the changes more easily. The general argument here is that individual country characteristics matter a great deal. The problem with these rules, however, is that the source of the shocks to an economy are likely to vary from episode to episode and, as a consequence, the basic rules outlined above provide less practical guidance than desired.

One interpretation of these two rules is that smaller economies that are open to the world economy will do better with more flexible exchange rates. Flexibility will help to minimize the potentially negative effects of shocks that originate in the world economy by allowing changes in the exchange rate to absorb some of the shock and to act as a buffer between the domestic economy and the rest of the world. Given that the actual trend for many small, open, developing economies has been toward greater use of flexible exchange rate systems, theory and practice seem to confirm each other.

On the other hand, exchange rate pegs are still popular, particularly with many developing countries. There are a couple of reasons for this. First, all economists agree that one of the most important elements of an exchange rate system is its credibility. That is, no matter what type of exchange rate is adopted, a successful system must generate confidence and the widespread belief that it is sustainable. Exchange rate systems that lack credibility are guaranteed to fail in their basic job of providing a smooth and reliable conversion between domestic and foreign money. Under some conditions, exchange rate pegs may offer greater credibility. One of the conditions, and the second reason why some countries continue to peg their currencies, is a relatively high degree of trade dependence on a single, major, economy. Consider the case of Mexico, with about 80 percent of its trade with the United States. Given its trade dependence on the United States, Mexico pegged its peso to the U.S. dollar for many years. Because Mexican inflation ran higher than the U.S. rate, a crawling peg was favored as the means of keeping the real exchange rate relatively constant. The purpose of the dollar peg was to provide benefits to Mexican businesses and consumers by eliminating some of the price variation in Mexican imports and exports. The rule seems to be that when a country is closely tied to the economy of a large, industrial country such as the United States, pegging to its currency may provide additional stability and help businesses to plan their futures with greater confidence.

This view is shared by many, but at the same time it is widely accepted that, in Mexico's case at least, the use of a flexible exchange rate has served it better than the pegged rates it used before 1994. The reason for the discrepancy between what might work in theory and what has worked in practice highlights the complexity of choosing an exchange rate system when every country has unique economic factors and its own set of institutions shaping its economic outcomes. In Mexico's case, due to a set of agreements between the business sector, organized labor, and government, it was unable to make the periodic adjustments to its nominal exchange rate that are required with a crawling peg. In effect, Mexico's institutional inability to adjust its nominal exchange rate undermined the credibility of the exchange rate system. The lack of credibility led to periodic bouts of speculation against the peso whenever it was perceived to be overvalued and vulnerable. Several of these speculative bouts were followed by a peso collapse and economic recession. The lesson, in the end, seems to be that the first criterion for choosing an exchange rate system is that it must have credibility in currency and financial markets.

CASE STUDY

The End of the Bretton Woods System

The Bretton Woods system of exchange rates was enacted at the end of World War II. It included most nations outside the former Soviet Union and its allies. The exchange rate system was a major component of the institutions that were designed to manage international economic conflict and to support international economic cooperation. In addition to the exchange rate system, the other institutions that were created at the same time included the International Monetary Fund (IMF), the International Bank for Reconstruction and

(continues)

Development (IBRD) or World Bank, and the General Agreement on Tariffs and Trade (GATT). (See Chapter 2.)

Each institution had its own role in the management of world economic affairs. The roles of the exchange rate were to provide stability by eliminating excess currency fluctuations, to prevent nations from using exchange rate devaluations as a tactic for gaining markets for their goods, and to ensure that there was an adequate supply of internationally accepted reserves so that nations could meet their international obligations.

In the Bretton Woods exchange rate system, the dollar was fixed to gold at the rate of $1 equalling 1/35 of an ounce of gold, or $35 per ounce. Every other currency within the system was fixed to the dollar and, therefore, indirectly to gold. Unlike a pure gold standard, however, countries could use U.S. dollars as their international reserve and did not have to accumulate gold or tie their money supply to their gold reserves.

The Bretton Woods exchange rate system had one fatal flaw—the dollar. The United States was in a privileged position since its currency was treated the same as gold. This meant that the United States could simply increase its money supply (the supply of dollars) and gain increased purchasing power over European, Japanese, and other countries' goods. Other nations preferred the United States to maintain a relatively robust supply of dollars, since this insured that there was an adequate supply of international reserves for the world economy.

Problems with this arrangement began when the U.S. economy expanded at a different rate than the economies of its trading partners. In the mid-to-late 1960s, the United States deepened its involvement in the Vietnam War while it simultaneously created the "War on Poverty" at home. Both policies generated large fiscal expenditures that stimulated the economy. While U.S. expansion raced ahead of expansion elsewhere, Europeans found themselves accumulating dollars more rapidly than they desired. The dollars were a by-product of U.S. economic expansion and partially reflected the price increases that were accompanying the expansion.

Under a different type of exchange rate system, it would have been appropriate for the United States to devalue its currency. U.S. prices had risen relative to foreign prices, the real exchange rate had appreciated as a consequence, and trade deficits were beginning to become a permanent feature of the U.S. economy.

One policy would have been to devalue the nominal dollar exchange rate, but this was not an option. Since every currency was tied to the dollar, there was no way for the United States to selectively devalue against a group of other currencies. An alternative was for the United States to devalue against all currencies by changing the gold value of the dollar. By the late 1960s, it was becoming apparent that this would be necessary.

Persistent U.S. deficits had led to an accumulation of dollars outside the United States which greatly exceeded the United States's supply of gold. In other words, the United States lacked the gold reserves to back all of the dollars that were in circulation. Official recognition of this fact led to the **Smithsonian Agreement** of December, 1971, in which the major industrialized countries agreed to devalue the gold content of the dollar by around 8 percent, from

$35 per ounce to $38.02. In addition, Japan, Germany, and other trade surplus countries increased the value of their currencies.

Although the Smithsonian Agreement was hailed by President Nixon as a fundamental reorganization of international monetary affairs, it quickly proved to be too little and of only temporary benefit. The gold value of the dollar was realigned again in early 1973, from $38.02 to $42.22. In addition, further devaluation occurred against other European currencies. The end of the system came in March, 1973, when the major currencies began to float against each other. A few currencies, such as the British pound, had begun to float earlier.

In each case, the strategy of allowing the exchange rate to float in response to supply and demand conditions was adopted as a means of coping with speculation. When speculators had perceived that the dollar was overvalued at $38 per ounce or $42 per ounce, they sold dollars in anticipation of a future devaluation. Nor was the dollar the only currency speculated against. Other weak currencies such as the pound and the Italian lira had also been correctly perceived as overvalued and had been sold off by speculators. In the end, the central banks of the weak-currency countries found it impossible to support an unrealistically high value of their currency. The costs of buying up the excess supply of their currencies at overvalued prices proved to be too great. The simplest solution was to let the currencies float.

SINGLE CURRENCY AREAS

On January 1, 1999, eleven of the fifteen members of the European Union adopted a new currency, the euro. Shortly thereafter, a twelfth member joined the euro group. Initially, the use of the euro was limited to government bonds and other financial instruments, and it served mainly as an accounting unit. By 2002, euro coins and paper money will be circulated, and shortly thereafter, the francs, marks, and pesetas of the twelve will be withdrawn from circulation. It has taken a while for the EU-12 to arrive at this point. The adoption of a single currency has been under serious consideration since at least the 1970s, and the official agreements between the member states have been in place since the early 1990s. Given that one of the strongest symbols of national independence is a nation's money, the thirty years it has taken to arrive at the point where the citizens and policymakers of the European Union are willing to give up their centuries-old forms of money may not seem so long.

The EU's experience with the euro is examined in more detail in Chapter 14, but any discussion of single currency areas has to recognize that it has excited the imagination of people all over the world. Researchers have begun to analyze other regions to see if they are suitable areas for the use of a single currency, and within the EU itself, there has been a huge amount of discussion of the single currency. The starting point for the economic analysis of the pros and cons of adopting a single currency is the work by the Nobel Prize–

winning economist Robert Mundell, whose work on the theory of **optimal currency areas** developed the criteria used to determine if two or more countries would be economically better off sharing a currency rather than maintaining their own national moneys.

There are at least four potential reasons why a group of countries might want to share a common money. First, a single currency eliminates the need to convert each other's money and thereby reduces transaction costs in a number of ways. It eliminates the fees paid to banks or to the currency brokers that arrange the conversion, it simplifies accounting and bookkeeping, and it enables consumers and investors to more accurately compare prices across international boundaries. Each of these advantages provide some gain in efficiency and a reduction in business costs. Second, a single currency eliminates price fluctuations that are caused by changes in the exchange rate. When speculators move their money into or out of a country, or when temporary interest rate changes in one country alter the supply and demand for foreign exchange, one country may become (temporarily) cheaper or more expensive for business. As a result, business decisions may reflect temporary shifts in currency values rather than underlying issues of economic efficiency. The elimination of misleading price signals that result from exchange rate fluctuations is also a potential gain in efficiency.

Third, the elimination of exchange rates through the adoption of a single currency can help increase political trust between countries seeking to increase their integration. A single currency removes some of the friction between integrating nations by eliminating the problems that are caused by exchange rate misalignments. An example may help clarify this point. On the EU's way to a single currency, it experienced a speculative episode that was directed against the British pound and the French franc, among other currencies. After some initial attempts to fend off the speculation against the pound, Britain let it depreciate. France, on the other hand, raised its interest rates in order to increase the demand for the franc. As a result, the pound was suddenly, significantly, depreciated against the franc. European businesses in France and elsewhere noted this development and moved several factories from the continent to England and Scotland. As you can imagine, this did not sit well with politicians in France and Holland (which also lost jobs to Britain). This episode illustrates the benefits of eliminating exchange rate misalignments, or sudden dramatic changes in exchange rates. For most pairs of countries, this is not an important issue, but for members of a regional trade alliance, particularly one that is seeking deeper levels of integration than simply free trade, it can be a very important political benefit from a single currency.

Fourth, and finally, for some developing countries, the adoption of a common currency may give their exchange rate system greater credibility. This is particularly applicable if the common currency is the dollar or the euro or some other widely traded currency. Use of such a currency can reduce exchange rate fluctuations and create greater confidence in the financial system of the adopting country, possibly leading to lower interest rates and an increased availability of credit, although this depends on the overall soundness of the financial system.

Nations that give up their national money do not do so without cost. In addition to its political symbolism, the adoption of a common currency also means that the country no longer has its own money supply as a tool for managing its economic growth. The topic of monetary policy is taken up in more detail in Chapter 11, but the basic point is easy to grasp. Countries with their own currency can influence the rate of growth of the economy in the short run (but not in the long run) through a change in the supply of money. While these policies are somewhat controversial, most countries use changes in the money supply to counteract an economic slowdown. When a country adopts a common currency with one or more other countries, it gives up this tool. After the introduction of the common currency, there is only one money supply and, consequently, one rate of growth of the money supply. New York, for example, shares a common currency with California and, as a consequence, both states experience the same changes in the money supply. If New York is growing fast and California is growing slowly, it would be impossible for the Federal Reserve to alter the money supply in a way that would speed up growth in California and slow it down in New York. With a single currency, there is a "one-size-fits-all" monetary policy.

Conditions for Adopting a Single Currency

Economic analysis offers four conditions for determining if the gains from a single currency will outweigh the costs of giving up a national money. None of these conditions is absolute, and if one is not met, it may be compensated for in one of the other three. Ultimately, the desirability of a single currency is not subject to hard and fast rules and it is a judgment call for the economists, politicians, and citizens of the affected nations.

The first criterion relates to the cost just noted. If countries have relatively similar economic experiences; they tend to enter expansions and recessions at more or less similar points in time then a one-size-fits-all policy for expanding or contracting the money supply will be appropriate for all members of the currency area. In this case, there is little or no cost associated with the loss of the national money as a tool to expand or contract the national economy. The multi-country currency area requires the same expansion or contraction in its money supply as the individual countries, and there is no conflict between the currency area and individual national needs. In fact, however, few countries are that well synchronized in their business cycles. Even the states of the United States enter and leave recessions at different points in time, and the national figures on growth only reflect an average across all fifty states.

The second condition is a high degree of labor and capital mobility between the member countries. This allows workers and capital to leave countries or regions where work is scarce and to join the supply of labor and capital in booming regions. In effect, free migration of the factors of production smooths out some of the differences in the business cycle by taking unemployed inputs and moving them to where they are needed. This is how the fifty states of the United States compensate for a lack of complete synchronization in the business cycles of individual states. When conditions are bad in one region, workers and investors move their labor and capital to another region, freeing inputs from areas where they are not needed and providing them to areas where they are.

While capital tends to be relatively mobile, labor is less so, even within countries. Therefore, a third condition is that there are regional policies capable of addressing the imbalances that may develop. Depressed areas may remain depressed if people cannot move or choose not to because the psychological or other costs are too high. Insofar as the economics of regional policies are concerned, they may be determined at any level, from the currency area (multi-country) to individual nation-states, to subnational units (provinces or cities). The key point is not the agency responsible, but that there are effective policies for assisting regions that may not be synchronized with the majority of the currency area's economy.

Finally, the first three conditions point to the fourth: The nations involved must be seeking a level of integration that goes beyond simple free trade. Free trade requires that nations remove their tariffs, quotas, and other border barriers that inhibit the flow of goods. If this is the goal, a common currency is unnecessary. If something much deeper is sought, however, such as a greater harmonization of national economies and much closer economic and political ties, then a single currency can be helpful, provided the other three conditions are observed. This condition is admittedly ambiguous and is part of the reason why policymakers do not always agree in their analysis. It is somewhat circular reasoning, but true nevertheless, that the desirability of a single currency partly depends on the goals of the countries involved.

CASE STUDY

Is the NAFTA Region an Optimal Currency Area?

The European Union is one model for the creation of a single currency. In the EU model, an entirely new currency is created and each joining country gives up its national money. The discussion of a single currency in the NAFTA countries has favored a different model. So far at least, discussion has centered on the adoption of the U.S. dollar by all three countries instead of the creation of an entirely new currency. Either model leads to the same outcome: a single currency area.

Is the discussion realistic? That is, are the proponents of a single currency dreaming or is there something to be gained in such a move? Whether a single currency for the NAFTA region will be created in the near future or not, its proponents are very serious. Even before taking office in 2000, Mexico's President Vicente Fox began talking about the possibility of more integration among Canada, Mexico, and the United States, including the opening of international borders to a freer movement of workers and wider use of the dollar. In 1999, Senator Mack from Florida introduced into the U.S. Senate the International Monetary Stabilization Act to encourage other countries to adopt the U.S. dollar, and corporate heads in Mexico continue to press the Mexican government on the issue. While interest in a single currency for the NAFTA region has waxed and waned, it is likely that over the long term it will continue to increase. Indeed, there is a great deal of interest throughout Latin America in the pros and cons of adopting the dollar.

It is clear that whatever the long-run advantages or disadvantages of a single currency might be, there is a long way to go before the NAFTA countries meet the four conditions necessary for a single currency area to be an optimal policy. First, the business cycles of the three countries are not very similar. While Canadian and American cycles are somewhat more synchronized, cycles of recession and expansion in Mexico are very different. In part, this is due to the fact that Mexico is a developing country, and changes in the world economy that create shocks for its economy are different than the factors that influence the United States. Second, given the current legal restrictions on labor mobility, there is little scope for overcoming the lack of synchronization with labor flows. Third, there are no regional policies within the NAFTA framework as there

are within the European Union. In the EU, national governments tax themselves to create a regional fund that is used to provide assistance to areas that lag in economic growth. This is useful for overcoming regional imbalances and removes some of the sting that a region might feel if the EU's other policies are not supportive. And finally, NAFTA was originally conceived as a means to reduce border barriers. While its ultimate goal will surely evolve over time, at present there does not appear to be a consensus that it should be something more than a free-trade area.

As it is presently constituted, the NAFTA region is clearly not an optimal currency area. Nevertheless, it is a safe bet that dollarization will continue to be explored, particularly in Mexico. In part, this is because there are counterarguments to each of the above objections: a single currency will help synchronize the three economies; it is possible to formulate an agreement that allows a guest worker program such as the United States and Mexico had in the 1940s, 1950s, and 1960s; regional policies are simply a matter of political will and financial means, but they would not require huge expenditures; and closer integration of the NAFTA partners is inevitable. The counterarguments are, in turn, debatable, but a second reason why discussion will continue is that there are potentially significant gains for Mexico.

It is inevitable that if Mexico dollarized, its economy would become more tied to the United States. In the view of some economists, this would have a number of positive effects, including a dramatic increase in trade, lower interest rates, more credit for small and medium-sized firms, and less inflation. If

(continues)

this is correct, then dollarization could significantly enhance Mexico's rate of growth. No one can say for certain at this point in time whether this analysis is correct. It is a tantalizing prospect, however, and is therefore guaranteed to generate further discussion.

Summary

- People hold foreign currency in order to buy goods and services, to take advantage of interest rate differentials, and to speculate. The primary institutions in the exchange-rate market are commercial banks and foreign exchange brokers.

- Exchange rates can be analyzed with supply and demand analysis, as if they are just another commodity in the economy. Increases (decreases) in the supply of foreign exchange cause the domestic currency to appreciate (depreciate). Increases (decreases) in the demand for foreign exchange cause the domestic currency to depreciate (appreciate).

- Exchange rates are unpredictable, because they are simultaneously influenced by long-run, medium-run, and short-run factors. In the long run, purchasing power parity is important. In the medium run, the business cycle is important, and in the short run, interest-rate differentials and speculation are important.

- The interest parity condition says that the interest rate differential between two countries is approximately equal to the percentage difference between the forward and spot exchange rates.

- Firms use forward exchange rate markets to protect against exchange rate risk.

- Real exchange rates are equal to nominal or market exchange rates adjusted for inflation. They give a better picture of the purchasing power of a nation's currency.

- Fixed exchange rate systems were thought to help limit the growth of inflation, but there is little evidence of this over the last two decades. Fixed exchange rates eliminate the ability of governments to use monetary policies to regulate the macroeconomy.

- Flexible exchange rate systems were thought to help increase growth, but there is little evidence of this over the last two decades. Flexible exchange rates free a nation's macroeconomic polices from the need to maintain a fixed exchange rate.

- All exchange rate systems are on a continuum between fixed and flexible rates. Pegged exchange rates, crawling pegs, and a managed float are examples of intermediary-type systems. The most important rule for countries is that their exchange rate system is credible.

■ Optimal currency areas are geographical regions within which it is optimal for countries to adopt the same currency. The criteria for an optimal currency area are a synchronized business cycle, complete factor mobility, regional programs for lagging areas, and a desire to achieve a higher level of economic and political integration.

Vocabulary

appreciation

Bretton Woods exchange rate system

covered interest arbitrage

crawling peg

currency board

depreciation

dollarization

exchange rate

exchange rate risk

fixed exchange rate

flexible (floating) exchange rate

forward exchange rate

forward market

gold standard

hedging

interest rate arbitrage

interest parity

managed float

nominal exchange rate

optimal currency area

pegged exchange rate

purchasing power parity

real exchange rate

Smithsonian Agreement

spot market

Study Questions

1. Draw a graph of the supply of and demand for the Canadian dollar by the U.S. market. Diagram the effect of each of the following on the exchange rate, state in words whether the effect is long, medium, or short run, and explain your reasoning

   a) More rapid growth in Canada than in the United States.
   b) A rise in U.S. interest rates.
   c) Goods are more expensive in Canada than in the United States.
   d) A recession in the United States
   e) Expectations of a future depreciation in the Canadian dollar.

2. Suppose the U.S. dollar–French franc exchange rate is 0.17 dollars per franc, and the U.S. dollar–German mark rate is 0.58 dollars per mark. What is the franc–mark rate?

3. Suppose the dollar–yen exchange rate is 0.01 dollars per yen. Since the base year, inflation has been 2 percent in Japan and 10 percent in the United States. What is the real exchange rate? In real terms, has the dollar appreciated or depreciated against the yen?

4. Which of the three motives for holding foreign exchange are applicable to each of the following?

    a) A tourist.
    b) A bond trader.
    c) A portfolio manager.
    d) A manufacturer.

5. If a visitor to Mexico from the United States can buy more goods in Mexico than they can in the United States when they convert their dollars to pesos, is the dollar undervalued or overvalued? Explain.

6. In a fixed exchange rate system, how do countries address the problem of currency market pressures that threaten to lower or raise the value of their currency?

7. In the debate on fixed versus floating exchange rates, the strongest argument for a floating rate is that it frees macroeconomic policy from taking care of the exchange rate. This is also the weakest argument. Explain.

8. Brazil, Argentina, Paraguay, and Uruguay are members of MERCOSÚR, a regional trade area that is trying to become a common market. What issues should they consider before they accept or reject a common currency?

9. Suppose that U.S. interest rates are 4 percent more than rates in the European Union.

    a) Would you expect the dollar to appreciate or depreciate against the euro, and by how much?
    b) If, contrary to your expectations, the forward and spot rates are the same, in which direction would you expect financial capital to flow? Why?

10. Why do some economists claim that the most important feature of any exchange rate system is its credibility?

APPENDIX: THE INTEREST RATE PARITY CONDITION

The following variables are defined the same as in this chapter:

   i = home country interest rate,
   i^* = foreign interest rate,
   R = the nominal exchange rate in units of home country currency per unit of foreign currency,
   F = the forward exchange rate, and
   the forward rate and the interest rates have the same term to maturity.

An investor has a choice between i and i^*. Letting the dollar be the home currency, \$1 invested today will return $\$1(1 + i)$ next period if invested at home. To make the comparison with a foreign investment, the dollar first has to be converted into the foreign currency, then invested, and the earnings must be converted back into dollars. The equivalent of \$1 in foreign currency is $1/R$. If $1/R$ is invested abroad, at the end of next period it returns $(1/R)(1 + i^*)$, which is in units of foreign currency. The reconversion to dollars can be done in the forward market where the exchange rate for a forward contract is F. Therefore, in dollars, $1 invested abroad will return $(1/R)(1 + i^*)F$ next period.

The interest parity condition states that investors will be indifferent between home and foreign investments (of similar risk), implying that they will move their funds around and cause interest rates and exchange rates to change until the returns are the same in the two cases:

$$1 + i = (1/R)(1 + i^*)F = (1 + i^*)(F/R).$$

Divide by $(1 + i^*)$:

$$(1 + i)/(1 + i^*) = F/R.$$

Subtract 1 from both sides:

$$[(1 + i)/(1 + i^*)] - [(1 + i^*)/(1 + i^*)] = F/R - R/R,$$
$$[(1 + i) - (1 + i^*)]/[(1 + i^*)] = (F - R)/R,$$
$$(i - i^*)/(1 + i^*) = (F - R)/R.$$

The left-hand side denominator is close to 1 for small values of i^* (this is why we state the interest parity condition as an approximation). The right-hand side is the percentage difference between the forward and spot rates. If it is negative, markets expect an appreciation in the home currency. Rewriting the last equation:

$$i - i^* \approx (F - R)/R.$$

In words, this says that the difference between home country and foreign interest rates is approximately equal to the expected depreciation in the home country currency.

Chapter 11

AN INTRODUCTION TO OPEN ECONOMY MACROECONOMICS

INTRODUCTION

The last two chapters introduced the concepts of the balance of payments and the exchange rate. In this chapter we look more closely at their relationship to each other and to the overall national economy. After a brief review of a few key macroeconomic concepts, the chapter focuses on the interactions among the current account, exchange rates, and key components of the macroeconomy—consumption, investment, and government spending. National governments are important to this chapter since they rarely take a passive role in the economy. Indeed, since the worldwide Great Depression of the 1930s, and especially since the end of World War II, national governments have shouldered a significant share of the responsibility for keeping the growth of the economy on track, the unemployment rate low, and prices stable. Whether this role for government is desirable or not, and whether they have succeeded or not, most people expect their government to do something during a recession. A major focus of this chapter, then, is the impact of macroeconomic policies on the exchange rate and current account.

While the impacts of activist macroeconomic policies are one focus of this chapter, it is also important to recognize that these are not the only links between a nation's macroeconomy and the rest of the world. Governments usually control a significant share of the national product and as a consequence, their normal, day-to-day operating decisions affect exchange rates and the current account. In addition, the same is true for consumers and businesses. In most economies, expenditures on consumption goods and services make up the largest single component of the macroeconomy, and as we have already seen, an increase in economic growth causes consumers to draw in a greater quantity of imports, increasing the demand for foreign exchange and pushing the current account toward the deficit side.

THE CIRCULAR FLOW OF EXPENDITURE AND INCOME

Table 11.1 shows the four main economic agents in the macroeconomy: households, businesses, government, and foreigners. In our simplified model of the macroeconomy, households supply all the factors of production (land, labor, and capital) that businesses need to produce the nation's output. In return, the revenue that businesses earn when they sell their goods is used to pay for the factors supplied by households. Accordingly, all of the income generated in the economy accrues to households since they supply all of the factor inputs. In effect, the income received by households is equivalent to the value of the output produced by businesses. This is a fundamental identity in the macroeconomy: The income for the economy as a whole equals the value of its output.

When we track income and output, it is important to understand the position of **intermediate inputs**—goods purchased by one business from another to use in production. For example, a car manufacturer hires not only labor, land, and capital (for which it pays wages and salaries, rents, interest, and dividends) but it also purchases glass, tires, steel, and so forth. The payment for auto glass is not directly income to households because it is paid to another business, but if we trace it back, it ultimately becomes income. For example, the glass manufacturer receives payment from the car company and it uses the payment to pay wages, rent, interest, and dividends, as well as its suppliers. We can keep following the flow of payments, through the suppliers to the glass firms, or more simply, we can recognize that all of the payments are incorporated into the value of the car. That is, the purchase price of the car ultimately generates an equivalent amount of income. As a result, the fundamental identity holds between income and output.

TABLE 11.1	The Main Economic Agents in the Macroeconomy

Agent	Function
Households	1. Supply factors (land, labor, capital) to business.
	2. Purchase consumer goods and services.
	3. Save.
	4. Pay taxes.
Businesses	1. Use the factors supplied by households to produce the nation's output.
	2. Purchase investment goods.
Government	1. Purchase government goods and services.
	2. Collect taxes.
Foreigners	1. Purchase exports.
	2. Supply imports.

There are four main agents in the macroeconomy. Each one is a different source of demand for goods and services.

The relationship between income and output is conveniently summarized in the **circular flow** diagram shown in Figure 11.1. Households use the income generated in the economy to purchase consumer goods and services, to save, and to pay taxes. In this simplified model, savings passes through financial institutions (specialized businesses that act as intermediaries between savers and borrowers) where it is available to businesses seeking loans. The borrowed money is used to purchase investment goods and services. In the real world, most businesses finance their investment goods with what are called **retained earnings**. These are profits that are not paid out to the stockholders (households) that own the business, but are kept and used as an internal source of financing. Conceptually, firms with retained earnings borrow from themselves rather than a bank or other financial institution. In either case, the funds are used to purchase investment goods, which are the machinery and structures that businesses use to produce more goods and services. This is an important point and the key distinction between consumption, savings, and investment. Since economists use these words slightly differently than their everyday usage, it is worth spending a moment clarifying the meaning of each.

Savings is income that is not consumed. In the real economy, households (hopefully) put their savings to work by putting it into a bank or the stock market or some other financial institution. Since household savings do not directly increase the ability of the economy to produce goods and services, these acts of personal financial investment are not considered economic investments. Economic investment is done by businesses and, again, only includes the purchase of goods and services that increase the ability of the economy to make goods and services, such as machinery for a factory or an office building where business services can be produced. Consumption goods, on the other hand, are consumed, as the name implies, and are not used to produce more goods and services. There are many fine points to these definitions, but the basic distinction between savings, investment, and consumption is robust and leads to the situation depicted in Figure 11.1, where households and businesses are each responsible for purchasing a different component of the national output.

Following the flow of demand, consumption demand and investment demand are supplemented by the demand for exports that originates in the foreign sector. In addition, since some of the purchases made by consumers and businesses (and government) are not produced at home, but are imported from abroad, we subtract the value of imports, which is a necessary step in the determination of the value of the nation's output.

The final component of demand in the circular flow model is the purchase of goods and services by governments. Note that government demand in Figure 11.1 is not the same as total government expenditure since government also spends money on transfers that are not directly counted in total production. Transfers are a rearrangement of output (taxing one group to give to another) and not an increase in the overall demand for goods and services.

FIGURE 11.1   The Circular Flow

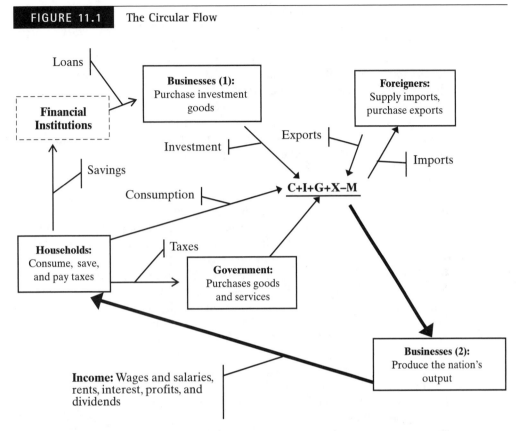

Total output is composed of consumer goods (C), investment goods (I), government goods and services (G), and exports (X), minus imports (M).

The top half of Figure 11.1 is the flow of demands for goods and services in the economy. Demand leads to the production of the nation's output by businesses, and the payment of incomes that are in the form of wages and salaries, rents, interest, dividends, and profits. These are shown with the arrow across the bottom of the diagram.

FISCAL AND MONETARY POLICIES

Macroeconomic policies generally fall into one of two categories, **fiscal policy** or **monetary policy**. Fiscal policy includes government taxation and expenditures, while monetary policy covers the money supply and interest rates. The institutions that enact fiscal and monetary policy vary across countries, but generally, the legislative and executive branches are responsible for tax policy and for determining spending priorities, while the central bank and the finance ministry set monetary policy, often with direct input from the executive branch of the national government. Recently, there has been a trend toward granting central banks complete independence in setting monetary policy, as has historically been the case in a number of countries, such as the United States. Generally, it is agreed that independent central banks are better at keeping inflation low and are more likely to make decisions for economic rather than political reasons. This is an important point that will come up again in the discussion of international financial crises in the next chapter.

Fiscal Policy

As defined above, fiscal policy covers government expenditure and taxation policies. Figure 11.1 is useful for conceptualizing the impacts on the macroeconomy of changes in fiscal policy, including the indirect effects on the other components of the macroeconomy. In Figure 11.1, government expenditures on goods and services constitutes one of the major demand components in the economy. All else equal, as businesses experience an increase in the demand for their products, they increase production, which, in turn, leads directly to an increase in household incomes. This happens because more people are employed to produce the additional goods, and many of those already employed work additional hours.

A decrease in taxes has a similar effect. Disposable household income—what is available to save or spend—increases because fewer taxes are taken out of paychecks. Note that in both this case and the case of an increase in government spending, we are assuming that nothing else changes. For example, there is no assumption that government budgets are balanced. Increases in spending are not offset by tax increases, and cuts in taxes are not countered by cuts in spending.

The increase in household income resulting from an increase in government spending or a cut in taxes is not the end of the story. Changes in household income have a feedback effect on production, as we see in Figure 11.1. One of the primary determinants of the quantity of consumer goods and services that households purchase is the level of after-tax household income. If after-tax income increases, more goods and services are demanded, and if it decreases, fewer goods and services are demanded. Therefore, when government expenditure or tax policies increase household income, the demand for consumer goods rises and businesses increase production. This, in turn, raises incomes again, and there is a second round effect, followed by a third round, a fourth round, and so forth.

Let Y stand for income, T for taxes, and C and G for consumption and government spending. Then the causal flow is as follows:

Increased government spending: $G\uparrow \Rightarrow Y\uparrow \Rightarrow C\uparrow \Rightarrow Y\uparrow \Rightarrow C\uparrow \ldots;$
Decreased taxation: $T\downarrow \Rightarrow Y\uparrow \Rightarrow C\uparrow \Rightarrow Y\uparrow \Rightarrow C\uparrow \ldots.$

Looking at the flow diagrams, it appears that an initial change such as the increase in government spending or the decrease in taxes starts a set of effects that go on forever ($C\uparrow \Rightarrow Y\uparrow \Rightarrow C\uparrow\ldots$). In fact, however, the effects slowly dissipate as each additional change in consumption and income is smaller than the previous one. There are several reasons for this, three of which can be spotted in Figure 11.1. First, some of the increase in income will be lost through taxation. Second, some is saved and does not result in an increase in consumer demand. And third, some of the increase in consumption will be an additional demand for imported goods that are made abroad. Therefore, income taxes, savings, and imports make up three important leakages out of the economy, and each reduces the impact of rising household income on the additional demand for consumer goods and services.

Even though each move around the circular flow ($C\uparrow \Rightarrow Y\uparrow \Rightarrow C\uparrow\ldots$), from demand to income and back to demand, is smaller than the previous one, after all of the impacts on production are added up, it usually turns out that an initial increase in demand ultimately results in an even larger total increase in production and income after the effects work through the economy. Economists call this the **multiplier effect** of an increase in demand. Cutting taxes also has a multiplier effect since, dollar for dollar, a cut in taxes leads to a larger (multiple) effect on total income than the dollar amount of the tax cut.

So far, we have looked at increases in government spending and cuts in taxes. Both of these expand total output; hence, they are collectively referred to as **expansionary fiscal policy**. The opposite of expansionary fiscal policy is called **contractionary fiscal policy** and it includes policies designed to shrink, or contract, the economy. These are cuts in government spending and increases in taxes. Contractionary policy is symmetrical with expansionary policy, so that in the same way that tax cuts and increased government spending boost household income and have a positive multiplier effect on total output, tax increases and decreases in government spending reduce household income and have a negative multiplier effect on total output.

Causality in the contractionary fiscal policy case works as follows:

Decreased government spending: $G\downarrow \Rightarrow Y\downarrow \Rightarrow C\downarrow \Rightarrow Y\downarrow \Rightarrow C\downarrow \ldots$;

Increased taxation: $T\uparrow \Rightarrow Y\downarrow \Rightarrow C\downarrow \Rightarrow Y\downarrow \Rightarrow C\downarrow \ldots$.

For many macroeconomists of the 1940s and 1950s, the discovery of the multiplier effect was like finding the holy grail of macroeconomics. It seemed to offer a technique for managing the economy and, most importantly, for avoiding disasters such as the Great Depression of the 1930s. Needless to say, most economists today are much more cautious about the use of fiscal policy. The reasons are not hard to understand. First, expansionary policies tend to cause inflation, which offsets some of the increased consumer spending by absorbing it into higher prices instead of higher output. Second, there is a substantial margin of error in the estimation of the size of the multiplier. Does a $50 billion tax cut lead to a $50 billion, $75 billion, or $100 billion increase in income? Third, the use of fiscal policy is complicated by its variation in effects stemming from the different possibilities for financing an expansionary policy. If governments accommodate the expansionary fiscal policy with an expansion of the money supply, the multiplier is larger than if there is no accommodation. Taken together, the three technical problems of inflation, the margin for error in measuring the multiplier, and variation in the multiplier's size depending on the means of paying for the expansion make it difficult to use fiscal policy in a precise way.

But this is not all. In addition, the politics of turning government spending off and on, or turning taxes off and on, is a long, drawn out, and complicated process. By the time the legislation is passed, the purpose for which it is originally intended may have disappeared entirely. In other words, fiscal policy as a tool for managing the economy to avoid recessions and curtail inflation is politically cumbersome. Taken together, the political problem plus the technical problem of measuring its precise effects make fiscal policy a less used tool for managing the economy. Nevertheless, it is still important to study, since government spending and taxation policies have significant impacts on the macroeconomy and the current account, regardless of whether or not they are implemented to achieve a particular macroeconomic objective.

Monetary Policy

Monetary policy is the other main category of policies that national governments use to influence the macroeconomy. As noted, in the United States, the European Union, and a growing number of other nations, monetary policy is determined by an independent central bank. Therefore, it reflects the views of the central bank and its responses to economic conditions rather than the views of a particular political party or the executive branch of government.

Monetary policy works through a combination of changes to the supply of money and changes to interest rates. When the central bank changes the supply of money, it does so by changing the quantity of funds in financial institutions that are available for lending. The most frequently used technique for accomplishing this is called **open market operations**. Open market operations are simply the buying and selling of bonds in the open market. When a central bank sells bonds, banks and other financial institutions give up some of their cash. Consequently, cash reserves shrink throughout the financial system. Buying bonds has the opposite effect on the financial system's reserves of cash and is the primary technique for expanding the money supply.

Looking at Figure 11.1, it is apparent that as cash reserves in the financial system increase, there is likely to be more investment. That is, financial institutions such as banks need to generate revenue by making loans. Money sitting in the vaults earns the bank no revenue, so an increase in bank reserves leads banks to make more loans. In order to encourage businesses to borrow additional funds, however, interest rates must fall.

Figure 11.2 illustrates the process of a fall in interest rates with a simple supply and demand diagram showing an increase in the supply of money. The horizontal axis measures the quantity of money in the system, where money is defined to be cash, checking accounts, and other easily spendable assets such as money market accounts that allow check writing. In economic terminology, the easier it is to spend an asset, the more liquid it is considered to be. Cash is the most liquid asset, while checking accounts are slightly less liquid, but still highly liquid compared to, say, stocks or bonds.

The supply curve is represented with a vertical line instead of the more common upward sloping supply curve because we are assuming that the central bank fixes the quantity of money at a given level, and that the quantity does not vary with the level of interest rates, measured on the vertical axis. In a usual supply and demand diagram, the vertical axis would be the price of the good or service whose quantity is measured on the horizontal axis. This case is actually no different from normal supply and demand in this sense, since the interest rate can be considered the price of money. There are two reasons for this: it is the price you pay to borrow money and it is the opportunity cost of holding your assets in the form of money instead of some other, interest-earning, form. This is admittedly a simplification, since borrowing costs and the return on savings are always different, and since some types of money earn interest (e.g., money market accounts). Still, it is a simplification that is useful and one that captures the essential relationship between interest rates and the quantity of money in the economy.

The fall in interest rates illustrated in Figure 11.2 is the key to the increase in investment that comes about as a result of an expansionary monetary policy.

FIGURE 11.2   Money Supply and Demand

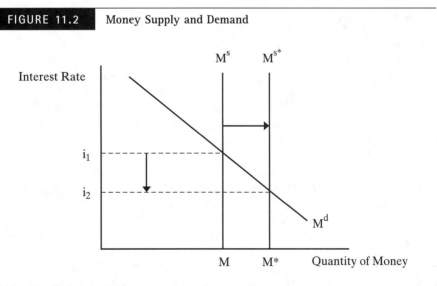

An increase in the supply of money reduces the rate of interest.

Once investment increases, total spending rises, and, in the short run and medium run, producers respond with more output. This is easy to spot looking back at Figure 11.1. Hence, an increase in the money supply will expand the economy and increase incomes. Not surprisingly, monetary policy is also symmetrical with respect to its contractionary and expansionary impacts, so a decrease in the money supply will result in a decline in production and incomes. Letting M stand for the money supply and i represent the interest rate, causality for expansionary policy runs as follows:

$$\text{Increase the money supply: } M\uparrow \Rightarrow i\downarrow \Rightarrow I\uparrow \Rightarrow Y\uparrow \Rightarrow C\uparrow \ldots;$$

and contractionary monetary policy starts by decreasing the money supply,

$$\text{Decrease the money supply: } M\downarrow \Rightarrow i\uparrow \Rightarrow I\downarrow \Rightarrow Y\downarrow \Rightarrow C\downarrow \ldots.$$

As shown, **expansionary monetary policy** involves an increase in the money supply and a fall in interest rates, leading to a positive expansion in income. **Contractionary monetary policy** is exactly the reverse, and involves a decrease in the money supply and a rise in interest rates, leading to a contraction in income. As with fiscal policies, both expansionary and contractionary monetary policies work through the multiplier process to raise or lower income, depending on whether the policy is expansionary or contractionary.

CASE STUDY

Fiscal and Monetary Policy During the Great Depression

The Great Depression is the name Americans give to the worst economic period in modern American history. It was a worldwide phenomenon, however, and most countries felt hard times. The onset of the crisis varied from country to country, but in the United States, it started during July of 1929, with an unnoticed modest decline in economic activity. Stock prices continued to rise through the summer of 1929, in spite of the overall decline in output and income. September and October were bad months for the market, culminating in the panic of Black Thursday, on October 24, when the market fell by more than one-third. Most people thought that the worst was over and many

argued that the stock market collapse was good for the economy since it squeezed out excess speculation.

The small recession that began during the summer of 1929 grew into one of the worst decades in American history. By 1933, over 25 percent of the labor force was unemployed and real GDP had fallen by nearly 26 percent. Out of the cauldron of the Great Depression came Social Security, the Fair Labor Standards Act to regulate working conditions and wages, the Securities and Exchange Commission to oversee stock trading, the Federal Deposit Insurance Corporation to protect bank deposits, the Tennessee Valley Authority, and a host of other programs that inserted the federal government much deeper into American economic life.

Most Americans probably think of the 1930s and the Great Depression as synonymous, but there were two separate recessions in the United States during the decade. The first and most severe, is the one that began in 1929 and lasted until 1933. The second began in 1937 and lasted into 1938. Between these two downturns in economic activity, there was a strong recovery, and by 1936, real GDP was above where it had been in 1929, the last year of overall positive growth until 1934. Figure 11.3 illustrates the annual rate of growth, 1930–1941.

In hindsight, it is easy to see the policy mistakes that prolonged the recession and made it far more severe than it needed to be. Based on what we know today about expansionary fiscal and monetary policy, the federal government should have done one or more of the following: raise government spend-

ing for goods and services, cut taxes, increase the money supply to lower interest rates. The problem in the 1930s was that no one was aware of the relations discussed in this chapter. In a very real sense, if you read the first part of this chapter, then you know more about fiscal policy than Presidents Roosevelt and Hoover and all of their advisors knew.

Instead of using increases in government spending and cuts in taxes to stimulate the economy, both Presidents Hoover (1929–1933) and Roosevelt (1933–1945) worried about the federal budget deficits that emerged during the 1930s. Roosevelt and Hoover both thought that budget deficits undermined business confidence and were a major reason for the recession. Consequently, the budget deficit became a major issue of the 1932 presidential election, in which Roosevelt successfully campaigned on the platform of a balanced federal budget. As it turned

---

FIGURE 11.3   Real GDP Growth, United States

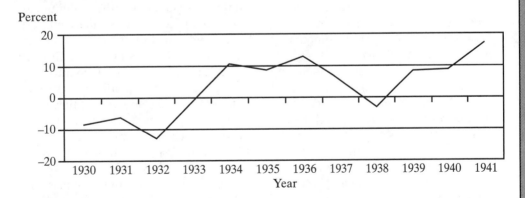

Source: Bueau of Economic Analysis.

(*continues*)

out, however, the federal budget was in deficit during every year of Roosevelt's presidency.

Hoover and Roosevelt both tried to balance the budget. Both presidents unsuccessfully opposed legislation to offer war veterans early payment of the retirement money they were owed, and both presidents supported tax increases when deficits began to appear after 1929. Hoover introduced a dramatic tax increase in 1932, while Roosevelt increased taxes at several points in time, most dramatically with the beginning of social security taxes in 1937. Given the contractionary impact of tax increases, it is not surprising that 1932 was the worst year of the depression, nor that the economy slipped back into recession in 1938 after the implementation of the new Social Security tax.

If fiscal policy was not helpful during the 1930s, monetary policy was a disaster. Between 1929 and 1933, the money supply (currency, checking accounts, and savings deposits) fell by nearly 31 percent. Credit became scarce and investment disappeared. In other words, if fiscal policy could be considered more or less neutral during most years of the Great Depression (neither expansionary nor contractionary), then monetary policy was contractionary.

In retrospect, it is easy to understand the failure to use expansionary fiscal policy. No one in the 1930s understood the macroeconomy well enough to discern how to use fiscal policy to fight the recession. It is more difficult to justify the misuse of monetary policy, however, because more was known about the relationships between the money supply, bank reserves, and investment. For many years, prominent economists such

as Nobel Prize winner Milton Friedman argued that the Federal Reserve was simply incompetent. This view cannot be ruled out, but more recent scholarship has shed new light on this historical episode. Rather than incompetence, the Fed's actions reflected a different set of priorities. In particular, it may have been acting responsibly if its first priority was to protect the gold standard.

Under the rules of the gold standard, central banks are required to use interest rates and monetary policy to attract gold whenever gold reserves run low. This usually means an interest rate hike in order to increase the demand for the domestic currency and to reduce the demand for foreign currencies.

In 1928, U.S. monetary policy turned contractionary as the Fed was worried about speculation in the stock market and wanted to make it more difficult for brokers to borrow from banks. The Fed raised interest rates and, unintentionally, created an inflow of gold to the United States. U.S. policy put pressure on European countries, which began to lose their gold reserves. Consequently, the contractionary policy in the United States spread across the Atlantic as countries began to raise their interest rates and slow their rate of money growth in order to stop the outflow of gold. The irony is that each country was acting responsibly according to the dictates of the gold standard, but they were following polices that resulted in a worldwide economic catastrophe.

At several points during the years that followed, U.S. and foreign policies turned even more contractionary. In 1931, it was widely expected that the United Kingdom would leave the gold standard altogether, and speculation turned against the pound. In September 1931, Britain left the gold standard and speculators immediately shifted their attention to the dollar. Expecting a similar decline in the value of the dollar, they began to sell dollars and dollar-denominated assets, all of which resulted in gold outflows. Once again, the Fed responded by raising interest rates in September and October of 1931, and the U.S. economy continued its downward spiral.

It is no coincidence that the first countries to leave the gold standard (the United Kingdom and the countries that followed it out of the gold standard in September 1931) were the first to experience recovery. Once their policies were freed from the constraint of supporting a fixed rate of exchange, they could turn them toward economic expansion. In the United States, Roosevelt's first act after taking office in March 1933 was to suspend the gold standard. It seems unlikely that he completely understood the relationship of gold to the depression, but it was a good move, as the economy began its recovery from the worst economic crisis of the twentieth century.

CURRENT ACCOUNT BALANCES REVISITED

Chapter 9 described the identity between private savings, government budget balances, investment, and the current account:

$$S + (T - G) = I + CA.$$

We are ready now to look more closely at this identity, and to incorporate the links between monetary and fiscal policy, income, and the current account. The goal is to analyze how a change in income caused by a change in monetary or fiscal policy influences the country's current account. We will do this in two steps. In the first step, we explore the links between changes in monetary and fiscal policies, interest rates, and exchange rates. The link from monetary policy to interest rates has already been described, but as we will see, fiscal policies have interest rate effects as well. In the second step, we put together policy changes, interest rates, exchange rates, and the current account balance. Once we have done this, we will have a much clearer understanding of the policies a country must follow if it needs to eliminate a trade imbalance in its current account.

It is important to emphasize that we are looking at changes in income and other macroeconomic variables that are likely to take place over the span of a few years or less, while ignoring long-run impacts that may take many years, perhaps even a decade or longer, to materialize. We will return to this point later in the chapter when we try to distinguish long-run, permanent changes from short-run changes.

Fiscal and Monetary Policies, Interest Rates, and Exchange Rates

From Chapter 10 and the interest parity condition, we know that interest rate increases lead to an appreciation of the domestic currency (the exchange rate, R, falls) and interest rate decreases lead to a depreciation (the exchange rate rises). Recall that this occurs through changes in the demand and supply of foreign currency. As interest rates rise, it increases the supply of foreign currency since interest arbitrageurs are constantly searching for the highest possible rate of interest for their financial investments. Similarly, a decline in interest rates reduces the inflow of foreign financial capital, decreasing the supply of foreign currency. Demand side effects are present in both cases as well, since home country interest arbitrageurs have the same motivation to move their capital into the home country when interest rates rise and to move it out when they fall.

The exchange rate effects of monetary policy are easily identified. We have already seen how an expansion of the money supply increases bank reserves and pushes down interest rates. Consequently, in addition to increasing income, expansionary monetary policy must also cause a depreciation of the exchange rate:

$$\text{Increase the money supply: } M\uparrow \Rightarrow i\downarrow \Rightarrow R\uparrow.$$

Given the symmetry between expansionary and contractionary policies, monetary contraction reduces bank reserves and drives up interest rates, leading to an appreciation of the exchange rate:

$$\text{Decrease the money supply: } M\downarrow \Rightarrow i\uparrow \Rightarrow R\downarrow.$$

Since a rapidly depreciating currency is a feature of most international financial crises, contractionary monetary policy is a very common technique attempted to stop a depreciation. This is discussed more fully in the next chapter, but it should be noted that the downside of using monetary policy this way is a contraction in income and possibly even a recession. This illustrates once again that it is not unusual for a tradeoff to exist between a country's exchange rate goal and its goals for income growth and employment. For example, the Fed's action to raise interest rates to protect the dollar in 1931 is a classic example of a conflict between the needs of the domestic economy and the desire to protect the exchange rate.

The interest rate effects of fiscal policy are less easily identified, but they are present nonetheless. So far we know that expansionary fiscal policy raises income and contractionary policy lowers it. What remains unexplained is the impact of fiscal policy on interest rates and, through them, on exchange rates. The key to understanding these links lies in the behavior of households and the changes they make when their incomes rise or fall. Looking first at the case of a rise in household income, we know that consumption expenditures will also rise. Furthermore—and this is key—rising incomes cause households to reevaluate the division of their assets between liquid forms, such as money, and relatively less liquid forms such as stocks and bonds. When income rises, the average household will hold more money. In economic terms, the demand for money increases, as illustrated in Figure 11.4.

Why do households increase their demand for money when their incomes increase? The reasons are straightforward. First, at higher levels of income, they consume more. That is, they need a higher level of money holdings to pay for their purchases. Second, the opportunity cost of the interest they lose on holding money instead of an interest-paying asset becomes less burdensome. In other words, when households have more income, they can "afford" to hold more money.

Lest this seem too abstract and immaterial to your personal situation, think about what you might do if your income doubled. Most likely, you would increase the amount of money in your wallet and checking account. You would also probably put aside some of your increased income into long-term savings. The point is that if you are more or less average in your spending behavior, an increase in income would cause you to spend more and you would facilitate your increased spending by carrying around more cash and larger balances in your checking account.

Now we have all of the pieces to analyze the exchange rate effects of fiscal policy. Expansionary fiscal policy will raise incomes and consumption. One outcome of these effects is an increase in the demand for money which, as shown in Figure 11.4, leads to higher interest rates. Given the relationship

---

FIGURE 11.4   **An Increase in the Demand for Money**

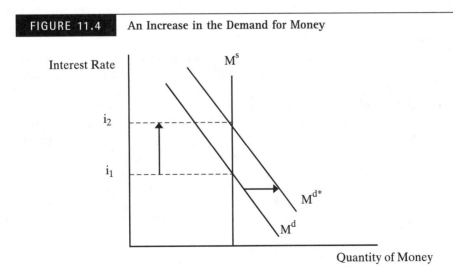

An increase in income causes households to increase their money holdings. As a consequence, interest rates rise.

---

between interest rates and exchange rates, we know that higher interest rates, all else equal, lead to an inflow of foreign capital and a fall in the exchange rate (an appreciation). The flow diagram for all these effects is as follows:

$$\text{Expansionary fiscal policy: } G\uparrow, T\downarrow \Rightarrow Y\uparrow \Rightarrow M^d\uparrow \Rightarrow i\uparrow \Rightarrow R\downarrow.$$

As usual, the flow diagram for contractionary policy is symmetrical:

$$\text{Contractionary fiscal policy: } G\downarrow, T\uparrow \Rightarrow Y\downarrow \Rightarrow M^d\downarrow \Rightarrow i\downarrow \Rightarrow R\uparrow.$$

Fiscal and Monetary Policy and the Current Account

Once the exchange rate effects of monetary and fiscal policy have been identified, it is relatively easy to describe their effects on the current account. As we shall see, the effect of fiscal policy on the current account is definite, while the effect of monetary policy is ambiguous. We turn now to the analysis of these impacts.

Taking the case of expansionary monetary policy first, we have seen that an increase in the money supply reduces interest rates and causes a depreciation in the domestic currency. Exchange rate depreciation switches some consumer spending from foreign goods (imports) to domestic goods, since foreign goods become relatively expensive. The effect of expenditure switching is to partially or completely offset the increase in imports caused by rising income. As a result, there is a more robust expansion of the domestic economy since less of the expansion of demand leaks out of the economy as an increase in imports. In other words, expansionary monetary policy is reinforced by the changes in the exchange rate.

Contractionary monetary policy has an opposite effect. Interest rates rise, causing an appreciation of the domestic currency, which makes imports relatively cheaper. As a consequence, consumers switch some of their expenditures away from domestic goods toward foreign ones. The reduction in demand for domestic goods reinforces the impact of contractionary monetary policy on income, consumption, and investment, and leads to a more vigorous decline in economic activity than would occur in a closed economy.

To summarize, the impact of monetary policy on income is magnified by its exchange rate effects. We cannot definitely say, however, what the effects are on the current account balance since the income effect of monetary policy on the current account is the opposite of the exchange rate effect. The current account balance could rise or fall with either expansionary or contractionary policy. However, a key idea in the chain of causation is the notion of expenditure switching. This refers to switching back and forth between domestic and foreign goods which, in this case, is in response to a change in the exchange rate. Expenditure switching magnifies the effects of monetary policy. Note, however, that this result depends on exchange rate flexibility. In an economy with a fixed exchange rate, the impact of changes in the money supply are weaker.

The effect of fiscal policy on the current account is more certain. As shown, expansionary fiscal policy increases interest rates, causing an exchange rate appreciation. Appreciation switches expenditures toward foreign goods since it makes them relatively cheaper, thereby increasing imports and reducing the current account balance. The expansionary fiscal policy leads to more imports, both from the rise in income and from exchange rate appreciation, which creates a feedback effect on domestic income. The shift in expenditures toward foreign goods offsets some of the increase in the demand for domestic goods and diminishes the impact of expansionary fiscal policy. Similarly, the exchange rate effect of contractionary fiscal policy switches expenditures away from foreign goods and toward domestic goods, diluting some of the contractionary effects of the policy.

The major short-run to medium-run effects of fiscal and monetary policy are summarized in Table 11.2. Differences between the two begin with their interest rate effects and carry over to exchange rates and current accounts. In the case of monetary policy, changes in the exchange rate and income have offsetting effects on the current account, but with fiscal policy, changes in the exchange rate and income have reinforcing effects on the current account. As a result, the impact of monetary policy on the current account is indeterminate, while the impact of fiscal policy is definite.

TABLE 11.2	The Main Effects of Fiscal and Monetary Policies			
	Monetary Policy		*Fiscal Policy*	
	Contractionary	Expansionary	Contractionary	Expansionary
Income and consumption	Fall	Rise	Fall	Rise
Interest rates	Rise	Fall	Fall	Rise
Exchange rates	Fall: appreciate	Rise: depreciate	Rise: depreciate	Fall: appreciate
Current account	Rise or fall	Rise or fall	Rise	Fall

Monetary and fiscal policies have different impacts on interest rates, exchange rates, and the current account. Monetary policy's impact on exchange rates counteracts some of the current account impact of the change in income.

The Long Run

How permanent are the effects? Economists are more or less agreed that in the long run, the level of output in an economy tends to fluctuate around a level that is consistent with full employment. Note that full employment does not mean that everyone has a job. No matter how strong the economy, there is always some unemployment from the entry of new workers into the labor force, or the return of workers after an absence from work. While searching for their jobs, both groups are considered unemployed. In addition, there are always a number of people who have voluntarily quit their jobs to look for better ones, and people who lack the job skills they need to find a job.

In a strong economy, unemployment may temporarily fall to a very low level, but this tends to resolve itself. Initially, employers may grab whoever is available to fill their job vacancies, but as the pool of the unemployed dries up, they raise wages and look for ways to get by with fewer workers. Ultimately, this returns the unemployment rate to its normal level. Conversely, in a weak economy, unemployed workers put downward pressure on wages, which ultimately resolves the problem of unemployment, since employers hire more workers when wages fall. The most controversial issue is how long these changes might take. Some observers believe they happen fast, while others are skeptical, particularly about the speed at which wages fall.

In one sense, the debate over the amount of time it takes an economy to reach its long-run equilibrium at full employment is a debate over the meaning of the long run. Is it two years, five years, or ten? Regardless of the time frame, economists agree that the impact of fiscal and monetary policies on income and consumption is not permanent.

In addition, the changes brought about in the exchange rate are not permanent either. In Chapter 10, we saw that in the long run, purchasing power parity determines exchange rates. Fiscal and monetary policy may cause deviations from purchasing power parity, but in the long run, a combination of exchange rate changes and changes in domestic prices will restore balance to the purchasing power of national currencies.

The current account must also tend toward balance in the long run. No nation can run deficits forever, nor can it run surpluses forever. Since deficits are equivalent to foreign borrowing and surpluses equivalent to foreign lending, there are limits in each direction. The limits are not well defined, however, and countries such as the United States have been able to run enormous deficits for long periods, while countries such as Japan have run surpluses.

CASE STUDY

The United States's Current Account Deficits of the 1980s and 1990s

Figure 11.5 shows the U.S. current account from 1980 through 2000. Two features stand out: the opening and closing of the deficit in the 1980s and its reopening in the 1990s. It is tempting to see these two episodes as essentially similar, yet they are very different in

their origin and in their potential to do harm to the U.S. economy. In both episodes, fiscal and monetary policies have played a key role, but so did events external to the United States.

In order to understand how the deficits of the 1980s differed from the

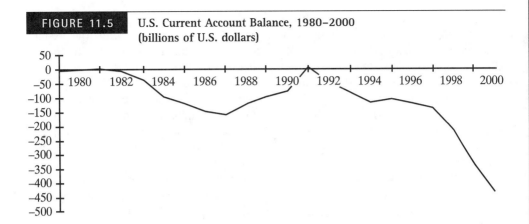

FIGURE 11.5 — U.S. Current Account Balance, 1980–2000
(billions of U.S. dollars)

The 1980s and 1990s were marked by large current account deficits, although the causes and consequences varied.

Source: Bureau of Economic Analysis. Online at http://www.bea.doc.gov

1990s, it is useful to look again at the identity between savings, investment, and the current account:

$$S + (T - G) = I + CA.$$

Rearranging the identity to isolate the current account on one side, we have:

$$CA = (S - I) + (T - G),$$

where the two terms in parentheses on the right-hand side represent the difference between savings and investment and the government budget balance.

Beginning around 1981, the budget of the federal government turned the governmental balance, T − G, into a large negative number, and CA turned negative. Both fiscal and monetary policy were key parts of the mechanism that made this happen. In the first place, interest rates in the early 1980s were driven up by an expansionary fiscal policy that resulted from large tax cuts plus a sizable increase in the military budget. In addition, monetary policy had been contractionary since 1979 as the Fed fought to bring down the rate of inflation by restricting the growth of the money supply. Both fiscal and monetary policy, then, drove up interest rates. The result for the exchange rate was a sharply appreciating dollar. Beginning in 1984, the United States's strong recovery from recession resulted in rising incomes and much greater demand for imports. Demand was facilitated by the sharply appreciated dollar, which made it cheaper for consumers to buy foreign goods.

The 1990s story is different in several ways, but perhaps most importantly in that over the course of the decade, the federal budget moved from a large negative to a positive. By itself, this should have resulted in a positive current account balance, but S and I were not constant. The decade saw sharp increases in investment spending as corporations bought new computer technology and the telecommunications equipment they needed to stay competitive. In addition, the stock market

(*continues*)

boom made consumers much wealthier while the long economic expansion relieved some anxieties about corporate downsizing and job layoffs. The net result for households was a consumption boom fueled in part by a significant drop in personal savings, one of the components of S. (Recall that the other component of savings is business savings, essentially the retained profits of firms.) Therefore, the changes in the government budget were overwhelmed by the increases in investment and by the decline in savings, resulting in a large and growing current account deficit.

In both the 1980s and 1990s, external events also played an important role. During the 1980s, much of Europe was stuck in a slow growth mode, so that U.S. exports to some of our largest trading partners were limited. During the 1990s, slow growth abroad was again a problem, particularly after the Asian crisis that began in 1997. The crisis caused investors to pull their money out of Asia, and to look for high-quality, low-risk, investments to replace them. U.S. government bonds were a good choice for many, and foreign capital poured into the United States, causing the dollar to appreciate. In addition, the deep recessions in parts of Asia and their spillover into Latin America curtailed U.S. exports to those regions.

A comprehensive discussion of the current account deficit, along with comparisons to the 1980s and a description of its impacts on particular economic sectors can be found in the testimony of economists and business people to the United States Trade Deficit Review Commission. They are located online at http://www.ustdrc.gov.

MACRO POLICIES FOR CURRENT ACCOUNT IMBALANCES

Fiscal, monetary, and exchange rate policies are essential tools for eliminating a current account imbalance. While any persistent imbalance can be portrayed as a problem, in practice the most dangerous imbalances are large current account deficits. Persistently large surpluses may bother a country's trading partners, but they rarely threaten a national economy the way that large deficits sometimes do. The macro policies for addressing a current account deficit are a combination of fiscal, monetary, and exchange rate policies, often collectively called **expenditure switching policies** and **expenditure reducing policies**. Both are essential.

We have already seen one type of expenditure switching policy when we talked about the exchange rate effects of fiscal and monetary policy. In general, an appropriate expenditure switching policy for eliminating a current account deficit is one that turns domestic expenditures away from foreign-produced goods and toward domestic goods. As discussed, an exchange rate depreciation is one way to do this. Recall that a depreciation raises the domestic price of foreign goods. An alternative type of expenditure switching policy is a trade barrier such as a temporary tariff to make foreign goods more expensive.

Expenditure reducing policies are simply contractionary fiscal or monetary policies that cut the overall level of demand in the economy. In most cases, they are necessary along with expenditure switching policies because without overall expenditure reductions, inflation ensues as home country domestic expenditures switch away from foreign producers and toward domestic producers. For this reason, expenditure switching policies must be accompanied by reductions in overall expenditures.

While expenditure shifts without expenditure reductions are inflationary, expenditure reductions without shifts toward domestic producers are recessionary. This makes the expenditure shifts necessary, since a shift in spending toward domestic producers offsets the decline in demand and leaves the economy with the same level of output but without a current account deficit. Given the need to use both types of policies simultaneously, expenditure reductions and expenditure shifts are not viewed as alternatives to each other but rather as two equally essential components of a macroeconomic policy designed to address a current account deficit.

The Adjustment Process

The **adjustment process** is the term used to describe changes in the trade deficit that are caused by a change in the exchange rate. We have already seen that a depreciation raises the real price of foreign goods, making domestic substitutes relatively more attractive. While this is an accurate description of the general pattern, depreciations often have delayed effects. In the United States, for example, there is a median average lag of about 9.5 months between a change in the exchange rate and an impact on U.S. exports. The median average lag for import responses is slightly less, but still more than 7 months. Consequently, it is a mistake to think that exchange rate changes will affect trade flows overnight.

In addition to the lag effects, the first impact of a depreciation on the current account may be a further deterioration rather than an improvement. This deterioration is known as the **J-curve**, and is illustrated in Figure 11.6.

After a depreciation, there is usually a short period of no noticeable impact on the flow of goods and services. When imports and exports begin to respond, the immediate change is an increase in the value of imports, pushing the current account balance deeper into deficit. The size of the deterioration and the length of time before there is an actual improvement varies from country to country. In the United States, a depreciation results in an improvement in the trade balance only after a year or more. The reasons are straightforward. A depreciation makes foreign goods immediately more expensive, but it takes time for households and businesses to find substitutes. In the short run they lack information, and it takes time to find new suppliers in the domestic

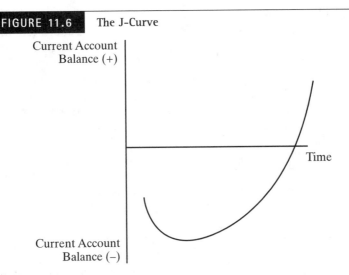

FIGURE 11.6   The J-Curve

Initially, depreciations often cause the current account balance to deteriorate further. With time, substitutions of domestic goods for foreign goods lead to an improvement in the balance.

economy, to check the quality of their products, and to negotiate contracts. Meanwhile, until the alternative suppliers are found, foreign goods continue to be used even though they cost more.

CASE STUDY

The Adjustment Process in the United States

From the third quarter of 1980 to mid-1987, the U.S. trade deficit widened from 0.48 percent of GDP to over 3.5 percent of GDP. In 1985, the Plaza Accord among the G-5 (France, Germany, Japan, the United States, and the United Kingdom) created a cooperative effort to bring down the value of the dollar. The dollar began to fall in early 1985 with the introduction of a new team of officials at the Treasury Department; from January, 1985, to January, 1987, it fell from an index of 152.83 to 101.13, or nearly 34 percent.

While the dollar was falling, the trade deficit continued to widen. This was unsettling to a number of politicians, economists, and others, who had predicted a significant decline in the U.S. trade deficit as a result of the depreciation. Some journalists and politicians began to argue that the trade deficit would never respond to a change in the value of the dollar, that foreign trade barriers would make it impossible for the United States to substantially expand exports, and that our own open market would ensure a growing volume of imports regardless of the dollar's value.

Nevertheless, after a little more than two years, the trade balance began to respond to the fall in the dollar. Figure 11.7 illustrates the change in the value of the dollar and the trade balance from 1980 to 1988. Note that the time scale for the trade deficit is offset two years to reflect the long lag in the adjustment process. This offset pairs the exchange rate with the value of the trade balance two years later. It is apparent that there is a striking similarity in their movement, once adjustment is made for the two-year lag.

The question economists have debated since this episode is why it took so long for trade balances to respond to the decline in the value of the dollar. There are several possible explanations.

One is that the prior increase in the dollar's value had padded the profit margins of foreign producers. From 1980 to 1985, their exports to the United States rose in terms of their domestic prices even though they sold in the United States for the same dollar prices. Consequently, when the dollar began to fall, foreign producers were initially able to keep dollar prices constant and absorb the decline in its value by realizing lower profits in terms of their domestic currency.

Another possible reason for the long lag is that there were still impacts from earlier appreciations working through the system. A third reason for the long lag is that exports began to increase from a much lower base than imports, and needed to increase much more rapidly in percentage terms in order for the trade deficit to begin to close.

FIGURE 11.7   The U.S. Trade Balance and the Exchange Rate, 1980–1988

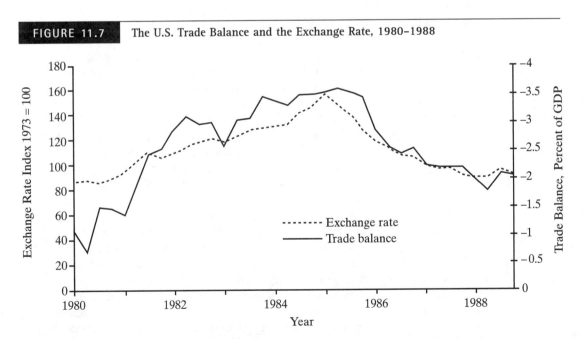

In the 1980s, changes in the U.S. trade balance mirrored changes in the exchange rate with a lag of two years.

Source: Business Cycles Indicators, BCI DataManager, Gary F. Langer; *Economic Report of the President.*

MACROECONOMIC POLICY COORDINATION IN DEVELOPED COUNTRIES

Coordination of macroeconomic policies is a frequent issue for the leading industrial economies. The annual meetings of the G-5 and the G-7 (G-5 plus Canada and Italy) are often an extended discussion about the need to coordinate fiscal, monetary, and exchange rate policies in order to accomplish mutually beneficial goals. Although coordination is rarely attained, it is easy to see why some countries would want it and why it is not particularly relevant for developing countries.

There are a variety of objectives for macroeconomic policy coordination, but the usual goal is to achieve a desirable level of world economic growth. The purpose of coordination is to avoid imposing a disproportionate burden on one of the major world economies. Unequal burdens result when one country pays a large share of the costs of economic adjustment. As an illustration, suppose that the world economy is in a period of relatively slow growth. Not every economy will experience this, but it may be the case that enough economies are in recession or growing slowly so that the average rate of growth throughout the world is too slow to raise living standards or to pull people out of poverty. If a group of industrial economies decide to jointly expand their economies with fiscal and monetary policies, then growth in their incomes raises incomes around the world as their demand for imports stimulates production in other countries. If all economies expand simultaneously, then no one country is burdened by a sudden excess of imports over exports—their exports grow along with their imports and with the growth in demand in their trading partner's economies. For a variety of reasons, such as existing large budget deficits, or fear of the inflationary effects of expansionary policy, some countries may choose not to expand their economies. In this case, the effectiveness of the expanding economies as engines of growth across the globe is reduced. Furthermore, the country or countries using expansionary policy will probably experience a deterioration in their current accounts since their trading partners are not growing at the same rate. If expansionary fiscal policies cause interest rates to rise, then a further deterioration in the current account is likely due to the appreciation of the currency as a result of the inflow of foreign capital.

The way out of this dilemma is for a coordinated effort at macroeconomic expansion. There are both political and economic problems with coordination, however. The political problem is that there is no international organization capable of arranging a multilateral agreement among nations, nor is one possible without a significant sacrifice of national sovereignty. The economic problem is that there is rarely a period in which nations find it in their own interest to pursue the same policies as their trading partners. Countries enter and leave slow growth periods and recessions at different points in time and it is rare that one policy is suitable for everyone. Coordination remains a topic of discussion among the world's leading economies, however, since it is always in one or more countries' interest.

Summary

- Households supply all the factors of production (land, labor, and capital) that businesses need to produce the nation's output. In return, they receive all the income, or factor payments, which are payments for the use of their land (rents), labor (wages and salaries), and capital (dividends, profits, and interest). The income received by households is equivalent to the value of the output produced by businesses.

- Businesses use financial institutions to borrow household savings. They use the savings to invest. Businesses also produce the nation's output. Governments spend on goods and services, using tax revenues from the income flow going to households. The foreign sector supplies imports and demands exports.

- Fiscal policies are government tax and expenditure policies. Monetary policies are for interest rates and the money supply. Expansionary policies raise GDP and national income, while contractionary policies do the opposite.

- Fiscal and monetary policies work by changing total demand. Fiscal policies either change government spending on goods and services, which is a direct change in demand, or they change household income through a change in taxes. This is an indirect change in total demand. Monetary policies work through a change in interest rates, which changes investment.

- The multiplier explains how an initial change in spending (demand) is multiplied through the economy into a larger change in spending.

- Fiscal policy is considered more difficult to implement than monetary policy because it requires Congress to pass legislation that must be signed by the president. Monetary policy is easier because it is conducted by the Federal Reserve.

- Both fiscal and monetary policy influence exchange rates and the current account balance. In each case, the effect is through a change in interest rates brought on by the fiscal or monetary policy. Neither policy is likely to have long-run effects on income

- In order to reduce or eliminate a current account deficit, countries must practice expenditure switching and expenditure reducing policies. Expenditure switching policies turn demand away from the foreign sector and toward domestic production. Expenditure reducing policies cut back on the overall level of demand.

- The J-curve describes how a policy designed to eliminate a current account deficit may initially make it larger before reducing it. The lag between a depreciation and a reduction in the size of a current account deficit is 1 to 2 years in the United States.

Vocabulary

adjustment process

circular flow

contractionary fiscal policy

contractionary monetary policy

expansionary fiscal policy

expansionary monetary policy

expenditure reducing policy

expenditure switching policy

fiscal policy

intermediate inputs

J-curve

monetary policy

multiplier effect

open market operations

retained earnings

Study Questions

1. Use a circular flow model to name the four main actors in an economy and their economic functions.

2. Explain the concepts of fiscal and monetary policy. Who conducts them and how do they work their way through the economy?

3. What are some of the problems in trying to use fiscal and monetary policies? Why can't economists and politicians make precise predictions about the effects of a policy change on income and output?

4. Describe the mechanism that leads from a change in fiscal policy to changes in interest rates, the exchange rate, and the current account balance. Do the same for monetary policy.

5. Analyze the differences in the United States's current account deficits of the 1980s and the deficits of the 1990s and 2000s.

6. Some countries have fixed exchange rate systems instead of flexible systems. How does the exchange rate system limit their ability to use monetary policy?

7. Suppose that the United States wanted to eliminate its current account deficit. How might it do that and what would be the effects on the rest of the economy?

8. During the second half of the 1980s, the United States depreciated the dollar in hopes that it would reduce the current account deficit. After a year, the deficit was actually larger and newspaper editorialists were writing columns claiming that there is no link between the exchange rate and the current account. Explain why they got this wrong.

9. Suppose the United States, Japan, and many other places around the world go into recession, but growth remains strong in Europe. Why would macroeconomic policy coordination help, who should coordinate, and what are some of the obstacles to coordination?

Chapter 12

INTERNATIONAL
FINANCIAL CRISES

INTRODUCTION

Increasing international economic integration has created opportunities for growth and development, but it has also made it easier for crises to spread from one country to another. In 1992, currency speculation against the British pound and a few other European currencies nearly caused the collapse of monetary arrangements in Europe, and inflicted high costs on a number of countries in the European Union. In late 1994, speculation against the Mexican peso led to its collapse, and spread a "Tequila effect" through South America. In 1997, several East Asian economies were thrown into steep recession by a wave of sudden capital outflows, and in 1998, Russia's default on its international debt sent shockwaves as far as Latin America.

Financial crises are not new, but the way they develop and spread continues to evolve with the world's financial and economic integration. In some instances, they are an almost predictable result of inconsistent or unrealistic macroeconomic policies, but in other cases, countries with fundamentally sound macroeconomic policies have been pulled into a currency or financial crisis for no obvious reason. This makes financial crises difficult to predict, but it also increases the value of a set of early warning indicators. The **contagion effects** of a crisis do not conform to a single pattern and they reinforce the idea that there are different types of crises with their own rules of behavior.

Financial crises have brought down governments, ruined economies, and destroyed individual lives. Their enormous costs have created an intense amount of research into causes, prevention, and treatment. This chapter reviews some of the basic themes of this literature. It begins by describing two types of crises that have been observed during the last 20 years. It then turns to a discussion of several key issues, including the steps countries might take to avoid or minimize a crisis, and the policy choices they face once one begins.

Much of the research in this area is designed to formulate sound principles for international financial reforms. The many reform proposals that have appeared in recent years are usually referred to as proposals for reform of the **international financial architecture**. Their contents often revolve around a set of proposed changes to the International Monetary Fund (IMF) and other multilateral institutions with a role in international financial relations. The final section of this chapter looks at two of the main issues in that discussion.

Specifically, does the world economy need a **lender of last resort**, and what type of conditions should a lender impose on the recipients of its assistance?

DEFINITION OF A FINANCIAL CRISIS

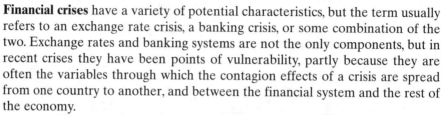

Financial crises have a variety of potential characteristics, but the term usually refers to an exchange rate crisis, a banking crisis, or some combination of the two. Exchange rates and banking systems are not the only components, but in recent crises they have been points of vulnerability, partly because they are often the variables through which the contagion effects of a crisis are spread from one country to another, and between the financial system and the rest of the economy.

A **banking crisis** occurs when the banking system becomes unable to perform its normal lending functions, and some or all of a nation's banks are threatened with insolvency. A bank, like any other business, is considered insolvent or bankrupt if its assets are less than its liabilities, or, to put it another way, if its net worth is negative.

The primary role of banks is to **intermediate** between savers and borrowers. Simply put, banks and other financial institutions pool the savings of households and make them available to businesses that want to invest. If the businesses that borrow from a bank go under, then the bank cannot pay back its depositors, and the bank may go out of business as well. **Disintermediation** occurs when banks are unable to act as intermediaries between savers and investors. Disintermediation is a serious problem with negative economic consequences.

When a bank fails, everyone that deposited money in the bank loses all or a portion of their money, unless the country has a functioning deposit insurance system. The loss of savings causes households to cut back on consumption and spreads the recessionary effect wider and wider through the economy. This is one way a crisis gets transmitted within an economy. Unaffected banks may stop making new loans as they take a cautious approach, new investment slows or stops altogether, layoffs occur, and the economy falls deeper into the vicious circle of a downward spiraling recession.

An **exchange rate crisis** is caused by a sudden and unexpected collapse in the value of a nation's currency. This can happen under either a fixed, flexible, or intermediate type of exchange rate. If the exchange rate system is some form of a fixed exchange rate, the crisis entails a loss of international reserves, followed by a sudden devaluation once it appears that the reserves will run out. Devaluation is intended to accumulate reserves, or to conserve existing reserves, by making the rate of exchange less favorable to people trying to convert their domestic currency to dollars or another international reserve currency. If a country uses some form of flexible exchange rate, an exchange rate crisis involves a rapid and uncontrolled depreciation of the currency. While no type of exchange rate system guarantees safety, current research favors the idea that countries that adopt a pegged exchange rate may be more vulnerable to an exchange rate crisis.

Similar to the effects of a banking crisis, an exchange rate crisis often results in a steep recession. There are several channels through which recessionary effects may be transmitted, but one of the most common channels is the banking system. For example, prior to the East Asian crisis of 1997 and 1998, banks borrowed dollars in international capital markets. When their home country currencies collapsed, the dollar value of their debt increased enormously. Consequently, many banks failed, disintermediation took place, new investment stopped, and the economies slid into a deep recession.

TWO TYPES OF INTERNATIONAL FINANCIAL CRISES

It is safe to say that every international financial crisis is unique in its origins and in the way it causes domestic economies to unravel. Nevertheless, it is useful to act as if there are two separate origins of crises. The first type is a result of definite and identifiable macroeconomic imbalances. For this type, the moment of crisis onset is difficult to predict, but unless the underlying conditions are corrected, it is almost certain to occur eventually. The second type is brought on by volatile flows of financial capital that quickly move into and out of a country. A sudden change in investor expectations may be a triggering factor, and underlying fragility in the banking and financial sector may be present. Still, this type of crisis can be puzzling since in several recent cases, it has affected countries with particularly strong international positions and stable macroeconomic policies.

Crises Caused by Macroeconomic Imbalances

During the last few decades, a number of crises have been triggered by severe macroeconomic imbalances, usually accompanied by an exchange rate system that intensifies the country's vulnerability. The best example of this type of crisis is the Third World debt crisis of the 1980s. The most common type of macroeconomic imbalances are overly expansionary fiscal policies that create large government budget deficits, often financed by a high growth rate of the money supply. When expansionary fiscal and monetary policies are joined with a crawling peg exchange rate system, the various components of economic policy often interact in ways that lead to a crisis followed by a severe recession.

Taking the budget deficit first, in the previous chapter it was argued that expansionary monetary and fiscal policies are intended to stimulate the economy and raise the level of output. After World War II, most developing countries experimented with industrial development strategies that used the government and its budget as a primary engine of economic development. That is, in addition to using the government budget as a way to stimulate demand and cure a recession, many developing countries made the government budget one of the primary tools of long-run, industrial development. Governments operated steel mills, airlines, phone companies, and many of the other pieces of a modern industrial economy. Furthermore, they were and are involved in providing social services, income support, and subsidies for groups of businesses and consumers.

In many cases, the potential problems of government spending are compounded by inefficient and unreliable tax systems. This means that government tax revenues may be insufficient for its expenditure programs. Under these circumstances, governments have resorted to selling bonds to finance expenditures. This has its own problems, however, as capital markets in many low- and middle-income countries are underdeveloped, and few people have the resources or the willingness to take on the risk of buying a bond (lending money to the government), particularly if they have safer places to put their savings. Consequently, governments sometimes require the central bank to buy the bonds. In effect, then, the money supply increases by the amount borrowed, leading to inflationary pressures.

At this point there is a deficit that is being financed by borrowed money. This has an inflationary impact through two possible channels. One is the increase in purchasing power from the added government spending and the other is the expansion of the money supply from the purchase of the bonds by the central bank. With either a fixed or crawling peg exchange rate system, higher inflation can have serious repercussions on the real value of the exchange rate. Recall from the chapter on exchange rates (Chapter 10) that if the nominal rate adjusts more slowly than the inflation differential between the home country and its trading partners, the real rate becomes overvalued.

 In particular, capital flight starts if people begin to suspect that the exchange rate is overvalued and that a correction is likely in the near future. The economic incentive is to sell domestic assets and convert them to foreign exchange, which people believe will be more valuable in the future after the domestic currency falls in value. As more people try to convert their domestic currency to a foreign one, the government begins to run out of international reserves and, in order to conserve its remaining supply, it devalues the currency.

An orderly devaluation may not be a problem, but one recent problem with crawling peg systems is that it has been difficult to arrange a smooth devaluation when it is necessary. Devaluations can undermine faith in the government's ability to manage the economy and they inevitably lead to political complications. Crawling pegs are designed to minimize currency fluctuations while keeping the real exchange rate relatively constant. Sudden devaluations can be politically difficult since they erode the purchasing power of the domestic currency and hurt some groups that depend on foreign goods. A delay in devaluing the currency, however, sometimes causes a deeper crisis when it eventually takes place, since a small devaluation may no longer be viewed as sufficient, and speculators may continue to expect further declines in the currency. In other words, a small devaluation may be insufficient to stem the outflow of capital since it does not change people's view of the currency, and can be viewed as a signal that policymakers do not understand the depth of the crisis. If exchange rate policies are not seen as credible, a crisis will continue to deepen.

In addition to large budget deficits, inflationary pressures, and an overvalued currency, the most common indicator of a potential crisis is a large and growing current account deficit. All of these symptoms share the same prescription for their treatment: austerity. In economic policy terms, **austerity** is composed of the same expenditure reduction and expenditure switching policies that were described in the previous chapter (Chapter 11) as appropriate for curing a current account deficit. Recall that expenditure reducing policies address the budget deficits through tax increases and expenditure cuts, while the expenditure switching policies address the current account deficit and the run on reserves through devaluation and, if necessary, temporary measures against imports. This treatment is relatively straightforward, but painful, as it usually results in a recession.

Crises Caused by Volatile Capital Flows

Not all crises are the result of unsustainable expansions in fiscal and monetary policies. National economies are increasingly vulnerable to the effects of technology that instantaneously shift vast sums of financial capital from one market to another. Together with the high degree of financial openness achieved in the last few decades, the contagion effects of crisis can spill across oceans and national borders. The best example of this kind of crisis is the one that hit some of the economies of East Asia in 1997 and 1998. While several economies had underlying weaknesses in their financial sectors, others such as Singapore, Hong Kong, and Taiwan were adversely affected even without the same weaknesses.

The fundamental cause of this type of crisis is that financial capital is highly volatile and technological advances have reinforced this volatility. The discovery of large emerging markets and the drive by financial investors in high-income countries to diversify their portfolios caused hundreds of billions of dollars to be invested throughout the world. While most savings in a nation never leaves, an increasingly large volume of savings has entered international capital markets, where it moves relatively freely in response to interest rates, exchange rate expectations, and economic activity. This creates opportunities as well as problems. For example, one of the main problems in financial markets is that portfolio managers look at the actions of each other for information about the direction of the market. This creates a kind of herd behavior that takes over at critical moments and intensifies a small problem, turning it into a major crisis as large numbers of investors simultaneously lose confidence in a country. What begins as a trickle of funds out of a country can be interpreted as bad news about underlying conditions and lead to an avalanche of capital flight. When that happens, international reserves disappear, exchange rates tumble, and the financial sector can suddenly look very weak.

A weak financial sector can also intensify the problems. A case in point is a banking sector that borrows internationally and lends locally. If the funds obtained in the international market are short term and are used to fund long-term loans such as real estate, problems arise when the international loans must be repaid. As long as international lenders are willing to roll over the debt and extend new loans, everything moves along smoothly. As soon as the lenders believe that there is a problem with a borrowing bank, they refuse to roll over the debt, creating a liquidity problem if the bank's assets are tied up in real estate loans. In the short run, real estate is relatively illiquid and cannot be used to make a payment. When a number of banks are confronted with similar problems, their attempt to unload real estate depresses prices even further and undermines the solvency of the banking system since every bank with real estate investments is suddenly holding a portfolio of declining value.

This type of scenario is particularly troubling because it can go either way. That is, it may resolve itself without a crisis if international lenders are willing to extend additional credit while banks sell their long-term assets. Alternatively, if international investors expect a crisis and as a result are unwilling to give domestic banks the time they need to convert illiquid assets into liquid ones, then the crisis becomes a self-fulfilling prophecy. The belief in a crisis causes lenders to refuse to rollover the banking debts, and the banks, which are illiquid, become insolvent.

Several parts of this scenario are unsettling to economists and policymakers. First, there are multiple possible outcomes, or in economic terms, there are *multiple equilibria*, depending on the responses of international lenders. Second, one of the possible outcomes is a crisis, but the crisis is self-fulfilling. It is not predetermined, nor is it necessary. Third, the crisis affects banks that are fundamentally sound, but that have mismatches between the maturities of their debts and their assets. In other words, they are illiquid, but not insolvent.

These factors seem to imply that it should be possible to avoid this type of crisis. In part, it requires that banks pay closer attention to the maturity match between their debts and assets. In some cases, this requires a higher degree of supervision and regulation on the part of the banking authorities. For their part, international lenders must be more informed about the activities of their borrowers. This requires greater information flows, the use of standard accounting practices, and overall greater transparency in domestic and international financial systems. And, as a final point, once a crisis occurs, international agencies such as the IMF that are called in to make emergency loans need to be able to distinguish between insolvency and illiquidity. This is more complex than it seems, but the distinction is crucial, since the appropriate response will vary depending on the short- to medium-run prospects of the borrowing country.

CASE STUDY

The Mexican Peso Crisis of 1994 and 1995

The collapse of the Mexican peso and the ensuing crisis that began at the end of 1994 has elements of both a crisis caused by macroeconomic imbalances and one caused by volatile capital flows and financial sector weakness. On the one hand, there were definite signs of macroeconomic imbalances, including an overvalued real exchange rate and a large current account deficit. On the other hand, the Mexican government operated a relatively austere fiscal policy, and, not counting foreign interest payments on its debt, the government budget was in surplus, not deficit. Similarly, inflation came down during the early 1990s and reached 7 percent overall in 1994, down from 22.7 percent in 1991. At the same time, huge capital flows entered Mexico from 1990 through 1993, and the volatility of those foreign flows, together with flows of Mexican-owned capital, ultimately subjected the country to a severe crisis and a deep recession, beginning in December, 1994. It is useful to pick up the story at the start of 1994.

On January 1, 1994, the North American Free Trade Agreement (NAFTA) between Canada, the United States, and Mexico, took effect. Throughout 1994, U.S.–Mexican trade expanded by almost a fourth (23.7 percent) and capital continued to flow into Mexico, much of it from Japan and the European Union. Between 1990 and 1993, Mexico experienced capital inflows of $91 billion, or an average of about $23 billion per year, the most of any developing country. The capital inflow was in the form of private portfolio investments ($61 billion), direct investments ($16.6 billion), and bank loans ($13.4 billion).

The administration of President Salinas (1988–1994) actively encouraged large inflows of foreign capital as a way to maintain investment rates far above the level that domestic Mexican savings could support. Recall from Chapter 9 the macroeconomic identity that private savings plus the government budget balance must equal domestic investment plus the current account balance:

$$S_p + (T - G) = I + CA.$$

Mexican savings of around 14 percent of GDP in 1994 could not support investment of more than 20 percent of GDP unless there was an inflow of savings from the rest of the world. Mexico ran large current account deficits, equal to 5 percent of GDP in 1991 and 6.5 percent in 1992 and 1993. The enormous inflow of foreign goods and services permitted more investment by providing capital goods that Mexico could not make itself, and by satisfying consumption through foreign goods and thereby allowing domestic factories to produce investment goods. This was the strategy of the Salinas government, and it seemed to be working. NAFTA inspired confidence in Mexico's institutional stability and guaranteed access to the wealthy U.S. market for any goods made in Mexico.

During 1994, the world capital market began to shift toward a more conservative, risk-averse stance. In February 1994, interest rate movements in the United States and exchange rate movements around the world led to large losses for a number of banks and other investors. Portfolio managers began to reassess their investments and to look for ways to reduce their exposure to risk. The January insurrection of subsistence farmers in the Mexican state of Chiapas raised the specter of political instability, and in March, the assassination of the presidential candidate Luis Donaldo Colosio added fuel to the fire.

Amid the growing perception that the Mexican peso was overvalued, the newly elected President of Mexico, Ernesto

(continues)

Zedillo, announced in early December 1994 that the government would devalue the peso by 15 percent. Figure 12.1 shows the movement of the peso from early December 1994 to late March 1995. The peso had been trading at about 3.5 to the dollar, and a 15 percent decline in value would have placed it at slightly more than 4 to the dollar. The news sparked a rush for the exit, however, as everyone tried to sell off the part of their portfolio that was denominated in pesos. No one wanted to be caught holding assets that were to lose 15 percent of their value in the next few days, and the huge inflow of portfolio investment during the previous years meant that there was a large volume of peso-denominated assets in the hands of non-Mexicans. At the same time that the supply of pesos increased, the demand declined, and the value of the peso fell dramatically. By early March, 1995, the peso had fallen to almost 8 to the dollar. As the dust settled, and a U.S.– IMF–Mexican stabilization plan was put into effect, the peso regained some of its lost value and, by the end of April 1995, it was trading at 6 to the dollar.

From Mexico's perspective, the problem was to maintain high investment rates when savings rates were low. The strategy of relying on large foreign inflows of world savings through a large financial account surplus (current account deficit) proved to be unstable given that so much of the foreign capital was invested in short-term portfolios rather than longer-term direct investment. The administration of President Zedillo addressed the short-run problem by seeking financial support from the IMF and the United States in order to prop up the value of the peso. The medium- to long-run issues were addressed with a package of austerity measures that cut government spending, increased taxes (T up, G down), and reduced consumption. Electricity prices and gasoline prices were raised (both supplied through government-owned enterprises) and credit was restricted through steep increases in interest rates and new lim-

---

FIGURE 12.1   Pesos Per Dollar: December 12, 1994 to March 22, 1995

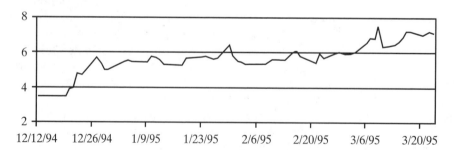

The peso lost over half its value between December 20, 1994, and March 9, 1995.

Source: Federal Reserve Board, http://www.federalreserve.gov/releases/H10/hist/

its on bank lending. These measures reduced consumption and increased savings, provided a greater pool of domestic funds for investment purposes, and reduced dependence on foreign capital inflows. In the short run, however, the fall in consumption and government expenditures caused a recession. The overall decline in Mexico's GDP was 6.2 percent in 1995, and more than 500,000 people lost their jobs in the first few months of the crisis.

DOMESTIC ISSUES IN CRISIS AVOIDANCE

Not all crises are avoidable. Nevertheless, there are steps countries can take to try to minimize their likelihood and the damage they cause when they happen. In addition to the need to maintain credible and sustainable fiscal and monetary policies, governments must engage in active supervision and regulation of the financial system and provide timely information about key economic variables such as the central bank's holding of international reserves.

In these areas, the design of effective policies is relatively straightforward, but in other areas, there is a wide array of expert opinion, and consensus remains elusive. Should countries bail out their banks if they fail, and what type of penalties should they impose if they do? Should they try to limit foreign capital inflows and outflows? Which type of exchange rate system is most stable? It is possible that in some areas, there is no single optimal policy for avoiding crisis and countries have a variety of equally viable options. In those cases, it is also possible that there are choices that are better for some countries, but not others, depending on the conditions inside the country.

Moral Hazard and Financial Sector Regulation

When a country's financial sector becomes dysfunctional, problems spread to the rest of the economy. Credit dries up, investment disappears, households worry about their lost savings, consumption falls, and the economy falls into recession. Hence, there is a big incentive to keep the financial sector operational, even if it means that governments have to spend revenues in order to keep the sector in working order.

This creates a dilemma for policymakers, since the knowledge that you will be bailed out if you fail usually leads people, including bankers, to take greater risks than are prudent. That is, if the costs of failure are removed, the incentive for the decision makers inside financial institutions to take normal precautions and to behave responsibly are also removed.

In economic terms, this is the problem of **moral hazard**. Moral hazards occur in many situations, and can be defined as an incentive to do the wrong thing. For example, when selling a used car, the seller has a financial incentive not to divulge negative information about the car, and people seeking life insurance have an incentive not to divulge negative information about their health. Similarly, in the financial sector, banks and other institutions have an incentive to make riskier investments that pay a higher return if they know they will be bailed out.

Moral hazard problems are particularly acute when the government of a country uses the credit system to make loans for specific economic development goals, or even worse, for satisfying important political constituencies. For example, a government may determine that the development of a particular steel plant is in the interests of the country, or that the economic enterprises of politically well-connected elites should be supported with easy credit. Many governments use state-owned banks to make such loans, or they provide financial incentives or threats to private banks to get them to make the loans. The result in either case is that the loans may not meet market criteria for lending, and there are either implicit or explicit guarantees to the banking sector that they will be bailed out if something bad happens. In the East Asian crisis of 1997 and 1998, these type of loans gave rise to the term **crony capitalism**. In several countries, a significant reform component is to remove politics from lending considerations.

The problem of moral hazard is inescapable if there is a general policy of protecting the financial system from collapse. In effect, no matter how it is administered, the policy of protecting the sector is a form of insurance, and all insurance systems have moral hazard elements. There is no way to completely eliminate the problem of moral hazard, but it can be minimized through various actions.

To this end, bank regulators from the industrial countries met in Basel, Switzerland, under the auspices of the Bank for International Settlements (or BIS; see Chapter 10 for a brief description of the Bank for International Settlements) to agree on a set of operational standards, including supervision and regulation, for internationally active banks. This led to the 1989 **Basel Capital Accord**, which was eventually adopted by more than 100 countries. In 2001, a New Basel Capital Accord was issued, updating the previous standards.

The New Basel Capital Accord is a set of recommended best practices that emphasize the three areas of capital requirements, supervisory review, and information disclosure. **Capital requirements** help to reduce moral hazard elements in the banking sector by requiring the owners of banking institutions to invest a percentage of their own capital in their bank so that bank losses are personal losses to shareholders and other bank owners, as well as losses to the bank's depositors. Bank **supervisory review** and regulations are designed to act as oversight to assist with risk management and to provide standards for daily business practices. The final area, **information disclosure**, is designed to encourage market discipline by requiring banks to disclose all the relevant information that lenders, investors, and depositors need to understand the full scope of a particular bank's operations.

All three of the elements are key to reducing the problem of moral hazard, and to ensuring that if a crisis strikes, the financial system will return to economic health as soon as possible. Since the Accord is a set of recommended practices without an enforcement component, countries are under no obligation to follow them. In addition, in many developing countries, the technical expertise required to implement some of the more complex supervisory functions may be in short supply. In other words, there is no guarantee that a country that adopts the standards set forth in the Accord is actually adhering to them, nor even that it is capable of implementing them.

Exchange Rate Policy

Through the 1970s and 1980s, many countries adopted a crawling peg exchange rate system, often as part of an anti-inflation strategy. Recall from Chapter 10 that the "pegged" part of a crawling peg involves fixing the exchange rate to a major world currency such as the dollar or the German mark, or to a basket of currencies that include the home country's major trading partners. The "crawling" part of the exchange rate involves regular—often daily—devaluations of a fixed amount. Theoretically, a crawling peg allows a country to periodically increase or decrease the value of its currency, but since pegs are usually intended to stabilize the real exchange rate in a country with higher inflation than its trading partners, most crawling pegs are set to a constant rate of devaluation rather than revaluation of the nominal exchange rate. That is, if domestic inflation is higher than foreign inflation, nominal devaluation keeps the real exchange rate constant. Given the definition of the real rate as,

$$R_r = R_n(P^*/P),$$

then if the change in P (domestic prices) is greater than the change in P* (foreign prices), the nominal rate, R_n, must rise (devalue) in order to keep the real rate constant. Maintaining the peg requires the monetary authority to exercise discipline in the creation of new money, and is anti-inflationary in that sense. In addition, many countries tried to reinforce the anti-inflation tendency of the crawling peg by intentionally devaluing at a slower pace than the difference between home and foreign inflation. This created real appreciation in the exchange rate, and was intended to act as a brake on domestic inflation. Foreign goods steadily became cheaper in real terms, limiting the price increases that domestic producers were able to impose. The use of the exchange rate in this manner had mixed success in helping to control inflation, but in a number of cases it led to severe overvaluation of the real exchange rate and increased the country's vulnerability to a crisis.

Another way in which a crawling peg exchange rate system increases a country's vulnerability to crisis is that it is politically difficult to find a way to exit from the system if it becomes overvalued. When a government announces a change in the system, it runs the risk of losing its credibility. Both domestic and foreign economic agents accommodate the existing system, and a sudden large devaluation leads to economic losses and a loss of confidence in the country's policymakers. Consequently, it is common for countries to delay addressing the problem of overvaluation, and when the correction comes, it has to be larger. The end of Mexico's crawling peg in 1994 is a good example.

The current consensus is that countries should adopt either a "hard peg," which is akin to a fixed exchange rate, or they should use a floating exchange rate, which is managed by the central bank. Hard pegs include fixed rates, dollarization, and the use of currency boards. In any of its possible forms, the monetary authority must exercise discipline in the creation of new money. Credibility of the peg is of the utmost importance to its survival, and it is only assured if there is a tight control on the money supply. Floating exchange rates allow more flexibility in the conduct of monetary policy, but they raise the specter of a lack of monetary discipline and a return to deficit financing through the printing of money. For this reason, many countries are reluctant to adopt flexible exchange rates.

Capital Controls

Many economists hold that the free movement of capital is a desirable objective because it allows investors to send their financial capital wherever the return is highest, which raises world welfare by putting financial capital to its most valuable use. At the same time, capital mobility allows countries to invest more than is possible with their domestic savings alone, which again raises world welfare when there are valuable investment projects and insufficient savings to realize them. Others, however, claim that the benefits of complete capital mobility are based on theory, but never fully demonstrated empirically. In addition, capital mobility generates very high costs in the form of macroeconomic crises, and these costs must be offset against any economic gain.

This issue is unsettled, and while economists agree that trade in goods and services raises a country's welfare, there is less agreement about the benefits of free capital movements. The sources of the disagreement cover not only the potential benefits of capital inflows versus the potential costs of sudden capital outflows, but include debates over the actual ability of **capital controls** to prevent capital movements, whether controls on the movement of capital can stop a crisis once it begins, and whether it is better to limit inflows, outflows, or both.

Through much of the twentieth century, countries guarded against the problems of capital mobility by restricting its movement. This seems to imply that countries are able to prevent capital from crossing their borders, but what may have been true in 1970 is much more doubtful today. The growth of emerging stock markets and the implementation of technology to facilitate capital transfers have created both the incentive and the means for investors to send their capital abroad.

Ordinarily, capital flow restrictions are imposed by limiting transactions that are part of the financial account of the balance of payments. (See Chapter 9 for a discussion of the components of the balance of payments.) Capital movements to support transactions on the current account are usually permitted since they are necessary for trade. Consequently, one of the primary ways in which firms can get around capital account restrictions is to overinvoice imports. This allows them to make payments abroad that are larger than necessary for the purchase of imports. Alternatively, they can underinvoice exports, so that the reported payments received are smaller than the actual payments, and the difference can be invested outside the country without reporting to authorities. While these techniques are common, and perhaps fraudulent, outright corruption in the form of bribes is also a possibility for getting money out of the country.

Whether these types of practices make controls on capital outflows completely ineffective is open to debate, but they clearly reduce the effectiveness of capital controls. For this reason, restrictions on inflows are seen as more workable than restrictions on outflows, as a general rule. Inflow restrictions can take a variety of forms, but they share the common goal of trying to reduce the inflow of volatile, short-run capital, which may add to the stock of liquid assets ready to flee the country.

Restrictions on capital inflows cannot stop a crisis once it begins, however. Consequently, there is an ongoing debate over the utility of imposing restrictions on capital outflows once a crisis starts. Since many crises include a speculative attack against the home country currency, some argue that a temporary limitation on capital outflows could help to stop a crisis by artificially reducing the demand for foreign exchange. In theory, this would prop up the value of the domestic currency and eliminate expectations of a large decline in its value.

In the midst of the Asian crisis, Malaysia followed this policy in spite of a number of warnings that it would undermine investor confidence in Malaysian policies, cut them off from international capital markets, and do long-term damage to the economy. None of the dire predictions materialized and Malaysia recovered from the crisis at about the same speed as Korea, which went the other way and eliminated some of its controls on capital flows. The fact that two different policies led to more or less similar outcomes is a measure of how much we do not know.

CASE STUDY

Chilean Taxes on Capital Inflows

One of the most discussed examples of a successful implementation of restrictions on capital inflows is Chile. Chile is not the only country to adopt this type of policy, but it has often been cited as a case in which controls on inflows suc-cessfully insulated the economy from the contagion effects of crises elsewhere in the world.

Chile experienced two periods of restrictions on capital inflows, the first lasting from 1978 through 1982, and the

(*continues*)

second from June 1991 through September 1998. Policy in both periods was oriented toward limiting short-term, portfolio investment, without causing a loss in longer term, foreign direct investment. Regulations varied between the two periods, but the main component was a rule forcing portfolio investors to deposit reserves into a noninterest-bearing account at the central bank. In 1991, foreign investors were required to deposit 20 percent of the value of their investment in the noninterest-bearing account, and in 1992, the reserve requirement was raised to 30 percent. In 1998, in the wake of the Asian crisis, as the government sought to protect the economy from a sudden loss of foreign investment due to the contagion effects of the crisis, they dropped the requirement to 10 percent, and then eliminated it altogether.

The forgone interest on the reserves is one way to measure the cost of investing in short-term, Chilean portfolios. Since reserves were legally tied up for a period of time in noninterest-earning accounts, the forgone interest is a way to measure the costs to the foreign private sector. For most of the period, 1991 to 1998, the reserves were required to remain on deposit for one year. Consequently, the implicit cost of investing declined as the maturity of the investment increased. For example, investments with a maturity of 180 days faced an implicit tax of 2 to 5 percent over the period from 1991 to 1998, while investments with a maturity of three years were taxed at a rate between $1/2$ and 1 percent.

Chile's objective of limiting short-term capital flows was relatively successful by most measures. The percentage of inflows with a maturity of one year or less declined steeply, while the overall inflow of foreign capital seems not to have suffered at all. Nevertheless, several other countries, Mexico and Argentina, for example, also experienced a lengthening of the term structure of foreign-held assets without resorting to capital controls.

In the longer run, the capital controls imposed in Chile seem to have isolated the country from some external shocks, such as the 1994–1995 Mexican crisis, but not from others. One hypothesis is that Chile's policies are adequate for a moderate disturbance in the international economy, but provide little or no protection against the turbulence of a major crisis, such as the one that occurred in East Asia in 1997 and 1998.

Source: Edwards, Sebastian, "How Effective Are Capital Controls," *The Journal of Economic Perspectives.* Fall, 1999.

DOMESTIC POLICIES FOR CRISIS MANAGEMENT

It is relatively easy to prescribe a cure for financial crises that result from inconsistent macroeconomic policies. For example, if a crisis is triggered by a collapsing currency, which, in turn is the result of large government budget deficits financed by money expansion with a fixed or crawling peg exchange rate, then the prescription is relatively straightforward in economic terms: Cut the deficit, raise interest rates to help defend the currency, and, perhaps, let the currency float. In other words, the solution to a fiscal crisis brought on by macroeconomic imbalances is to correct the imbalances.

The problem is that the economic austerity of budget cuts and higher interest rates may not be politically feasible. In addition, several economic problems are often present. Tax systems in many countries are unenforceable, meaning that tax increases may not generate more revenue. The adoption of a floating exchange rate system may undermine the credibility of the government's commitment to fighting inflation, since financial sector interests often fear that it will remove the last bit of restraint over money creation and lead to hyperinflation. Governments may not be able to cut expenditures easily, since government employees may be unionized with multiyear contracts, and other elements of the budget may support powerful domestic interests.

The case of a crisis brought on by sudden capital flight in the context of relatively stable and credible macroeconomic policies is even more difficult to resolve. Given that this type of crisis may have multiple equilibria outcomes, depending on the direction taken by expectations, there is a powerful argument for addressing the problem of a collapsing currency through interest rates hikes, sales of reserves, and other actions that might help convince investors that the currency is strong. On the other hand, high interest rates and other actions to defend the currency are likely to intensify bankruptcies and other contractionary forces that develop during a crisis. Hence, defending a currency may push a small downturn into a full blown depression.

In both a crisis caused by macroeconomic imbalances and one caused by sudden capital flows, there is a strong desire to avoid a recession. In the first type, however, both fiscal and monetary policies are usually so overextended that the crisis is partly a result of policies that are unsustainable and overly expansionary to begin with. In effect, this forecloses fiscal and monetary policies as tools to avoid the recessionary aspects of the crisis. The only way out is usually through some sort of recession.

In the second case, however, fiscal and monetary imbalances may not be part of the initial problem, so that the use of fiscal and monetary policies is not entirely ruled out. However, the dilemma faced by governments in this position is that expansionary policies include a reduction in interest rates, which can cause a further depreciation in the domestic currency. If domestic firms have debts that are denominated in dollars or another foreign currency, a depreciation implies a sudden increase in the size of their debts and spreads additional bankruptcies through the economy.

In effect, this implies that fiscal and monetary policies are limited if there is an international component to the crisis. It also creates a stark set of choices for handling the crisis. Either defend the currency with high interest rates and spread the recessionary effects of the crisis, or defend the domestic economy against the recessionary effects of a crisis and intensify the problems of a collapsing currency. Much of the debate over the policies recommended by the IMF during the Asian Crisis of 1997 and 1998 (raise interest rates to try to stabilize the collapsing currencies) turned on precisely this point. Clearly, if there was an easy, nonrecessionary, way to end a crisis, policymakers would use it.

CASE STUDY

The Asian Crisis of 1997 and 1998

The East Asian financial crisis began in Thailand, during July of 1997. From there, it spread to a number of other countries, including Malaysia, the Philippines, Indonesia, and South Korea. The outward symptoms of the crisis were fairly similar across countries: currency speculation and steep depreciations, capital flight, and financial and industrial sector bankruptcies. It is tempting to interpret these symptoms as signs of the region's weaknesses, but ironically, the causes are at least in part due to the region's great strengths.

Current Account Deficits and Financial Account Surpluses

The most severely affected countries all had large trade deficits. Table 12.1 shows current account deficits in 1996, the year before the crisis. For the five countries in the top panel, deficits averaged 5.2 percent of GDP in 1996. In Thailand, where the crisis began, the current account deficit was nearly 8 percent of GDP. The three countries in the bottom panel of Table 12.1 all felt reverberations from the crisis in spite of their small deficits (Hong Kong) or large surpluses (Singapore and Taiwan).

Large current account deficits necessarily imply large financial account surpluses, and the countries in the top half of Table 12.1 all experienced large capital inflows. Foreign investors were more than willing to send their capital to East Asia as the region had averaged about 5 percent growth per year in real GDP for the last 30 years, and there was no reason to believe that would change anytime soon. Furthermore, slow growth in Japan and Europe during much of the 1990s caused many international investors to scour the globe looking for higher returns, and the stable and dynamic economies of southeast Asia stood out prominently. Low inflation, small budget deficits or consistent government surpluses, and the high rates of economic growth made them highly desirable places to invest and to loan funds.

Exchange Rate Policies

Exchange rate policies in the region usually involved pegging to the dollar, so that as the dollar appreciated in the mid-1990s, it caused many exchange rates to appreciate along with it, resulting in a number of significant currency misalignments. The pegged exchange rates became harder and harder to sustain, partly because they made it more difficult for the pegged countries to export. According to some observers, this problem was exacerbated by China's devaluation of its fixed exchange rate in 1994, and the signifi-

TABLE 12.1	Current Account Balances and Currency Depreciations	
	Current Account Balance, 1996, Percent of GDP	*Currency Depreciation in Dollars, 7/1/97 to 12/31/97*
Countries with large deficits		
Indonesia	–3.4	–44.4
Malaysia	–4.9	–35.0
Philippines	–4.7	–33.9
South Korea	–4.9	–47.7
Thailand	–7.9	–48.7
Countries with small deficits or surpluses		
Hong Kong	–1.3	0.0
Singapore	+15.7	–15.0
Taiwan	+4.0	–14.8

Large current account deficits led to large depreciations. Nevertheless, some countries were hit with depreciations even when they had large surpluses.

Source: Goldstein, Morris, *The Asian Financial Crisis: Causes, Cures, and Systemic Implications,* Washington, DC: Institute for International Economics, June, 1998.

cant depreciation of the Japanese yen throughout the period of dollar appreciation. The movements in these two currencies made the exports of Thailand and several others less competitive.

Financial Sector Problems

The downturn in export revenues exposed several other weaknesses, including those in regulatory systems, corporate structures, and financial systems. Many countries in East Asia rely on corporate structures built around family ties and personal networks. This can have significant advantages for small and medium-size enterprises, but as firms grow, the lack of disclosure and transparency make it difficult for outside lenders to assess the microeconomic risks of lending. In addition, the lack of hard data and information make it difficult to implement the kinds of regulatory controls that all economies need for stability, especially in the financial sector. For example, many banks experienced the kind of mismatches between the maturities of their assets and liabilities that is described as a serious vulnerability earlier in the chapter. These firms took out short-term loans in international capital markets and used the money to finance real estate developments with long and risky payoffs.

Another major weakness in the financial sector stemmed from the politicization of the financial systems of many countries. Banks in many nations were forced to make loans to politically well-connected firms and favored industries. These loans were often at below-market interest rates and, in many cases, were a component of the industrial

(*continues*)

support policies implemented by the national government. In Indonesia, for example, industries that were favored with cheap bank credit were owned by family members of President Suharto and individuals with personal political connections.

As long as growth remained robust, the weaknesses in the economy stemming from a lack of regulatory oversight and financial sector misallocations were invisible. In a growing economy, there are always new opportunities to make profits, and banks with bad loans on their books made up for it by charging their other customers higher interest rates. As exchange rate misalignments accumulated, however, export revenues slipped, and current account deficits widened. The IMF and a number of private economists warned of the building instabilities and advised Thailand (and others) to reduce their trade deficits. The IMF is obliged to keep quiet about its warnings to a country in order to avoid setting off a crisis, and so most people were unaware of its concerns.

Crisis and Contagion

The event that triggers a crisis is often relatively unimportant. For example, some analysts blame the decline in Thailand's export earnings that stemmed from the downturn in prices for computer chips. In any case, the huge trade imbalance and the disappointment on export revenues undermined investor confidence in Thailand's ability to keep its exchange rate pegged to the dollar. People began to expect a devaluation and did not want to be holding the Thai baht when it came. Furthermore, many of the loans to the Thai financial sector were short-term loans obtained in inter-

national capital markets, and required repayment in dollars. This raised the cost of a devaluation, since Thai financial institutions earned revenue in baht, but owed a fixed amount of dollars. Any change in investor confidence could undermine the entire economy.

How the Thai crisis spread internationally is one of the less certain components of the overall crisis. One hypothesis is that Thailand served as a "wake up call" for investors to examine more closely their holdings in other countries. Another hypothesis is that the Thai devaluation made exports from several neighboring countries less competitive and forced them to engage in competitive devaluations. Regardless, there was a contagion element in the Thai crisis and it soon spread to countries as far away as Brazil and Russia.

Some of the consequences of the East Asian crisis are easily visible in Table 12.2, which shows the growth rate of real GDP in 1998 and 1999. With the exceptions of Singapore and Taiwan, every country affected by the crisis experienced a recession in 1998. Given their large trade surpluses and their ample international reserves, Singapore and Taiwan were able to focus on their domestic economies rather than trying to defend their currencies, thereby avoiding recessions. By the second quarter of 1999, every country had returned to positive growth.

The rapid recoveries in Table 12.2 caught most analysts by surprise, yet the flexibility and fundamental soundness of macroeconomic policies throughout East Asia facilitated swift recovery. Still, Table 12.2 does not tell the whole story since poverty rose significantly throughout the region and will take many years to return to its pre-crisis level. In addi-

TABLE 12.2	Real GDP Growth	1998	1999
Real GDP Growth in Countries with Large Current Account Deficits			
Indonesia		–13.2	+0.2
Malaysia		–7.5	+5.4
Philippines		–0.6	+3.3
South Korea		–6.7	+10.7
Thailand		–10.2	+4.2
Real GDP Growth in Countries with Small Current Account Deficits, or Surpluses			
Hong Kong		–5.1	+3.0
Singapore		+0.4	+5.4
Taiwan		+4.6	+5.7

Many countries experienced deep depressions in 1998, but by the second quarter of 1999, virtually every crisis country had returned to positive growth.

Source: Asian Development Bank, "Economic and Statistics, Regional Data," available http://www.adb.org/Statistics/regdata.asp [February 24, 2001].

tion, without fundamental financial sector reform, the chances of a repeat episode remain fairly high.

Crisis Management

Three issues in crisis management remain unresolved after this episode. First, did the IMF make a mistake in advising the borrowing countries to defend their currencies with interest rate hikes? Second, were there moral hazard elements present, perhaps as a result of the Mexican bailout in 1995? Third, are capital controls helpful as a temporary measure to stem a crisis?

The first issue is a specific instance of the dilemma referred to earlier. Should countries try to protect their domestic economies or must they defend their currencies? For countries with large trade surpluses and ample international reserves, defense of the domestic economy through lower interest rates seems feasible. The real question applies to the five countries with large current account deficits. Some critics of the IMF blame it for turning a financial panic in those countries into full blown depressions by counseling them to raise their interest rates. The critics charge that the IMF treated the crisis as if it were the same as the Latin American debt crisis of the 1980s, in which governments had large budget deficits and high rates of inflation. In East Asia, governments were running surpluses or small deficits, so there was no need to temporarily contract the economy with interest rate increases. Defenders of the IMF argue that interest rate hikes were necessary

(continues)

as a means to stop the slide in currency values. The temporary but harmful effects on economic activity caused by interest rate hikes were much smaller than the harm that would have been done if the currency depreciations were not stopped.

A second issue relates to the moral hazard of bailing out a bank or corporation. If banks know they will be bailed out if they make bad lending decisions, then they have less reason to exercise prudence and caution, and more reason to take greater risks that offer higher returns. Some critics allege that the IMF loans to Mexico set a precedent that taught lenders their mistakes would be covered by loans from the IMF, and consequently, the East Asian crisis became more likely. The counterargument is that "bailouts" are not really bailouts in the full sense of the word because they do not protect investors from losses.

Most investors in East Asia saw sizable reductions in the values of their portfolios, so they have plenty of reason to exercise caution when lending.

A final unresolved issue is the problem of capital flight. Can it be stopped, at least in the short term, with controls on capital outflows? Malaysia thought so, and implemented capital controls that appeared to have some success in removing pressures on the Malaysian ringgit to depreciate. Malaysia acted in spite of a number of warnings that it would lose its access to international capital markets, yet its recovery from the crisis was as rapid as in any of the other affected countries On the other hand, Korea went the other way and removed some of the controls it had on capital flows, and it also recovered quickly. Did capital controls make a difference? As with the previous two issues, an answer awaits further research.

REFORM OF THE INTERNATIONAL FINANCIAL ARCHITECTURE

The frequency of international financial crises coupled with their high costs has generated a great deal of interest in finding the right policies for avoiding a crisis and for handling one if it begins. Taken as a whole, the discussion of new international policies for crisis avoidance and management is referred to as reforming the international financial architecture. In particular, a lot of attention is focused on the role of the IMF and the conditions it imposes as part of its loan packages.

A number of ideas for reforming the international financial architecture have been advanced in recent years. Private think tanks such as the Council on Foreign Relations, the Overseas Development Council, and the Centre for Economic Policy and Research in London have each published proposals, as have multilateral agencies such as the United Nations Conference on Trade and Development (UNCTAD), and government appointed bodies such as the International Financial Institutions Advisory Commission of the U.S. Congress.

The proposals for international financial reform express a variety of conflicting viewpoints, but they agree that two issues are at the center of the discussion. The first is the role of an international lender of last resort, and the rules governing its lending practices. A second issue is the type of conditions such a lender might impose on its borrowers. If effect, both these issues are questions about the role of the IMF and its current practices.

A Lender of Last Resort

Recall from Chapter 2 that a lender of last resort is a source of loanable funds after all commercial sources of lending have disappeared. In a national economy, this role is usually filled by the central bank. In the international economy, it is filled by the IMF, often with the support of high-income, industrial economies such as Canada, France, Germany, Japan, and others. As a lender of last resort, the IMF is often asked to intervene when countries reach a crisis point in their finances and cannot make payment on their international loans, or cannot convert their domestic currency into dollars or another foreign currency due to an insufficiency of international reserves.

Not everyone agrees that there should be a lender of last resort, and some observers worry about the moral hazard problems of such lending. This is particularly problematic as a crisis begins to develop and some firms are on the verge of collapse. The moral hazard problem can intensify since managers of failing firms have a large incentive to gamble on high-stakes, high-risk, ventures, that, if they pay off, will cover all their losses. In response, those that favor maintaining the IMF in its current role as an international lender of last resort stress the importance of financial sector regulation, including the elements outlined in the Basel Capital Accord. If the owners of financial firms risk a substantial loss in the event of financial meltdown, they are less likely to take on excessive risk.

Three other issues that are central to the discussion of the IMF's role as a lender of last resort are the question of how high an interest rate it should charge when it makes loans, the length of the payback period, and the size of its loans. Taking the interest rate issue first, the traditional prescription for a lender of last resort is that it lends at a relatively high, or penalty level, interest rate. Most IMF loans are at a rate of interest that is equivalent to a weighted average of short-term government borrowing rates in leading industrial economies, plus a slight surcharge. In practice, these tend to be fairly low-interest loans and definitely not a penalty rate.

Some fear that this encourages countries to borrow, while others argue that the interest rate does not affect the incentive to borrow in a crisis. It may affect the length of time countries take to pay back the loan, however, and in this sense, a higher rate may encourage countries to get out from under their IMF debt. Some proponents of higher interest rates on IMF loans also believe it is necessary to shorten the loan period, while others point out that higher interest rates will encourage countries to pay off their loans more quickly. The length of IMF loans varies by type of loan, with some as short as a year, and others as long as ten years, depending on whether the loan is for immediate relief or long-term structural adjustment.

The final issue about the rules for IMF loans is the size of the loan. Countries pay a subscription, called a *quota*, to join the IMF. The size of the quota depends mainly on the size of the economy and its strength. The quota determines how much a country can borrow in a "normal" crisis, as well as how many votes the country has in setting IMF policy. Generally, countries can borrow up to 300 percent of their quota, but in extraordinary circumstances such as the Mexican peso crisis, the East Asian crisis, or other crises with the potential to spread, the limits on country borrowing are determined more or less by the needs at the time, as well as the amounts available directly from other governments.

While some countries have borrowed enormous sums that are well above 300 percent of their quota, the limits on borrowing have not kept up with the growth in the size of national economies. Some argue that borrowing limits should be greatly expanded, while others propose differentiating between crises that have a high probability of spreading, versus those that are contained within a single country. While in many cases it may not be possible to determine the difference, systemwide crises definitely have the potential to impose greater costs. Hence, there is a clear rationale for intervening with larger sums if they will stop a crisis more quickly.

Conditionality

The second set of issues surrounding the role of a lender of last resort such as the IMF is the issue of conditionality. IMF **conditionality** refers to the changes in economic policy that borrowing nations are required to make in order to receive IMF loans. Conditionality typically covers monetary and fiscal policies, exchange rate policies, and structural policies affecting the financial sector, international trade, and public enterprises. The IMF makes its loans in **tranches**, or installments on the total loan, with each additional tranche of the loan dependent on the completion of a set of reform targets. For example, a loan recipient may have to promise to develop a plan for privatization in order to receive the first tranche, have a workable plan in order to receive the second tranche, begin implementation for the third tranche, and so forth.

These types of reforms often generate significant opposition since they seem to override national sovereignty and generally impose contractionary macroeconomic policies. Some economists argue that conditionality requirements intensify the recessionary tendencies of a crisis, although there is a debate whether countries recover faster with IMF assistance than without it. Until the early 1990s, the IMF focused its efforts on economic policy reforms in a way that more or less ignored their social consequences. Public outcry against the effects of conditionality on the vulnerable members of societies forced a closer look at the social impacts of policies, and the IMF has tried to make adjustments. Even so, however, there are still widespread complaints that IMF conditionality is too punitive and too contractionary, and a few countries have refused IMF assistance when in crisis. The most notable example is Malaysia during the East Asian crisis of 1997 and 1998. Apparently, refusing to work with the IMF did not hurt, since they recovered from the crisis as fast as any other country.

Prior to the 1970s, IMF conditionality focused primarily on correcting the immediate source of the problem that led to a crisis, and avoided involvement with underlying economic issues, such as trade policy and privatization. This was criticized as too short-sighted, and it was agreed that the Fund should involve itself beyond short-run economic policy. New loan programs were developed to provide money and technical assistance to countries that needed help in restructuring their economies. This shift involved the IMF in far more than crisis resolution, as it took on an active role in assisting in privatization, the design of social policies, trade policy reform, agricultural policies, environmental policies, and a number of other areas.

By the late 1990s, there was growing recognition that "mission creep" had become a problem and that the Fund had taken on responsibilities that were better left to the World Bank, regional development banks, or some other agency designed to address the long-run issues of economic development. Several of the proposals for reforming the international financial architecture envision a reduced role for the IMF in this area.

In addition to dealing with the problem of "mission creep," several of the reform proposals argue in favor of a set of requirements that countries must pass before they will be allowed to borrow. These proposals favor a prequalifying examination of country policies as a means to avoid crises in the first place. Proponents argue that in order to receive assistance, countries should first demonstrate that they meet a number of requirements such as open financial markets, adequate bank capital, transparent reporting of financial sector data, and others. Those who propose this type of prequalification for IMF assistance argue that it will force countries to adopt fundamentally sound financial sector policies that will minimize the probability of a crisis.

Critics of the prequalification idea point out that prequalification will not avoid crises since they do not deter speculative attacks on a country's currency. They may even promote instability if they induce complacency about a country that prequalifies. In addition, it would be impossible for the IMF to ignore the needs of member countries that fail to prequalify, and this would lead to other, less open ways to handle a crisis. Finally, the IMF has already implemented a prequalification procedure for one type of loan, but to date no country has tried to prequalify since it might be interpreted as a signal to the rest of the world that problems are developing.

Two additional issues are worth mentioning as part of the reforms of the international financial architecture. First is the issue of a set of standards for transparency and data reporting in the financial sector. The purpose of greater transparency is to make a country's financial standing clearer to potential lenders. The issue of transparency and data reporting is moving forward with the Basel Capital Accord, and the IMF's own development of standards for data reporting, called the **data dissemination standards**.

A final issue is the need to find ways to coordinate private sector involvement in times of crisis. Less progress has been made on this issue than on the data dissemination issue, and it continues to be a serious concern. When a country reaches a crisis, the insistence by numerous private creditors that they be paid first can make it more difficult to resolve a crisis. Hence, proposals have been put forward for **standstills**, in which the IMF officially recognizes the need for a country in crisis to temporarily stop interest and principal repayments on its debt. This would also impose a burden on the country's creditors, and reduce the moral hazard element in their lending practices.

In addition, conflict between private creditors over who deserves first repayment has often been an obstacle to resolving a crisis. Consequently, many analysts see the need for **collective action clauses** in all international bond loans. A collective action clause would require each lender to agree to a collective mediation between all lenders and the debtor in the event of a crisis. To date, little progress has been made in inserting this type of clause into international loans.

Summary

- International financial crises are generally characterized by financial disintermediation in the crisis country, a collapsing currency value, and a steep recession.

- One type of crisis is caused by severe macroeconomic imbalances, such as large budget deficits, hyperinflation, overvalued real exchange rates, and large current account deficits.

- Another type of crisis is the result of a speculative attack on a currency that prompts large outflows of financial capital and a run on the country's international reserves. This type of crisis can be self-fulfilling since economic agents that believe an attack on the currency is imminent will abandon the currency, which is equivalent to an attack on the currency.

- The Mexican peso crisis of 1994–1995 had elements of both types of crises, as did the East Asian crisis of 1997–1998. However, several countries in East Asia were subjected to speculative attacks on their currencies even though their underlying macroeconomic fundamentals were very strong.

- Responding to a crisis is complicated by the problem of moral hazard. If the government or the IMF bail out the banks and other firms hit by crisis, it may encourage future risky behavior. The problem of moral hazard is particularly acute if the government has directed credit to specific enterprises for political or developmental purposes, since directed credit either explicitly or implicitly includes a government guarantee.

- The Basel Capital Accord and the New Basel Capital Accord are a set of recommendations for internationally active banks and financial enterprises. They cover the supervision and regulation of enterprises, minimum capital requirements, and standards for information disclosure.

- The current consensus among most economists is that crawling peg exchange rates make countries more vulnerable to a crisis since they become overvalued more easily and there is no smooth way to abandon them when a crisis begins to brew.

- Capital controls on capital outflows are generally viewed as ineffective, although there is some debate about their temporary efficacy in times of crisis. Capital controls on the inflow of short-term financial capital have more supporters, although there is no consensus on their efficacy in avoiding crisis. Some research shows that they can help a country avoid a small crisis, but are less effective at avoiding a large crisis.

- The optimal response to a crisis depends on its causes. If it is caused by macroeconomic imbalances, then changes in macroeconomic policies are essential. If it is caused by sudden, unexplained capital flight, then the optimal response is less certain. Some economists, particularly those at the IMF, argue that stabilizing the currency with high interest rates will lead to a quicker recovery, even though this intensifies the contractionary elements of the crisis in the short run. Others favor expansionary fiscal and monetary policies to minimize the short-run effects of a recession.

- Reform of the international financial architecture includes a revaluation of the role of the IMF and other international agencies. A few favor abolishing the IMF as a lender of last resort, while most favor keeping it but reconsidering some of its policies. In particular, questions have been raised about the interest rates it charges on its loans, the length of the loan period, and the limits on the size of loans.

- The most contentious element of IMF lending policies is conditionality. In particular, there is widespread agreement that the IMF tries to support too many different types of reform, and that it should refocus on its core competencies which include financial sector reform, balance of payments assistance, and exchange rate policies. There is some discussion about whether it should require countries to prequalify before they are eligible for its lending programs.

- Other issues in the international financial reform discussion include standards for data dissemination and policies to create greater involvement of private creditors in working out the solutions to international financial crises when they occur.

Vocabulary

austerity

banking crisis

Basel Capital Accord

capital controls

capital requirements

collective action clauses

conditionality

contagion effects

crony capitalism

data dissemination standards

disintermediation

exchange rate crisis

financial crisis

information disclosure

intermediation

international financial architecture

lender of last resort

moral hazard

standstills

supervisory review

tranches

Study Questions

1. What is an international financial crisis, and what are the two main causes?

2. In the text, the point is made that the expectation of a crisis from volatile capital flows is sometimes a self-fulfilling crisis. How can a crisis develop as the self-fulfillment of the expectation of a crisis?

3. What are three things countries can do to minimize the probability of being hit by a severe international financial crisis?

4. Why are crises associated with severe recessions? Specifically, what happens during an international financial crisis to create a recession in the affected country or countries?

5. What type of exchange rate is associated with a higher probability of experiencing a crisis? Why?

6. In a crisis not caused by macroeconomic imbalances, economists are uncertain whether a country should try to guard against recession or try to defend its currency. Why are these mutually exclusive, and what are the pros and cons of each alternative?

7. Explain the moral hazard problems inherent in responding to a crisis.

8. Some people argue that U.S. loans to Mexico in 1995 led to the East Asian crisis. Explain the logic of this argument.

9. Some countries impose capital controls as a means of preventing a crisis. Evaluate the pros and cons of this policy.

10. How has the role of the IMF come under scrutiny in the recent discussion of reforms in the international financial architecture?

Part 4

REGIONAL ISSUES IN THE GLOBAL ECONOMY

Chapter 13

ECONOMIC INTEGRATION IN NORTH AMERICA

INTRODUCTION

After several years of negotiations, the North American Free Trade Agreement (NAFTA) began life on January 1, 1994. In Mexico, NAFTA was greeted by a group of armed rebels that seized several towns in the southern state of Chiapas. In the United States, NAFTA was ratified by Congress after a close and bitter debate in which both the proponents and opponents had exaggerated (and misread) the likely impacts. The debate in Canada was not nearly so dramatic, but then Canadians had just gone through a similarly divisive struggle over the Canadian–United States Trade Agreement (CUSTA) that began in 1989, and Canadian commerce with Mexico is relatively small.

For many U.S. economists, it seemed odd that a relatively dry and straightforward agreement should turn into one of the most contentious issues of the 1990s. After all, U.S. barriers to Mexican imports were already low; if Mexico decided to lower its barriers to U.S. and Canadian products, then what could possibly be controversial? Plenty, as it turns out, and as this chapter explores.

ECONOMIC AND DEMOGRAPHIC CHARACTERISTICS OF NORTH AMERICA

Before we turn to the history and controversy over NAFTA, it is useful to have an idea of the size of the combined North American market. Table 13.1 shows population and GNP comparisons that are measured in two different ways. By any measure, the combined market is enormous. In 1999, it had approximately 25 million more people than the fifteen members of the European Union, and more than 190 million more than MERCOSÚR, the South American customs union of Brazil, Argentina, Paraguay, and Uruguay.

International income comparisons are more complicated than population comparisons. The third column in the table is one (typical) way to make comparisons. Mexican and Canadian incomes are converted to U.S. dollars, using the average exchange rate over the entire year. This method shows that the average Canadian income is about 63 percent of the United States's average income, and the average Mexican income is around 14 percent. The first problem with this comparison is that regardless of changes in either nation's output, fluctuations in the exchange rate can lead to dramatically different values for

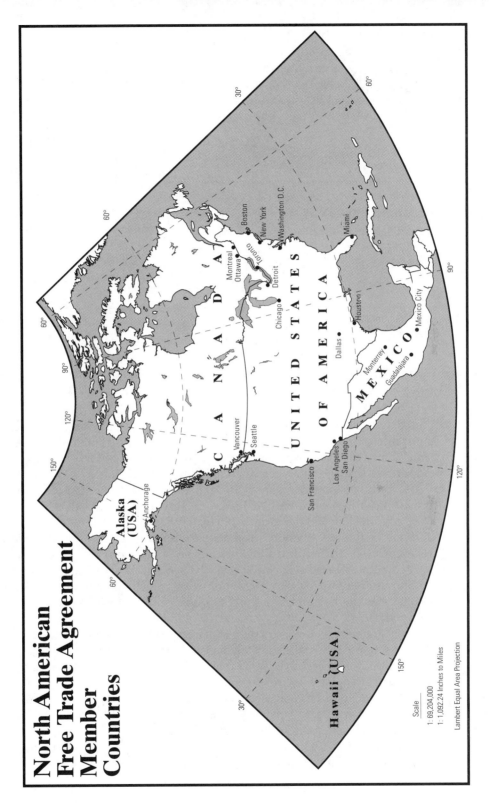

North American
Free Trade Agreement
Member
Countries

CANADA

UNITED STATES OF AMERICA

MEXICO

Alaska (USA)

Hawaii (USA)

Boston
New York
Washington D.C.
Montreal
Ottawa
Toronto
Detroit
Chicago
Miami
Houston
Dallas
Monterrey
Guadalajara
Mexico City
Vancouver
Seattle
San Francisco
Los Angeles
San Diego
Anchorage

Scale
1: 69,204,000
1: 1,092.24 Inches to Miles

Lambert Equal Area Projection

30°
60°
90°
120°
150°
60°

TABLE 13.1	Population and GNP for Canada, Mexico, and the United States, 1999			
	Population (millions)	GNP ($U.S. market exchange rates, billions)	GNP per Capita ($U.S. market exchange rates)	GNP per Capita ($U.S., PPP*)
Canada	30.5	591.4	19,390	23,725
Mexico	97.4	428.8	4,402	7,719
United States	272.7	8,351.0	30,623	30,623
Total	400.5	9,371.2	23,399	

The NAFTA market is over 400 million people and $9.3 trillion.

*Purchasing power parity.
Source: The World Bank, *World Development Report, 2000/2001.*

Mexican or Canadian GNP when measured in dollar terms. A second problem is that real prices vary across countries. Haircuts, restaurant meals, and maid services, to name just a few, cost far less in real terms in Mexico than in the United States. These goods and services are not traded, and Mexico's relative abundance of labor makes production of labor-intensive goods cheaper. As a consequence, the average annual income in Mexico of $4,402 buys more goods and services than a similar income would in the United States.

The fourth column shows income comparisons in **purchasing power parity** terms. Purchasing power parity comparisons use an artificial exhange rate to make adjustments for differences in prices. It can be interpreted as the U.S. dollar value of the real quantity of goods and services that a typical Mexican income buys. In other words, GNP per person in Mexico is enough income to buy goods and services that would cost $7,719 in the United States. However, if a Mexican citizen took that amount of pesos, converted them to dollars, and brought them to the United States, they would only get $4,402 worth of goods and services.

Measurements of GNP per capita at market exchange rates and at purchasing power parity prices both convey important information. Market exchange rates tell what a nation can buy externally (outside the nation), while purchasing power parity prices tell what it can buy internally (inside the nation). As an exporter, I would be more interested in the former, but as someone interested in knowing how Mexico's living standards compare to those of the United States, I would want to know the latter.

Two more points about Table 13.1 are worth considering. First, even though Mexico is a developing country, the NAFTA market is very rich. Few countries have a higher GNP per capita than the weighted average of Canada, Mexico, and the United States, and total GNP at market exchange rates is over $10 *trillion*. Second, NAFTA combines nations that are at very different levels of economic development. Even though Mexico is one of the wealthiest nations in Latin America, the gap between its per capita income and that of the United States adds a layer of political and social tension to NAFTA. Issues such as immigration and environmental and labor standards are more contentious than in other trade blocs.

Table 13.2 shows the importance of trade between each pair of countries. Note that the trade between each pair of countries is an important share of each nation's overall trade, with the exception of Canada–Mexico. Both Canada's and Mexico's trade with the United States is far greater than their trade with any other country, while in the United States, Canada is the number one trading partner, and Mexico is number three, after Japan.

Mexico and Canada both depend on trade more than the United States does. Recall that one way to measure how much a country depends on trade is to calculate its openness ratio ((Exports + Imports) / GDP). Using this measure, 1998 trade was equal to nearly 82 percent of Canada's GDP, 68 percent of Mexico's GDP, and 25 percent of the United States's GDP. These numbers reflect the general proposition that the smaller a nation, the more it must trade in order to achieve a given level of prosperity. Small markets are less able to realize the economies of scale that come from producing in large volume, and they cannot produce the variety of products that large markets can. Through trade, they overcome the limitations of size. The relative importance of trade is a good indicator of Canada's and Mexico's interest in maintaining unobstructed access to the U.S. market and in negotiating lower trade barriers.

TABLE 13.2	Merchandise Trade within the NAFTA Region, 1999 (millions of U.S. dollars)

| | *Exports by* | | | |
Imports by:	Canada	Mexico	United States	World
Canada	—	2,391	163,913	219,963
Mexico	2,949	—	87,044	141,975
United States	198,324	109,706	—	1,029,900
World	242,703	136,391	684,000	—

Canadian and Mexican trade is highly concentrated with the United States.

Sources: Statistics Canada; Instituto Nacional de Estadística, Geografía, e Informática; U.S. Department of Commerce, *U.S. Foreign Trade Highlights, 1999.*

THE MANAGEMENT
THE RIGHT TO
LICENSE GRA
TICKET BY
TICKET PRI
OF PERF

RELA...

The United States and ...
world. In 1999, for example, the combined ...
imports from Canada was $362 *billion* (U.S.). Figure 13.1 illustr...
stant upward trend in U.S.–Canada trade. On average, from 1989 to
Canadian exports to the United States increased 9 percent per year, while U.S.
exports to Canada grew 7.8 percent per year. Since 1989, the value of exports
and imports has increased 112 percent and 136 percent, respectively, a remarkable achievement. In addition to the world's largest trade relationship, the
United States's political and military relationship to Canada is closer than with
any other nation. Canadian defense firms, for example, may bid on U.S. defense
contracts as if they were U.S. firms.

Given the history of close ties and the importance of trade, it is not surprising that the United States and Canada would join together to form a free-trade
area and that they would do so before NAFTA was created. The
Canadian–United States Trade Agreement, or **CUSTA**, was signed in 1988 and
implemented on January 1, 1989, exactly five years before NAFTA. CUSTA,
however, was not the first important trade agreement between Canada and the
United States. In 1965, twenty-four years before the implementation of
CUSTA, Canada and the United States signed an agreement on trade and
investment in automotive products, the single largest component of U.S.–
Canadian trade.

The Auto Pact of 1965

Although the **Auto Pact** agreement was limited to trade in automotive products, it is a very successful example of gains from trade. By removing barriers
to trade, the Pact permitted the big three Detroit automakers (General
Motors, Ford, and Chrysler) to produce for a single, combined market. Prior to
the agreement, Canadian content laws required that cars sold in Canada had
to be mostly produced there as well. The relatively small market size caused
factories in Canada to lose some of the economies of scale of their American
counterparts, and, not surprisingly, Canada's productivity in automotive products was around 30 percent below the U.S. level.

With the coming of free trade in cars and car parts, Detroit automakers
(who were also Canadian automakers) were able to reoganize production in
Canada and the United States, and both locations began to produce for both
markets. The impact on trade was stunning. Between 1963, when firms began
to anticipate an opening of Canada–U.S. auto trade, and 1969, Canadian
exports to the United States grew 169 percent, while U.S. exports to Canada
grew 114 percent. Most of the trade growth was in automotive products, and
even today, they remain the single largest component of trade between the
United States and Canada.

The Canadian–U.S. Trade Agreement (CUSTA) of 1989

From the Canadian viewpoint, the 1980s brought to the foreground two tr
that had to be addressed. First the United States began to be a less relia
trade partner. The problem was the United States's expanded use of count
vailing and antidumping duties, and "voluntary" export restrictions that wes
imposed on a number of U.S. imports. In addition, U.S. rhetoric indicated a
greater willingness to use these measures as a means of gaining political support from declining U.S. industries. Although VERs and antidumping and
countervailing duties did not directly affect an important share of U.S.–
Canadian trade, the specter of the United States turning increasingly protectionist was a problem for Canada. Their dependence on international trade
means that protectionism in the United States is a direct threat to their standard of living.

The second problem facing Canada in the 1980s was the need to restructure
many of its firms and industries in order to keep them competitive in a more
global environment. Many observers inside Canada felt that Asian manufacturing was beginning to exert strong competitive pressures on Canadian firms
and without significant modernization and rebuilding, Canadian firms were
likely to lose markets at home and abroad.

Creating a free-trade agreement with the United States was one solution to
the problem of growing U.S. protectionism and increasing Asian competitiveness in manufacturing industries. This solution locks the United States into an

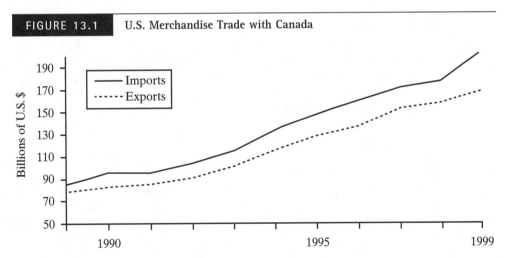

FIGURE 13.1 U.S. Merchandise Trade with Canada

Since the implementation of the Canada–United States Free Trade Agreement in 1989, trade between
the two countries has more than doubled.

Source: U.S. Department of Commerce, International Trade Administration. Available: http://www.ita.doc.gov.

international agreement requiring it to keep its market open and, at the same time, puts pressure on Canadian manufacturers to make the necessary changes.

The impacts of CUSTA were more or less as expected. Between 1989 and 1994, Canadian exports to the United States grew 55 percent, ($47 billion increase), while U.S. exports to Canada grew 46.6 percent ($36.5 billion increase). In percentage terms, this growth is not quite as rapid as the period before and after the implementation of the Auto Pact, but given that trade was already at a high level in 1987, a fifty percent increase represents an enormous volume of trade.

The debate over U.S.–Canadian free trade was low key and dispassionate in the United States. In Canada, however, a heated public discussion erupted when it was announced that the United States and Canada were negotiating an agreement. The opponents of the trade agreement feared that (1) Canada might not be able to compete with U.S. firms, which had the advantages of economies of scale; (2) expanded trade might force Canada to jettison many of its social programs; and (3) Canadian culture might come to be dominated by U.S. news, information, arts, and entertainment industries.

The issue of Canadian competitiveness is largely one about the need to gain economies of scale and to increase productivity through organizational or technological changes within firms. For the most part, the real issue for a high-income, industrialized country such as Canada is the length of time over which the changes can be expected to occur, and not whether firms are capable of competing.

The Canadian opponents of CUSTA also argued that it would erode Canada's social programs. For many citizens, Canada's more extensive social programs, such as universal health care and income maintenance, are part of a national identity that make Canada unlike the United States. The opponents of CUSTA argued that the intensification of competition with the United States would undermine these social programs. They reasoned that social programs would be cut in order to reduce business taxes and make Canadian firms more competitive. Given that taxes are but one component of business costs and that in some cases there are offsetting reductions in cost elsewhere, it is not at all certain what the final impact of free trade will be on Canadian social programs. In the case of health care, for example, it makes more sense to argue that the United States's system is a competitive disadvantage, since it raises the cost of hiring workers when they must be provided with health care benefits by their employer. In Canada, by contrast, health care coverage is universal and is paid for out of general government revenues and individual taxes. A complicating factor for examining the impact of free trade on social spending is that by the mid-1990s, Canada's federal and provincial deficits had grown to the point where governments were forced to scale back some social programs. The cuts are a result of large and unsustainable deficits at both the provincial and federal levels, however, and are not caused by increased trade.

The final, and most contentious, issue from the Canadian point of view is the possibility of U.S. cultural domination. A very wide spectrum of opinion,

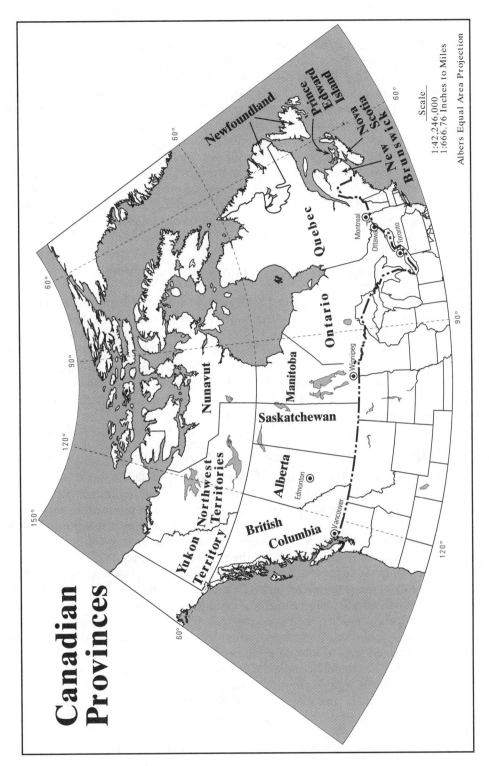

Canadian Provinces

Newfoundland

Prince Edward Island

Nova Scotia

New Brunswick

Quebec

Ontario

Montreal

Ottawa

Toronto

Manitoba

Winnipeg

Saskatchewan

Nunavut

Alberta

Edmonton

Northwest Territories

Yukon Territory

British Columbia

Vancouver

Scale

1:42,246,000

1:666.76 Inches to Miles

Albers Equal Area Projection

60°

60°

60°

60°

60°

60°

90°

90°

90°

120°

120°

120°

150°

297

including both opponents and proponents of expanded free trade, argue that the combination of Canada's smaller population and its proximity to the United States will destroy its national identity if it allows completely free trade in the cultural industries. These industries include music in all of its venues, as well as radio, television, newspapers, book publishing, magazines, drama, cinema, and painting. Under the rules of CUSTA, Canada is allowed to protect its national identity by imposing quantitative restrictions on imports of "cultural products." In most cases, the rules allow Canada to impose domestic content requirements on television, radio, and theater. The content requirements make it illegal for a radio or TV station to program twenty-four hours a day of U.S.-origin material. Cable TV companies give preferences to Canadian-based TV networks, and there are national rules that favor Canadian theater companies, artists, and writers.

RECENT MEXICAN ECONOMIC HISTORY

While Canada's interests in CUSTA were relatively straightforward, Mexico's interests in signing NAFTA were more complex. Like Canada, Mexico wanted to guarantee its access to the U.S. market; unlike Canada, however, Mexico needed to fundamentally alter its economic strategy. The decision to seek closer economic ties to the United States was one of many major policy changes that Mexico made between the late 1980s and early 1990s. By the time the agreement was ratified in 1993, Mexico had completely abandoned the economic policies it had followed since the end of World War II.

Import Substitution Industrialization (ISI)

Until the mid-1980s, Mexico's economic policy and development strategy was inward rather than outward oriented. Inward orientation meant that Mexico favored self-sufficiency over trade and that domestic production was used to replace imported goods. The name for this policy is **import substitution industrialization**, or **ISI**. ISI was the dominant economic strategy throughout Latin America from World War II until the 1980s (see Chapter 15).

ISI policies target the development of manufacturing sectors, particularly those that compete against imported goods. Supporters of ISI theorized that a country should be able to begin by producing simple consumer nondurables such as toys, clothing, food products (e.g., beverages, canned goods) and simpler consumer durables, such as furniture. Gradually, the focus of industrial targeting would shift to include more complex consumer goods (appliances and autos) and intermediate industrial goods (pumps, generators, basic metals). In the third stage, complex industrial goods would be produced (chemicals, electronic equipment, machine tools). In practice, ISI policies had mixed success and attainment of the third stage was elusive.

From 1950 to 1973, Mexico's GDP per capita grew at the rate of 3.1 percent per year when measured in purchasing power parity terms. By comparison,

Canadian and American growth rates over the same period, and measured in the same way, were 2.9 percent and 2.2 percent, respectively. Mexico's growth was also favorable when compared to Asia, Europe, and the rest of Latin American. By the criterion of growth in GDP per capita, ISI policies were relatively successful. In addition, the policies helped shift the structure of the Mexican economy toward greater industrial production. Between 1950 and 1980, industry rose from 21.5 percent to 29.4 percent of GDP.

Although ISI policies seem to have succeeded in stimulating GDP growth and a shift toward industry, they also created a number of long-term problems in Mexico and elsewhere. Most seriously, ISI policies reduced the flexibility of the economy by reducing its ability to generate exports. Equally serious was the fact that ISI created conditions that fostered corruption. We will take up these issues in more detail in Chapter 15, when we look at Latin American reforms.

In the 1980s, the nations of Latin America began to abandon the inward-oriented, antitrade policies they had followed since the 1930s. In most cases, the shift in economic policy favored stronger markets, more trade, and a reduced role for industrial policies. In many cases, the changes were triggered by the inability of the nations to continue to make payments on the enormous debt that had been accumulated in the 1970s and early 1980s. Mexico's role in the historic shift of Latin American policies was to be a leader, both in the sudden appearance of a severe debt crisis and in the shift of its policies away from ISI.

The Onset of the Debt Crisis of 1982

When Lopez Portillo became president of Mexico in 1976, he entered office with a number of constraints. Mexico was operating under the terms of an agreement with the IMF. In 1976, Mexico was a fairly typical case of a government that had borrowed in world financial markets and then found that it could not keep up with its commitments. In order to receive assistance from the IMF and other lenders, the Mexican government was required to make substantial cuts in expenditures and programs. Consequently, during Portillo's first year in office, he was forced to continue the program of austerity and budget cuts.

By 1978, little more than a year after Portillo's election, Mexico's rich reserves of petroleum were coming into production, and the budget crisis was solved. In 1979, the second world oil crisis began and oil prices rose dramatically, bringing up government revenues as well. (Pemex, or Petroleos Mexicano, is owned by the Mexican government and has a monopoly on oil exploration, development, and sales.)

In 1979, the Portillo administration responded to the high and rising oil prices by pouring money into economic and social programs in an attempt to restart the economy. Portillo declared that the era of scarcity was over and that the problem for Mexico was to "manage the abundance." The ambitious expenditure and investment programs required the government to seek capital from international financial markets because the domestic level of savings was insufficient, despite the high oil revenues. The oil reserves, however, caused Mexico's credit worthiness to be solid, as future oil sales were almost a guarantee that debt could be repaid. By 1982, the deficit of the federal government reached 14.1 percent of the GDP, an extraordinarily high level.

It should be noted that people and economies around the world acted as if the oil crisis and high prices were a permanent feature of the world economy. Economic forecasters predicted that crude oil prices were headed ever upward and that by the year 2000 they could easily reach $100 per barrel. In retrospect, it is easy to understand their mistake: New oil takes time to discover and to come into production, and it takes time for businesses to find new, less oil-intensive equipment and to look for oil substitutes. Most individuals cannot immediately buy more fuel-efficient cars or adjust their demands for heating oil. Over time, however, all these changes take place in response to an increase in oil prices, thus moderating or even reversing the increase in prices.

In 1981, the situation for Mexico began to unravel. First, world oil prices started to fall. At the time, few people inside or outside Mexico believed that it was the beginning of a trend. By 1982, however, it was apparent that oil prices were not going to stay high and that Mexico's credit worthiness was under serious pressure. At the same time, a second problem was beginning to bedevil Mexico's finances. The Mexican government's international debt was mostly from commercial banks and was at variable interest rates. In 1979, the U.S. Federal Reserve began to fight inflation in the United States with monetary policies that caused interest rates to reach extraordinarily high levels. Each upward tick of U.S. and world interest rates caused a significant increase in the interest charges on Mexico's debt, so that at precisely the same time that oil revenues were falling, Mexico was required to pay more on its debt.

There was a certain amount of reluctance on the part of the U.S. government and international lenders to acknowledge the severity of the problem as it developed through 1982. By August of 1982, however, it was unavoidable. Mexico's holdings of dollars and other international reserves had fallen below what they needed in order to make repayment possible. On August 12, 1982, the government announced that it was temporarily suspending repayment of the principal it owed. The **debt crisis** had begun.

The Lost Decade: 1980s

The 1980s are known as the **Lost Decade** in Mexico (and throughout Latin America), because GDP growth was nearly nonexistent during that time. Foreign capital stopped flowing into the country, credit became scarce, and investment declined. These factors, along with the budget cuts, peso devaluations, and debt repayment, brought on a severe recession. The debt crisis of 1982 was a more severe repeat of the crisis of 1976. At bottom, both crises were the result of macroeconomic mismanagement, and both stemmed from levels of government expenditure that required significant foreign borrowing. When the government's capacity to make payment on its debts declined, the crises began.

In response to the 1982 crisis, Mexico worked out an agreement with the U.S. government, a group of U.S. banks, and the International Monetary Fund. In essence, Mexico agreed to significant budget cuts and a peso devaluation, the latter to boost the country's exports. In return, Mexico's debt repayment was restructured, and a small amount of new loans were made for the purposes of helping with temporary liquidity shortfalls. A downside to the devaluation of the peso was that it caused inflation. Imported goods became more expensive, and Mexican producers that relied on imported parts or capital equipment were forced to raise prices in order to cover their higher costs. In addition, producers that directly competed with imports could raise their prices without losing sales, since the imported goods had gone up in price.

Partly as a result of the inflation, partly due to the budget cuts, the real incomes of the middle class fell dramatically. The wage data are striking: between 1983 and 1988, real wages fell by 40 to 50 percent. Overall, inflation adjusted per capita GDP fell by about 15 percent between 1982 and 1986. (In the United States, a "normal" recession causes a decline in per capita GDP of 1 to 3 percent.) In addition, as the government sought to reduce its expenditures, spending on health care and education was cut.

Structural Reforms in the Mexican Economy

There were three main lessons from the debt crisis of 1982. First, it was clear that Mexico's management of its macroeconomy had to change. Both the 1976 and 1982 crises had resulted in large part from poor handling of the macroeconomy, and the consequences had been disastrous. Second, and related to the first point, the government could no longer use public expenditures as a way to start economic growth. Third, it was necessary to give markets a much larger role (and state intervention a smaller role) in order to attract the capital needed for investment and growth.

In 1982, newly elected President Miguel De la Madrid began the process of reducing the economic role of the state. Trade barriers slowly began to diminish (especially after 1985), and the budget deficit was eventually reduced. By the end of his presidency in late 1988, the policies were in place to bring inflation under control.

President Carlos Salinas entered office in December 1988. Growth had been poor throughout much of the decade, but Salinas understood the impossibility of using government expenditures to stimulate a recovery. The additional problem he faced was that the private sector was hesitant to invest because it lacked confidence in the economy and the government. Salinas's key tasks were to reduce the costs of servicing Mexico's international debt, to create a climate in which Mexicans would bring home the financial capital they had sent abroad during the turmoil of the 1980s, and to attract foreign capital for investment in Mexico.

CASE STUDY

Mexico's Export Processing Industry

A large share of the trade between the United States and Mexico is intrafirm (25 to 35 percent) and occurs in the context of Mexico's special export processing sector. Mexico began its program in 1965, when the government initiated the Border Industrialization Program (BIP) with its Decree for the Development and Operation of the Maquiladora Export Industry. The primary purpose of the plan was to generate employment along its northern border, where large numbers of workers had suddenly become unemployed due to the termination of the agricultural guest worker program (called the *bracero* program) in the United States.

The BIP created an **export processing zone**, or **EPZ**, in which foreign firms could set up an assembly-type operation and escape Mexican tariffs on the parts and materials they imported as long as they exported the assembled goods. In addition, U.S. tariffs on imports from the EPZ were usually limited to the share of the value of the product created in Mexico. In other words, American firms such as General Motors or 3M could set up assembly operations in Mexico and pay no Mexican tariffs on the inputs the assemblers brought into Mexico as long as they exported the output. When the output was shipped back to the United States, it qualified for special U.S. tariff treatment, which allowed them to avoid tariffs on the share of the value that was created outside Mexico.

The firms that located in the export processing zone became known as *maquila* (mah-kee′-lah), and the indus-try as a whole is referred to as the *maquiladora* (mah-kee-lah-dor′-ah) industry. Although there are many areas outside the border region that qualify for free-trade status, the greatest concentrations of *maquila* are across the border from El Paso in Ciudad Juarez and across from San Diego in Tijuana.

The *maquiladora* industry grew steadily during the 1970s, and by 1980, there were 620 plants employing 120,000 workers. After the crisis of 1982, a decision was made in Mexico City to diversify exports away from oil, and greater encouragement was given to *maquiladora* operations. In addition, the depreciation of the peso and the proximity to the U.S. market made these operations more attractive to foreign investment. As a result, the period of most rapid growth began after 1983.

In mid-2000, the *maquiladora* industry employed over 1.3 million Mexican workers in more than 3600 firms. Their output was about 40 percent of total Mexican manufacturing and the source of about 40 percent of total trade. In addition, the *maquiladora* industry is the largest earner of foreign exchange, with a trade surplus of almost $12 billion in 1999.

Non-Mexican firms are motivated to locate a branch of their production in the *maquiladora* industry by several factors in addition to tariffs. Labor costs are a primary consideration. In 1999, total compensation costs averaged $3.90 versus $13.90 for production workers in United States manufacturing. The differences in labor costs indicate that much of the intrafirm trade between U.S. firms and their subsidiaries or affiliates in the *maquiladora* industry is an example of trade based on comparative advantage and factor cost differences.

In many low-wage countries, low labor costs are more than offset by the lack of nearby suppliers and the poor condition of roads, sewer hookups, and other critical pieces of infrastructure. In the case of the *maquiladora*, most firms are close to the U.S. market, where suppliers are also located and poor road conditions are less of an aggravation. In addition, Mexico has built many full-service industrial parks that provide good infrastructure to the firms that locate in them. Many *maquiladora* are owned by multinational firms such as General Motors and Sony, which make a differentiated product with significant economies of scale. Consequently, much of the output of the industry reflects conditions of trade and growth based on internal economies of scale.

The *maquiladora* industry is responsive to conditions inside the United States more than macroeconomic conditions in Mexico. For example, during the recession of 1995, Mexico's GDP fell by 6.2 percent, but employment in the *maquiladora* industry grew by 9.4 percent. Given that about 80 percent of the industry is located in the northern Mexican states adjacent to the border, the business cycle in northern Mexico is more synchronized with the United States than are those in the interior and southern parts of the nation.

Critics of the industry point to the fact that it has not created linkages to domestic Mexican suppliers. It is estimated that in 1999, less than 3 percent of the intermediate inputs came from domestically owned, Mexican producers. Nevertheless, provisions in NAFTA that eliminated the duty-free import status of the *maquiladora* industry on January 1, 2001, provided incentives for manufacturers of final products such as cars and televisions, to help their suppliers locate nearby in order to qualify for free-trade status under the rules of origin provisions of NAFTA.

The key to Salinas's strategy was capital for investment. Without investment, there could be no growth and no modernization of Mexico's economy. Traditionally, the government had been one of the primary sources of investment capital, but that role was foreclosed by the debt crisis. In the future, Mexico would have to rely on private sources for its investment, both at home and abroad.

In order to attract domestic and foreign investment, Salinas and his advisors argued that they had to strengthen the role of markets. Investors needed to perceive that their economic fortunes would depend on product quality and production efficiency. In the past, economic success or failure often depended on arbitrary government rules that changed prices and limited supplies of key goods throughout the economy.

Salinas carried forward the reforms begun under De la Madrid and added several of his own. Progress continued to be made on bringing the government budget under control. To help with this, and to demonstrate the reality of the change in Mexico's policies, Salinas began to speed up the privatization of state-owned enterprises. In 1982, the government owned 1155 enterprises, ranging in size from the nation's largest firm, Pemex, all the way down to small retail outlets. By 1992, the number of state-owned enterprises had fallen to 217. Most significantly, Salinas announced in May 1990 that he was privatizing the banking sector, which had been nationalized in 1982 by one of his predecessors.

Salinas needed to tackle the debt problem in order to reduce the outflow of Mexican savings going to pay interest and principal on debts contracted in the 1970s and 1980s. The flow of savings out of the country reduced the pool of funds available for investment inside Mexico and was one of the reasons why growth had been slow. In 1989, when the United States announced the introduction of the **Brady Plan** for debt relief, Salinas acted quickly to put Mexico first in line. Named after Nicholas Brady, U.S. secretary of the treasury, the goal was to address the international debt crisis throughout the developing world. (See Chapter 15 for more details.) Mexico was the first case and ultimately received a reduction in its debt of about 10 percent. Perhaps more important than the modest amount of debt relief, Mexico's participation in the Brady Plan, along with other policy measures such as the privatization of the banks, began to significantly alter international perceptions about the country and its future prospects.

On the trade front, Salinas carried forward De la Madrid's reforms by continuing to reduce tariff levels and by freeing more imports from licensing requirements. These reforms had been slowed under the De la Madrid presidency because the dropping of import restrictions caused the trade deficit to increase, and Mexico's shortage of international reserves made it costly to have a large excess of imports over its exports.

Reprivatizing the banks, reducing trade barriers, curbing inflation, cutting the budget deficit, and renegotiating Mexico's international debt were key components in the reorientation of Mexico's economic strategy. It was still not enough, however, in the eyes of many potential investors inside and outside Mexico. One problem was that the reforms in the Mexican economy were not permanent. While people might applaud the Salinas administration, what would the next president do? As long as the reforms were the policies of a single presidential administration, they could be reversed.

In order to provide credibility and permanency for the economic reforms, Salinas took the bold step of proposing a trade agreement with the United States. His goal was to tie up many of the reforms in an international treaty, making it much harder, if not impossible, to reverse them in the future. The proposal for a **North American Free Trade Agreement (NAFTA)** with the United States was a bold break with Mexico's recent past. Although the United States and Mexico had come to agreement on several important issues during the 1980s, U.S.–Mexican relations had been lukewarm at best through most of the twentieth century. The memory of the bitter dispute over Mexico's nationalization of its oil industry in 1938, the historical loss of about one-third of the country to the United States in the nineteenth century, and the different languages and cultures created misunderstanding and a lack of trust on both sides.

Closer economic ties with the United States seemed to offer Mexico the guarantees that international investors wanted. Not only would it make future policy reversals more difficult, it also offered full access to the wealthy American market for anyone that produced their goods in Mexico. The proposal seemed to accomplish its goals: Capital began to pour into Mexico, both from foreign investors and from Mexican nationals who had sent their savings out of the country during the turmoil of the debt crisis. Between 1990 and 1993, Mexico attracted over $90 billion in outside capital, or about one in every five dollars that went to developing countries from private sources.

THE NORTH AMERICAN FREE TRADE AGREEMENT (NAFTA)

Trade flows between the United States and its NAFTA partners increased significantly in the 1990s. Given that trade flows were growing before the implementation of NAFTA, and that they have continued to grow afterward, it is impossible to say how much of the increase in trade is directly due to the trade agreement. Some of the increase before NAFTA's implementation may have been in anticipation of freer trade, while much of the growth since then may have occurred without the agreement. Given that tariffs on about half of the goods traded between the United States and Mexico were eliminated immediately in 1994, it makes sense to think that NAFTA caused at least some of the growth in trade. United States–Canadian trade also expanded, even though there was little change in trade barriers. In part, the growth in trade among NAFTA partners was a reflection of the overall growth of the three economies. NAFTA, however, facilitated the trade growth.

The first important feature of NAFTA is that most forms of trade barriers came down. Since the United States and Canada were relatively open economies with few trade barriers before NAFTA, most of the change has come on the Mexican side. For example, between 1993 and 1996, average U.S. tariffs on Mexican goods fell from 2.07 to 0.65 percent. By contrast, Mexican tariffs on U.S. goods fell from 10 to 2.9 percent. These reductions in tariffs under NAFTA were a continuation of the decline in Mexican tariffs that began in the mid-1980s during the De la Madrid presidency. Between 1982 and 1992, the percentage of Mexico's imports that required import licenses from the government declined from 100 to 11 percent. At the same time, tariffs were falling from an average level of 27 to 13.1 percent. By 1994, at the beginning of the implementation of the agreement, Mexico's economy was substantially open to the world.

The phase-out period for the remaining tariffs and investment restrictions varies from sector to sector. In cases where there is expected to be significant new competition, industries were given a longer grace period to prepare themselves. Some sectors do not reach zero tariffs or become completely open to foreign investment until 2004. Although each country wants the gains from trade, they also want to avoid a sudden disruption of their economies.

A second feature of NAFTA is that it specifies North American content requirements for goods that are subject to free trade. That is, in order to qualify for free trade or the reduced tariff provisions of the agreement, a specified percentage (usually 50 percent) of the value of the good must be made in North America. The purpose of local content requirements is to prevent non-NAFTA countries from taking advantage of low tariffs in one NAFTA country in order to gain access to all three. Most trade economists dislike these provisions because they increase the likelihood of trade diversion. Production of inputs in lower-cost, nonmember countries could be reduced if firms move their operations to NAFTA countries in order to meet the content requirements. Nevertheless, content requirements were politically necessary in order to pass the agreement in Canada and the United States.

A third feature of the agreement is that it establishes a system of dispute resolution. When a disagreement arises, any country may request an investigation. This will set in motion a binational panel that investigates the issue and makes a report. Both countries are bound by the results of their analysis. It is hoped that this will lead to greater consultation and cooperation between countries and prevent trade disputes from escalating.

THE NAFTA DEBATE
IN THE UNITED STATES

The proposal for a trade agreement with Mexico reignited the debate over free trade in the United States. In particular, organized labor and environmental groups opposed the agreement, along with a handful of specific industrial and agricultural interests that feared stiffer competition with Mexico. Noneconomic opposition to NAFTA came from a number of politicians and citizens who expressed doubts about signing a trade agreement with a country that lacked strong democratic institutions.

Labor Issues

Blue-collar industrial labor unions were the most vocal opponents of NAFTA. Their reasons parallel the dicussion of trade, jobs, and labor standards in Chapters 7 and 8. Recall that the labor argument rejects free trade because of the fear that competition with low-wage countries will drive down wages at home, cause jobs to migrate overseas, and create a race to the bottom in labor standards. The relevant ideas have been disussed in the earlier chapters, but it is worth repeating that the core mistake of this view is the failure to take into account the productivity differences between U.S. and foreign workers. Labor in Mexico, for example, earns less for three reasons: (1) average Mexican education and skill levels are lower than in the United States; (2) the average Mexican worker has less capital at work; and (3) the public infrastructure of roads, ports, water systems, communication systems, and power and waste disposal systems is less reliable and less developed than in the United States. The net outcome of these three fundamental differences in human and physical capital is that productivity levels are lower in Mexico, and, as a consequence, wages are lower.

Recall, however, that the Stolper-Samuelson theorem predicts that U.S. workers with skills that are in abundance in Mexico may be hurt by the agreement. In the model of Chapter 4, trade favors the abundant factors that are used intensively to make the export good and trade hurts the scarce factors that are used intensively in the production of the import good. Given that Mexico is relatively well endowed with low-skilled labor and that the United States is relatively well endowed with skilled labor, trade between the United States and Mexico is likely to exert downward pressure on the wages of low-skilled U.S. labor. Garment workers, low-skilled and semiskilled autoworkers, and low-skilled assembly line workers may find their wages held down or their jobs moved out of the country. As always, the key question is how big an effect there will be, particularly in comparison to the macroeconomic policies of the Federal Reserve, which, in the short run, exert far more influence over wages and jobs than trade. In addition, since Mexico's GDP is only about 5 percent as large as that of the United States, its ability to absorb capital investment is limited.

Organized labor in the United States is still a significant political force, even though a relatively small share of the workforce belongs to industrial unions. During the NAFTA debate, industrial unions formed the core of a pressure group that pushed the Clinton administration to seek a separate agreement that paralleled NAFTA but focused solely on labor issues. The agreement came to be known as the side agreement on labor, or, more formally, the **North American Agreement on Labor Cooperation**. It was one of two such agreements, the other dealing with environmental issues. The labor side agreement requires both the United States and Mexico to enforce their own labor laws, especially laws pertaining to child labor, minimum wages, and workplace safety. Countries are required to permit investigators to examine alleged infringements of these protections, and fines may be levied. The agreement does not permit investigations into the rights of workers to organize, nor does it cover this aspect of labor law.

In the United States, labor interests sought the side agreement in order to prevent U.S. companies from fleeing to Mexico in order to take advantage of lax enforcement of labor laws. In addition, they wanted to be certain that Mexico did not gain a competitive advantage over U.S. firms and workers by using child labor, by paying less than minimum wage, or by cost cutting that allowed unsafe and unhealthy working conditions. Ironically, the first instance in which the international panel was called to investigate the nonenforcement of workplace health and safety rules was in the United States. In 1996, Mexican unions protested that a U.S. firm was abusing Hispanic telemarketers in San Francisco and that the U.S. government had failed to enforce U.S. workplace health and safety laws.

In the final analysis, most industrial labor groups expressed complete dissatisfaction with the labor side agreement and continued to oppose ratification of NAFTA. In essence, they remain unconvinced that U.S. workers can compete with Mexican workers without lowering their own wages. In their view, much, if not all, of U.S. trade with developing countries is unfair to U.S. workers and is responsible for a significant erosion in living standards in the United States.

Recall from the discussion in Chapter 4 about trade and income inequality that the bulk of the increase in inequality in the 1970s, 1980s, and 1990s is attributable to technological changes that reduced the demand for low-skilled workers. NAFTA has little to do with this trend. Nevertheless, it is fair to say that while the NAFTA countries benefited from increased trade, the agreement has caused some economic restructuring, and in this sense, not every individual has benefited.

In another sense, however, trade unionists may be correct. The labor side agreement does not seem to be an effective mechanism for creating change and has done little to address labor issues inside any of the partner countries. Since it does not give anyone significant power to compel the release of information, investigators often have a hard time obtaining evidence. Critics argue that this is by design, that the labor side agreement is only for show and that its real purpose was to win votes in the United States Congress during the ratification process in 1993.

Environmental Issues

The second major side agreement is called the **North American Agreement on Environmental Cooperation**. This agreement was motivated by two main concerns. One was the desire to prevent U.S. and Canadian firms from relocating to Mexico where they might take advantage of less stringent environmental enforcement. The second concern was the growth of environmental pollution along the U.S.–Mexico border. Like its labor laws, Mexico's environmental laws are quite good in general, but enforcement has often been lacking, due either to a lack of resources or corruption. The high visibility of this issue in North America has required Mexico to get tougher in its enforcement, and in this way, NAFTA has helped generate some desirable environmental outcomes.

Recall from the discussion in Chapter 8 about trade and the environment the distinction between transboundary and non-transboundary environmental problems. In the context of the NAFTA, transboundary pollution along the United States–Mexico border is an issue of considerable importance to both countries. Since the 1980s, rapid population growth on both sides of the border has created a number of environmental challenges that have been compounded by the rapid growth of manufacturing in northern Mexico. A significant share of the manufacturing is located in cities on the border, as close as possible to the U.S. market and the U.S. transportation network. In many cases, U.S. and Mexican cities share watersheds, air basins, and ecological habitats, making whatever happens on one side of the border of concern to the other side.

The rapid influx of population to the border region, coming from elsewhere in the United States to take advantage of the warm climate and sunny weather, and coming from the interior of Mexico to find jobs and a decent income, has put a heavy burden on the public infrastructure of roads, sewers, water systems, and so forth. Unfortunately, a large increase in population and manufacturing growth on the Mexican side of the border occurred in the 1980s, during the debt crisis in Mexico, when there were few resources for urban development. Consequently, sewage and water capacity have been strained beyond capacity and there is a backlog of projects needing attention and resources.

As noted in Chapter 8, it is unrealistic to expect environmental standards, clean-up preferences, or resource commitments to be identical in high- and low-income countries. Nevertheless, NAFTA provides an excellent opportunity to address the issue of transboundary environmental problems. Most notably, the agreement provides a formal, institutional framework in which issues and problems can be discussed and resolved. Without the institutional framework, each problem is addressed on an ad hoc basis in which lines of authority and responsibility are less clearly defined. Specifically, the side agreement on the environment creates a mechanism for investigating environmental disputes, such as cases where it is alleged that Mexico (or the United States or Canada) is gaining competitive advantages by not enforcing environmental laws. Investigation of these cases is followed by a resolution of the dispute through binding arbitration if both sides cannot agree.

The side agreement also established the **North American Development Bank (NADBank)** to help finance border cleanup costs. NADBank has several hundred million dollars of initial funds provided by the United States and Mexico, but the majority of funds are expected to come from either international agencies or private sources. Estimates of border cleanup costs vary widely, from $2 billion to $8 billion. In addition to the NADBank, the environmental side agreement created the Border Environmental Cooperation Commission (BECC) to analyze and certify the technical and scientific components of border cleanup proposals for NADBank funding. The NADBank, the BECC, and other binational, cooperative, border environmental programs (e.g., Border XXI) are targeted at issues such as increasing the availability of clean drinking water, wastewater treatment, air quality monitoring and improvement, solid and hazardous waste disposal, and so forth.

Like the labor side agreement, the environmental side agreement has not had much effect to date. This ineffectiveness, coupled with the fact that the NADBank has been slow in distributing funds for projects, has led many to complain that the positive institutional features of the side agreements are little more than window dressing and that—furthermore—they do not confront the real problems of trade between industrial United States and developing Mexico.

Immigration

Probably the most contentious issue in U.S.–Mexico relations in the 1990s was illegal immigration. While the vast majority of border crossings are by persons with the legal right to enter the United States, it is estimated that around 300,000 illegal immigrants from Mexico cross into the United States each year. Around 40 to 45 percent of these people settle in California; the remainder go to Illinois, New York, Texas, and a few other states. The total number of illegal border crossings is much higher because many people cross more than once, and most return to Mexico after a short visit or a few months' work.

Three factors are involved in the determination of the number of migrants. First, **demand-pull factors** refer to the attraction of U.S. jobs. When the U.S. economy booms, it exerts a stronger pull on foreign labor. Jobs are more plentiful, and labor supply in the United States is relatively scarce. In some sectors, labor shortages may appear. The second set of factors are **supply-push factors**. These are the forces inside Mexico that are pushing people to leave. They include recessions but also the structural changes taking place in the Mexican economy that have temporarily dislocated workers from jobs. For example, Mexico's agricultural policy has become more laissez faire, with fewer subsidies for farmers. These and other changes are part of an effort to modernize agriculture and to attract more investment in agricultural capital. One effect of the policy changes is that Mexico hopes to reduce its agricultural labor force from 26 percent of the total labor force in the early 1990s to 16 percent during the first decade of the twenty-first century. Ten percent of the labor force represents around 10 million people if you include the families of those workers. Some, perhaps many, of these people may eventually try to find temporary employment in the United States. A third factor determining migration is the existence of **social networks**. California attracts a larger share of immigrants (both legal and illegal) than other states because there are already a large number there, and the newcomers have contacts or family on whom they can rely while they are establishing themselves.

Taken together, the impacts of demand-pull, supply-push, and social networks imply that illegal immigration from Mexico will continue, all else equal. The increase may be averted if the United States puts more resources into controlling the border, but this is uncertain. For example, Operation Gatekeeper, started in 1994 in the San Diego sector of the U.S.–Mexico border, more than doubled resources spent on border control. The outcome of this effort is that would-be immigrants were pushed east, out into the relatively inhospitable terrain of the desert and mountains. In the last few years hundreds of migrants have perished from exposure to the heat of the desert or the cold of the mountains, while the supply of immigrant workers in the state of California did not seem to diminish. Mexico's role as a sender of migrants will continue because modernization and change within the economy will create more dislocated workers, and many of them will seek economic relief outside their home country.

For political reasons, many proponents of NAFTA chose to emphasize the claim that it would reduce immigration. President Salinas, for example, picked up this theme, and when addressing U.S. audiences, he often rallied support by stating, "Mexico wants to export goods, not people." His point was that NAFTA would give Mexico greater access to the U.S. market and would create faster growth in Mexico. As a result, the nation would experience a greater capacity to absorb labor into the national economy. Most simulations of the effects of NAFTA found a similar effect: the faster the Mexican economy grows, the weaker the supply-push factors will be. Nevertheless, in the short run, the immigration-increasing supply-push factors are probably stronger than the long-run immigration-reducing supply-push factors. That is, in the short run, agricultural reorganization and market opening probably have a bigger impact in the determination of the number of Mexican migrants than does overall economic growth and the spread of jobs and opportunities across the country. The net effect is that NAFTA probably causes migration from Mexico to the United States to be less than it would have been if there were no agreement, but changes in the Mexican economy cause migration to increase.

THE IMPACT OF NAFTA

The most common issue in the internal U.S. debate over NAFTA was its effects on U.S. jobs. Many trade economists were discouraged by this because the key effect of any trade agreement is the increased productive efficiency that comes with a reallocation of resources, not job gains or job losses. Placing the focus of the debate on workers who might be dislocated was politically inevitable, but it ignored the real economic advantages of expanded trade.

Many people also lost sight of the fact that Mexico's economy is less than 5 percent as large as the United States's economy. This makes it roughly the same size as Illinois, Pennsylvania, or Florida in terms of gross output. Consequently, it is unlikely that expanded trade can have a large economic impact on the United States. This point is well illustrated by an examination of the predicted effects of NAFTA on the U.S. economy. Before its implementation, a number of forecasts were made by academic economists and various interest groups. In each category (employment effects, wage effects, impact on overall U.S. current account balance), a majority of forecasts predicted either no effect on the national economy or effects too small to be measured. Note that this does not imply that there are no local effects, particularly along the border or in states that have a relatively large share of their overall trade with Mexico— for example, Texas. In more general terms, however, U.S.–Mexico trade under NAFTA was predicted to grow but not in a way that had a significant impact on the overall U.S. trade balance.

U.S.–Mexico trade since 1989 is shown in Figure 13.2. Two features stand out. First, trade has been expanding since 1989, the first year of data in the table. Given the trend toward expanded trade prior to the implementation of NAFTA, it is difficult to know the independent effects of the trade agreement. Growth in U.S.–Mexico trade started with the reforms of the mid-1980s that opened the Mexican economy, and NAFTA has been a part of the continued trend.

The second notable feature in Figure 13.2 is the decrease in exports in 1995. The peso crisis of late 1994 and 1995 caused a 6.2 percent decline in Mexico's GDP. The peso's collapse and the recession were caused by a combination of an overvalued exchange rate, political turmoil, and a weak banking sector. (See Chapter 12.) In the early 1980s, when faced with a similar crisis, Mexico responded by imposing quotas and import duties of up to 100 percent. As a result, U.S. exports to Mexico in the early 1980s fell by 50 percent and did not return to their 1981 level for nearly seven years. This time, however, the Mexican economy and U.S.–Mexico trade resumed growth within one year.

Some aspects of Mexico's recent economic history are a clear illustration of trade and growth driven by economies of scale (see Chapter 5). The inward orientation of Mexican economic policy up until the mid-1980s meant that production for the internal market was favored over exports. Consequently, firms with high fixed costs and high transport costs tried to locate near the internal Mexican market, leading to the rapid growth of Mexico City and its environs. In the 1980s, as policy changes made it more profitable to export, firms began to locate as close as possible to foreign markets, in this case the United States.

FIGURE 13.2   U.S. Merchandise Trade with Mexico

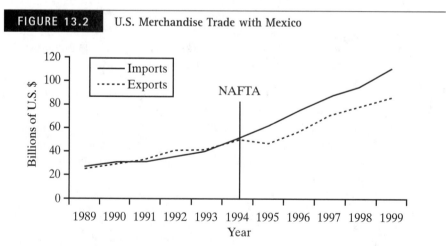

Since the start of NAFTA in 1994, U.S. exports to Mexico have grown more than 70 percent (in spite of the collapse of the Mexican economy in 1995), and U.S. imports from Mexico have grown over 120 percent.

Source: See Table 13.1.

The result is the extremely rapid growth of population and manufacturing production in northern Mexican states along the U.S.–Mexico border. In the medium to long run, this rapid northern growth is perhaps the most dramatic effect of the opening of the Mexican market through trade liberalization and NAFTA.

Turning to analyses of the impact of NAFTA on U.S. jobs, recent careful analysis has concluded that most estimates have exaggerated both the number of job displacements due to imports and the number of jobs created due to exports. Measurement is difficult because Mexican imports usually do not displace U.S. goods one for one. Imported goods are often complementary to domestic goods, not substitutes. They may enter distinct market niches that complement the demand for domestically produced goods, or they may satisfy a part of the increase in overall domestic demand. As the U.S. and Mexican economies become more integrated, we should expect to see increased complementarities in production. For example, Detroit automakers find it profitable to maintain product lines within Mexico that it would abandon if produced entirely in the United States and Canada. Maintenance of these product lines can easily increase the demand for related U.S. parts and components. In addition, imports from Mexico may in many cases displace imports from other Latin American or Asian nations. In that case, an increase in imports from Mexico is offset by a reduction in imports from another country. Similarly, job creation due to exports has probably been exaggerated by the pro-NAFTA side. A good deal of U.S. "export" business consists of intermediate inputs that are incorporated into final products that are shipped back to the United States. Consequently, as production of a final good moves to Mexico, shipments of intermediate inputs from the United States to Mexico are often misinterpreted as an increase in the number of jobs supported by exports.

Careful analysis has concluded that the impact of NAFTA on net job creation in the United States has been very small but positive, on the order of magnitude of a few tens of thousands of jobs in the first few years of the agreement. In order to put this into perspective, it should be noted that the United States currently generates about 2.25 million new jobs (net) a year. In other words, the jobs effect of three years' worth of NAFTA was a small percentage of one month's worth of job creation.

The politics of trade make discussion of job impacts necessary even though the ability of an economy to generate jobs is determined by labor market policies and fiscal and monetary policies, not by trade policies. Furthermore, there is widespread agreement among economists that the real test of success or failure for a trade agreement is whether it leads to a more efficient allocation of resources. By this criterion, the growth in trade between all three NAFTA partners is a positive indicator of increasing specialization, economies of scale, and efficiency. It is interesting that this tendency predates NAFTA and has simply continued since its implementation.

In sum, it is tempting to downplay the importance of the NAFTA agreement, at least in the United States and Canada. From the Canadian perspective, trade with Mexico is growing, but it is still a relatively small share of Canadian trade, and the 1989 CUSTA locked in most of the gains from trade with the United States. From the United States's perspective, Mexico's relatively small economy, about 5 percent of the U.S. economy, means that it is unlikely that trade can have a major impact on the national economy, even if there are pockets of the United States that feel the effects, both positive and negative. In Mexico, however, NAFTA has solidified the openness of the Mexican economy and acted as an impetus for a broad set of economic reforms in trade, in agriculture, in industrial policy, and increasingly, in the legal system. From a purely economic perspective, the conclusion seems to be that NAFTA is important to Mexico, and relatively unimportant to the United States and Canada. It is a mistake, however, to limit our view in this way.

Mexico is the most populous Spanish-speaking country in the world, and as the country with the second largest GDP in Latin America, it is viewed as a leader throughout the hemisphere. It has been at the forefront of economic reform in Latin America, and currently holds the distinction of having signed more free-trade agreements than any other nation. It is clearly in the long-run interests of all three NAFTA partners to share a cooperative and collaborative political and economic environment. Historically, the possibility for close relations has been limited by U.S. aggression and Mexican nationalism. Given that most of the U.S. southwest was taken from Mexico in the nineteenth century, and given the desire of most Mexican governments to act independently from the United States, relations have often been strained.

NAFTA represents a break with this historical pattern. Since its creation, a number of new binational and trinational institutions have been created with the purpose of addressing mutual problems. These include the labor and environmental institutions discussed earlier in the chapter, as well as numerous governmental and private organizations in the areas of business, education, the environment, labor, sports, and the arts. In the long run, the widening of the channels of communication between Mexico and the United States may be one of NAFTA's most important effects since it has given the two countries a set of institutional linkages that enable greater cooperation in finding solutions to common problems.

Nowhere is this more true for the United States than along the border with Mexico. Historically, the border region has been either ignored or viewed as a law enforcement problem having to do with the smuggling of drugs, guns, and undocumented workers. The relative poverty of the U.S. border region (outside of San Diego) went largely ignored, and the binational, shared problems of inadequate infrastructure, particularly water and sewage treatment, remained beyond the ability of border residents to address. The pattern of settlement along the border created a set of "twin cities" with a U.S. and Mexican counterpart, which often form a single urban space divided by an international border. Since cities such as Laredo and its counterpart, Nuevo Laredo, are in separate nations, considerations of national sovereignty require local city governments to communicate with each other through their respective national governments. In effect, cooperation and collaboration on shared problems was extremely limited.

While the formal rules of contact between cities and states in separate nations have not changed, NAFTA and the changes it represents have stimulated both U.S. and Mexican citizens to search for new institutional and organizational structures. The result has been a flowering of border-based local governmental, business, civic, and grassroots organizations that are creating new solutions to transboundary problems of water pollution, air quality, civic education, infrastructure development, and others.

In the long run, the opportunities for U.S.–Mexico dialogue may be the most important effect of NAFTA. Without doubt, the institutional linkages between the two countries, both on the border and elsewhere, are an important reason why a narrow economic view of the trade agreement is incomplete.

CASE STUDY

The Free Trade Agreement of the Americas

Soon after the NAFTA negotiations began, concerns were raised that Mexico's preferential access to the U.S. market might harm the economic interests of several Latin American economies. If trade were diverted from the Caribbean or other area, or if U.S. foreign direct investment were diverted to Mexico, it might come at the expense of other developing regions. In response, the United States launched the **Enterprise of the Americas Initiative (EAI)** in June, 1990.

The purposes of the EAI were to ensure that capital continued to flow to Latin America, to provide relief from the debt crisis of the 1980s, to liberalize trade, and to create incentive for Latin countries to continue with the economic and political reforms they began in the latter half of the 1980s. Latin America embraced the EAI for reasons similar to the ones that motivated Canada and Mexico to seek the CUSTA and the NAFTA. In all cases, U.S. trading part-

ners were looking for assurances of continued access to the U.S. market. Unfortunately for the EAI, it was forced to take a back seat to first the NAFTA and then the Uruguay Round negotiations.

In December of 1994, leaders from 34 countries in the Western Hemisphere met in Miami, Florida, at the First Summit of the Americas, to discuss a number of common concerns. Twenty-three initiatives were proposed and adopted, touching on political, cultural, social, and economic issues, including the possibility for a Western Hemispheric free trade pact. The governments committed themselves to negotiate a **Free Trade Agreement of the Americas (FTAA)**, and to conclude all negotiations no later than 2005.

The Miami Summit, as it came to be called, set the agenda for an action plan leading to the FTAA. Trade officials from the thirty-four countries worked out the preliminary details, and in 1998, the official negotiations began in

(continues)

Santiago, Chile, at the Second Summit of the Americas. This was followed in April, 2001, by the Third Summit of the Americas, in Quebec City, Canada, where the thirty-four leaders reconfirmed their commitment to the FTAA.

The scope of the negotiations was worked out through the efforts of twelve negotiating groups and periodic meetings of trade ministers that began to take place regularly after the Santiago Summit. Nine key areas of negotiations have emerged since Santiago:

- removing technical barriers to increased market access;
- reducing subsidies and non-tariff barriers in agriculture;
- consistent and uniform rules for antidumping duties, subsidies, and countervailing duties;
- creation of a minimum required set of competition policies;
- opening trade in services;
- creation of rules for foreign investment;
- protection of intellectual property rights;
- greater transparency and openness in government procurement;
- a method for resolving disputes.

In addition, three consultative groups have formed within the negotiating process to provide information and monitor the effects of the negotiations on small economies, civil society, and electronic commerce.

One obstacle is that the President of the United States has not had fast-track negotiating authority since 1994. Recall that the United States Congress must approve all trade agreements, and when it grants fast-track authority to the President, it agrees to vote yes or no on the agreement without seeking to amend it. The President's failure to obtain the authority to negotiate without worrying about future Congressional amendments has delayed negotiations, since it makes countries hesitant to agree on tough issues, and it makes the United States hesitant to compromise as any compromise is likely to be questioned by Congress. At the Quebec City Summit, President Bush assured the other leaders that he would soon obtain fast-track authority.

Latin interests in the FTAA are not hard to understand. The United States is the main trading partner of the Caribbean, Central America, and the Andean Community (a free trade area of Venezuela, Colombia, Peru, Ecuador, and Bolivia). Forty to sixty percent of the trade of those countries is with the United States. In other parts of South America, trade patterns are more diversified, but with the partial exception of Brazil—which is interested in the idea of a South American Free Trade Area—countries agree about the benefits of greater access to North American markets. Chile, for example, has signed free-trade agreements with both Canada and Mexico, and opened negotiations with the United States in December of 2000.

The interests of the United States in pursuing a FTAA can be viewed partly as a reflection of U.S. commercial interests and partly as a strategic interest in supporting policies that might produce greater prosperity. Clearly, the United States and other countries also view the FTAA as a political tool for reinforcing the democratic reforms that have occurred throughout the Western Hemisphere. Evidence of this includes the exclusion of Cuba from the FTAA, and affirmation of the "Democratic Clause" asserting that countries will be denied the benefits of the FTAA in the event that their governments become undemocratic.

If the FTAA remains on track and is implemented at the end of 2005, it is too early to know how far it will go to liberalize trade and investment relations. It seems likely, however, that it may go much farther than the WTO in a number of areas, including agriculture, antidumping duties, competition policies, investment rules, trade in services, and electronic commerce. Each of these areas is high on the list of topics the WTO wants to negotiate, and the FTAA could break new ground here.

Summary

- Canada is the United States's closest ally. In addition, it is mostly English speaking, has a similar standard of living, and a long democratic tradition. Mexico, on the other hand, is a vastly different society with historical reasons for wariness toward the United States. Furthermore, economic integration with Mexico is much more contentious than with Canada: labor and environmental standards, worker displacement, poorly developed infrastructure, corruption in the political and judicial systems, immigration, and the drug trade are areas of existing or potential conflict.

- The United States and Canada have had a free-trade agreement since 1989 (CUSTA). It was preceded by an agreement in 1965 (the Auto Pact) to allow free trade in autos and automobile parts between the two countries.

- Mexico's long process of opening its economy began in the mid-1980s and was a result of the collapse of its traditional economic policy of import substitution industrialization (ISI). ISI stresses self-sufficiency and independence from world markets. The collapse of the Mexican economy in 1982 was due to its inability to repay its international loans; that episode began the Third-World debt crisis. The recessions that followed came to be known throughout Latin America as the Lost Decade.

- The most contentious issues in the United States related to the signing of the NAFTA agreement were issues of labor policy, environmental policy and enforcement, and migration.

- To date, the main impact of NAFTA has been to continue an ongoing trend toward increased trade. It is impossible to accurately measure the effects of NAFTA on jobs and wages, but most economists estimate a small, positive effect on job creation.

- Mexico's recession of 1995 was severe but short. It had nothing to do with NAFTA, but it was caused by macroeconomic mismanagement that let the trade deficit balloon under an overvalued peso. It is likely that

NAFTA played a positive role in helping Mexico to escape from recession through increased exports. U.S. exports to Mexico fell in 1995 but rose above 1994 levels in 1996.

- U.S. benefits from NAFTA are political as well as economic. It offers the opportunity to develop institutions that provide formal mechanisms for discussion, consultation, and resolution of issues. An example is the NADBank, which was created to deal with the long-festering problem of the border environment. Without these institutions, problems were addressed on an ad hoc basis, outside regularized, formal channels, and in political contexts where the discussants often had no power to take action. By creating new institutions such as the consultative bodies on trade, harmonization of standards, labor, and the environment, the two largest populations of North America have begun working toward greater cooperation and understanding.

Vocabulary

Auto Pact

Brady Plan

Canada–U.S. Trade Agreement (CUSTA)

debt crisis

demand-pull factors

Enterprise of the Americas Initiative (EAI)

export processing zone (EPZ)

Free Trade Agreement of the Americas (FTAA)

import substitution industrialization (ISI)

Lost Decade

maquiladora

North American Development Bank (NADBank)

North American Agreement on Environmental Cooperation

North American Agreement on Labor Cooperation

North American Free Trade Agreement

purchasing power parity

social networks

supply-push factors

Study Questions

1. How does Mexico's GDP per person compare to that of the United States? Discuss the different approaches economists can use to make this calculation.

2. Why is the openness indicator for Canada greater than that for the United States?

3. Explain how an increase in U.S. and Canadian intraindustry trade altered the level of productivity in the Canadian sector affected.

4. What were Canada's motives for proposing and signing the Canadian–United States Free Trade Agreement?

5. What were the forces at work in the Mexican economy that led to the market reforms and market opening of the mid-1980s?

6. What were Mexico's motives for proposing and signing the North American Free Trade Agreement?

7. In what areas are there NAFTA side agreements? Discuss the pros and cons of these agreements.

8. What are the three main categories of factors that determine the number of immigrants to the United States from Mexico? Give specific examples of each.

9. Explain why claims about job creation and job destruction due to NAFTA are likely to be misleading and inaccurate.

Chapter 14

THE EUROPEAN UNION: MANY MARKETS INTO ONE

INTRODUCTION: THE EUROPEAN UNION

In 1987, the twelve members of the **European Community (EC)** embarked on an ambitious program to capture additional gains from trade. The members passed legislation amending the treaty that had originally brought them together after World War II. The 1987 legislation was named the **Single European Act (SEA)** because it sought to create a single European identity that would form an umbrella over the various national cultures, economies, and political systems.

The centerpiece of the Single European Act is the "four freedoms," which are defined as the free movement of goods, services, capital, and labor. Not only would Italian and other firms be able to sell their goods in France on the same basis as domestic French firms, but workers from Spain would be free to compete for jobs in Germany on an equal basis with German citizens. There was a great deal of excitement through the late 1980s and the early 1990s leading up to the implementation of the Single European Act in January 1993. In fact, the SEA enjoyed support from the citizens of the twelve countries, the national political parties, and the business community. In essence, there was no major opposition.

Despite this lack of opposition, it still required over five years of tough negotiations among the twelve, and at the end, not all the steps necessary for complete implementation had been taken. This raises an interesting question. If citizens, governments, and businesses are united in their desires to open their economies and to achieve greater gains from trade, then why is it so difficult to accomplish? If trade liberalization is contentious and uncertain even when everyone desires it, you can imagine how tough it is when constituencies are divided. The fight over the Single European Act is a graphic illustration of the fact that trade issues are rarely about trade only. In the rest of this chapter we will look at the process of economic integration in Western Europe and in parts of Central and Eastern Europe. One feature that will stand out is that the process underway in Western Europe has political, social, and cultural dimensions as well as economic ones.

Before moving on, it is useful to clarify the name *European Union*. **European Union (EU)** is the name of a group of fifteen West European countries, formerly known as the European Community (EC) or as the European Economic Community (EEC). As the EEC took on more responsibilities of a social and political nature, the community began to consider itself as more than an economic community, and the use of the name *European Community* came into common usage. Then, with the ratification of the Maastricht Treaty on November 1, 1993, "Community" was replaced with "Union." Technically, the EC still exists within the expanded framework of the EU, and the term *EC* is still encountered when the discussion is focused on exclusively economic

European Union

Norway
Estonia
Latvia
Lithuania
Sweden
Finland
Denmark
Netherlands
Belgium
Ireland
United Kingdom
Germany
Poland
Luxembourg
Czech Republic
Slovakia
Switzerland
Austria
Hungary
France
Slovenia
Italy
Portugal
Spain
Greece

Text Size Denotes

Members of the European Union
Leading Candidates for Membership in the European Union
Others

Scale

1: 26,423,000
1: 417.02 Inches to Miles

Lambert Equal Area Projection

issues. In this chapter, *EC* refers to events before the Maastricht Treaty, and *EU* to events thereafter.

THE SIZE OF THE MARKET IN WESTERN EUROPE

Before discussing the history or economics of economic integration in Western Europe, let us define the nations and groups that are important and get an idea of the size of the market. The European Union has the potential to become the largest integrated market in the world. By implication, the EU is likely to have a major role in determining future international political arrangements, trade patterns and rules, and international economic relations in general. Few countries will be able to grow and prosper without selling their goods in the European market, and this is a powerful incentive to accept European leadership on international issues.

Table 14.1 lists the members of the European Union (EU), their populations, and their gross national products. GNP is measured in current 1999 U.S. dollars, at market exchange rates. Comparisons at market exchange rates are a less accurate indicator of living standards than comparisons at purchasing power parity rates, but they are a more accurate indicator of the size of each market in terms of its ability to buy goods and services that are imported. Several features of Table 14.1 are worth highlighting. First, notice that not all West European nations are members. Despite the addition in 1995 of three new members, Norway (who voted not to join in 1970 and in 1995) and Switzerland are noticeably absent. In addition, a number of the supersmall nations, such as Iceland, Liechtenstein, San Marino, and Monaco, are not members, nor are any countries from the former East Bloc, such as Poland, Hungary, or the Czech Republic. Second, many non-Europeans are probably surprised at the small average population size of most West European nations. By most measures, only five nations are large: Germany, Italy, France, the United Kingdom, and Spain. The four largest (minus Spain) were each approximately sixty million until West Germany merged with East Germany and became the single largest country. The fact that Germany is now over one-third larger than its nearest rival has implications that we will examine. Third, the nations of the EU form a combined market worth more than U.S. $8 trillion. In terms of external purchasing power and population, the EU is about the same size as the North American market created by NAFTA. In 1999, the NAFTA market had approximately 400 million people and around $10,400 billion in GNP at market exchange rates (see Chapter 13, Table 13.1).

Two additional facts about the size of the EU market are worth keeping in mind. The countries listed in Table 14.1 are not the full extent of the current free-trade area since the EU has formally included Iceland, Norway, and Liechtenstein in its common market area. This gives citizens in those countries the same rights as citizens of the EU to move, invest, and trade freely through-

| TABLE 14.1 | 1999 Population and GDP in the EU |

Original Members	*Population (millions)*	*Total GNP ($U.S., market rates, billions)*	*Per Capita GNP ($U.S. market rates)*
Belgium	10.2	250.6	24,569
France	59.1	1,427.2	21,149
Germany	82.1	2,079.2	25,325
Italy	57.3	1,136.0	19,825
Luxembourg	0.4	19.3	44,676
Netherlands	15.8	384.3	24,323
New Members, 1973–1986			
Denmark (1973)	5.3	170.3	32,132
Greece (1981)	10.6	124.0	11,698
Ireland (1973)	3.8	71.4	18,789
Portugal (1986)	10.0	105.9	10,590
Spain (1986)	39.4	551.6	14,000
United Kingdom (1973)	58.7	1,338.1	22,796
New Members in 1995			
Austria	8.2	210.0	25,610
Finland	5.2	122.9	23,634
Sweden	8.9	221.8	24,921
Totals	374.9	8,212.6	21,906

The EU is nearly the same size as the NAFTA region.

Source: World Bank, *World Development Report, 2000/2001.* (Tables 1, 1a).

out the EU. Second, several former East Bloc countries in Central Europe have applied for membership in the EU and have an "associate member" status providing them with enhanced market access. Several nations are likely to join the EU over the next decade, including Poland, Hungary, The Czech Republic, Estonia, and Slovenia (and the Mediterranean island nation of Cyprus), and others are waiting in the wings. Membership depends on the ability of the countries to continue their political and economic reforms. The issue of widening the membership will be examined in greater detail toward the end of this chapter, but note that the EU is still under construction. In addition, the effective sizes of its free-trade area and common market are much larger than the list of official members.

BEFORE THE EUROPEAN UNION

The European Economic Community was born on March 25, 1957, with the signing of the **Treaty of Rome** by the original six members. The Treaty entered into force about nine months later, on January 1, 1958. The Treaty remains the fundamental agreement between the fifteen members, and more recent agreements such as the Single European Act and the Maastricht Agreement were passed as amendments to the original treaty. The six founding members were the Benelux countries (Belgium, Netherlands, and Luxembourg), along with France, West Germany, and Italy.

The Treaty of Rome

The European Economic Community grew out of the reconstruction of Europe at the end of World War II. The goals of the founders of the EEC were to rebuild their destroyed economies and to prevent the destruction from happening again. The original vision of the founders of the EEC was for a political union that they hoped to create through economic integration. The first step was a 1950 proposal by Robert Schuman, the foreign minister of France, to pool the European coal and steel industries. Coal and steel were chosen because they were large industrial activities that served as the backbone of military strength. Schuman's plan was to pool the industries of Germany and France, the two largest West European antagonists, but Luxembourg, Belgium, the Netherlands, and Italy signed on as well. The **European Coal and Steel Community (ECSC)** Treaty was signed in 1951 and included provision for the establishment of the ECSC High Authority, an international agency with regulatory powers. Coal and steel trade between the six members grew by 129 percent in the first five years of the treaty.

The success of the ECSC led to early attempts at integration in political and military areas (the European Defense Community and the European Political Community), but these efforts failed when they were rejected by the French Parliament in 1954. At that point, European leaders decided to focus their efforts on economic integration. In 1955, the six foreign ministers of the ECSC countries launched a round of talks in Messina, Italy, to discuss the creation of a **European Economic Community** and a **European Atomic Energy Community (EAEC or Euratom)**. The goal of the former was to create a single, integrated market for goods, services, labor, and capital, and the latter sought to jointly develop nuclear energy for peaceful purposes. Two separate treaties were signed in 1957 in Rome, creating the EEC and Euratom.

Institutional Structure of the EEC

The founders of the EEC envisioned a federation in which local, regional, national, and European authorities cooperate and complement one another. The model was similar to the interaction between the cities, counties, states, and federal government in the United States, or local, provincial, and federal governments in Canada. An alternative view, called *functionalism*, favors a gradual transfer of national sovereignty to the European level. The functionalist approach is more controversial and has generated a great deal of resistance by those who fear a loss of national power and culture.

Both of these approaches can be seen today, however, and the actual performance of the European Union is a blend of both. In EU jargon, **subsidiarity** describes the relationship between national and EU areas of authority, and between national and EU institutions. Subsidiarity is defined as the principle that the Union will only have authority to tackle issues that are more effectively handled through international action than by individual nations acting alone. In some cases, these issues are easily defined, but in others they are not. Current thinking places under EU control the responsibility for environmental and regional policy, research and technology development, and economic and monetary union.

Areas that are less clear cut and where there continues to be some degree of controversy include the issues of labor market policies, social policies, and competition policies. The presence of controversy, however, has not prevented the EU from agreeing to a common competition policy and a common set of labor market policies, called the Social Charter. Both areas continue to be sources of significant disagreement and political maneuvering as national policies reflect fundamental philosophical differences in values and choices. The conflict between policies that reflect national values and the desire to obtain greater gains from trade through economic integration is a pervasive problem in every instance of economic integration. Given that nations rarely speak with a single voice but are themselves composed of factions and special interests, the struggle over the transfer of sovereignty is all the more contentious.

Decision making within the EU is split between four governmental bodies. These are the European Commission, the Council of Ministers, the European Parliament, and the European Council. Table 14.2 shows how votes are allotted in the first three branches.

The European Commission.

The executive body of the EU is the **European Commission**. Each of the five largest countries (France, Germany, Italy, Spain, and the United Kingdom) has two seats, and the remaining ten countries have one commissioner each for a total of twenty members. Commissioners serve five-year terms that are renewable, and they are appointed by national governments with the mutual approval of the member states. The Commission elects one of its own members to serve as the president of the European Commission. Work is divided in a way that gives each commissioner responsibility for one or more policy areas, but all decisions are a collective responsibility.

The Commission's primary responsibility is to act as the guardian of the treaties, ensuring that they are faithfully and legally enforced. This role includes responsibility for creating the rules for implementing treaty articles and for EU budget appropriations. As the executive branch, the Commission

TABLE 14.2	Member Country Votes in the Main Institutions of the EU		
	European Commission	*Council of Ministers*	*European Parliament*
Germany	2	10	99
France	2	10	87
Italy	2	10	87
United Kingdom	2	10	87
Spain	2	8	64
Netherlands	1	5	31
Belgium	1	5	25
Greece	1	5	25
Portugal	1	5	25
Sweden	1	4	22
Austria	1	4	21
Denmark	1	3	16
Finland	1	3	16
Ireland	1	3	15
Luxembourg	1	2	6
Total	20	84	626

has the sole right to initiate EU laws and the same right as the national governments to submit proposals.

The Council of Ministers. The **Council of Ministers** serves as the legislative branch of the EU and enacts laws based on proposals submitted by the Commission. It is composed of ministers from each nation, depending on the subject under discussion. For example, farm issues are discussed by agricultural ministers from each nation, and any labor issues are handled by labor and economic affairs ministers. Representation is more or less proportional to national population, with eighty-seven total votes. Most decisions of the Council of Ministers require a majority vote (called a *qualified majority*) of sixty-two of the eighty-seven votes and at least ten of the fifteen states. A few issues that are sensitive—for example, tax law changes—require unanimity for passage.

The Council's leadership rotates among the member states in six-month terms. The chance to serve as president of the Council for six months is an important mechanism for individual member states to bring up their own legislative agendas and has been instrumental in the adoption of key EU regulations.

The European Parliament. The **European Parliament** has 626 members, directly elected by the people for five-year terms and apportioned among the member states according to population. Members associate by political affiliation rather than national origin. One traditional function of the Parliament is to act as the representative of popular interests with the power to question the Council of Ministers and Commission and to issue nonbinding opinions. Parliament's lack of real legislative clout has raised concerns that there was a **democratic deficit** in EU governance. Proponents of the democratic deficit view have succeeded in the last few years in significantly increasing the real power of Parliament from the ability to amend some legislation to veto powers over new membership and "Associate Agreements" with nonmembers. The **Maastricht Treaty**, signed in 1991, carried this evolution farther, and gave Parliament the right to change the budget of the EU. Prior to Masstricht, it could only approve or disapprove the budget.

The European Council. Throughout the 1980s and the first half of the 1990s, the European Commission was the main policymaking body of the EU. Commission members are appointed by national governments but they are expected to adopt a European outlook rather than a national one. By the late 1990s, the Commission's role had changed, and the **European Council** emerged as the more important body. The European Council (not to be confused with the Council of Ministers) is a four-times-a-year meeting of the heads of state of the member countries. It has taken the primary policymaking function out of the hands of the Commission, in part due to the Commission's own ineptness (some members of the Commission were implicated in a budgetary corruption scandal), but also as a reflection of the importance that national governments place on issues such as monetary union. Some observers argue that a significant degree of democracy has been restored to the EU since this has placed the primary policymaking function closer to the national governments. Others worry that government leaders will take too nationalistic a view of matters, to the detriment of the EU.

Other Institutions. In addition to these four, several other institutions are important in the EU's governance. For example, the **Court of Justice** is the EU's supreme court. Composed of one member appointed by each nation, the Court's job is to interpret the treaties and to ensure that they are correctly followed by the other EU institutions. The Court's rulings are binding and take precedence over the fifteen national courts.

Since the implementation of the Maastricht Treaty, the Committee on Regions has taken on a larger role. In part, this reflects a natural economic evolution, as increasing economic integration has caused national economies to lose some of their importance and regional economies to gain in importance.

There are 226 officially recognized regions in the EU, and some of them, such as Catalonia, Baaden Wurtemberg, Rhone Alps, and Lombardy, have become important centers of economic growth and innovation. The Committee on Regions' responsibility is to defend the interest of communities and regions in the EU decision making, and to serve as an information conduit between the EU and local communities.

The institutions and programs of the EU are paid for with money from import duties (about 15 percent of the 2001 budget), the EU's 1.2 percent share of the value added taxes collected by each country (36 percent of the budget), and the contributions of national governments (about 49 percent of the budget). One might expect that such a large and ambitious undertaking would have an enormous budget, but the overall budget of the EU is quite small. The 2001 budget is about 97 billion euros, or around 82 billion U.S. dollars at the rate of one **euro** equals $0.85. This is equal to 1.1 percent of the EU's total GDP, or about 250 euros per person. Another way to express this amount is that the EU's budget is more than the government of Finland's, but less than Denmark's. Nevertheless, the EU is the first regional trade agreement with its own financing sources.

DEEPENING AND WIDENING THE COMMUNITY IN THE 1970s AND 1980s

When Europeans speak of increasing the level of cooperation between member countries, they use the term *deepening*. Deepening refers to both economic and noneconomic activities that have the effect of increasing the integration of the national economies. For example, the movement from a free market to a customs union, or the harmonization of technical standards in industry, or agreements to develop a common security and defense policy are deepening activities that increase interactions between the member states. On the other hand, when Europeans speak about extending the boundaries of the EU to include new members, they use the term *widening*. Between the signing of the Treaty of Rome in 1957 and the Single European Act in 1987, six new members were admitted to the EC. These were Denmark, Ireland, and the United Kingdom in 1973, Greece in 1981, and Portugal and Spain in 1986. Three more members, Austria, Finland, and Sweden, joined in 1995. The issue of future widening remains very contentious throughout Europe, and we will look at it more closely later in this chapter. For now, however, we turn to the issue of deepening in the period before the Single European Act.

Before the Euro

In 1979, the members of the European Economic Community began to link their currencies in an effort to prevent radical fluctuation in currency values.

Recall from Chapter 10 that a devaluation in a country's currency results in more exports, while a rise in the currency's value creates more imports. The EC wanted to prevent competitive devaluations in which one country devalues in order to capture the export markets of another country. **Competitive devaluations** inevitably generate conflict and lead to a breakdown in cooperation, since the devaluing country is viewed as gaining exports and jobs at the expense of others. Nations sometimes find it difficult to resist devaluation, especially during recessions. This tactic is viewed as unfair, however, and in the medium to long run, it is usually ineffective since the nondevaluing countries are obliged to follow suit and retaliate with their own devaluations.

In addition to looking for a mechanism that might discourage competitive devaluations, the EC sought to remove some of the uncertainty and risk from trading and investing across national boundaries. While forward markets can be used to protect against exchange rate risk, they only work about six months into the future.

The goal was to create an environment in which trade and investment throughout the EC was determined by considerations of comparative advantage and efficient resource allocation rather than by changes in exchange rates. The result was the **European Monetary System (EMS)** with its **exchange rate mechanism (ERM)**. (Since the ERM was the central component of the EMS, the two terms are used interchangeably by most writers and commentators. Technically, however, a country could belong to the EMS and not participate in the ERM. The United Kingdom was an example.) The formation of the EMS in 1979 was a significant deepening of the EC and served to prepare the way for the eventual introduction of a single currency. It was designed to prevent extreme currency fluctuations by tying each currency's value to the weighted average of the others. The group average, the **European currency unit (ECU)**, was used as a unit of account, but not in actual day-to-day transactions.

The ERM system was an example of an exchange rate band. Each currency in the band was fixed to the ECU, but was allowed to fluctuate several percentage points up or down. (Initially, fluctuations of ±2.25 percent were permitted. This was changed after the crisis of 1992 to ±15.0.) For example, if 1 ECU equaled 0.9 British pounds or 3 German marks, then the mark equaled 0.3 pounds. Each currency was allowed to fluctuate 2.25 percent around its parity, so the pound could move between 0.9202 and 0.8798 ECU before the British central bank was obligated to intervene and pull its currency back within the exchange rate band. In September 1992, for example, the United Kingdom spent an estimated $30 billion in just a few days trying to protect the British pound from market speculators who had become convinced that it was going to fall in value. (The speculators were right, and the Bank of England lost a bundle of money trying to move against the market.)

Given the ineffectiveness of market intervention in the face of a strong and determined market movement, most analysts predicted that the ERM would fail as a mechanism for maintaining stable European currency values. An ERM-type arrangement was tried out in 1973, but it soon collapsed as a result of the first oil shortage and its effects on national inflation rates. When the EC proposed a similar arrangement in 1979, many were skeptical that it would survive for very long or that it would effectively stabilize currencies. To most economists' surprise, the ERM effectively linked EC exchange rates for two decades.

The ERM experienced several adjustments, but none of them threatened the functioning of the system until 1992. Oddly enough, it was the reunification of Germany that caused the system to nearly collapse, and that resulted in a much weaker linkage between exchange rates. Because German reunification had a profound effect on the ERM, and because it is an interesting lesson in the costs of tying currencies together, it is useful to look at this episode in more detail.

Problems began in 1990 with Germany's decision to speed up its reunification with the German Democratic Republic (East Germany) after the fall of the Berlin Wall in November 1989. Economic conditions in East Germany were worse than expected, and it was soon apparent that the costs of building a productive economy would be enormous. The infrastructure (roads, bridges, ports, utilities, schools, hospitals, and so forth) was in worse shape than most people realized, and environmental pollution was significant. In order to build a prosperous economy in its eastern region, Germany had to raise the productivity levels of the people living there, and this required huge investments in infrastructure and the environment. The unexpectedly large expenditures to raise the productivity of the East resulted in a very large fiscal stimulus to the German economy. Such large expenditures (both by the government and by the private sector) were also expected to have an inflationary impact, and the Bundesbank (Germany's central bank) acted to counteract the increased probability of future inflation by raising German interest rates. This is a normal policy move whenever it is thought that aggregate demand is rising too fast, as it was in the unified Germany. The increase in interest rates is expected to slow the economy by increasing the costs of using borrowed capital. Germany, therefore, had an expansionary fiscal stimulus that was partially offset by a contractionary monetary policy.

High German interest rates made German financial instruments more attractive and caused capital to flow into Germany from the other EC countries. This resulted in the selling of British pounds, French francs, and other currencies in order to buy German marks (and then German bonds) and caused the pound, the franc, and other currencies to fall in value. At first, the movement was within the 2.25 percent bandwidth, and most of the EC hoped that they would somehow muddle through without making any drastic changes in the ERM or the EMS.

One solution would have been for the countries with falling currencies to raise their interest rates to match Germany's. This would have stemmed the outflow of financial capital looking for better rates of return in Germany. Some of the countries, the United Kingdom for example, were entering recessions in

1990 and 1991 and did not want to raise interest rates just as a recession was taking hold. The likely effect would have been to hasten and deepen the recession—something no policymaker wants to be accused of doing. Other countries, such as France, were not yet entering the recessionary phase of their business cycle, but they had very high unemployment rates, and contractionary monetary policy was not desirable.

The dilemma faced by the EC countries is a good example of a recurring theme in the history of exchange rate systems. By tying their exchange rates to each other, the EC countries gave up a large measure of independence in their monetary policies. Because Germany was the largest country and the one with the most influential central bank, its monetary policy set the tone for the rest of the EC, and, at a time when many of the members wanted expansionary monetary policy, they were forced to adopt contractionary policies. The 1992 episode illustrates the recurrent tension that occurs between the appropriate external policies (exchange rate management) and the appropriate internal policies (full employment, reasonable growth, low inflation) when nations tie their exchange rates together. Since the "right" policy choice for meeting the exchange rate problem was diametrically opposite to meeting the needs of the internal economy, EC members were left with a tough decision: Honor their commitments to the ERM and make their unemployment and growth rates worse, or do the right thing for internal growth and watch the ERM fall apart. In the French case, an interest rate increase threw the country into recession, but France remained within the ERM. In the cases of Italy and the United Kingdom, the ERM was abandoned, and their currencies were allowed to freely float against other EC currencies. A third option was chosen by Spain, where the parity, or center of the band, was shifted. In order to lessen the probability of future repeats of this problem, the bandwidth was widened in 1993 from ±2.25 percent to ±15 percent.

THE SECOND WAVE OF DEEPENING: THE SINGLE EUROPEAN ACT

Other than the creation of the European Monetary System in 1979, the changes in the EC were minor through the 1970s and the first half of the 1980s. In the early 1980s, most West European countries suffered through a recession that left their unemployment rates high even as they recovered their economic growth in 1984 and 1985. The European economies seemed stale and incapable of new dynamism and many in the United States began to refer to the European situation as "Eurosclerosis," signifying a permanent hardening of the arteries of commerce and industry.

By the late 1980s, people in North America and Europe had stopped using Eurosclerosis and begun to speak of "Europhoria." While both terms were exaggerations, dramatic events had reshaped the EC in the intervening years.

What was previously dismissed in the early 1980s as a hopeless case of bureaucratic inefficiency was now regarded as a dynamic, forward-looking, integrated regional economy. Europe seemed to be "on the move."

The Delors Report

Reshaping the EC got under way with the selection of the former French finance minister, Jacques Delors, to serve a five-year term as president of the European Commission. Delors was a compromise candidate, and no one expected unusual or dramatic changes in the EC under his stewardship. Delors's vision of the EC, however, was of a fully integrated union, and as president of the EC's executive branch, he had a platform from which he could initiate significant change. In retrospect, it seems that his vision was shaped in part by the belief that the institutions of the EC could help to return the individual national economies to economic prosperity and in part by the desire to complete the task of building an economic and political union.

Delors's first step, and perhaps his most significant one, was to issue a report called "Completing the Internal Market," which detailed 300 specific changes necessary for the EC to move from a quasi-customs union to an economic union. It laid out a timetable for completing the changes and, importantly, removed the need for unanimous voting in the Council of Ministers. Most analysts agreed that the requirement of unanimous voting had created gridlock in the governing institutions. Delors proposed that most measures be allowed to pass with a "qualified majority" (fifty-four out of the seventy-six votes in the Council of Ministers—the EC had twelve members and the Council was smaller than it is now) and that unanimity be reserved for only the most momentous issues, such as taxes. Although the qualified majority still allowed as few as three countries to block a measure (assuming that they include one large nation with ten votes), it prevented any single country from blocking a proposed change.

After some relatively minor changes in the **Delors Report**, it was adopted in its entirety in 1987, as the Single European Act (SEA). Legally it is a series of amendments to the Treaty of Rome. Of the 300 steps, or "directives," 279 were included in the SEA. Many of the twenty-one not included were considered too difficult to accomplish in the time period the EC gave itself, but were taken up as goals of the next round of deepening. For example, monetary union under a single currency was moved forward to the next round of deepening.

The date for implementation of the SEA was January 1, 1993. By the end of 1992, it was expected that the "four freedoms" (freedom of movement for goods, services, capital, and labor) spelled out in the SEA would be instituted and, as a result, the EC would be at the common market level of economic integration. In order to accomplish these goals, it was necessary to determine the method of implementation of each of the 279 directives and for each of the twelve member nations to make the necessary changes in their internal laws, standards, and customary practices. While some areas remain incomplete, the vast majority of the directives were put into practice by the end of 1992, and the EC achieved common market status.

The steps taken to implement the SEA can be broadly divided into three areas: (1) the elimination of physical barriers, such as passport and customs controls at the borders between member countries; (2) the elimination of technical barriers, such as differences in product and safety standards; and (3) the elimination of fiscal barriers, such as differences in taxes, subsidies, and public procurement. Each of these poses its own benefits and challenges and will be discussed in more detail. First, we will consider the gains that the EC hoped to reap from the elimination of these barriers.

Forecasts of the Gains from the Single European Act

One of the central reasons for supporting the SEA was to achieve gains in economic efficiency. These gains had three main sources. First was the gain from removing customs and passport checks at internal national borders. Although tariffs and other customs-type inspections have been restricted or eliminated altogether, the gains from the elimination of border barriers have yet to be completely realized, since customs inspections have been replaced by "tax inspections" as a result of the failure of the EC to establish a uniform system of taxing goods. Still, substantial progress has been made in eliminating the long queues of trucks waiting to cross borders. The result is speedier, less costly distribution of goods throughout the EC.

Integration also created economic benefits from greater economies of scale and increased competitiveness. Economies of scale are possible because EC firms are able to produce at one site (or in a fewer number of sites) for the entire European market and will not have to duplicate production facilities across national boundaries. This enables some companies to consolidate their operations and to avoid duplication in their production and support services, such as accounting. The increase in competitiveness comes from several sources. For example, the increased pressure of competition will force some firms to make productive investments that they would not otherwise have made. In addition, the openness of the competitive environment will generate a larger, more mobile pool of labor that carries skills from one firm to another. Finally, the free flow of goods and services will generate a greater flow of information and ideas so that firms have easier access to the best new ideas.

In sum, internal EC analysis predicted increases in GDP in the range of 4 to 6.5 percent, with additional positive impacts on prices, employment, trade balances, and government budgets. There was no precise specification of the time frame over which these effects would be realized, but five to ten years seemed to be implied. As with all forecasts of future economic activity, the results are based on a great number of assumptions about the actual behavior of firms, industries, and nations. For example, the forecast assumes that each of the (then) twelve members of the EC would fully implement the changes negotiated in the Single European Act and that the adversely affected firms and industries could not stall or impede their implementation. In general, this has turned out to be the case in the years since January 1993; however, there remain a few sectors where goods and services are not freely traded, and many of the expected benefits have so far failed to materialize. This is probably due not so much to bad forecasts as it is to the recession that gripped most of Western Europe in 1993. Still, the often cited increase in GDP of 4 to 6.5 percent was viewed as overly optimistic by many analysts.

Problems in the Implementation of the SEA

One of the most interesting lessons of the Single European Act is that it is still difficult to reduce barriers to trade and investment even when the citizens, businesses, and governments of the involved countries are united in their desire to do so. According to all the polls, the SEA enjoyed very broad support throughout the EC. Still, from the time when it was first proposed in 1985 until its final implementation in 1993, there were very difficult negotiations among the member countries. In several cases, such as taxes and the harmonization of standards, the EC either set aside its attempts at reaching an accord or is still in the process of looking for agreement.

The Effects of Restructuring. As we saw in Chapter 3, when a national economy goes from a relatively closed position to a relatively open one, economic restructuring takes place. The less efficient firms are squeezed out, and the more efficient ones grow; overall economic welfare expands as countries concentrate on what they do best, but that inevitably means abandoning some industries and expanding others. In the case of the EC, it was forecast that almost all manufacturing industries would see a shrinkage in the number of firms. The most extreme case was the footwear industry, which was predicted to lose 207 of its 739 firms. In some cases, the majority of the disappearing firms were concentrated in one or two countries, such as the UK carpet industry, where it was predicted that thirty-one of fifty-two manufacturers would go out of business.

The firms that go under are part of the economy-wide shift to a more efficient use of labor and capital resources, but it is obvious that there are immediate human costs. In the long run, it is easy to show that the gains in efficiency and the improvement in living standards outweigh the costs of restructuring, but in the short run, individuals and communities can feel acute pain. Due to the inevitable costs from restructuring, many people predicted that adversely affected firms and labor unions, along with the communities and regions that depend on the firms, would fight to prevent the full implementation of the SEA.

The auto industry is the best example of an economic interest that fought to prevent the full realization of the goals of the SEA. Car prices vary throughout the EU by as much as 50 percent due to a lack of harmonization of national technical standards, documentation requirements, and rates of taxation. Ordinarily, such large price differences would present an opportunity for consumers and distributors to move cars from the low-price countries to the high-price ones and, in the process, bring about a reduction in price differences. The auto industry is covered by a separate set of tax laws, however, that require buyers to pay the tax rate of the country where they register the car, not where they buy the car. This effectively discourages buyers from crossing national borders in order to search out the best deal on car prices and helps maintain the status quo in automobile production. Furthermore, Japanese-brand cars produced inside the EC will continue to be treated as Japanese imports while practices vary a great deal with respect to the rules governing Japanese car imports. Some members permit very few imports and others have very open markets. The agreement reached in the SEA was to set EU-wide quotas that would be phased out gradually

The automobile industry in the EU lags behind the United States and especially Japan in its switch to new, more flexible production systems that generate higher levels of productivity. As one of the largest industrial employers inside the EU, it has successfully argued that the complete elimination of all internal barriers would significantly reduce the overall size of the industry and create regional pockets of extreme distress. Because of its size, it is atypical in the political clout it can wield. Most industries have not been able to successfully make similar arguments, and the lowering of barriers throughout the EU has proceeded much more rapidly than the skeptics thought likely.

One significant reason why there have not been more exceptions to the dropping of trade barriers is that the EU has a broad array of programs to address the problems of structural change. Some of these programs are funded out of the EU budget, and others are national in origin. Programs include the EU's Regional Development Funds, which can be used to address problems of structural unemployment, and the member nations' income maintenance, education, and retraining funds. The latter vary across the member countries, but, in general, they reduce the costs to individuals and communities of unemployment and structural change by providing a generous social safety net for laid-off workers. They probably reduce political opposition to economic change as well, because workers in a factory that is shut down may not fight the closing as strenuously given the economic support system for laid-off employees. At the same time, the society-wide perception that workers who have been hurt by restructuring will be taken care of may effectively reduce opposition to change from the rest of the society on the grounds of "fairness."

It should be noted that although the generosity of the social safety net in the EU may be politically instrumental in reducing opposition to economic restructuring, many economists and politicians argue that the social safety net's generosity creates its own problems. In particular, many see it as a primary reason for the high unemployment rates of the late 1980s and 1990s. By providing many benefits to the unemployed, the EU has reduced the cost to individuals of unemployment and removed some of the incentives to look for work. In addition, taxes for these social programs often fall on employers. As a consequence, many firms are reluctant to hire new employees during an economic expansion. This is an ongoing debate within the EU.

Harmonization of Technical Standards.   A second major obstacle to the creation of the four freedoms was the problem of harmonizing standards. These include everything from building codes, to industrial equipment, to consumer safety, to health standards, to university degrees and worker qualifications. The EU estimated that there were more than 100,000 technical standards that required harmonization in order to realize the benefits of a completely integrated market. Many of the technical standards involved rules that touched directly on cultural identities. Nowhere was this more true than in the case of food processing. For example, there were discussions around the allowable level of bacteria in French cheese, the type of wheat required to make Italian pasta, the ingredients of German beer, and the oatmeal content of English bangers (breakfast sausages). In the end, the EU recognized that complete harmonization of standards would generate significant hostility and that the work required to agree on a set of common standards was beyond its capacity. Consequently, a combination of harmonization and mutual recognition of standards was adopted. In particularly sensitive cases, mutual recognition is the rule, but individual nations are allowed to keep their own national production requirements. For example, German beer must be certified as having been made according to the German standards, but Germany must allow all brands of beers to be sold within its borders.

As the discussion in Chapter 8 noted, standards do not have to be the same in order to create a single market, but the gains in economic efficiency that come from sharing the same standard can be significant. Shared standards permit manufacturers to produce to one standard, rather than fifteen, and to capture important economies of scale in the process. These economies also pass outside the EU, since U.S. or Japanese manufacturers share the benefits of being able to produce to one set of standards, and non-EU-based firms only have to get their product certified once in order to be able to sell in all fifteen countries. For this reason, the United States has had a keen interest in the standards-setting process and has looked to create joint U.S.-EU agreements on standards and the procedures by which they are set. The United States's preference has been to use the procedures of the International Standards Organization (ISO) to streamline the process of harmonization. (The ISO is an international organization that provides technical standards and whose ISO-9000 is a set of certifications applying to nearly all types of economic activity.)

Value-Added Taxes.   A third difficulty standing in the way of completely realizing the four freedoms is the issue of value-added taxes (VAT). These taxes function essentially like sales taxes and are levied by each of the EU members but at a wide variety of rates and coverage. When the SEA was first proposed in 1987, there were significant differences in the dependence of the member governments of the EU on value-added taxes, ranging from 19 to 35 percent of total government revenue. The European Commission studied the United States to determine the effects of different rates of sales taxation on the states sharing common borders and found that once the difference in sales taxes exceeded 5 percent, the higher-tax state lost revenues (and sales and jobs) to the adjoining lower-tax state. In other words, a 5 percent difference was sufficient to cause consumers to cross state boundaries to make purchases. The standard VAT rate in the EU before the SEA varied from 12 percent at the low end (Luxembourg and Spain) to 20 percent in the Netherlands, 22 percent in Denmark, and 25 percent in Ireland. In addition, there were special rates for sensitive goods, and these varied a great deal more than the standard rates.

VAT rates proved impossible to completely harmonize because they go to the heart of national political philosophy. High-tax countries expect the state to play a relatively greater role in national economic life, while low-tax countries are closer to the laissez-faire end of the political economy spectrum. The level of value-added taxes, and the degree to which the national government depends on them are in large part determined by the political philosophy of the nation. In turn, these philosophical attitudes are shaped by complex historical, cultural, and social factors, as well as economics.

The upshot of the attempt to harmonize value-added taxes was an inability to agree on a single rate. What was accomplished, however, was the creation of minimum and maximum rates that were set at 15 and 25 percent. Since the difference still exceeds the 5 percent differential that is the threshold at which high-tax countries lose revenue and sales, a number of controls were established to prevent revenue loss, even though these controls prevent the complete realization of the four freedoms. Among the controls are the previously mentioned tax on autos that is levied at the rate of the country where the purchaser intends to register and use the car, rather than at the rate of the country where the car is sold. A similar rule applies in a few countries (e.g., Denmark) to many appliances and other costly consumer goods.

Despite these obstacles, however, there are still significant incentives for cross-border shopping. Although the SEA has not brought a 100 percent free flow of goods and services, it is important to keep the exceptions in perspective. For most goods and services, in most border regions, consumers are perfectly free to cross national boundaries to bring back unlimited quantities of goods, and they will not be stopped at a border inspection station.

Public Procurement. Public procurement is the purchase of goods and services by governments or government-owned enterprises, such as state-run television companies, utilities, or hospitals. Most nations of the world tend to use procurement processes that discriminate in favor of nationally owned suppliers, although there are limits on their ability to do so if they belong to the WTO.

Since 1970, the EU has attempted to eliminate discrimination in public procurement but this has proved difficult. It is particularly a problem in the areas of telecommunications, pharmaceuticals, railway equipment, and electrical equipment. In many instances, national governments have attempted to create firms that would serve as "national champions" in world competition. One method was to favor those firms in the government procurement process so that they would have a guaranteed market for their output while they were still learning the most efficient methods of production. Needless to say, firms and industries that receive favorable treatment often develop effective lobbying efforts, particularly if there are a large number of jobs in the industry or if it shares the glamour of high technology and can raise concerns about national security if it is allowed to disappear.

Discrimination in public procurement, however, limits the benefits of restructuring and the gains from trade. If the EU countries are able to successfully develop a common security and foreign policy, the national security argument for discrimination in public procurement begins to lose a great deal of its justification.

THE THIRD WAVE OF DEEPENING: THE MAASTRICHT TREATY

By 1989, planning for the implementation of the Single European Act in January 1993 was well under way. Europe had seen several years of economic expansion, and the excitement of the SEA seemed to signal that the time was ripe to consider some of the directives proposed in the Delors Report that had been set aside because they were too complex to accomplish by 1993. In 1990, the European Commission convened an Intergovernmental Conference on Economic and Monetary Union. The purpose of the conference was to bring together the leaders of the twelve nations to discuss the steps necessary to create a monetary union under a single currency. There were other issues on the agenda, but this was the one that attracted the most interest, both inside and outside the EU.

The Intergovernmental Conference continued through most of 1991. The final draft of the proposed agreement was completed in December in the Dutch town of Maastricht and, ever since, has been known as the **Maastricht Treaty**. Many of the provisions in the agreement are technical and cover such arcane issues as the tax treatment of holiday homes in Denmark or the status of the pope in trade disputes with the Vatican. Other issues are much more fundamental, dealing with basic EU social policy. For example, Maastricht calls for the creation of a "Social Charter" defining a uniform set of labor laws and worker rights; it defines the right of all residents in a community to vote and to stand for election in local contests, regardless of the resident's nationality; it puts more control over health, education, cultural, and consumer safety issues in the hands of the European Commission; it calls for a common defense and security policy along with a common military force; and it defines the steps for achieving a common currency under the control of a European Central Bank by the year 1999 at the latest.

It is the last goal that has attracted the most attention. Achieving a single currency requires each country to give up its ability to set its own monetary policy and to accept whatever contractionary or expansionary policy the European Central Bank chooses. This is the most controversial feature of the Maastricht Treaty, both within and without the EU. The controversy stems from the fact that no group of countries has ever given up their national money to create a single currency, there is significant political opposition to its realization, and there are economic risks associated with voluntarily giving up one of the few tools that governments have to counteract recessions. If, for example, Germany is booming, but Spain is slumping, there is no common monetary policy that will be suitable to both countries. Germany would need a contractionary policy to cool off the economy and to prevent the ignition of inflation, while Spain needs an expansionary policy to create employment and growth.

These controversies have led to a very different public reception for the Maastricht Treaty than that received by the Single European Act. Whereas citizens, businesses, and governments were solidly behind the SEA, support for the Maastricht Treaty has been much more tentative. It is interesting to speculate why it was proposed at all, given its controversial extension of EU powers at the expense of national sovereignties and given that implementation of the SEA was still two years into the future.

One explanation for the timing of Maastricht is that it is simply a consideration of all the directives that were dropped from Delors's original proposal of 1985. According to this view, Maastricht includes all the final steps necessary to create a single market, and the enthusiasm and momentum leading up to 1993 made it an opportune time to propose the controversial final steps. A second explanation for the timing of Maastricht is that it was in response to the rapid pace of German unification. According to this view, European fears of a united Germany, which would be about one-third larger in population than the next most populous state, pushed forward the timetable for a single currency. Furthermore, both Germany's close ties to Eastern Europe and the collapse of the Soviet Bloc threatened to focus German attention eastward rather than westward. The solution to a potentially dominant German economy was to bind it so tight into the European Union that its ability to act independently would be severely limited.

A third possibility for the timing of Maastricht is that the goal of a single currency became politically necessary as a result of the changes that occurred under the Single European Act. In this view, the lifting of controls on the free movement of financial capital in 1990 made it more likely that weak currency countries would experience speculative attacks, leading inevitably to currency devaluations. Ultimately, the impacts would be felt through the movement of industries and jobs, pitting nations against each other as they tried to keep or attract new industries and leading to serious strains on cooperation. In order to explain this point and to see its logic more clearly, however, it is necessary to examine the pros and cons of monetary union.

MONETARY UNION AND THE EURO

The timetable for monetary union under a single currency is scheduled to occur in three separate stages. Stage one began in 1990 with the lifting of controls on the movement of financial capital within the EU. Stage two began in 1994 with the creation of the European Monetary Institute, based in Frankfurt, Germany. The Institute was charged with the responsibility for coordinating the move to monetary union and gradually took on elements of a supranational central bank. Stage 3 began in 1999 with the phased-in introduction of the euro and the European Central Bank.

During Stage 1 and Stage 2, nations were expected to bring their monetary and fiscal policies into harmony so that the introduction of the euro would not happen under wildly different sets of monetary and fiscal policies. In order to judge when individual national policies were in agreement, the EU developed a set of **convergence criteria**. These were objective measures that signalled whether the national policies were in conflict or in agreement and whether individual nations were ready for monetary union. Table 14.3 lists the specific monetary and fiscal variables that are required to be coordinated and the target ranges for each.

Initially, nations were expected to meet all five goals for monetary union. The experience of the first half of the 1990s, however, indicated that no nation (except perhaps Luxembourg) could consistently maintain each of these targets and that some countries would never meet them. For example, Italian and Belgian central government debts were well over 100 percent of their annual GDP, and there was no way to change this in the span of a few years. Some economists questioned why these particular criteria were chosen in the first place, since a country that can maintain its interest rates, debts, deficits, inflation, and exchange rates in the target range is already doing what the EU hopes to achieve with monetary union. In other words, meeting the convergence criteria was an indicator that the nation can do what monetary union does but without actually giving up its currency. Why, then, should countries surrender control over monetary policy, and why should they give up their national currency, particularly since there are hidden costs?

Costs and Benefits of Monetary Union

There is no doubt that there are benefits to having one currency in a market as large as the EU's. For example, the average cost of currency conversion for travelers is 2.5 percent of the amount converted. A trip from Portugal to Sweden, with stops along the way, can quickly eat up a sizable portion of one's vacation money. Businesses fare much better, however, and if they buy in quantities greater than the equivalent of U.S. $5 million, then the costs are a much smaller 0.05 percent, or $5000 to convert $10 million. One estimate combining both tourists and businesses puts the total costs of currency conversion at 0.4 percent of the European Union's GDP. This is not a trivial sum, but it is not

TABLE 14.3	Convergence Criteria for Monetary Union

Goals	Targets
1. Stabilize exchange rates	Maintain currency within the ERM band
2. Control inflation	Reduce it to less than 1.5 percent above the average of the three lowest rates
3. Harmonize long-term interest rates	Bring to within 2 percent of the average of the three lowest rates
4. Government deficits	Reduce to less than 3 percent of national GDP
5. Government debt	Reduce to less than 60 percent of national GDP

These five goals were designed to harmonize fiscal and monetary policies in preparation for the single currency.

huge either. The 0.4 percent figure could certainly be higher, however, given the costs of maintaining separate accounting systems and separate money management processes for the different currencies.

A second reason for desiring monetary union is to reduce the effects of exchange-rate uncertainty on trade and investment. Since orders for goods are often placed long before delivery occurs, traders face a good deal of uncertainty about both their earnings (if they export) and their payments (if they import). A single currency eliminates this uncertainty, in the same way, for example, that California manufacturers can always be certain of the value of payments they will receive when they ship goods to Ohio. Recall from Chapter 10 that traders and investors can protect themselves from currency fluctuations with forward markets. Therefore, it should not be surprising that until fairly recently there was no evidence whatsoever that the elimination of currency fluctuations through a monetary union would increase cross-border trade and investment. On the other hand, tests of this idea were difficult because there are few examples of monetary unions. Recently, however, evidence has emerged that shows large positive effects on trade and investment flows from the creation of a single currency. Ultimately, the European Union's experience will prove to be a valuable case study.

Given these considerations, the benefits of a single currency appear to be uncertain. The same cannot be said for the potential costs. A single currency does not allow individual nations to pursue an independent monetary policy, in the same way that the state of New York cannot have a monetary policy that differs from New Jersey's or the rest of the United States. In other words, in a single-currency area, there is a "one size fits all" monetary policy. It is optimal to have a single currency, and to eliminate the costs of currency conversion and other transaction costs, as long as the regions in the single currency area have synchronized business cycles and mobile labor forces. Synchronization of business cycles means that there is a single monetary policy—expansionary, neutral, or contractionary—that is appropriate for everybody. A mobile labor force guarantees that if some regions are not well synchronized, labor will move from the shrinking region to the expanding one, making the business cycles move together. If, however, the business cycles are not synchronized and labor is relatively immobile, then the single monetary policy will be right for some areas but wrong for others.

Business cycles in Europe have never been synchronized, although the convergence criteria were partly designed with this goal in mind. In addition, the Single European Act's guarantee of freedom for labor mobility does not seem to have created significantly more continent-wide labor mobility, and Europeans are far less mobile than Americans. Given that most conventional measures show that the EU fails both criteria for being an optimal currency area, it seems natural to ask why they are taking this momentous step.

The Political Economy of a Single Currency

Most policies that offer uncertain benefits and potentially large costs should be rejected. Why, then, is monetary union pushing ahead? This is the question that many economists have asked, and the answers are less than clear. The easiest answers are that the leaders of the EU believe that monetary union will create substantial trade and investment flows or that the leaders of the EU are simply swept up in a euphoric rush to greater political and economic unity. The latter explanation suffers from the defect that the EU has been unable to forge a consensus around a common defense and security policy, as evidenced by the divisions over the conflict in the former Yugoslavia.

The best explanation for the push to monetary union seems to be that it is politically necessary in the wake of the capital market liberalization required under the Single European Act. Prior to 1990, many countries had controls on the movement of foreign exchange into their country. Regulatory measures were common, such as taxes on foreign currency holdings, or on assets denominated in foreign currencies, and limitations on the uses of foreign currencies were widespread. The removal of these controls made it easier to speculate in foreign currency markets. One outcome of the removal of capital controls was the turmoil of 1992, when speculators became convinced that a number of currencies in the ERM would ultimately have to be devalued, prompting them to sell off large quantities of the currencies. During the sell-off, Portugal, Ireland, and Spain all devalued; Italy temporarily suspended participation in the ERM; and the United Kingdom dropped out permanently. Ultimately, the British pound fell by 25 percent from its peak before the speculative attacks. Soon after it left the ERM, there were several cases of firms that announced their intentions to close plants inside EU countries and move to the United Kingdom. For example, Philips Electronics, the giant Dutch firm, closed plants in Holland, and S.C. Johnson and the Hoover Company closed French plants, all in order to open new plants in the United Kingdom where French and Dutch currencies bought more land, labor, buildings, and machinery.

Needless to say, political friction increases and cooperation decreases when one country loses jobs to another as a result of currency depreciations. The desire to reduce these types of frictions is the reason why the European Monetary System, with its Exchange Rate Mechanism, was created in 1979. Consequently, it is the reason why a flexible exchange rate system is not an option. Although floating exchange rates have the advantage of permitting the greatest amount of flexibility in a nation's monetary policies, the EU's economic integration plans have closed the door on the use of flexible exchange rate systems.

Given that flexible rates are ruled out, it seems logical to ask why the EU did not choose to institute a system of fixed exchange rates. In fact, the ERM acted somewhat like a fixed exchange rate system because it tied each country's currency to a weighted average of the other currencies. Exchange rates were not completely fixed, however, and we saw that there were bands that the currencies tried to stay within. The EU's problem with a fixed exchange rate system is that it lacked the ability to keep the currencies within their bands, let alone to completely fix them. International currency markets know that there are definite limits to the resolve and the resources of member countries trying to defend their currencies. The EU partially solved this by changing the band-widths from ±2.25 percent to ±15 percent, which removed the minor short-run speculative pressures against particular currencies by letting them float down more before intervention became required. This, however, did nothing about the serious pressure against a currency that the United Kingdom and Italy experienced in 1992. In other words, the EU is not willing to defend their fixed rates if the costs grow too high, which means that fixed rates are not really "fixed."

Implementation of the Single Currency

The inability of the EU to maintain a set of fixed rates, coupled with the political undesirability of floating rates, made the single-currency option an attractive choice. Membership in the monetary union, however, is a subset of the EU. The United Kingdom has left the ERM and, along with Denmark and Sweden, did not join the move to a single currency. Few, if any, of the countries met the convergence criteria by the 1998 deadline for compliance. Nevertheless, in May of 1998, it was announced that eleven countries (the fifteen members of the EU, minus the United Kingdom, Sweden, Denmark, and Greece) would adopt the single currency on January 1, 1999. Greece adopted the euro one year later, in 2000.

In the first stage of the implementation process, countries keep their national currencies, but fix their exchange rates to each other. Until euro coins and notes begin to circulate in 2002, each of the euro area countries continues to use its own national money, which is fixed in value to the euro and, therefore, to the money of the other member countries. Table 14.4 shows the fixed euro rates for each of the member countries. During the transition period before the introduction of euro coins and notes, national currencies are managed as separate, national manifestations of the euro. In other words, the German mark is worth about one-half a euro, just as two quarters are worth one-half a U.S. dollar. Consequently, speculation against any one currency is equivalent to speculating against all of them. The euro itself is on a flexible exchange rate system, so it is free to move up or down against the dollar, the yen, and other currencies. Given the absolute fixity of the member countries' currency, a movement in the value of the euro is implicitly a proportional movement in each of its constituent currencies. The euro is managed by the European Central Bank (ECB), which also conducts monetary policy in the euro region.

Since its introduction in January, 1999, at $1.18, the euro has lost about a fourth of its value. Many observers anticipated that it might be weak at first, but no one predicted such a significant slide over its first two years. The euro's weakness caused some to question its long-term viability, but most economists remained sanguine about its future prospects. The weakness was largely written off as a result of high and rising U.S. interest rates during late 1999 and 2000, and the United States's high economic growth rate, which made it a good

TABLE 14.4	Fixed Euro Rates

Currency	Euro Equals
Austrian schillings	13.7603
Belgian francs	40.3399
Finnish markkas	5.94573
French francs	6.55957
German marks	1.95583
Irish pounds	0.787564
Italian lire	1936.27
Luxembourg francs	40.3399
Netherlands guilders	2.20371
Portuguese escudos	200.482
Spanish pesetas	166.386

These are the fixed rates during the transition period, lasting from January, 1999, until the euro coins replace the national monies in 2002.

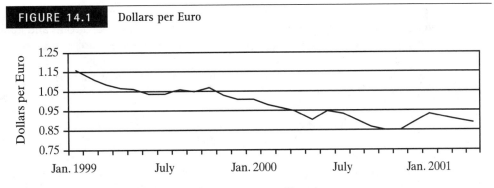

FIGURE 14.1   Dollars per Euro

In its first year and a half, the euro lost about 25 percent of its value.

Source: Board of Governors of the Federal Reserve Bank.

place to invest. Meanwhile, throughout the EU, new waves of mergers took place as firms looked to increase their size and attain greater scale economies, and price differences began to narrow significantly as the fixed euro rates made it easier for consumers and businesses to compare prices around the EU.

While the problems are real, it is also remarkable that there seems to be a strong determination to implement the program of monetary union. In fifty years, a short period in historical terms, the nations of Western Europe have moved from world war to a common market. Now, they stand at the beginning of an economic union that has elements that may eventually lead to a political union. The achievement is remarkable.

WIDENING THE EUROPEAN UNION

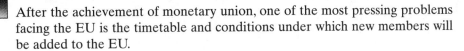

After the achievement of monetary union, one of the most pressing problems facing the EU is the timetable and conditions under which new members will be added to the EU.

Central and Eastern Europe

There are twelve applicants for membership in the EU. Ten are transition economies in Central Europe, and two are the small Mediterranean nations of Malta and Cyprus. The transition economies are in the middle of their transformation from state-controlled, authoritarian nations to market-oriented democracies. In 1997, the EU invited Cyprus, Poland, Hungary, the Czech Republic, Estonia, and Slovenia (formerly a part of Yugoslavia) to begin negotiations for accession, and in 1999, it opened negotiations with the other six, Latvia, Lithuania, the Slovak Republic, Romania, Bulgaria, and Malta.

There are three criteria for membership. First, each of the countries must be stable, functioning democracies. Second, they must have market-based economies, and third, they must formally adopt the EU-wide rules, called the ***acquis communautaire***. These include technical standards, environmental and technical inspections, banking supervision, public accounts, statistical reporting requirements, and other elements of EU law. The *acquis* is sovereign over national laws and must be completely adopted by each new member before it is granted full membership.

In the years prior to accession, the EU is actively involved in monitoring and providing technical assistance to prospective members. For example, several countries in Central and Eastern Europe lack the administrative structures necessary to apply for and administer the *acquis*. Judges must be trained in EU law, environmental inspectors need to know how to assess hazardous conditions, banking supervisors must learn accounting standards, and so forth. These are significant hurdles for countries that are still adapting their economic and political systems to capitalism and democracy.

The eastern movement of the EU began in 1991 when it signed free-trade agreements with each of the **Visegrad Four** (Poland, Hungary, the Czech Republic, and the Slovak Republic). Similar agreements were negotiated with Romania and Bulgaria in 1993 and the **Baltic Republics** in 1994. The agreements provide for an "associate member" status in the EU and phase in free trade in most, but not all, goods and services. These agreements are asymmetrical in the sense that the EU lifts its barriers before the other countries. The idea is to give them time to complete their transitions to market-based economies. The short-run effect of the free-trade agreements has been positive, and most of the applicants have experienced strong growth in their trade with Western Europe (see Chapter 17).

There are three major problems with the planned expansion. The first is agriculture and agricultural policies. Several of the prospective members in Central and Eastern Europe have large agricultural sectors. Poland, for example, is a large country (39 million) and has about 27 percent of its labor force in agriculture. Agriculture is important to several of the other applicants as well because it generates exports and earns badly needed foreign exchange. Large agricultural sectors are a problem for the EU, however, because of the EU's agricultural policies, known collectively as the **Common Agricultural Policy**, or **CAP**. The CAP is the world's most extensive set of farm price supports and farm income maintenance programs. One indicator of the CAP's importance is that despite recent and ongoing reforms, it is still taking 41 percent of the entire EU budget in the year 2001.

The CAP sets farm prices and guarantees a market for farm produce. It also provides direct-income payment to EU farmers. Among its many effects are that it keeps the farm sector in the EU larger than market forces would make it, and it has created large stockpiles of excess products. It seems unlikely that the EU can absorb more agricultural products itself, but the political and economic realities in the EU make it difficult to reduce subsidies paid to farmers. Extension of the subsidies to Poland and the other applicants is even less feasible. Full membership in the CAP would entail an enormous flow of payments to Central European farmers and an output response that would significantly add to the unwanted stockpiles of agricultural commodities. Similarly, but on a smaller scale, other EU programs will be stretched thin by the addition of countries with much lower incomes.

This situation has its own tensions, however. While it is politically difficult to permit Central Europeans to penetrate EU markets with their agricultural commodities, it is also in the political and economic interests of the EU to support the transition to a stable and prosperous Central Europe. If Eastern and Central European transitions to market economies fail, the consequences for Western Europe include an unstable eastern border, fewer markets for manufactured goods, and the possibility of significant East-West migratory flows.

It is difficult to measure accurately the pool of potential migrants from all of Central and Eastern Europe. Within the ten countries of Central Europe that have applied for EU membership, the total population is approximately 103 million. Russia and the states of the former Soviet Union add more than 280 million more people to the pool of potential migrants. Estimates of the actual number of migrants among these nearly 300 million people vary widely, from as low as 1 million people to as high as 15 million. The latter number is probably way too high, but no one really knows. Factors such as social networks and the evolution of the economies on Western Europe's eastern border will determine the actual number of migrants.

The rules of movement within the EU are also an important factor. The Single European Act legalized the migration of workers within EU states as long as the migrant has a means of support. Anyone can travel outside his or her country of origin to another EU country for three months as a tourist, and retirees can move to another nation if their pension is adequate to support them. Students may cross international boundaries to study as long as they have support, but most countries do not allow portability of government support. Workers can move to another country to look for a job, but they must find a job and become part of the local system before they can collect social insurance. In other words, migrants cannot move with the intent of collecting social insurance in a richer country. After the EU is widened, many observers believe that it might actually reduce migration because it will regularize and bring above ground the illegal migration that already exists.

A second problem with expansion is the governance structure of the EU. As the original six of the EEC evolved into the fifteen members of the EU, institutions changed and adapted so that they could accommodate the new members. The European Commission, Council of Ministers, and Parliament grew in size in order to provide fair representation in EU decision making. With the addition of six new members, and six after them, followed by possibly another group of ten or fifteen, the governance structure of the EU becomes unwieldy. A simple expansion of the number of seats in the main institutions makes some of the bodies too large to be effective, while it dilutes the importance of the larger countries in Western Europe. Leaders in Western Europe believe that they should continue to exercise power in proportion to the size of their economies and populations rather than on a one-country, one-vote, basis. In essence, the problem confronting the EU is identical to the problem faced by the United States during the creation of its constitution. Large states feel that their representation should be proportional to their size, while small states prefer not to be completely dominated by the more populous ones.

It has been difficult to reach an agreement on specific changes for determining the number of votes each country will have in each governing body. One proposal, introduced in December of 2000, calls for each nation to have only one seat on the European Commission, and for the allocation of votes in the Council of Ministers and the European Parliament to remain proportional to population.

A third problem with expansion is that entering countries are significantly less well-off than most of the existing members. As the EU expanded to include Portugal, Ireland, and Greece, the gap between poorest and richest members widened, but these countries are relatively small. This meant that programs that target EU expenditures in poorer regions were stretched, but still able to provide funds for infrastructure and other needs in the low-income areas. Not only are the gaps wide between the incomes of many of the potential entrants and the EU average, there are also some fairly large countries, beginning with Poland and its 39 million people. Extension of all EU expenditure programs, as they now exist, to all new entrants, is likely to stretch the EU budget beyond its means.

The problems of agriculture, governance, and income gaps are real threats to EU expansion. Nevertheless, the EU has shown an ability to overcome graver problems, and has continued to move forward in the creation of its economic union. These problems are not likely to be resolved swiftly, but fifty years ago, few thought that there would be a functioning economic union in the first decade of the twenty-first century.

A Possible Direction for Institutional Evolution

As Western Europe contemplates the widening of its economic union, there are a number of additional institutional complications that it must consider. First, the Baltic Republics, the Visegrad Four, and a number of other states have special economic and cultural ties to individual EU countries and to each other. The Baltic states and the Visegrad Four, for example, have a free-trade area among themselves. The individual Baltic Republics have each signed free-trade agreements with both non-EU countries (Switzerland, Liechtenstein, and Norway) and with EU countries (Sweden and Finland). Swedish and Finnish memberships in the EU take precedence over their ties to the Baltic Republics, but it is unlikely that either Sweden or Finland will back away from the close relationship it has formed with the Baltic Republics.

From the EU's perspective, expansion becomes a more difficult task as all of the formal and informal ties are considered. Does inclusion of Sweden and Finland in 1995 mean, for example, that Russian goods transshipped through

Lithuania will have a greater opportunity to enter the EU market through Lithuania's ties to Sweden and Finland? In most cases, the EU can probably prevent this sort of unwanted occurrence by tracking the location of production of the goods it imports, but the boundaries between EU and non-EU countries begin to blur.

Even within the formal boundaries of the EU, not all countries have equal participation. Denmark, Ireland, and the United Kingdom have chosen to continue their passport controls on intra-EU travel. Denmark has limitations on cross-border shopping for autos and major household appliances. The United Kingdom stressed that it will not accept EU standards for workers' rights or other labor legislation, a stand that it reversed with the election of a Labor party majority in 1997. And three countries will not adopt the euro in the forseeable future.

As these examples indicate, the general rules of the EU permit countries to opt out of institutions in which they do not want to participate. This attribute led many to believe that the future will involve several layers of participation, ranging from core members that follow all or nearly all the institutional rules to peripheral members that have the loosest of institutional ties. At the core will be the countries that share the single currency as well as the four freedoms. The next tier of participation will include the rest of the EU, all of whom share the four freedoms. Outside this group will be the remainder of Western Europe, including Liechtenstein, Iceland, and Norway, who share the four freedoms, but have no voting rights in EU institutions, nor do they participate in the most important EU programs, such as the CAP and the Regional Development Fund. The next layer of participants includes the countries sharing free-trade agreements with the EU, including the Baltic Republics, Poland, the Czech Republic, Slovakia, Hungary, Bulgaria, Romania, and Turkey. The extent of their participation in EU institutions is yet to be determined.

An arrangement with a core group and then several layers of membership categories would solve many of the institutional issues facing the EU. In particular, it would create a series of stages that allow new members to progress from distant to full participants if their own political and economic institutions warrant greater inclusion. It would remove the risk to the EU of admitting potentially unstable members, while offering an incentive for new democracies to strengthen their democratic institutions. It also solves the problem within the EU of the differences in the willingness and ability of states to participate in the changes called for by the Maastricht Treaty, such as the single currency.

Summary

- The EU has been created in several stages. The earliest stage involved agreements over open trade for coal and steel (ECSC) and cooperation over the peaceful development of nuclear energy (Euratom).
- The main institutions of the EU are the Council, the Commission, the Council of Ministers, the Court of Justice, and the European Parliament.

The role of the institutions has evolved, and the Council and Parliament are gaining greater power.

- The Treaty of Rome was signed in 1957 (it was put in force in 1958), creating a six-country free-trade area that was gradually phased in over the next ten years.

- The next wave of deepening was the creation of the European Monetary System in 1979, linking exchange rates.

- Following the EMS, the Single European Act was passed, creating a common market by 1993. While preparations were taking place for the implementation of the SEA, the Maastrict Treaty, or Treaty on European Union, was signed in 1991 and approved by the national governments in late 1993.

- The Maastricht Treaty's main item calls for a common currency. In preparation for the common currency, a set of convergence criteria was developed to determine which countries would be ready to change over. The criteria set targets for interest rates, inflation, government spending, and government debt.

- While the EU was undergoing its several rounds of deepening its integration, it was also widening its membership to nearly all of Western Europe. Between 1958 and 1995, it expanded from the original six members to fifteen.

- Several Central European nations have applied for membership, and at least five are expected to join by 2003. Eastward expansion of the EU has created three major problems in the areas of agricultural policy, governance, and income differences.

Vocabulary

acquis communautaire

Baltic Republics

Common Agricultural Policy (CAP)

competitive devaluation

convergence criteria

Council of Ministers

Court of Justice

Delors Report

democratic deficit

Euratom

euro

European Coal and Steel Community (ECSC)

European Commision

European Community (EC)

European Council

European currency unit (ECU)

European Monetary System (EMS)

European Parliament

European Union (EU)

exchange rate mechanism (ERM)   subsidiarity

Maastricht Treaty   Treaty of Rome

Single European Act (SEA)   Visegrad Four

Study Questions

1. What were the three main stages of deepening that occurred in the European Community after the passage of the Treaty of Rome?

2. What are the four main institutions of the EU, and what are their responsibilities?

3. The Single European Act was cited as a case in which it was difficult to create an agreement, despite the fact that there was near unanimity in support of an agreement. If everyone wanted the agreement, why was it hard to negotiate?

4. How did the EU expect to create gains from trade with the implementation of the Single European Act?

5. A sudden sharp increase in the demand for the mark almost destroyed the Exchange Rate Mechanism in 1992. Explain how a rise in the demand for a currency can jeopardize a target zone or exchange rate band.

6. Discuss the pros and cons of the single currency.

7. What are the pressures on the EU to admit new members? What pressures are there if it goes ahead with its plan to let in five more countries

Chapter 15

TRADE AND POLICY REFORM IN LATIN AMERICA

DEFINING A "LATIN AMERICAN" ECONOMY

Latin America stretches from Tijuana on the U.S.–Mexico border all the way to Cape Horn at the southern tip of South America. Within this vast geographic area lies such a diversity of languages and cultures that any definition of Latin America must have exceptions and contradictions. For example, *Webster's Tenth New Collegiate Dictionary* defines the region as Spanish America and Brazil, a standard view that must leave out a few small countries in Central and South America (Belize, Suriname, Guyana, and French Guiana) and the island nations of the Caribbean that were outside the region of Spanish and Portuguese settlement. Webster's second definition is "All of the Americas south of the United States," but it is perhaps less important to give a precise definition than it is to recognize the variety of physical geography, cultures, and income levels that coexist within any definition. In fact, the variety is so great that it is worth asking if these nations can truly be said to constitute a single world region. In other words, what is the "Latin American" experience, and how does it allow us to group together nations as different as Argentina, with its European culture and relative prosperity, and Guatemala, with its indigenous culture and great poverty?

The diversity within Latin America should make us careful not to overgeneralize. Nevertheless, there are several common themes shared by all, or nearly all, the nations in the region. First, there are common historical threads, beginning with the fact that a great many nations share a heritage of Spanish and Portuguese colonization, and a common linguistic base. We should be aware, however, that in some countries the languages of indigenous people are important as well. A second part of their shared histories is that many Latin American countries gained their national independence from Spain and Portugal during the nationalist revolutions of the early and middle nineteenth century. This differentiates them from the colonial experiences of Africa and Asia, and implies that the national identities of Latin Americans are perhaps deeper than in many parts of the developing world.

During the twentieth century, Latin American nations had much in common. The Great Depression of the 1930s, for example, caused most nations to shift their policies away from an outward, export orientation toward an inward, targeted industrial strategy. The new strategy eventually developed its own theoreticians and came to be known as "import substitution industrialization." More recently, most nations were borrowers in the 1970s, and severely indebted in the 1980s. Finally, beginning in the 1980s and continuing through to the twenty-first century, the region began a wide-ranging set of economic policy reforms, similar in scope to the transformation of Central and Eastern Europe after the collapse of communism.

In this chapter, we examine the origins and extent of the economic crisis that hit Latin America in the 1980s and analyze the responses. Before we examine the crisis of the 1980s and the economic reforms of the late 1980s and 1990s, we must first step back and look at the long-run performance of the economies of Latin America. When seen in the light of history, it is understandable why the miserable economic growth record of the 1980s gave rise to a dramatic shift in policies.

POPULATION, INCOME, AND ECONOMIC GROWTH

Table 15.1 is a snapshot of the current levels of income and population. The nations of Latin America include approximately 500 million, or 100 million more people than the three nations of NAFTA, and almost 125 million more than the fifteen nations of the European Union.

Table 15.1 shows the extent to which five countries account for the bulk of the population and production in Latin America. These are, in order by size of population, Brazil, Mexico, Colombia, Argentina, and Peru. Taken together, they add up to about 74 percent of the population of Latin America and nearly 85 percent of the GNP. In fact, Brazil, Mexico, and Argentina by themselves account for more than three-fourths (76 percent) of the GNP and three-fifths of the population.

If we were to focus exclusively on the 1980s, Latin America's ability to create economic growth and rising living standards seems limited. The obvious and natural comparison with the high-growth nations of East Asia—South Korea, Singapore, Hong Kong, Taiwan, Malaysia, Thailand, Indonesia—paints a picture of persistent failure in Latin America. Fortunately, this picture would be wrong.

For long stretches of the twentieth century, Latin America was one of the fastest-growing regions of the world. In particular, from 1900 to 1960, the region's real GDP per capita grew as fast or faster than that of Europe, the United States, or Asia. Individual experiences varied, but most countries saw adequate to excellent growth along with rising living standards. As shown in Table 15.2, growth continued from 1960 to 1980, when it kept up with all but the fastest-growing Asian economies. As world economic growth slowed after 1973, the experiences of the main Latin American economies became more varied. Some grew faster or nearly as fast, while some experienced a dramatic slowdown.

| **TABLE 15.1** | Population and GNP for Latin America and the Caribbean, 1999 | | |

Country	Population (millions)	GNP per Capita ($U.S., market exchange rates)	GNP per Capita ($U.S., PPP*)
Andean Community			
Bolivia	8.1	1,010	2,193
Colombia	41.6	2,250	5,709
Ecuador	12.2	1,310	2,605
Peru	25.2	2,390	4,387
Venezuela	23.7	3,670	5,268
Central American Common Market			
Costa Rica	3.6	2,740	5,770
El Salvador	6.2	1,900	4,048
Guatemala	11.1	1,660	3,517
Honduras	6.4	760	2,254
Nicaragua	4.9	430	2,154
MERCOSÚR			
Argentina	36.6	7,600	11,324
Brazil	161.8	4,420	6,317
Paraguay	5.4	1,580	4,193
Uruguay	3.3	5,900	8,280
Other Latin America/Caribbean			
Chile	15	4,740	8,370
Cuba	11.1	na	na
Dominican Republic	8.33	1,910	4,653
Haiti	7.8	460	1,407
Mexico	97.4	4,400	7,719
Panama	2.8	3,070	5,016
Total Population and (Weighted) Average GNP per capita	492.5	3,778.6	6,212.8

Latin America has nearly 500 million people. The five largest economies—Argentina, Brazil, Colombia, Mexico, and Peru—have nearly three-fourths of the population and produce 85 percent of the GNP.

*Purchasing power parity.

Source: World Bank, *World Development Report, 2000/2001.* (Tables 1, 1a).

Latin America: Income Classification

INCOME CLASSIFICATIONS

- [ ] N.A.
- [ ] Low (less than $756)
- [ ] Low Middle ($756–2995)
- [ ] Upper Middle ($2996–9265)

Income Classification is
based on GNP per Capita
1999 $. *Source:* World Bank,
World Development Report 2000/01

Scale
1:46,578,000
1:735.14 Inches to Miles
Robinson Projection

TABLE 15.2	Average Annual Growth in Real GDP, 1960-1999		

Annual Growth in Real GDP per Capita

Country	1960–1980	1980–1990	1990–1999
Argentina	1.9	–2.2	3.6
Brazil	4.5	0.7	1.5
Chile	1.5	2.6	5.7
Colombia	2.8	1.5	1.2
Mexico	3.9	–1.0	0.9
Peru	1.8	–2.5	3.7
Venezuela	0.7	–1.5	–0.5
Latin America		–0.3	1.7

Growth slowed in the 1980s, but picked up again in the 1990s.

Source: Penn World Tables (Mark 5.6); World Bank, *World Development Report, 2000/2001*; author's calculations.

Then the crisis struck. The Lost Decade of the 1980s was a disaster through-out Latin America. The entire region experienced negative per capita growth from 1980 to 1985. A few countries, notably Chile and Colombia, began to emerge from the crisis by the middle of the decade, but the largest economies continued to have negative growth over the entire decade. By the late 1980s, most were emerging from the crisis, with the notable exceptions of Brazil and Peru, which were late to begin reforms. The effects of the crisis were profound. Nearly fifty years of economic strategy came to an end as each nation began to abandon the inward-oriented, closed, and interventionist policies. The degree and timing of these changes varied from country to country, and there are questions about their permanency, but there is no question that the crisis of the 1980s triggered a major shift in economic policies throughout Latin America.

GENERAL CHARACTERISTICS OF LATIN AMERICAN ECONOMIES, 1950-2000

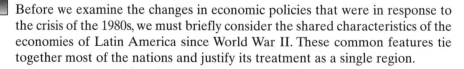

Before we examine the changes in economic policies that were in response to the crisis of the 1980s, we must briefly consider the shared characteristics of the economies of Latin America since World War II. These common features tie together most of the nations and justify its treatment as a single region.

Inward Orientation

The nations of Latin America relied on a common economic development strategy, called **import substitution industrialization**, or **ISI**, from the 1930s until the debt crisis of the 1980s. Recall from Chapter 13's review of Mexico's recent economic history, that ISI policies aim at reducing imports by producing the same or similar goods at home. An unintended consequence of this policy is a reduction in exports, which, together with the reduction in imports, left the economies of Latin America less economically integrated with the world economy. Contrary to the intent of many Latin American leaders, and perhaps somewhat paradoxically, the relatively weak integration with the world economy left Latin America more vulnerable to sudden shifts in worldwide economic conditions.

Inequality

As a group, the nations of Latin America have levels of inequality that are higher than any other region of the world. This is partly an historical legacy, but is also intimately connected to low levels of productivity in subsistence agriculture and a lack of educational and economic opportunity, particularly for women. One of the challenges over the last two decades has been to stimulate growth while simultaneously reducing inequality. The record is very mixed, at best.

Macroeconomic Instability

A third feature of the economies of Latin America over the last fifty years is the periodic reoccurrence of macroeconomic crises, typically characterized by high rates of inflation, overvalued real exchange rates, and large trade and budget deficits. Crisis response calls for the adoption of expenditure-reducing policies (cuts in government spending, wages, and consumption) and expenditure-switching policies (devaluations of the currency and termporary tariff barriers), which, in turn, result in recession and rising inequality and poverty.

The Debt Crisis of the 1980s

A fourth shared feature is the severe crisis brought on in the early 1980s by the collapse in oil prices and the rise in world interest rates. The **debt crisis** initiated nearly a decade of economic depression and rising poverty, and it forced a reevaluation of the economic policies of the previous 50 years.

Reform Movements of the 1980s and 1990s

The economic depression spawned by the debt crisis led directly into the reform movements of the last twenty years. The timing, pattern, and extent of reform has varied from country to country, but every country has been affected. In many cases, economic policies were changed from highly protectionist to aggressively export oriented; Mexico and Chile are two outstanding examples. In addition, the role of the state in economic affairs is being reassessed, and most countries started to privatize large parts of their state-owned economies.

These five features of Latin America are common threads throughout the region. There are exceptions, such as Cuba, which remains largely outside these currents of world history, but the vast majority of the people in Latin America live in countries that share these features. We turn now to look at some of them in more detail.

IMPORT SUBSTITUTION INDUSTRIALIZATION

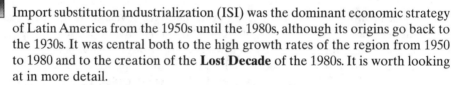

Import substitution industrialization (ISI) was the dominant economic strategy of Latin America from the 1950s until the 1980s, although its origins go back to the 1930s. It was central both to the high growth rates of the region from 1950 to 1980 and to the creation of the **Lost Decade** of the 1980s. It is worth looking at in more detail.

Origins and Goals of ISI

From the second half of the nineteenth century until the middle of the twentieth century, most of Latin America relied on exports of agricultural commodities (tropical fruits, coffee, cotton, grains) and minerals (petroleum, copper, tin) to earn foreign revenue. These export sectors were often developed or controlled by foreign capital and had few economic linkages to the domestic economy, functioning instead as foreign enclaves within the nation. In cases where the export sector was domestically owned, it usually brought wealth to a relatively small number of people and added greatly to the inequality of power and money that is pervasive in Latin American society. As a result of this history, powerful proindustrial interests have often viewed the traditional export sector with suspicion and hostility. Nevertheless, the exports produced in these sectors were important sources of foreign revenue.

The disruption of world trade caused by World War I and the Great Depression was particularly hard on countries that depended on primary commodity exports as a major source of income. In particular, the Depression was harmful because it caused a large reduction in demand and falling prices for the agricultural and mineral commodities that Latin America exported. In the 1940s, however, primary commodity producers in Latin America found that many of the effects of the Depression were reversed by World War II. While it created new risks for shipping, many nations earned large reserves of foreign currency from the materials they sold during the war.

This trend ended after the war with a sudden decrease in the demand for primary commodities from Latin America. The United States no longer needed as many raw materials, and Europe was unable to buy. The Argentine economist Raul Prebisch argued that raw materials such as copper, cotton, tin, coffee beans, and other exports from Latin America would experience declining prices over the long run. In particular, prices would fall in relation to the prices of manufactured goods, so that the ratio of raw material prices to manufactured goods prices would decline. In trade analysis, the ratio of average export prices to average import prices is called the **terms of trade** (**TOT**):

TOT = (Index of export prices)/(Index of import prices).

Since Latin America exported raw materials and imported finished goods, Prebisch's prediction was that the terms of trade for the region would decline. In effect, this prediction amounted to stating that over time, each unit of exports would earn a smaller and smaller unit of imports. For obvious reasons, this view was given the label **export pessimism**.

The reasoning behind Prebisch's export pessimism included both statistical studies and economic theory. Statistical analysis showed raw material prices falling over periods as long as several decades. (More recent analysis shows that while prices may fall for extended periods of time, there is no long-run trend up or down.) Economic theory holds that as incomes rise, people spend a smaller and smaller share of their overall income on foodstuffs and other raw material based goods such as textiles and apparel, while they spend more and more on manufactured items. Consequently, the demand for raw materials would decline in relation to the demand for manufactured goods.

Export pessimism formed the basis of economic policy from roughly the 1950s through the 1980s. As the head of the United Nations' **Economic Commission on Latin America** (**ECLA** in English; **CEPAL** in Spanish), Prebisch guided economic policies throughout Latin America. Prebisch's policy prescriptions reinforced a shift that had begun with the destruction of trade in the 1930s. The loss of markets during the Great Depression temporarily forced Latin America away from dependence on raw material exports and toward industrial development through the replacement of imported manufactured goods with domestically produced ones—hence the name "import substitution industrialization." Ironically, domestic production of manufactured import substitutes required the importation of large quantities of capital goods (factory machinery and parts), and, in order to earn the revenues needed to buy these imports, most nations continued to depend on raw material exports in the decades after World War II. Primary commodities still make up a significant share of today's exports from Latin America.

ISI is a form of industrial policy. Its answer to the question about which industries to target is that developing countries should focus on those industries that produce substitutes for imported goods. According to Prebisch, the inevitable decline in the terms of trade for primary commodities means that the biggest constraint on industrial development is the shortage of foreign exchange. Lower export prices mean that countries find it harder and harder to earn the foreign exchange they need in order to buy the machinery and other capital goods they cannot produce themselves. One of the most important roles of import substitution is to reduce the need for foreign exchange that is used to buy goods that could be made at home.

ISI theorists argued that a country should begin by producing inexpensive and relatively simple consumer items, such as toys, clothing, food products (e.g., beverages, canned goods, etc.), and furniture. Gradually, the focus of industrial targeting should move on to more complex consumer goods (appliances and autos) and intermediate industrial goods (pumps, generators, basic metals, etc.). In the third stage, complex industrial goods would be produced (chemicals, electronic equipment, machine tools, etc.).

Criticisms of ISI

The economic tools for implementing ISI are the same as those for industrial policies discussed in Chapter 5. These include a variety of different types of government support, from subsidies of all kinds to trade protection and monopoly power in the domestic market. In retrospect, import substitution industrialization generated a number of unintended consequences that caused inefficiencies and wasted resources. Among the many criticisms that have been leveled at ISI are the following: (1) governments misallocated resources when they became too involved in production decisions; (2) exchange rates were often overvalued; (3) policy was overly biased in favor of urban areas; (4) income inequality worsened; and (5) ISI fostered widespread rent seeking. These issues will be taken up in turn.

Foremost among the problems of ISI are those related to an overconfident and naive belief in the ability of the state to efficiently direct resources into their best uses. In the 1950s and 1960s, it was often assumed that **market failures** were far more common in developing nations than in industrial ones, and that one of the main goals of any state should be to correct these through selective and careful state intervention in the economy. In this context, ISI can be interpreted as a set of policies in which government uses its economic and political power to improve on the market. (Recall from Chapter 5 how difficult it is to measure market failures and to know the required corrective action.)

While this model is not altogether wrong, it does overestimate the technical ability of government officials to identify market failures and their solutions. It also assumes that government bureaucrats are selfless individuals who ignore political considerations and focus only on economic efficiency and what is best for the nation as a whole. This naive model of political reality caused an underemphasis on problems related to the implementation of economic policies, such as corruption and the lobbying power of economic elites. It also failed to take into account the slow accumulation of special provisions, favors, and economic inefficiencies that built up over time when policies were heavily influenced by politics. Naturally, this problem was magnified by the inequality in wealth and income throughout Latin America. Powerful interest groups were able to use ISI policies to their own ends rather than in the national interest.

A second problem of ISI was the development and persistence of overvalued exchange rates. Overvaluation was a deliberate policy in some countries, while in others it was a chronic problem stemming from the maintenance of a fixed exchange rate under conditions of higher inflation than among the countries' trading partners. Overvaluation developed into a particularly serious obstacle to economic growth after world inflation picked up in the 1970s. As a deliberate policy, overvaluation of the exchange rate accomplished several goals. In particular, it made it easier for the targeted industries to obtain the imported capital goods they needed. It also helped to maintain political alliances between the urban working classes and the political parties in power. It did this by providing access to relatively less expensive foreign goods, which kept living standards higher than they would have been otherwise. As evidence of this point, when governments were forced to depreciate in the 1980s and 1990s, they often lost the political support of the urban classes.

Although overvalued exchange rates had some benefits, they also had costs. Most importantly, they made it difficult to export because they raised the foreign price of domestic goods. The effects were harmful to agriculture and the traditional export sectors, but it hurt industry as well by making exports less attractive and reducing the pressures of international competition. Since agricultural exports were less profitable, capital investment was directed away from that sector which, in turn, held down the growth of agricultural productivity and caused incomes to be relatively stagnant in rural areas. Overvalued exchange rates also made foreign machinery cheaper and caused industrial investment to be too capital intensive and insufficiently labor intensive. Consequently, industry did not create enough new jobs to absorb the growing labor force and the labor that left agriculture for the cities. Furthermore, since most industry is located in urban areas, government investment in infrastructure improvements—such as transportation, communication, and water—were heavily targeted toward cities and their environs. The share of the population that lives in urban areas varies across countries, but in many nations the failure to develop rural infrastructure, from roads to schools to power supply systems, meant that subsistence farmers and their families did not benefit from (or contribute to) national economic development. The human costs are high, since rural inhabitants are far more likely to live below poverty lines.

In addition to a persistent tendency toward overvalued exchange rates, ISI trade and competition policies were heavily protectionist and often favored the creation of domestic monopolies. The lack of foreign and domestic competition meant that manufacturing remained inefficient and uncompetitive. With profits from a protected domestic market, many producers saw no reason to invest in modern equipment, further reinforcing the uncompetitiveness of their products. It is ironic that as a consequence many countries became more vulnerable to economic shocks that originated outside of Latin America, which was precisely the opposite effect from the one that motivated ISI in the first place.

CASE STUDY

ISI in Mexico

The Mexican constitution of 1917 established the power and the responsibility of the federal government to intervene in the economy in order to act as the leading agent of economic growth and as the referee of social conflict. This role was not institutionalized inside the Mexican government until the Mexican revolution was consolidated in the 1930s under the presidency of Cárdenas (whose son was a leading opponent of the dismantling of ISI during the reforms of the 1980s and 1990s).

In order to lead and direct economic growth, government could legitimately claim the need to be powerful—otherwise, powerful social classes could resist the government's directives and initiatives, particularly those with distributional goals or consequences. Therefore, economic policy served not only to meet the needs of the country for economic growth and a fairer distribution but also to increase the political power of government. Mexico nationalized its oil industries in 1938, and throughout the twentieth century, a number of sectors were nationalized and turned into state-run monopolies (telephones, airlines, banks, railroads, mineral development companies). The use of the government budget in this manner guaranteed access to investment funds, while monopoly markets ensured that the favored firms would succeed, at least within the nation.

The government also offered loans and loan guarantees to many firms in targeted industries. Loans and loan guarantees helped firms obtain capital at interest rates that were below what they would have paid otherwise. Similarly, the government sold foreign exchange at artificially low prices to targeted firms who needed to buy imports. Mexican exporters were required to convert their foreign exchange earnings into pesos at an overvalued peso rate (too few pesos per dollar), which made exporting relatively less profitable; the government then sold the cheaply acquired foreign exchange to targeted industries. In effect, exporters were subsidizing the development of the targeted industries.

Unlike many ISI nations, Mexico limited foreign investment. Like most ISI nations, however, when investment was permitted (e.g., autos), performance requirements were placed on the foreign firms. A common requirement was that the foreign firm balance its foreign exchange requirements so that each peso of imports was matched by a peso of export earnings. Further interventions occurred in the area of commercial policy where import licenses limited many types of imports. Recall that import licenses are essentially quotas. About 60 percent of all imports were subject to licensing by the 1970s.

From 1950 to 1973, Mexican real GDP per capita grew at the rate of 3.1 percent per year. By comparison, the United States grew 2.2 percent per year; the fourteen largest OECD nations grew 3.5 percent per year; and growth in the six largest Latin American economies was 2.5 percent. At the same time that the economy was undergoing relatively rapid economic growth, industrialization was changing the structure of the economy. Mexican manufacturing expanded from 21.5 percent of GDP to 29.4 percent. Growth began to slow in the 1970s, as it did in many parts of the world.

One widely shared view is that Mexican growth began to stall because the country was running out of easy targets for industrial development. Light manufacturing and simple consumer goods industries are relatively easy to start up, and the conversion of a part of the nation's economy from subsistence agriculture to apparel manufacturing makes growth rates look good. The next stages require more sophisticated manufacturing, however, and are relatively harder to start up. According to this view, Mexico had run out of simple industries to start and was inevitably having a harder time producing more sophisticated goods that were further from its comparative advantage.

In spite of rapid economic growth during the 1950s and 1960s, poverty and income inequality continued. Large numbers of Mexicans, many of them indigenous people living in rural areas, did not participate in the growth of the economy. This is evidenced by the fact that in the 1980s, much of agriculture was still at a subsistence level, using 26 percent of the nation's labor force to produce just 9 percent of the nation's GDP. The urban bias in Mexico's development strategy turned Mexico City into one of the largest metropolises in the world, with more than 15,000,000 people in the greater metropolitan area by the late 1980s. The sensational growth and crowding of people and industry into the basin that holds Mexico City resulted in serious pollution problems.

There is no consensus among economists as to the role played by ISI in the Mexican debt crisis of the 1980s. Certainly, ISI policies expanded the role of the federal government in economic activity and increased government expenditures and borrowing during the 1970s. Nevertheless, overall economic growth remained fairly robust until the mid-1970s. One widespread view is that the easy gains of ISI were gone by the 1970s, and in order to keep growth on track, Mexican presidents used their power over public finances to dramatically increase expenditures. At first, the government argued that it could easily afford to borrow in foreign capital markets because the nation had recently (1978) become a major oil exporter. Ultimately, the government's fiscal policies generated enormous public sector deficits, fears of devaluation, and capital flight. By 1982, a year after the price of oil fell, the nation had run out of international reserves and could no longer service its international debt. If the government had not resorted to unsustainable macroeconomic policies, would it have fallen into the debt crisis and rejected ISI policies in the mid-1980s?

A final problem of ISI behavior is the development of widespread rent seeking behavior. When governments intervene in the planning and directing of industrial development, they give government officials and bureaucrats a wide range of valuable commodities to distribute. These include the many subsidies and licenses that are a part of ISI policies. For example, in order to protect the domestic market and to ensure access to needed imports, governments often required import licenses and at the same time, provided foreign exchange at subsidized prices to the importer. When government policy creates something of value, such as the license to import or a subsidy to buy foreign exchange, the private sector will spend resources to obtain it. In the absence of strong institutions to ensure the independence of the bureaucracy (and, often, even when they are present), bribes and corruption become a part of the decision making. Ultimately, some decisions are made for the wrong reasons, and economic waste is the result.

MACROECONOMIC INSTABILITY AND ECONOMIC POPULISM

Many economists are convinced that while ISI policies are suboptimal, they had less of a direct effect in creating the economic crisis of the 1980s than did misguided macroeconomic policies. The reasons are relatively straightforward. ISI policies involve trade barriers and government support for selected industries. Collectively, these policies may lower a nation's income by a few percentage points, but they rarely lead to a full-blown economic crisis. Faulty macroeconomic policies, on the other hand, often lead to hyperinflation, depression, and balance of payments crises. In addition, while most of Latin America used ISI policies from the 1950s through the 1980s, economic growth remained at fairly high levels for most countries until the early 1980s when growth turned negative in nearly all countries. While it is entirely possible that the 1980s crisis was the culmination of several decades of ISI policies, it is certain that the crisis was directly linked to the faulty macroeconomic policies of the late 1970s and early 1980s.

Populism in Latin America

Many Latin America specialists blame the faulty macroeconomic policies of the region on **populist** or **economic populist** political movements that use economic tools to reach specific goals, such as obtaining support from labor and domestically oriented business, or isolating rural elites and foreign interests. Examples of populist leaders abound: in Argentina, Juan Perón (1946–1955 and 1973–1976) and Raúl Alfonsín (early 1980s); in Brazil, Getúlio Vargas (1951–1954), Joaõ Goulart (1961–1964), and José Sarney (1985–1990); in Chile, Carlos Ibáñez (1952–1958) and Salvador Allende (1970–1973); in Peru, Fernando Belaúnde Terry (1963–1968), Juan Velasco Alvarado (1968–1975), and Alan García (1985–1990); in Mexico, Luis Echeverría (1970–1976) and José Lopez Portillo (1976–1982). Populist movements in Latin America share nationalistic ideologies and a focus on economic growth and income redistribution. The central economic problem generated by these movements is the

CASE STUDY

Peronism in Argentina

Juan Perón served as president of Argentina during two separate periods: 1946 to 1955 and throughout 1973 until his death in 1974. After his death, his second wife and vice president, Isabel Perón, took over the presidency and continued his policies until she was overthrown in 1977. Perón's two terms demonstrate the shift in populist economics from a more traditional or classical version to a cruder economic version. Classical populism was more aware of the limits imposed by budgets and the availability of foreign exchange, whereas the more recent versions of economic populism have largely ignored these constraints. Perón's presidency is also significant because it was a dramatic statement of the policies that led to much slower growth in Argentina and that caused the country to fall farther behind the industrial nations of the world. Early in the century, Argentina was one of the ten or fifteen richest countries in the world, and although it continued to grow economically, its rate of growth was so slow by comparison to the rest of the world that by the end of Perón's first term, it had fallen into the ranks of developing nations.

Perón's early policies were built on two core ideas. First, the powers of the state should be used to ensure that growth did not lead to increased inequality. Second, the terms of trade for Argentina were going to deteriorate, so the nation should seek economic independence from world trade. Perón's rhetoric called for a "New Argentina" in which workers would receive their fair share, foreign influences would be eliminated, and owners of businesses would receive favorable credit policies. This required heavy state involvement, and the government asserted itself by nationalizing foreign trade, communications, railroads, docks, and banking. A five-year economic plan was established, consisting of subsidized credit, wage increases, and an expansion of federal expenditures and the fiscal deficit.

The policies of the five-year economic plan were initially successful, with significant growth in GDP between 1946 and 1948, moderate inflation, and rising real wages. The data in Table 15.3 illustrate the typical populist pattern of rapid growth in 1946 through the first half of 1948, the early years of the policy. The fiscal deficit also rose steadily, along with real wages. The increase in wages caused inflation to begin rising, however, and the sizable trade surpluses of 1945 and 1946 deteriorated quickly, resulting in a serious decline in foreign reserves in 1949. In 1949, Perón was forced to name a new finance minister, who implemented an orthodox stabilization plan consisting of tight credit, reduced government expenditures, and wage and price controls. By 1952, the plan began to work, prompting a new five-year plan that froze wages for two years and focused on attracting foreign capital. At the end of 1952, wages were still higher than in 1945, despite the fact that many of the gains between 1945 and 1952 were given back.

(continues)

TABLE 15.3	Economic Indicators During the First Perón Administration							
	1945	*1946*	*1947*	*1948*	*1949*	*1950*	*1951*	*1952*
GDP growth	–3.2%	8.9%	11.1%	5.5%	–1.4%	1.2%	3.1%	–6.6%
Real wage index	100	103	129	156	162	172	145	128
Deficit/GDP	4.6	6.9	5.8	13.4	9.8	5.5	4.5	5.6
Inflation	8.6	15.7	3.6	15.3	23.2	20.4	49.0	31.2
Trade balance (millions of U.S. $)	$429	$568	$107	$90	–$160	$143	–$305	–$455

Populist policies produce temporary economic growth at the expense of large budget and trade deficits and inflation.

Source: Gerchunoff, "Peronist Economic Policies, 1946–1955," in *The Political Economy of Argentina, 1946–1983*, edited by di Tella and Dornbusch, 1983.

The second Perón administration began in 1973 with the election of a caretaker president, Hector Campora. Campora was a stand-in until new elections could be held to reelect Perón. Between his election and his resignation, Campora launched an economic plan that consisted of a one-time wage increase followed by a two-year wage freeze and a freeze on prices. Perón, with his wife, Isabel, as his vice presidential running mate, was easily elected in September 1973 with 62 percent of the vote. Meanwhile, Campora's economic program showed early success, as the GNP grew in 1973 and 1974, inflation fell, and real wages increased (see Table 15.4).

TABLE 15.4	Economic Indicators During the Second Perón Administration			
	1973	*1974*	*1975*	*1976*
GDP growth	5.8%	6.5%	–1.3%	–2.9%
Real wage index	100	109	106	63
Deficit/GDP	6.3	5.9	14.4	7.9
Inflation	44	40	335	364
Current account balance (Millions of U.S. $)	$731	$94	–$1,094	$125

The second Perón administration left workers much worse off after temporary modest wage gains.

Source: di Tella, Guido, "Argentina's Economy Under a Labour-Based Government, 1973–6," in The *Political Economy of Argentina, 1946–1983*, edited by di Tella and Dornbusch, 1983.

Perón died in July 1974, and Isabel assumed the presidency. Unions, which were an important component of the Perón constituency, negotiated 100 percent nominal wage increases, and inflation increased to 335 percent. Exports declined significantly, and the government adopted a stringent stabilization plan in March 1976 in return for help from the IMF. By 1977, the inflation rate had declined from 364 to 160 percent, the fiscal deficit declined, and GNP began growing once again. The end result of the economic policies of the second Perón administration was a significant decline in real wages, and a reduction of labor's share of national income—the exact opposite of what was intended.

use of expansionary fiscal and monetary policies without regard for the importance of inflation risks, budget deficits, and foreign exchange constraints.

Economic populism is usually triggered by three initial conditions. First, there is a deep dissatisfaction with the status quo, usually as a result of slow growth or recession. Second, policymakers reject the traditional constraints on macro policy: Budget deficits financed through printing money are justified by the existence of high unemployment and idle factories, which offer room for expansion without inflation. Third, policymakers promise to raise wages while freezing prices and to restructure the economy by expanding the domestic production of imported goods, thereby lessening the need for foreign exchange. In the words of one analyst, the policies call for "reactivating, redistributing, and restructuring" the economy.

Early in the populist regime, there is a vindication of the policies. The economic stimulus of government expenditures and newly created money leads to rising growth rates and rising wages. Soon, however, bottlenecks begin to set in. For example, construction firms run out of particular inputs, such as cement or specialized steel products, and manufacturing firms cannot find the parts they need to repair their machinery. Prices begin to rise, and the budget deficit grows. In the next stage, inflation begins an extreme acceleration, and shortages become pervasive throughout the economy. The budget falls into serious deficit as policies become unsustainable, and wage increases cease keeping up with inflation. In the final stage, countries experience massive capital flight as fears of a devaluation develop. The flight of capital out of the country depresses investment and further depresses real wages.

After all is over, real wages are often lower than before the cycle began, and there is an international intervention under the sponsorship of the IMF, which is designed to stop the high inflation and end a balance of payments crisis. Typically, the IMF oversees the implementation of stabilization and structural reform policies that call for serious budget cuts, a slowdown in the growth of the money supply, a reduction in trade barriers, and, in general, greater reliance on market mechanisms and less government intervention. While these stages of the populist cycle are an idealization, they capture the essence of the populist experience as it has occurred in many Latin nations.

CASE STUDY

Alan García and Peru

Alan García became president of Peru in July 1985. As part of the fallout from the debt crisis, the country suffered through a serious recession in 1983, but by 1985 it was on the mend. García's policies were a textbook case of economic populism. He immediately began a program to raise real wages in order to stimulate demand and redistribute income. The economy responded to the stimulus of higher consumption with very robust increases in the GDP in 1986 and 1987. The presence of idle factory capacity along with unemployed workers enabled the GDP to expand without initially creating inflation. By mid-1987, however, some essential imported inputs became scarce and began to act as bottlenecks on further increases in production. Consequently, inflation rekindled. See Table 15.5.

Government policy for the exchange rate was based on a controlled rate that was periodically devalued. Inflationary price increases were greater than the exchange rate devaluations and thereby caused an appreciation in the real exchange rate, which led to a significant increase in the current account deficit.

The rise in 1987's budget deficit, trade deficit, and rekindling of inflation late in the year would have been enough to cause a more cautious government to rein in expenditures. García's administration responded to the deterioration in economic indicators by nationalizing the property of the financial services sector (banks, insurance companies, etc.) and expanding credit subsidies for favored groups in the agricultural and industrial sectors. In 1988, the government tried to tackle the problem of

TABLE 15.5	Economic Indicators During the García Administration						
	1984	*1985*	*1986*	*1987*	*1988*	*1989*	*1990*
GDP growth	4.8%	2.3%	9.2%	8.5%	−8.3%	−11.7%	−5.1%
Real wage	−8.0	−8.4	26.6	6.1	−23.1	−46.7	−14.4
Deficit/GDP	6.7	3.4	5.7	7.9	8.1	8.5	5.9
Inflation	110	163	78	86	667	3339	7482
Current account balance (Millions of U.S. $)	−$221	−$137	−$1,077	−$1,481	−$1,091	$396	−$766

Alan García's policies produced temporary wage gains followed by enormous declines, large deficits, runaway inflation, and unsustainable current account imbalances.

Source: Inter-American Development Bank, *Economic and Social Progress in Latin America,* various years.

inflation through devaluations and price freezes, but in order to protect incomes and to bring relative prices into agreement, it simultaneously permitted selected price increases and compensating wage increases.

By 1990, the economy reached the deepest point in its recession. In July, a new government took office and implemented a relatively orthodox stabilization program of fiscal and monetary austerity in order to end inflation and curb the budget deficit. By then, however, real wages were well below the level they had attained when the previous government took power in 1985.

THE DEBT CRISIS OF THE 1980s

In August 1982, Mexico announced that it lacked the international reserves it needed to pay the interest and principal due on its foreign debt. Mexico was not the first country to declare its inability to service its debt, but it was the biggest up to that point. Its announcement soon led to the realization that a number of other countries, including most of Latin America, were in similar circumstances. Thus began the Lost Decade.

Proximate Causes of the Debt Crisis

In Mexico's case, the collapse of oil prices in 1981 undermined its ability to earn the revenue it needed to service its debt. The problem was compounded by the fact that a significant portion of its debt was owed in dollars at variable interest rates and that efforts to combat inflation in the United States and elsewhere had resulted in a higher level of world interest rates. Consequently, interest payments on Mexico's debt rose at the same time that the nation's ability to earn dollars shrank.

The collapse of oil prices in 1981 and the rise in world interest rates were not the only external shocks to the economies of Latin America. In 1981–1982, the world's industrial economies entered a deep recession that reduced world demand and prices for many of the raw materials produced in Latin America and elsewhere. In Mexico's case, oil was the critical commodity, but a number of other primary commodity exports experienced a similar decline in their world price.

The price decline for Latin America's exports and the rise in interest rates were significant parts of the mix of events that led up to the debt crisis. These external economic shocks probably would not have caused a generalized debt crisis without some additional factors, however. Historically, debt crises require a set of external shocks to the indebted countries but also an acceleration of international lending which occurred between 1974 and 1982. Added to theses two factors was the complicating problem of mismanagement of national macroeconomic policies in the late 1970s and early 1980s.

During the 1970s, financial institutions throughout the developed world were awash in money that they were anxious to lend. The rise in oil prices in 1973 and 1974 (and again in 1979) led to an enormous expansion of bank deposits by the oil-rich nations of the world. Banks in New York, London, Paris, and Frankfurt were anxious to lend these deposits and aggressively sought out new borrowers beginning in 1974. For Latin America and the Caribbean, long-term, publicly guaranteed debt rose from slightly over $37 billion in 1973 to more than $261 billion in 1983. The sudden acceleration in commercial bank lending and the rise in the amount of debt made the economies vulnerable to a sudden and unforeseen economic shock.

Table 15.6 shows the size of the debt for some of the most heavily indebted countries after the first year of the crisis. The second column of numbers expresses the debt in net terms (gross debt minus debt owed by foreigners) as a percentage of GDP. The third column shows the net interest payments owed as a percentage of exports of goods and services. This is a useful indicator because nations ultimately have to pay the interest on their international debts out of the revenues they earn from their exports. What we see is that between 10 and 63 percent of the revenue earned by exports went to pay interest and, consequently, was unavailable for purchasing imports or for investing domestically.

Responses to the Debt Crisis

Initially, most analysts in the United States and in the international financial institutions such as the IMF perceived the debt crisis to be a temporary, short-run liquidity problem. Under this assumption, the reasonable response is to increase capital flows to Latin America and other indebted regions so that they would have the financial resources to service their debts. If additional capital flows can stimulate higher rates of economic growth, then it is a reasonable policy since an adequate growth rate would allow the countries to outgrow their debt.

From the standpoint of U.S. policy, the key to growth was viewed as increased investment, which was only possible if capital flows into the region were restored. The first policy proposal along these lines was that of U.S. Treasury secretary, James Baker, in 1985. The **Baker Plan** tried to organize a renewed lending program by commercial banks. The problem was that most banks that had Latin American loans in their portfolios were trying to reduce their exposure to the region, not increase it. Consequently, few resources were forthcoming under this plan.

Without capital flows from developed country banks, the choices were not attractive. Outright default and disavowal of the debt would cut off most of a nation's trade and investment linkages. The consequences for investment and growth would be risky and potentially disastrous, depending on the reaction of the United States and other governments. On the other hand, if they continued to make interest payments (and, potentially, principal repayment), it would require huge trade surpluses in order to earn the revenue they needed to pay for imports plus interest on the debt.

TABLE 15.6	Debt Indicators at the Onset of the Debt Crisis, 1983		
	Gross External Debt (millions of U.S. $)	*Net External Debt as a Percentage of GDP*	*Net Interest Payments as a Percentage of Exports*
Argentina	43,634	75.3	62.8
Bolivia	3,328	141.9	38.5
Brazil	92,961	48.3	38.7
Chile	17,315	87.6	32.9
Colombia	10,306	25.1	18.8
Costa Rica	3,646	137.8	45.4
Mexico	86,081	63.8	32.1
Peru	10,712	52.4	20.1
Venezuela	32,158	38.8	9.6

A large percentage of the exports of indebted countries went to pay interest on their debts.

Source: Cline, William, *International Debt Reexamined,* 1995; World Bank, *World Debt Tables,* 1987.

Interest payment on the debt owed to foreigners enters the current account as a debit in the category of income paid abroad (Chapter 9). Consequently, interest payments severely increased the current account deficits of many countries. Recall from Chapter 9 the fundamental accounting balance of an open economy:

$$S_p + T - G = I + CA,$$

where S_p is private savings, $T - G$ is government (public) savings, I is investment, and CA is the current account balance. Without financial capital inflows to finance their current account deficits, countries must eliminate the deficit through a combination of increased exports and reduced imports. The policies that accomplish this are expenditure-switching and expenditure-reducing policies. Recall from Chapter 11 that expenditure-switching policies such as devaluations of the currency turn the demand for foreign goods into a demand for domestic goods and raise CA directly. Expenditure-reducing policies, such as tax increases and cuts in government spending, raise $T - G$ and, indirectly, reduce consumption, investment, and imports. The net effect of expenditure-reducing policies is often a recession in which the demand for domestic and imported goods falls due to a fall in domestic income.

In other words, in order to accumulate the resources they needed for their interest payments, Latin governments were forced to follow contractionary policies that caused deep recessions throughout the region. Between 1982 and

1986, the average rate of growth of real per capita GDP was –1.8 percent per year in Latin America and the Caribbean.

By 1987, it was apparent to analysts throughout the world that restoring capital flows was not enough. There was a need for deep reform in the economies of Latin America. First, it was observed that the faulty macroeconomic policies of the region consistently left aggregate national expenditure above national income and that the likelihood of a return to growth was small as long as the gap between the two remained. Second, in their attempt to keep government expenditures higher than warranted, many countries had resorted to printing money, which resulted in high and increasing rates of inflation. Third, the burden of the debt itself was becoming apparent to everyone inside and outside Latin America. After the interest and principal payments were made, insufficient export earnings remained for domestic investment and consumption. Hence growth was stunted. By 1988–1989, both creditors and the multilateral lending agencies such as the IMF were in agreement that debt relief was in everyone's interest.

The growing consensus on the need for debt relief led to the **Brady Plan** (1989), named after the secretary of the treasury during the Bush Administration, Nicholas Brady. Essentially, the Brady Plan gave something to everyone. Creditors were expected to restructure some of the old debt into longer-term debt with a lower interest rate and to make some additional new loans. The multilateral lending agencies, such as the IMF, were expected to provide additional loans on concessional terms (i.e., below market interest rates), and borrowers were required to provide evidence of their willingness to begin serious economic reform before any new loans would be forthcoming. The Brady Plan did not end the debt crisis, but it was a significant step toward greater stability in the region. Countries that renegotiated their debt with the Brady Plan package were perceived to have greater credibility and sounder finances by the international financial community. Consequently, after 1989, capital flows began to return to Latin America but this time not in the form of bank loans. Rather, savers and investors in the United States, Europe, and Asia began to increase their direct investment in Latin America, as well as their holdings of various financial assets, such as stocks and bonds issued by private companies doing business there. While large inflows of capital can present problems (particularly if they reverse and flow out), they are the additional savings and investment that are needed if the region is to return to its historical levels of growth. To a large degree, the new capital that has been flowing into the region since 1989 is a vote of confidence by investors around the world.

From the vantage point of the first decade of the twenty-first century, the most lasting effects of the debt crisis (other than the forgone output due to the recessions of the 1980s) are the deep economic reforms that have taken place in country after country. These reforms are key to explaining the return of capital flows to Latin America. Reforms vary by country, both in kind and degree, but they mark a historical shift away from the protectionist and interventionist policies of ISI and economic populism and toward more open and market-oriented policies.

ECONOMIC POLICY REFORM AND THE "WASHINGTON CONSENSUS"

By the late 1980s, most countries in Latin America had started a series of economic policy reforms that began to alter the fundamental relationships between business and government and between their national economy and the world. After 1989, the reforms intensified and became more general. In most cases, the reforms consisted of three separate but interrelated features. First, and with varying degrees of success, governments implemented stabilization plans to stop inflation and to control their budget deficits. Second, most countries began privatizing the government-owned parts of their economies, such as manufacturing enterprises, financial and other services, mining operations, tourism, and utility companies. Third, trade policies became more open and less discriminatory against exports.

Throughout Latin America, this package of reforms has come to be known as the "**neoliberal model**" or **neoliberalism** because it represents a partial return to classic nineteenth-century European liberalism that favored free markets and minimal government intervention in the economy. By 1992, growth had returned to most countries.

In spite of the benefits of policy reform, however, many problems persist. Poverty and inequality continued to increase in many countries, since growth did not filter down into all the sectors. The problem of poverty was compounded by the lack of adequate infrastructure, which made it harder for all segments of society to benefit from economic growth. The absence of schools, health clinics, roads, clean water, and other infrastructure elements, particularly in rural areas where poverty is greatest, limits the reach of restored economic growth.

Stabilization Policies to Control Inflation

Many countries sought to avoid the recessionary consequences of the onset of the debt crisis by increasing government spending. The only way to finance government spending, however, was through the printing of more money, since tax systems were inadequate and government borrowing abilities were limited by the debt crisis. The reckless printing of money to finance government spending drove a number of nations into periods of hyperinflation, as detailed in Table 15.7.

The solution to the hyperinflation experienced by Argentina, Bolivia, Brazil, and Peru is simple to prescribe: cut government spending and stop printing money. The implementation of this prescription was difficult, however. In the short run, if price increases outstrip wage increases (as is often the case in a period of disinflation), then the burden of bringing down the rate of infla-

TABLE 15.7	Inflation Rates, 1982–1992

| | Inflation (in Percents) | | |
Country	Average 1982–1987	Average 1987–1992	Highest 1982–1992
Argentina	316	447	4924 (1989)
Bolivia	776	16	8170 (1985)
Brazil	158	851	1862 (1989)
Chile	21	19	27 (1990)
Colombia	21	27	32 (1990)
Mexico	73	48	159 (1987)
Peru	103	733	7650 (1990)
Venezuela	10	40	81 (1989)

High rates of inflation were a common problem of the 1980s.

Source: Edwards, Sebastian, *Crisis and Reform in Latin America*, 1995.

tion falls mainly on wage earners who experience a fall in their real wages. Consequently, anti-inflation policies create economic hardship and alienate the political support of many wage earners, making governments unpopular with a large share of the population.

A further complication was the lack of agreement over the causes of inflation. Some argued that it was caused by inertia since everyone expected future inflation to be high, and this caused producers to raise prices in anticipation of higher future input costs. The problem of inflation developing a momentum of its own and a lack of empirical information about the depth of this problem led to two different policy prescriptions for controlling inflation: the orthodox model and the heterodox model.

The **orthodox** model minimizes government involvement in the economy. Consequently, its anti-inflation prescription is straightforward: cut government spending, reform the tax system to increase compliance and revenues, and limit the creation of new money. The **heterodox** model calls for the same actions plus the freezing of wages and prices. In the heterodox view, inflationary expectations are so embedded in economic decision making that price increases will continue even if government spending and new money creation cease. In practice, heterodox plans often ignored the budget deficits that were part of the problem.

Between 1986 and 1992, Brazil implemented five separate heterodox stabilization plans to end inflation, and not one of them worked. Similarly, heterodox plans in Argentina (1985) and Peru (1985) succeeded for approximately a year but then failed, as inflation returned with a vengeance. Nevertheless, Brazil and Mexico each ultimately controlled inflation using heterodox methods.

One issue that neither the heterodox nor orthodox models address directly is institutional reform. In Mexico's case, the freezing of wages and prices was an outcome of a formal agreement between labor interests, business interests, and the government, known as the *Social Solidarity Pact* (Pacto de Solidaridad Social, or "El Pacto"), which was passed in 1987. Brazil's successful plan under President Cardoso (the Real Plan, 1994) was widely discussed in Congress before it was implemented, and Argentina's plan (The Convertibility Plan, 1991) was part of a set of institutional reforms that limited the ability of the central bank to print new money. Bolivia was able to control its hyperinflation without the extensive use of price and wage freezes, but it depended on a series of financial reforms that significantly lessened direct government control over the financial services sector and reformed the tax system to make revenue collection more reliable.

One last issue still confronting many nations is the problem of inconsistency between inflation stabilization and exchange rate policy. Mexico's experience is a good example of the problem and stems from the fact that the exchange rate is a powerful weapon in the fight against inflation. Mexico fixed its peso to the dollar in the mid-1980s as part of its anti-inflation strategy. (Argentina and Brazil did the same under their stabilization plans of 1991 and 1994, respectively.) Domestic producers that compete with U.S. goods were forced to avoid price increases so they would remain competitive. Furthermore, prices did not increase on imports of U.S.-made capital goods, which were essential to Mexican industry, thereby helping to hold down Mexican prices for finished manufactured goods. Since Mexican inflation was still slightly higher than U.S. inflation, the peso became overvalued over a period of time. Ultimately, this contributed to a serious trade imbalance and the collapse of the peso in December 1994, followed by a deep recession in 1995. Since 1994, Mexico has let the peso float against the dollar and has stopped trying to use the exchange rate as an anchor against the current of inflation.

In Argentina's case, the peso remained fixed against the dollar, but when turmoil in international financial markets spread to Latin America in the fall of 1998, Brazil devalued. In effect, this made Brazil's currency cheaper and its industries more competitive against Argentine industries. As a result, Argentina faced an economic slowdown and the regional trade agreement that includes both countries (MERCOSÚR) came under pressure.

Structural Reform and Open Trade

Stabilization policies to control inflation and curtail large budget deficits are usually one part of a package that also includes **structural reform policies**. One way to keep the two types of policies separate is to recognize that stabilization generally focuses on macroeconomic policies (e.g., inflation and government budgets), while structural reform tends to be more microeconomic, dealing with issues of resource allocation. For example, structural reform policies include the privatization of government-owned enterprises, deregulation and redesign of the regulatory environment of overregulated industries such as financial services, and the reform of trade policy.

The many initiatives to privatize and reform the regulatory environments of the economies of Latin America are quite remarkable, but this section will focus on the most impressive area of structural reform to date: the economic integration of the region with the world economy. Prior to the onset of the debt crisis, the economies of Latin America had the most restricted trade systems of all the nations in the noncommunist world. In many countries, the debt crisis reinforced the belief that isolation from the world economy was the only way to protect a nation from shocks that originated in the external environment.

In the 1970s, Chile broke with this tradition and began to reform its trade policies. Mexico and Bolivia followed in 1985 and 1986, and by 1987–1988, it was apparent throughout Latin America that trade had to be more open if economic growth were to be restored. In the late 1980s and early 1990s, nearly all the countries of Latin America began reducing both the level of tariffs and nontariff barriers (NTBs) and the variability of tariff rates across industries and goods. Table 15.8 shows the changes in tariffs that occurred between the mid-1980s, when the reforms began, and the early 1990s. As large as the tariff reductions were, the effect of the elimination of nontariff barriers such as quotas and import licensing requirements was even more dramatic, as many countries eliminated all or nearly all these barriers. By the early 1990s, most of the

TABLE 15.8	Average Tariff Rates in Latin America		
	Average Tariff Rate		
	1985	1992	2000
Argentina	28.0	14.8	13.5
Bolivia	20.0	9.8	9.7
Brazil	80.0	17.6	14.3
Chile	36.0	11.0	9.8
Colombia	83.0	11.6	11.6
Costa Rica	92.0	16.0	7.2
Mexico	34.0	13.1	16.2
Peru	64.0	17.6	13.7
Uruguay	32.0	18.3	12.3
Venezuela	30.0	11.8	12.0

Latin America dramatically reduced trade barriers in the latter part of the 1980s.

Source: Inter-American Development Bank.

tariff and nontariff changes had been implemented, and countries began to turn to alternative forms of market opening.

New regional integration efforts were begun, along with a number of initiatives to revitalize older trade agreements that had ceased to function by the early 1980s (see Table 15.9). In 1991, four nations signed an agreement (implemented in 1994) creating the Common Market of the South (Mercado Común del Sur, or MERCOSÚR), which combines two of the largest economies in Latin America (Argentina and Brazil) with two small economies (Paraguay and Uruguay). In 1993, Mexico, the United States, and Canada signed NAFTA (implemented in 1994), largely at the instigation of Mexico, which sought broader access to the U.S. and Canadian markets. In addition to new agreements, previously existing regional agreements such as the Andean Pact, the Caribbean Community (CARICOM), and the Central American Common Market (CACM) became the basis for new efforts toward regional integration and export promotion.

A third set of regional integration initiatives developed out of the trade policies of a number of individual countries, most notably Chile and Mexico. These two countries began negotiating and signing a number of bilateral free-trade agreements with other countries, as well as agreements with other trade blocs. For example, Mexico signed free-trade agreements with 28 countries, including each of the Andean Pact nations, Chile, CARICOM, and the European Union. Chile has signed agreements with the Andean Pact nations, and with MERCOSÚR, and is negotiating with the EU. Perhaps the most dramatic example of regional integration is the Free Trade Area of the Americas, currently being negotiated by 34 countries in the Western Hemisphere (see the case study in Chapter 13).

The three main goals of trade reform were to reduce the anti-export bias of trade policies that favored production for domestic markets over production for foreign markets, to raise the growth rate of productivity, and to make consumers better off by lowering the real cost of traded goods. In response to the changes in trade policy, the growth rate of exports picked up in most countries, while nontraditional exports increased dramatically. Furthermore, productivity rose in a majority of countries for which there are data. The productivity increase is at least partly the result of trade opening due to the impact of technology transfers, the improved investment climate, and the pressures on local firms to remain competitive.

It is difficult to judge whether more open trade has, as yet, contributed to an increase in the standard of living of consumers throughout Latin America. As long as productivity is rising, living standards will follow, although often with a lag. It may also be the case that the benefits of rising productivity are limited to specific sectors, however, where productivity growth occurs or where unions have more bargaining power over wages. Overall, economic growth in the 1990s surpassed the experience of the 1980s, but in many countries, growth has not reached into all sectors of society.

TABLE 15.9	Regional Trade Blocs		
	Year	*Members*	*Goals*
Andean Community	1969	Bolivia, Colombia, Ecuador, Peru, Venezuela	Common market
Caribbean Community	1973	Antigua and Barbuda, Bahamas, Barbados, Belize, Dominica, Guyana, Grenada, Jamaica, Montserrat, St. Kitts and Nevis, St. Lucia, St. Vincent and the Grenadines, Suriname, Trinidad and Tobago	Common market
Central American Common Market	1961	Costa Rica, El Salvador, Guatemala, Honduras, Nicaragua	Customs union
MERCOSÚR	1994	Argentina, Brazil, Paraguay, Uruguay	Common market
NAFTA	1994	Canada, Mexico, United States	Free-trade area

CASE STUDY

The Washington Consensus on Economic Policy Reform

The **Washington Consensus** is the term coined by the economist John Williamson for a set of economic policies that constitute a broad consensus among conservative and liberal economists. Williamson developed the list while thinking about Latin America in particular, but the elements are applicable to other parts of the world as well. The "Washington" part of the name refers not only to the site of the U.S. government but also the site of the leading institutions in the international financial community (IMF and World Bank) and the unofficial community of think-tanks that is centered there. The "Consensus" part of the name refers to the fact that these are elements that a majority of economists in those institutions (U.S. government, IMF, World Bank, and Washington, DC think tanks) believe to be good economic policy.

The consensus has ten elements:

1. Fiscal discipline: Central government surplus of several percent of GDP (not including interest on the debt) and an operational deficit (including interest) of no more than approximately 2 percent of GDP.

2. Public expenditure priorities: Favor

(continues)

efforts to improve income distribution via health, education, and infrastructure expenditures over administration, defense, indiscriminate subsidies, white elephants.

3. Tax reform: Lower marginal rates, increase effectiveness of overall system, broaden the base.
4. Financial liberalization: Ensure positive real rates; abolish preferential interest rates for favored borrowers.
5. Exchange rates: Set at a level to ensure competitiveness; make it credible.
6. Trade liberalization: Replace quantitative restrictions with tariffs, and progressively reduce them.
7. Foreign direct investment: Encourage it; allow foreign and domestic firms to compete on equal footing.
8. Privatization: State enterprises should be privatized.
9. Deregulation: Abolish barriers to entry or restrictions on competition; ensure an environmental, safety, or prudential rationale for remaining regulations.
10. Property rights: Make them secure for both the formal and informal sector.

Not surprisingly, some economists outside of Washington question the need for some of these policies—particularly those relating to numbers 6 through 10, which might be considered more micro and less macro in scope. We will take up this issue in the next chapter when we look at the success stories of East Asia. It should also be noted that even within the Washington Consensus there is ample room for disagreement.

Disagreements include the following:

1. The use of capital controls
2. The need to target the current account
3. How fast, how far to reduce inflation
4. Whether to try to stabilize the business cycle
5. The use of incomes policies
6. The need to eliminate indexation
7. The best technique to try to correct market failures
8. The size of the tax burden and the size of government (as measured by GDP)
9. Whether to engage in deliberate income redistribution policies
10. Whether to use industrial policies
11. The correct model of the market economy (Anglo-Saxon versus social market economy or "Japanese style")
12. Priority of population control
13. Priority of environmental preservation

Source: John Williamson, "In Search of a Manual for Technopols," in *The Political Economy of Policy Reform.* Washington D.C.: Institute for International Economics. 1994.

The effects of both stabilization and structural reform policies on the welfare of Latin Americans is crucial to the long-run sustainability of the reform programs. Ultimately, if economic policy reforms do not make a majority of the people better off, then there is no point in keeping to the reforms. Economic theory predicts that the reforms that have been set in place will eventually lead to more efficient allocations of resources, higher productivity, and higher living standards. Yet, many factors may stand in the way, not the least of which is the need for deep reform in the political systems of many nations.

Summary

- Latin America has been one of the fastest-growing regions of the world throughout most of the twentieth century. Growth came crashing to a halt in the 1980s, however, and only began to return in the late 1980s and early 1990s.

- Until the recent reforms, Latin American economic growth has tended to focus on inward development rather than outward orientation. Productivity in subsistence agriculture has lagged behind overall growth, leading to much higher rates of poverty in rural areas than in urban ones.

- The primary development strategy of Latin America was adopted in the 1930s, 1940s, and 1950s. It came to be called import substitution industrialization and focused on the inward-oriented development of industries that could produce goods that would substitute for imports. This model of development was favored because it was thought that Latin America would suffer ever-declining terms of trade for its primary commodity exports, and that ISI would reduce the need for foreign exchange and imports, thereby making the region less vulnerable to economic shocks from outside.

- Economic growth under ISI was adequate, but ultimately it led to an inefficient manufacturing sector, excessive rent seeking, a persistent tendency toward overvalued exchange rates, and too great a concentration of resources on the urban sector.

- ISI policies were often made worse by the tendencies of many countries to elect or support economic populists. Populists favored economic growth and redistribution while, in the extreme, they ignored economic constraints such as government budgets and foreign exchange shortages.

- Populist policies generated macroeconomic instability, which often led to hyperinflation and falling real wages.

- The debt crisis that began in 1982 affected every country of the region, even those without high levels of debt or debt problems. As a result of the crisis, it became extremely difficult to borrow internationally.

- The main causes of the debt crisis were the increases in lending during the 1970s and the external shocks of interest rate hikes and primary commodity price decreases, especially oil. The faulty macroeconomic policies of many Latin American governments during the late 1970s and early 1980s made them more vulnerable to the shocks.

- The debt crisis resulted in negative growth throughout the region for most of the period from 1982 through 1987. By 1987–1988, the need for significant reforms in economic policy was apparent to almost all governments.

- From the mid-1980s up to the present, the governments of Latin America have engaged in serious reforms of economic policy. The reforms have first tried to create macroeconomic stability through controlling inflation and reducing budget deficits. Stabilization policies have been followed by structural reforms that have opened trade, privatized, and reduced and redesigned the regulatory environment.

■ Growth has returned to most of Latin America, but dissatisfaction with the economic reforms is widespread. Job creation is less than desired, inequality persists, and economic growth is below the rate necessary to significantly reduce poverty.

Vocabulary

Baker and Brady Plans	market failure
debt crisis of the 1980s	neoliberalism
Economic Commission on Latin America (ECLA, or CEPAL in Spanish)	orthodox and heterodox stabilization policies
economic populism	structural reform
export pessimism	terms of trade (TOT)
import substitution industrialization (ISI)	Washington Consensus
Lost Decade	

Study Questions

1. What were the main characteristics of economic growth in Latin America from the end of World War II until the debt crisis of the 1980s?

2. What is import substitution industrialization? Explain its goals and methods.

3. What are the main criticisms of import substitution industrialization? Did ISI fail?

4. Describe a typical cycle of economic populism. Why does it often leave its supporters worse off than before the cycle begins?

5. Explain how economic populist policies usually lead to overvalued exchange rates and large trade deficits.

6. What were the proximate causes of the debt crisis? How did the United States and other industrial countries respond?

7. Why did the Latin American debt crisis of the 1980s cause recessions in each country?

8. What is the difference between stabilization policies and structural adjustment policies? Give examples of each.

9. What is neoliberalism? Why do some people consider it a negative term?

10. What was the content of Latin American trade reforms of the late 1980s and 1990s? How do the actions taken relate to the desired goals?

Chapter 16

EXPORT-ORIENTED GROWTH IN EAST ASIA

THE HIGH-PERFORMANCE ASIAN ECONOMIES

One of the most interesting stories of the last 50 years is the take-off of the high-growth economies of East Asia. The World Bank coined the term **High Performance Asian Economies**, or **HPAE**, to refer to the eight countries of Hong Kong, Indonesia, Japan, Malaysia, Singapore, South Korea, Taiwan, and Thailand. They vary in their income levels and living standards, but they share a number economic policies, including an outward orientation and extremely rapid growth by world standards. These eight countries form the core of what has also been called the *East Asian Miracle*, and their success continues to have a profound impact on the formation of economic policy around the world, particularly in Latin America and other developing regions.

After the severe economic and financial crisis that hit the HPAE region in the summer of 1997, it is reasonable to ask whether their success is a long-run trend, or a temporary economic bubble. The worst hit countries were Indonesia, Malaysia, South Korea, and Thailand. While problems continue to linger several years later, in many respects the crisis highlights the robust strength of these economies. By 2000, they were all on positive growth paths in the range of 5 to 10 percent per year in real terms. The crisis of 1997–1998 was severe and exposed the need for change, but it did not put an end to the story of their remarkable economic growth and development. Understanding their experiences continues to be well worth the effort, particularly because they illustrate a case where developing countries use international trade and the international economy to achieve high rates of economic growth.

Before proceeding, it is useful to explain some of the terms used to describe this part of the world. A common name for one group of countries that began its rapid economic growth period shortly after Japan took off in the 1950s is the **Four Tigers**. This group includes the two city-states of Hong Kong and Singapore, plus Korea and Taiwan. They are also sometimes referred to as the *Four Dragons*, or the *Little Dragons*, and all four are classified by the World Bank as either high income or upper middle income. Another group, which is broader and not confined to East Asia, is the **Newly Industrializing Economies**, or **NIEs**. There are a number of these economies in Latin America as well as East Asia (e.g., Argentina, Brazil, Chile, and Mexico). NIEs among the HPAEs are Indonesia, Malaysia, and Thailand. China may also be considered an NIE, but

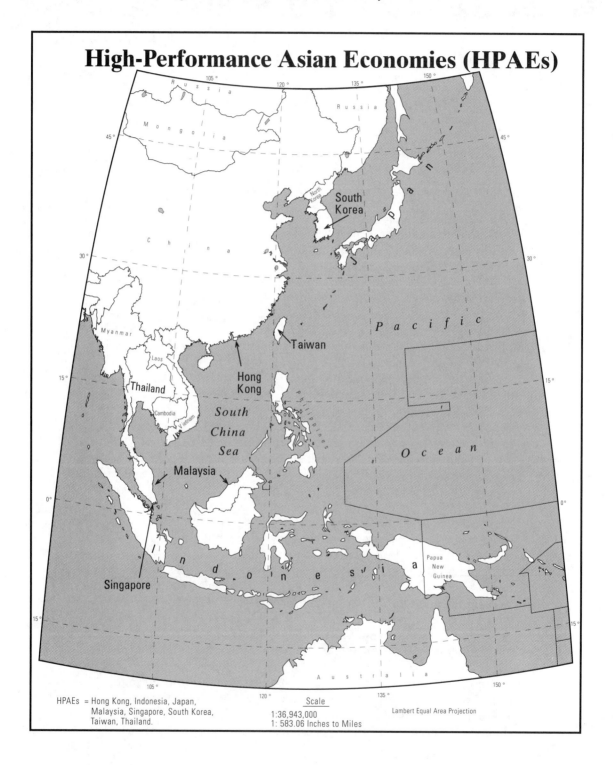

High-Performance Asian Economies (HPAEs)

HPAEs = Hong Kong, Indonesia, Japan, Malaysia, Singapore, South Korea, Taiwan, Thailand.

Scale

1:36,943,000
1: 583.06 Inches to Miles

Lambert Equal Area Projection

it is generally not included among the HPAE because its economic system is radically different from a market-based system. All of the NIEs began their high rates of economic growth after the take-off of the Four Tigers.

Economists agree on several of the keys to the growth of the HPAE. For example, unlike the experience of Latin America, and in spite of their own recent financial chaos, macroeconomic stability has been a high priority of their economic policies. A second fact that stands in contrast to other regions is that there is a strong and credible commitment to sharing economic growth with all layers of society, in part through access to education, health care, and land reform. This proved to have numerous benefits, including the rapid creation of a skilled workforce. A third difference is that the HPAE nations promoted their export sectors while at the same time they were more open to imports than most developing countries. This, too, had numerous advantages, including access to technology, high export earnings, and an implicit incentive to foreign investment.

Several questions about the HPAE experience remain unanswered. For example, the importance of industrial policies (industrial targeting) is unclear. Were these policies incidental, or were they instrumental in creating growth? Another series of questions revolves around the use of interventionist government policies and the avoidance of rent seeking. Specifically, in the various government interventions in economic activity, how did HPAE nations avoid the problem of rent seeking that has been so costly to Latin America? On the other hand, some have argued that they did not avoid it, and that is one of the reasons for the collapse of the financial sector in several countries during the summer and fall of 1997. This is a big unknown, particularly in light of the crisis. Finally, does the "East Asian Miracle" represent a new model for economic growth or are the HPAEs doing fundamentally the same thing that the United States and other industrialized nations did to achieve high incomes?

This chapter examines these and several other questions as it explains the issues surrounding the successes of the East Asian high-growth economies. In particular, the contrast with Latin America is emphasized, along with East Asian trade and international economic relations.

POPULATION, INCOME, AND ECONOMIC GROWTH

Table 16.1 illustrates the size and income levels of the HPAEs along with several other large Asian economies. In contrast to Latin America, income levels are high in the HPAEs. Measured in either market exchange rates or purchasing power parity terms, GNP per person is high in Singapore, Japan, Hong Kong, Taiwan, and South Korea, while the three remaining countries, Thailand, Malaysia, and Singapore, began their period of rapid growth later and are considerably behind the other five.

A Note on Hong Kong

On July 1, 1997, Great Britain officially returned the colony of Hong Kong to China after more than 150 years of British rule. China has pledged itself to follow the policy of "one country, two systems" in its relations with Hong Kong. In practical terms, this means that China will allow Hong Kong to keep its own currency, will limit migration between Hong Kong and the mainland, and will generally try to preserve Hong Kong's current system. No one can say whether they will adhere to this policy or not. Insofar as this book is concerned, Hong Kong will be treated as a separate nation, as it was under British colonial rule.

Table 16.2 is arranged so that it is directly comparable to Table 15.3 in Chapter 15. Note that there is no growth slowdown in the 1980s and that, in fact, several of the HPAEs (as well as several other Asian economies) experienced accelerated growth. This is one of the biggest contrasts between the recent experiences of East Asia and Latin America, and it is one of the primary reasons why East Asia has attracted attention in Latin America. China's growth record might also qualify it as a member of the "high-performance" club, but the differences in its policies and institutions make it unlike any other Asian economy in Tables 16.1 and 16.2, so it is treated separately in Chapter 17.

According to the "Rule of 72," if a variable (income, for example) grows at the rate X, then it doubles in approximately $72/X$ years. In other words, Singapore's 7.5 percent growth rate for real GDP per capita between 1960 and 1980 implies that per capita income doubled every $72 / 7.5 = 9.6$ years. Over the span of twenty years, income doubled and then doubled again, so that average income per person rose more than four times. While Singapore, 1960–1980, is one of the most outstanding examples of rapid growth, each of the other HPAEs saw its income at least double between 1960 and 1980. Since 1980, growth has slowed somewhat, yet with the exception of Japan, which was mired in a slow growth period during the 1990s, each of the HPAEs continues to enjoy rates of growth that are envied elsewhere in world.

GENERAL CHARACTERISTICS
OF GROWTH IN THE HPAES

Recall from Chapter 15 that from the end of World War II until the mid- to late 1980s, economic growth in Latin America was characterized by high levels of inequality, periods of macroeconomic instability, and an inward orientation. The contrast with the HPAEs could not be more striking, since their growth was built around falling inequality, generally sound macroeconomic funda-

		GNP per Capita	GNP per
	Population	*($U.S., market*	*Capita*
Country	*(millions)*	*exchange rates)*	*($U.S. PPP*)*
High-Performance Asian Economies			
Hong Kong	7.0	23,520	20,939
Indonesia	221.1	580	2,439
Japan	126.3	32,230	24,041
Malaysia	21.3	3,400	7,963
Singapore	4.0	29,610	27,024
South Korea	47.0	8,490	14,637
Taiwan	22.0	13,235	
Thailand	60.7	1,960	5,599
Other Asian Economies			
Bangladesh	127.1	370	1,475
China	1,250.5	780	3,291
India	997.9	450	2,149
Pakistan	138.5	470	1,757
Philippines	79.5	1,020	3,815

TABLE 16.1 Population and GNP for the HPAEs and Selected Asian Economies, 1999

Asia contains the most populous countries in the world and a wide variation in income levels.

Sources: United States Census Bureau, *International Data Base*; World Bank, *World Development Report, 2000/2001*; Republic of China (Taiwan), Director General of Budget, Accounting, and Statistics.
*Purchasing power parity.

mentals, and the promotion of exports. It is worth looking at each of the elements in more detail.

Shared Growth

One of the most remarkable features of growth in the HPAEs is that it was accompanied by rising economic equality. This feature is even more remarkable when it is realized that inequality in income and wealth was already relatively low at the start of the period of high growth. Since the 1950s pioneering work of the economist Simon Kuznets, it was thought that growth in developing countries would first result in falling economic equality, followed later by rising equality. While Kuznets's work was based on measurements from a large

TABLE 16.2	Average Annual Growth in Real GDP per Person, 1960-1999		
	Annual Growth in Real GDP per Capita		
Country	1960–1980	1980–1990	1990–1999
High-Performance Asian Economies			
Hong Kong	7.0	5.7	1.8
Indonesia	3.5	4.3	3.0
Japan	6.3	3.4	1.1
Korea	6.3	8.2	4.7
Malaysia	5.0	2.5	3.8
Singapore	7.5	5.0	6.1
Taiwan	6.5	6.7	5.3
Thailand	4.3	5.9	3.5
Other Asian Economies			
Bangladesh	0.7	1.9	3.2
China	2.7	8.5	9.6
India	0.7	3.7	4.3
Pakistan	2.8	3.6	1.5
Philippines	2.6	–1.6	0.9

Growth in many Asian countries accelerated during the 1980s when growth in the rest of the world was slowing.

Source: Penn World Tables (Mark 5.6); World Bank, *World Development Report, 2000/2001*; Republic of China (Taiwan), Director General of Budget, Accounting, and Statistics; author's calculations.

number of countries, the East Asian experience has called into question the idea that economic growth in developing countries follows a "Kuznets's curve," in which equality first declines and then rises.

Table 16.3 compares income distribution in the HPAEs with Latin America. The last three columns show the percent of the nation's income received by the poorest 20 percent of households, the percent received by the richest 20 percent, and the ratio of the two. The poorest households in the five Latin American nations receive an average of 3.4 percent of society's income, while in the HPAEs, the poorest receive 6.8 percent, or twice as large a share of national income. The richest 20 percent receive 57.4 percent in the Latin American sample and 44.6 percent of total income in the HPAEs. In other words, by comparison to Latin America, the rich receive a smaller share in the HPAEs, and the poor receive a larger share.

The conditions that led to greater income equality were rooted in the

TABLE 16.3		Measures of Income Distribution, East Asia and Latin America		
	Year*	*Income Share of Bottom 20 Percent*	*Income Share of Top 20 Percent*	*Ratio of Top 20 Percent to Bottom 20 Percent*
HPAEs				
Hong Kong	1980	5.4	47.0	8.7
Indonesia	1996	8.0	44.9	5.6
Japan	1993	10.6	35.7	3.4
Malaysia	1995	4.5	53.8	12.0
Singapore	1983	5.1	48.9	9.6
South Korea	1993	7.5	39.3	5.2
Taiwan	1999	7.1	39.2	5.5
Thailand	1998	6.4	48.4	7.6
Average		6.8	44.6	6.6
Latin America				
Brazil	1996	2.5	63.8	25.5
Colombia	1996	3.0	60.9	20.3
Mexico	1995	3.6	58.2	16.2
Peru	1996	4.4	51.2	11.6
Venezuela	1996	3.7	53.1	14.4
Average		3.4	57.4	16.9

Income is distributed much more equally among the HPAEs than in Latin America.

*Comparisons of income distribution must rely on country studies that are done in different years.

Source: World Bank, *World Development Report, 2000/2001*; Republic of China (Taiwan), Director General of Budget, Accounting, and Statistics; Campos and Root, *The Key to the East Asian Miracle*, p. 11.

unique historical experiences of each country. Nevertheless, each nation had a similar set of highly visible wealth-sharing mechanisms. Specifically, these included land reform, free public education, free basic health care, and significant investments in rural infrastructure, such as clean water systems and transportation and communication systems. These policies did not equalize incomes, but they provided people with the tools they needed to raise their individual incomes and gave hope for the future. This had several positive effects. For example, when purchasing power is spread more widely through a society, it increases the opportunities for small- and medium-scale entrepreneurs that produce for the local market. The experiences gained in meeting local demand may help them develop their firms into larger enterprises and may carry over into numerous other activities. In addition, rising incomes across a broad spectrum of socioeconomic groups raise everyone's hopes for future improvements and encourage cooperation among the different classes of society while conferring legitimacy on the ruling governments. Both factors contribute to political stability as well as the willingness by the business elites to commit to long-term investments.

Rapid Accumulation of Physical and Human Capital

Rising levels of equality were closely tied to very rapid rates of accumulation of physical and human capital. Rapid accumulation of physical capital is synonymous with high levels of investment. Investment, in turn, depended on high savings rates. The level of savings in the HPAEs is considerably higher than in many other parts of the world. The explanations for high savings are varied. In part, it is a result of the rapid **demographic transition** experienced by those nations after World War II. The demographic transition is the shift from high birth rates and high death rates to low birth and death rates that accompanies modernization. Countries that have completed a demographic transition have fewer children below working age and a larger percentage of the population engaged in economically productive work. Hence, they tend to have higher savings rates.

Another factor that increased both the level of savings and the level of investment was the absence of high inflation and the presence of stable financial institutions. The crisis of 1997 calls into question whether people will continue to have confidence in their financial institutions and whether this will affect savings rates, but until the crisis, most investors acted as if they believed that their financial savings were protected both against loss of value through high inflation and against a collapse in the banking system.

While the rapid demographic transition, low inflation rates, and stable financial institutions appear to have caused savings rates to be high, probably the most important factor was simply the rapid rate of income growth. That is, savings and income growth are interdependent, and the HPAEs seemed to have created a "virtuous cycle" in which rapid income growth caused high savings. Savings led to high rates of investment, which fed back into a second round of income growth and high savings.

Investment in people was as important as the accumulation of physical capital. One of the key features of the HPAEs' educational policy is that public investment in education was focused on the primary and secondary levels. Educational dollars go farther at this level, and the social impact is much greater per dollar spent than at the university level. These investments raised literacy rates dramatically and laid the foundation for a highly skilled workforce that was capable of tackling increasingly sophisticated forms of production. In effect, the continuous rise in human capital endowments of the HPAEs constituted an ongoing shift in the comparative advantages of those nations, so that new investments could continually push into new product lines.

Rapid Growth of Manufactured Exports

Each of the eight HPAEs actively and successfully promoted exports, although each began its development pushes with import substitution policies. ISI policies, however, were quickly replaced with an emphasis on export promotion. The timing of the switch from ISI to export promotion varied by country. Japan began promoting exports in the late 1950s and early 1960s, the 4 Tigers (Hong Kong, Korea, Singapore, Taiwan) started in the late 1960s, and the newly industrializing economies (NIEs—Indonesia, Malaysia, and Thailand) began in the early 1980s.

Table 16.4 shows the results of the export push. Between 1965 and 1998, the HPAEs more than doubled their share of total world exports and total world manufactured exports. If we leave out the two richest HPAEs, Japan and Singapore, and consider the six others, in 1998, they were responsible for 56 percent of the manufactured goods exports from developing countries.

In part, the success of the export promotion drives was the result of education policies that favored primary and secondary schooling. These policies created widespread literacy and an adaptable and easily trained labor force. In addition, each of the HPAEs pursued various export promotion policies. For example, Japan and the 4 Tigers made export financing credit readily available; they required export targets for firms that wished to receive favorable credit terms or tax benefits; and they provided tariff-free access to imports of capital equipment used to manufacture exports. Policies in the NIEs were somewhat less interventionist and relied to a greater extent on attracting foreign direct investment in export activities.

The connection between export promotion and high rates of growth is an area of some controversy in economics. There are several possible connections

TABLE 16.4   The Share of HPAEs in World Exports, 1965–1998

	HPAE Share of World Exports		
	1965	1980	1998
Total Exports	7.9	13.1	18.5
Exports of Manufactures	9.4	17.3	23.3

HPAE exports have significantly increased their share of world exports.

Source: World Bank, *The East Asian Miracle*; and World Bank, *World Development Report, 2000/2001.*

that are explored in greater detail later in the chapter. A second controversy is the possibility of other nations using similar export promotion strategies. In many cases, these policies generate trade conflicts and may be at odds with the rules for fair trade agreed to by the members of the WTO.

Stable Macroeconomic Environments

A fourth and final characteristic of the HPAE economies is the maintenance of stable macroeconomic environments. Chapter 15 argued that one of the persistent problems of Latin America has been the frequent reoccurrence of macroeconomic crises. Even before the crisis of 1997, the high-performance economies of East Asia were not completely free of macroeconomic crises, but when they occurred, policy responses were usually quick and appropriate. Responses to the 1997 crisis were no different in this regard. Macroeconomic stability can have several components, and the factors that are usually emphasized in this context are a commitment to keeping inflation under control, good management of both internal government debt and externally owed foreign debt, and the quick resolution of crises when they occurred. In general, macroeconomic policy has been characterized as "pragmatic and flexible."

On average, budget deficits and foreign debt were not dramatically smaller than in other regions of the world although there was a significant amount of variation across countries. The difference in the HPAEs, however, is that with the exception of the recent crisis, they were kept within the limits of the ability of the government to finance without having to print money or to borrow excessively. High growth rates helped ease the constraints imposed by a given level of debt, while foreign debts remained within acceptable limits, partly because of the high levels of exports that earned the foreign assets necessary for debt servicing. The crisis of 1997 is the exception that proves this rule, since one of the key triggers of the crisis was a significant reduction of export earnings in a couple of countries and the growth of large current account deficits. To many foreign investors, these deficits began to seem larger than was warranted, and this triggered significant capital flight.

The commitment to low inflation helped keep real interest rates stable and enabled firms to take a longer-run view of their investments. In addition, low inflation helped to avoid severe real appreciations in the exchange rate. Low inflation also meant that variations in the real exchange rate, the real interest rate, and the inflation rate were relatively low. In turn, this helped to foster a greater security in the minds of investors and probably encouraged them to take a long-run view of their activities.

THE INSTITUTIONAL ENVIRONMENT

Economic success stems from an ability to mobilize and allocate resources. In the HPAEs, large flows of savings were generated, they were channeled into the financial system, and they were lent to business enterprises that used them productively. Simultaneously, governments emphasized education and universal literacy. Ultimately, an efficient mobilization and allocation of resources is based on the decisions of individuals and businesses that own resources. In order to ensure that individuals and businesses use their resources in the most productive manner, governments must create rules that foster efficient outcomes. In this regard, the institutional environments of the HPAEs are essential to their success.

Several components of the institutional environment are critical insofar as they help to make government policy credible. In particular, property rights are relatively secure and free from the threat of nationalization. Bureaucracies are generally competent; individuals and businesses are free to make contracts that will be enforced; access to information is widespread; and regulations tend to be clear and well publicized. Of course, there are exceptions to each of the above, depending on the time and place, but, in general, these features characterize the institutional environments of the HPAEs.

These characteristics should not be confused with the characteristics of open, democratic societies. Measures of political rights and civil liberties (e.g., those of the Freedom House) place the HPAEs, other than Japan, in the middle of their rankings along with many African dictatorships. The general lack of political and civil liberties raises a question about the relationship between authoritarian rule and economic growth. Specifically, do the lack of political and civil liberties and the concentration of power in the executive branch of government confer advantages for economic development?

The answer to this question is complex and beyond the scope of this book. Nevertheless, it should be noted that many dictatorships have failed in their bid to mobilize and allocate resources. Dictatorships or authoritarian regimes may be as likely to prey upon society as they are to foster its economic development. However authoritarian they are, the HPAEs fostered growth rather than the enrichment of a small elite at the expense of the majority.

A second issue that arises from the general lack of traditionally defined democratic rights is the relevancy of the HPAE experience to other regions of the world, such as Latin America. Some social scientists argue that the context of authoritarian rule makes the HPAE experience irrelevant to nations such as Bolivia and Argentina, where policy reform is taking place within an institutional setting that allows far more dissent.

Both issues, the relationship between authoritarian rule and economic growth and the applicability of the HPAE experience to the rest of the developing world, are contentious and lack consensus. Generally speaking, there does not seem to be a correlation between the type of government (democratic or authoritarian) and the ability to put good policies into place.

Fiscal Discipline

Whether democratic or not, governments must create a stable macroeconomic environment in order for economic growth to succeed. The characteristic of macroeconomic stability has already been discussed, but it is worth revisiting because of its central importance and because of its contrast with the experiences of other regions such as Latin America.

The maintenance of a stable macroeconomic environment requires fiscal discipline and an acceptance of the resource constraints that limit government actions. Budget deficits and foreign debt must be kept manageable, and the real exchange rate must be relatively stable. The benefits of accepting these limitations are that it increases the credibility of government policy and builds the private sector's confidence. The result is more investment and less capital flight.

Business-Government Relations

Stable macroeconomic policies are necessary for growth, but they are no guarantee. For example, macroeconomic stability does not address the very significant problem in all developing countries of the coordination of interdependent investment projects. The coordination problem results from the fact that many private sector investments are interdependent. That is, their profitability depends on the simultaneous or prior creation of a complementary investment. The same often holds true for private sector/public sector investments. For example, profitable investment in warehousing facilities at a seaport depends on the prior investment in sufficient port infrastructure to provide an adequate flow of goods through the warehouses. Yet, the port and related transportation linkages may not be worthwhile unless there is a simultaneous investment or a guarantee of future investment in the warehouses.

CASE STUDY

Deliberation Councils in the Ministry of International Trade and Industry (MITI)

Japan's use of deliberation councils has been more extensive than any other country's. In Japan, the councils are attached to a particular ministry, or bureaucracy, such as the Ministry of International Trade and Industry (MITI). Since MITI is one of the largest bureaucracies in Japan, and because it has more control over Japanese economic policy than any other bureaucracy (with the exception of the Ministry of Finance), it has numerous deliberation councils. According to one account, in 1990, there were seventeen major regular deliberative councils attached to MITI.

Councils in MITI are of two basic types: they are either industry specific, such as the Textile Industry Council, or they are thematic, such as the Industrial Structure Council. Thematic councils deal with a broad range of issues and, consequently, are composed of numerous committees. For example, the Industrial Structure Council had eighteen committees in 1990, ranging from the

Industrial Finance Committee to the Industrial Labor Committee to the Industrial Location Committee.

The method for using deliberation councils involves a feedback process in which the first step is for MITI officials to call a hearing and invite comments from various interested parties. Based on the information it collects, MITI officials issue a draft report that is then forwarded for discussion to a deliberative council. The council may include affected industry representatives, academics, journalists, consumer and labor representatives, former bureaucrats,

financial representatives, and politicians. Representation is not proportional in any sense, nor are representatives elected. Based on the feedback that MITI gets from the council, it makes changes in its draft plan and issues a final document that details the steps that will be taken, such as policy changes or new policy initiatives. The final action taken by MITI is essentially a public relations campaign to sell the plan to the wider public.

Source: Campos and Root, *The Key to the East Asian Miracle.*

The coordination of interdependent investment activities is difficult in a purely free-market framework. The difficulty stems from the fact that the flow of information is not sufficient to let all investors know of the intentions of each other. Six of the eight HPAEs surmounted this problem through the creation of **deliberation councils**, a set of quasi-legislative bodies that bring together representatives from the private and the public sectors. In effect, deliberation councils coordinate the information flow between businesses and policymakers.

Individual councils are usually created to deal with a limited set of issues involving one industry or a particular set of policy issues, such as the government budget. By bringing together government officials and affected business groups, the councils reduce the cost of acquiring information about new policies, they provide a forum for bargaining over policies, they instill greater investor confidence, and they raise the level of credibility of the government's policies. More than perhaps any other function, however, deliberation councils serve as a vehicle for the business elites to have a strong voice in the setting of government policy and thereby ensure their cooperation in the overall economic strategy.

Avoiding Rent Seeking

Economic policy in the HPAEs has been relatively interventionist. That is, the laissez-faire ideology of letting markets determine outcomes has not been followed. Hong Kong is somewhat of an exception, but even in Hong Kong, government has directed and actively participated in the creation of extensive public housing. In the next section, we examine some of the issues related to the effectiveness and extent of government intervention in the economy. Whether extensive or not, however, one of the biggest puzzles surrounding HPAE economic policy was the degree to which most countries were able to avoid the costs and inefficiencies associated with private sector rent seeking.

When governments intervene to help specific industries or to channel resources in a particular direction, they create benefits that are of value to someone. Generally speaking, when private interests perceive the possibility of obtaining something of value from government (e.g., credit subsidies, import protection, business licenses, etc.), they will devote scarce resources to obtaining those benefits. The result, as discussed in several earlier chapters, is wasteful rent seeking.

Government policies in the HPAEs created numerous benefits of value to specific industries, yet in spite of this, there was relatively little rent seeking by those interests. To be sure, rent seeking still occurs, and there is significant variation by HPAE nations. Nevertheless, there seems to have been less overall rent seeking than in many other societies.

It is unlikely that there is a single, simple explanation for this lack of rent-seeking behavior, but the deliberation councils probably played a key role. By providing a policy forum in which various interests can make their views known and have a chance to argue in favor of policies that are particularly beneficial, the need to hire lobbyists is reduced. Furthermore, given that industrial and business interests meet with government officials as a group, rather than single interests by themselves, there is greater transparency and less worry about what competing interests may be doing behind the scenes.

In addition to the role played by deliberation councils, some analysts point to the fact that whenever governments offer something of value, they usually attach performance requirements. For example, firms receiving credit subsidies or import protection are usually required to meet specific targets—often export targets—or else the subsidies are taken away. What is remarkable, and not clearly understood, is how HPAE governments are able to enforce the performance requirements they lay down. Many nations outside East Asia, including many Latin American governments, have used performance requirements as incentive mechanisms, but often they have proven to be unenforceable. That is, when firms have not met their production or export targets, governments outside the HPAEs have often been unable to withdraw the special considerations they are providing to the noncompliant firms.

Two key elements that have played a role in enforceability are the presence of a well-educated bureaucracy along with its insulation from the political process. In most of the HPAEs, civil service careers are highly respected and well paid. Consequently, bureaucrats are well educated and competent. In addition to ability, their insulation from the political process gives them the room to make decisions based on merit rather than on the basis of special interests.

A final explanation for the relative lack of rent seeking is the commitment to shared growth that we saw at the beginning of the chapter. The fact that business elites are convinced that they will share the benefits of economic growth reduces the pressure for them to seek added benefits through the manipulation of the political process. In effect, greater equality in the HPAEs reduces the number of individuals and groups that feel left out of the growth process and eliminates the underlying cause of much rent seeking.

CASE STUDY

Japanese Keiretsu

Many of the most prominent and best known Japanese firms are organized into groups called *keiretsu*. Firms within a *keiretsu* are legally separate entities tied to each other through their ownership structure, business relations, and interlocking directorates (shared membership on their boards of directors). Many observers outside Japan argue that the *keiretsu* form of industrial organization gives Japanese firms an unfair advantage in international trade. The United States raised the issue of *keiretsu* in the WTO, but to date, it has been unsuccessful in its attempt to have them declared an unfair trade advantage. Unfair or not, they are a major source of trade friction between Japan and a number of other nations.

There are two types of *keiretsu*: horizontally organized and vertically organized. Horizontally integrated *keiretsu* have family or group members that are spread out across the economy and not concentrated in one type of production. The most important and largest examples of horizontal *keiretsu* are integrated around a major financial institution and usually include life and casualty insurance companies, trading companies, and manufacturing companies. The largest are relatively well known in the United States, for example, Mitsui, Sumitomo,

Sanwa, and Mitsubishi. In the mid-1990s, the six largest included approximately one-half of the 200 largest Japanese firms, and accounted for approximately 15 percent of all sales in Japan.

Firms in vertical *keiretsu* are usually organized around a single large industrial corporation and include allied firms, subcontractors, and important consumers. In the automobile industry, Toyota and Nissan are examples; in electrical equipment, Hitachi, Toshiba, and Matsushita; and in steel, Nippon Steel. Although they tend to be concentrated in a single industry (autos, electronics, etc.), they often have ties to distributors and to a financial institution.

One of the distinguishing features of *keiretsu* is the cross-ownership of firms. Cross-ownership means that a majority share of each firm is owned by the other firms in the family, and, as a result, a minority share of the stock is independently owned. A second common feature is that the companies have interlocking directorates in which the boards of directors share a common pool of members. Third, the management of the firms in a *keiretsu* jointly plan their economic strategies and regularly meet to discuss conditions and business practices.

Trade economists have attempted to gather data on the extent to which

(*continues*)

keiretsu control production in a sector of the economy, such as automobiles, and then have tried to see if imports by Japan are less than expected, after all other factors that determine imports have been accounted for. Some economists have concluded that *keiretsu* do cause imports to be less, while others have shown that they have no effect. In other words, the results of the statistical analysis are inconclusive and do not provide a clear answer to whether this form of industrial organization discriminates against foreign trade and investment.

Those that believe that *keiretsu* are harmful to trade and investment usually make several interrelated points about the economic incentives they create. First, the cross-shareholding of firms within a group prevents foreigners from directly acquiring major Japanese firms. Since direct acquisition of firms is one of the main avenues of foreign direct investment, the overall rate of foreign investment is lower in Japan. Second, members of a *keiretsu* conduct the majority of their business with other members—not with outsiders. As a result, suppliers of intermediate parts, such as automobile parts manufacturers, find it difficult to break into the Japanese economy. Toyota, Nissan, and others, have their own parts manufacturers, with whom they have long-term relationships and share proprietary information.

For outsiders, one solution might be to establish their own production facilities. That is, instead of trying to buy existing Japanese firms, U.S. and European companies could set up their own factories. At this point, however, they run into another feature of *keiretsu*, which is the control of existing distribution channels. For example, in the dispute between the U.S. film producer, Kodak, and its Japanese counterpart, Fuji, Kodak complained that Fuji signed exclusive contracts with the four main distributors of photographic film and effectively denied outsiders access to the normal distribution channel in Japan. Kodak lost this dispute when it took it to the WTO, but many observers continue to believe that the control of the distribution system by Japanese *keiretsu* limits foreign trade and investment.

An underlying problem for anyone who studies the effects of *keiretsu* on the Japanese economy is that they are difficult to define once you go beyond the most obvious examples. Relationships between firms tend to be fluid over time, and it is difficult to specify which firms are in which corporate groups. In addition, firms within a vertical *keiretsu* may rely on firms in a separate horizontal *keiretsu* for some of their business, as when Toyota uses Mitsui for its banking. For this reason, some analysts have argued that *keiretsu* are little more than social clubs, a vehicle for managers of different firms to get to know one another so that they will have golf partners and drinking buddies.

More recently, research has turned from trying to measure whether *keiretsu* discriminate against foreign firms, goods, and services, to examining whether they played a significant role in Japan's relative economic stagnation during the 1990s. The fact that most *keiretsu* have a large bank as part of their group means that many lending decisions are based on group membership rather than market principles. In the 1990s, as the banking sector teetered on the edge of collapse, some share of its problems may have resulted from bad loans made to group members.

THE ROLE OF INDUSTRIAL POLICIES

The most influential study to date of the high-performance Asian economies is the World Bank's policy research report entitled *The East Asian Miracle: Economic Growth and Public Policy*. The World Bank's research team concluded that government interventions were common in three areas: (1) targeting of specific industries, that is, industrial policies narrowly defined; (2) directed credit; and (3) export promotion. In this section, we examine the debate over the effectiveness of industrial policies and offer a word of caution about the use of directed credit.

Targeting Specific Industries in the HPAEs

Recall from Chapter 5 that industrial policies can be defined in broad or narrow terms. The broad definition is policies that alter a nation's endowment in a way that does not favor particular industries. For example, we have already seen that the East Asian success story involves high rates of primary and secondary schooling that altered the characteristics of the labor force and the high rates of savings and investment that created the infrastructure and capital goods necessary to enter more sophisticated lines of manufacturing.

The narrow definition of industrial policies is the targeted development of specific industries. In effect, targeted industrial policies attempt to change the comparative advantage of a nation through the alteration of its industrial structure. These policies channel resources to favored industries and are often criticized as "government bureaucrats picking winners and losers."

With the exception of Hong Kong, every HPAE has had or still has some form of targeted industrial policy. They were strongest in Japan, Korea, and Taiwan (the "northern tier" of HPAEs), but they were significant in the other countries as well. In Japan, the focus has been on steel, autos, textiles, shipbuilding, aluminum, electronics, and semiconductors, among others. The height of Korean policies was between 1973 and 1979 with the Heavy and Chemical Industries (HCI) program, which targeted steel, shipbuilding, petrochemicals, and other heavy industries. While lacking the same clear focus as Japan and Korea, Taiwan's programs have provided research institutes, science parks, and basic infrastructure for a variety of industries and seem to have targeted the development of import substitutes.

Malaysian policies took off in the early 1980s with the Look East policy, which emulated Korea's and Japan's industrial development. Malaysia created the Heavy Industries Corporation of Malaysia (HICOM) to develop steel, nonferrous metals, machinery, paper and paper products, and petrochemicals, but it ran into financial constraints in the late 1980s when a number of the firms under HICOM proved to be unprofitable and required government bailouts. Since then, Malaysia has privatized many firms and reduced the degree of state control in others. Indonesia and Thailand did not make systematic efforts such as Japan and Korea did, but the Thai Board of Investment has promoted industries that it deemed to have the potential for technological learning. Indonesia has attempted to use large state-run enterprises to leapfrog from labor-intensive to high-technology industries. Singapore's policies have focused largely on encouraging technology transfer from firms in industrial nations through the promotion of foreign direct investment.

The tools that nations use to promote specific industries include the instruments of trade policies. Restrictions on imports, through licensing, quotas, or tariffs, and export subsidies were all used. In many cases, protection from foreign competition enabled firms to earn high profits in domestic markets, which compensated for the losses they suffered in foreign markets. In addition to trade policy, the HPAEs used numerous other mechanisms to channel resources to targeted industries. Directed credit was one of the most important tools, because even when it was small in size, it signaled the private sector that government policy favored the industry receiving the funds. This official stamp of approval was an important device for encouraging private lending to new and potentially risky industries. Other tools included subsidies, market information, especially with respect to foreign markets, infrastructure construction, and research and development funds.

There are two essential elements to these policies that make them different from most other national attempts to promote specific industries. First, resources were usually only provided as long as the companies receiving them met specific export targets. If the targets were not met, the resources (protection, credit, etc.) were withdrawn. Export targets are argued to be a better criterion than profits because many firms had monopolies or significant market power in their domestic markets; hence, profitability may be unrelated to efficiency. Second, governments placed macroeconomic stability above industrial policies. If they began to experience fiscal problems that were caused by the industrial promotion programs, they scaled back or abandoned them.

The World Bank view of these programs is that they were insulated from purely political influences so that industrial targeting decisions were based on technical analysis rather than politics. The collapse of the financial sectors in many countries in 1997 and 1998 has called this assumption into question. For example, government use of directed credit programs appears to be one of the main causes of the financial crisis. Government involvement in credit allocation forced financial institutions to make unsound loans. In turn, the failure to apply business criteria led to a mountain of bad debt, which ultimately sank many banks and whole financial sectors. In the future, conventional economic wisdom will undoubtedly be much more cautious about the benefits of directed credit programs to target industrial development.

Did Industrial Policies Work?

The role of industrial policies in the story of HPAE growth is controversial. Ideally, we would like to know the answers to two simple questions. First, did they work? A successful policy would be one that increases the overall rate of GDP growth or the rate of productivity growth. Second, if they worked, were they important? That is, was their contribution to economic growth significant enough to be considered one of the reasons for East Asian success?

With respect to the question of whether they made a positive contribution to growth, opinion ranges from "no effect" to "positive effect." The reason for the lack of consensus on this important issue is that, in general, it is difficult to measure the effects of policy interventions on growth rates. There are conceptual disagreements about the measurements that should be made, and few countries have data of sufficient quality. In the World Bank's view, "reasoned judgments" must be used to settle the issue. Unfortunately, the paucity of data, together with disagreements over measurement techniques, results in the use of qualitative judgments of the sort that inevitably lead researchers to confirm the opinions that they began with.

In spite of these obstacles to assessing industrial policies, the variety of opinions among researchers can be characterized as falling into two camps. One camp is represented by the World Bank's research. In their view, some government interventions fostered economic growth (export promotion and directed credit), but, in general, industrial policies did not. They assert that industrial policies usually targeted the same industries that market forces were developing and, therefore, were unnecessary. In the cases where the "wrong" industries were targeted, pragmatic and flexible policymakers of the HPAEs managed to quickly change policies before any damage was done to the rest of the economy.

The World Bank's analysis rests on two pieces of evidence. First, they compare the growth rates of productivity in the targeted and nontargeted sectors in the three countries with sufficient data (Japan, Korea, and Taiwan). In general, they find that productivity change in the promoted sectors was high but no higher than in the rest of the economy. Possible exceptions to their general finding are Japan's chemical and metalworking industries and Korea's chemical industry. One problem for the advocates of industrial policies is that the unpromoted textile sector did as well as any of the promoted sectors. Second, they examine the change over time in the industrial structure of the HPAEs. If industrial policies worked, they should have led to a different pattern of industrial growth than the pattern that is caused by a change in factor endowments. They conclude that industrial policies were at most marginally effective, since the sector-by-sector growth pattern is as expected, given the national endowments of labor and the high savings and investment rates.

Critiques of the World Bank's findings usually rest on two points. First, the fact that productivity growth was generally no faster in promoted sectors is irrelevant, according to the critics. The important issue is what the growth rates would have been without promotion. It is conceivable that without industrial policies, growth in the targeted industries would have been much slower than with the policies. Second, the critics point out that the World Bank analysis is overly general. In their view, it is based on industry groupings that are too broad to uncover the details of selective targeting. For example, some components of the textile industry were heavily promoted in both Japan and Korea in the early period of their industrial policies. Therefore, it is not surprising that textiles overall have experienced a rapid increase in productivity and that they remain a larger than expected component of Japanese and Korean industry.

At present, there is no way to resolve this debate. Consequently, there are a variety of opinions about the relevance of industrial policies for developing countries outside the HPAE group. To the extent that there is agreement, most analysts share the view that if industrial policies are to be successful, they should have three key characteristics. Countries must have (1) clear performance criteria such as export targets; (2) institutional mechanisms to monitor compliance and enforce compliance; and (3) low costs so that nontargeted sectors do not suffer.

CASE STUDY

HCI in Korea

Most observers agree that Korean industrial policies have at least partially succeeded. The most enthusiastic observers argue that they have accelerated the rate of overall growth without creating offsetting inefficiencies elsewhere in the economy. Less optimistic observers concede success in generating exports and in changing the industrial structure of the country, but they offset many of those gains with the huge financial costs of the Heavy and Chemical Industries (HCI) promotion in the 1970s.

Korea's industrial promotion drive began a few years after the Korean War in the early 1960s. Early efforts at industrial targeting focused on key industrial materials such as cement, fertilizer, and petroleum refining. The government typically supported large-scale conglomerates, called *chaebol*, which were given monopolies in the domestic market. Trade policy in the form of an aggressive promotion of exports along with high levels of protection was the main tool for targeting industries, but

directed credit and tax breaks were important as well.

Industrial targeting evolved into the Heavy and Chemical Industries program, which was at its most active from 1973 to 1979. HCI targeted six specific industrial groups: steel, petrochemicals, and nonferrous metals for enhanced self-sufficiency, and shipbuilding, electronics, and machinery (especially earth-moving equipment and autos) for export. The tools used to promote these industries were the same as previously described but with a different emphasis. By the mid-1970s, trade policy had become somewhat more liberal, although most industries still received significant protection. Greater emphasis was placed on subsidies, directed credit through loans at below-market interest rates, and special tax exemptions.

The cost of promotion during the HCI period was significant. Direct funds provided to targeted industries were around 5 percent of the overall budget, and tax exemptions amounted to about 3 percent of total tax revenues. In 1977, around 45 percent of the banking system's total provision of domestic credit went to the targeted industries. Gradually, bottlenecks and large debts began to accumulate.

By 1979, when the second oil crisis hit, inflation was high, the exchange rate had appreciated, causing exports to falter, and the targeted industries had significant idle capacity. In addition, the labor-intensive sectors (which had not been targeted) were starved for credits, and bad debts and financial insolvencies were growing in the HCI sector.

Policymakers quickly switched course. HCI promotion was curtailed, the currency was devalued, and financial market and import liberalization were hastened. One of the main efforts of policymakers in the 1980s was to restructure a number of the distressed industries that were overpromoted in the 1970s. The cost to the government

budget has been significant, as it has been forced to bail out bankrupt firms and dispose of nonperforming loans.

Was HCI promotion worth it? It is impossible to answer this question definitively because we can never know what would have happened under an alternative set of policies. During the height of the HCI program and its immediate aftermath, Korea's growth rate dipped slightly (from the mid-1970s through the mid-1980s), but the change was slight, and growth overall remained extremely high, even by HPAE standards. Korea achieved classification as a high-income nation, a feat that only Japan and the city-states of Singapore and Hong Kong have accomplished in the twentieth century.

Source: World Bank, *The East Asian Miracle*; and Westphal, "Industrial Policy in an Export-Propelled Economy: Lessons from South Korea's Experience," in *The Journal of Economic Perspectives*, Summer 1990.

THE ROLE OF MANUFACTURED EXPORTS

The promotion of manufactured exports played a significant role in the industrial strategies of each of the HPAEs. These policies were largely successful, and the exports of each country grew even faster than their GDP. Given these facts, it is reasonable to assume that there might be a connection between the two. That is, a number of studies of the HPAEs and other regions have shown that higher rates of growth of exports are correlated with higher rates of growth of GDP. What is the mechanism that causes this?

The Connections Between Growth and Exports

It is true by definition that exports are part of the GDP, so it would seem that growth in exports is simply a part of overall GDP growth. Export growth may not add to GDP growth, however, if it crowds out growth in the output of goods for domestic consumption, such as consumer goods or investment. In effect, the idea that export growth causes faster GDP growth is an assertion that export growth causes the overall capacity of the economy to grow faster than it would have if production was focused on goods for the domestic market.

If production focused on exports results in greater overall growth, then there must be something in the production process or its links to the rest of the economy that is absent from domestically focused production. One possibility is that because exports are produced for the world market, economies of scale come into play in a way that is absent when firms produce for a small domestic market. Larger firms often have lower average costs because they can spread their fixed costs for capital and machinery over a larger volume of output. Another possible reason why exports might foster growth is that as firms produce for a world market, there are added incentives to increase R&D. Economies of scale may make it more worthwhile, and the need to keep up with foreign competition may make it more necessary.

Other connections between export growth and GDP growth are possible as well. Exports may speed up the adoption and mastery of international best practices. Firms that operate in global markets are not protected from competition. In fact, they are going up against the world's best, and the competitive pressures may force firms to stay abreast of the latest developments in their product area and production process. Measurement of this possible effect is complicated by the presence of some form of export promotion in the HPAEs. An exporter does not have to be among the world's best if it receives subsidies (for example, direct payment or access to low-interest loans or tax breaks). Firms can be competitive due to subsidies received at home, which may reduce the pressures to compete based on efficiency or quality. Successful export promotion programs, such as those in Korea, are well aware of this problem, and since their goal is to develop firms that are capable of head-to-head international competition without special breaks, they carefully monitor the programs to ensure that the subsidies granted to the exporters do not become the reason for competitive success abroad. In addition, subsidies are gradually reduced. Note, however, that since 1995, the international rules for subsidies have tightened considerably, and it is much harder for countries to provide them within the WTO framework.

Production of exports has several other potential advantages. Exports make possible the purchase of imports. Developing countries are not usually on the technology frontier, and the creation of an efficient manufacturing enterprise is often dependent on imports of machinery and other capital goods. A scarcity of exports impairs a country's ability to purchase imports, with the result that firms are unable to obtain the imported inputs they need in order to raise their efficiency. A related advantage of exports is that the need to meet export targets tied the HPAEs to policies that openly encouraged inward foreign direct investment (FDI) and the acquisition of new technology. One way to overcome the backwardness of domestic manufacturing is to encourage foreign firms to invest. Most of the HPAEs welcomed FDI; Singapore went so far as to build its industrial policies around it. At the same time that FDI was encouraged, several countries also sought to provide incentives for the foreign firm to license its technology to potential domestic rivals. This was a particularly common strategy in Japan, where the incentive of access to the large Japanese market was sufficient to encourage many firms to sign technology licensing agreements.

The ability to import capital and modern technology is seen by some as the most critical ingredient in policies that successfully close the gap between developing and developed countries. Export promotion can encourage the acquisition of new technologies because in order to succeed, governments must allow access to whatever imports firms need to become efficient. Most of the HPAEs selectively protected their domestic markets, but they also adjusted their policies so that exporters were given access to needed imports. In general, they used less protection than other developing areas.

Is Export Promotion a Good Model for Other Regions?

The export promotion model has succeeded so well in East Asia that, inevitably, it is being prescribed for other developing areas. In Latin America, for example, the economic crisis of the 1980s, together with the very visible counterexample of East Asia, has propelled many nations into similar types of policies. A serious question is whether other areas can duplicate the export successes of the HPAEs.

If developing countries around the world begin to emphasize export promotion policies, an issue arises whether the world's industrial nations can absorb the exports of a series of newly industrializing countries. One possibility is that these exports will undermine industries in industrial nations and lead to renewed trade conflicts and calls for protection. While trade conflict appears to be a permanent part of the international landscape, developing countries currently account for only 21 percent of the world's manufactured exports. Of this 21 percent of the world's manufactured exports, developing country HPAEs produce about 12 percent, meaning that the rest of the developing world produces only 9 percent of the world's export of manufactures. Clearly, the problem of saturating the markets of industrial economies does not appear to be close on the horizon, even if developing economies were to expand their exports at a furious rate.

Perhaps the greatest obstacle for countries that wish to replicate the export promotion policies of the HPAEs is the Uruguay Round of the GATT. Under the rules that went into effect in 1994, developing countries must eliminate any subsidies that are contingent on export performance. The phase-out period is eight years, and no new subsidies may be provided in the intervening years. Extremely poor countries with per capita GDP less than $1000 are exempted. Essentially, the new GATT rules eliminate the possibility that developing countries can use the same tools—credit subsidies, tax breaks, direct payments—that the HPAEs used. The only exceptions are the poorest of the poor, who do not export manufactured goods in any quantity. In all countries, subsidies for noncommercial R&D, regional development, and promoting compliance with environmental regulations are allowed.

CASE STUDY

East Asian Trade Blocs

East Asia is the one region of the world without significant trade blocs. While there are numerous informal agreements, the only formal bloc is the Association of South East Asian Nations, or ASEAN. ASEAN was founded in 1967 as mainly a political cooperation and security agreement. Its current membership includes the nine nations of Brunei, Indonesia, Laos, Malaysia, Myanmar, Philippines, Singapore, Thailand, and Vietnam. Cambodia has observer status and is expected to join in the near future.

In 1977, ASEAN negotiated preferential trade among its members, but barriers did not begin to fall until 1987. In 1992, the nations negotiated a free-trade agreement, known as the ASEAN Free Trade Area, or AFTA, which has a fifteen-year time frame for the elimination of tariffs. As part of the process of reducing trade barriers, quantitative restrictions were converted to tariffs, and all countries were required to reduce tariffs on intra-ASEAN trade to 20 percent by the year 2001.

The ASEAN nations are one component of a far vaster trade region known as Asia Pacific Economic Cooperation, or APEC. In addition to most of the ASEAN, APEC includes the HPAEs plus China, Russia, New Zealand, Aus-

tralia, Canada, the United States, Mexico, and Chile. APEC was created in 1989. Its twenty-one members have a combined GDP of more than $17 trillion (1999) and account for approximately 45 percent of world exports. The goal of APEC, as set forth in the 1994 Declaration of Common Resolve, is "free and open trade and investment in the region no later than 2010 for the industrialized economies and 2020 for the developing economies." APEC is not a trade bloc in the normal sense. Its goal, as just stated, does not commit the members to forming a free-trade area. Rather, it does something even more amazing: It commits members to implement free-trade and open-investment flows as part of their overall trade and investment policy, not just for other APEC countries but for all of the world's nations. No one can say if every member nation will honor its commitments to create free trade, but at annual meetings of each nation's finance ministers, along with the numerous working groups and committees, progress is slowly being made on a wide range of issues.

Another issue is the question of whether there is a trade bloc developing in East Asia that is centered around Japan. There seems to be a widespread popular belief that the world is forming into three blocs centered around the European Union, the United States, and Japan. In this view, Japan is using not only its foreign trade with East Asia, but also its foreign aid and extensive foreign investment ties to cement its role as the center of a developing Asian bloc. Empirical analysis of Japan's trade and investment, along with the growing role of the yen, argues against the idea. Europe, the Western Hemisphere, and East Asia each have trade patterns that are biased toward their own regions. In the 1980s, the bias toward intraregional trade (i.e., trade within the region) increased in Europe and the Western Hemisphere. There was no increase in the East Asian intraregional bias. In fact, the most potent trade grouping for explaining the regional bias in East Asian trade seems to be APEC—a region that includes the NAFTA countries as well as Australia, New Zealand, and the leading economies of East Asia.

In terms of the use of the yen and the creation of a "yen bloc," the available evidence shows that yen usage, while growing, is not expanding as fast as Japan's economy and trade. As a leading industrial nation, it is reasonable to expect that the yen will inevitably play a greater role in world trade and finance. Indeed, the yen has grown as a percentage of official Asian reserves and as a percentage of Asian invoices for imports and exports. Nevertheless, neither the share of reserves nor the share of invoices has kept pace with the growth in Japan's trade.

Sources: Both ASEAN and APEC have Web sites: *http://www.aseansec.org.id* and *http://www.apecsec.org.sg.* Empirical analysis of the role of Japan in Asian trade and the absence of a "yen bloc" can be found in Frankel, Jeffrey, "Is Japan Creating a Yen Bloc in East Asia and the Pacific?" in *Regionalism and Rivalry: Japan and the United States in Pacific Asia,* edited by Frankel and Kahler.

IS THERE AN ASIAN MODEL OF ECONOMIC GROWTH?

The East Asian "Miracle" has given rise to a large number of studies that seek to explain rapid growth in the HPAEs and China. While the issue may superficially appear academic, it has become one of the more interesting and heated debates in recent popular economics. Proponents of laissez-faire economics have used the relative openness of the East Asian economies, their use of private markets, and their strong macroeconomic fundamentals to argue for government policies that are less activist. Proponents of a more activist government have pointed to selective interventions, such as export promotion, industrial policies, and deliberation councils, to argue in favor of a larger government role in the economy. Some Asian politicians have pointed to their restrictions on civil and political liberties as laying a foundation for order and the avoidance of chaos.

Is there an Asian model of the economy? That is, have the HPAEs managed to achieve their extraordinary growth rates through policies that are fundamentally different from the policy advice dispensed by proponents of the Washington Consensus (see Chapter 15)? At stake are the paths followed by today's developing economies and the future role of government policy in the industrial countries. Naturally, with a question so controversial, there are a variety of answers and opinions. Recent work, however, seems to be pointing toward a robust set of conclusions.

In order to describe some interesting recent studies, we must briefly review the idea of growth accounting. Recall that labor productivity is a measurement that is defined as output per worker. The growth in labor productivity is highly correlated with the growth in income (or output) per member of the population, but they are not the same thing. East Asian growth is remarkable for its growth in per capita income and its growth in labor productivity.

Any given rate of growth of labor productivity can be broken down into the share that is due to more capital and the share that is due to more skills or education. In the economics literature, such an exercise is called a *growth accounting*. When growth accounts are constructed for a country or a region, there is always some share of the growth in labor productivity that cannot be explained by the amount of additional capital or education. This share is a measure of the effects of using the available inputs more efficiently. That is, if more growth occurs than can be explained by the growth of capital or education, it must be due to a more productive use of the available inputs. For example, the organization of production may have changed so that people are working more efficiently, or the quality of technology may have changed so that each unit of capital and labor input produces more units of output.

Another name for the share of labor productivity that is not explained by capital or education is *total factor productivity*, or TFP. TFP growth reflects changes in output that are unrelated to changes in capital or labor inputs but that are related to new technologies, innovation, and organizational improvements. According to most estimates, over the long run, the lion's share of per capita income growth in high-income countries has resulted from increases in total factor productivity.

Growth accounting may seem a long way from the debate on East Asia, but it is actually very relevant. As it turns out, the vast bulk of Asian growth since 1960 can be accounted for by increases in capital and education, while TFP plays a much smaller role. Table 16.5 provides the details and some comparisons over the same period.

What we observe in Table 16.5 is that in the sample of six HPAEs, TFP growth accounts for between 24 and 36 percent of overall growth. In the slower-growing United States, it accounts for 27 percent, and in the other industrial nations, the figure is 37 percent. The fact that TFP growth accounts for about the same overall share of growth in the HPAEs was surprising to many observers for two reasons: First, the HPAEs are not on the frontier of new technologies as are the United States and the rest of the industrial world.

| TABLE 16.5 | Sources of Growth, 1960–1994 (Percent) | | | |

| Country | Growth of Output per Worker | Contribution of | | |
		Capital per Worker	Education per Worker	Total Factor Productivity
Indonesia	3.4	2.1	0.5	0.8
Korea	5.7	3.3	0.8	1.5
Malaysia	3.8	2.3	0.5	0.9
Singapore	5.4	3.4	0.4	1.5
Thailand	5.0	2.7	0.4	1.8
Taiwan	5.8	3.1	0.6	2.0
Latin America	1.5	0.9	0.4	0.2
United States	1.1	0.4	0.4	0.3
Industrial Nations*	2.9	1.5	0.4	1.1

Economic growth in East Asia is mainly a result of capital accumulation.

*Including Japan, excluding the United States.

Source: Collins and Bosworth, "Economic Growth in East Asia: Accumulation Versus Assimilation," in *Brooking Papers on Economic Activity,* 2: 1996.

Consequently, they should be able to more easily borrow techniques that increase their TFP. Second, the proponents of a new Asian model of economic growth have argued that the selective interventions such as industrial policies and export promotion have increased productivity. In fact, what they appear to have done, if anything, is to increase the quantity of capital per worker.

The last point is key to understanding this debate. When growth is decomposed into its various causes, what appears to account for the bulk of HPAE growth is capital accumulation and not increased total factor productivity. These results appear to be fairly strong, since several other researchers have done similar growth accounting exercises and have reached the same conclusions. The growth accounts for East Asia are important because they paint a consistent, if surprising, picture of the East Asian "Miracle." They tell us that there may be no miracle at all, just the hard work and sacrifice that comes from forgoing today's consumption in order to raise savings and investment rates. For example, between 1966 and 1985, Singapore raised investment from 11 percent of GDP to 40 percent. It is no surprise, then, that capital accumulation accounts for the bulk of its growth.

If these measures are accurate, then the argument for a distinct Asian model looks weak. Rather than selective interventions that target specific industries, the keys were high savings and high investment, together with the other factors outlined in this chapter.

Summary

- The major characteristics of economic growth in the high-performance Asian economies are (1) increasing equality, (2) rapid accumulation of savings and high rates of investment, (3) rapid increases in levels of schooling, (4) rapid growth of manufactured exports, and (5) stable macroeconomic environments.

- The institutional environment is instrumental in creating confidence in policymakers. The policymaking bureaucracy tends to be insulated from the push and pull of the political system. This leads some to decry the lack of representation of the population in policy decisions, but it allows decisions to be made on technical merit rather than political expediency. The voice of business and industry, and to a lesser extent other groups such as consumers, is often heard through consultative bodies known as *deliberation councils*. Deliberation councils are a mechanism for the private sector and government policymakers to exchange information and discuss policies.

- One of the key elements of policy is fiscal control over inflation, the budget, foreign debt, and exchange rates. While inflation, budgets, and foreign debt all vary country by country, inflation is kept under control, and budget deficits and foreign debt are kept within the boundaries defined by the government's and the economy's ability to finance them.

- With the exception of Hong Kong, each of the HPAEs followed industrial policies that targeted the development of particular industries. These policies were most focused in the "northern tier" of Japan, Korea, and Taiwan. The effects of these policies are difficult to measure, and there is a long and contentious debate about their efficacy.

- Each of the HPAEs promoted manufactured exports. These policies largely succeeded, although the mechanisms that link export growth to faster GDP growth are still uncertain.

- Recent empirical work shows that the main contributor to economic growth in the HPAEs is the extremely rapid accumulation of physical capital. Consequently, the argument that the HPAEs have pioneered a model that leads to more rapid total factor productivity growth appears false, and the keys to growth should be looked for in the policies that raise savings and investment.

Vocabulary

deliberation councils

demographic transition

4 Tigers

high-performance Asian economies (HPAEs)

keiretsu

newly industrializing economies (NIEs)

total factor productivity (TFP)

Study Questions

1. Contrast the characteristics of economic growth in the HPAEs with those characteristics in Latin America.

2. How can passage through a demographic transition lead to high savings and investment rates?

3. What are the characteristics of East Asian institutional environments that contributed to rapid economic growth?

4. Economists are divided over the effectiveness of East Asian industrial policies. Provide a balanced assessment of the issues relevant to understanding the role of industrial policies in fostering growth. Do you think one point of view is better than another? Why?

5. How might manufactured exports contribute to economic growth?

6. Is there a uniquely Asian model of economic growth? What are the issues, and how might we go about answering that question?

Chapter 17

ECONOMIC INTEGRATION IN THE TRANSITION ECONOMIES

INTRODUCTION: ECONOMIES IN TRANSITION

The Berlin Wall fell in the fall of 1989. It was impossible to mistake the historical symbolism: The Cold War was over. Two years later, in December 1991, the USSR divided itself into fifteen separate nations. These events catapulted those regions into an ocean of political and economic reforms. Unlike the Chinese economic reforms that began in December 1978, in the former Soviet Union, political reform and democracy were also on the agenda.

The term **transition economy** refers to a country that is moving away from socialism and toward capitalism. This transition requires a common set of reforms, no matter how the histories and the cultures of nations vary. Macroeconomic policies must strive to create stability; domestic prices must be linked to world prices; labor markets and financial markets must be created; property rights have to be defined; and institutional structures to support markets must be developed. The transition may be fast or slow, macroeconomic policies may differ depending on initial conditions (debt or no debt, inflation or no inflation), and the privatization of state-owned assets may go forward or stall, but the necessary changes are qualitatively similar in each country.

At one time or another, every nation has gone through an economic reform process. What is different about these economic reforms is that they go far beyond anything in recent history. Even the deep Latin American reforms that began in the mid-1980s (Chapter 15) are small by comparison. A description of each of the steps that must be taken to complete the transition to market economies is far beyond the scope of this book. Instead, this chapter provides a general characterization of the transition process and focuses on trade issues. Along the way, it describes some of the similarities and differences between countries, especially the East Asian reformers (China and Vietnam), the nations of the former Soviet Union (FSU), and the **Central and East European (CEE)** countries.

One word of caution is appropriate here: Change is constant. Countries that seem to be making little or no progress can quickly turn into rapid reformers, and vice versa. Consequently, the path of reform is uncertain, and what may be true today about a country's trade regime or external relations could be false tomorrow.

412

Central and Eastern European Countries

Former Yugoslavia = Bosnia and Herzegovina, Croatia, Macedonia, Montenegro, Yugoslavia
Baltic Republics = Estonia, Latvia, Lithuania
Visegrad Four = Poland, Czech Republic, Slovakia, Hungary

Scale

1: 9,512,000
1:150.12 Inches to Miles
Lambert Equal Area Projection

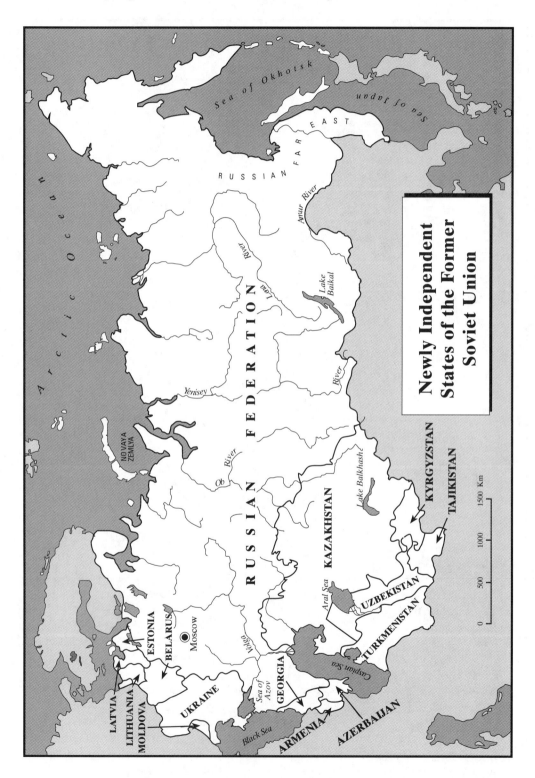

THE LEGACY OF CENTRAL PLANNING

The socialist economies of the former Soviet Union, Central and Eastern Europe, and China were **centrally planned economies**. Vietnam, Cuba, and a few other small countries shared this form of economic decision making as well. All countries (including Cuba) are moving away from central planning. Some, such as several nations in Central Europe, have become market-based economies, while others lag. In a centrally planned economy, the fundamental decisions of what to produce, how to produce it, and who gets it are decided by a central planning authority. The central planning bureaucracy is usually staffed with production engineers who use mathematical models to set output targets for each industry. Prices reflect political as well as economic decisions. Markets have little or no role in allocative decisions. In theory, the central economic authority surveys the available inputs and production sites and formulates a production plan. Most enterprises are state owned, so implementation of the plan takes the form of distributing production targets (quotas) to the various production sites. Since enterprises have more specific information about their own capabilities, there is usually a bargaining process between the central state authority, the regions, and the local enterprises over the allotment of inputs and the output targets.

Centrally planned economies differ from market economies in some fundamental ways. First, production, prices, and external trade are all controlled by the central economic authority. In other words, there are no goods markets where quantities and prices respond to demand and supply. Prices are administratively set and have little or no relationship to the scarcity or abundance of goods. Second, there are no asset markets, since most wealth is state owned (no need for stock markets) and financial flows to firms respond passively to the demands of the plan (no need for bond markets or other capital markets for lending). Third, there are no labor markets in the normal sense. Wages are set along with other prices in the economy, workers are allocated to firms like other inputs, and there is a prohibition on dismissals.

The promise of central planning was that it could free society from the volatility and uncertainty of markets through conscious control over economic development. Income distribution could be made more equal since the planning authority determines the level of economic rewards that each person receives. Basic economic necessities, such as jobs, education, health care, housing, and food are treated as economic rights.

The reality of central planning is more complex. On the positive side, unemployment was low, income distribution relatively more equal than in industrial market economies, and education and health care were high relative to the levels of income. Furthermore, at least in its early years, massive investment in heavy industry led to rates of economic growth that were very high. On the negative side, all this depended on the coercive power of the state to create forced savings that were invested in areas deemed important by the central planners and the political elite. Over time, economies became more and more distorted as the plan poured vast amounts of resources into heavy industry while it neglected light industry, consumer goods, and service industries. Without prices to guide them, many manufacturing industries ended up creating negative value added. That is, the real value of the inputs (i.e., what they would command at world prices) was greater than the value of the output. As time went on, the cumulation of inefficiencies began to have a profound effect on overall economic growth, and the Soviet Union, Central Europe, and China fell farther and farther behind the West.

One core problem of central planning is that it does not provide incentives for efficiency or innovation. In addition it is impossible for planners to absorb enough information to coordinate all economic decisions as well as markets can. Firms have no hard bottom line, since inputs are allocated based on the set targets, and financial resources are forthcoming whenever necessary. Even firms that do not meet their targets never go out of business. Consequently, there is no reason to consider quality, profits, customer service, or innovation. In order to ensure that they meet their targets, enterprise managers hoard excess labor and inputs, further eroding productivity growth.

A further complication for centrally planned economies is that they require authoritarian political systems in order to enforce the dictates of the plan. In practice, this means that every centrally planned economy had a powerful political elite that could intervene and demand changes in the plan whenever it suited their political or personal interests. Consequently, the practice of central planning was never truly in the hands of technocrats or engineers, but remained under the political control of the governing class. "Special plans" were layered on top of the official plan, and production decisions were often redirected to meet the needs of these powerful interests. Even if it were theoretically possible to rationally plan an entire economy, the problem of political interference would undermine the results.

International trade in centrally planned economies is limited and controlled through state trading monopolies. Under this system, a branch of the central economic authority controls the flow of all imports and exports. Prices and currency values are irrelevant, since much of the trade is a form of government-to-government barter agreements. Most foreign trade is limited to other centrally planned economies, thereby limiting the interaction of these economies with markets and the world economy. When trade occurs with market economies, the state trading monopoly keeps the foreign currency earned on exports and uses it to purchase non-bartered imports. Quotas and tariffs are irrelevant since prices are administratively set and in many cases have no relationship to the economic value of goods. Given the ability to set a price at any level, a tariff can always be offset by a change in the set price.

ECONOMIC INDICATORS

The transition economies of Tables 17.1 to 17.3 are divided into three groups: Central and Eastern European countries (CEE) in Table 17.1; the **Newly Independent States (NIS) of the former Soviet Union** in Table 17.2; and the Asian

TABLE 17.1	Transition Economies: Central and Eastern European Countries (CEE), 1999

Country	Population (millions)	GNP per Capita ($U.S., market exchange rates)	GNP per Capita ($U.S., PPP*)
Albania	3.4	870	2,892
Bulgaria	7.9	1,380	4,914
Romania	22.5	1,520	5,647
Baltic Republics			
Estonia	1.4	3,480	7,826
Latvia	2.4	2,470	5,938
Lithuania	3.6	2,620	6,093
Visegrad Four			
Czech Republic	10.3	5,060	12,289
Hungary	10.2	4,650	10,479
Poland	38.7	3,960	7,894
Slovak Republic	5.4	3,590	9,811
Former Yugoslavia			
Croatia	4.3	4,580	6,915
Macedonia	2.0	1,690	4,339
Slovenia	1.9	9,890	15,062

Most CEE countries are relatively well off compared to the other transition economies.

*Purchasing power parity.

Sources: United States Census Bureau, *International Data Base*; World Bank, *World Development Report, 2000/2001*.

transitional economies in Table 17.3. Economic statistics for the transition economies should be treated with caution. Statistical agencies are grappling with the problem of measuring economic output in an entirely new system, often at a time of significant economic decline and scarce resources for data collection. The transition has also altered the structure of production and requires new statistical measures. For example, services, which are hard to measure in any economy, are a fast-growing share of total output and easy to miss, since they are often provided by small microenterprises. In addition, high inflation in some countries made it difficult to disentangle price and output increases. A revision of Russia's national accounts, for example, showed that officials overestimated the 1990–1994 decline in the level of GDP by 12 percent.

While China has had longer to develop reliable economic statistics, there are still problems. Because of its size and strategic importance, its economic num-

TABLE 17.2	Transition Economies: Newly Independent States of the Former Soviet Union (NIS), 1999

Country	Population (millions)	GNP per Capita ($U.S., market exchange rates)	GNP per Capita ($U.S., PPP)
Russian Federation	146.5	2,270	6,339
Caucasus Region			
Armenia	3.4	490	2,210
Azerbaijan	7.7	550	2,322
Georgia	5.1	620	3,606
Central Asian Republics			
Kazakstan	16.7	1,230	4,408
Kyrgyz Republic	4.6	300	2,223
Tajikistan	6.3	290	981
Turkmenistan	4.4	660	3,099
Uzbekistan	24.4	720	2,092
Western Region			
Belarus	10.4	2,630	6,518
Moldova	4.4	370	2,358
Ukraine	49.6	750	3,142

The NIS are relatively poor, developing countries.

Sources: See Table 17.1.
*Purchasing power parity.

bers have generated considerable interest and scrutiny. One result is that there is a wide range of opinions about the real purchasing power of Chinese income. One expert has estimated it to be about three times the official exchange rate estimate, or about $2400, considerably below the World Bank estimate in Table 17.3 ($3291).

Most of the countries in Tables 17.1–17.3 are developing countries classified as low income (GNP per person less than $755) or lower middle income ($756 to $2995) by the World Bank. The exceptions are the **Visegrad Four** (Poland, Hungary, Czech Republic, Slovakia), which are all upper middle income ($2996–$9265), and Slovenia, which is high income (≥$9266). The normal set of development issues are applicable, although at times, it is difficult to disentangle the general problem of economic development from the issues of economic

TABLE 17.3	Transition Economies: Asia, 1999		
Country	Population (millions)	GNP per Capita ($U.S., market exchange rates)	GNP per Capita ($U.S., PPP*)
China	1,250.5	780	3,291
Mongolia	2.6	350	1,496
Vietnam	77.6	370	1,755

Asian transition economies are the least developed of all the transition economies.

*Purchasing power parity.
Sources: See Table 17.1.

transition. Both development and transition aim at generating economic growth and raising living standards, and both call for policies to develop financial systems, build new infrastructure, and so forth. Nevertheless, in the discussion that follows, the focus is on the shift from central planning to a market orientation, and not on development. It would be a mistake, however, to interpret this as implying that development issues are unimportant.

The beginning date for the transition to market economies varies by country. China announced the beginning of its reforms in December 1978 and began to implement them gradually in 1979. Vietnam began gradual reforms in 1986, but after a period of few results, it switched to a faster pace in 1989. Most of the CEE countries and NIS began their reforms between 1990 and 1994. Poland, for example, implemented a large number of deep reforms all at once in 1990. The experiences of the NIS have varied widely. A few nations began immediate and deep reforms and have moved relatively quickly to market economies, for example the Baltic republic of Estonia and the Central Asian Kyrgyz Republic. Others moved slowly and are only recently beginning their reform processes, for example Ukraine. And still others, such as the Central Asian republics of Turkmenistan and Uzbekistan, have resisted the introduction of reforms and have done little to start the transition to market economies.

Given that the transition is not simply an economic reform but also involves the breakup of the Soviet empire and the establishment of independent nations, it is not surprising that politics continues to hold back many countries. For example, in the early 1990s, many analysts predicted that Ukraine and Belarus would do very well as independent nations. Ukraine's rich soil gives it a comparative advantage in agriculture; it has well-developed seaports and inland transportation networks, shipbuilding, and other heavy industry. Both Ukraine and Belarus are in the center of Europe, and both have a well-educated labor force with relatively low labor costs. Unfortunately, neither country has done as well as hoped, since the reforms have been inconsistent, arbitrary, and very partial.

In addition to domestic policy confusion, a number of countries have been wracked by civil wars, secessionist movements, and fighting over territorial boundaries. In the NIS, Russia, Armenia, Azerbaijan, Tajikistan, Georgia, and Moldova fall into this category, while in the former Yugoslavia, war touched every region except Slovenia (which did experience a large influx of refugees). As is always the case, the wars proved expensive in human and financial terms, and with the exception of the Russian conflict in Chechnya, they delayed the onset of reforms.

With the breakup of the Soviet Union and the beginning of the reform process in Central and Eastern Europe, every country experienced a deep recession. The depth and timing of the bottoming out varied, but in general, the recessions were less severe and over sooner in the CEE countries, followed by the Baltic republics and the NIS.

Figure 17.1 and Table 17.4 summarize the regional growth experiences of the transition economies. What is not apparent in the data is the wide variation between countries, even those in the same region. For example, there are a few countries that reached or surpassed their pretransition output levels by 1999. Foremost among them are Poland, at 128 percent of pretransition output, and Slovenia at 105 percent. Several other countries are at or near their pretransition levels, although none of them are in the NIS. At the other end of the per-

---

FIGURE 17.1   Average Annual Growth of GDP

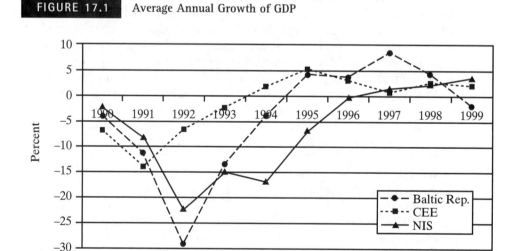

Deep recessions were common in the early years of the transition.

Source: Economist Intelligence Unit, *Country Reports.* Various years.

TABLE 17.4	Economic Performance, 1989–1999		
	Cumulative Output Decline to Lowest Level (%)	*Year Output Hit Bottom*	*Output in 1999 Relative to Output in 1989 (%)*
CEE Countries	27.9	1992	90
Baltic Republics	43.4	1994	70
NIS	54.2	1995	60

Most economies have not recovered from the recessions of the transition period.

Source: International Monetary Fund, *Finance and Development*, September 2000.

formance spectrum, in 1999, Moldova produced only 38 percent of its pretransition output, Ukraine 41 percent, and Russia 59 percent.

THE TASKS OF REFORM

The transition to a market economy requires the central planning authority to relinquish its control over the economy while market forces become established. As less and less of the economy is directly controlled, there is greater scope for markets to grow, but unfortunately they do not magically appear when needed. Consequently, as the central plan's forced allocation of resources disappears, there is a period of uncertainty before clear market signals appear. The result is that many industries sit idle, especially those that are grossly inefficient or that produce goods no one wants. The machines and equipment may never be used, and the labor has no immediate place to go. In other words, there is a steep depression.

Negative growth lasts until enough of the transition process has been completed so that growth in the new economy outweighs the disappearance of the old. The time this takes depends on numerous factors, including the speed of reform, the degree of competency with which it is managed, and the ability of society to tolerate the uncertainty and change that result. The term *reform fatigue* has been coined to describe countries that have become exhausted from the loss of income and the associated uncertainty and that have slowed or partially reversed their transitions.

No matter what the culture or the history of a nation is, there are several tasks it must accomplish to become a stable market economy. First, the government must implement macroeconomic policies that will stabilize the economy. Second, it must liberalize the domestic market and external trade, and allow for the entry of new businesses. Third, it must clearly define property rights. Fourth, it must create the institutions it needs to support the market economy.

Economic Stabilization

In Chapter 15, on economic policy reform in Latin America, economic stabilization was defined as controlling inflation, budget deficits, and the external debt. The same definition applies to the transitional economies. Chapter 15 also singled out stabilization as one of the first steps in the reform process. In addition, Chapter 16, on the high-performance Asian economies, showed the important role of stable macroeconomies in the extraordinary growth performance of those nations. The same reasoning applies to the CEE countries, the NIS, and the other transitional economies.

In every transitional economy, the socialist legacy of overinvestment in heavy industry and state ownership placed a heavy burden on the central government's budget. The problem was compounded by the relative isolation of socialist economies from world trade and investment, as isolation severely limited competitive pressures and the incentive for efficiency improvements. One result is that a large part of the industrial sector in every country requires subsidies to stay afloat. One option was to let the enterprises collapse, but in some cases, this may cost more, since it leads to greater spending on social support programs for the people thrown out of work.

In most market economies, there are tax systems with fully developed legislative and administrative structures for levying, collecting, and enforcing the tax code. In addition, most countries have securities markets in which the government can borrow private savings to finance its expenditures. Initially, the transition economies had neither tax systems nor financial markets in which governments could borrow. There were essentially two options for financing their growing deficits: The transition economies could seek to borrow abroad, most likely from international agencies such as the IMF, or they could print money. Most countries did both, especially the printing of money. The predictable result was a rapid rise in inflation in the early years of the transition. In some economies, that was followed by restrictions on the issuance of new money, curbs on government expenditures, the development of effective systems of taxation, and ultimately, a market for government securities. In others, it has been politically difficult to limit subsidies to industry, and the government budget has continued to run up large deficits, with the corresponding inflationary effects. In the Russian case, for example, the use of money creation to finance government deficits led to a financial crisis in 1998 and the collapse of Russia's currency.

Liberalization

In general, *liberalization* refers to the replacement of administrative controls with market-based allocative mechanisms. This is equivalent to saying that prices and outputs are left up to markets rather than the central plan. In practice, it means that domestic prices are free from bureaucratic control and that individuals and enterprises are free to buy and sell and to import and export. Liberalization also requires that the barriers to new firms entering a market must be lifted. As long as entry is controlled, prices and outputs will not reflect the value of goods and services.

Lifting the barriers to entry has an international dimension because firms may find it profitable to import foreign goods or to export domestic ones. In effect, this means an end to the state's total control of foreign trade and the replacement of the state monopoly with an explicit trade regime. The introduction of foreign goods in the domestic market also serves to link foreign and domestic prices. Their linkage has an important impact on inflation control, since the presence of foreign goods limits the amount of price increase that domestic producers can ask for.

Liberalization refers not just to markets for goods and services but to input markets as well. Labor markets and financial markets are more difficult to create but important nonetheless. Labor markets require provisions for unemployment, pension systems, and a social safety net separate from employment. Financial markets require a host of supporting measures, from tax and security laws to development of financial service firms. These issues are beyond the scope of this chapter.

Defining Property Rights

Property rights refer to the legal rights to use an asset, to exclude others from its use, to collect income from it, and to dispose of it. Market economies specify property rights in great detail, since they are a fundamental underpinning of market relations. Well-functioning markets require a clear definition of property rights. When property rights are ambiguous or subject to political whim, there is a built-in reluctance to exchange (labor, goods, or financial assets), as one's economic interest is uncertain. Property rights that are not clearly specified are major obstacles to generating new economic activity.

Property rights in transition economies are usually unclear and often not recognized. Most assets were owned by the state, so there was little need to specify them. In order for markets to play a greater role, this obstacle must be overcome. Obviously, it requires a large number of supporting actions, such as the development of contract and commercial law, privatization of state-owned assets, and explicit recognition of the commercial rights of individuals and enterprises. In many countries, there is a scarcity of people with the knowledge and skills necessary to create the needed legal systems.

Institutional Development

The transition to market economies has proven to be more difficult and to take longer than most people initially anticipated. Naively, many people thought that once input and output prices were freed, markets would magically begin to allocate inputs to their highest-valued uses. The reason for the disappointment is that most people who thought the transition would be quick—a couple of years at most—failed to recognize that there are a large number of market-supporting institutions that must be created if markets are to work as desired. In the industrial market economies, these institutions have evolved over decades or even centuries. In the transition economies, they were expected to spring fully formed from economic texts.

Recall that institutions are the "rules of the game" that limit human behavior. They include legal systems, the definitions of property rights and entitlements, social support programs, enforcement mechanisms, and information systems. Until regulatory and enforcement institutions are created, transition economies lack a large number of goods and services that are important to markets. Some examples may be useful. Credit reports, business directories, market research, and actuarial data are important pieces of information in market economies. Efficient provision of these services requires clearly specified rules with respect to personal privacy, business practices, and intellectual property. Once an enterprise or an individual has the required business information, it is important to also have a clear idea of the rules governing fair trade, foreign commerce, environmental impacts, taxation, and so forth. If a party to an economic enterprise fails to deliver, there must be a credible set of enforcement procedures within which to seek redress. Along the way, economic agents must rely on a significant number of institutions. In the advanced industrial economies, we tend to take these things for granted, but in the transition economies, the institutions must be created. As long as the rules are unspecified or ambiguous, or appear to be subject to somebody's whim, it raises the level of risk and discourages economic initiative.

CASE STUDY

Should the Transition Be Fast or Slow?

No issue is more controversial or has generated more debate than the question about the speed of the reforms. Two metaphors are often repeated. The proponents of a fast, "big bang" transition are fond of a saying that has been attributed both to a Russian proverb and to Václav Havel, former president of the Czech Republic: "You can't cross a chasm in two leaps." The gradualist preference is summed up in the quote from Deng Xiao-ping, the late Chinese leader and initiator of its reforms: Reforms are like "feeling the stones to cross the river."

The proponents of slow reforms point to China. Chinese reforms were first proposed in late 1978 and got under way in 1979. Until the mid-1980s, they mainly affected the agricultural sector, but since China had such a large share of its population in rural areas, the positive effects on food output and rural incomes were significant. Primarily, the agricultural reforms let families and villages take individual responsibility for meeting their production quotas and allowed them to keep for consumption or for sale whatever amount they produced above the quota. Villages and communes were allowed to disband the collectivist system of production, and individual incentives began to rule the efforts and decision making of producers.

In the mid-1980s, China extended its market-based reforms to a number of **special economic zones (SEZs)**, economic and technology development zones (ETDZs), high-technology development zones (HTDZs), and other special developmental areas, mostly located along the coast. The rules of each type of zone varied, but in general, they allowed far more independent, profit-oriented, market-based decision making. The SEZs, in particular, were encouraged to experiment with new forms of economic organization and to develop joint ventures by attracting foreign investment. These areas began to account for the bulk of Chinese growth, exports, and foreign investment.

China's transition strategy is considered a gradualist strategy because it has not attempted to reform the entire economic structure in one fell swoop. Rather, it has used a "dual-track strategy," which localizes reforms to certain areas or sectors (e.g., agriculture) while maintaining traditional, central planning structures in the remainder of the economy. Slowly, subsidized prices were raised to the market level, and the mandatory production targets were reduced to a small share of the total output or zero. By the early to mid-1990s, more than 90 percent of retail prices and 80 to 90 percent of agricultural and intermediate goods prices were decontrolled. China has been much slower to privatize its state-owned sector, and state-owned enterprises continue to be a significant share of the economy.

Unlike the other transition economies, China's output never declined during its transition. (Vietnam's economy is the only other exception besides China.) Many proponents of the gradualist point of view argue that the phasing in of reforms relieves the pressure to instantaneously develop new institutions and economic relations. By adopting a dual-track approach, China has allowed the market economy to develop alongside the centrally planned economy and to gradually take over more and more of its functions as it matured. Perhaps even more importantly than avoiding an economic downturn, it gave the Chinese people time to adjust their expectations to a market-based system, reducing the shock of change.

The proponents of rapid reform view China as a special case. First, central planning was less extensive in China, with the result that its economy was less distorted and less overconcentrated on heavy industry. Second, and most importantly, China's economy is much more agricultural. In 1978, when China began its reforms, 71 percent of the labor force was in agriculture. The figure for Russia in 1990, at the beginning of its transition, was 13 percent. Most of the CEE countries are more like Russia than China. China's heavier concentration in agriculture gives it a large rural labor force that has very low productivity. If these workers leave the countryside, the resulting loss of output is very small, but the offsetting productivity gains from employment in urban and village industrial enterprises are significant. Hence, China can move labor from agriculture into the new enterprises, while the CEE countries and most of the NIS must take labor out of heavy industry to staff the new enterprises.

Proponents of the "big bang" approach to the transition cite Vietnam.

(*continues*)

Vietnam began its reforms gradually in 1986, then suddenly switched to an "all-at-once" strategy in 1989 when the gradualism failed to produce results. Agriculture and trade were liberalized; prices throughout the economy were decontrolled; foreign investment was encouraged; the fiscal deficit was cut along with subsidies to state enterprises; and new business enterprises were encouraged. The result was a jump in the growth rate. Like China, low-productivity agriculture employs the bulk of Vietnam's labor force.

Gradualists counter with the argument that rapid transitions lead to "reform fatigue." The psychological and social costs of the transition can be high: Workers are confronted with the possibility of getting laid off for the first time in their lives; fundamental necessities such as shelter, health care, and bread are suddenly expensive and unobtainable for some; and crime, alcoholism, and other social ills increase. The uncertainty of it all produces enormous stress and a high social cost. It is at least conceivable that the reforms might actually be undone in some cases.

Empirical measures seem to support the proponents of a fast transition. Although there is no final word as yet, there seems to be an emerging consensus that the more consistent and rapid the reform policies, the quicker the return to growth. Data from the World Bank (remember that data on the transition economies are suspect) show a smaller average decline in GDP and a quicker return to growth for the rapid reformers. For example, the Visegrad Four (Poland, Hungary, Czech Republic, Slovakia) in Table 17.4 have a shallower decline and a quicker return to growth than the other CEE countries and the NIS. They are among the most rapid and consistent reformers. Countries that reversed or partially reversed their reforms, or that applied them in a stop-and-go fashion (e.g., Russia), have had a harder time restoring growth.

During the first half of the 1990s, several studies seemed to show that radical stabilization policies (inflation control and reductions in government spending) were the causes of the depressions. More recent analysis points to three factors as having caused the depressions: (1) the disruption of traditional trading patterns; (2) the shift in internal demand away from the state-produced goods toward the as-yet-small consumer goods sector; and (3) disruptions in the supply of inputs that were brought on by the collapse of central planning and the absence of its replacement with market institutions. The debate continues.

It is increasingly clear, however, that whether governments adopt a "big bang" or a "go slow" approach, different tasks of transition require different time dimensions, and not all reforms can be done quickly. For example, while prices can be liberalized quickly, the building of new institutions such as legal structures or securities markets requires more time. In part, this stems from the fact that there are scarcities of people with the relevant skills and experience, and training takes time. Privatization of state-owned enterprises can be accomplished relatively fast when the assets are small, such as houses and retail shops. Large industrial enterprises have been more complex, however, and take longer to privatize successfully.

János Kornai is a Hungarian economist and one of the foremost experts on the transition process. Kornai recently observed

I am convinced that speed, while important, is not the primary measure of success. The transformation of society is not a horse race.

The transition from socialism to capitalism has to be an organic process. It is a curious amalgam of revolution and evolution, a trial-and-error process in which some old companies survive while others vanish, and new firms are tested before being accepted or rejected. Some developments are rapid, others slow. Some call for a one-stroke intervention, while many others come about through incremental changes.... The emphasis has to be on consolidation, stability, and sustainability, not on breaking speed records (Finance and Development, *September, 2000).*

OLD AND NEW TRADE RELATIONS

One of the most remarkable features of the transition has been the shift in trading patterns. The most dramatic changes have come in the CEE countries and in China. The shift in the CEE countries' trading pattern has affected both the direction of trade and, to a lesser degree, the composition of trade. When Soviet domination ended, the trade it had created disappeared, and new trade relations quickly developed. The shift in the commodity composition of CEE countries' trade illustrates the difficulties many countries have in trying to make their manufacturing sectors competitive in the world market.

The Council for Mutual Economic Assistance (CMEA)

After World War II, as relations between the Allies deteriorated and the Cold War began to heat up, the Soviet Union tried to create organizations of economic cooperation within its sphere of power. In trade, the result was the **Council for Mutual Economic Assistance (CMEA)**. In the West, it has also been known by the acronym **COMECON**. Originally, the CMEA included the CEE countries and the Soviet Union. The former Yugoslavia was never a member, nor was China. Vietnam and Cuba joined later.

The CMEA was a trade bloc in which none of the countries had currencies that were freely convertible. Partly for this reason, trade between the CMEA countries was a form of barter, known as **counter-trade**. Counter-trade took several forms, including pure barter. A more common form, known as **counter-purchase trade**, occurred when an exporting country was required to spend its earnings on imports of equal value from the country receiving its exports. In this way, trade was always balanced.

The pattern of commodity trade within the CMEA was for the CEE countries to export machinery and equipment to the Soviet Union in exchange for raw materials and oil. The goal of the CMEA was to organize the coordination of national economic plans. Trade flows were built into the plan and different countries and regions specialized in products for the whole bloc. The CMEA was only partially successful in coordinating economic plans. One major problem was the determination of prices for trade. Domestic prices were entirely artificial and conveyed no information about scarcity. Beginning in the mid-1970s, the CMEA attempted to set trade prices at world levels, but the application of an "adjustment factor" led to the valuation of most goods at levels far below world prices. Undervaluation became an especially acute problem for oil as world energy prices rose.

In 1991, the rules were changed to reflect the reform processes that had begun in many countries. Beginning in January of 1991, all countries were required to pay hard currency for imports, and prices were set at prevailing world market prices. Trade shrank dramatically, and the CMEA was formally ended later in 1991.

The collapse of trade had a negative impact on the CEE countries and the NIS. There are differing estimates of the decline in trade among the NIS (intra-NIS trade), but they all show a dramatic fall. Unlike the NIS, and after a few

---

FIGURE 17.2   Visegrad Four Exports to Industrial Nations

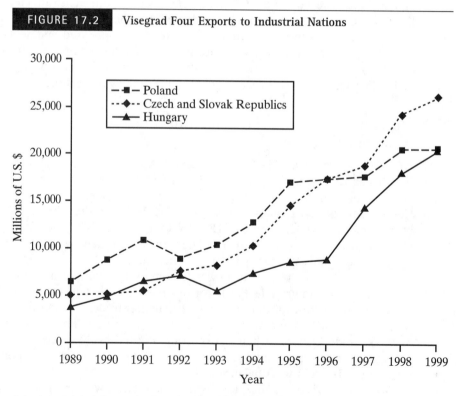

Exports to industrial countries have increased more than four times since 1990.

Source: International Monetary Fund, *Direction of Trade Statistics.*

years of falling trade, most of the CEE countries were able to offset the loss of CMEA trade with new markets in the high-income, industrial economies. Figures 17.2 and 17.3 for the Visegrad Four illustrate the decline of trade with the CMEA and the rise of trade with the advanced market economies. The patterns for the other CEE countries are essentially similar.

Figure 17.3 shows a rise in CMEA trade after 1992, although trade shrank again in 1998 and 1999. The CEE countries have signed a number of regional trade agreements, and it is possible that they can explain the reemergence of trade. These agreements are discussed later in the chapter.

Figures 17.2 and 17.3 are for exports alone, but imports show a similar pattern: a breakoff in trade with the former CMEA countries and a rise in imports from the industrial market economies. Import flows tend to be greater than the increase in exports, and many of the CEE countries have begun to run sizable trade deficits. Nevertheless, the remarkable increase in overall trade, both imports and exports, has raised living standards and is a strong indicator of their integration into the world trading system.

In addition to worries over deficits, the growth of trade has presented several additional challenges. Under the old system of CMEA trade, the CEE countries exported machinery and equipment to the Soviet Union in exchange for Soviet fuel and raw materials. This was particularly true for the Visegrad

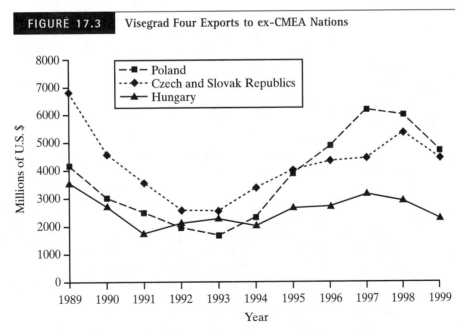

FIGURE 17.3 Visegrad Four Exports to ex-CMEA Nations

Exports to CMEA nations declined sharply in the early years of the transition.

Source: International Monetary Fund, *Direction of Trade Statistics.*

Four. Trade with Western Europe and North America was more balanced and included a larger share of basic metals, food and other agricultural products, chemicals, and apparel and textiles. The expansion of trade with the West required the CEE countries to expand their exports of these items since equipment and machinery could not be as easily redirected from the old Soviet Union to Western Europe because CEE countries' industrial plants were significantly less competitive, and there were serious questions about the quality of machinery they produced.

One problem with this composition of trade is that basic metals, food and agricultural products, chemicals, and textiles and apparel are in abundant supply around the world. They tend to be labor intensive (except chemicals), and they are relatively highly protected. For example, Western Europe's system of agricultural subsidies limits their market to outsiders (Chapter 14), and protection in the United States is highest in the textile and apparel industry (Chapter 7). Furthermore, steel and iron have had off-and-on quantitative restrictions in the United States and Europe over the last few decades. Nevertheless, most industrial economies have dropped the trade barriers they had that were aimed specifically at centrally planned economies.

Recent surveys of exporters in the CEE countries have shown that the greatest barriers to export are domestic problems inside the CEE countries. Undoubtedly, the same is true of the NIS economies as well. The main obstacles according to exporters are the lack of domestic infrastructure, particularly the poor condition of telecommunications and the inefficiency in border crossings. In addition, exporters cite their lack of information about Western markets and their own government's policies, particularly changes in domestic regulations that affect exports.

TRADE POLICY AND THE TRANSITION

Trade policy in centrally planned economies tends to be simple. Imports fill gaps in central plans, and exports are above-target outputs that are exchanged for imports. Furthermore, both inward and outward foreign investments are highly controlled and, consequently, there is a limited need for foreign currencies. In most cases, domestic currencies were not convertible, meaning that they could not be freely exchanged for foreign money. Hence, balance of payments problems, such as capital flight or prolonged periods of trade deficits, were not possible. The goal of trade and exchange rate policies is to help manage the transition through greater interaction between the domestic economy and the rest of the world. Greater integration with the world trading system is expected to bring the benefits of foreign trade and investment, including larger markets and the opportunity to specialize, technology transfer, foreign investment, and a wider variety of consumer goods. It can also bring currency instability and balance of payments crises if the policies are inappropriate or lack credibility.

Steps to Trade Liberalization

The earlier discussion of China's case illustrates most of the steps involved in the opening up of trade. One of the first is to end the state monopoly on trade. Centrally planned economies allow only a handful of designated state-owned enterprises to engage in trade. Rather than acting independently, these firms are required to be purchasing agents of the central plan. With the removal of the barriers to entry in the trade sector, private firms can enter and become trading firms. This is only the beginning, however, and market economies require several additional steps.

In order for firms to know which goods to trade, domestic prices must convey information about relative scarcities. Under central planning, prices are artificial and do not convey real information. Therefore, a key component of trade liberalization is the linking of domestic prices to world prices. That is, fluctuations in world prices that convey information of either greater scarcity or greater abundance should be felt inside the economy. In China's case, prices were liberalized on a gradual "dual-track" plan. Over time, the artificial prices set by the central plan and used for internal transactions were limited to a smaller and smaller share of the economy, while they were simultaneously raised gradually to world levels. In Poland's case, price controls were abolished on January 1, 1990, along with many other controls over the economy.

CASE STUDY

China's Economic Reform, Foreign Trade, and Investment

China's gradualist reforms began in late 1978. Its go-slow approach, "feeling the stones to cross the river," was not the result of an overarching strategy as much as it was a response to the political constraints of the Chinese system. Proponents of reform were not certain how to proceed, and at the same time, they feared a reaction from the hardline, conservative antireformers. Under the old system of foreign trade, there were twelve Foreign Trading Corporations (FTCs) that were attached to the various branches of government. All exports and imports went through these twelve FTCs. As in other centrally planned economies, trade was a balancing item in the central plan. Imports were sought only when domestic enterprises were incapable of filling the targets set by the plan. They were paid for out of surplus production that was also built into the plan. The FTCs were required to sell to the Bank of China the foreign exchange they earned on exports. Imports were paid for with foreign currency provided by the Bank according to the central plan. No considerations were given to China's comparative advantage.

A critical feature of China's reforms was the decentralization of this system, leading to the opening of trade and the reintegration of China into the world

(continues)

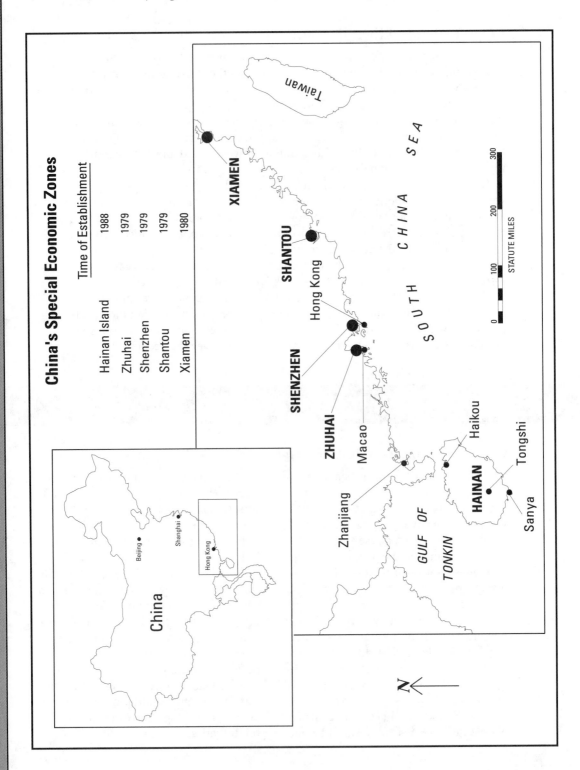

trading system. First, China allowed the creation of additional FTCs in the hands of national, provincial, and local authorities. In addition, large state-run enterprises were given the right to trade. Second, price reforms were implemented. Under the old system, the domestic price of imports was arbitrarily set equal to the price charged for similar goods produced domestically. Consequently, Chinese manufacturers were completely isolated from fluctuations in world prices. Gradually, larger and larger shares of import prices have been set equal to the world price (i.e., the dollar price converted to yuan at the official exchange rate). Tariffs and other barriers keep domestic prices from equaling the world price, but there is no longer a complete separation of the two. A third element of trade reform was the curtailment of mandatory targets for exports. These have been reduced in stages so that required exports were a decreasing share of total exports and then disappeared altogether. At the same time, subsidies for exports have fallen as China has tried to bring its trade policy into alignment with the requirements for membership in the World Trade Organization.

In order to limit the initial impact of reforms on the domestic economy and to prevent a political backlash, China turned to an innovative concept that they labeled *special economic zones* (SEZs). SEZs were modeled on the export-processing zones of some East Asian economies, but they went far beyond in scope. Export-processing zones are special regions in which manufacturers are given rebates on tariffs they pay for imported goods if the imports are incorporated into an export. SEZs go beyond this by giving provincial and local authorities a wide latitude to experiment with economic and trade policies that are radically different from national policies. In China's view, SEZs are "windows and bridges" to the outside world. Foreign enterprises "looking in" can see the Chinese market through the SEZ and are given incentives to build production facilities. Chinese firms "looking out" can learn about technology and world markets. Special incentives to form joint ventures and set up production facilities (tax breaks, relaxed rules on tariffs, licensing, foreign exchange conversion, and so forth) create a "bridge" between China and the rest of the world.

China created its first SEZ in 1979 and its fifth and final one in 1988. The enormous success of these regions in attracting foreign investment (particularly from Taiwan, Hong Kong, and the overseas Chinese business communities) and in generating exports and economic growth created a demonstration effect for the rest of China. Additional regions began to push for similar treatment, and the central government has responded with a number of new designations (eg., ETDZs, HTDZs). These areas are more restricted than the SEZs but still more open than the rest of the country. The special regions have been so successful that many now fear that China's next big problem is its growing regional inequality. Most of the regions that have received favorable treatment are coastal, so there is regional inequality in overall Chinese economic development. The coastal regions, for example, have absorbed the overwhelming majority of foreign direct investment received by China.

In the long run, the reforms must move beyond the coastal regions and

(continues)

they must also involve the many state-run enterprises that continue to function outside of the market economy. State ownership, often in the hands of the Red Army, gives firms political clout and has helped them avoid hard budget constraints. Large numbers of these firms operate at a loss even in good years, but their soft budgets ensure that they receive the financing necessary for continued operation. This places stress on the government's budget, however, and makes the macroeconomy less stable. The Chinese government has made it a priority to reform its state-owned sector, but there continues to be a significant degree of uncertainty about its political feasibility.

China's technique for economic opening has, so far, been unable to reform loss-making state-owned enterprises and has led to the creation of growing regional inequality. Neverthe-less, at the national level, its policies must be seen as a major success. Over the last decade, the national economy grew nearly 11 percent per year, while exports grew an even faster 13 percent. By 1998, China was the fourth largest exporter in the world and the second largest recipient of foreign investment. One of the main reasons for the phenomenal growth of China's exports is that the reforms have shifted production toward its comparative advantage: labor-intensive products and assembling and processing firms. In the past, comparative advantage was never considered. In the current system, firms must be more responsive to world prices and profitability. While barriers to imports remain a concern to industrial economies, China's "open door" policy for trade, investment, and technology transfers has successfully linked the economy to the world trading system.

A third step is to formulate an explicit trade policy. Decisions must be made about import substitution strategies, export promotion strategies, and key industries that might need protection. If protection is adopted, governments must decide which form of protection to use: tariffs, quotas, licensing, or some other nontariff barrier. Additional considerations are membership in the WTO and the constraints it imposes on trade policy. Fourth, nations must adopt rules governing foreign investment. For many countries—China, for example—foreign investment is an important supplement to domestic savings. Key considerations are how it will be encouraged, how it is affected by the other parts of the trade regime, and whether capital controls should be used to limit financial flows into and out of the country. Fifth, nations must formulate an exchange rate policy, including decisions about convertibility, both in timing and degree. Exchange rate policy has direct links to trade balances, foreign investment, domestic inflation, and macroeconomic stability. Consequently, it is one of the most important policy decisions.

Commercial policy and the exchange rate play such central roles in the transition process that each is discussed in greater detail in the following two sections.

Transitional Protection and Balance of Payments Problems

Trade policy reform in the CEE countries was fast and deep. Quantitative restrictions disappeared along with most other nontariff barriers (NTBs), and tariff rates were set at fairly low levels. Exceptions have occurred mainly in cases where there was a need to protect the current account from unsustainable import surges. All of the CEE countries in Table 17.1 are members of the WTO, except Macedonia, which is still negotiating the terms of its accession.

The NIS lag behind the CEE countries in the opening of their economies, and many still maintain extensive NTBs and relatively high tariffs. A couple, Turkmenistan and Uzbekistan, have adopted explicit import substitution (ISI) policies similar to those recently rejected by Latin America (see Chapter 15). To date, only Georgia and Armenia have joined the WTO, although most of the others are negotiating their membership. The opening of trade in many countries is complicated by the continuation of state ownership in many branches of economic activity. Infant industry arguments are widespread, but, as always, it is difficult to separate legitimate claims for protection from rent seeking by powerful political interests. As the transition moves into its second decade, it becomes more and more difficult to take the infant industry argument seriously.

In the early stages of the reform process, import surges are common. There are two reasons. First, consumers in centrally planned economies lived under regimes that channeled too many resources into heavy industry and capital goods production. Consequently, there is an excess demand for consumer goods that can be met only through imports. Second, the modernization of infrastructure and industry requires imported technology and capital goods. Increased imports raise social welfare because they provide consumers with access to the goods they desire and producers with the tools they need to become competitive. Nevertheless, import surges can also lead to large trade deficits and balance of payments problems that undermine the economy's overall macroeconomic stability.

Recall that trade deficits must be financed through capital inflows—borrowing, foreign investment, or aid. When capital inflows are insufficient to sustain the trade deficit (or, more accurately, the current account deficit), the economy enters a crisis. Mexico at the end of 1994 and Thailand in July of 1997 are examples. The usual solution to the crisis is an emergency loan from the IMF and a steep devaluation of the currency (expenditure switching).

The problem of trade balances in the early stages of the transition is compounded by three interrelated factors. One, most countries implemented stabilization policies to control inflation and reduce budget deficits. Stabilization policies often entailed a squeeze on bank credit that made it difficult for firms to gain the financing they needed to export. This fed into the second factor: the collapse of trade within the former CMEA countries. Stabilization reduced overall aggregate demand, including the demand for foreign goods, so that stabilization in, say, Poland, reduced the demand for goods produced in the Czech Republic. Third, the time lag in institutional development, especially regulatory and legal institutions, created a climate of uncertainty and made it difficult to export. As mentioned earlier, surveys of exporters have shown that the biggest obstacles to exports included the lack of information about regulatory and legal changes. Stabilization policies, the collapse of traditional export markets, and the institutional lag each limited the supply response of exporters and contributed to export growth that was weaker than the growth in imports. This was not true in every case, but even in cases such as Poland, the trade surpluses during the first year of radical reform (1991) proved to be fragile, and large deficits opened thereafter. One bright spot, however, was the rapid growth in trade with high-income industrial market economies, as illustrated in Figure 17.2.

Exchange Rate Regimes and Convertibility

Most transitional economies began their stabilization and transition programs with large devaluations. Devaluation was usually done to protect the balance of payments during the transition and is preferred to tariffs or quotas because it is neutral in its effects on specific industries while providing incentives to export. Furthermore, tariffs, quotas, and other quantitative restrictions, if used selectively, provide a protective wall around domestic producers that delays their adjustment to world prices and perpetuates the misallocation of resources that has plagued those economies.

For most countries, it has proven difficult to maintain a devalued exchange rate in real terms. Higher rates of inflation led to real appreciation and undid the initial effects of the nominal devaluation. Consequently, there was increased pressure to use tariffs and nontariff barriers to address the macroeconomic problem of trade balances and the microeconomic problems of competitiveness in specific sectors. For example, Czechoslovakia (prior to its breakup in 1993) and Hungary supplemented their devaluations with import surcharges, which are a uniform tax on all imports, and import quotas on consumer goods. These types of protection are generally viewed as temporary. Within the NIS and China, liberalization of imports has not progressed as far, and various quantitative restrictions are in place, including the very common requirement that importers obtain a government-issued license.

Along with devaluation of the official exchange rate, transitional economies were required to unify their exchange rates, choose an exchange rate regime, and agree on a timetable for convertibility. Most countries operated with multiple exchange rates prior to the transition. Official exchange rates generally overvalued the domestic currency. Under normal conditions, overvalued currencies lead to large trade deficits and balance of payments problems, but since trade and the purchase of foreign exchange was strictly controlled, this was not as great a problem under central planning.

In addition to the official exchange rate, the monetary authority usually set a rate for so-called swaps. The **swap rate** was the rate at which two monetary authorities settled claims on each other. For example, suppose that counter-trade between Romania and Bulgaria resulted in each country's monetary authority acquiring the currency of the other country. The rate of exchange between the two currencies is the swap rate, and it usually differed from the official exchange rate. Multiple exchange rates imply that there are potential differences in the domestic price of foreign goods, depending on which exchange rate is used. Consequently, unification of the official rate and the swap rate into one exchange rate is a necessary step in the elimination of resource misallocations caused by arbitrary and inaccurate prices.

There is considerable debate about the type of exchange rate regime appropriate for the transition process. Both flexible and fixed rates have been successful. Fixed rates require consistent fiscal and monetary policies in order to maintain the credibility of the exchange rate and to avoid inflation and real appreciation. Overly loose macroeconomic policy can feed the self-fulfilling perception of speculators that a devaluation is unavoidable. Floating rates, on the other hand, while appropriate in the long run, are less powerful than pegged rates or fixed rates as signals of the monetary authority's determination to end the period of inflation that is common in the initial stages of the transition. Given the liabilities of completely fixed and freely floating rates, pegged exchange rates have been adopted in a number of countries.

In addition to unifying the exchange rate and choosing an exchange rate regime, individuals and enterprises must be granted the right to freely purchase foreign currencies at the official, unified exchange rate. Generally, **currency convertibility** has been limited to transactions within the current account. Either unrestricted convertibility or current account convertibility is necessary for trade liberalization, and each is complementary to it. Importing is impossible if individuals and enterprises are not permitted to purchase foreign exchange, and, conversely, convertibility is meaningless if they are not allowed to import.

One complication that delayed the introduction of convertibility in many of the NIS and CEE countries was the presence of a **monetary overhang**, also called a *liquidity overhang*. Monetary overhang is another of the legacies of central planning and is simply the accumulation of a large amount of unspent domestic currency. It exists because consumers cannot find the goods and services they want to buy while the government has resorted to excess money creation to finance its deficits. Movement to a convertible exchange rate usually fails if the monetary overhang has not been disposed of or if government spending is excessive. The reasons are that convertibility requires a sufficient inflow of capital to finance the current account deficit, if there is one, and a sufficient stock of foreign exchange reserves to meet the expected day-to-day variation in demand. Either a large monetary overhang or excessive government spending can unravel the implementation of convertibility by raising the level of domestic demand for imports above the level that can be sustained out of existing reserves and inflows of new reserves.

Under the policy of current account convertibility, the purchase of foreign currencies is limited to transactions that fall into the current account, for example, exporting and importing, tourism, and remittances of investment and labor income. The point of limiting convertibility to this level is to avoid large and sudden flows of capital out of the country (capital flight) and the resulting macroeconomic instability. Current account convertibility does not necessarily discourage inward foreign investment as long as there are assurances of the right to repatriate profits.

The Links Between Trade Policy and Other Areas of Reform

International trade and the exchange rate have numerous effects on each of the areas of reform discussed in this chapter. Probably the most important effect is to act as an accurate source of information about prices and scarcities. The resource misallocations of centrally planned economies cannot be corrected without price signals that accurately convey information to producers and consumers. Accurate prices allow producers to correctly decide what to produce, as well as how to produce it, and help consumers decide how to allocate their income. Trade, therefore, helps in the task of industrial restructuring and furthers the process of modernization. Even in sectors where trade is relatively inconsequential or nonexistent, the potential to trade ensures that domestic prices are more or less equivalent to world prices after adjustments for transportation, tariffs, and so forth. More importantly, the potential to trade ensures that changes in the world economy that result in price changes are also felt in the domestic economy. Trade is the vehicle by which the isolation of national economies is broken.

While international trade's strongest effect may be to help with the process of liberalization, it also has important effects on institutional reform, such as privatization, legal reform, and regulatory changes. The freeing of trade from the government's monopoly is a first step in the creation of new businesses. The freedom to export and import encourages new entrepreneurs, and the competitive pressures of imports can be an added incentive for governments to sell off enterprises that demand large subsidies to stay afloat. In addition, trade puts pressure on the authorities to move forward with regulatory and legal reforms. Exporters and importers need to know the rules of the game in order for them to be willing to take risks. When trade opportunities exist, businesses lobby for more transparency and less arbitrariness in regulatory structures, putting pressure on governments to design new institutions.

INTEGRATION INTO THE WORLD TRADING SYSTEM

Many of the trade reforms of the NIS, CEE countries, and the Asian transitional economies are motivated by their desire to become full members of the world trading system. Access to foreign goods, foreign technology, and foreign investment are essential to raising their living standards. The most direct route to becoming fully integrated in the world economy is through full membership in the multilateral organizations, such as the GATT, the WTO, the IMF, and the World Bank. In addition, several countries have sought closer ties with their most important trading partners, for example Western Europe and the former members of the CMEA.

The WTO and the Transitional Economies

As of 2001, all but one of the countries in Table 17.1 (Macedonia) are members of the WTO. Czechoslovakia (the dissolved union of the present-day Czech and Slovak Republics) was one of the original twenty-three GATT members, while Poland, Romania, and Hungary joined between 1967 and 1973. Most of the other transitional economies have applied for membership and currently have "observer" status.

Membership is granted on a case-by-case basis after a period of consultations to determine the **accession protocol**. The accession protocol is a set of steps that new members must take in order to put their economic policies in compliance with the rules of the WTO. During the period of negotiation, the applicants have observer status that allows them to participate in most functions without having a voice in any decisions. It is a period of observation, in which the applicants learn the rules and procedures of the WTO.

In the past, it was possible for a country to join even if its economy was radically at odds with the spirit of GATT. For example, Poland, Romania, and Hungary joined while their economies were centrally planned. They were so far from market-based economies that many of the rules and privileges of GATT membership made no sense. For example, exports and imports discriminated heavily in favor of the CMEA area and were completely controlled by the central plan. Consequently, key values of the GATT, such as MFN status and national treatment, were impossible. In compensation, their accession protocols required them to make commitments to import from outside the CMEA and to submit to periodic reviews of their compliance. Furthermore, other members were permitted to discriminate against them on a selective basis. The experiment of admitting centrally planned economies under restrictive conditions is generally considered a failure, and countries will not be admitted in the future unless their trading systems are substantially market driven.

One of the key requirements for membership in the WTO is transparency in the trade regime. Recall that transparency means that all the rules and regulations relating to importing and exporting are readily available and clearly stated. In economies with large state-owned sectors or state-owned trading corporations, the lack of transparency can lead to favorable treatment for state-owned enterprises and discrimination against foreign and domestic firms that are privately owned. Another membership requirement is that countries adjust their economic policies to eliminate all export subsidies and most direct production subsidies. In some cases—China, for example—this is a complex issue, since accounting procedures and ownership structures differ greatly from the norms in industrial market economies. Determining whether a state-owned enterprise is subsidized is difficult and has various answers, depending on the procedure used to measure subsidies.

Compliance with GATT and WTO rules is more easily accomplished in the areas of tariffs and quotas. Nations must adopt an acceptable timetable for converting quantitative restriction to tariffs and "bind" their tariffs. Tariff binding refers to the fact that once the tariffs are set, they may be lowered, but they cannot be raised without first seeking an exception through the WTO.

The advantages of membership in the WTO are significant, which is why all but two (Tajikistan and Turkmenistan) transitional economies are in the WTO or have observer status. With membership comes the guarantee of MFN status and low tariff rates for exported products. (By 1995, most transitional economies had been granted MFN status by the industrial market economies. Membership in the WTO would guarantee that this will not be revoked.) Other benefits include the binding of tariffs, which reduces rent seeking by domestic producers, and access to the dispute settlement body of the WTO. In addition, it is a strong positive signal to the rest of the world that a country's trade policies are acceptable. In the long run, membership is valuable because it gives a nation a voice in the creation of future rules.

Integration with Western Europe

The natural trading partner for the CEE countries and the westernmost NIS is Western Europe. Proximity, culture, and history all point in this direction, and the rapid growth of trade with the industrial nations has already begun to take place. Formal integration is moving forward on several tracks. In 1992, the EU signed free-trade agreements with each of the Visegrad Four; in 1993, agreements were concluded with Romania and Bulgaria; and in 1994, with each of the Baltic Republics. The terms varied somewhat, but each called for an asymmetrical opening in which EU barriers to CEE countries' goods were lifted more quickly than CEE countries' barriers to EU goods. These agreements, sometimes referred to as the **Europe Agreements**, opened the door to eventual EU membership for the CEE countries participants.

Membership requirements for the transition economies are spelled out in a number of EU documents, and most of the CEE countries have applied. Albania and the war-torn areas of the former Yugoslavia are the exceptions. The EU has laid down three basic criteria. Transitional economies must be stable democracies that protect minorities and respect human rights, they must have functioning market economies, and they must be willing and able to implement EU policies. Following these criteria, in July 1997, the EU released a list of applicants that it expected to meet these criteria in the next few years. The list included Estonia, Poland, the Czech Republic, Hungary, and Slovenia. In June, 2001, the EU reaffirmed that this group would enter in 2004. In addition, a second group of applicants began negotiations for EU membership in 1999. The second group includes the two remaining Baltic Republics, Latvia and Lithuania, as well as the Slovak Republic, Romania, and Bulgaria. The timetable for concluding their accession agreements is open ended, but it is unlikely to happen before 2007.

Several problems stand in the way, some of which are in the EU and some of which are in the CEE countries. In the CEE countries, the most difficult problem is the creation of the institutions necessary to apply and enforce EU rules. Recall from Chapter 14 that the *acquis communautaire* is the body of legislation governing EU-wide health, safety, technical, environmental, and administrative rules. To date, many countries lack the administrative and judicial capacity to apply and enforce the laws.

In the EU, the most difficult problems are budgetary, including the current system of agricultural supports, along with regional development funds. EU enlargement requires a redirection of current spending, as well as changes in the formulae that determine spending, both of which are contentious. In addition, the EU is currently engaged in internal negotiations to change the number of votes each member state has in the various EU institutions. Small countries have relatively more votes than their populations warrant, and large countries would like to see this changed, but, naturally, the small countries do not want to give up some of their power.

Over the next two decades, it is not unreasonable to expect that the EU will take in more of the CEE countries and the western states of the NIS, if they care to join. The speed of membership will most likely be determined by the consistency and progress of reforms, both economic and political, in the countries seeking membership.

In addition to the Europe Agreements with individual CEE countries, the EU has signed a number of **Partnership and Cooperation Agreements (PCAs)** with individual NIS. These agreements have given the NIS access to the EU market within a GATT/ WTO framework. The PCAs usually begin with the granting of MFN status to the NIS. By adhering to the GATT/WTO framework, discrimination against third-party countries is avoided, and no obstacles are placed in the way of membership in the WTO.

Other Regional Agreements

Several other regional agreements have been concluded both within the group of transitional economies and between transitional economies and "outsiders." The CEE countries, for example, wanted to revive trade within the region, and also found it necessary to strike deals among their own members in order to compensate for the preferential opening they made to the EU. In 1992, the agreement creating the Central European Free Trade Area (CEFTA) was signed. CEFTA includes the Visegrad Four, along with Slovenia and Romania. In addition, the Baltics and Bulgaria are negotiating membership and will likely join in the near future. The CEFTA, along with a number of bilateral agreements within the CEE countries, are factors behind the partial recovery of trade among the former CMEA, as shown in Figure 17.3. A large number of additional agreements have been signed between pairs of CEE countries. Finally, Western European nations not in the EU (Switzerland and Norway) have signed free-trade agreements with most of the individual CEE countries.

Outside of the CEE countries, there were several strands of negotiations to revive trade through preferential trade agreements. One strand focused on the revival of trade within the NIS, while the other looked to develop new trade patterns, particularly between the Central Asian Republics and the Middle East. In 1992, Russia, Ukraine, and several other NIS signed bilateral agreements with each of the other NIS to continue state-to-state trade. The success of these agreements depended on the ability of governments to compel enterprises to deliver the goods that governments contracted to sell, which no state could do any longer. In essence, these agreements were an attempt to hold onto central planning in the area of international trade, while the rest of the economy was changing into a market economy.

All of these agreements failed, and trade within the NIS continued to collapse. Russia, which dominates the exports and imports of every NIS except Turkmenistan, turned to another strategy to revive trade. The strategy was patterned after the EU and took institutional form through the Treaty on Economic Union, signed in 1993 by eleven of the twelve NIS. There was no timetable and no implementation procedure, and there appears to be no practical effect on trade. A third Russian strategy was a customs union with Belarus and Kazakstan, signed in 1995. This agreement appears to have had little practical effect as well. The problem for each of these agreements is that they try to reestablish trade when the reforms are very incomplete. In particular, prices are still set at artificially low levels in many countries, and this necessitates controls on exports. If there were no controls, entrepreneurs could buy up subsidized goods at the artificially low prices and sell them outside the country at world prices, draining the government's budget and contributing to macroeconomic instability. The solution is to press forward with reforms, particularly the decontrol of prices. Furthermore, trade between republics in the former Soviet Union was overintegrated as Soviet policy had intentionally produced intermediate and final goods in different locations in order to increase economic interdependence between regions. It is unclear at this point in time what the right level of integration might be.

The desire to break out of the overintegrated NIS showed itself in another strand of trade agreements, this time within the Central Asian republics. This group of five republics recognized that rebuilding trade within the NIS was less desirable than the creation of new trade patterns that took advantage of their own proximity and cultural similarities, as well as their nearby neighbors in Iran, Pakistan, and Turkey. In 1991, all five Central Asian republics signed the Organization for Economic Cooperation with Iran, Pakistan, and Turkey. It does not appear to have had a practical effect as yet, but geography and a shared Islamic heritage will most likely lead to growth in trade between these two groups. In 1994, the Central Asian Economic Community was formed between Kazakstan, Uzbekistan, and the Kyrgyz Republic, and Tajikistan joined in 1998. As with many Latin American attempts with preferential trade agreements in the 1960s and 1970s, high levels of tariffs between member countries have hampered trade development, and attempts by Uzbekistan to dominate the regional arrangement have generated resistance in the other countries.

Finally, a number of the Central Asian republics have begun to develop trade relations with China. Given China's Islamic west and its more developed consumer goods sector, it is probably the best bet for future trade in the region.

THE IMPACT OF THE TRANSITION ECONOMIES ON THE WORLD ECONOMY

China is so large—1.3 billion people—that it is difficult to imagine a scenario in which it does not have a significant impact on the world trading system and world economy. When its rapid rate of economic growth over the last two decades is added to the mix, it seems certain that its impact is likely to be profound. Even if the rate of real GDP growth slows from its current level above 10 percent per year, as most analysts expect, the economy is still likely to become the largest in the world sometime in the middle of the twenty-first century. (If China grows twice as fast as the United States, its GDP surpasses the United States's sometime around 2040. It does not approach U.S. living standards, however, until around the year 2200—a long way into the future.)

In the short to medium run, the economic impacts of Chinese economic growth show up in two areas. First, China now attracts more foreign investment than any other developing nation. In fact, it is safe to say that while its own savings rate compares favorably with the high rates of the other rapidly growing Asian economies, China depends more on foreign savings. Foreign investment has been particularly central to the development of export goods and the introduction of modern technology. In addition to direct investment, however, China is a major borrower from the World Bank and the IMF, which it joined in 1980, and the Asian Development Bank. The fact that China has become a large consumer of foreign capital means that other developing countries are forced to settle for smaller shares of foreign savings.

The second area of international economic impacts stems from its development into a major trading nation. For example, China's successful export drive has emphasized goods for which it has a comparative advantage. These are labor-intensive goods and are similar to the ones produced in other developing economies, particularly in other parts of East Asia. In other words, China's rising share of world markets for labor-intensive products has come at the expense of Taiwan and Hong Kong. These countries rightly recognized that they would be challenged by China and other low-wage producers and have successfully moved into more complex forms of manufacturing and services. In future years, it is likely that there will be greater competition between China and other East Asian producers of labor-intensive goods, for example, Thailand, the Philippines, Indonesia, and so on. Ultimately, this is one reason why it is important that China's internal market be opened further. If China promotes exports but limits imports, trade conflicts will inevitably get worse. Given its size and its capacity to both produce and consume, it is difficult to imagine that the world's nations will grant market access without a reciprocal opening in China.

The CEE countries and NIS transitional economies, while smaller than China, could still have a significant impact on the world trading system. First, several of them are quite large in their own right. Poland, Romania, Russia, Ukraine, and Uzbekistan are each over 20 million people. Their markets are significantly large already, and their demand for capital and production of tradeable goods will undoubtedly grow over time. Several of the NIS are well endowed with natural resources, including minerals and petroleum. Several countries, both in the NIS and CEE, are rich agricultural regions, and incorporation of some of the production in those states into Western Europe through inclusion in the EU (Poland, for example) will require a significant alteration in European agricultural policies to deal with the potential surplus. While trade and petroleum reserves are important, probably the most significant impact from the end of the relative isolation of the CEE countries and NIS is the possibility for peaceful development free from the cloud of military conflict. While peace remains an elusive goal in some countries, the ending of the Cold War, the reduction in East–West tensions, and the development of market economies have made it possible to address economic issues without filtering them through the lens of East–West relations and Cold War strategy.

CASE STUDY

China's Accession to the WTO

China applied to join GATT in 1986, and has been negotiating the terms of its accession since 1988. Barring an unforeseen political blow-up, it is likely to join the WTO in 2001 or 2002, since negotiations for its membership were nearly complete by the start of 2001. Membership in the WTO is accomplished through a series of steps that are the same for all countries. First, a prospective member must provide a complete description of its trade and economic policies that may affect the WTO agreements. The WTO forms a working party to examine in detail the prospective member's policies and to work out the changes necessary for membership. Parallel to the WTO's work, the prospective member is required to negotiate bilaterally with individual countries. The purpose of these talks is to address the specific issues that are important to individual member countries and to design policy changes that address their needs, such as greater access or special safeguards against import surges. In the end, the provisions in each of the bilateral agreements are extended to all members, so that no particular country has preferential access, and the MFN principle is preserved. Membership is granted by a two-thirds vote. During 2000, China concluded its bilateral negotiations with the United States, and the U.S. Congress voted to accept the outcome of the negotiations. This clears the way for Chinese membership in the WTO, although China was still negotiating with a handful of other countries in 2001.

While China was outside the GATT and the WTO, the United States and other countries had no obligation to extend MFN status. United States–China trade relations were complicated by the **Jackson-Vanik Amendment** to the U.S. Trade Act of 1974, which applies special trade rules to communist countries. Normally, the United States grants MFN status to non-WTO nations, but the Jackson-Vanik Amendment is a piece of Cold War legislation targeting the former Soviet Union and other communist countries. The Amendment forbids the granting of MFN status to communist countries that prevent emigration of their citizens. Under the terms of the Amendment, the President can ask Congress for a waiver, which permits the granting of MFN status, but Congress must vote on the waiver. Since 1980, Congress has never denied the waiver request for China. Nevertheless, the annual review of the waiver request became a forum for Congressional criticism of China's trade and non-trade policies. Once China joins the WTO, the annual Jackson-Vanik review will end.

China is more than willing to let people emigrate, except for a few high-profile political dissidents who are in jail.

The reason there are not large flows of people out of China and into the United States is strict U.S. immigration policies. In practice, however, when Congress voted every year on whether to grant MFN status to China (which the U.S. relabeled **Permanent Normal Trade Relations**, or **PNTR**, for domestic political reasons), three sets of issues arose: trade issues, national security issues, and human rights issues. In effect, the U.S. debate over MFN has nothing to do with Chinese emigration policy, but is a device to try to influence China on these three issues. One school of thought argues that if the United States withholds MFN trading status, it provides an incentive for China to improve its human rights record. The counterargument is that meddling in internal Chinese affairs is more likely to harden Chinese policies, and that the authorities would interpret this as a challenge to national sovereignty that cannot be accommodated.

Security issues revolve around Chinese sales of missile technology and other strategic military hardware. Some U.S. politicians prefer not to trade with China at all since it has the world's largest army and, in their view, poses a threat to security and stability in East Asia. Again, the counterargument is that "constructive economic engagement," that is, trade and investment, is the best way to encourage a more cooperative and less aggressive China.

On the trade side, China's export growth has intensified the scrutiny it gets from the U.S. Congress. Over the last decade, Chinese exports grew about 13 percent per year, and manufactured exports grew even faster, as China has become the fourth largest exporter in the world. Although China does not run

(continues)

chronic, overall export surpluses, its bilateral surplus with the United States expanded from $12.7 billion in 1991 to $68.7 billion in 1999 (although if re-exports through Hong Kong are taken into account, it appears to be about $25 billion less).

U.S. imports from China are of two types. The first type consists of labor-intensive, low-tech goods such as textiles, apparel, sporting goods, and toys. The second type is also labor intensive but requires larger capital investment. These include radios, telephones, and large household appliances, all of which are standardized goods that have moved through the product cycle. Most of these goods are assembled in China from imported components, usually in factories that are partly foreign owned.

In their bilateral negotiations, both the United States and the European Union noted the lack of clarity in China's import rules. Virtually all areas of Chinese economic administration were cited as inconsistent, nontransparent, and subject to arbitrary decision making. For example, tariffs were levied in an unpredictable way so that some goods paid the published rate, others paid less than the published rate, and some paid a zero rate. Similarly, nontariff barriers such as quotas and import licenses were widespread and administered in an arbitrary and nontransparent manner. For example, there were complaints by both U.S. and EU businesses that China never made public a number of rules that limited its imports.

The United States–China bilateral negotiations for China's accession to the WTO focused on six areas. These were

- tariffs reductions
- elimination of nontariff barriers

(NTBs) such as import quotas and licensing requirements
- services industry access to the Chinese market, including distribution rights, banking, insurance, telecommunications, professional services (accountancy and legal), consulting, business and computer-related services, motion pictures, and sound recording services
- investment and intellectual property as embodied in existing WTO agreements
- safeguards for import surges and dumping cases and special rules for safeguarding the U.S. textile and clothing industries
- anti-competitive behavior by state-owned enterprises (SOEs)

Estimates vary for the impact of WTO membership on Chinese exports and imports. The United States International Trade Commission estimated that the U.S.–China bilateral agreement would result in a 12 percent increase in U.S. imports from China, and a 14 percent increase in exports. Since imports are currently larger than exports, the absolute value of the trade deficit with China could widen even though exports grow faster. Much of the growth in imports, however, is a displacement of imports from other markets, so the overall U.S. trade deficit is not expected to increase.

In general, the bilateral agreements appear to increase Chinese transparency and foreign access to their market. Although this will put competitive pressures on many Chinese firms, and especially the uncompetitive state-owned enterprises, it also makes them more competitive in the end. This seems to be a key element of China's strategy, as the relatively uncompetitive state-owned enterprise sector has been a drain on government budgets and yet difficult to reform. A more open market will put outside pressure on these firms and, most likely, speed up the reform process.

China's other interests in joining the WTO include the credibility it gains through its membership in the most important trade organization in the world and the access it will have to the dispute resolution mechanism of the WTO. This frees it from bilateral negotiations over disputes and provides a fairer mechanism for their resolution.

Summary

- Economic reform of the formerly socialist economies of Central and Eastern Europe (CEE) and the Newly Independent States (NIS) of the former Soviet Union requires four sets of actions. First, nations must stabilize their economies by reducing the rate of inflation and cutting the budget deficit. Second, they must liberalize markets by freeing prices to create a market for goods and services, create labor and financial markets, and end barriers to the entry of new businesses. Third, they must clearly define property rights. Fourth, they must develop the institutions, such as legal and regulatory rules, which support markets and without which they cannot function.

- There is a lack of consensus about the speed of the overall transition. Go-slow proponents point to China's gradualist reforms and argue that reforms must allow people time to adjust their ways of thinking and allow institutions time to develop. Go-fast proponents argue that speed is necessary to prevent backsliding and that once central planning ceases to work, a quick transition to markets is the only alternative.

- Before 1989, trade in the CEE countries and the NIS was regulated by the Council for Mutual Economic Assistance (CMEA), which coordinated the individual central plans of nations in the trade area. During the transition, trade between the CMEA countries broke down. The CEE nations were largely successful in creating new trade with Western Europe and other industrial areas, but the NIS remained much more isolated.

- China was not part of the CMEA, and it began its reforms a decade earlier, in 1978. China adopted a dual-track strategy of trying to develop a market-based economy alongside the traditional state-controlled economy. It relied heavily on Special Economic Zones it created in five coastal areas, along with a number of other targeted development areas, to act as "windows and bridges" to the outside world. One key reason for the success of China's gradualist approach is that it has a large supply of low-productivity agricultural labor that can be redirected to new enterprises in the special zones without losing output in the countryside.

- The steps that every country must take to liberalize its trade are (1) end the government monopoly on trade by permitting new enterprises to enter; (2) link domestic prices to world prices; (3) adopt an explicit trade policy concerning tariffs, quantitative restrictions, and so forth; (4) develop polices toward foreign investment; and (5) unify the exchange rate while choosing an exchange rate system.

- Many countries experience balance of payments problems when they open their economies. Usually, they devalue the exchange rate to keep the trade deficit from soaring. However, if inflation is high or if residual barriers to imports remain, the effect of a nominal devaluation can quickly disappear with real appreciation. Hence, some countries prefer to impose import controls even though it potentially puts them at odds with the requirements for WTO membership.

- Nearly every transition economy has applied to join the WTO. Most CEE countries are already in, while the NIS are negotiating the terms of their membership. In addition, most of the individual CEE countries have signed free-trade agreements with the EU, and five are slated to join by 2003 followed by a second wave of five some years later. Trade agreements in the NIS have been much less effective at restoring trade.

Vocabulary

accession protocol

Baltic Republics

central planning

Central and East European countries (CEE)

Council for Mutual Economic Assistance (CMEA or COMECON)

counter-trade

counter-purchase trade

currency convertibility

Europe Agreements

Jackson-Vanik Amendment

monetary overhang

Newly Independent States of the former Soviet Union (NIS)

Partnership and Cooperation Agreements (PCAs)

Permanent Normal Trade Relations (PNTR)

special economic zones (SEZs)

swap rate

transition economies

Visegrad Four

Study Questions

1. What is a centrally planned economy? What are the main ways in which it differs from a market-based economy?

2. What are the main tasks in the transition from central planning to a market-based economy?

3. Should countries go fast or slow in the transition? Describe the pros and cons of each.

4. How did the end of communism in Central and Eastern Europe, and in the Former Soviet Union, alter the trade patterns of the countries in those regions?

5. What steps must be taken by the formerly centrally planned economies in order to liberalize their trade?

6. Why does trade liberalization in the transition economies usually lead to import surges? What can countries do to avoid the balance of payments problems that these surges create?

7. How does trade reform in the transitional economies impact reforms in other parts of the economy?

8. What is currency convertibility? Why is it desirable?

9. What steps are being taken by the transitional economies to join the world trading system?

Suggested Readings

Chapter 1: The United States in a Global Economy

Bordo, Michael, Barry Eichengreen, and Douglas Irwin, "Is Globalization Today Really Different than Globalization a Hundred Years Ago?" National Bureau of Economic Research Working Paper. WP7195. June, 1999.

Dollar, David, and Aart Kraay, "Growth *Is* Good for the Poor." World Bank Working Paper, Development Research Group. March, 2000.

Edwards, Sebastian, "Openness, Trade Liberalization, and Growth in Developing Countries," *Journal of Economic Literature*. September, 1993.

Feenstra, Robert C., "Integration of Trade and Disintegration of Production in the Global Economy," *Journal of Economic Perspectives*. Fall, 1998.

Frankel, Jeffrey, and David Romer, "Does Trade Cause Growth?" *American Economic Review*. June, 1999.

Friedman, Thomas, *The Lexus and the Olive Tree: Understanding Globalization*. New York: Farrar, Straus, Giroux. 1999.

Irwin, Douglas, "The United States in a New Global Economy? A Century's Perspective." *The American Economic Review*. May, 1996.

Krugman, Paul, "The Localization of the World Economy," *Pop Internationalism*. Cambridge, MA: MIT Press. 1997.

Maddison, Angus, *The World Economy in the 20th Century*. Paris: OECD. 1989.

————, *Monitoring the World Economy, 1820–1992*. Paris: OECD. 1995.

Chapter 2: International Economic Institutions Since World War II

Bhagwati, Jagdish, "Preferential Trade Agreements: The Wrong Road," in *A Stream of Windows: Unsettling Reflections on Trade, Immigration, and Democracy*. Cambridge, MA: MIT Press. 1998.

Bhagwati, Jagdish, and Anne O. Krueger, *The Dangerous Drift to Preferential Trade Agreements*. Washington, DC: The American Enterprise Institute. 1995.

Fischer, Stanley, "On the Need for a Lender of Last Resort," *Journal of Economic Perspectives*. Fall, 1999.

Frankel, Jeffrey, *Regional Trading Blocs*. Washington DC: Institute for International Economics. 1997.

Helliwell, John, *How Much Do National Borders Matter?* Washington, DC: The Brookings Institute. 1998.

Kenen, Peter B., editor, *Managing the World Economy: Fifty Years after Bretton Woods*. Washington, DC: Institute for International Economics. 1994.

Kindleberger, Charles, *The International Economic Order: Essays on Financial Crisis and International Public Goods*. Hertfordshire, England: Harvester-Wheatsheaf. 1988.

Krueger, Anne O., "Are Preferential Trading Arrangements Trade-Liberalizing or Protectionist?" *Journal of Economic Perspectives*. Fall, 1999.

Robinson, Joan, "Beggar-My-Neighbour Remedies for Unemployment," in *Readings in the Theory of International Trade*, H.S. Ellis and L.M. Metzler, editors. Homewood, Ill: Irwin. 1950.

Schott, Jeffrey, *The Uruguay Round: An Assessment*. Washington, DC: Institute for International Economics. 1994.

————, editor, *The WTO after Seattle*. Washington, DC: Institute for International Economics. 2000.

Stiglitz, Joseph, "What I Learned at the World Economic Crisis," *The New Republic*. April 17, 2000. Available online at http://www.tnr.com/041700/stiglitz041700.html

Williamson, Jeffrey, "Globalization, Labor Markets, and Policy Backlash in the Past," *Journal of Economic Perspectives*. Fall, 1998.

Chapter 3: Comparative Advantage and the Gains from Trade

Balassa, Bela, "An Empirical Demonstration of Classical Comparative Cost Theory," *Review of Economics and Statistics*. August, 1963.

Blaug, Mark, "Adam Smith," and "David Ricardo," *Economic Theory in Retrospect*. New York: Cambridge University Press. 1978.

Chipman, J.S., "A Survey of the Theory of International Trade," *Econometrica*. July, 1965.

Greenaway, David, editor, *Current Issues in International Trade*. New York: St. Martin Press. 1996.

Irwin, Douglas, *Against the Tide: An Intellectual History of Free Trade*. Princeton, New Jersey: Princeton University Press. 1996.

King, Philip, editor, *International Economics and International Economic Policy: A Reader*. New York: McGraw-Hill. 1995

Krugman, Paul, "Competitiveness: A Dangerous Obsession," *Pop Internationalism*. Cambridge, MA: MIT Press. 1996.

————, "What Do Undergrads Need to Know about Trade?" *op. cit.*

MacDougall, G.D.A., "British and American Exports: A Study Suggested by the Theory of Comparative Costs," *Economic Journal*. December, 1951 (Part 1), and September, 1952 (Part 2).

Ricardo, David, *Principles of Political Economy and Taxation*. New York: Dutton. 1911.

Smith, Adam, *An Inquiry into the Nature and Causes of the Wealth of Nations*. New York: Modern Library. 1965.

Viner, Jacob, *Studies in the Theory of International Trade*. London: Allen & Unwin. 1964.

Chapter 4: Comparative Advantage and Factor Endowments

Baldwin, Robert, "The Effects of Trade and Foreign Direct Investment on Employment and Relative Wages," *OECD Economic Studies,* No. 23. Winter, 1994.

Belassa, Bela, "The Changing Pattern of Comparative Advantage in Manufactured Goods," *Review of Economics and Statistics*. May, 1979.

Cline, William, *Trade and Income Distribution*. Washington, DC: Institute for International Economics. 1997.

Deardorff, Alan, "Testing Trade Theories and Predicting Trade Flows," in *Handbook of International Economics*, Ronald Jones and Peter Kenen, editors. New York: North Holland. 1984.

Freeman, Richard, "Are Your Wages Set in Beijing?" *Journal of Economic Perspectives*. Summer, 1995.

Lawrence, Robert, *Can America Compete?* Washington, DC: The Brookings Institute. 1984.

Grant, Richard, Maria Papadakis, and J.David Richardson, "Global Trade Flows: Old Structures, New Issues, and Empirical Evidence," *Pacific Dynamism and the International Economic System*, C. Fred Bergsten and Marcus Noland, editors. Washington, DC: Institute for International Economics. 1993.

Heckscher, Eli, "The Effect of Foreign Trade on the Distribution of Income," in *Readings in the Theory of International Trade,* H.S. Ellis and L.M. Metzler, editors. Homewood, Ill: Irwin. 1950.

Samuelson, Paul, "The Gains from International Trade," *Canadian Journal of Economics and Political Science.* May, 1939. Reprinted in *Readings in the Theory of International Trade,* H.S. Ellis and L.M. Metzler, editors. Homewood, Ill: Irwin. 1950.

Stolper, Wolfgang, and Paul Samuelson, "Protection and Real Wages," *Review of Economic Studies.* November, 1941.

Vernon, Raymond, "International Investment and International Trade in the Product Cycle," *Quarterly Journal of Economics.* May, 1966.

Chapter 5: Beyond Comparative Advantage

Grubel, H.G., and P.G. Lloyd, *Intra-Industry Trade: The Theory and Measurement of International Trade in Differentiated Products.* New York: Halstead. 1975.

Hanson, Gordon, "Increasing Returns, Trade, and the Regional Structure of Wages," *The Economic Journal.* January, 1997.

Krugman, Paul, "Scale Economies, Product Differentiation and the Pattern of Trade." *American Economic Review.* 1980.

———, "Is Free Trade Passé?" *Journal of Economic Perspectives.* Fall, 1987.

———, "Increasing Returns and Economic Geography." *Journal of Political Economy.* June, 1991.

———, "What's New About the New Economic Geography." *Oxford Review of Economic Policy.* 1999.

Krugman, Paul, and Livas Elizondo, Raul, "Trade Policy and the Third World Metropolis," *Journal of Development Economics.* 1996.

Krueger, Ann O., "Government Failures in Development," *The Journal of Economic Perspectives.* Summer, 1990.

Norton, R.D., "Industrial Policy and American Renewal," *Journal of Economic Literature.* 24:1. 1986.

Ottaviano, Gianmarco, and Diego Puga, "Agglomeration in the Global Economy," *The World Economy.* 21:6, 707-731. 1998.

Ostroy, Sylvia, and Richard Nelson, *Techno-Nationalism and Techno-Globalism: Conflict and Cooperation.* Brookings Institute. 1995.

Tyson, Laura D'Andrea, *Who's Bashing Whom?: Trade Conflict in High-Technology Industries.* Institute for International Economics. 1992.

Venables, Anthony, "The Assessment: Trade and Location," *Oxford Review of Economic Policy.* 14:2, 1-6. 1999.

Chapter 6: The Theory of Tariffs and Quotas

Baldwin, Robert, "Trade Policies in Developing Countries," in *Handbook of International Economics*, Ronald Jones and Peter Kenen, editors. New York: North Holland. 1984.

Bhagwati, Jagdish, "On the Equivalence of Tariffs and Quotas," in *Trade, Growth, and the Balance of Payments: Essays in Honor of Gottfried Haberler,* Robert Baldwin, et. al., editors. Chicago: Rand McNally. 1965.

Bhagwati, Jagdish, and Marvin Kosters, *Trade and Wages: Leveling Wages Down?* Washington, DC: American Enterprise Institute. 1994.

Corden, W.M., *Trade Policy and Economic Welfare.* Oxford: Oxford University Press. 1974.

Crandall, Robert, *Regulating the Automobile*. Washington, DC: The Brookings Institute. 1986.

Destler, I.M., *American Trade Politics*. Washington, DC: Institute for International Economics. 1995.

Dornbusch, Rudiger, "The Case for Trade Liberalization in Developing Countries," *Journal of Economic Perspectives*. Winter 1992.

Hufbauer, Gary Clyde, Diane T. Berliner, and Kimberly Ann Elliott, *Trade Protection in the United States: 31 Case Studies*. Washington, DC: Institute for International Economics. 1986.

Martin, L., and L. Alan Winters, *The Uruguay Round*. Washington, DC: The World Bank. 1995.

Rodrik, Dani, "The Limits of Trade Policy Reform in Developing Countries," *Journal of Economic Perspectives*. Winter 1992.

Chapter 7: Commercial Policy

Bhagwati, Jagdish, *Protectionism*. Cambridge, MA: MIT Press. 1988.

Feenstra, Robert, "How Costly is Protectionism?" *Journal of Economic Perspectives*. Summer, 1992.

————, "Estimating the Effects of Trade Policy," in *Handbook of International Economics, Volume III*. Gene Grossman and Kenneth Rogoff, editors. Amsterdam: Elsevier. 1995.

Hufbauer, Gary Clyde, and Kimberly Ann Elliott. *Measuring the Costs of Protection in the United States*. Washington DC: Institute for International Economics. 1994.

Krugman, Paul, "Free Trade and Protection," in *The Age of Diminished Expectations*. Cambridge, Massachusetts: The MIT Press. 1994.

Laird, S, and A. Yeats, *Quantitative Methods for Trade-Barrier Analysis*. New York: NYU Press. 1990.

Rodrik, Dani, "Political Economy of Trade Policy," in *Handbook of International Economics, Volume III*. Gene Grossman and Kenneth Rogoff, editors. Amsterdam: Elsevier. 1995.

————, *Has Globalization Gone Too Far?* Washington DC: Institute for International Economics. 1997.

Salvatore, Dominick, *National Trade Policies*. New York: Greenwood Press. 1992.

Sazanami, Yoko, and Shujiro Urata, and Hiroki Kawai, *Measuring the Costs of Protection in Japan*. Washington DC: Institute for International Economics. 1995.

Shugang, Zhang, Zhang Yansheng, and Wan Zhongxin, *Measuring the Costs of Protection in China*. Washington DC: Institute for International Economics. 1998.

Chapter 8: International Trade and Labor and Environmental Standards

Bhagwati, Jagdish, "Trade Liberalisation and 'Fair Trade' Demands: Addressing the Environmental and Labour Standards Issues," in *A Steam of Windows: Unsettling Reflections on Trade, Immigration, and Democracy*. Cambridge, MA: MIT Press. 1998.

Bhagwati, Jagdish, and Robert Hudec, editors, *Fair Trade and Harmonization: Prerequisites for Free Trade?* 2 vols. Cambridge, MA: MIT Press. 1996.

Elliott, Kimberly Ann, "The ILO and Enforcement of Core Labor Standards." Washington, DC: Institute for International Economics. July, 2000. http://www.iie.com/NEWSLTR/news00-6.htm. Accessed 10-9-00.

Esty, Daniel C., *Greening the GATT: Trade, Environment and the Future*. Washington DC: Institute for International Economics. 1994.

Graham, Edward M., *Fighting the Wrong Enemy: Antiglobal Activists and Multinational Enterprises.* Washington, DC: Institute for International Economics. 2000.

Human Rights Watch, *Fingers to the Bone: United States Failure to Protect Child Farmworkers.* New York: Human Rights Watch. 2000.

International Labor Office, "Child Labour: Targeting the Intolerable." International Labor Conference. 86th Session. Geneva. 1996.

———, *Child Labour: What is to be Done?* ILO: Geneva. 1996.

Krugman, Paul, "What Should Trade Negotiators Negotiate About?" *Journal of Economic Literature.* V35n1: 113-120. March, 1997.

Siddiqi, Faraaz, and Harry Patrinos, "Child Labor: Issues, Causes, and Interventions," Human Capital Development and Operations Policy Working Paper 56. Washington, DC: World Bank. No date.

Stern, Robert, "Labor Standards and International Trade," *Integration and Trade.* 3:7/8. January-August, 1999.

Chapter 9: International Trade and the Balance of Payments

Dunning, J. H., *Multinational Enterprises and the Global Economy.* Reading, MA: Addison Wesley. 1993.

Graham, Edward, and Paul Krugman, *Foreign Direct Investment in the United States.* 3rd Edition. Washington, DC: Institute for International Economics. 1995.

Grunwald, Joseph, and Kenneth Flamm, *The Global Factory.* Washington, DC: Brookings Institute. 1985.

Heath, Jonathan, and Sidney Weintraub, *Mexico and the Sexenio Curse: Presidential Successions and Economic Crises in Modern Mexico.* Washington, DC: CSIS Press. 1999.

International Monetary Fund, *Balance of Payments Statistics.* Washington, DC: IMF. Quarterly.

Krugman, Paul, "The Trade Deficit," and "Global Finance," *The Age of Diminished Expectations.* 3rd Edition. Cambridge, MA: MIT Press. 1997.

Lancaster, Carol, *Transforming Foreign Aid: United States Assistance in the 21st Century.* Washington, DC: Institute for International Economics. 2000.

Mann, Catherine, *Is the US Trade Deficit Sustainable?* Washington, DC: Institute for International Economics. 1999.

Meade, James, *The Balance of Payments.* London: Oxford University Press. 1951.

United States Department of Commerce, *Survey of Current Business.* Washington, DC: Government Printing Office. Monthly.

Chapter 10: Exchange Rates and Exchange Rate Systems

Dominguez, Kathryn, and Jeffrey Frankel, *Does Foreign Exchange Intervention Work?* Washington, DC: Institute for International Economics. 1993.

Dornbusch, Rudiger, "Expectations and Exchange Rate Dynamics," *Journal of Political Economy.* December, 1976.

Eichengreen, Barry, editor, *The Gold Standard in Theory and History.* New York: Methuen, Inc. 1985.

———, "The Origins and Nature of the Great Slump Revisited," *Economic History Review.* May, 1992.

Feldstein, Martin, "Does One Market Require One Money?" *Policy Implications of Trade and Currency Zones.* A Symposium Sponsored by the Federal Reserve Bank of Kansas City. 1991.

Frankel, Jeffrey, and Andrew Rose, "Empirical Research on Nominal Exchange Rates," in *Handbook of International Economics, Volume III.* Gene Grossman and Kenneth Rogoff, editors. Amsterdam: Elsevier. 1995.

Jennings, Thomas, "Dollarization: A Primer." *International Economic Review*. USITC Publication 3298. April/May 2000. Available at http://www.usitc.gov/ier.htm.

Jennings, Thomas, and Souphala Chomsisengpet, "Nafta: An Optimum Currency Area? *International Economic Review*. USITC Publication 3331. June/July 2000. Available at http://www.usitc.gov/ier.htm.

Krugman, Paul, *Has the Adjustment Process Worked?* Washington, DC: Institute for International Economics. 1991.

Melvin, Michael, *International Money and Finance*. 5th edition. Reading, MA: Addison Wesley. 1996.

Rogoff, Kenneth, "The Purchasing Power Parity Puzzle," *Journal of Economic Literature*. June, 1996.

Chapter 11: An Introduction to Open Economy Macroeconomics

Friedman, Milton, and Anna Jacobson Schwarz, *The Great Contraction: 1929-1933*. Princeton, NJ: Princeton University Press.

Kindleberger, Charles, *The World in Depression: 1929-1933*. Berkeley, CA: University of California Press. 1986.

Krugman, Paul, *The Age of Diminished Expectations*. Cambridge, MA: MIT Press. 1997.

——, *Peddling Prosperity: Sense and Nonsense in the Age of Diminished Expectations*. New York: W.W.Norton. 1994.

Meulendyke, Ann-Marie, *U.S. Monetary Policy and Financial Markets*. New York: Federal Reserve Bank of New York. 1998.

Schulze, Charles, *Memos to the President: A Guide through Macroeconomics for the Busy Policymaker*. Washington, DC: Brookings. 1992.

Stein, Herbert, *The Fiscal Revolution in America: Policy in Pursuit of Reality*. Washington, DC: American Enterprise Institute. 1996.

——, *Presidential Economics: The Making of Economic Policy from Roosevelt to Clinton*. Washington, DC: American Enterprise Institute. 1994.

Temin, Peter, *Did Monetary Forces Cause the Great Depression?* New York: W.W.Norton. 1976.

——, *Lessons from the Great Depression*. Cambridge, MA: MIT Press. 1989.

Chapter 12: International Financial Crises

Eichengreen, Barry, *Globalizing Capital: A History of the International Monetary System*. Princeton, NJ: Princeton University Press. 1996.

——, *Toward a New International Financial Architecture: A Practical Post-Asia Agenda*. Washington, DC: Institute for International Economics. 1999.

Federal Reserve Bank of Kansas City, *Policy Implications of Trade and Currency Zones: A Symposium Sponsored by The Federal Reserve Bank of Kansas City*. Kansas City: FRB. 1991.

Goldstein, Morris, *The Asian Financial Crisis: Causes, Cures, and Systemic Implications*. Washington, DC: Institute for International Economics. 1998.

——, "IMF Structural Conditionality: How Much is Too Much?" Institute for International Economics, Working Paper 01-4. 2001.

——, "Strengthening the International Financial Architecture: Where Do We Stand?" Institute for International Economics, Working Paper 00-8. 2000.

Kindleberger, Charles, *Manias, Panics, and Crashes*. New York: John Wiley and Sons. 2000.

Krugman, Paul, *The Return of Depression Economics*. New York: W.W.Norton. 2000.

Mann, Catherine, "Market Mechanisms to Reduce the Need for IMF Bailouts." Institute for International Economics, Policy Brief, 99-4. 1999.

Mishkin, Frederic, "Global Financial Instability: Framework, Events, Issues." *The Journal of Economic Perspectives*. Fall, 1999.

Rogoff, Kenneth, "International Institutions for Reducing Global Financial Instability." *The Journal of Economic Perspectives*. Fall, 1999.

Woo, Wing Thye, Jeffrey D. Sachs, and Klaus Schwab, editors, *The Asian Financial Crisis: Lessons for a Resilient Asia*. Cambridge, MA: MIT Press. 2000.

Chapter 13: Economic Integration in North America

Freeman, Alan, and Patrick Grady, *Dividing the House: Planning for a Canada without Quebec*. Toronto: Harper Collins. 1995.

Hufbauer, Gary Clyde, and Jeffrey J. Schott, *North American Free Trade: Issues and Recommendations*. Washington DC: The Institute for International Economics. 1992.

—— and ——, *NAFTA: An Assessment*. Washington DC: The Institute for International Economics. 1993.

Hufbauer, Gary Clyde, Daniel C. Esty, Diana Orejas, Luis Rubio, and Jeffrey J. Schott, *NAFTA and the Environment: Seven Years Later*. Washington DC: The Institute for International Economics. 2000.

Lustig, Nora, *Mexico: The Remaking of an Economy*. Washington DC: The Brookings Institute. 1992.

Lustig, Nora, Barry Bosworth, and Robert Lawrence, editors, *North American Free Trade: Assessing the Impact*. Washington DC: The Brookings Institute. 1992.

Martin, Philip, *Trade and Migration: NAFTA and Agriculture*. Washington DC: The Institute for International Economics. 1993.

Pastor, Robert, *Integration with Mexico: Options for US Policy*. New York: Twentieth Century Fund Press. 1993.

US Congress, Office of Technology Assessment, *US–Mexico Trade: Pulling Together or Pulling Apart?* Washington DC: U.S. Government Printing Office. 1992.

Weintraub, Sidney, *NAFTA at Three: A Progress Report*. Washington, DC: CSIS. 1997.

Weintraub, Sidney, and Christopher Sands, editors, *The North American Auto Industry under NAFTA*. Washington, DC: CSIS Press. 1998.

Wonnacott, Paul, *The United States and Canada: The Quest for Free Trade*. Washington DC: Institute for International Economics. 1987.

United States Congress, House Committee on Ways and Means, Subcommittee on Trade, "President's Comprehensive review of the NAFTA : Hearing before the Subcommittee on Trade of the Committee on Ways and Means, House of Representatives, One Hundred Fifth Congress, first session, September 11, 1997." Washington, DC: U.S. G.P.O. 1999.

Chapter 14: The European Union: Many Markets into One

Bakker, A.F.P., *International Financial Institutions*, Chapters 9-11. New York: Longman. 1996.

Baun, Michael J., *A Wider Europe: The Process and Politics of European Union Enlargement*. Lanham, MD: Rowman & Littlefield Publishers. 2000.

Crouch, Colin, *After the Euro: Shaping Institutions for Governance in the Wake of European Monetary Union*. New York: Oxford University Press. 2000.

Dinan, Desmond, editor, *Encyclopedia of the European Union*. Boulder, CO: Lynne Rienner Publishers. 2000.

Eichengreen, Barry, and Jeffry Frieden, editors, *The Political Economy of European Monetary Unification*. Boulder, CO: Westview Press. 2001

Henning, C. Randall, "Cooperating with Europe's Monetary Union." Washington, DC: Institute for International Economics. 1997.

Henning, C. Randall, and Pier Carlo Padoan, *Transatlantic Perspectives on the Euro*. Pittsburgh, PA: European Community Studies Association; Washington, DC: Brookings Institution Press. 2000.

Hirtis, T., *European Community Economics*. New York: St. Martin's Press. 1991.

United States Congress, House Committee on Ways and Means, Subcommittee on Trade, "Trade relations with Europe and the new transatlantic economic partnership: hearing before the Subcommittee on Trade of the Committee on Ways and Means, House of Representatives, One Hundred Fifth Congress, second session, July 28, 1998." Washington, DC: U.S. G.P.O. 2000.

Wallace, William, *Regional Integration: The West European Experience*. Washington, DC: Brookings Institute. 1994.

Chapter 15: Trade and Policy Reform in Latin America

Barber, William J., "Chile con Chicago: A Review Essay." *Journal of Economic Literature*. December, 1995.

Birdsall, Nancy, Carol Graham, and Richard Sabot editors, *Beyond Tradeoffs: Market Reform and Equitable Growth in Latin America*. Washington, DC: Inter-American Development Bank and Brookings Institute Press. 1998.

Birdsall, Nancy, and Frederick Jaspersen, editors, *Pathways to Growth: Comparing East Asia and Latin America*. Washington, DC: Inter-American Development Bank. 1997.

Cardoso, Eliana, and Fishlow, Albert, "Latin American Economic Development: 1950-1980," *Journal of Latin American Studies*. Quincentenary Supplement, 1992.

Ffrench-Davis, Oscar Muñoz, and Ricardo Palma, "The Latin American Economies, 1950-1990," in *Latin America: Economy and Society since 1930*, Bethell, Leslie, editor. New York: Cambridge University Press. 1998.

Franko, Patrice, *The Puzzle of Latin American Development*. Lanham, MD: Rowman and Littlefield. 1999.

Sokoloff, Kenneth, and Stanley Engerman, "Institutions, Factor Endowments, and Paths of Development in the New World," *Journal of Economic Perspectives*. Summer, 2000.

Stallings, Barbara, and Wilson Peres, *Growth, Employment and Equity: The Impact of the Economic Reforms in Latin America and the Caribbean*. Washington, DC: The Brookings Institute and the United Nations. 2000.

Williamson, John, "What Should the World Bank Think about the Washington Consensus?" Institute for International Economics, unpublished paper. Available at: http://www.iie.com/papers/williamson0799.htm. 1999.

Chapter 16: Export-Oriented Growth in East Asia

Campos, Jose Edgardo, and Hilton L. Root, *The Key to the East Asian Miracle: Making Shared Growth Credible*. Washington, DC: The Brookings Institution. 1996.

Choi, Inbom, and Jeffrey J. Schott, *Free Trade between Korea and the United States?* Washington, DC: Institute for International Economics. 2001.

Collins, Susan, and Barry Bosworth, "Economic Growth in East Asia: Accumulation versus Assimilation," in *Brooking Papers on Economic Activity*, 2:1996.

Fishlow, Albert, Catherine Gwin, Stephan Haggard, Dani Rodrik, and Robert Wade, *Miracle or Design: Lessons from the East Asian Experience*. Washington, DC: Overseas Development Council. 1994.

Frankel, Jeffrey, "Is Japan Creating a Yen Bloc in East Asia and the Pacific," in *Regionalism and Rivalry: Japan and the United States in Pacific Asia*, Jeffrey Frankel and Miles Kahler, editors. Chicago: University of Chicago Press. 1993.

Posen, Adam, "Japan 2001—Decisive Action or Financial Panic?" Institute for International Economics Policy Brief 01-4. March, 2001.

Stiglitz, Joseph, "Some Lessons from the East Asian Miracle," in *The World Bank Research Observer.* August, 1996.

Westphal, Larry, "Industrial Policy in an Export-Propelled Economy: Lessons from South Korea's Experience," in *The Journal of Economic Perspectives.* Summer, 1990.

World Bank, *The East Asian Miracle: Economic Growth and Public Policy.* New York: Oxford University Press. 1993.

Chapter 17: Economic Integration in the Transition Economies

Drysdale, Peter, editor, *Achieving High Growth: Experience of Transitional Economies in East Asia.* New York: Oxford University Press. 2001.

Lardy, Nicholas, *China in the World Economy.* Washington, DC: Institute for International Economics. 1994.

Moran, Theodore, *Foreign Direct Investment and Development: The New Policy Agenda for Developing Countries and Economies in Transition.* Washington, DC: Institute for International Economics. 1999.

Naughton, Barry, "China's Emergence and Prospects as a Trading Nation," *Brookings Papers on Economic Activity:2.* 1996.

OECD, Centre for Co-operation with the Economies in Transition, *Integrating Emerging Market Economies into the International Trading System.* Paris: OECD. 1996.

OECD, Centre for Co-operation with the Economies in Transition, *Trade Policy and the Transition Process.* Paris: OECD. 1996.

Rosen, Daniel, *Behind the Open Door: Foreign Enterprises in the Chinese Marketplace.* Washington, DC: Institute for International Economics. 1999.

———, "China and the World Trade Organization: An Economic Balance Sheet." Institute for International Economics Policy Brief 99-6. June, 1999.

Woo, Wing Thye, Parker, Stephen, and Sachs, Jeffrey, *Economies in Transition: Comparing Asia and Eastern Europe.* Cambridge, MA: MIT Press. 1997.

World Bank, *From Plan to Market: World Development Report, 1996.* New York: Oxford University Press. 1996.

Glossary

Absolute productivity advantage, or absolute advantage. A country has an absolute productivity advantage in a good if its labor productivity is higher; that is, it is able to produce more output with an hour of labor than its trading partner can.

Acquis communautaire. The European Union rules governing technical standards, environmental and technical inspections, banking supervision, public accounts, statistical reporting requirements, and other elements of EU law.

Adjustable peg exchange rate. An exchange rate that is fixed in value to a foreign currency, but that is periodically devalued or revalued as conditions warrant.

Adjustment process. Usually refers to the changes in a country's current account that occur as a result of a fall in the value of its currency.

Agglomeration. Regional or local concentrations of firms that are in the same or a related industry.

Antidumping duty (ADD). A tariff levied on imports in retaliation for selling below fair value. *See also* Fair value.

Appreciation. An increase in a currency's value under a floating exchange rate system. *See also* Revaluation.

Asia Pacific Economic Cooperation (APEC). A grouping of Pacific-region nations founded in 1989 with the purpose of creating free trade among all its members by 2020. APEC includes the United States, Japan, and China, among others. APEC's goal is not a free trade area; instead, it is to get all members to commit to free trade and open investment flows as a part of their trade policies toward all nations.

Association of Southeast Asian Nations (ASEAN). Mainly a political and security grouping of seven nations in Southeast Asia. ASEAN was founded in 1967 and has recently begun a slow movement toward creating a free trade zone.

Austerity. Usually refers to the cuts in government spending and increases in taxes that are implemented to reduce or eliminate a government budget deficit.

Autarky. The complete absence of foreign trade; total self sufficiency of a national economy.

Auto Pact. The 1965 agreement between the United States and Canada that created free trade in the automotive sector.

Baltic Republics. Latvia, Lithuania, and Estonia.

Banking crisis. A common feature of international financial crises, a banking crisis occurs when banks fail and disintermediation spreads.

Basel Capital Accords. A set of recommended "best practices" designed to help countries avoid banking and financial crises. The accords emphasize the three areas of capital requirements, supervisory review, and information disclosure.

Brady Plan. A 1989 plan of U.S. Treasury Secretary Nicholas Brady intended to help indebted developing countries. Unlike previous plans, the Brady Plan offered a modest amount of debt relief.

Bretton Woods. A small town in New Hampshire that was, in July 1944, the site of talks establishing the international financial and economic order after World War II. The International Monetary Fund and the World Bank came out of the Bretton Woods conference.

Bretton Woods exchange rate system. The exchange rate system that emerged out of the Bretton Woods Conference at the end of World War II. See Smithsonian Agreement.

Canada–United States Free Trade Agreement (CUSTA). A 1989 free trade agreement between the United States and Canada, and a precursor of the NAFTA.

Capital account. A record of the transactions in highly specialized financial assets and liabilities between the residents of a nation and the rest of the world.

Capital controls. National controls on the inflow and/or outflow of funds.

Capital requirements. Requirements that owners of financial institutions invest a percentage of their own capital, so that any losses are personal losses to shareholders and other bank owners, as well as losses to depositors.

Centrally planned economy. An economy in which the fundamental decisions of what to produce, how to produce it, and who gets it are decided by a central planning authority.

Circular flow. A model of a country's macroeconomy showing the flow of demand across the top and the flow of income across the bottom.

Collective action clauses. A requirement that each international lender agrees to collective mediation between all lenders and the debtor in the event of an international crisis.

Common Agricultural Policy (CAP). The system of support payments and other forms of assistance that is the main agricultural program of the European Union.

Common external tariff. The policy of customs unions in which the members adopt the same tariffs towards nonmembers.

Common market. A regional trade agreement whose member nations allow the free movement of inputs as well as outputs, and who share a common external tariff towards nonmembers.

Comparative productivity advantage, or comparative advantage. A country has a comparative productivity advantage in a good, or simply a comparative advantage, if its opportunity costs of producing a good are lower than those of its trading partners.

Competition policy. A rule within a nation that governs economic competition. Competition policies are primarily concerned with the limits to cooperation between firms, especially mergers, acquisitions, collusion, and joint ventures.

Competitive advantage. The ability to sell a good at the lowest price. Competitive advantage may be the result of high productivity and a comparative advantage. Alternatively, it may be the result of government subsidies for inefficient industries.

Competitive devaluation. A devaluation or depreciation in a currency with the intent to gain export markets.

Conditionality. See IMF conditionality.

Consumer surplus. The difference between the value of a good to consumers and the price they have to pay. Graphically it is the area under the demand curve and above the price line. *See also* Producer surplus.

Contagion effects. The spread of a crisis from one country to another. This may happen through trade flows, through currency and exchange rate movements, or through a change in the perceptions of foreign investors.

Contractionary fiscal policy. Tax increases and/or cuts in government spending.

Contractionary monetary policy. A cut in the money supply and a rise in interest rates.

Convergence criteria. The five indicators of readiness to begin the single currency in the European Union. They are (1) stable exchange rates, (2) low inflation, (3) harmonization of long-term interest rates, (4) reduction of government deficits, and (5) reduction of government debt.

Core labor standards. Eight core labor rights developed and advocated by the ILO, and embodied in eight ILO conventions. They cover such areas as freedom from coercion, minimum work age, freedom to bargain collectively, and others.

Council of Ministers. The legislative body of the EU.

Council for Mutual Economic Assistance (CMEA). The economic assistance and trade agreement between the former Soviet Union and allied nations, primarily in Central and Eastern Europe.

Counter-trade, and counter-purchase trade. Counter-trade includes pure barter (goods exchanged directly for goods) and counter-purchase trade, in which the proceeds from sold exports must be spent on imports from the country receiving the exports. A third, less common, form is buy-back trade, in which the sale of exports is tied directly to the purchase of imports.

Countervailing duty (CVD). A tariff on imports that is levied in retaliation against foreign subsidies. *See also* Subsidy.

Court of Justice. The judicial body of the EU.

Covered interest arbitrage. Interest rate arbitrage that includes the signing of a forward currency contract to sell the foreign currency when the foreign assets mature. *See* Interest rate arbitrage.

Crawling peg exchange rate system. A system in which a country fixes its currency to another currency (or a basket of currencies) and makes regular periodic adjustments in the nominal exchange rate in order to offset or control movement in the real exchange rate.

Crony capitalism. A term used to describe conditions in which resources such as bank loans are allocated for political and personal reasons rather than on the basis of market-oriented criteria.

Currency board. A government board that strictly regulates the creation of new money.

Currency convertibility. A currency that is freely exchangeable for another.

Current account. A record of transactions in goods, services, investment income, and unilateral transfers between the residents of a country and the rest of the world.

Current account balance. The broadest measure of a nation's commerce with the rest of the world.

Customs union. An agreement among two or more member countries to engage in free trade with each other and to share a common external tariff toward nonmembers.

Data dissemination standards. The IMF's standards for reporting macroeconomic data.

Deadweight loss. A pure economic loss with no corresponding gains elsewhere in the economy. *See also* efficiency loss.

Debt crisis. Usually refers to the period between 1982 and 1989 when many indebted developing countries were unable to make interest or principal amortization payments.

Deep integration. The elimination or alteration of domestic policies when they have the unintended consequence of acting as trade barriers. Major examples include labor and environmental standards, investment regulations, the rules of fair competition between firms, and allowable forms of government support for private industry.

Deliberation councils. Quasi-legislative bodies that combine representatives from industry with government and that have the purpose of discussing government policy and private sector investment. Japan, Korea, Malaysia, Singapore, and Thailand use deliberation councils.

Delors Report. Named after the President of the European Commission during the 1980s, the report contained 300 steps that the EU needed to follow in order to become a common market. The report was adopted in 1987 and led to the creation of a common market under the Single European Act.

Demand pull factors in migration. Economic conditions in the receiving country that "pull" in migrants. *See also* Supply push and Network factors in migration.

Democratic deficit. The EU is described as having a democratic deficit because its only popularly elected body, the European Parliament, is not a real parliament and therefore lacks the authority to serve as a legislature.

Demographic transition. The shift from high birth rates and high death rates (characteristic of nearly all pre-industrial societies) to low birth and death rates, characteristic of high-income, industrial societies.

Depreciation. A decrease in a currency's value under a floating exchange rate system. *See also* Devaluation.

Derived demand. Demand for a good or service that is derived from the demand for something else. For example, the demand for labor is derived from the demand for goods and services.

Devaluation. Equivalent to a depreciation, except that it refers to a decline in a currency's value under a fixed exchange rate system. *See also* Depreciation.

Disintermediation. A failure on the part of the banking system that prevents savings from being channeled into investment.

Dollarization. The use of the dollar in place of a country's domestic currency. Technically, dollarization can refer to the use of any currency not the country's own.

Dumping. Selling in a foreign market at less than fair value. *See also* Fair value.

Economic nationalism. The modern form of mercantilism. Nationalists discount the benefits of trade. They share the fallacious belief that national welfare can be improved by limiting imports and curtailing foreign investment.

Economic populism. Economic policies emphasizing growth and redistribution that simultaneously de-emphasize (or deny the importance of) inflation risks, deficit finance, external constraints (i.e., trade and exchange rate issues), and the reactions of economic agents.

Economic restructuring. A movement from one point to another along a country's production possibilty curve.

Economic union. The most complete form of economic integration, these unions are common markets that also harmonize many standards while having the same or substantially similar fiscal and monetary policies. Economic unions may include a common currency.

Economies of scale. A decline in average cost while the number of units produced increases.

Effective rates of protection. Effective rates of protection take into account levels of protection on intermediate inputs as well as the nominal tariff levied on the protected good. Effective rates are measured as the percentage change in the domestic value added after tariffs on the intermediate and final goods are levied. *See also* Nominal rates of protection.

Efficiency loss. A form of deadweight loss that refers to the loss of income or output occuring when a nation produces a good at a cost higher than the world price.

Enterprise of the Americas Initiative (EAI). An initiative by the United States, launched in 1990 with the purpose of ensuring that the NAFTA did not harm the interests of Latin America outside Mexico. Its objectives were to ensure continued capital flows, relief from the debt crisis of the 1980s, support for trade liberalization, and incentives for continuing the economic and political reforms begun in the latter half of the 1980s. The EAI ultimately took a backseat to NAFTA, but can be seen as a precursor for the FTAA.

Escape clause relief. Temporary tariff protection granted to an industry that experiences a sudden and harmful surge in imports.

Euratom. An agreement concurrent with the Treaty of Rome that committed the six countries to the peaceful and cooperative development of nuclear energy.

Euro. The new currency of the EU. Formally introduced as the unit of account in 1999, the euro currency will appear in January, 2002.

Europe Agreements. Partial free trade agreements between the EU and countries in Central and Eastern Europe.

European Coal and Steel Community (ECSC). A 1951 agreement among the six countries that eventually formed the EEC, creating free trade in the coal and steel industries.

European Commission. The executive branch of the EU.

European Community (EC). The name for the EU prior to the signing of the Maastricht Treaty and the creation of the economic union.

European Council. The EU body consisting of the leaders of each country. The Council has taken some power from the Commission in recent years.

European currency unit (ECU). The artificial currency that was a weighted average of the currencies of the EU prior to the introduction of the euro.

European Economic Community (EEC). The original name for the community founded by the Treaty of Rome. The EEC eventually became the EC, and then the EU.

European monetary system (EMS). An exchange rate system started in 1979 linking the currencies of each of the members of the EC. The EMS was replaced in 1999 by the euro.

European Parliament. A quasi-advisory body of the EU. The Parliament is the only directly elected government body in the EU, and it has been moving toward becoming a true legislature.

European Union. Fifteen Western European nations that are an economic union.

Exchange rate. The price of one currency expressed in terms of a second currency. Exchange rates may be measured in real or nominal terms.

Exchange rate crisis. A collapse of a country's currency.

Exchange rate mechanism (ERM). The system adopted by the EC when it used the EMS. The ERM was a target zone exchange rate that allowed some limited flexibility in an otherwise fixed set of exchange rates.

Exchange rate risk. Risk occuring when an individual or firm holds assets that are denominated in a foreign currency. The risk is the potential for unexpected losses (or gains) due to unforeseen fluctuations in the value of the foreign currency.

Expansionary fiscal policy. Tax cuts and/or increases in government spending.

Expansionary monetary policy. Increases in the money supply and cuts in interest rates.

Expenditure reducing policies. Policies that reduce the overall level of domestic expenditure. These are appropriate for addressing the problem of a trade deficit, and they include cuts in government expenditures and/or increases in taxes.

Expenditure switching policies. Policies designed to shift the expenditures of domestic residents. If the problem is a trade deficit, they should shift toward domestically produced goods; if the problem is a trade surplus, they should shift toward foreign goods. Examples of these policies are changes in the exchange rate and changes in tariffs and quotas.

Export pessimism. The views of Argentine economist Raul Prebisch and his followers, who believed that the real prices received by Latin American countries for their exports would fall over time.

Export processing zone (EPZ). A geographical region in which firms are free from tariffs so long as they export the goods that are made from imports. Rules and regulations governing EPZs vary by country but all are aimed at encouraging exports, often through encouragement given to investment.

External economies of scale. Scale economies that are external to a firm, but internal to an industry. Consequently, all the firms in an industry experience declining average costs as the size of the industry increases.

Externality. A divergence between social and private returns.

Factor abundance, factor scarcity. These are relative terms since, strictly speaking, all factors are scarce. Relative factor abundance implies that an economy has more of a particular factor, in relation to some other factor, and by comparison to another economy. Relative factor scarcity implies the opposite.

Fair value. A standard for determining whether dumping is occurring or not. Generally, in the United States, fair value is the average price in the exporter's home market or the average price in third country markets. Definitions vary by country, making fair value a source of disagreement.

Financial account. The part of the balance of payments that tracks capital flows between a national economy and the rest of the world.

Fiscal policy. Policies related to government expenditures and taxation.

Fixed exchange rate. An exchange rate that is fixed and unchanging, relative to some other currency or group of currencies.

Flexible (floating) exchange rate. When supply and demand for foreign exchange determine the value of a nation's money.

Foreign direct investment (FDI). The purchase of physical assets such as real estate or businesses by a foreign company or individual. It can be outward (citizens or businesses in the home country purchase assets in a foreign country) or inward (foreigners purchase assets in the home country). *See also* Foreign portfolio investment.

Foreign exchange reserves. Assets held by the national monetary authority that can be used to settle international payments. Dollars, euros, yen, and monetary gold are all examples of reserves.

Foreign portfolio investment. The purchase of financial assets such as stocks, bonds, bank accounts, or related financial instruments. As with FDI, it can be inward or outward.

Forward exchange rate. The exchange rate in a forward market.

Forward markets. Markets in which buyers and sellers agree on a quantity and a price for a foreign exchange or other transaction that takes place in (usually) 30, 90, or 180 days from the time the contract is signed. *See also* Spot markets.

Four Tigers. Hong Kong, Korea, Singapore, and Taiwan. Their economic growth began shortly after Japan's post-World War II development. They are all classified by the World Bank as either high-income or upper-middle-income economies. (The Four Tigers are sometimes called the Four Dragons or the Little Dragons.) *See also* High-performance Asian economies and Newly industrializing economies.

Free riding. Occurs when a person lets others pay for a good or service, or lets them do the work when they know they cannot be excluded from consumption of the good or from the benefits of the work.

Free trade area. A preferential trade agreement in which countries permit the free movement of outputs (goods and services) across their borders as long as they originate in one of the member countries.

Free Trade Area of the Americas (FTAA). An agreement currently under negotiation to create a free trade area among thirty-four countries in the Western Hemisphere.

Gains from trade. The increase in consumption made possible by specialization and trade.

General Agreement on Tariffs and Trade (GATT). The main international agreement covering the rules of trade in most, but not all, goods. The GATT's origins can be traced back to negotiations that took place in 1946, after World War II.

General Agreement on Trade in Services (GATS). An attempt to extend the rules and principles of the GATT to trade in services. GATS was one of the outcomes of the Uruguay Round.

Gold standard. A fixed exchange rate system that uses gold as its standard of value.

Gross domestic product (GDP). The market value of all final goods and services produced in a year inside a nation.

Gross national product (GNP). The market value of all final goods and services produced by the residents of a nation, regardless of where the production takes place. GNP equals GDP minus income paid to foreigners plus income received from abroad.

Grubel-Lloyd index. A measure used to determine the importance of intraindustry trade.

Harmonization of standards. Occuring when two or more countries negotiate a common standard or policy. Harmonization can occur with respect to safety standards, technical standards, environmental standards, legal standards, certification, or with respect to any requirement set forth by national policies. *See also* Mutual recognition of standards.

Heckscher-Ohlin Theorem. A trade theorem that predicts the goods and services countries export and import. It states that countries will export goods with production requirements that intensively use its relatively abundant factors, and import goods requiring its relatively scarce factors.

Hedging. Eliminating risk. For example, exchange rate risk can be eliminated, or hedged, by signing a forward contract.

Heterodox stabilization policies. A heterodox stabilization policy is designed to cure inflation by (1) cutting government spending, (2) limiting the creation of new money, (3) reforming the tax system, and (4) freezing wages and prices. *See also* Orthodox stabilization policies.

High-performance Asian economies (HPAE). The eight high-performance Asian economies of Hong Kong, Japan, Indonesia, Korea, Malaysia, Singapore, Taiwan, and Thailand. *See also* Four Tigers and Newly industrializing economies.

IMF conditionality. The changes in economic policy that borrowing nations are required to make in order to receive International Monetary Fund loans. The changes usually involve policies that reduce or eliminate a severe trade deficit and/or a central government budget deficit. In practical terms, they involve reduced expenditures by the government and by the private sector (to reduce imports) and increased taxes. *See also* International Monetary Fund.

Import substitution industrialization (ISI). An economic development strategy that emphasizes the domestic production of goods that substitute for imports. ISI policies decrease both imports and exports.

Index of openness. A measure of the importance of trade to a national economy, consisting of exports plus imports divided by GDP.

Industrial policy. A policy designed to create new industries or to provide support for existing ones.

Infant industry argument. An argument for tariff protection based on the belief that a particular industry is incapable of competing at present but that it will soon grow into a mature and competitive industry that no longer needs protection.

Informal economy. The part of a national or local economy that is unmeasured, untaxed, and unregulated.

Information disclosure. One of the three areas emphasized by the Basel Accord in its list of recommended practices, information disclosure is intended to encourage market discipline by requiring banks to disclose all the relevant information that lenders, investors, and depositors need to understand the full scope of a particular bank's operations.

Institution. A set of rules of behavior. Institutions set limits, or constraints, on social, political, and economic interaction. An institution may be informal (e.g., manners, taboos, customs) or formal (e.g., constitutions or laws).

Interest parity. The notion that the interest rate differential between two countries is approximately equal to the percentage difference between the forward and spot exchange rates.

Interest rate arbitrage. The transfer of funds from one financial asset and currency to another to take advantage of higher interest rates. *See also* Covered interest arbitrage.

Intermediate inputs. Parts and materials that are incorporated into a final good such as a consumer good or investment good.

Intermediation. The role of banks as institutions that concentrate savings from many sources and lend the money to investors.

Internal economies of scale. The idea that an individual firm experiences a decline in its average cost of production as it increases the number of units produced.

International financial architecture. The complex of institutions, international organizations, governments, and private economic agents that together make up the international financial system.

International investment position. The value of all foreign assets owned by a nation's residents, businesses, and government, minus the value of all domestic assets owned by foreigners.

International Labor Organization (ILO). The international organization charged with responsibilities for researching international labor conditions and providing technical assistance in the area of labor conditions and standards.

International Monetary Fund (IMF). One of the original Bretton Woods institutions, IMF responsibilities include helping member countries that suffer from instability or problems in their balance of payments. It also provides technical expertise in international financial relations.

Intra-firm trade. International trade between two or more divisions of the same company which are located in different countries.

Intraindustry trade. Exports and imports of the same category of goods and/or services.

Investment income. A subcomponent of the current account; income received or paid abroad.

J-curve. A currency depreciation often results in a worsening of the trade deficit in the short run and an improvement in the long run.

Keiretsu. Groups of Japanese firms tied together into family-like relationships through cross-ownership, business relations, and interlocking directorates.

Labor argument. The argument for trade protection based on the false belief that high-wage countries will be harmed by imports from low-wage countries.

Labor productivity. The amount of output per unit of labor input.

Large country case for a tariff. A country that purchases a significant share of the world's output of a particular good may improve its welfare by imposing a tariff that causes import prices to fall.

Lender of last resort. In international economics, a place where nations can borrow after all sources of commercial lending have dried up. Today, the IMF (International Monetary Fund) fills this role.

Lost Decade. The period of recession in Latin America brought on by the region-wide debt crisis beginning in August 1982. There is no official date ending the Lost Decade, but 1989 is a useful benchmark, since it coincides with a new strategy for handling the crisis.

Low-, lower-middle, upper-middle, and high-income countries. Categories used by the World Bank to classify countries by their level of per capita income. The borders between categories change over time. Currently, low income is less than $755 per year, lower middle is $756 to $2995, upper middle is $2996 to $9255, and upper income is above $9255 per person per year.

Maastricht Treaty. Also sometimes called the Treaty on Economic and Monetary Union. Ratified in 1991 by the members of the European Union, its most visible provision includes the single currency program that began in 1999. It will create an economic union among the members of the European Union.

Magnification effect. The idea that a rise or decline in goods prices has a larger effect in the same direction on the income of the factor used intensively in its production.

Managed float. A floating exchange rate in which the monetary authority occasionally intervenes to cause a rise or fall in the value of the country's currency.

Maquiladora. Mexican manufacturing firms, mostly along the U.S.–Mexico border that received special tax breaks until 2001.

Market failure. A situation in which markets do not produce the most beneficial economic outcome. Market failure has numerous causes, including externalities and monopolistic or oligopolistic market structures.

Mercantilism. The economic system that arose in Western Europe in the 1500s, during the period in which modern nation states were emerging from feudal monarchies. Mercantilism has been called the politics and economics of nation building because it stressed the need for nations to run trade surpluses to obtain revenues for armies and national construction projects. Mercantilists favored granting monopoly rights to individuals and companies, they shunned competition, and they viewed exports as positive and imports as negative. Today, the term *mercantilism* is sometimes used to describe the policies of nations that promote their exports while keeping their markets relatively closed to imports.

Merchandise trade balance. Exports of goods minus imports of goods.

MERCOSÚR. The Mercado Común del Sur, or Common Market of the South, is the largest regional trade grouping in South America. It includes four countries: Brazil, Argentina, Uruguay, and Paraguay.

Monetary overhang. The large stock of unspent domestic money that was present in most transitional economies. (China is a major exception to this generalization.) Monetary overhang existed because consumers could not find the goods and services they wanted to buy, because consumer goods prices were kept below equilibrium levels, and because too much money was created.

Monetary policy. National macroeconomic policies related to the money supply and interest.

Monopolistic competition. Competition between differentiated products, combining elements of perfect competition and monopoly.

Moral hazard. A financial incentive to withhold information, take on excessive risk, or behave in manner that generates significant social costs.

Most favored nation (MFN). The idea that every member of WTO (World Trade Organization) is required to treat each of its trading partners as well as it treats its most favored trading partner. In effect, MFN prohibits one country from discriminating against another.

Multilateralism. An approach to trade and investment issues which involves large numbers of countries. Multilateralism stands for the belief that market openings should benefit all nations. Multilateral institutions include the World Trade Organization, the World Bank, and the International Monetary Fund.

Multiplier effect. The macroeconomic concept that a change in spending has an impact on national product that is ultimately larger than the original spending change.

Mutual recognition. An alternative to the harmonization of standards. Under a mutual recognition system, countries keep different standards while agreeing to recognize and accept each other's standards within their national jurisdictions.

National income and product accounts. A nation's set of accounts measuring macroeconomic activity.

National treatment. The idea that foreign firms operating inside a nation should not be treated any differently than domestic firms.

Neoliberalism. Market fundamentalism that became common throughout Latin America in the late 1980s and 1990s.

Newly industrializing economies (NIE). The most recent wave of rapidly growing and industrializing developing nations. There are a number of these economies in Latin America (e.g., Argentina, Brazil, Chile, and Mexico) as well as in East Asia (among the HPAE, Indonesia, Malaysia, and Thailand fall into this category).

Nominal exchange rate. The price of a unit of foreign exchange. *See also* Real exchange rate.

Nominal rates of protection. The amount of a tariff (or the tariff equivalent of a quota) expressed as a percentage of the good's price. *See also* Effective rates of protection.

Nominal tariff. The tax on imports of a particular good, expressed in either percentages or absolute amounts. See effective rate of protection.

Nondiminishable. A good or service that is not reduced by consumption. For example, listening to a radio broadcast does not reduce its availability to others.

Nondiscrimination. The notion that national laws should not treat foreign firms differently than domestic firms.

Nonexcludable. When people who do not pay for a good or service cannot be excluded from its consumption. National defense is an example.

Nonrival. See nondiminishable.

Nontariff barriers (NTBs). Any trade barrier that is not a tariff. Most important are quotas, which are physical limits on the quantity of permitted imports. Nontariff barriers include red tape and regulations, rules requiring governments to purchase from domestic producers, and a large number of other practices that indirectly limit imports.

Nontransparent. Not easily interpreted or understood. For example, some countries use red tape and bureaucratic rules to block imports.

North American Agreement on Environmental Cooperation. The environmental "side agreement" to the NAFTA.

North American Agreement on Labor Cooperation. The labor "side agreement" to the NAFTA.

North American Development Bank (NADBank). A financial institution responsible for raising private funds and providing its financing for development projects along the U.S.-Mexico border.

North American Free Trade Agreement (NAFTA). The free trade area formed by Canada, Mexico, and the United States. NAFTA began in 1994.

Official reserve assets. Assets held by governments for use in settling international debts. Official resource assets consist primarily of key foreign currencies.

Oligopoly. A market with so few producers that each firm can influence the market price.

Open market operations. The main tool of monetary policy, consisting of the buying and selling of government debt (bills, notes and bonds) in order to influence bank reserves and interest rates.

Openness. See index of openness.

Opportunity cost. The value of the best forgone alternative to the activity actually chosen.

Optimal currency area. A region of fixed exchange rates or a single currency. A currency area is optimal in the sense that it is precisely the right geographical size to capture the benefits of fixed rates without incurring the costs.

Orthodox stabilization policies. A orthodox stabilization policy is designed to cure inflation by (1) cutting government spending, (2) limiting the creation of new money, and (3) reforming the tax system. *See also* Heterodox stabilization policies.

Partial trade agreement. An agreement that covers only some goods and/or services and is less than a free trade agreement.

Pegged exchange rate. A form of fixed exchange rate; see crawling peg.

Permanent normal trade relations (PNTR). The U.S. term for most favored nation (MFN).

Pollution havens. Countries that compete for investment by advertising their low environmental standards.

Price line. The rate at which one good trades for another in a two good model; the slope of the price line is the relative price. The same as a trade line.

Private returns. The value of all private benefits minus all private costs, properly adjusted to take into account that some costs and benefits are in the future and must be discounted to arrive at their value in today's dollars. *See also* Social returns.

Producer surplus. The difference between the minimum price a producer would accept to produce a given quantity and the price they actually receive. Graphically it is the area under the price line and above the supply curve. *See also* Consumer surplus.

Product cycle. The idea that manufactured goods go through a cycle of heavy research and development requiring experimentation in the product and the manufacturing process, followed by stabilization of design and production, and a final stage of complete standardization.

Product differentiation. Two products that serve similar purposes but that are different in one or more dimension. Most consumer goods are differentiated products.

Production possibilities curve (PPC). This curve shows the maximum amount of output possible, given the available supply of inputs. It also shows the tradeoff that a country must make if it wishes to increase the output of one of its goods.

Public goods. Goods that share two characteristics: nonexcludability and nonrivalry or nondiminishability. If they are excludable but nondiminishable goods, they are sometimes called collective goods.

Purchasing power parity. An adjustment to exchange rates or incomes that is designed to keep constant the real purchasing power of money when converted from one currency to another.

Quota. A numerical limit on the volume of imports.

Quota rents. The excess profits earned by foreign producers (and sometimes domestic distributors of foreign products) in an export market. Quota rents occur whenever a quota causes a price increase in the market receiving the exports.

Race to the bottom. Downward pressure on labor, environmental, or other standards, that comes about through price competition.

Real exchange rate. The inflation-adjusted nominal rate. The real rate is useful for examining changes in the relative purchasing power of foreign currencies over time.

Regional trade agreement (RTA). Agreements between two or more countries, each offering the others preferential access to their markets. RTAs provide varying degrees of access and variable amounts of deep integration.

Relative price. The price of one good in terms of another good. It is similar to a money price, which expresses the price in terms of dollars and cents; but relative price is in terms of the quantity of the first good that must be given up in order to buy a second good.

Rent seeking. Any activity by firms, individuals, or special interests that is designed to alter the distribution of income to their favor. Political lobbying, legal challenges, and bribery are common forms of rent-seeking behaviors, which use resources (labor and capital) but do not add to national output. For this reason, rent seeking is a net loss to the nation.

Retained earnings. Profits that a firm keeps as a source of financial capital for future investment.

Revaluation. An increase in the value of a currency under a fixed exchange rate system. *See also* Appreciation.

Section 301. A clause in U.S. trade legislation that requires the United States Trade Representative to take action against any nation that persistently engages in what the U.S. considers unfair trade practices. *See also* Super 301.

Separate standards. Environmental, labor, or other standards that are unique to each country.

Shallow integration. The elimination or reduction of tariffs, quotas, and other border-related barriers (such as customs procedures) that restrict the flow of goods across borders. *See also* Deep integration.

Single European Act (SEA). The act that created a common market among the members of the European Community. The SEA was implemented in 1993.

Smithsonian Agreement. A 1971 agreement by the major industrialized countries to devalue the gold content of the dollar. This was the beginning of the end for the Bretton Woods exchange rate system.

Social networks. Members of a migrant's family or village that provide support in the migrant's new location.

Social returns. Social returns include private returns, but they add costs and benefits to the elements of society that are not taken into consideration in the private returns. For example, a firm that generates pollution that it does not have to clean up imposes costs on society, which causes social returns to be lower than private returns.

Special drawing right (SDR). The unit of account and artificial currency used by the International Monetary Fund (IMF). The SDR is a weighted average of several currencies and serves an a official reserve asset.

Special economic zone (SEZ). A special region in China, in which local officials are encouraged to experiment with new economic policies. SEZs are designed to encourage foreign investment and exports.

Specific factors model. A trade model that allows for mobile and immobile factors of production.

Spot markets. Market transactions that are concluded at the same time the price is agreed upon. In the currency spot market there is usually a day's lag before the currency is actually delivered. *See also* Forward markets.

Stabilization polices. National macroeconomic policies designed to cure inflation and reduce a government deficit. Stabilization policies are usually a first step in compliance with IMF conditionality during a macroeconomic crisis. *See also* Structural adjustment policies, Orthodox stabilization, and Heterodox stabilization.

Standstills. An agreement between international creditors and debtors to allow a temporary halt to the payment of interest and principal on previous loans.

Statistical discrepancy. The sum of the current, capital, and financial accounts (times minus one).

Stolper-Samuleson Theorem. A corollary of the Heckscher-Ohlin Theorem stating that changes in import or export prices lead to a change in the same direction of the income of factors used intensively in its production.

Strategic trade policy. The use of trade barriers, subsidies, or other industrial support policies designed to capture the profits of foreign firms for domestic firms.

Structural adjustment policies. Policies that are designed to increase the role of market forces in a national economy. Structural adjustment policies are mainly microeconomic in nature and include privatization, deregulation, and trade reform. *See also* Stabilization policies.

Subsidiarity. The principle that the authority of the European Union (EU) to involve itself in individual national affairs is limited to those issues that are transnational in scope. In current practice, this includes environmental policies, regional policies, research and technology development, and economic and monetary union.

Subsidy. Government assistance for industry. The Uruguay Round of the GATT defined subsidies as direct loans or transfers, preferential tax treatments, a direct supply of goods, or income and price supports.

Super 301. A 1988 addition to U.S. trade law requiring the United States Trade Representative (USTR) to publicly name countries that, in the opinion of the United States, systematically engage in unfair trade practices. Super 301 requires the USTR to open negotiations with the targeted country and to recommend retaliation if the negotiations are unsuccessful. *See also* Section 301.

Supervisory review. One of the areas of reform emphasized by the Basel Accord, dealing with the supervision of risk management and standards for daily business practices for banks engaged in international borrowing.

Supply push factors in migration. The factors that "push" migrants out of their home country. *See also* Demand pull and Network factors in migration.

Swap rate. The rate of exchange used when the monetary authorities of two countries exchange the assets they have acquired against each other. In centrally planned economies, the swap rate is different from the official exchange rate.

Target zone exchange rate. An exchange rate system in which currencies are allowed to float against another currency or group of currencies, so long as it stays within a pre-defined band. Once the currency begins to move out of the band, the nation must intervene to pull it back.

Tariffs. Taxes imposed on imports. Tarrifs raise the price to the domestic consumer and reduce the quantity demanded.

Terms of trade (TOT). The average price of a country's exports divided by the average price of imports: TOT = (index of export prices)/(index of import prices). A decline in the terms of trade means that each unit of exports buys a smaller amount of imports.

Total factor productivity (TFP). A measurement of the quantity of output per unit of input. Increases in TFP mean that overall productivity has improved and that a given level of inputs will create more output; hence, technology or enterprise organization must have improved.

Trade adjustment assistance. Government programs that offer temporary assistance to workers who lose jobs because of foreign trade or their firms moving abroad.

Trade bloc. Two or more countries sharing a regional trade agreement.

Trade creation. The opposite of trade diversion, trade creation occurs when trade policies cause a shift in production from a higher cost producer (often a domestic one) to a lower cost producer.

Trade deficit. A negative merchandise trade balance; the deficit may or may not include measurement of services trade.

Trade diversion. The opposite of trade creation, trade diversion occurs when trade policies cause a shift in production and imports from a lower cost producer to a higher cost producer.

Trade line. See price line.

Trade rounds. Multilateral negotiating rounds under the auspices of the GATT or the WTO.

Tranches. The parts of an IMF loan which is made in several pieces.

Transaction costs. The costs of gathering market information, arranging a market agreement, and enforcing the agreement. Transaction costs include legal, marketing, and insurance costs, as well as quality checks, advertising, distribution, and after-sales service costs.

Transboundary and non-transboundary environmental problems. Environmental externalities that do or do not cross international borders.

Transition economies. Countries that are in the process of moving from bureaucratically controlled economies to market-based economies. Transition economies include most of those that adopted socialist or communist ideologies during the twentieth century.

Transparency. Any trade barrier that is clearly defined as a barrier. Tariffs have the most transparency—are the most transparent—because they are usually clearly specified and published in each country's tariff code. Any disguised or hidden trade barriers cause a country's trade policy to be nontransparent.

Treaty of Rome. The funding document of the European Economic Community (EEC), the Treaty of Rome was signed by six nations in 1957 and went into force in 1958. The EEC has since become the European Union (EU) and includes fifteen members, but the Treaty of Rome remains its core legal document.

Unilateral transfers. A component of the current account that measures the grants from one country to another.

Uruguay Round. The latest round of tariff negotiations within the GATT framework, the Uruguay Round began in 1986 in Punta del Este, Uruguay, concluded in 1993, and was ratified in 1994. Among other things, it created the World Trade Organization.

Value added. The price of a good minus the value of intermediate inputs used to produce it. Value added measures the contribution of capital and labor at a given stage of production.

Visegrad Four. Poland, Hungary, the Czech and Slovak Republics.

Voluntary export restraint (VER). An agreement between nations in which the exporting nation voluntarily agrees to limit its exports in order to reduce competition in the importing country.

Washington Consensus. A set of policies prescribed for developing countries by the U.S. government, the International Monetary Fund and World Bank, and the unofficial community of think-tanks centered in Washington D.C. In general, they favor the use of market forces over government direction as allocative mechanism.

World Bank. A Bretton Woods institution, originally charged with the responsibility for providing financial and technical assistance to the war-torn economies of Europe. In the 1950s, the World Bank began to shift its focus to developing countries.

World Trade Organization. An umbrella organization created by the Uruguay Round of the GATT talks, the WTO houses the GATT and many other agreements. The WTO is the main international body through which multilateral trade talks take place.

Zero sum. The costs and benefits of an activity cancel each other (equal zero).

Index